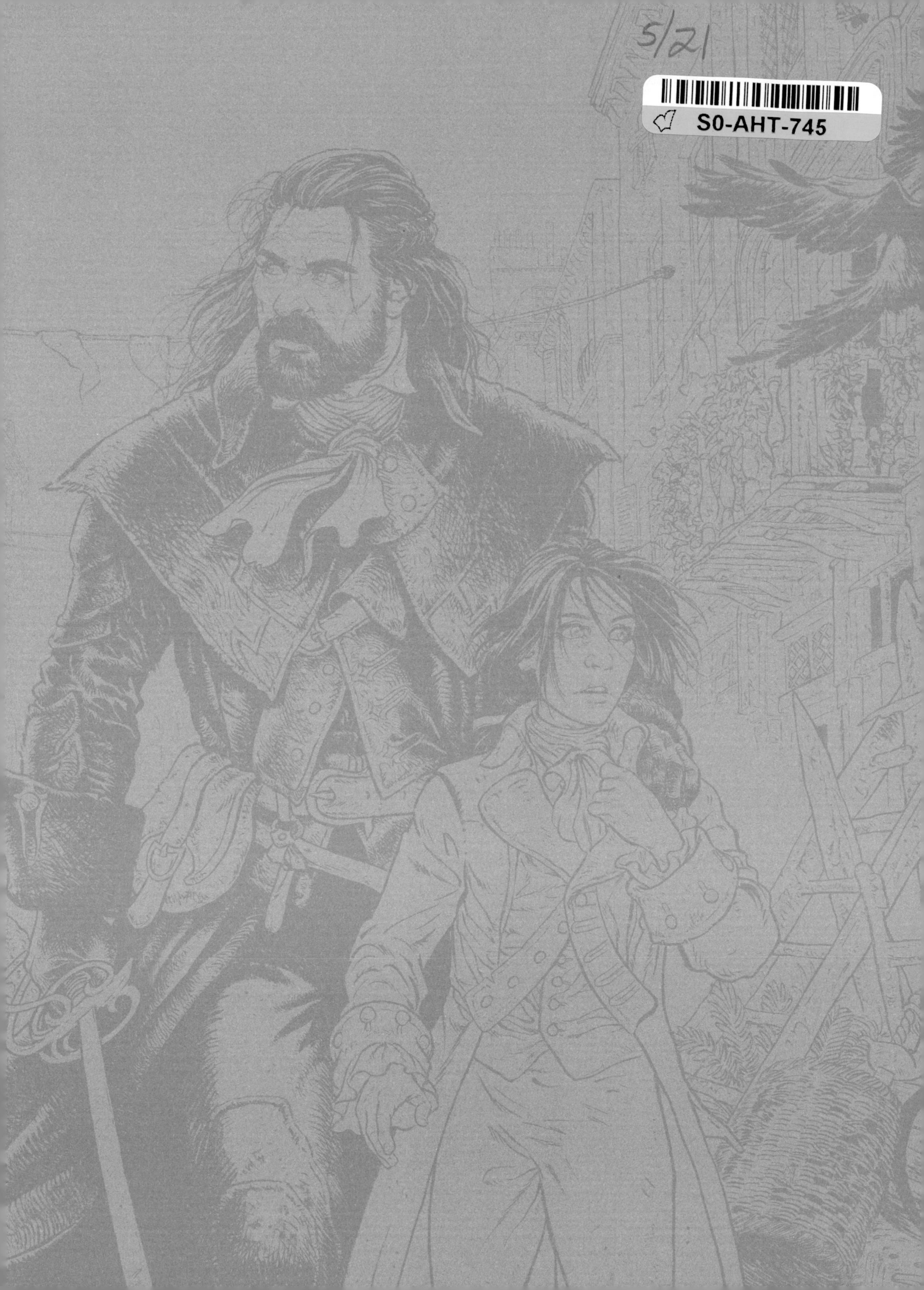

KNIGHTS OF HELIOPOLIS

TITAN®
COMICS

MORE JODOROWSKY TITLES FROM TITAN

Royal Blood

Showman Killer vol. 1:
Heartless Killer

Showman Killer vol. 2:
The Golden Child

Showman Killer vol. 3:
The Invisible Woman

TITAN COMICS

SENIOR EDITOR / Jake Devine
DESIGNER / Donna Askem

MANAGING EDITOR / Martin Eden
ASSISTANT EDITOR / Phoebe Hedges
SENIOR CREATIVE EDITOR / David Leach
SENIOR DESIGNER / Andrew Leung
ART DIRECTOR / Oz Browne
PRODUCTION CONTROLLER / Caterina Falqui
SENIOR PRODUCTION CONTROLLER / Jackie Flook
SALES & CIRCULATION MANAGER / Steve Tothill
MARKETING & ADVERTISEMENT ASSISTANT / Lauren Noding
DIRECT MARKETING ASSISTANT / George Wickenden
PUBLICIST / Imogen Harris
MARKETING MANAGER / Ricky Claydon
EDITORIAL DIRECTOR / Duncan Baizley
OPERATIONS DIRECTOR / Leigh Baulch
PUBLISHERS / Vivian Cheung & Nick Landau

KNIGHTS OF HELIOPOLIS
ISBN: 9781787736085
Published by Titan Comics
A division of Titan Publishing Group Ltd.
144 Southwark St.
London SE1 0UP

A CIP catalogue record for this title is available from the British Library.

First edition: April 2021

10 9 8 7 6 5 4 3 2 1

Printed in China.

www.titan-comics.com
Follow us on Twitter @ComicsTitan
Visit us at facebook.com/comicstitan

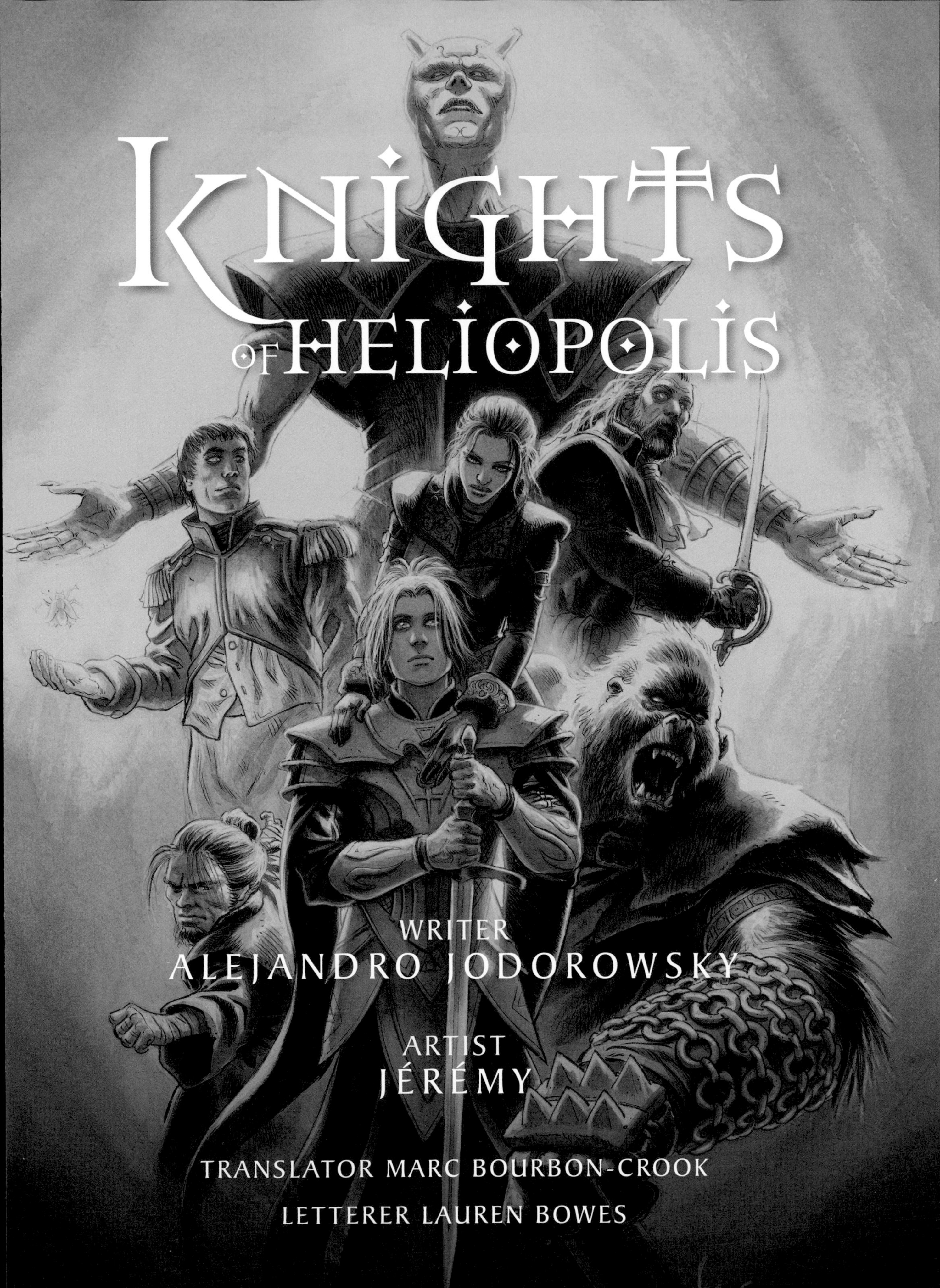

KNIGHTS OF HELIOPOLIS

WRITER
ALEJANDRO JODOROWSKY

ARTIST
JÉRÉMY

TRANSLATOR MARC BOURBON-CROOK

LETTERER LAUREN BOWES

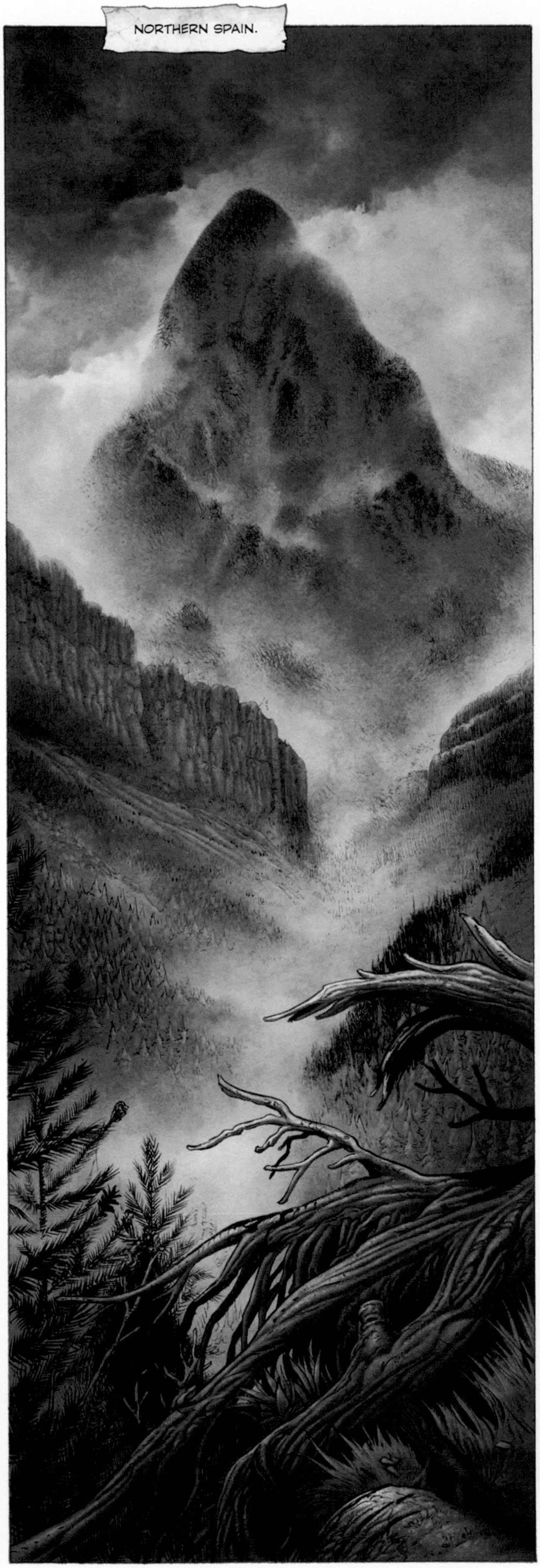
NORTHERN SPAIN.

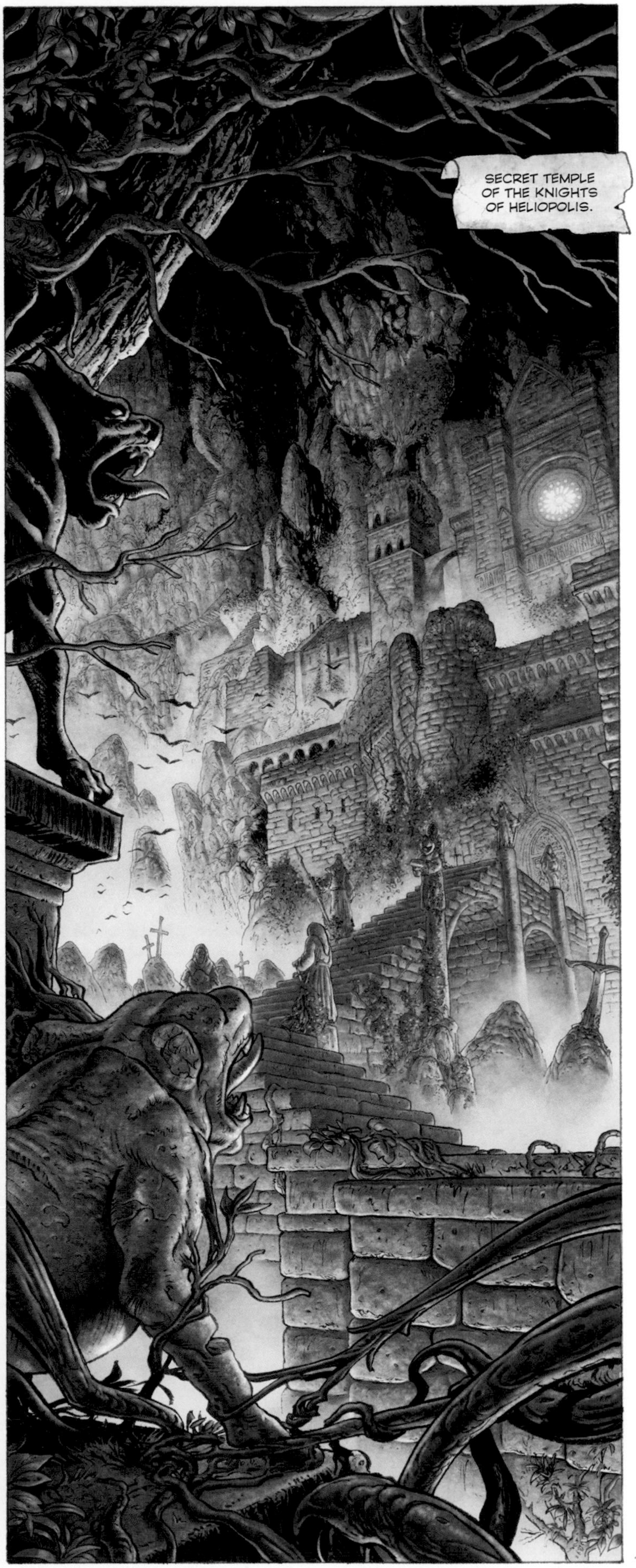
SECRET TEMPLE OF THE KNIGHTS OF HELIOPOLIS.

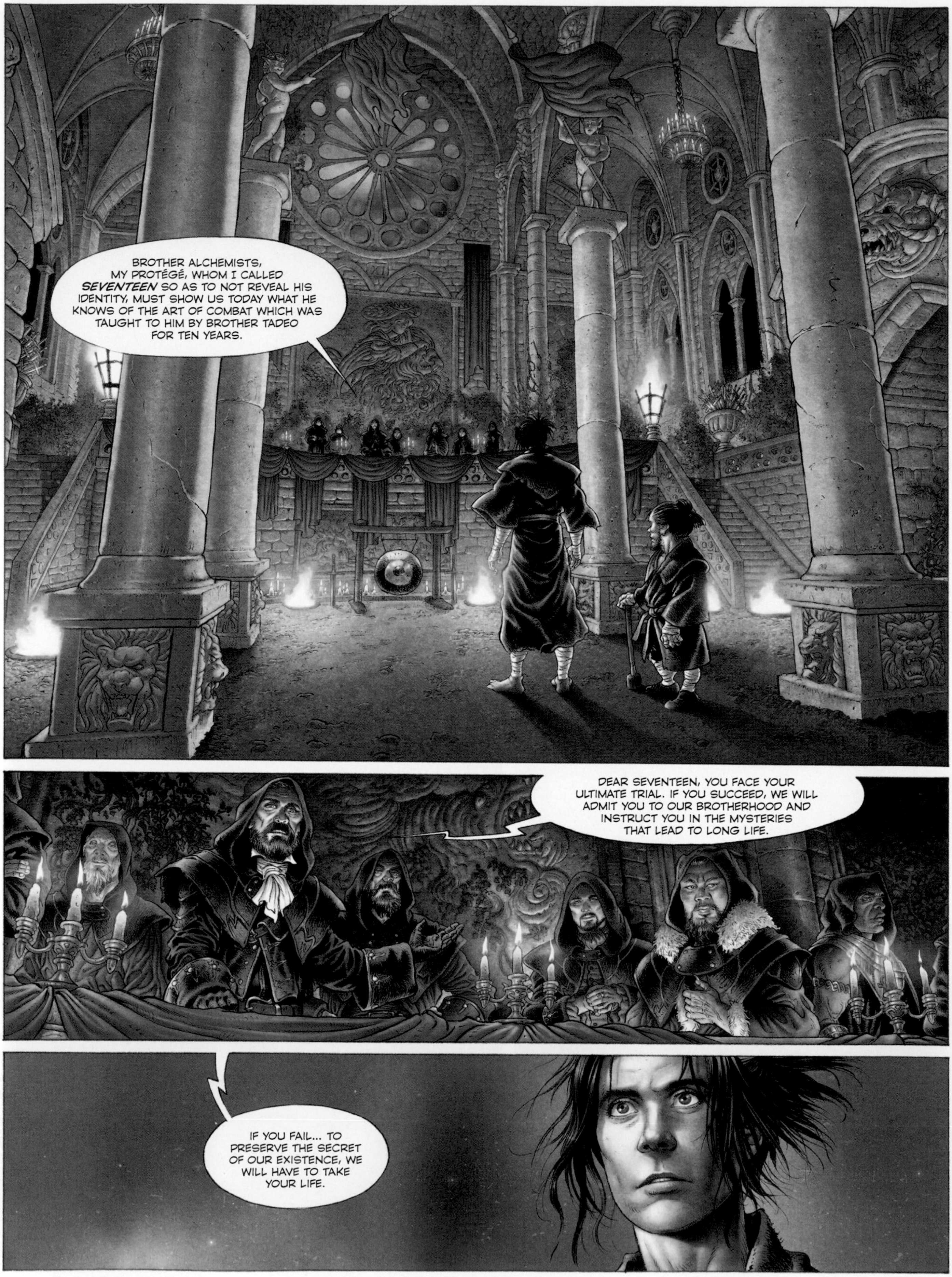
BROTHER ALCHEMISTS, MY PROTÉGÉ, WHOM I CALLED SEVENTEEN SO AS TO NOT REVEAL HIS IDENTITY, MUST SHOW US TODAY WHAT HE KNOWS OF THE ART OF COMBAT WHICH WAS TAUGHT TO HIM BY BROTHER TADEO FOR TEN YEARS.
DEAR SEVENTEEN, YOU FACE YOUR ULTIMATE TRIAL. IF YOU SUCCEED, WE WILL ADMIT YOU TO OUR BROTHERHOOD AND INSTRUCT YOU IN THE MYSTERIES THAT LEAD TO LONG LIFE.
IF YOU FAIL... TO PRESERVE THE SECRET OF OUR EXISTENCE, WE WILL HAVE TO TAKE YOUR LIFE.

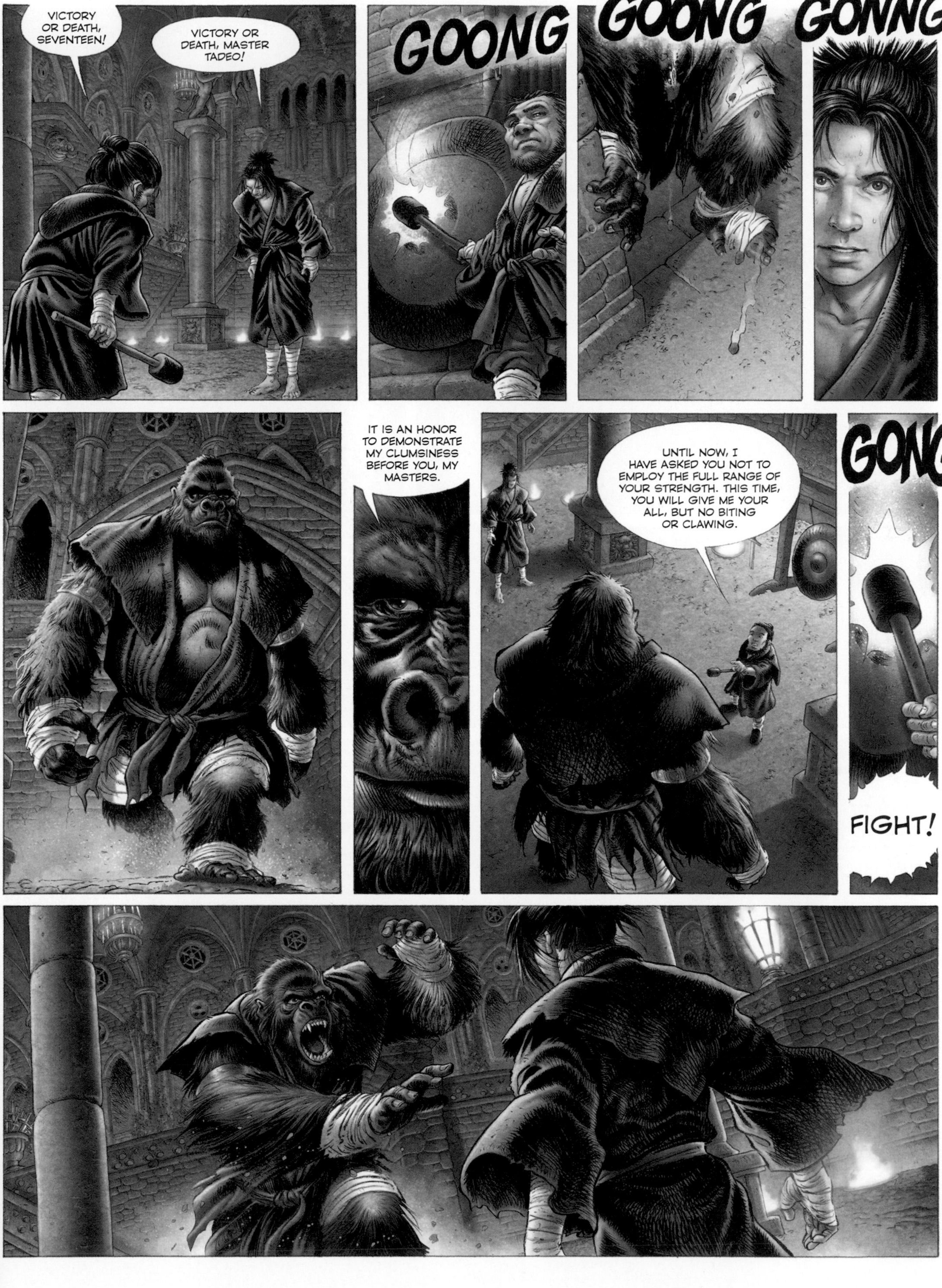
VICTORY OR DEATH, SEVENTEEN!
VICTORY OR DEATH, MASTER TADEO!
GOONG
GOONG
GONNG
GONG
IT IS AN HONOR TO DEMONSTRATE MY CLUMSINESS BEFORE YOU, MY MASTERS.
UNTIL NOW, I HAVE ASKED YOU NOT TO EMPLOY THE FULL RANGE OF YOUR STRENGTH. THIS TIME, YOU WILL GIVE ME YOUR ALL, BUT NO BITING OR CLAWING.
FIGHT!

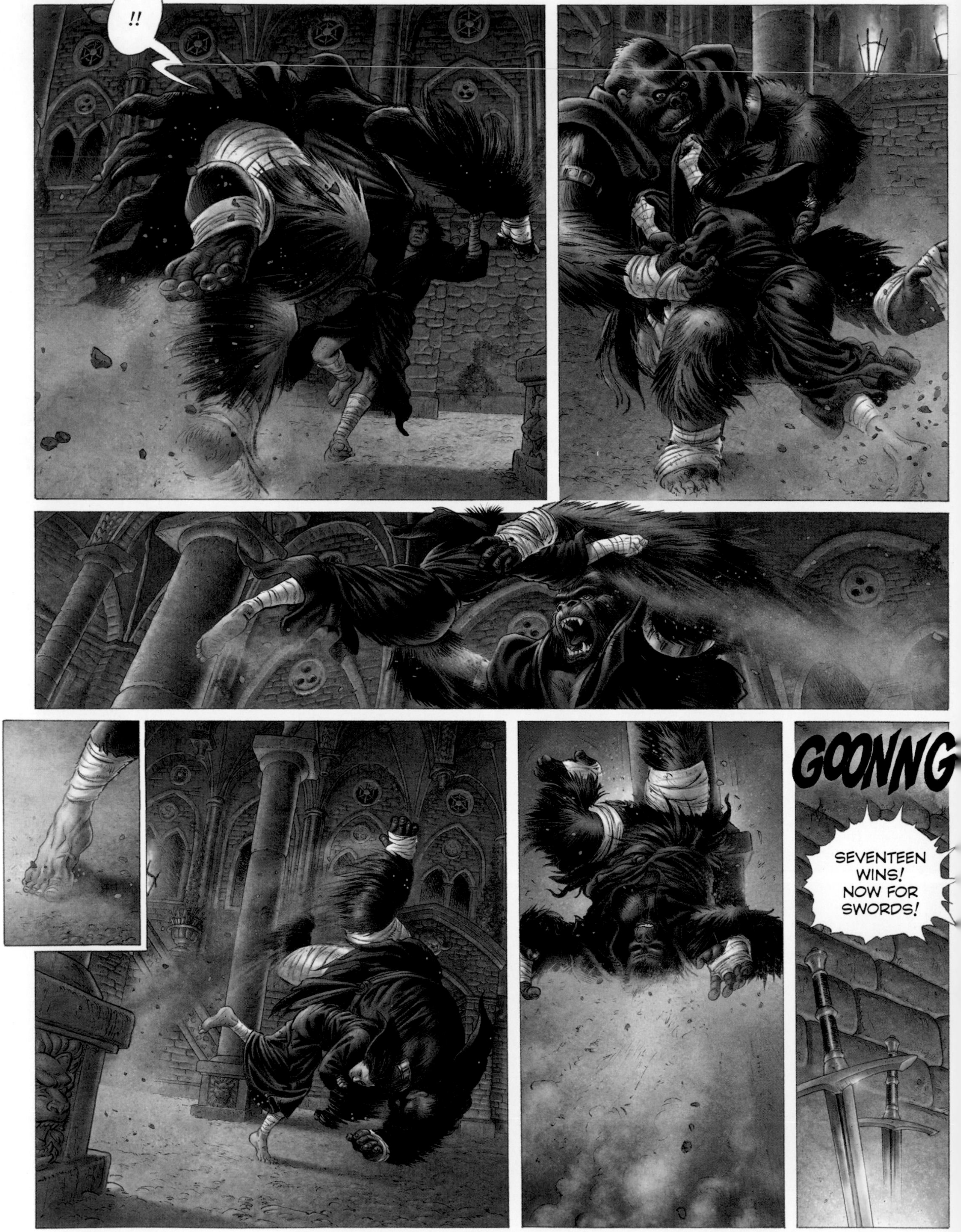
!!
GOONNG
SEVENTEEN WINS! NOW FOR SWORDS!

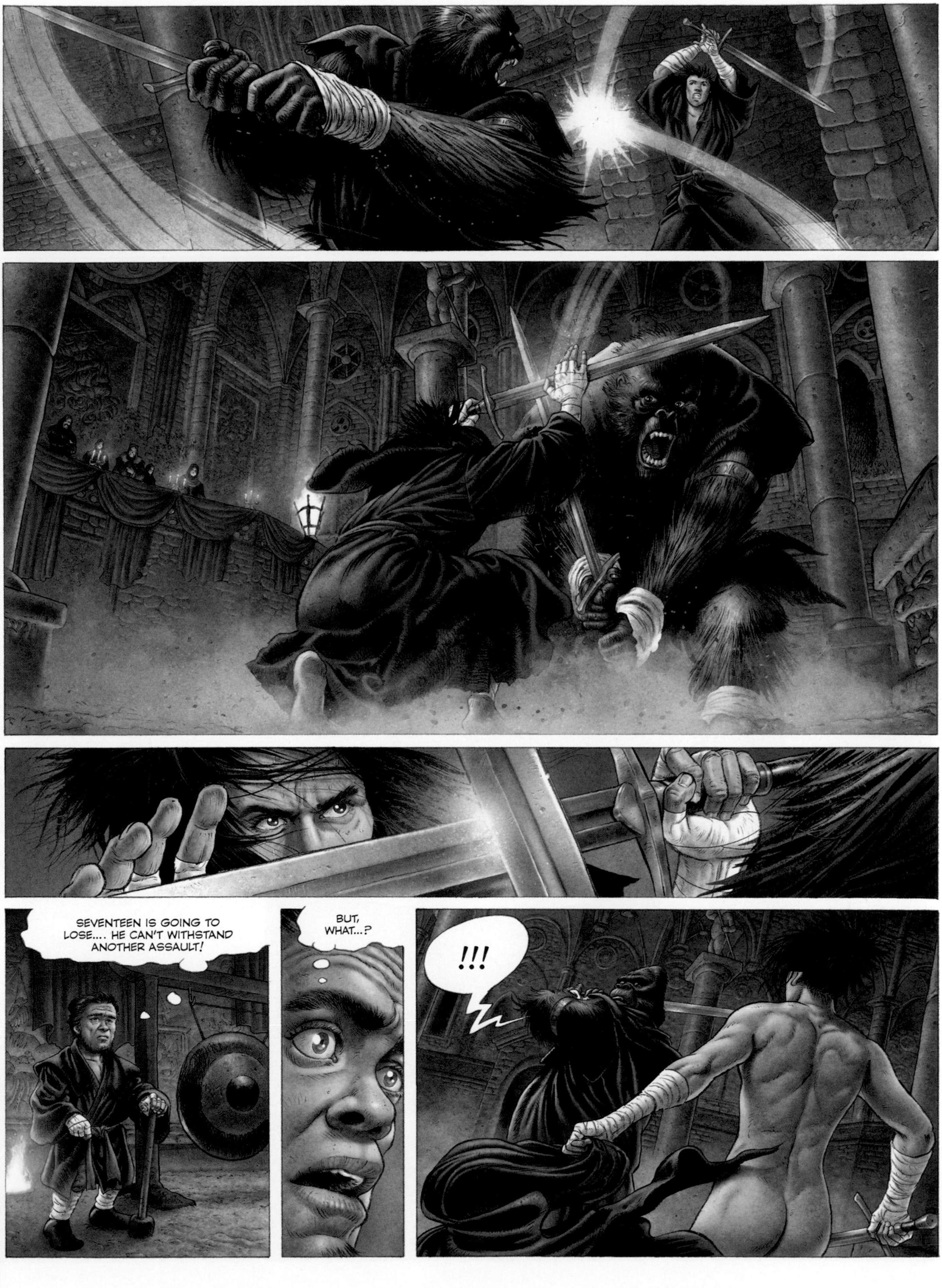
SEVENTEEN IS GOING TO LOSE.... HE CAN'T WITHSTAND ANOTHER ASSAULT!
BUT, WHAT...?
!!!

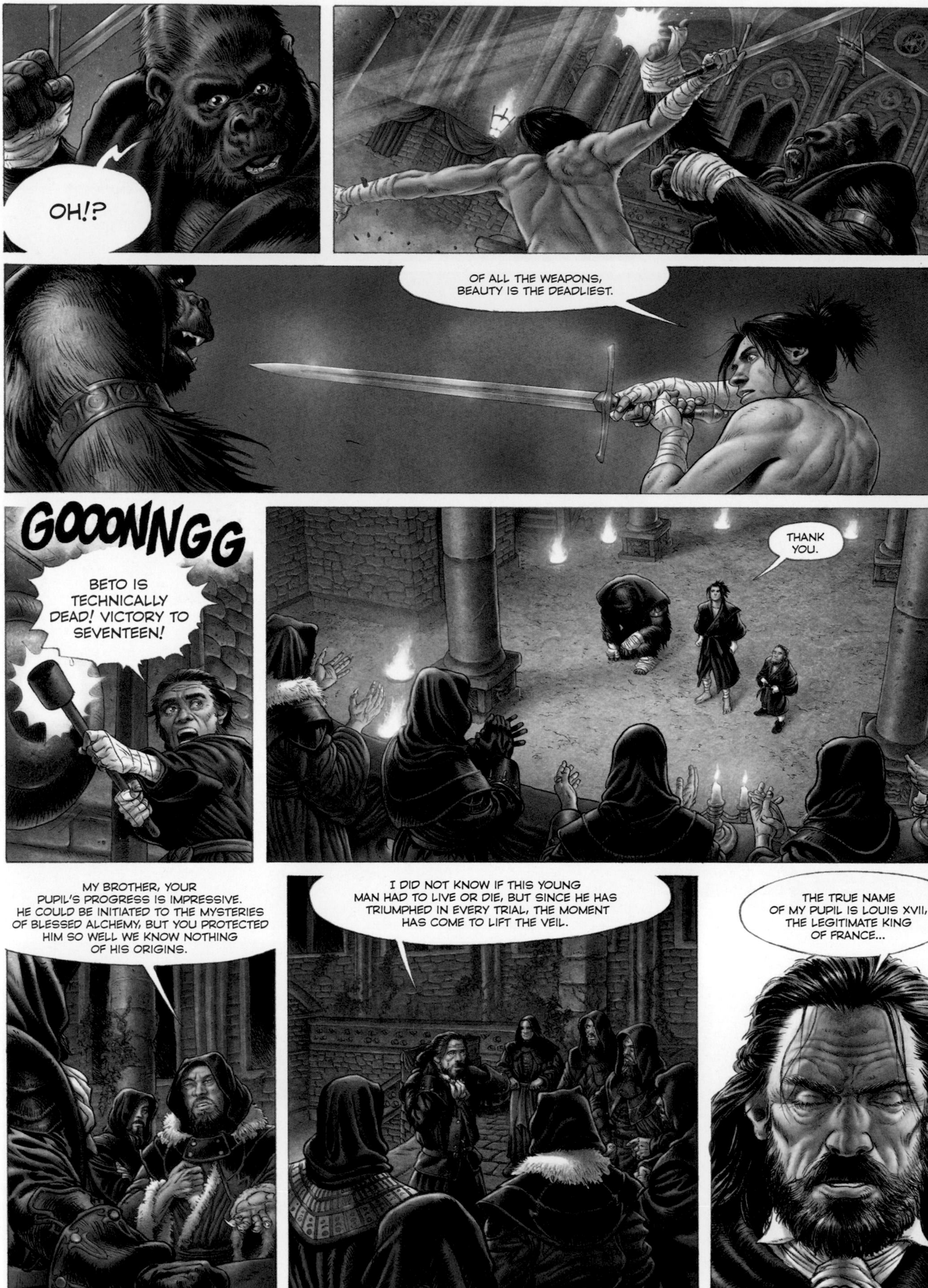
OH!?
OF ALL THE WEAPONS, BEAUTY IS THE DEADLIEST.
GOOONNGG
BETO IS TECHNICALLY DEAD! VICTORY TO SEVENTEEN!
THANK YOU.
MY BROTHER, YOUR PUPIL'S PROGRESS IS IMPRESSIVE. HE COULD BE INITIATED TO THE MYSTERIES OF BLESSED ALCHEMY, BUT YOU PROTECTED HIM SO WELL WE KNOW NOTHING OF HIS ORIGINS.
I DID NOT KNOW IF THIS YOUNG MAN HAD TO LIVE OR DIE, BUT SINCE HE HAS TRIUMPHED IN EVERY TRIAL, THE MOMENT HAS COME TO LIFT THE VEIL.
THE TRUE NAME OF MY PUPIL IS LOUIS XVII, THE LEGITIMATE KING OF FRANCE...

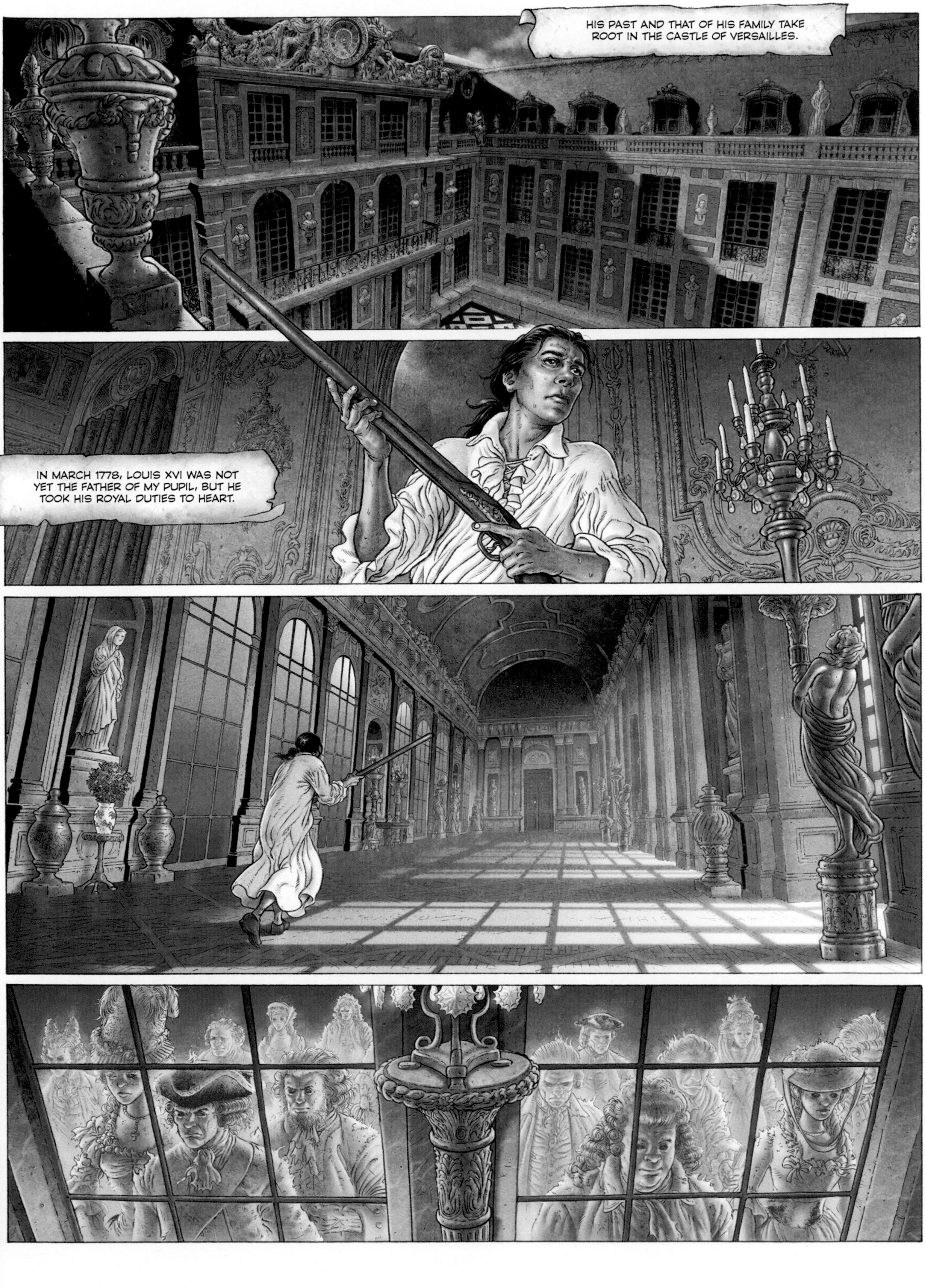
HIS PAST AND THAT OF HIS FAMILY TAKE ROOT IN THE CASTLE OF VERSAILLES.
IN MARCH 1778, LOUIS XVI WAS NOT YET THE FATHER OF MY PUPIL, BUT HE TOOK HIS ROYAL DUTIES TO HEART.

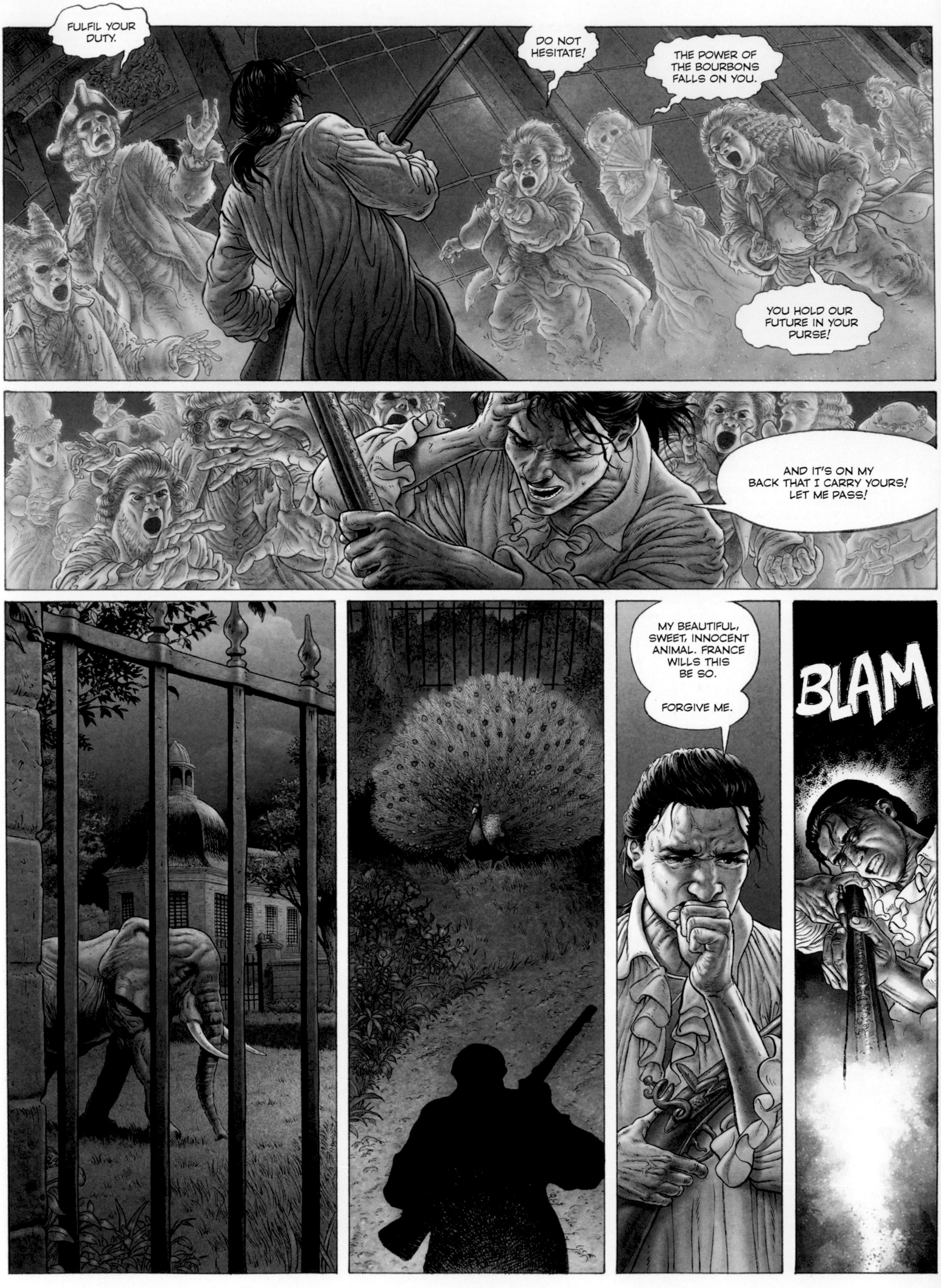
FULFIL YOUR DUTY.
DO NOT HESITATE!
THE POWER OF THE BOURBONS FALLS ON YOU.
YOU HOLD OUR FUTURE IN YOUR PURSE!
AND IT'S ON MY BACK THAT I CARRY YOURS! LET ME PASS!
MY BEAUTIFUL, SWEET, INNOCENT ANIMAL. FRANCE WILLS THIS BE SO.
FORGIVE ME.
BLAM

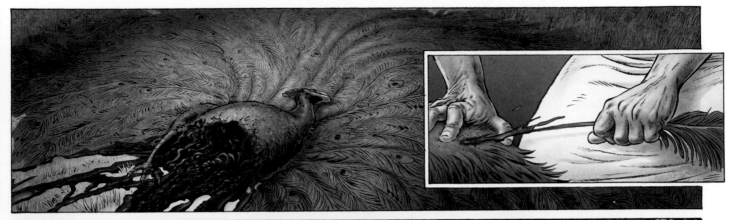

HAVE YOU DONE IT, YOUR MAJESTY?

I KILLED IT... HERE IS THE FEATHER, MARIE-ANTOINETTE.

TAKE OFF YOUR CLOTHES.

NOW CALMLY KEEP YOUR LEGS OPEN FOR THE FOLLOWING HOUR.

9

JUST AS HE ADVISED, I NEED TO STROKE YOUR INTIMACY UNTIL SIX THIRTY. HAVE YOU TAKEN YOUR DROPS OF WINE?

LET'S MAKE THIS HAPPEN, MY FRIEND... BUT STOP TALKING, CONCENTRATE... AND BE GENTLE... HMMM...

THE PREVIOUS DAY.

MISTER FULCANELLI, WE HAVE CONFIDENCE IN YOUR ALCHEMICAL KNOWLEDGE...

WE HAVE BEEN MARRIED OVER SEVEN YEARS BUT HAVE NEVER KNOWN INTIMATE CONTACT.

WHAT'S WRONG WITH US?

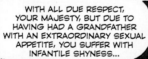

WITH ALL DUE RESPECT, YOUR MAJESTY, BUT DUE TO HAVING HAD A GRANDFATHER WITH AN EXTRAORDINARY SEXUAL APPETITE, YOU SUFFER WITH INFANTILE SHYNESS...

WITH ALL DUE RESPECT, YOUR MAJESTY, BUT DUE TO HAVING HAD A MOTHER WHO GAVE LIFE TO 16 CHILDREN, AND OUT OF FEAR OF BECOMING LIKE HER, YOU HAVE REPRESSED YOUR DESIRES...

THESE TRAUMAS THAT YOU HAVE INHERITED FROM YOUR FAMILIES HAVE TAKEN ROOT IN YOU, TO THE POINT WHERE THEY HAVE BECOME CHAINS SHACKLING YOU DOWN... WE MUST FREE YOU OF THEM...

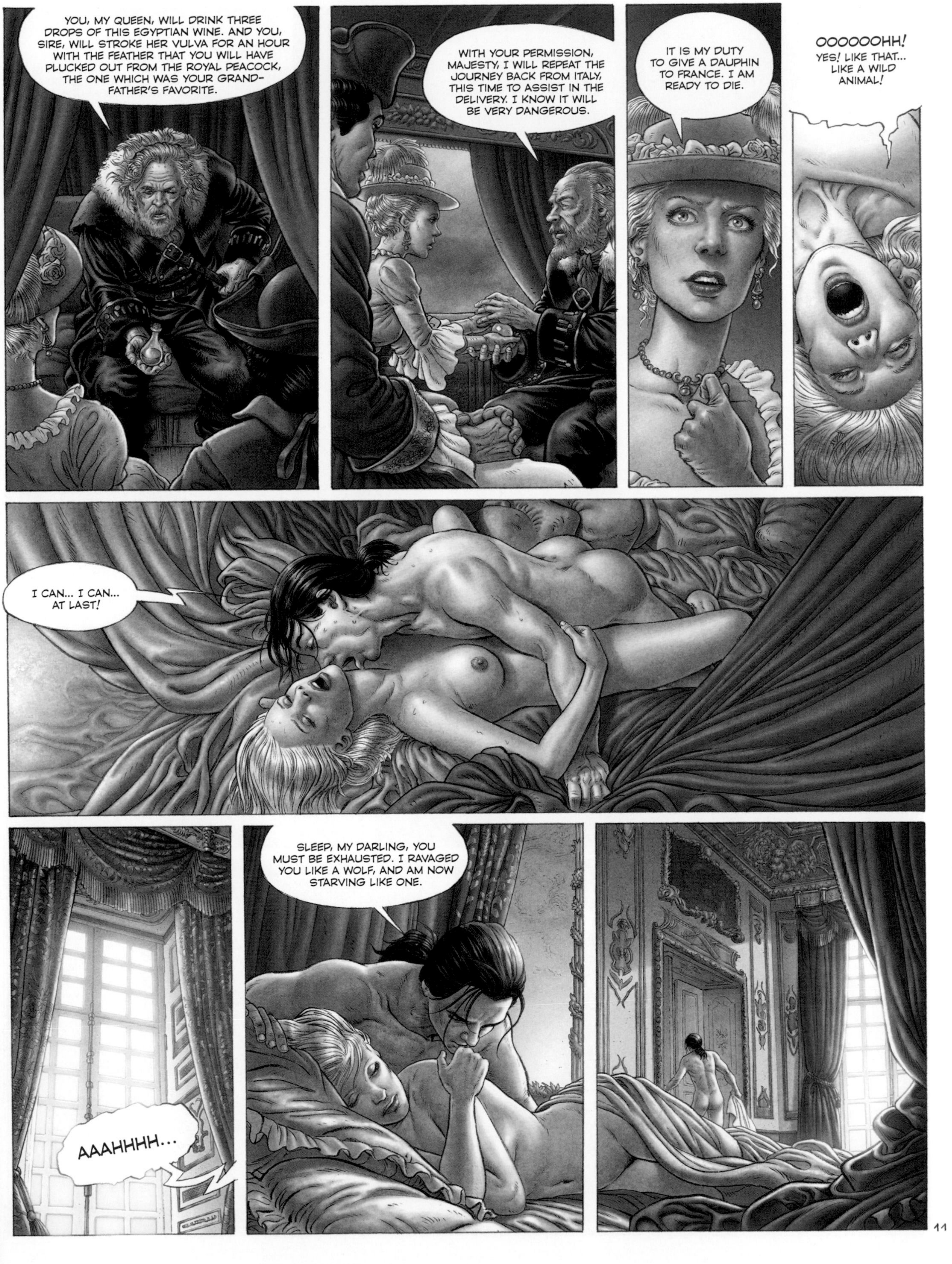
YOU, MY QUEEN, WILL DRINK THREE DROPS OF THIS EGYPTIAN WINE. AND YOU, SIRE, WILL STROKE HER VULVA FOR AN HOUR WITH THE FEATHER THAT YOU WILL HAVE PLUCKED OUT FROM THE ROYAL PEACOCK, THE ONE WHICH WAS YOUR GRAND-FATHER'S FAVORITE.
WITH YOUR PERMISSION, MAJESTY, I WILL REPEAT THE JOURNEY BACK FROM ITALY, THIS TIME TO ASSIST IN THE DELIVERY. I KNOW IT WILL BE VERY DANGEROUS.
IT IS MY DUTY TO GIVE A DAUPHIN TO FRANCE. I AM READY TO DIE.
OOOOOOHH! YES! LIKE THAT... LIKE A WILD ANIMAL!
I CAN... I CAN... AT LAST!
AAAHHHH...
SLEEP, MY DARLING, YOU MUST BE EXHAUSTED. I RAVAGED YOU LIKE A WOLF, AND AM NOW STARVING LIKE ONE.

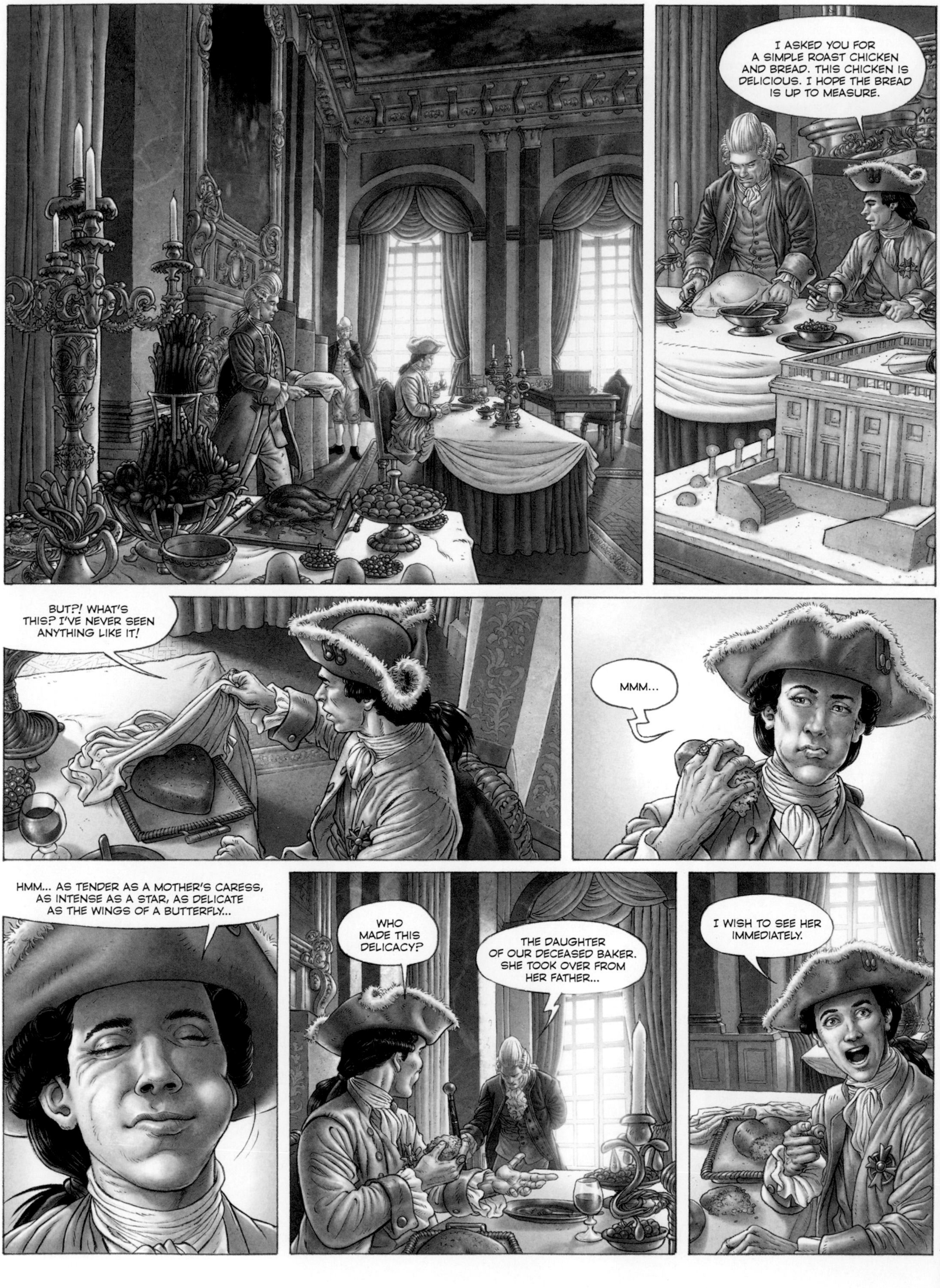
I ASKED YOU FOR A SIMPLE ROAST CHICKEN AND BREAD. THIS CHICKEN IS DELICIOUS. I HOPE THE BREAD IS UP TO MEASURE.
BUT?! WHAT'S THIS? I'VE NEVER SEEN ANYTHING LIKE IT!
MMM...
HMM... AS TENDER AS A MOTHER'S CARESS, AS INTENSE AS A STAR, AS DELICATE AS THE WINGS OF A BUTTERFLY...
WHO MADE THIS DELICACY?
THE DAUGHTER OF OUR DECEASED BAKER. SHE TOOK OVER FROM HER FATHER...
I WISH TO SEE HER IMMEDIATELY.

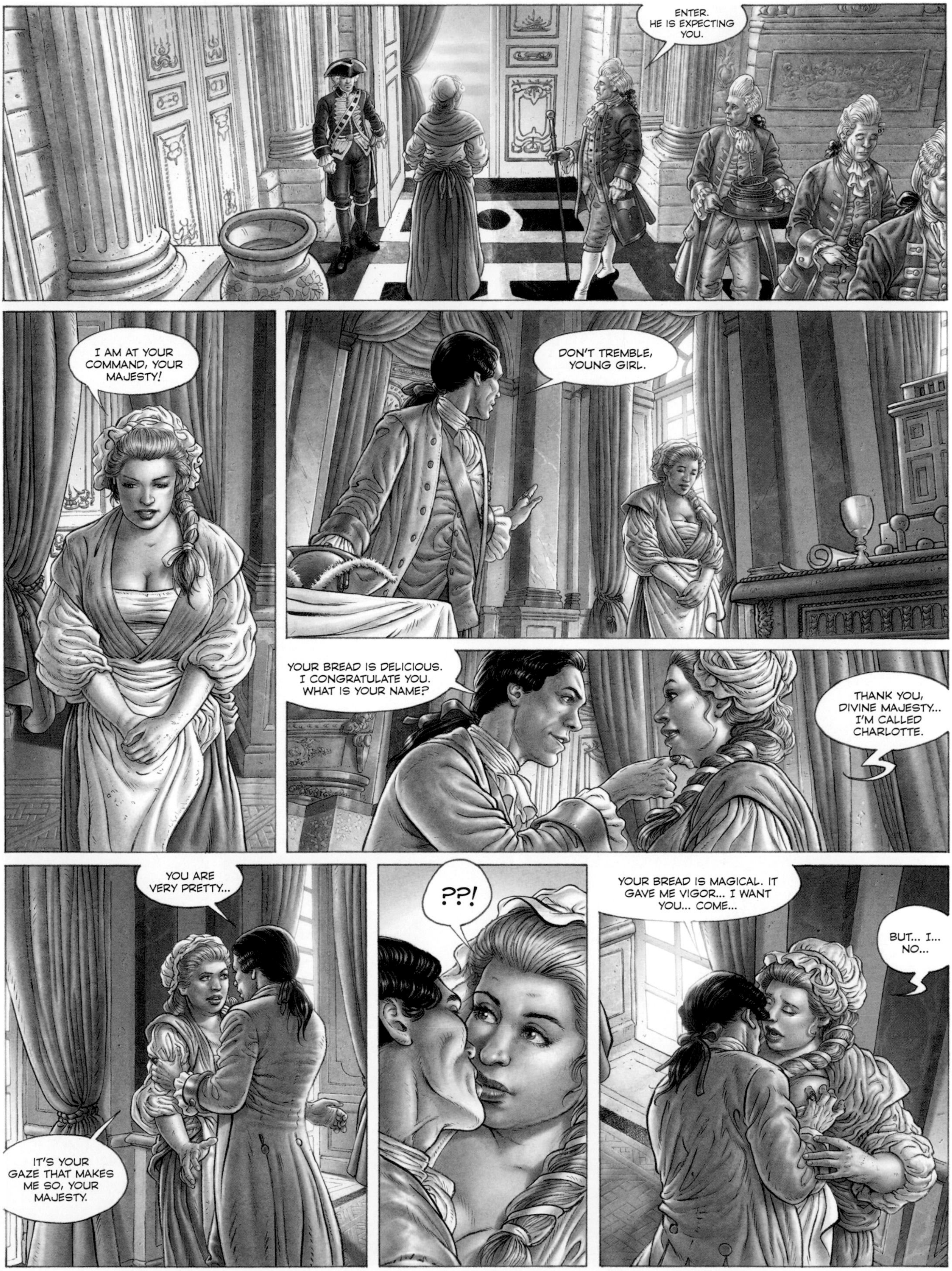
ENTER. HE IS EXPECTING YOU.
I AM AT YOUR COMMAND, YOUR MAJESTY!
DON'T TREMBLE, YOUNG GIRL.
YOUR BREAD IS DELICIOUS. I CONGRATULATE YOU. WHAT IS YOUR NAME?
THANK YOU, DIVINE MAJESTY... I'M CALLED CHARLOTTE.
YOU ARE VERY PRETTY...
IT'S YOUR GAZE THAT MAKES ME SO, YOUR MAJESTY.
??!
YOUR BREAD IS MAGICAL. IT GAVE ME VIGOR... I WANT YOU... COME...
BUT... I... NO...

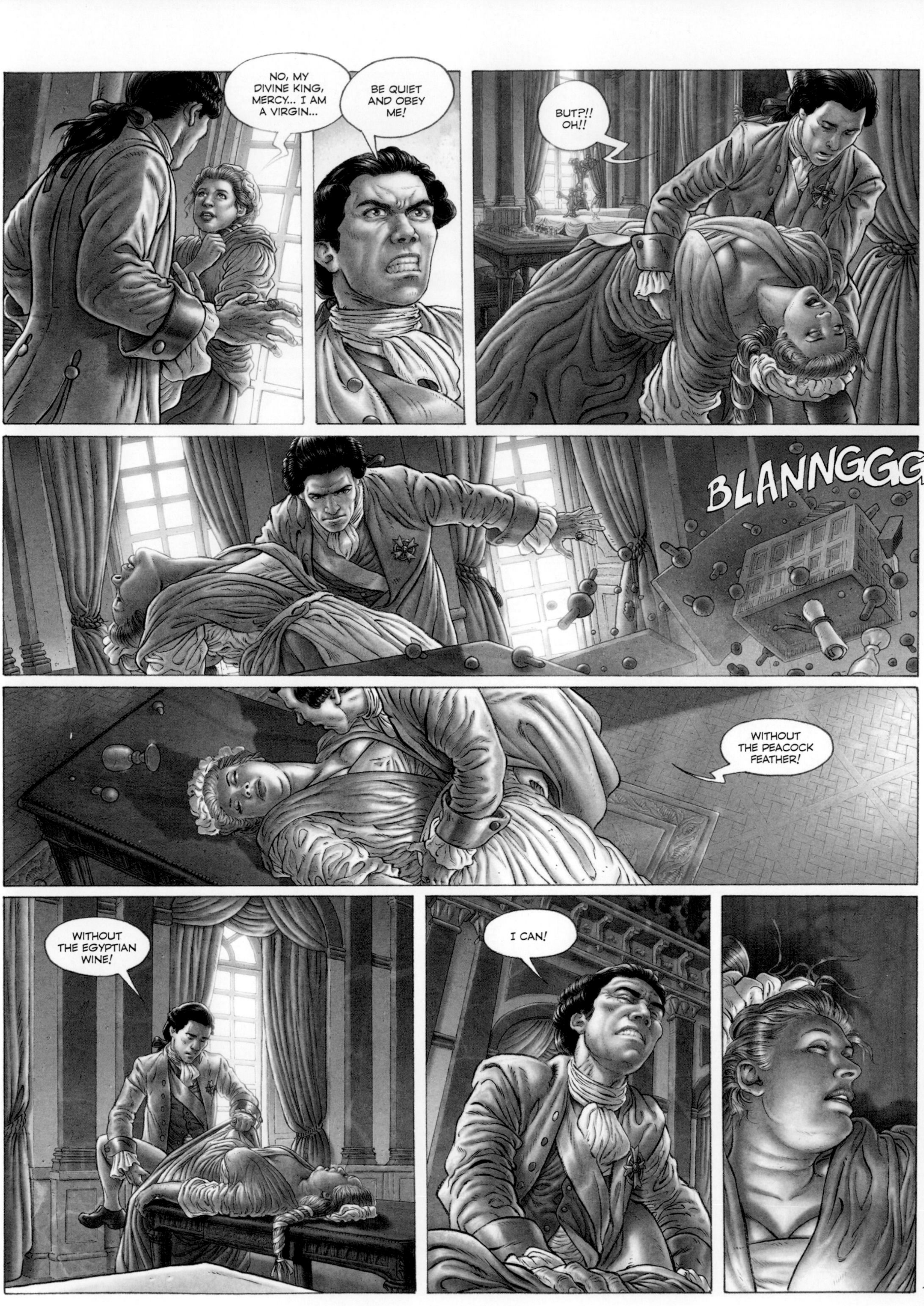
NO, MY DIVINE KING, MERCY... I AM A VIRGIN...
BE QUIET AND OBEY ME!
BUT?!! OH!!
BLANNGGG
WITHOUT THE PEACOCK FEATHER!
WITHOUT THE EGYPTIAN WINE!
I CAN!

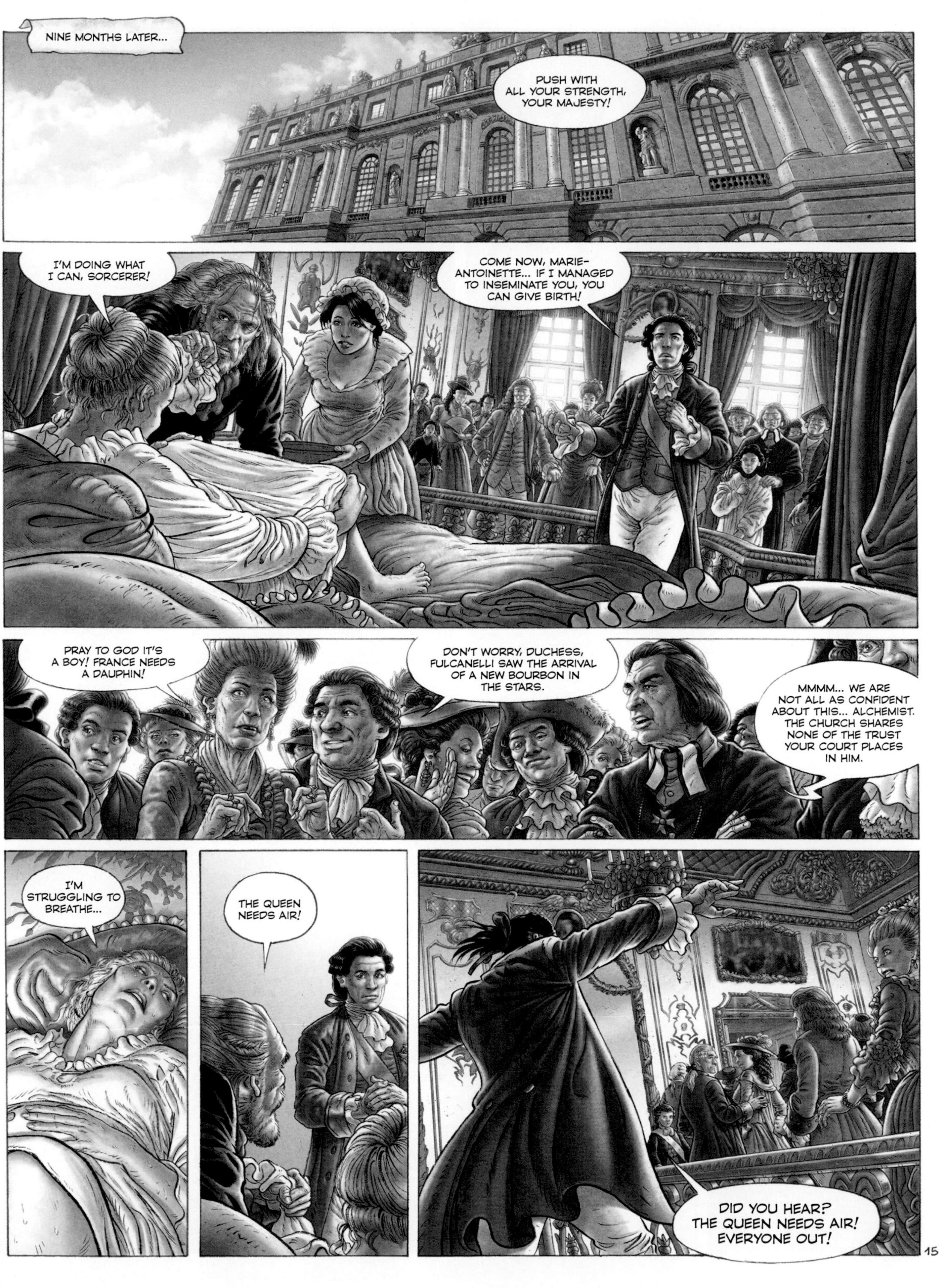
NINE MONTHS LATER...
PUSH WITH ALL YOUR STRENGTH, YOUR MAJESTY!
I'M DOING WHAT I CAN, SORCERER!
COME NOW, MARIE-ANTOINETTE... IF I MANAGED TO INSEMINATE YOU, YOU CAN GIVE BIRTH!
PRAY TO GOD IT'S A BOY! FRANCE NEEDS A DAUPHIN!
DON'T WORRY, DUCHESS, FULCANELLI SAW THE ARRIVAL OF A NEW BOURBON IN THE STARS.
MMMM... WE ARE NOT ALL AS CONFIDENT ABOUT THIS... ALCHEMIST. THE CHURCH SHARES NONE OF THE TRUST YOUR COURT PLACES IN HIM.
I'M STRUGGLING TO BREATHE...
THE QUEEN NEEDS AIR!
DID YOU HEAR? THE QUEEN NEEDS AIR! EVERYONE OUT!

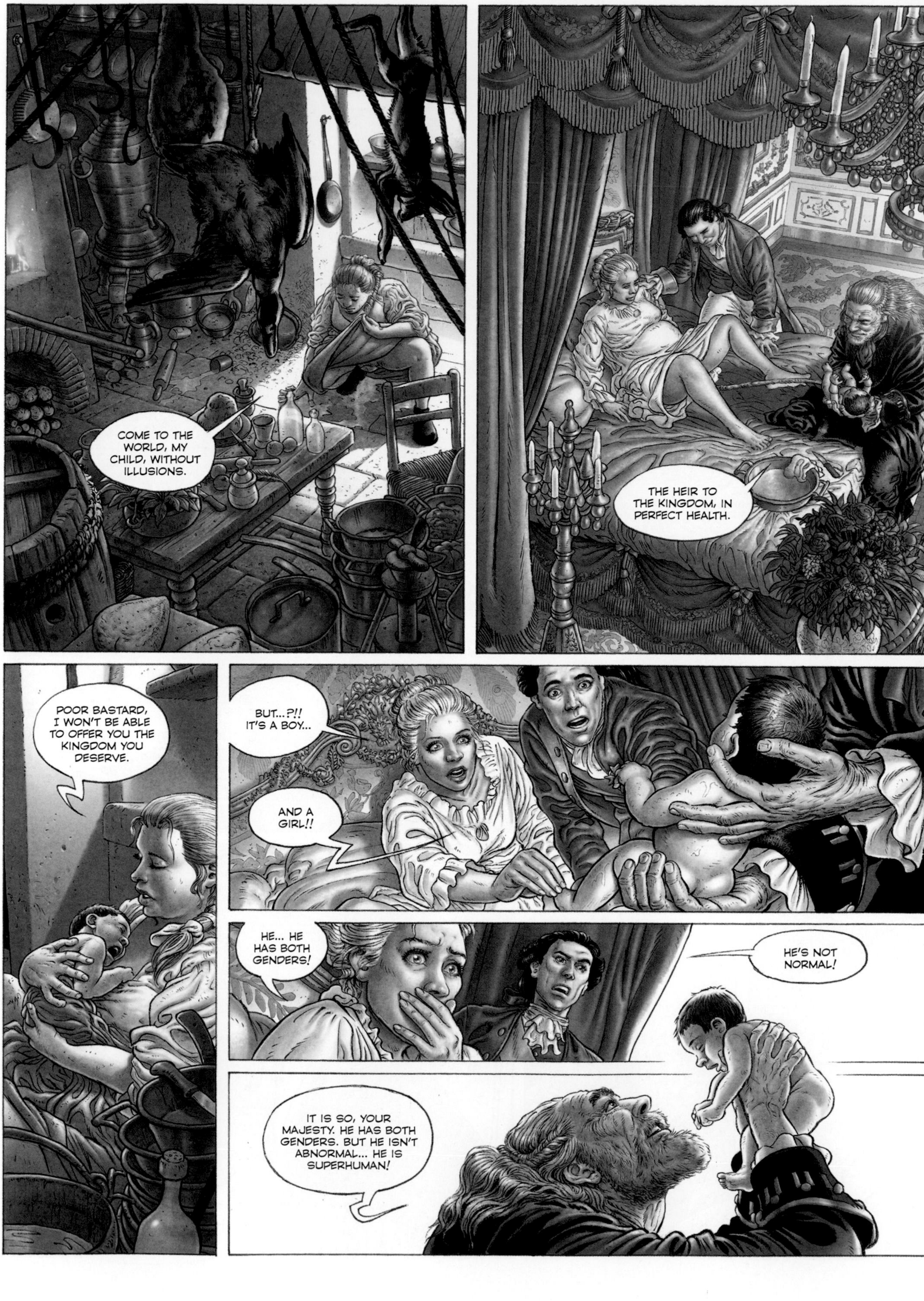
COME TO THE WORLD, MY CHILD, WITHOUT ILLUSIONS.
THE HEIR TO THE KINGDOM, IN PERFECT HEALTH.
POOR BASTARD, I WON'T BE ABLE TO OFFER YOU THE KINGDOM YOU DESERVE.
BUT...?!! IT'S A BOY...
AND A GIRL!!
HE... HE HAS BOTH GENDERS!
HE'S NOT NORMAL!
IT IS SO, YOUR MAJESTY. HE HAS BOTH GENDERS. BUT HE ISN'T ABNORMAL... HE IS SUPERHUMAN!

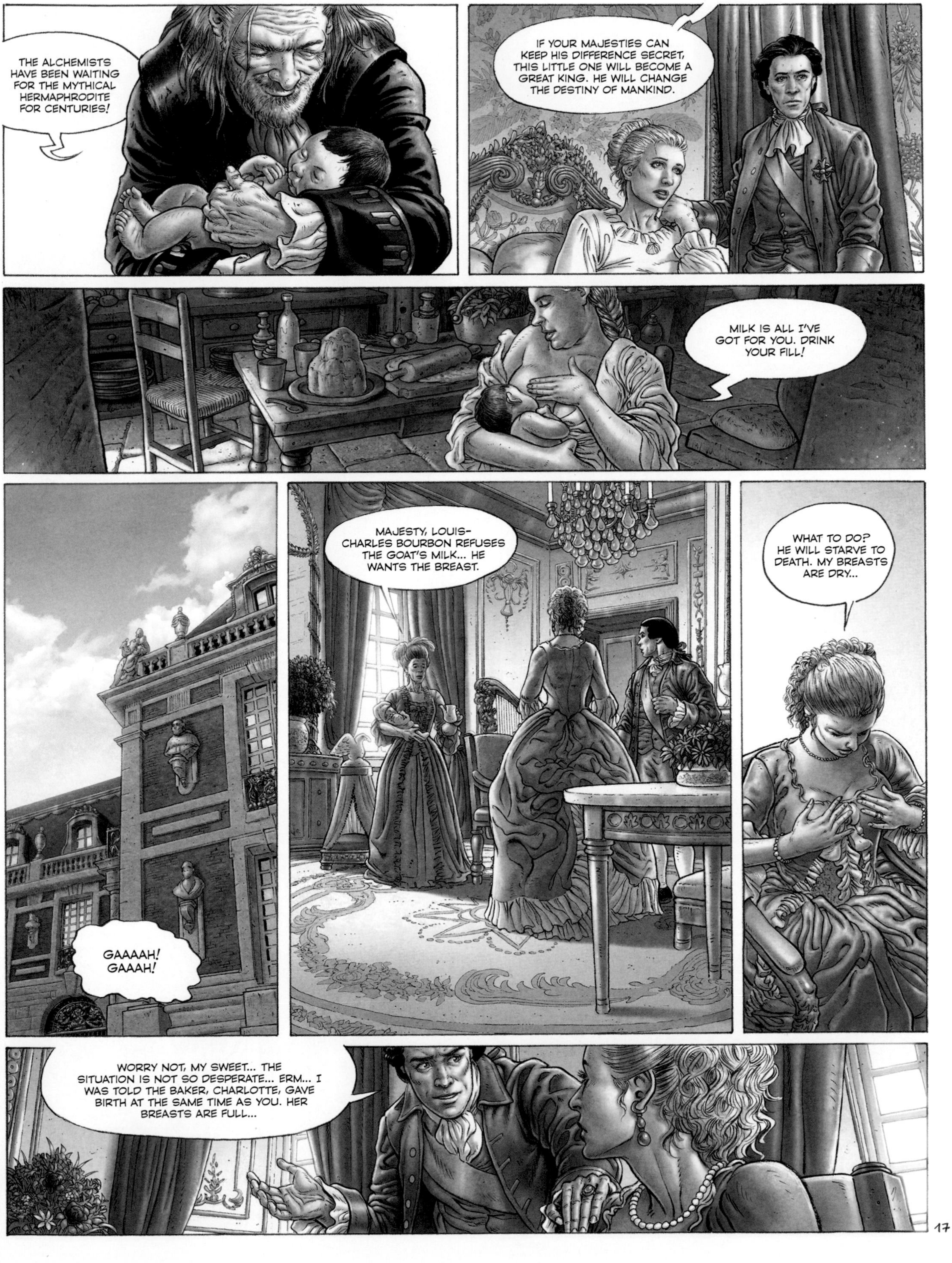
THE ALCHEMISTS HAVE BEEN WAITING FOR THE MYTHICAL HERMAPHRODITE FOR CENTURIES!
IF YOUR MAJESTIES CAN KEEP HIS DIFFERENCE SECRET, THIS LITTLE ONE WILL BECOME A GREAT KING. HE WILL CHANGE THE DESTINY OF MANKIND.
MILK IS ALL I'VE GOT FOR YOU. DRINK YOUR FILL!
GAAAAH! GAAAH!
MAJESTY, LOUIS-CHARLES BOURBON REFUSES THE GOAT'S MILK... HE WANTS THE BREAST.
WHAT TO DO? HE WILL STARVE TO DEATH. MY BREASTS ARE DRY...
WORRY NOT, MY SWEET... THE SITUATION IS NOT SO DESPERATE... ERM... I WAS TOLD THE BAKER, CHARLOTTE, GAVE BIRTH AT THE SAME TIME AS YOU. HER BREASTS ARE FULL...

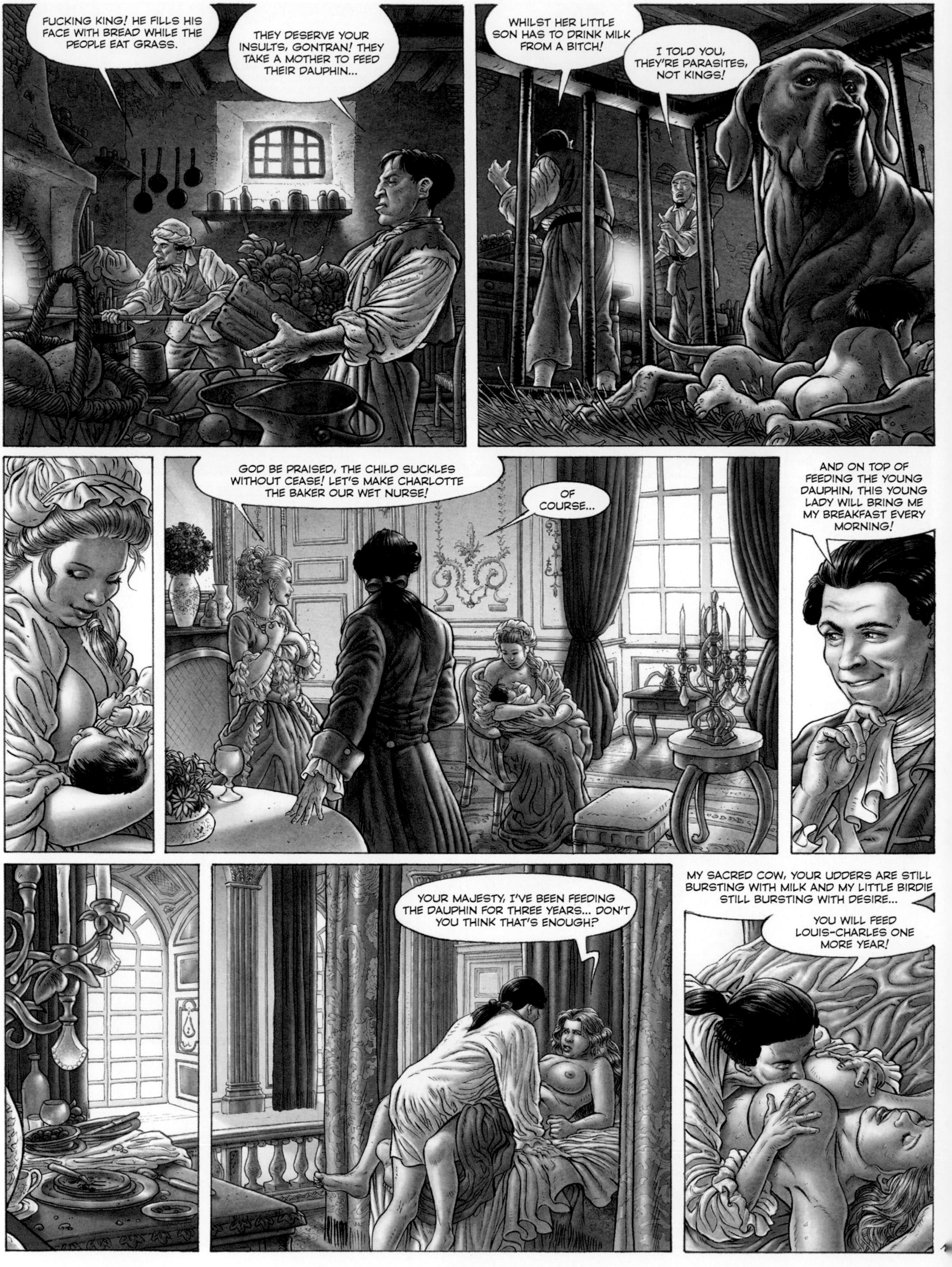
FUCKING KING! HE FILLS HIS FACE WITH BREAD WHILE THE PEOPLE EAT GRASS.
THEY DESERVE YOUR INSULTS, GONTRAN! THEY TAKE A MOTHER TO FEED THEIR DAUPHIN...
WHILST HER LITTLE SON HAS TO DRINK MILK FROM A BITCH!
I TOLD YOU, THEY'RE PARASITES, NOT KINGS!
GOD BE PRAISED, THE CHILD SUCKLES WITHOUT CEASE! LET'S MAKE CHARLOTTE THE BAKER OUR WET NURSE!
OF COURSE...
AND ON TOP OF FEEDING THE YOUNG DAUPHIN, THIS YOUNG LADY WILL BRING ME MY BREAKFAST EVERY MORNING!
YOUR MAJESTY, I'VE BEEN FEEDING THE DAUPHIN FOR THREE YEARS... DON'T YOU THINK THAT'S ENOUGH?
MY SACRED COW, YOUR UDDERS ARE STILL BURSTING WITH MILK AND MY LITTLE BIRDIE STILL BURSTING WITH DESIRE...
YOU WILL FEED LOUIS-CHARLES ONE MORE YEAR!

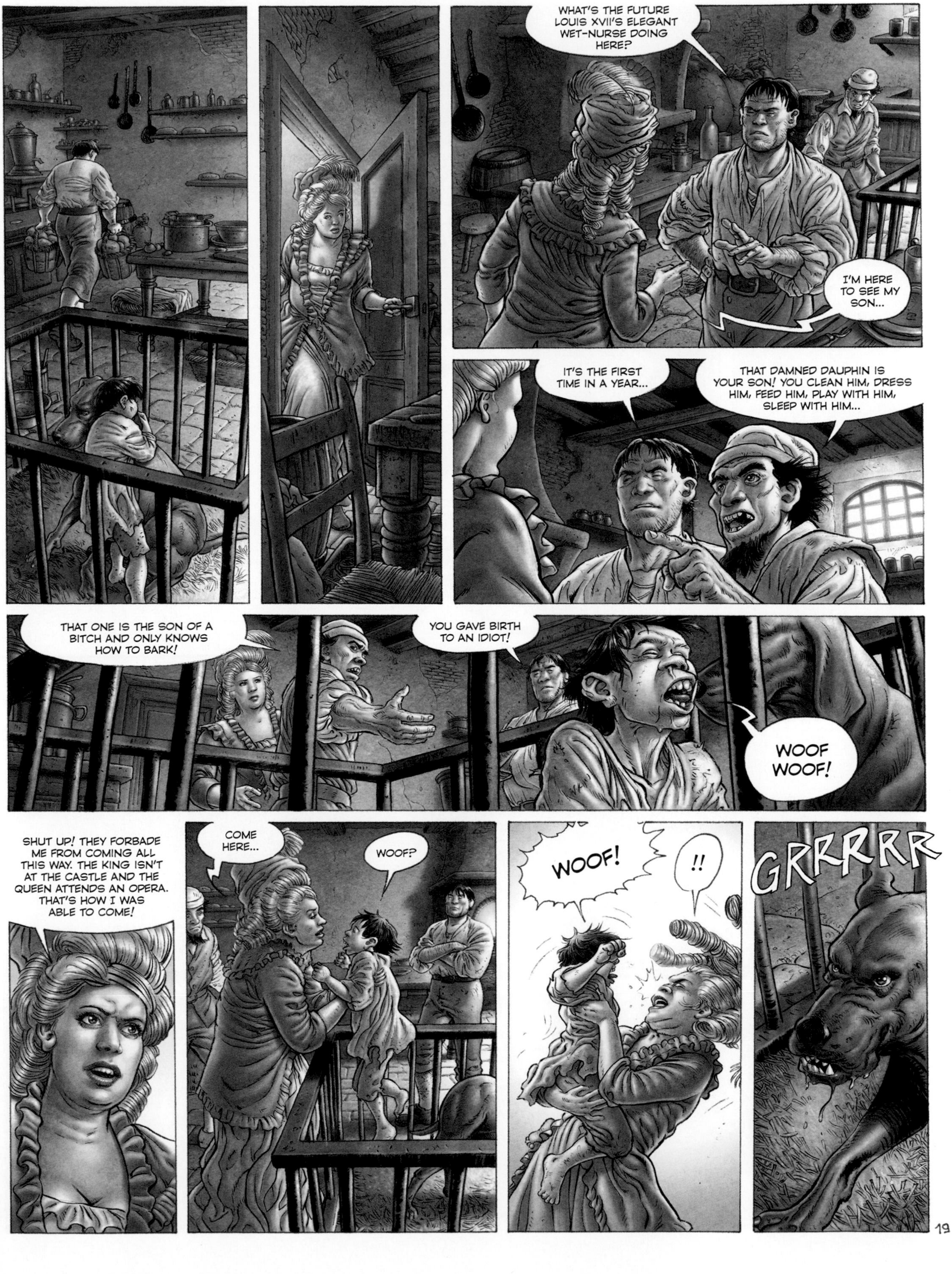
WHAT'S THE FUTURE LOUIS XVII'S ELEGANT WET-NURSE DOING HERE?
I'M HERE TO SEE MY SON...
IT'S THE FIRST TIME IN A YEAR...
THAT DAMNED DAUPHIN IS YOUR SON! YOU CLEAN HIM, DRESS HIM, FEED HIM, PLAY WITH HIM, SLEEP WITH HIM...
THAT ONE IS THE SON OF A BITCH AND ONLY KNOWS HOW TO BARK!
YOU GAVE BIRTH TO AN IDIOT!
WOOF WOOF!
SHUT UP! THEY FORBADE ME FROM COMING ALL THIS WAY. THE KING ISN'T AT THE CASTLE AND THE QUEEN ATTENDS AN OPERA. THAT'S HOW I WAS ABLE TO COME!
COME HERE...
WOOF?
WOOF!
!!
GRRRRR

CALM, LÉONE.

I'M NOT ONLY THE DAUPHIN'S WET-NURSE, I'M ALSO THE KING'S WHORE... WHAT CAN I DO?

TAKE YOUR SON AND FLEE.

YOU COULD LIVE IN PARIS, AND TAKE UP BEING A BAKER AGAIN.

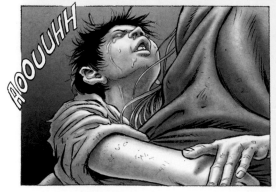

AOOUUHH

STOP HOWLING AT THE MOON. IT WON'T BRING LÉONE BACK.

IT'S ME, YOUR MOTHER...

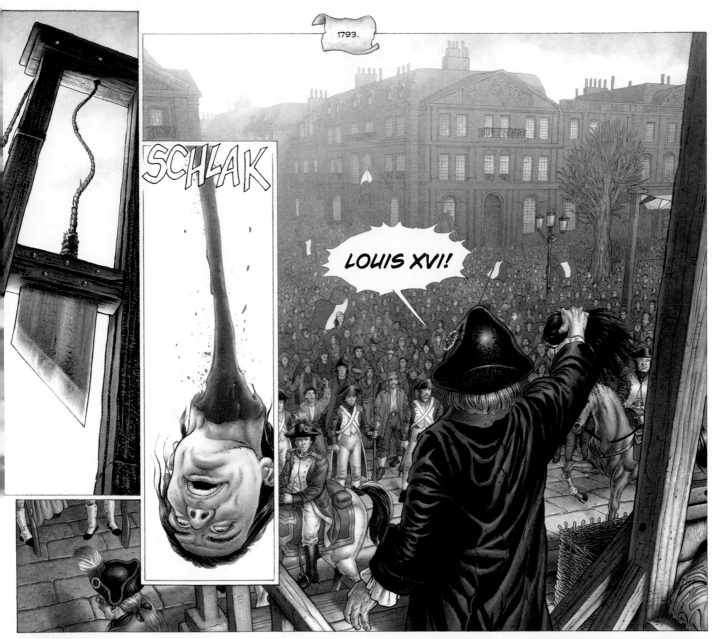

1793.

SCHLAK

LOUIS XVI!

FILTH! LONG LIVE THE REPUBLIC!

BRAVO!

ASSHOLE!

PARASITE!

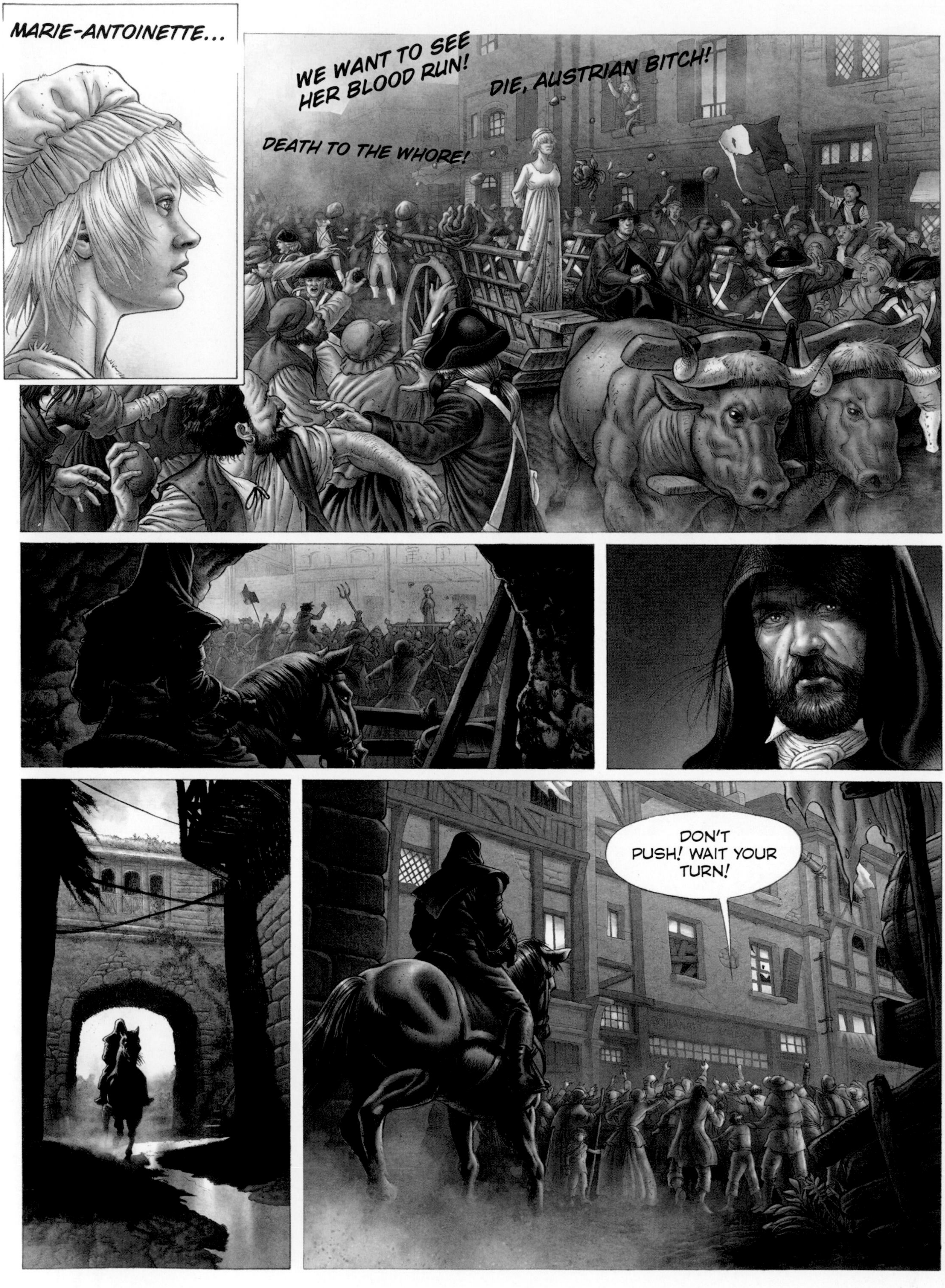
MARIE-ANTOINETTE...
WE WANT TO SEE HER BLOOD RUN!
DIE, AUSTRIAN BITCH!
DEATH TO THE WHORE!
DON'T PUSH! WAIT YOUR TURN!

SURELY NOT! THERE'S TOO MANY OF US!
THERE WON'T BE ENOUGH FOR EVERYONE.
CALM DOWN!
HHHUUUU...
???
STOP THERE! THERE'S NO SKIPPING TO THE FRONT. YOU QUEUE LIKE EVERYONE ELSE!
I AM YOUR MASTER. LET ME THROUGH!
OF COURSE, MY LORD. GO IN!

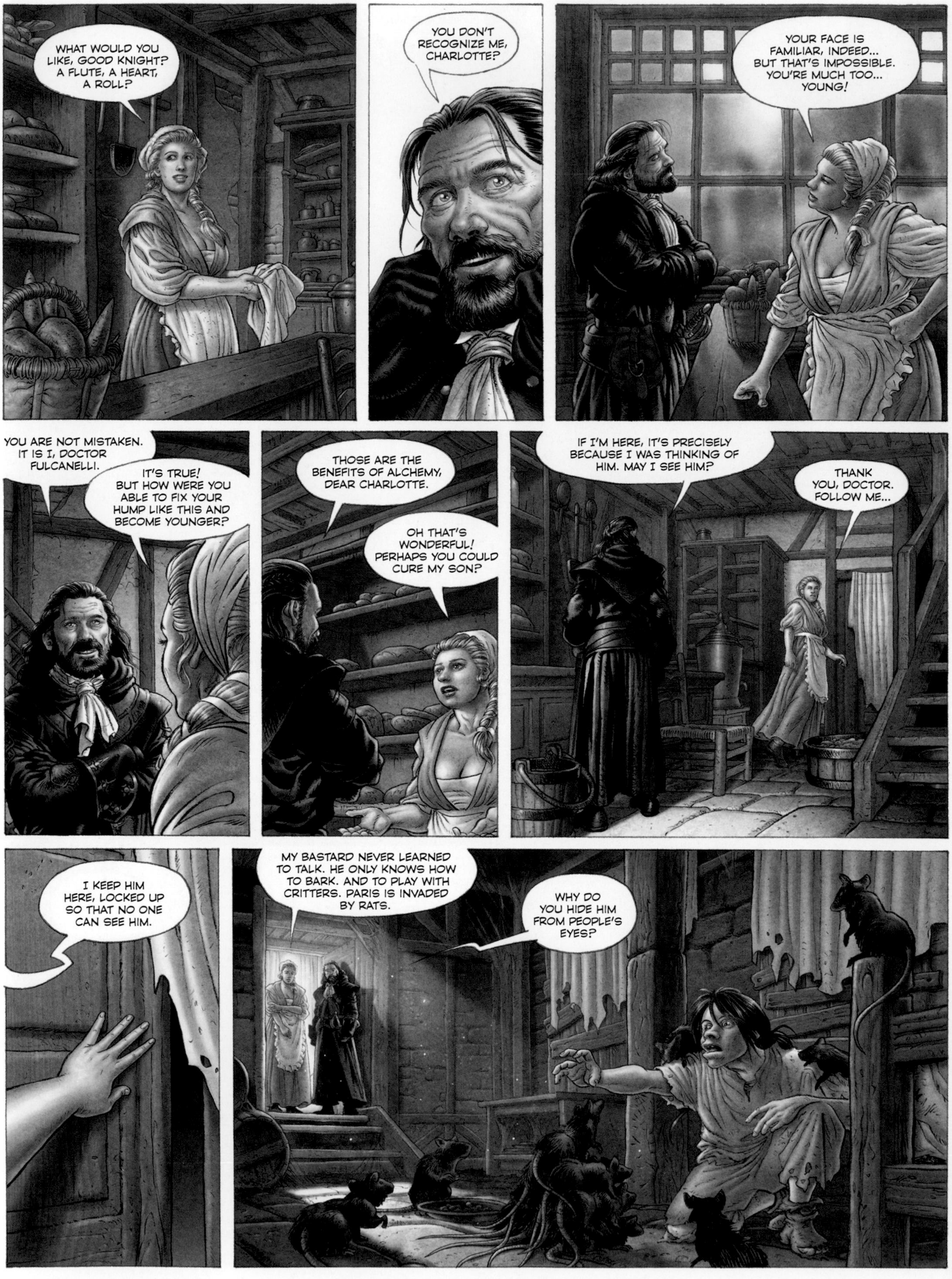
WHAT WOULD YOU LIKE, GOOD KNIGHT? A FLUTE, A HEART, A ROLL?
YOU DON'T RECOGNIZE ME, CHARLOTTE?
YOUR FACE IS FAMILIAR, INDEED... BUT THAT'S IMPOSSIBLE. YOU'RE MUCH TOO... YOUNG!
YOU ARE NOT MISTAKEN. IT IS I, DOCTOR FULCANELLI.
IT'S TRUE! BUT HOW WERE YOU ABLE TO FIX YOUR HUMP LIKE THIS AND BECOME YOUNGER?
THOSE ARE THE BENEFITS OF ALCHEMY, DEAR CHARLOTTE.
OH THAT'S WONDERFUL! PERHAPS YOU COULD CURE MY SON?
IF I'M HERE, IT'S PRECISELY BECAUSE I WAS THINKING OF HIM. MAY I SEE HIM?
THANK YOU, DOCTOR. FOLLOW ME...
I KEEP HIM HERE, LOCKED UP SO THAT NO ONE CAN SEE HIM.
MY BASTARD NEVER LEARNED TO TALK. HE ONLY KNOWS HOW TO BARK. AND TO PLAY WITH CRITTERS. PARIS IS INVADED BY RATS.
WHY DO YOU HIDE HIM FROM PEOPLE'S EYES?

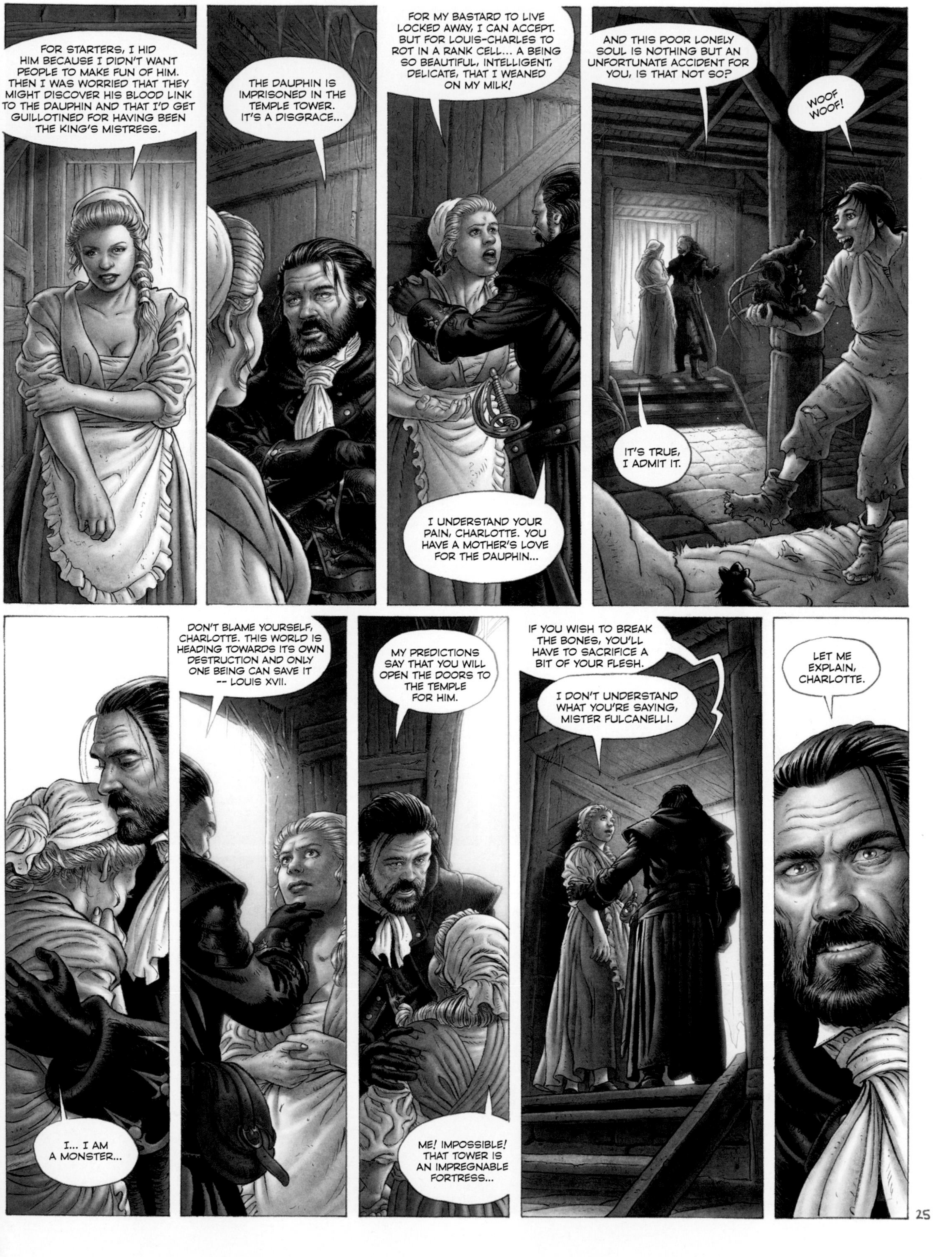
FOR STARTERS, I HID HIM BECAUSE I DIDN'T WANT PEOPLE TO MAKE FUN OF HIM. THEN I WAS WORRIED THAT THEY MIGHT DISCOVER HIS BLOOD LINK TO THE DAUPHIN AND THAT I'D GET GUILLOTINED FOR HAVING BEEN THE KING'S MISTRESS.
THE DAUPHIN IS IMPRISONED IN THE TEMPLE TOWER. IT'S A DISGRACE...
FOR MY BASTARD TO LIVE LOCKED AWAY, I CAN ACCEPT. BUT FOR LOUIS-CHARLES TO ROT IN A RANK CELL... A BEING SO BEAUTIFUL, INTELLIGENT, DELICATE, THAT I WEANED ON MY MILK!
I UNDERSTAND YOUR PAIN, CHARLOTTE. YOU HAVE A MOTHER'S LOVE FOR THE DAUPHIN...
AND THIS POOR LONELY SOUL IS NOTHING BUT AN UNFORTUNATE ACCIDENT FOR YOU, IS THAT NOT SO?
WOOF WOOF!
IT'S TRUE, I ADMIT IT.
I... I AM A MONSTER...
DON'T BLAME YOURSELF, CHARLOTTE. THIS WORLD IS HEADING TOWARDS ITS OWN DESTRUCTION AND ONLY ONE BEING CAN SAVE IT -- LOUIS XVII.
MY PREDICTIONS SAY THAT YOU WILL OPEN THE DOORS TO THE TEMPLE FOR HIM.
ME! IMPOSSIBLE! THAT TOWER IS AN IMPREGNABLE FORTRESS...
IF YOU WISH TO BREAK THE BONES, YOU'LL HAVE TO SACRIFICE A BIT OF YOUR FLESH.
I DON'T UNDERSTAND WHAT YOU'RE SAYING, MISTER FULCANELLI.
LET ME EXPLAIN, CHARLOTTE.

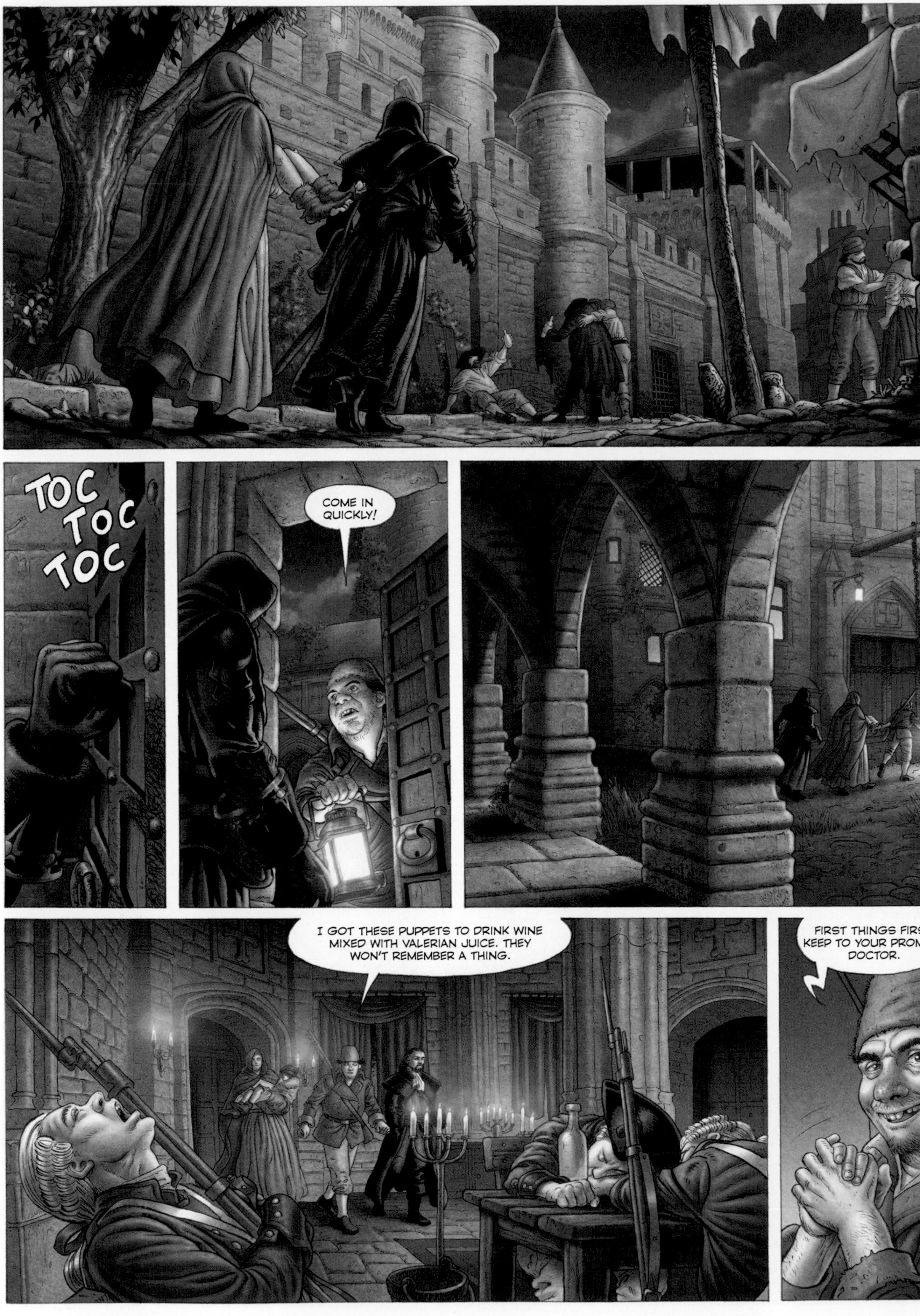
TOC TOC TOC
COME IN QUICKLY!
I GOT THESE PUPPETS TO DRINK WINE MIXED WITH VALERIAN JUICE. THEY WON'T REMEMBER A THING.
FIRST THINGS FIRST, KEEP TO YOUR PROMISE, DOCTOR.

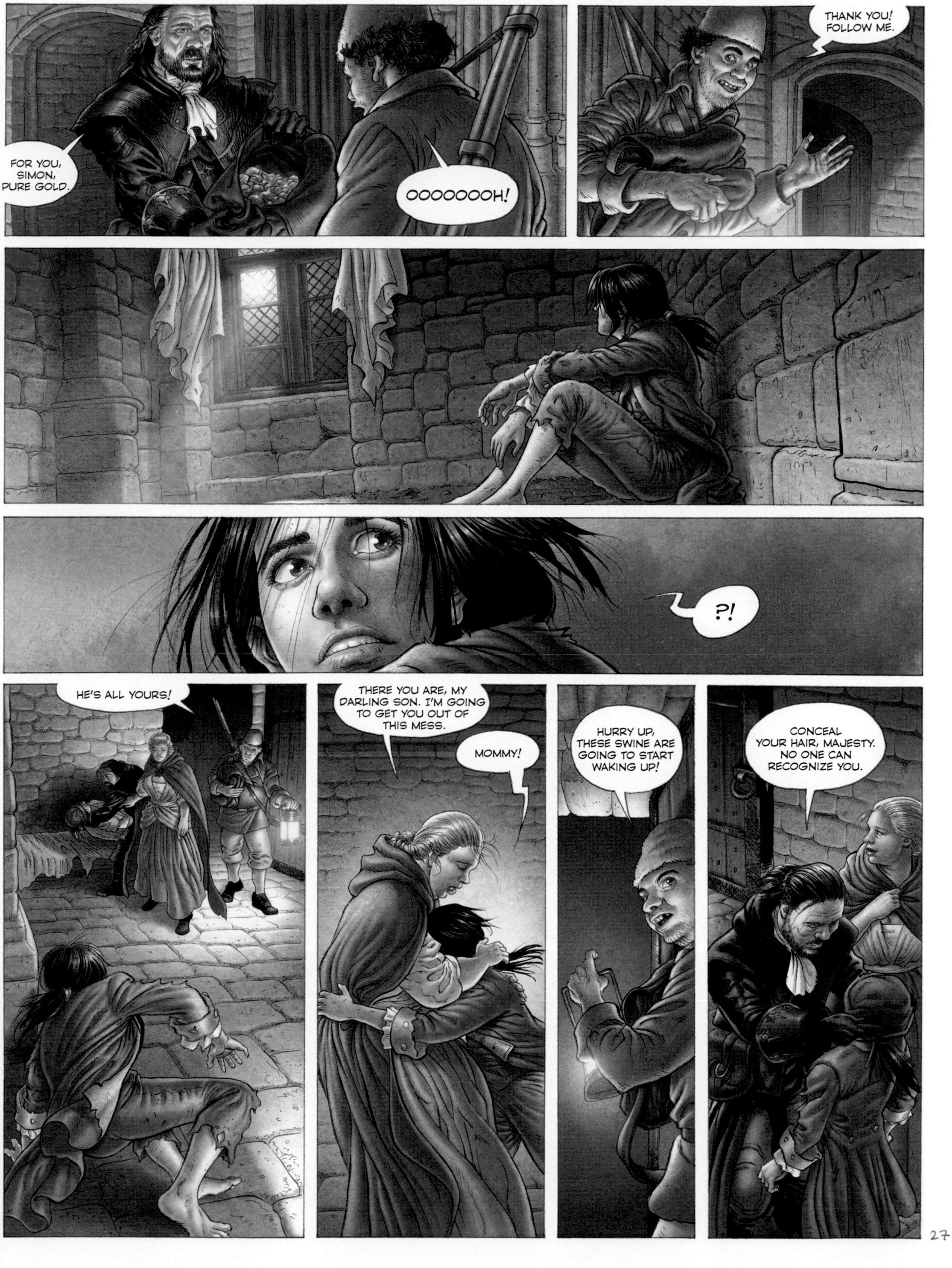
FOR YOU, SIMON, PURE GOLD.
OOOOOOOH!
THANK YOU! FOLLOW ME.
?!
HE'S ALL YOURS!
THERE YOU ARE, MY DARLING SON. I'M GOING TO GET YOU OUT OF THIS MESS.
MOMMY!
HURRY UP, THESE SWINE ARE GOING TO START WAKING UP!
CONCEAL YOUR HAIR, MAJESTY. NO ONE CAN RECOGNIZE YOU.

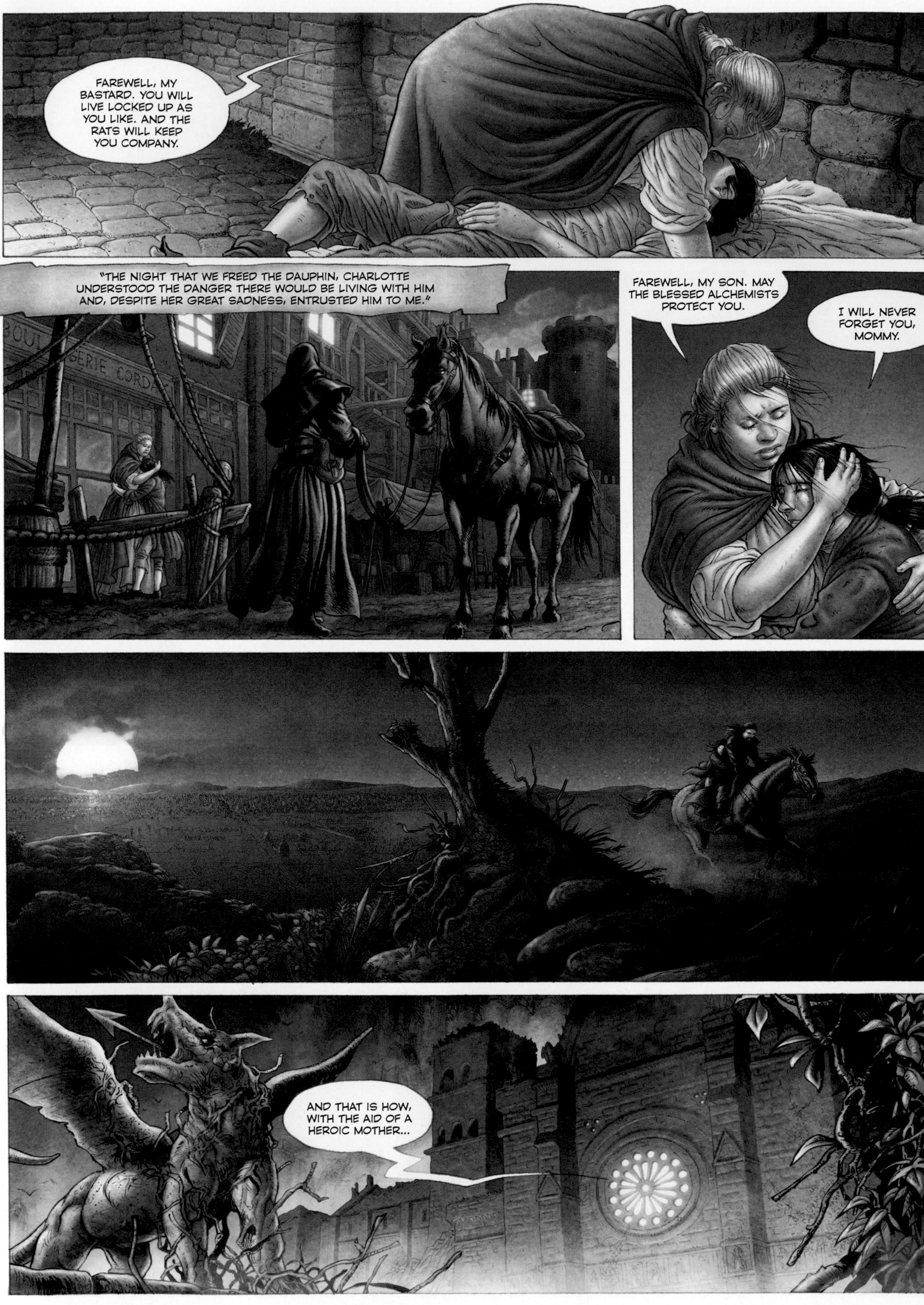
FAREWELL, MY BASTARD. YOU WILL LIVE LOCKED UP AS YOU LIKE. AND THE RATS WILL KEEP YOU COMPANY.
"THE NIGHT THAT WE FREED THE DAUPHIN, CHARLOTTE UNDERSTOOD THE DANGER THERE WOULD BE LIVING WITH HIM AND, DESPITE HER GREAT SADNESS, ENTRUSTED HIM TO ME."
FAREWELL, MY SON. MAY THE BLESSED ALCHEMISTS PROTECT YOU.
I WILL NEVER FORGET YOU, MOMMY.
AND THAT IS HOW, WITH THE AID OF A HEROIC MOTHER...

I WAS ABLE TO SAVE THE DAUPHIN.

BROTHER FULCANELLI, YOU DESERVE OUR CONGRATULATIONS. BUT ALTHOUGH TEN YEARS HAVE PASSED, THE BAKER CAN STILL REVEAL HOW THE CHILDREN WERE SWAPPED AND JEOPARDIZE OUR EXISTENCE.

NO, BROTHER IMHOTEP. IF I DUBBED HER HEROIC, IT'S BECAUSE THIS WOMAN DIED WITH OUR SECRET.

"SEVERAL DAYS AFTER SEVENTEEN AND I ARRIVED HERE, MARAT, A REBEL JOURNALIST, CONSIDERED THE EXISTENCE OF LOUIS XVII TO CONSTITUTE A THREAT TO THE REVOLUTION AND DECIDED TO ASSASSINATE HIM."

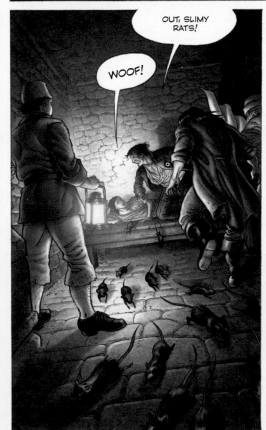

OUT, SLIMY RATS!

WOOF!

WAAAAHH!!!

THE KING IS DEAD!

LONG LIVE MARAT!

MY TROPHY! WE'RE DONE WITH THE BOURBONS!

29

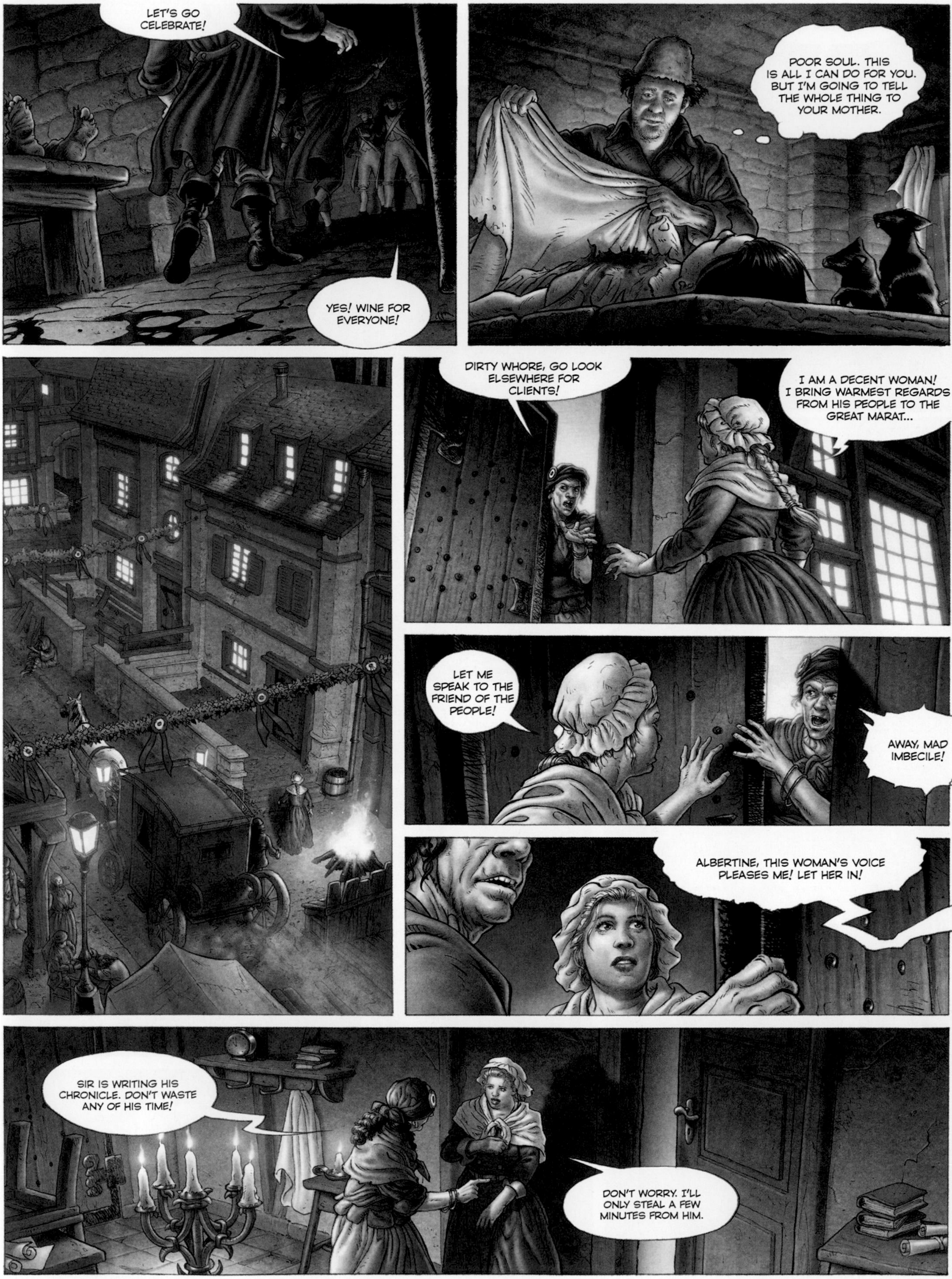
LET'S GO CELEBRATE!
YES! WINE FOR EVERYONE!
POOR SOUL. THIS IS ALL I CAN DO FOR YOU. BUT I'M GOING TO TELL THE WHOLE THING TO YOUR MOTHER.
DIRTY WHORE, GO LOOK ELSEWHERE FOR CLIENTS!
I AM A DECENT WOMAN! I BRING WARMEST REGARDS FROM HIS PEOPLE TO THE GREAT MARAT...
LET ME SPEAK TO THE FRIEND OF THE PEOPLE!
AWAY, MAD IMBECILE!
ALBERTINE, THIS WOMAN'S VOICE PLEASES ME! LET HER IN!
SIR IS WRITING HIS CHRONICLE. DON'T WASTE ANY OF HIS TIME!
DON'T WORRY. I'LL ONLY STEAL A FEW MINUTES FROM HIM.

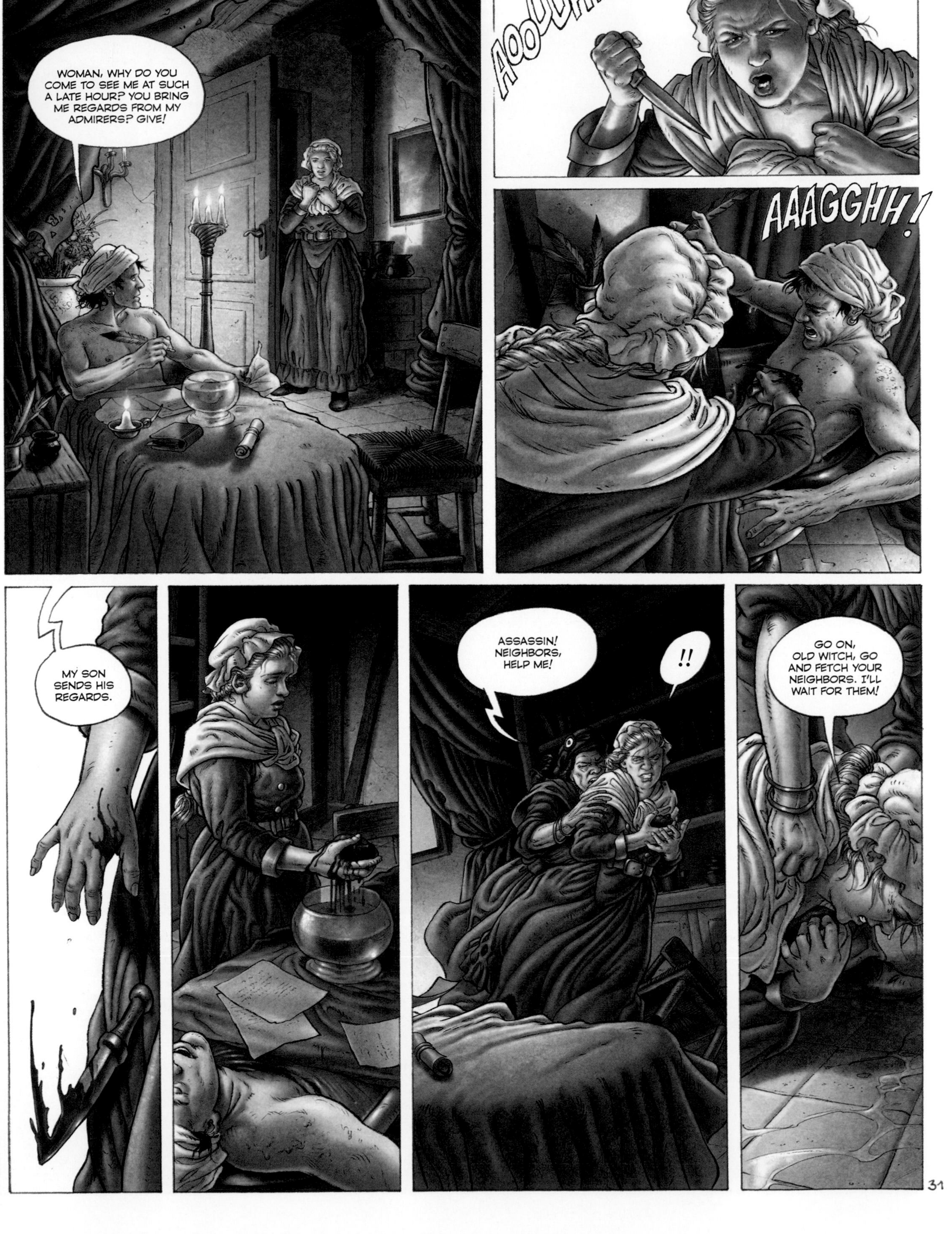
WOMAN, WHY DO YOU COME TO SEE ME AT SUCH A LATE HOUR? YOU BRING ME REGARDS FROM MY ADMIRERS? GIVE!
AOOUUHH!
AAAGGHH!
MY SON SENDS HIS REGARDS.
ASSASSIN! NEIGHBORS, HELP ME!
!!
GO ON, OLD WITCH, GO AND FETCH YOUR NEIGHBORS. I'LL WAIT FOR THEM!

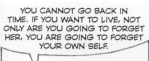

CHARLOTTE CORDAY WAS GUILLOTINED ON JULY 17TH 1793.

MARIE-ANTOINETTE NEVER SHOWED ME THE SLIGHTEST TENDERNESS, THE SLIGHTEST ATTENTION. CHARLOTTE WAS MY TRUE MOTHER, THE ONE WHO REMAINS IN MY MEMORY.

YOU CANNOT GO BACK IN TIME. IF YOU WANT TO LIVE, NOT ONLY ARE YOU GOING TO FORGET HER, YOU ARE GOING TO FORGET YOUR OWN SELF.

PHEW, I CAN'T GO ON! MY FEET ARE BLOODY, MASTER NOSTRODAMUS... AND THIS SACK IS SO HEAVY IT'S SAWING THROUGH MY SHOULDERS...

HANG ON, SON. THIS SACK WEIGHS EXACTLY THE SAME AS YOUR BODY. AND YOUR FEET ARE BLEEDING LIKE YOUR MEMORY... IF YOU WANT TO BE FREE, TO BECOME WHAT YOU TRULY ARE, YOU MUST BECOME AWARE OF WHAT IT IS THAT SHACKLES YOU.

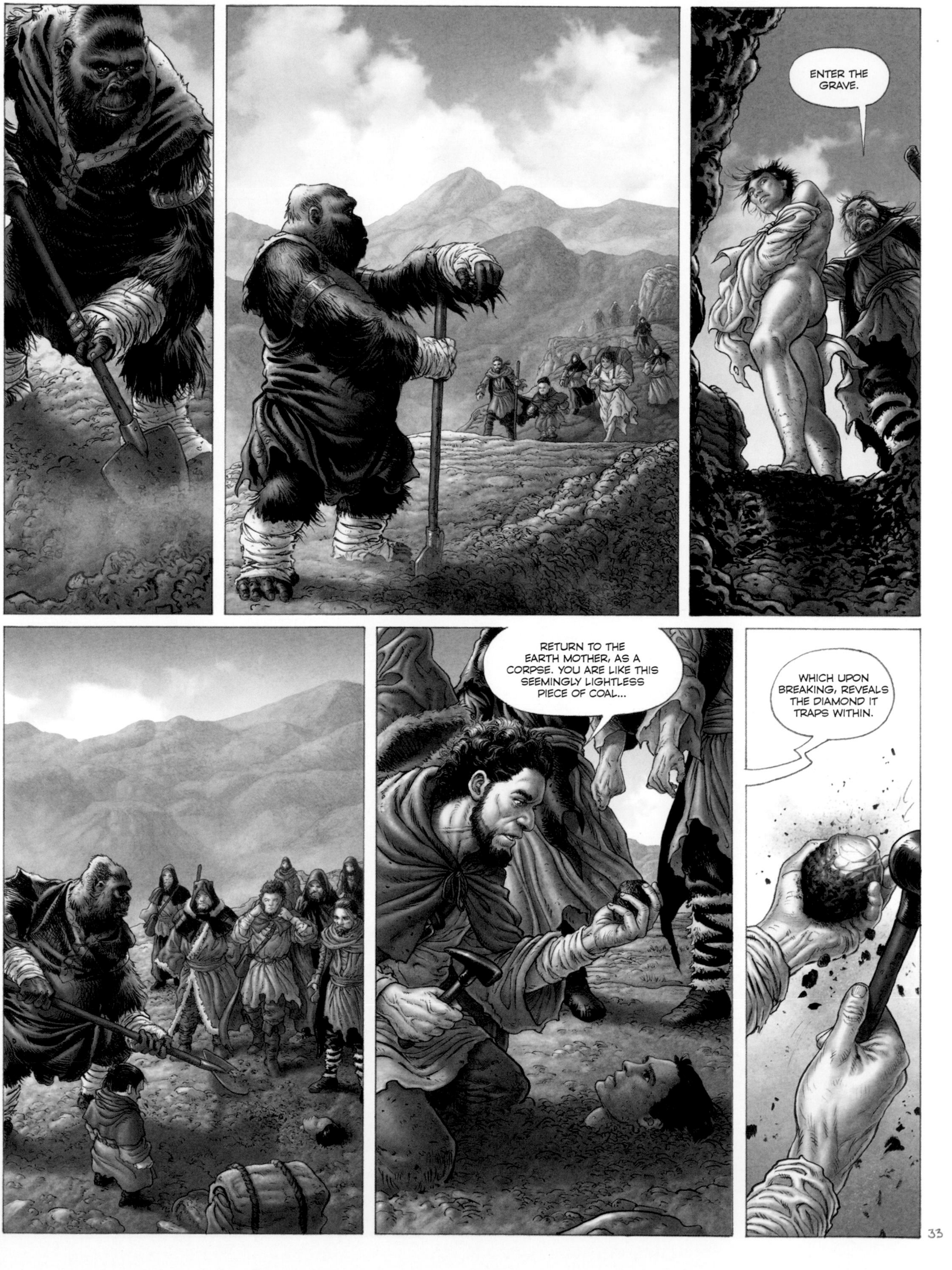
ENTER THE GRAVE.
RETURN TO THE EARTH MOTHER, AS A CORPSE. YOU ARE LIKE THIS SEEMINGLY LIGHTLESS PIECE OF COAL...
WHICH UPON BREAKING, REVEALS THE DIAMOND IT TRAPS WITHIN.

YOU, UNDEAD, DO LIKEWISE -- FREE YOURSELF FROM YOUR MEMORY, CEASE BEING THAT UNHAPPY KING LOUIS XVII.

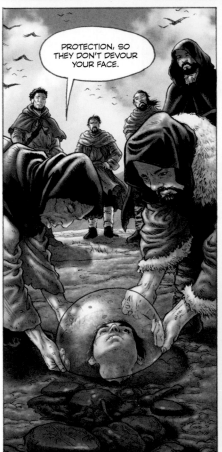

PROTECTION, SO THEY DON'T DEVOUR YOUR FACE.

THIS MEAT THE RAVENS ARE EATING, IMAGINE IT'S THE FLESH WHICH IMPRISONS YOUR PURER SPIRIT, YOUR CLEAR CONSCIOUSNESS. UNMAKE THESE ILLUSIONS TO FINALLY BE YOURSELF!

WE WILL COME DIG YOU OUT IN SEVEN HOURS. LEARN TO DIE!

3

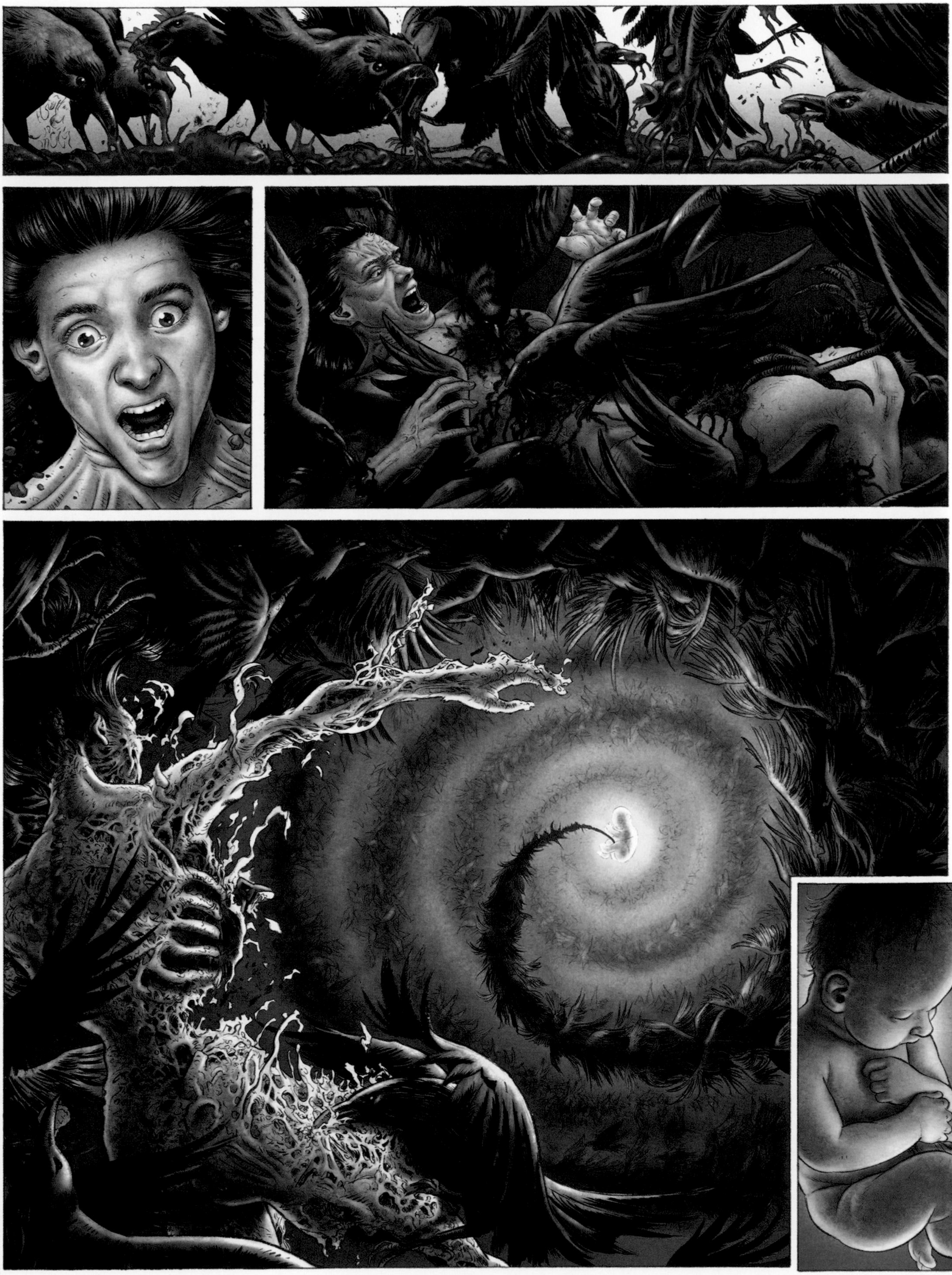

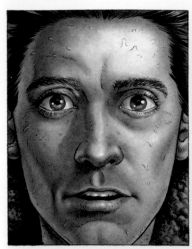

THANK YOU... THANK YOU FOR PULLING ME FROM THIS WOMB WHERE I DIED AND WAS RESURRECTED A THOUSAND TIMES...

MAY YOU BE BLESSED BY THIS WATER, AS YOU ARE BY YOUR TEARS... YOU CAN BE PROUD...

YOU LIVE AGAIN IN A NEW BEING, WITHOUT PAST AND WITHOUT NAME, WITHOUT NATION, WITHOUT AGE, WITHOUT DEFINITION. FREE!

IN THE NAME OF THE UNIVERSAL AGENT, OUR UNIQUE GOD, WE WILL CALL YOU COUNT ASLAMAR, OR COUNTESS, DEPENDING.

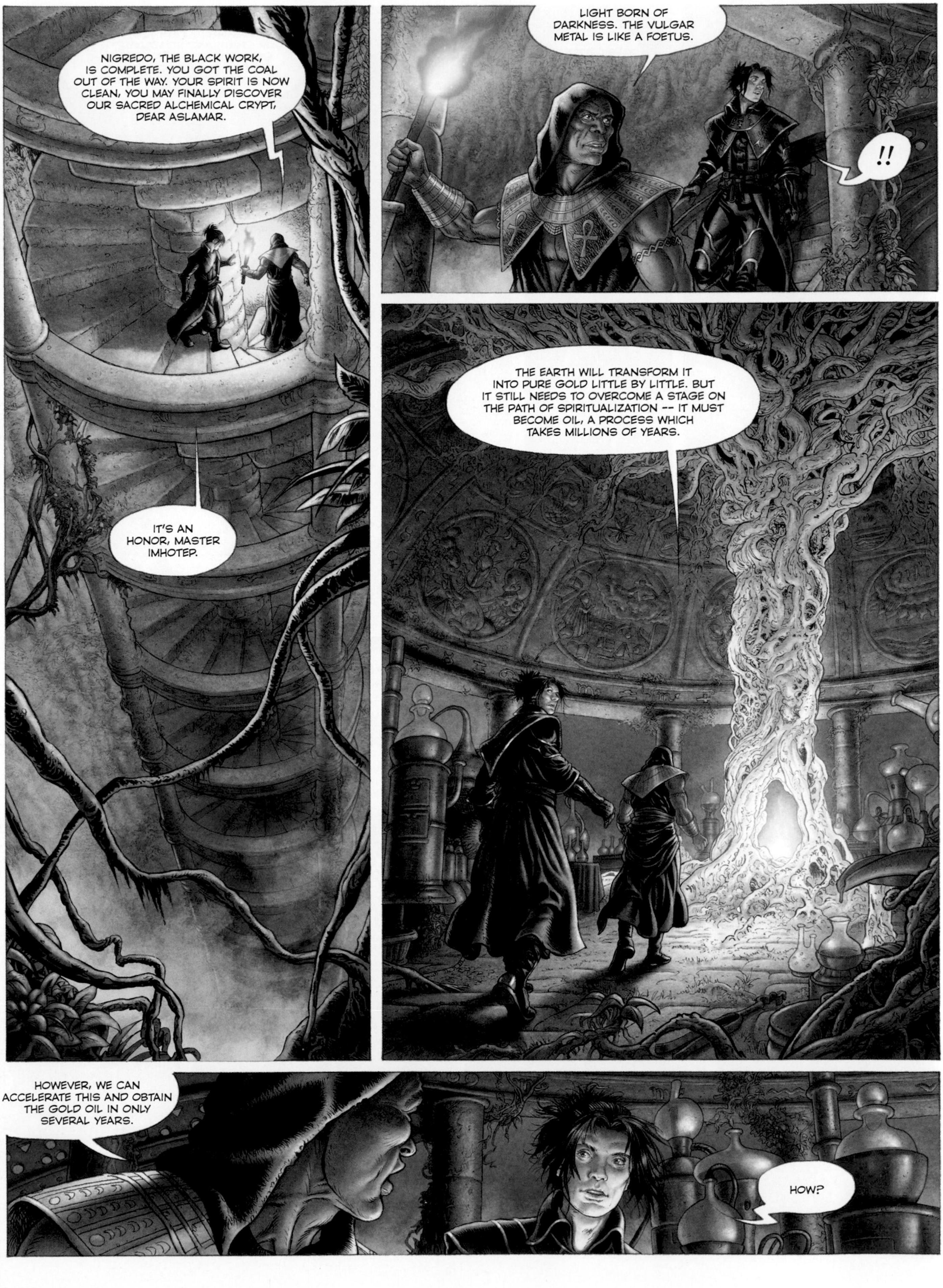

NIGREDO, THE BLACK WORK, IS COMPLETE. YOU GOT THE COAL OUT OF THE WAY. YOUR SPIRIT IS NOW CLEAN, YOU MAY FINALLY DISCOVER OUR SACRED ALCHEMICAL CRYPT, DEAR ASLAMAR.
IT'S AN HONOR, MASTER IMHOTEP.
LIGHT BORN OF DARKNESS. THE VULGAR METAL IS LIKE A FOETUS.
!!
THE EARTH WILL TRANSFORM IT INTO PURE GOLD LITTLE BY LITTLE. BUT IT STILL NEEDS TO OVERCOME A STAGE ON THE PATH OF SPIRITUALIZATION -- IT MUST BECOME OIL, A PROCESS WHICH TAKES MILLIONS OF YEARS.
HOWEVER, WE CAN ACCELERATE THIS AND OBTAIN THE GOLD OIL IN ONLY SEVERAL YEARS.
HOW?

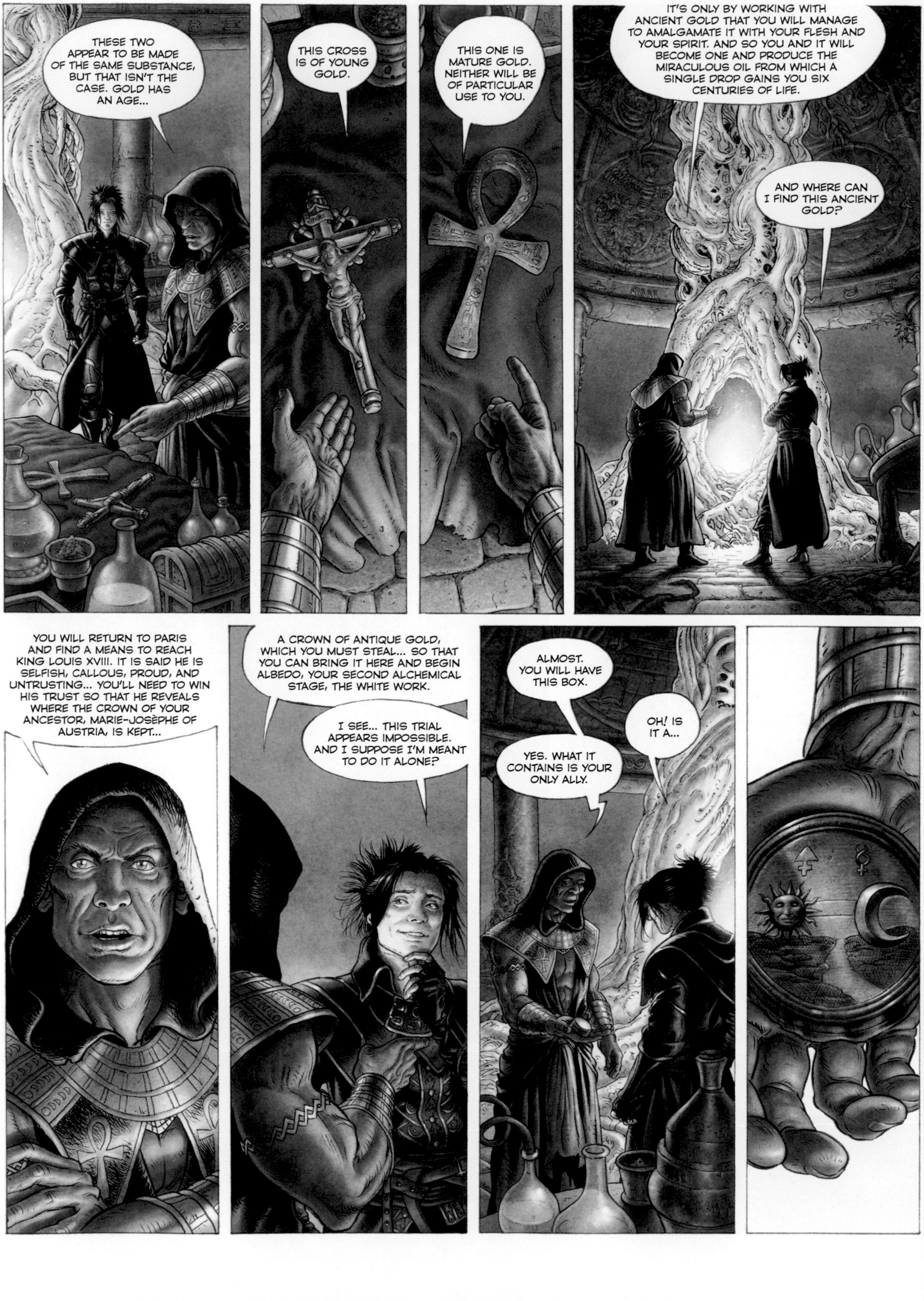
THESE TWO APPEAR TO BE MADE OF THE SAME SUBSTANCE, BUT THAT ISN'T THE CASE. GOLD HAS AN AGE...
THIS CROSS IS OF YOUNG GOLD.
THIS ONE IS MATURE GOLD. NEITHER WILL BE OF PARTICULAR USE TO YOU.
IT'S ONLY BY WORKING WITH ANCIENT GOLD THAT YOU WILL MANAGE TO AMALGAMATE IT WITH YOUR FLESH AND YOUR SPIRIT. AND SO YOU AND IT WILL BECOME ONE AND PRODUCE THE MIRACULOUS OIL FROM WHICH A SINGLE DROP GAINS YOU SIX CENTURIES OF LIFE.
AND WHERE CAN I FIND THIS ANCIENT GOLD?
YOU WILL RETURN TO PARIS AND FIND A MEANS TO REACH KING LOUIS XVIII. IT IS SAID HE IS SELFISH, CALLOUS, PROUD, AND UNTRUSTING... YOU'LL NEED TO WIN HIS TRUST SO THAT HE REVEALS WHERE THE CROWN OF YOUR ANCESTOR, MARIE-JOSÈPHE OF AUSTRIA, IS KEPT...
A CROWN OF ANTIQUE GOLD, WHICH YOU MUST STEAL... SO THAT YOU CAN BRING IT HERE AND BEGIN ALBEDO, YOUR SECOND ALCHEMICAL STAGE, THE WHITE WORK.
I SEE... THIS TRIAL APPEARS IMPOSSIBLE. AND I SUPPOSE I'M MEANT TO DO IT ALONE?
ALMOST. YOU WILL HAVE THIS BOX.
OH! IS IT A...
YES. WHAT IT CONTAINS IS YOUR ONLY ALLY.

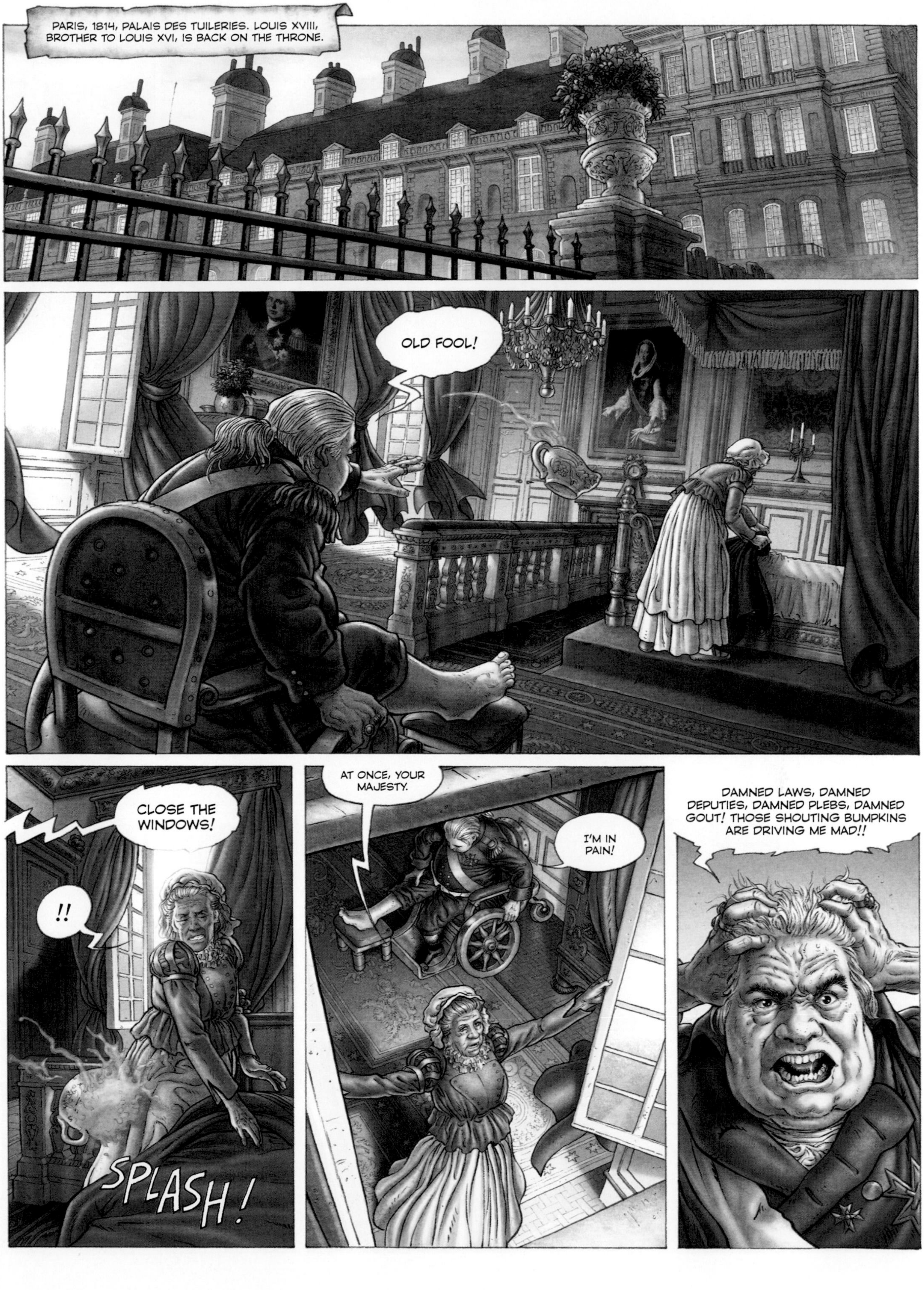
PARIS, 1814, PALAIS DES TUILERIES. LOUIS XVIII, BROTHER TO LOUIS XVI, IS BACK ON THE THRONE.
OLD FOOL!
CLOSE THE WINDOWS!
!!
SPLASH!
AT ONCE, YOUR MAJESTY.
I'M IN PAIN!
DAMNED LAWS, DAMNED DEPUTIES, DAMNED PLEBS, DAMNED GOUT! THOSE SHOUTING BUMPKINS ARE DRIVING ME MAD!!

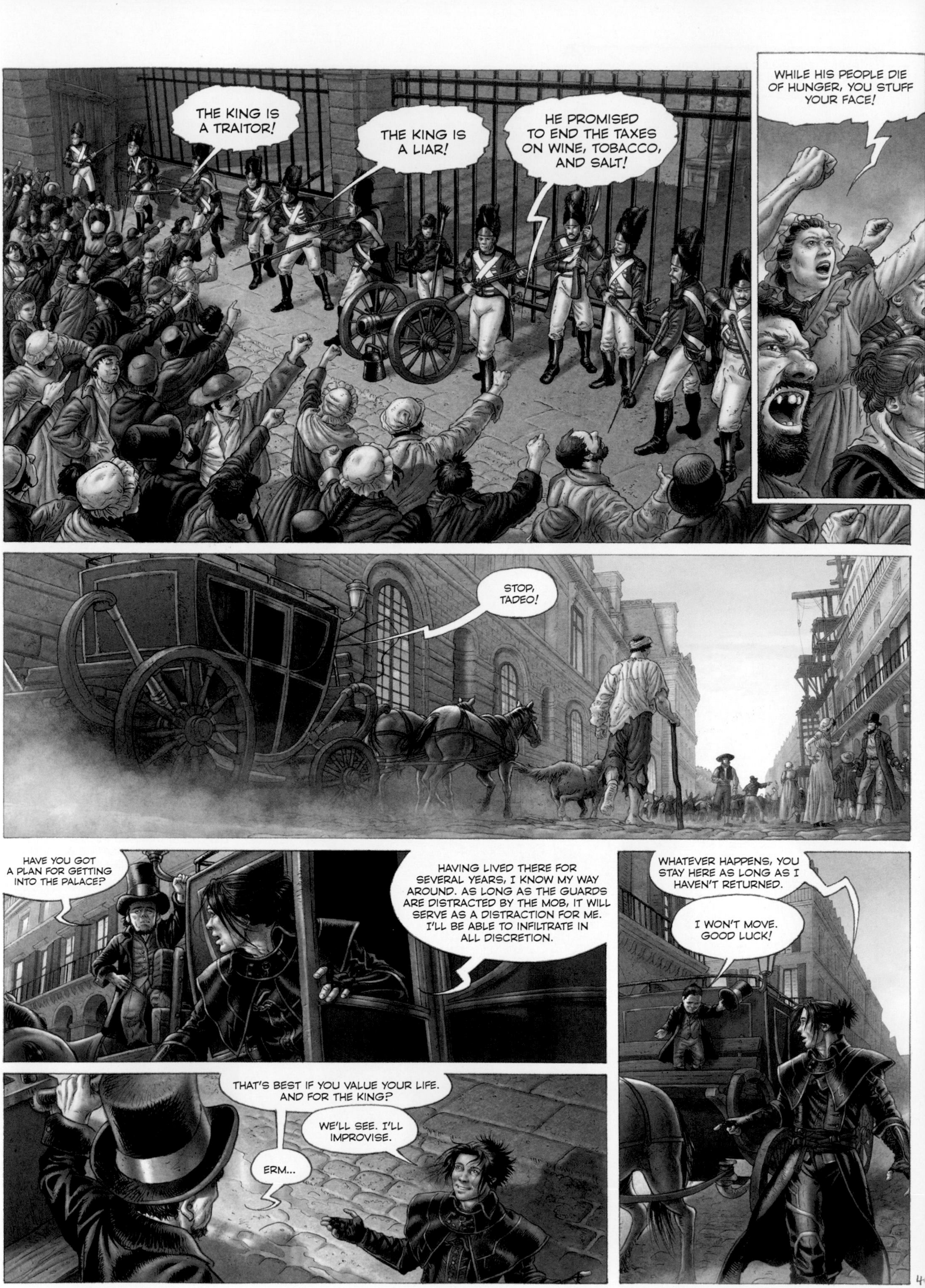
THE KING IS A TRAITOR!
THE KING IS A LIAR!
HE PROMISED TO END THE TAXES ON WINE, TOBACCO, AND SALT!
WHILE HIS PEOPLE DIE OF HUNGER, YOU STUFF YOUR FACE!
STOP, TADEO!
HAVE YOU GOT A PLAN FOR GETTING INTO THE PALACE?
HAVING LIVED THERE FOR SEVERAL YEARS, I KNOW MY WAY AROUND. AS LONG AS THE GUARDS ARE DISTRACTED BY THE MOB, IT WILL SERVE AS A DISTRACTION FOR ME. I'LL BE ABLE TO INFILTRATE IN ALL DISCRETION.
THAT'S BEST IF YOU VALUE YOUR LIFE. AND FOR THE KING?
WE'LL SEE. I'LL IMPROVISE.
ERM...
WHATEVER HAPPENS, YOU STAY HERE AS LONG AS I HAVEN'T RETURNED.
I WON'T MOVE. GOOD LUCK!

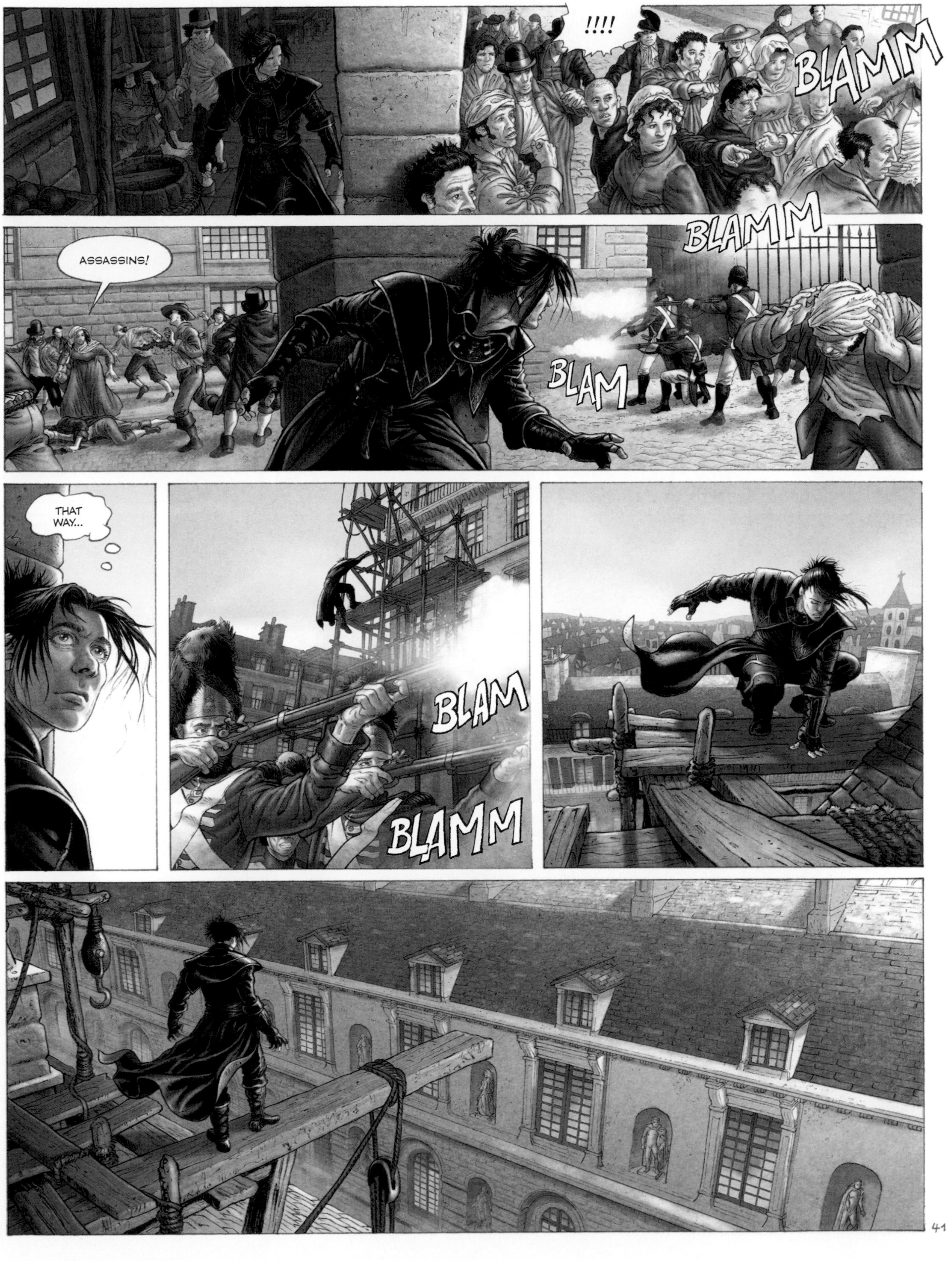
!!!!
BLAMM
ASSASSINS!
BLAMM
BLAM
THAT WAY...
BLAM
BLAMM

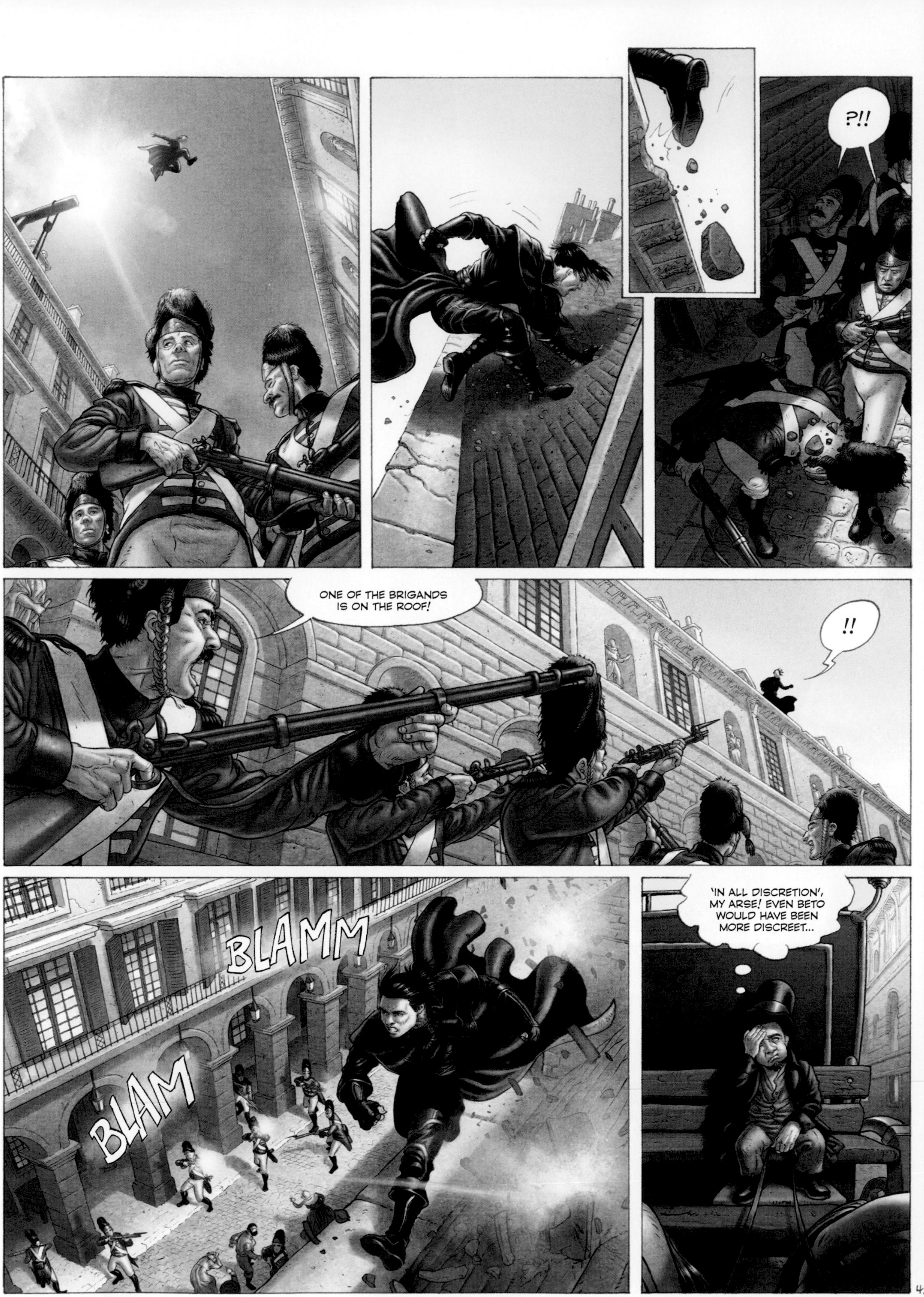
?!!
ONE OF THE BRIGANDS IS ON THE ROOF!
!!
BLAMM
BLAM
'IN ALL DISCRETION', MY ARSE! EVEN BETO WOULD HAVE BEEN MORE DISCREET...

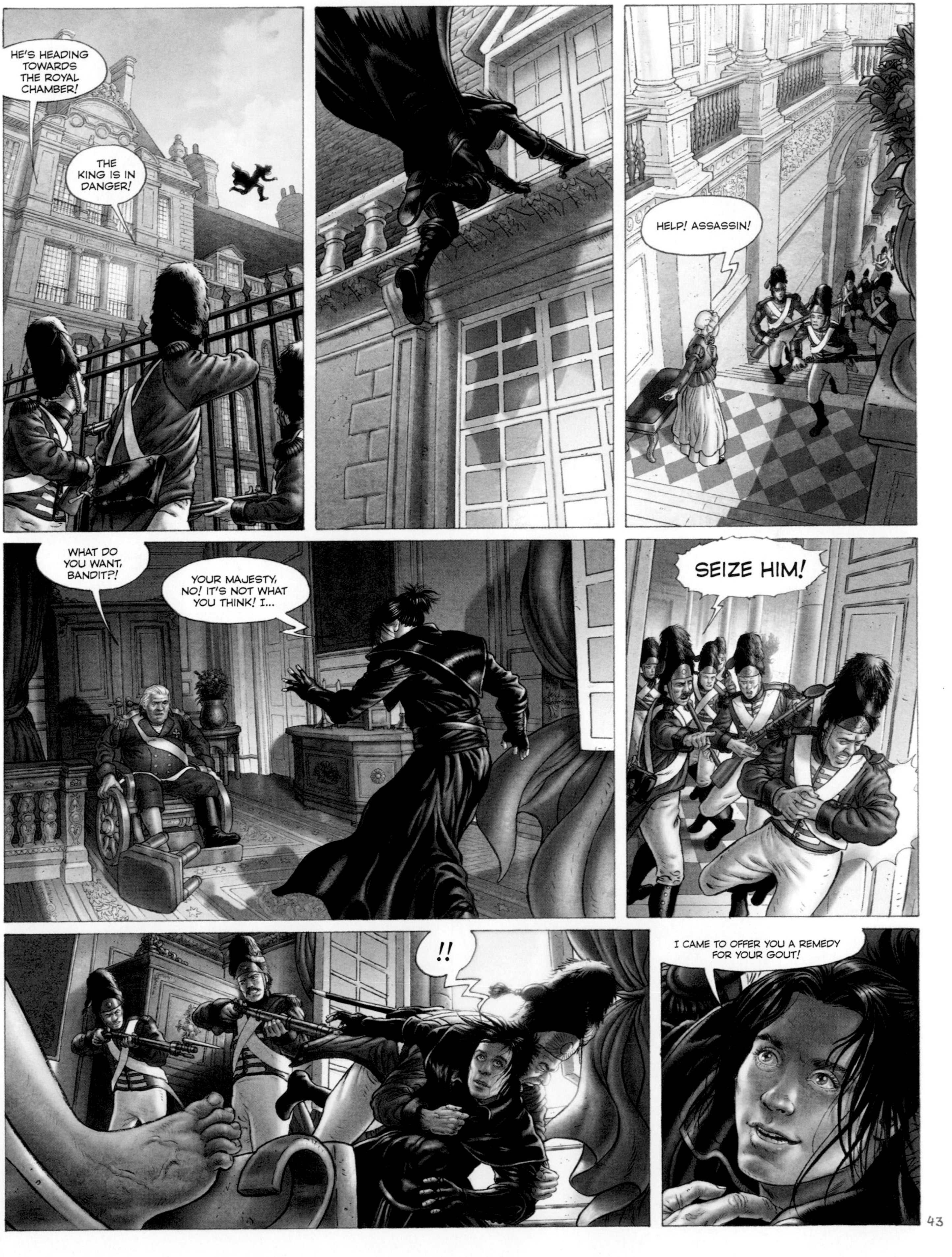
HE'S HEADING TOWARDS THE ROYAL CHAMBER!
THE KING IS IN DANGER!
HELP! ASSASSIN!
WHAT DO YOU WANT, BANDIT?!
YOUR MAJESTY, NO! IT'S NOT WHAT YOU THINK! I...
SEIZE HIM!
!!
I CAME TO OFFER YOU A REMEDY FOR YOUR GOUT!

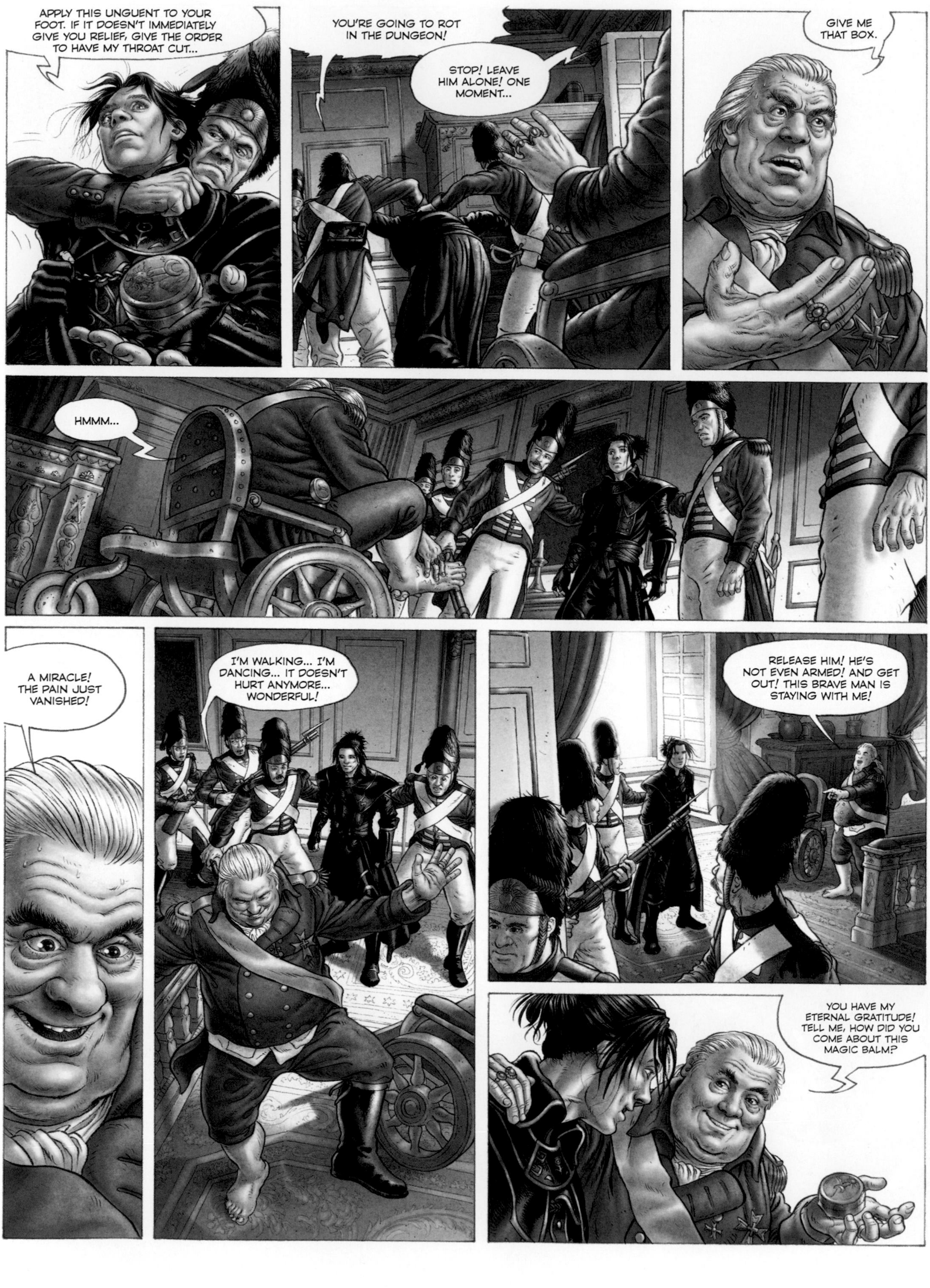
APPLY THIS UNGUENT TO YOUR FOOT. IF IT DOESN'T IMMEDIATELY GIVE YOU RELIEF, GIVE THE ORDER TO HAVE MY THROAT CUT...
YOU'RE GOING TO ROT IN THE DUNGEON!
STOP! LEAVE HIM ALONE! ONE MOMENT...
GIVE ME THAT BOX.
HMMM...
A MIRACLE! THE PAIN JUST VANISHED!
I'M WALKING... I'M DANCING... IT DOESN'T HURT ANYMORE... WONDERFUL!
RELEASE HIM! HE'S NOT EVEN ARMED! AND GET OUT! THIS BRAVE MAN IS STAYING WITH ME!
YOU HAVE MY ETERNAL GRATITUDE! TELL ME, HOW DID YOU COME ABOUT THIS MAGIC BALM?

ERM... MY GRANDFATHER WAS AN ALCHEMIST, YOUR MAJESTY. HE CONFIDED IT TO ME ON HIS DEATHBED, AND TOLD ME, 'THIS REMEDY IS FOR THE GOOD KING'.

AND YOU RISKED YOUR LIFE TO BRING IT TO ME! WHAT DO YOU WISH IN EXCHANGE FOR THIS ENORMOUS FAVOR?

SIRE... I WISH ONLY TO SERVE YOU...

BECOME YOUR BODYGUARD!

A SCRAWNY WEAKLING LIKE YOURSELF? WOULD THAT YOU COULD EVEN MANAGE THE WEIGHT OF A SWORD?

SIRE, I AM THE FINEST SWORDSMAN IN THE KINGDOM... I CAN SHOW YOU!

HA! HAHAHA! AND HOW?

GIVE THE ORDER TO ARRANGE A COMBAT BETWEEN YOUR BEST FENCING MASTERS AND MYSELF.

HAHAHAHA! I OWE YOU THIS FAVOR! EVEN IF YOU END UP CRIPPLED FOR LIFE!

I'M GOING TO COMMAND MY CHAMBERLAIN TO SUMMON THEM IMMEDIATELY. THE COMBAT WILL TAKE PLACE IN OUR THEATER, THIS VERY DAY!

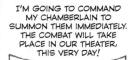

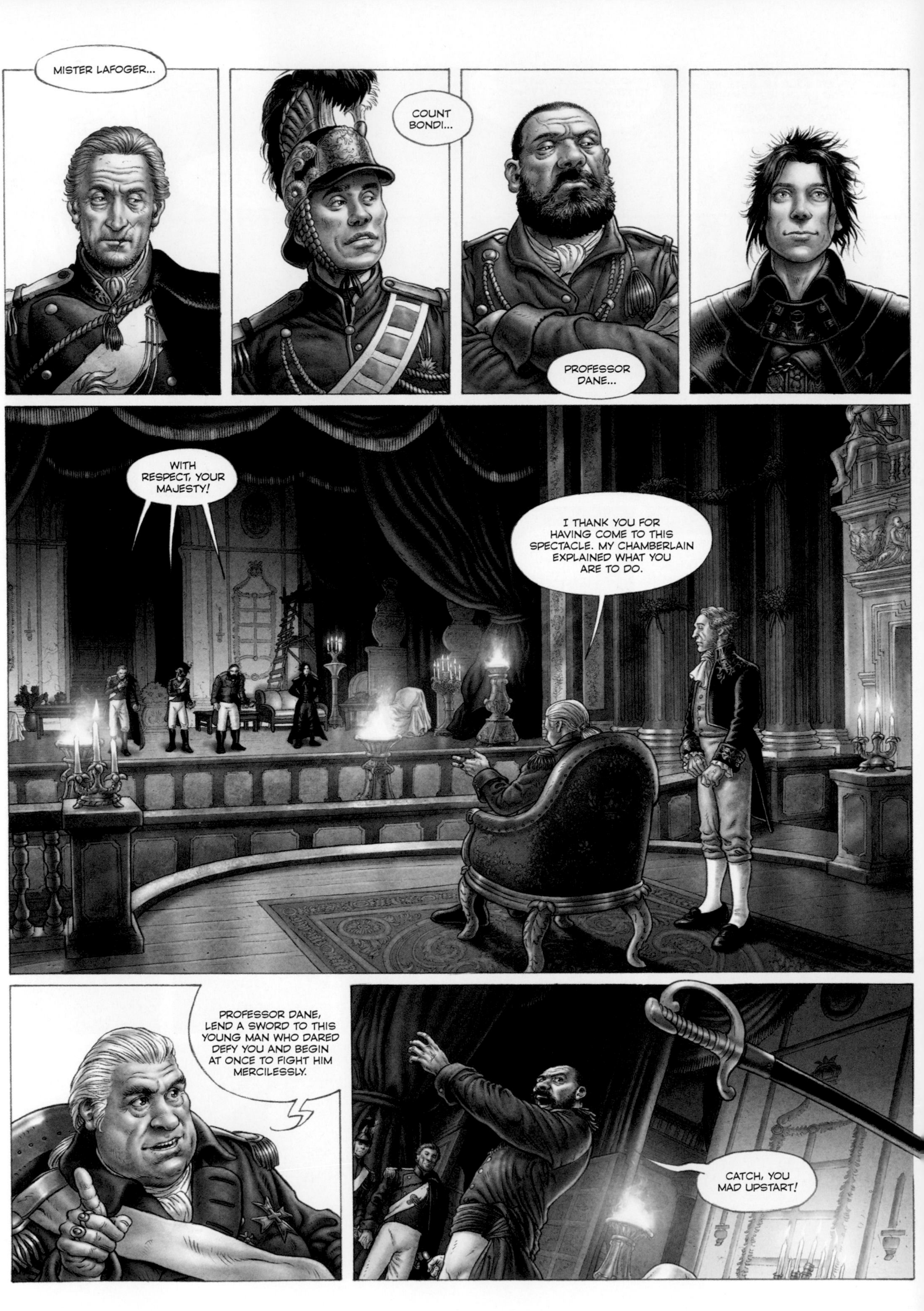
MISTER LAFOGER...
COUNT BONDI...
PROFESSOR DANE...
WITH RESPECT, YOUR MAJESTY!
I THANK YOU FOR HAVING COME TO THIS SPECTACLE. MY CHAMBERLAIN EXPLAINED WHAT YOU ARE TO DO.
PROFESSOR DANE, LEND A SWORD TO THIS YOUNG MAN WHO DARED DEFY YOU AND BEGIN AT ONCE TO FIGHT HIM MERCILESSLY.
CATCH, YOU MAD UPSTART!

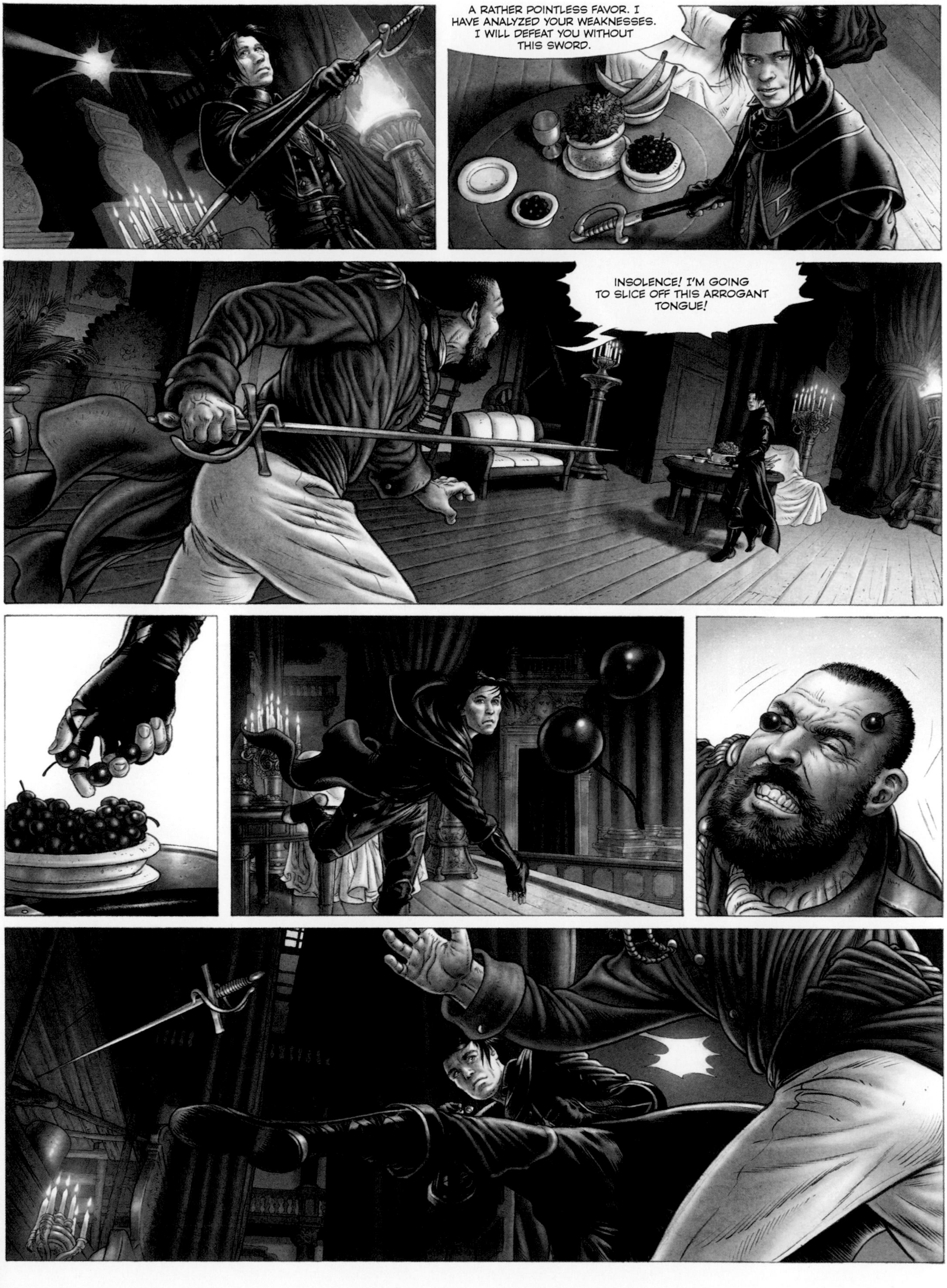
A RATHER POINTLESS FAVOR. I HAVE ANALYZED YOUR WEAKNESSES. I WILL DEFEAT YOU WITHOUT THIS SWORD.
INSOLENCE! I'M GOING TO SLICE OFF THIS ARROGANT TONGUE!

KLING!

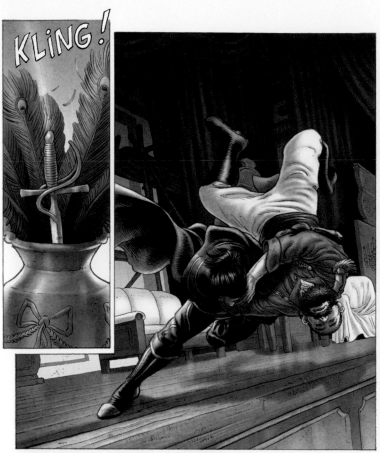

SCOUNDREL! YOU TRICKED ME!

FORGIVE ME YOUR MAJESTY, BUT PERMIT ME TO RENOUNCE THIS COMBAT. IF IT'S ALLOWED TO BE WON AT ANY COST, THEN WHY NOT JUST ARM THIS INSOLENT WITH A MUSKET?

SIRE, I ACCEPT THIS COMBAT BY SWORD IF THE LORD BONDI CEASES TO HIDE BEHIND THESE COWARDLY EXCUSES AND IS WILLING TO GO UP AGAINST ME.

NO ONE CALLS COUNT BONDI A COWARD! YOU'RE GOING TO PAY FOR THIS INSULT WITH YOUR LIFE! EN-GARDE!

EN-GARDE!

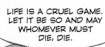

EVEN IF I USE IT LIKE A MACE, A SWORD IS A SWORD...

BRAVO, YOUNG MAN! YOU'RE BEGINNING TO CONVINCE ME! YOUR TURN, MISTER LAFOGER.

IT IS MY DUTY, YOUR MAJESTY, TO WARN YOU THAT THIS LITTLE GAME IS HENCEFORTH A DUEL TO THE DEATH.

LIFE IS A CRUEL GAME. LET IT BE SO AND MAY WHOEVER MUST DIE, DIE.

49

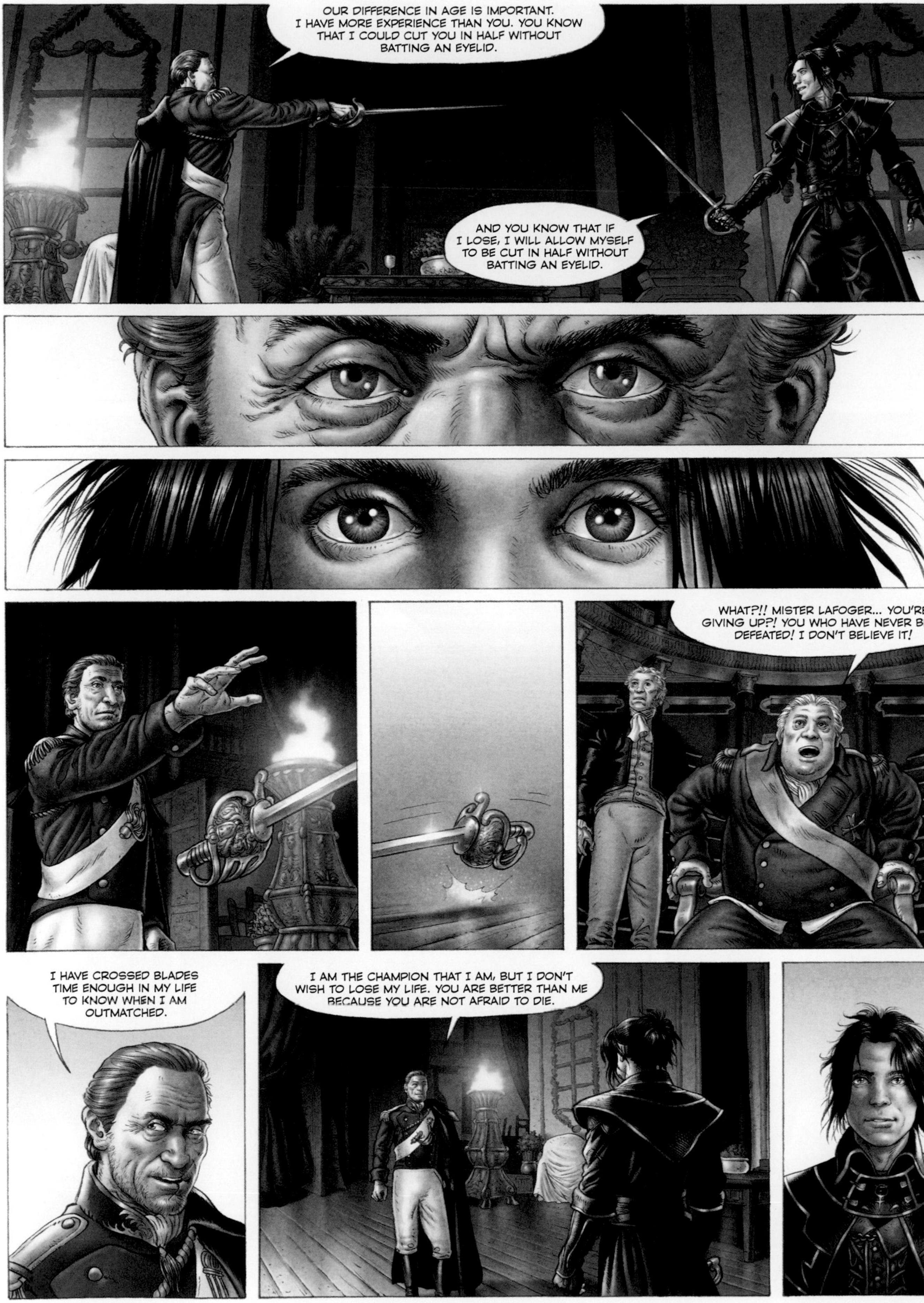
OUR DIFFERENCE IN AGE IS IMPORTANT. I HAVE MORE EXPERIENCE THAN YOU. YOU KNOW THAT I COULD CUT YOU IN HALF WITHOUT BATTING AN EYELID.
AND YOU KNOW THAT IF I LOSE, I WILL ALLOW MYSELF TO BE CUT IN HALF WITHOUT BATTING AN EYELID.
WHAT?!! MISTER LAFOGER... YOU'RE GIVING UP?! YOU WHO HAVE NEVER BEEN DEFEATED! I DON'T BELIEVE IT!
I HAVE CROSSED BLADES TIME ENOUGH IN MY LIFE TO KNOW WHEN I AM OUTMATCHED.
I AM THE CHAMPION THAT I AM, BUT I DON'T WISH TO LOSE MY LIFE. YOU ARE BETTER THAN ME BECAUSE YOU ARE NOT AFRAID TO DIE.

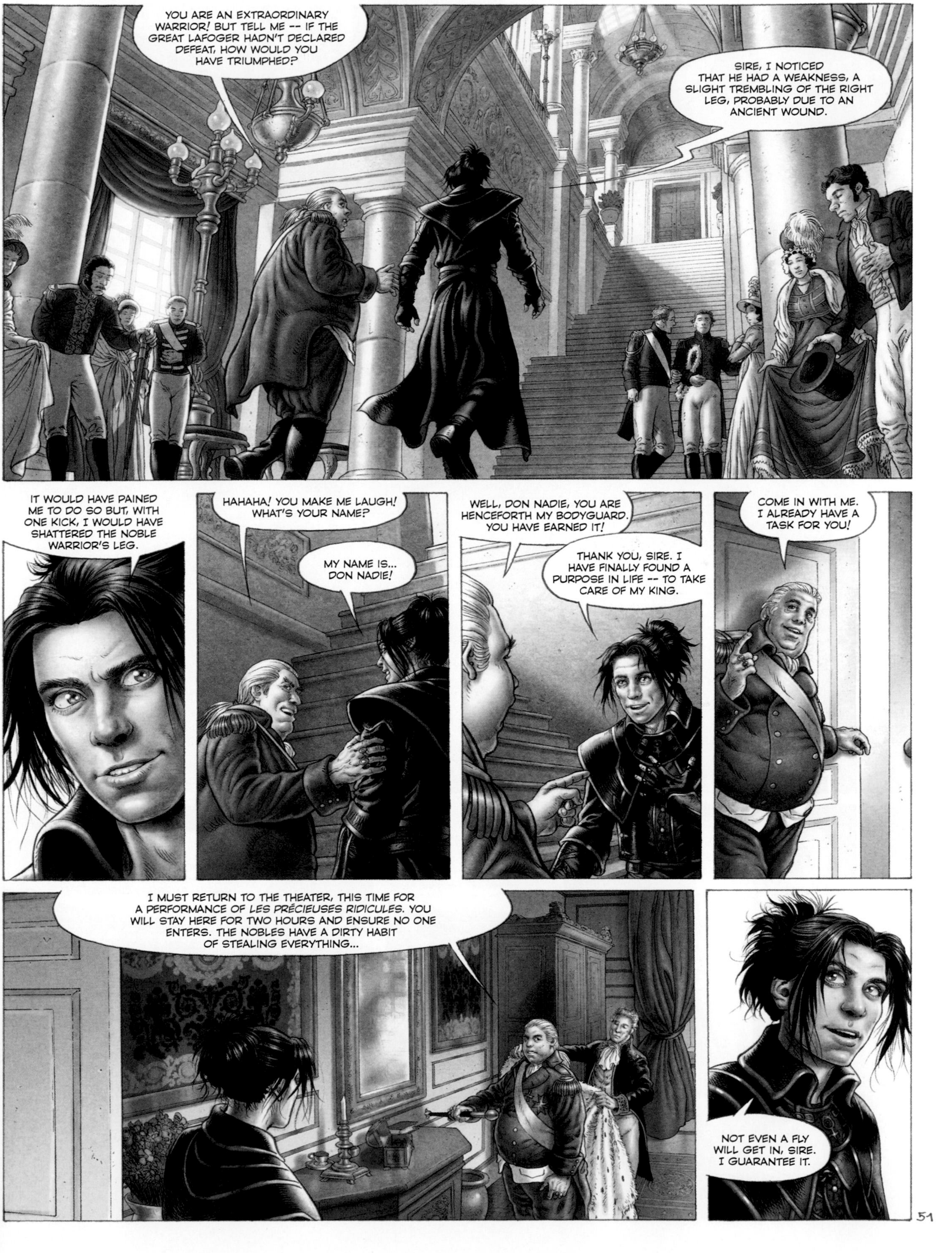
YOU ARE AN EXTRAORDINARY WARRIOR! BUT TELL ME -- IF THE GREAT LAFOGER HADN'T DECLARED DEFEAT, HOW WOULD YOU HAVE TRIUMPHED?
SIRE, I NOTICED THAT HE HAD A WEAKNESS, A SLIGHT TREMBLING OF THE RIGHT LEG, PROBABLY DUE TO AN ANCIENT WOUND.
IT WOULD HAVE PAINED ME TO DO SO BUT, WITH ONE KICK, I WOULD HAVE SHATTERED THE NOBLE WARRIOR'S LEG.
HAHAHA! YOU MAKE ME LAUGH! WHAT'S YOUR NAME?
MY NAME IS... DON NADIE!
WELL, DON NADIE, YOU ARE HENCEFORTH MY BODYGUARD. YOU HAVE EARNED IT!
THANK YOU, SIRE. I HAVE FINALLY FOUND A PURPOSE IN LIFE -- TO TAKE CARE OF MY KING.
COME IN WITH ME. I ALREADY HAVE A TASK FOR YOU!
I MUST RETURN TO THE THEATER, THIS TIME FOR A PERFORMANCE OF *LES PRÉCIEUSES RIDICULES*. YOU WILL STAY HERE FOR TWO HOURS AND ENSURE NO ONE ENTERS. THE NOBLES HAVE A DIRTY HABIT OF STEALING EVERYTHING...
NOT EVEN A FLY WILL GET IN, SIRE. I GUARANTEE IT.

I ASSURE YOU, YOUR MAJESTY, THESE ARE MATURE TOMATOES, FULL OF JUICE...

VERY GOOD! I WILL BOMBARD THE ACTORS WITH THEM. THAT WAY, AT LEAST, I AM CERTAIN TO LAUGH AT THIS COMEDY!

NOTHING... NOTHING... NOTHING... AND HALF AN HOUR BEFORE THE KING RETURNS... WHERE IN THE DEVIL COULD HE HAVE HIDDEN THE CROWN?

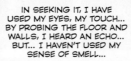

THINK... MASTER FULCANELLI WOULD ADVISE ME TO... MAKE FULL USE OF MY SENSES.

IN SEEKING IT, I HAVE USED MY EYES, MY TOUCH... BY PROBING THE FLOOR AND WALLS, I HEARD AN ECHO... BUT... I HAVEN'T USED MY SENSE OF SMELL...

SNIFF... SNIFF... PERFUMES... CONCEALING WITHIN THEIR PLEASANT SMELLS THE NAUSEATING ODOR OF... SNIFF... SNIFF... EXCREMENT?!!

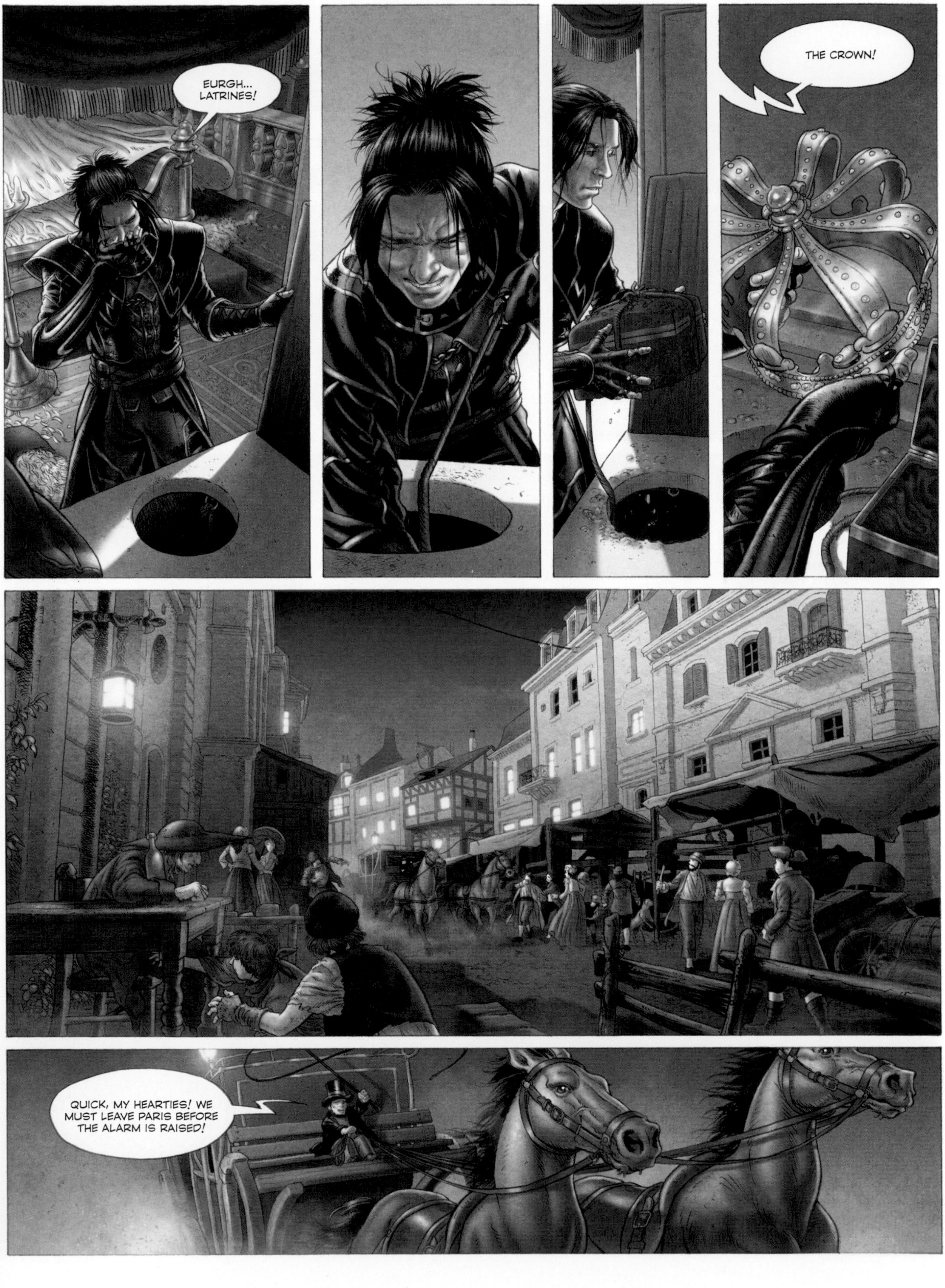
EURGH... LATRINES!
THE CROWN!
QUICK, MY HEARTIES! WE MUST LEAVE PARIS BEFORE THE ALARM IS RAISED!

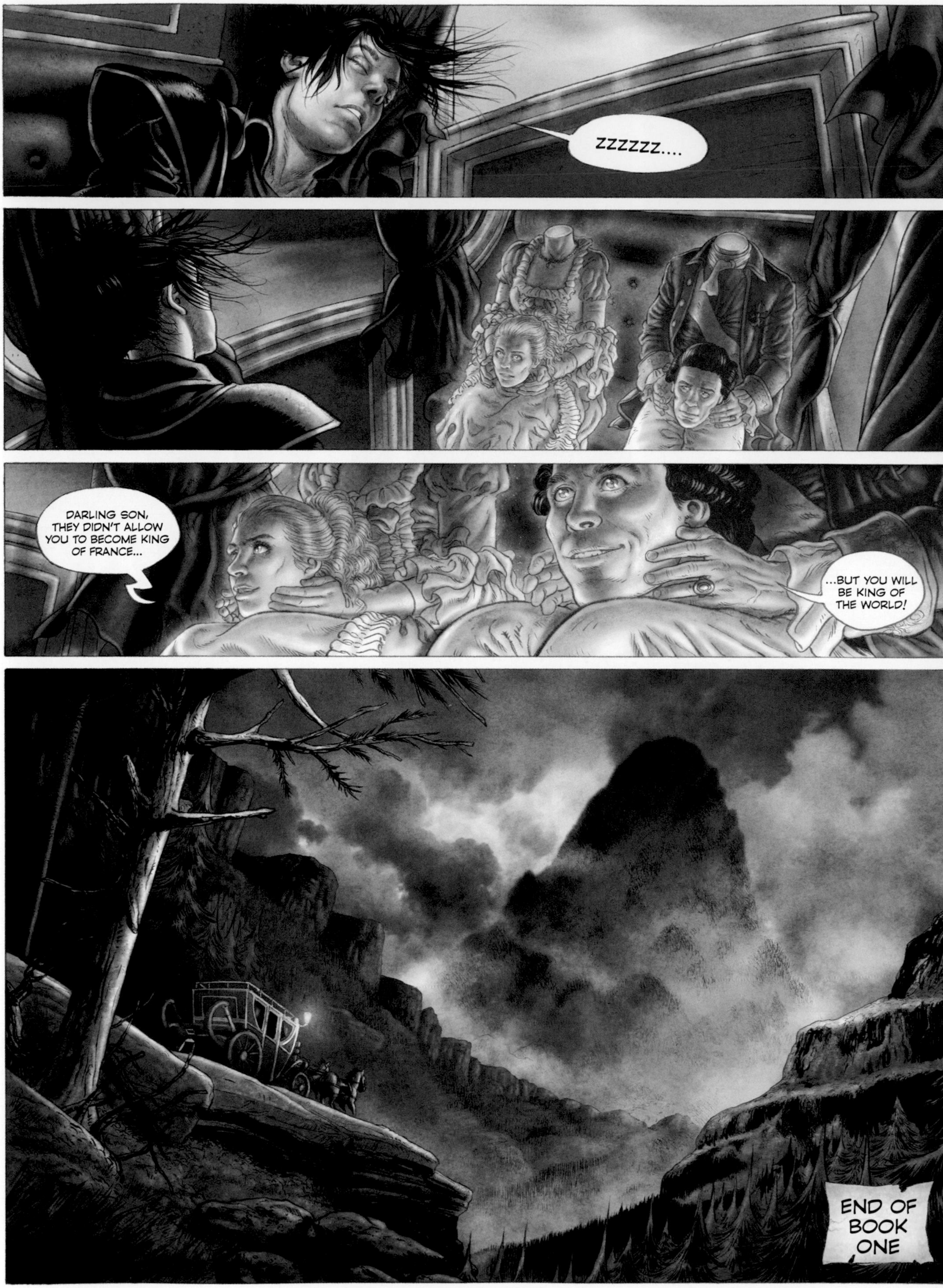
ZZZZZZ....
DARLING SON, THEY DIDN'T ALLOW YOU TO BECOME KING OF FRANCE...
...BUT YOU WILL BE KING OF THE WORLD!
END OF BOOK ONE

THE KNIGHTS OF HELIOPOLIS

NINE ALCHEMISTS WHO, BY BREWING THE ELIXIR
OF LONG LIFE, CAN LIVE FOR 300 CENTURIES.

FUXI, BORN IN 2852 BC, ONE OF THE FIRST
KINGS OF CHINA, INVENTOR OF WRITING
AND THE I CHING HEXAGRAMS.

IMHOTEP, BORN IN 2700 BC, GRAND
PRIEST OF THE SACRED CITY OF HELIOPOLIS,
IN EGYPT. AUTHOR OF THE OLDEST TEXTS
IN MEDICINE AND ASTRONOMY.

LAO TZU, BORN IN THE 4TH CENTURY BC,
THE GREATEST PHILOSOPHER IN CHINESE
HISTORY. HE WROTE THE TAO TE CHING,
AN ESSENTIAL WORK OF TAOISM.

EZEKIEL, BORN IN 595 BC, A HEBREW
PROPHET, AUTHOR OF THE BOOK OF EZEKIEL,
IN WHICH HE MADE IMPORTANT REVELATIONS
IN THE FORM OF SYMBOLIC VISIONS.

JOHN, APOSTLE, AUTHOR OF THE APOCALYPSE
(NEW TESTAMENT). THE YOUNGEST DISCIPLE
AND THE MOST LOVED BY JESUS.

NOSTRADAMUS, BORN IN 1503, DOCTOR AND
ASTROLOGIST OF JEWISH ORIGIN, AUTHOR OF
PROPHECIES IN WHICH HE PREDICTS SEVERAL
GLOBAL DISASTERS, FROM 1555 TO 3797.

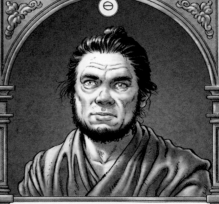

THE COUNT DE SAINT-GERMAIN, BORN IN
1712, OF UNKNOWN NATIONALITY, SPOKE 11
LANGUAGES TO PERFECTION, CARRIED ON HIS
PERSON NUMEROUS DIAMONDS THAT HE USED
AS MONEY, WAS ADVISOR TO LOUIS XV.

FULCANELLI, AGE UNKNOWN, AUTHOR
OF BOOKS ON ALCHEMY, RESTORER OF
FRENCH GOTHIC CATHEDRALS.

TADEO, AGE AND ORIGIN UNKNOWN, MASTER
OF MARTIAL ARTS. HE COULD BE THE APOSTLE
JUDE THADDAEUS, WHOM THE EVANGELISTS
IDENTIFIED AS THE BROTHER OF JESUS.

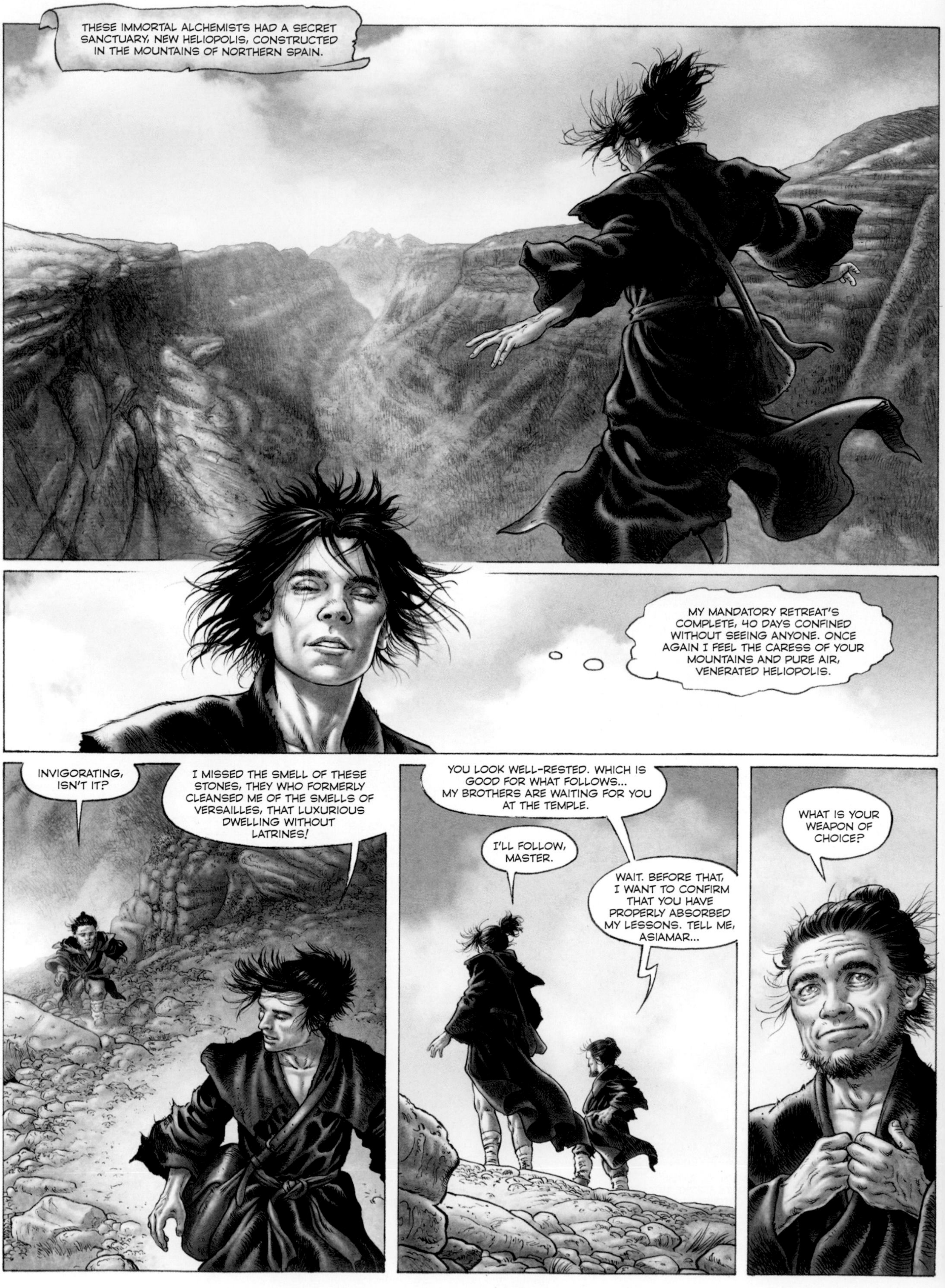
THESE IMMORTAL ALCHEMISTS HAD A SECRET SANCTUARY, NEW HELIOPOLIS, CONSTRUCTED IN THE MOUNTAINS OF NORTHERN SPAIN.
MY MANDATORY RETREAT'S COMPLETE, 40 DAYS CONFINED WITHOUT SEEING ANYONE. ONCE AGAIN I FEEL THE CARESS OF YOUR MOUNTAINS AND PURE AIR, VENERATED HELIOPOLIS.
INVIGORATING, ISN'T IT?
I MISSED THE SMELL OF THESE STONES, THEY WHO FORMERLY CLEANSED ME OF THE SMELLS OF VERSAILLES, THAT LUXURIOUS DWELLING WITHOUT LATRINES!
YOU LOOK WELL-RESTED. WHICH IS GOOD FOR WHAT FOLLOWS... MY BROTHERS ARE WAITING FOR YOU AT THE TEMPLE.
I'LL FOLLOW, MASTER.
WAIT. BEFORE THAT, I WANT TO CONFIRM THAT YOU HAVE PROPERLY ABSORBED MY LESSONS. TELL ME, ASIAMAR...
WHAT IS YOUR WEAPON OF CHOICE?

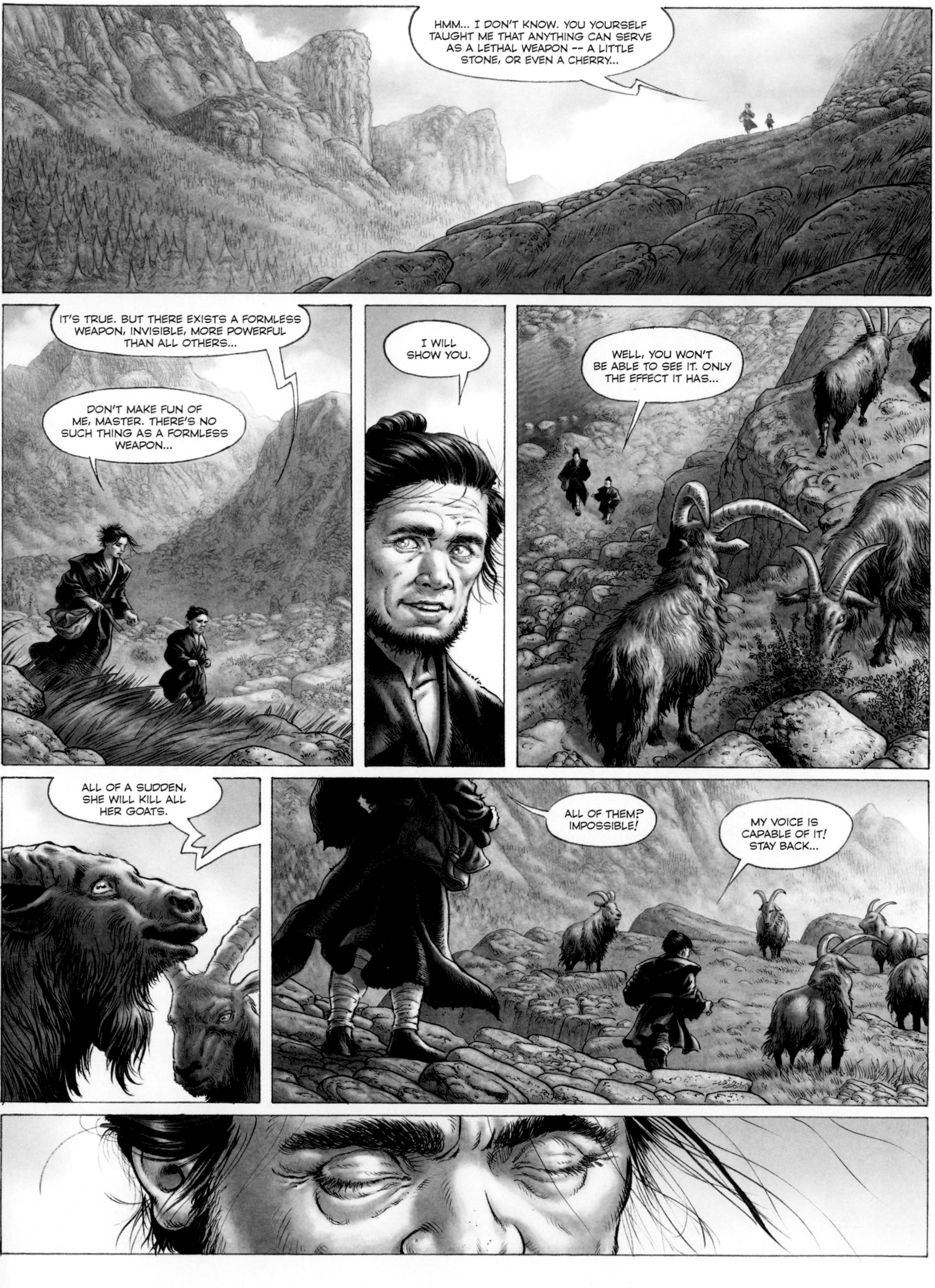
HMM... I DON'T KNOW. YOU YOURSELF TAUGHT ME THAT ANYTHING CAN SERVE AS A LETHAL WEAPON -- A LITTLE STONE, OR EVEN A CHERRY...
IT'S TRUE. BUT THERE EXISTS A FORMLESS WEAPON, INVISIBLE, MORE POWERFUL THAN ALL OTHERS...
DON'T MAKE FUN OF ME, MASTER. THERE'S NO SUCH THING AS A FORMLESS WEAPON...
I WILL SHOW YOU.
WELL, YOU WON'T BE ABLE TO SEE IT. ONLY THE EFFECT IT HAS...
ALL OF A SUDDEN, SHE WILL KILL ALL HER GOATS.
ALL OF THEM? IMPOSSIBLE!
MY VOICE IS CAPABLE OF IT! STAY BACK...

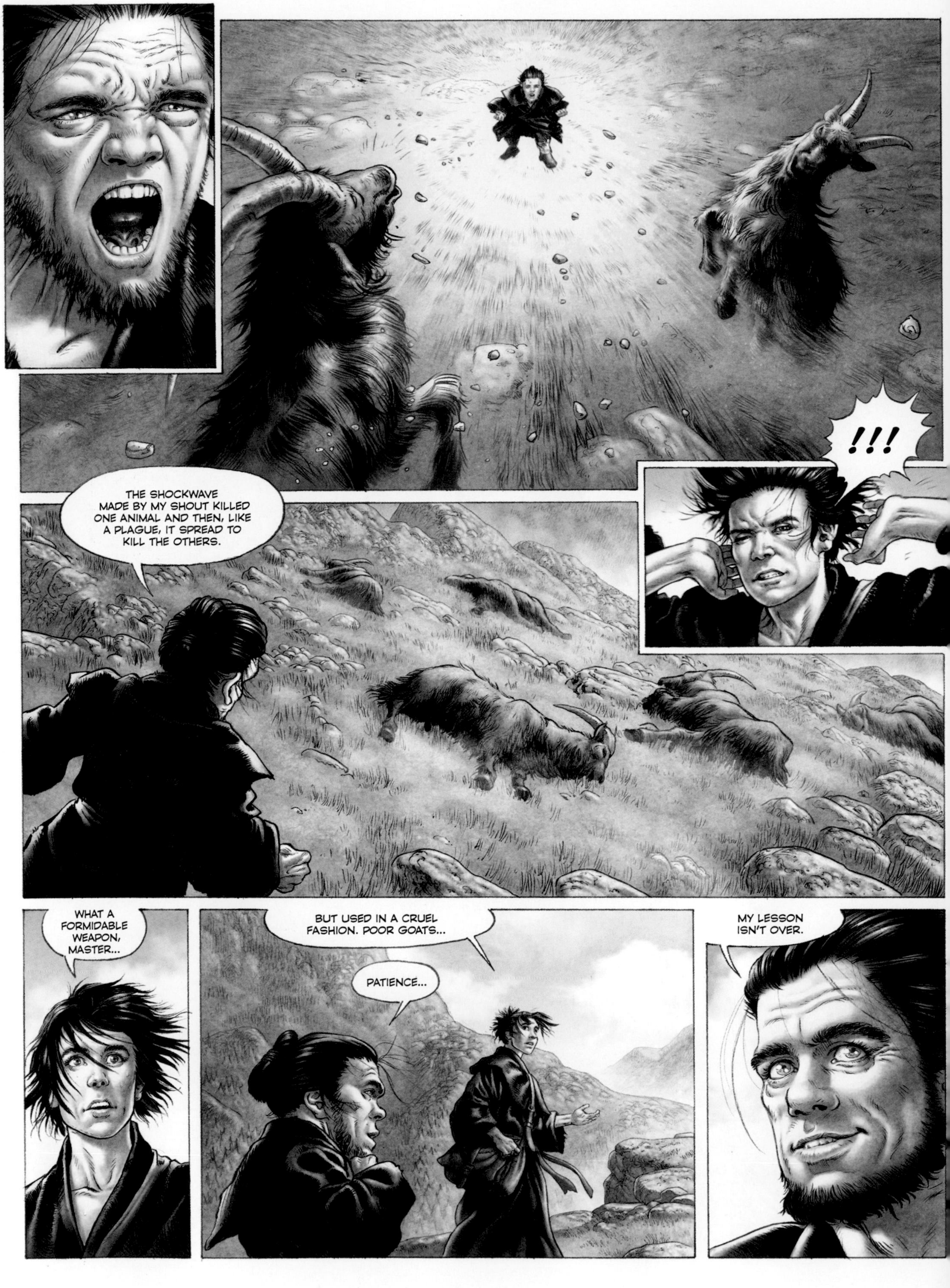
!!!
THE SHOCKWAVE MADE BY MY SHOUT KILLED ONE ANIMAL AND THEN, LIKE A PLAGUE, IT SPREAD TO KILL THE OTHERS.
WHAT A FORMIDABLE WEAPON, MASTER...
BUT USED IN A CRUEL FASHION. POOR GOATS...
PATIENCE...
MY LESSON ISN'T OVER.

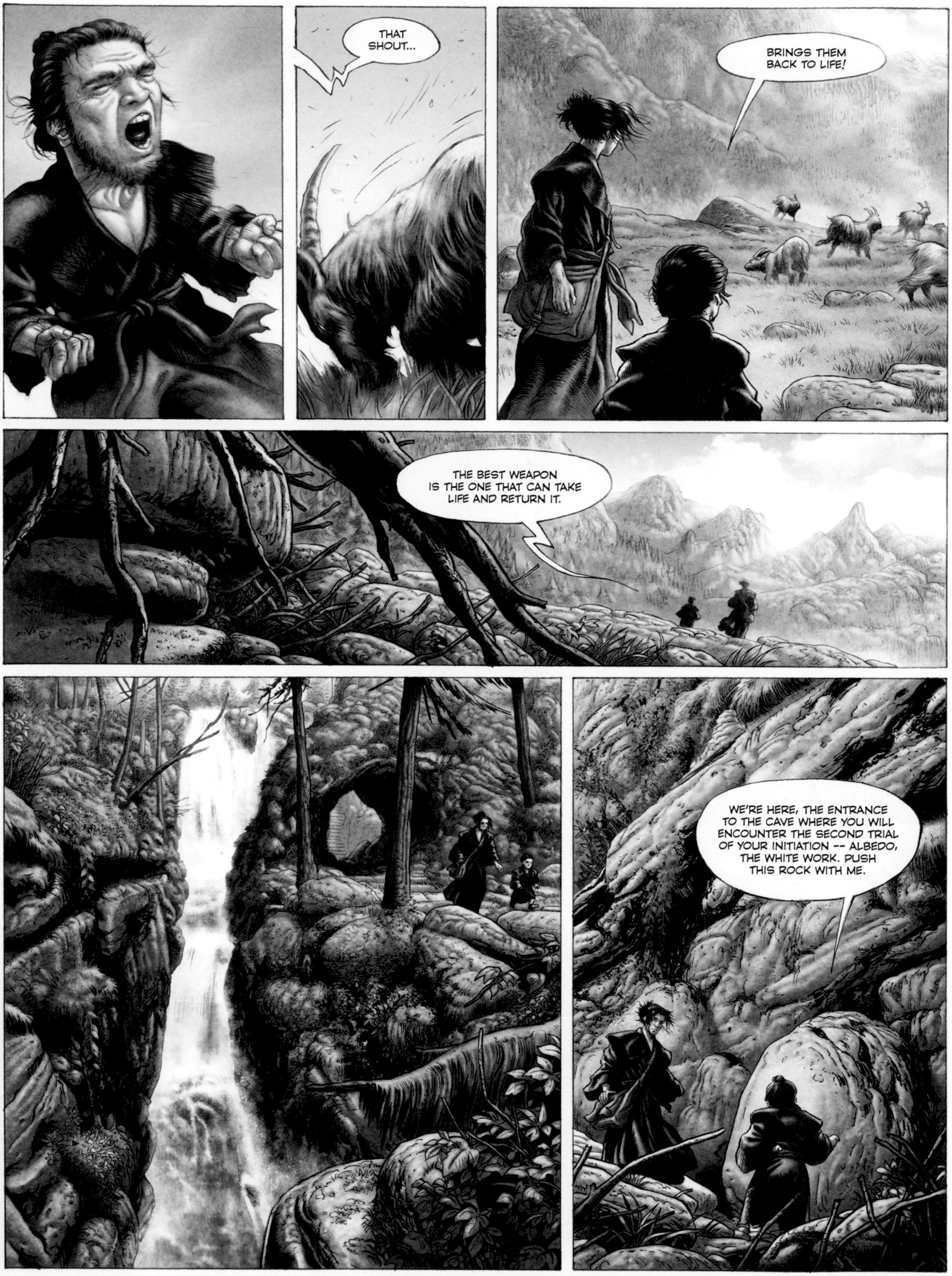
THAT SHOUT...
BRINGS THEM BACK TO LIFE!
THE BEST WEAPON IS THE ONE THAT CAN TAKE LIFE AND RETURN IT.
WE'RE HERE, THE ENTRANCE TO THE CAVE WHERE YOU WILL ENCOUNTER THE SECOND TRIAL OF YOUR INITIATION -- ALBEDO, THE WHITE WORK. PUSH THIS ROCK WITH ME.

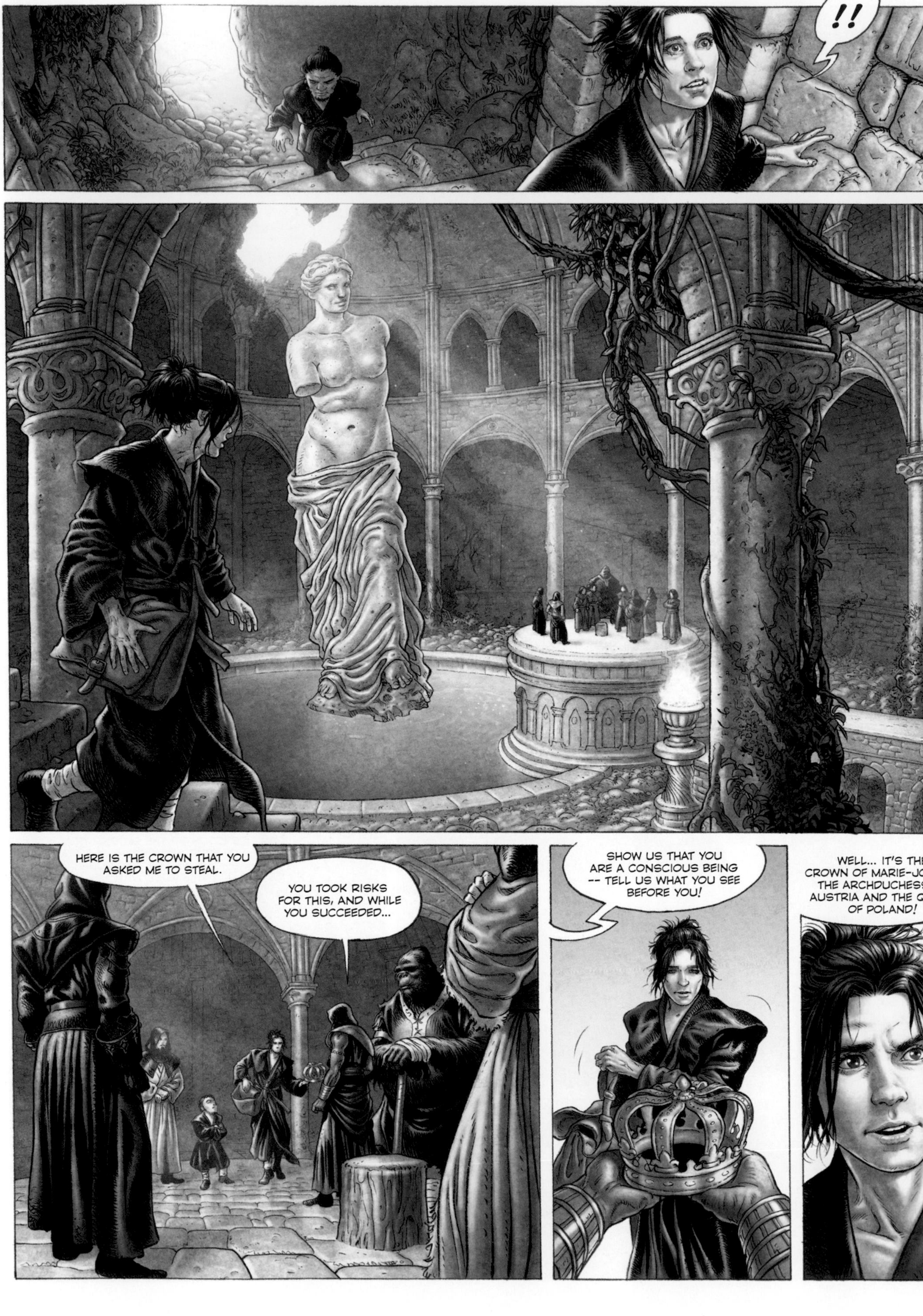
!!
HERE IS THE CROWN THAT YOU ASKED ME TO STEAL.
YOU TOOK RISKS FOR THIS, AND WHILE YOU SUCCEEDED...
SHOW US THAT YOU ARE A CONSCIOUS BEING -- TELL US WHAT YOU SEE BEFORE YOU!
WELL... IT'S THE CROWN OF MARIE-JOSEPH, THE ARCHDUCHESS OF AUSTRIA AND THE QUEEN OF POLAND!

YOU DON'T DESERVE TO LIVE 300 CENTURIES! YOU DO NOT KNOW HOW TO SEE!

??

SEE WHAT? I DON'T UNDERSTAND, IMHOTEP...

OH BROTHERS, THIS BEING DISAPPOINTS ME. HE HAS BEFORE HIM TRUTH, BEAUTY AND GOODNESS... AND ALL HE SEES IS A 'CROWN', AN OBJECT OF DESIRE FOR THE VAIN, A DANGER FOR HUMANITY.

YOU SHOULD KNOW BETTER THAN ANYONE -- ROYAL CROWNS ARE FUNERAL WREATHS FOR BILLIONS OF HUMAN BEINGS TRANSFORMED INTO SLAVES!

THESE CROWNS ADORN THE LEADER OF THIEVES, OF CRIMINALS, OF PREDATORS WHO THINK THEMSELVES OWNERS OF THEIR PEOPLES!

YOU ARE STILL NOT FREE OF YOUR CHAFF. IN A PART OF YOUR BRAIN YOU REMAIN LOUIS XVII.

YOU PERCEIVE ONLY THE SHAPE. YOU DON'T SEE THE TRUE VALUE OF THINGS!

WE WILL SHOW YOU WHAT THE COST OF ALL THAT WORK AND RISKS ACCOMPLISHED.

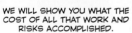

BETO, DO YOUR DUTY!

MY DUTY AND MY PLEASURE, MASTER.

BAM BAMM BAMMM BAM BAM

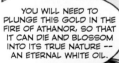

HERE IS WHAT YOU STOLE -- A PRECIOUS PEACE OF ANCIENT GOLD, THE PUREST MATERIAL ON EARTH.

IT BELONGS TO YOU, FREED OF THE HEINOUS SHAPE GIVEN TO IT BY THESE INSATIABLE ARISTOCRATS!

YOU WILL NEED TO PLUNGE THIS GOLD IN THE FIRE OF ATHANOR, SO THAT IT CAN DIE AND BLOSSOM INTO ITS TRUE NATURE -- AN ETERNAL WHITE OIL.

THAT ALSO WILL BELONG TO YOU, ASIAMAR. THIS TIME, YOU WON'T BE PRETENDING TO DIE, LIKE WHEN YOU ALLOWED YOURSELF TO BE BURIED...

YOU WILL HAVE TO TRULY DIE SO THAT YOUR TRUE NATURE CAN IN TURN BLOSSOM.

?!

YOUR DESTINY DEPENDS ON YOUR WILL. WILL YOU BE STRONG ENOUGH TO RETURN TO LIFE? DEATH IS THE GREATEST ENEMY. BUT ALSO YOUR ALLY -- IT WILL TURN YOUR SOUL TRANSPARENT.

WILL YOU DO THIS?

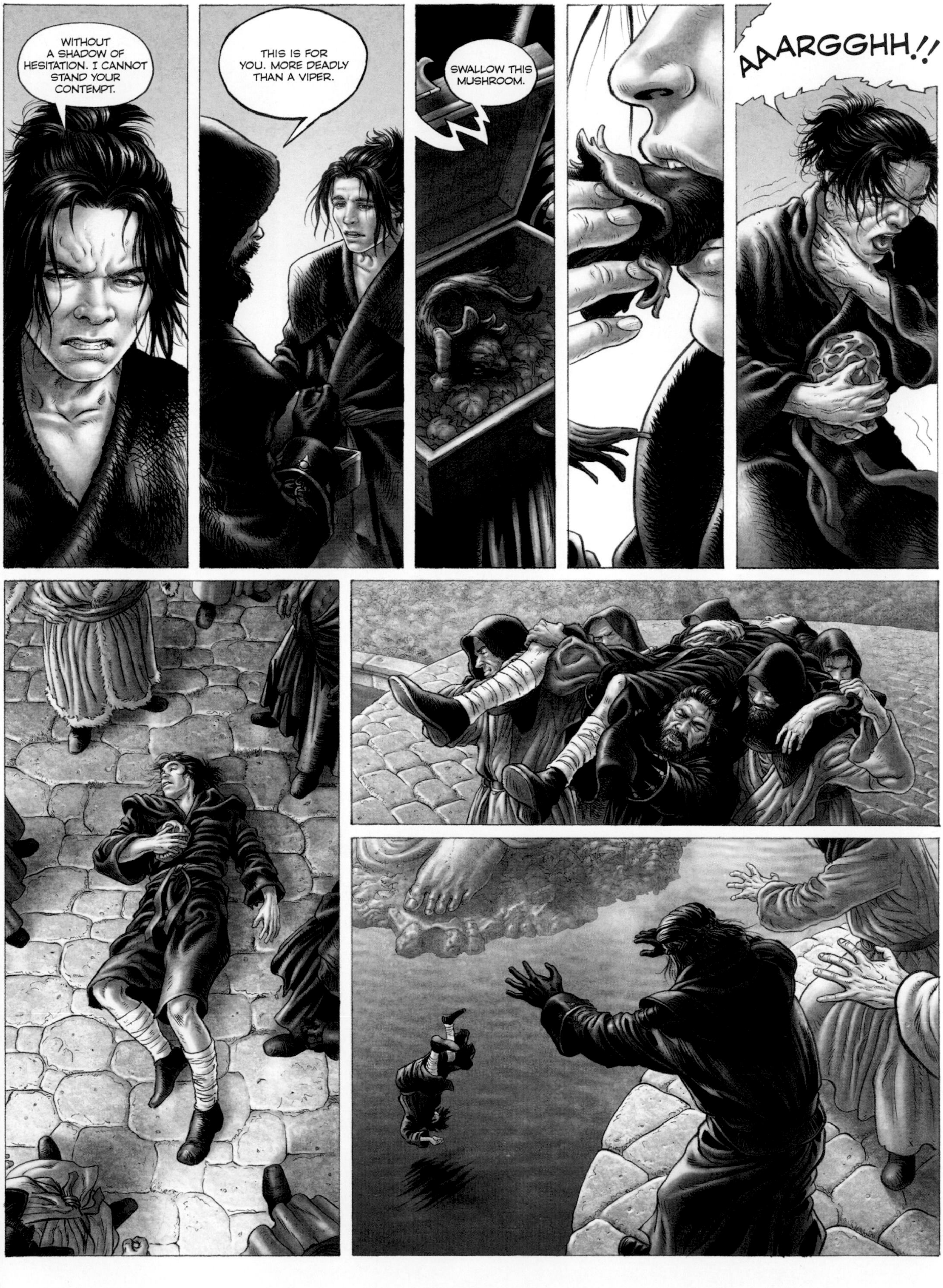
WITHOUT A SHADOW OF HESITATION. I CANNOT STAND YOUR CONTEMPT.
THIS IS FOR YOU. MORE DEADLY THAN A VIPER.
SWALLOW THIS MUSHROOM.
AAARGGHH!!

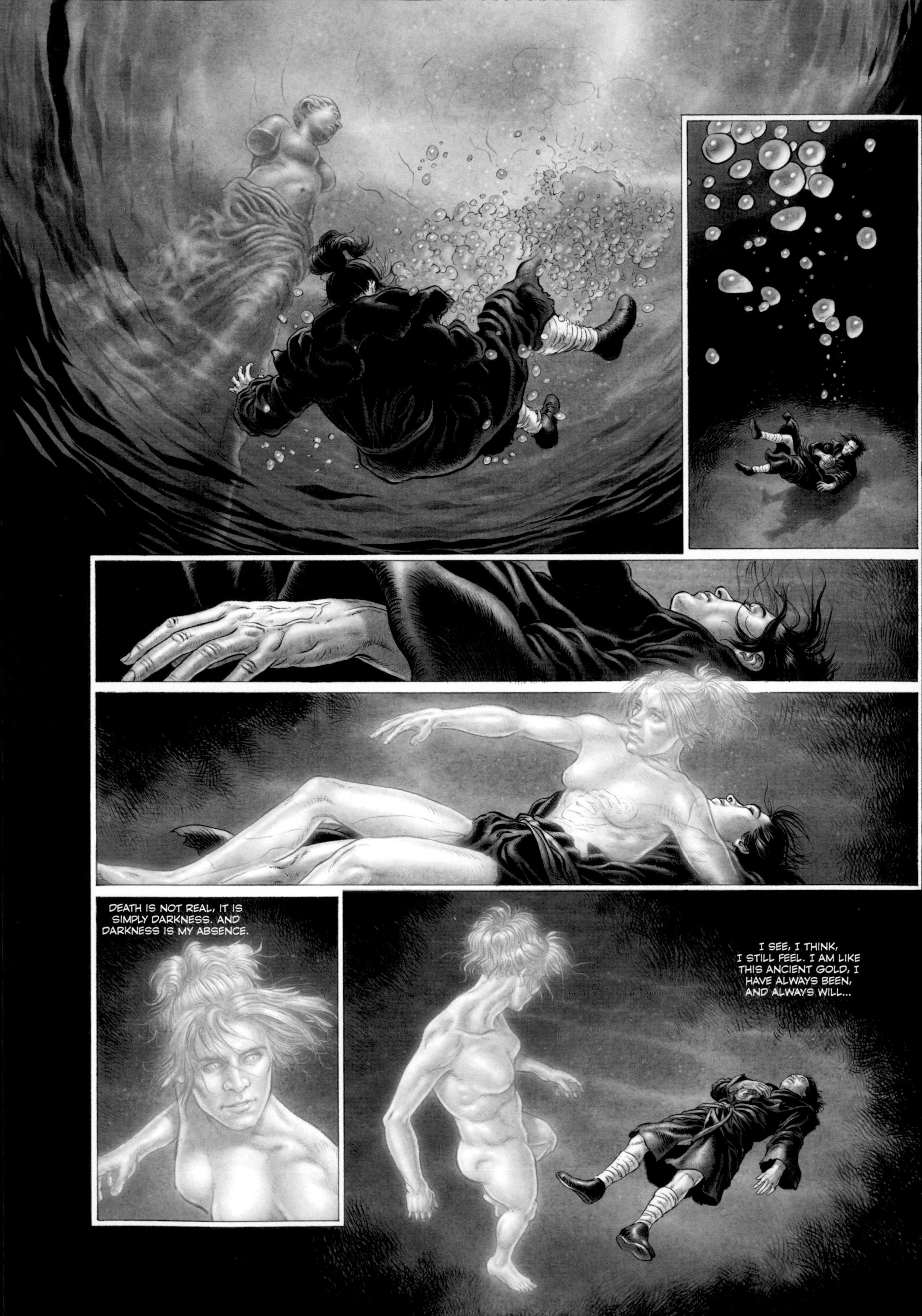
DEATH IS NOT REAL, IT IS SIMPLY DARKNESS. AND DARKNESS IS MY ABSENCE.
I SEE, I THINK, I STILL FEEL. I AM LIKE THIS ANCIENT GOLD, I HAVE ALWAYS BEEN, AND ALWAYS WILL...

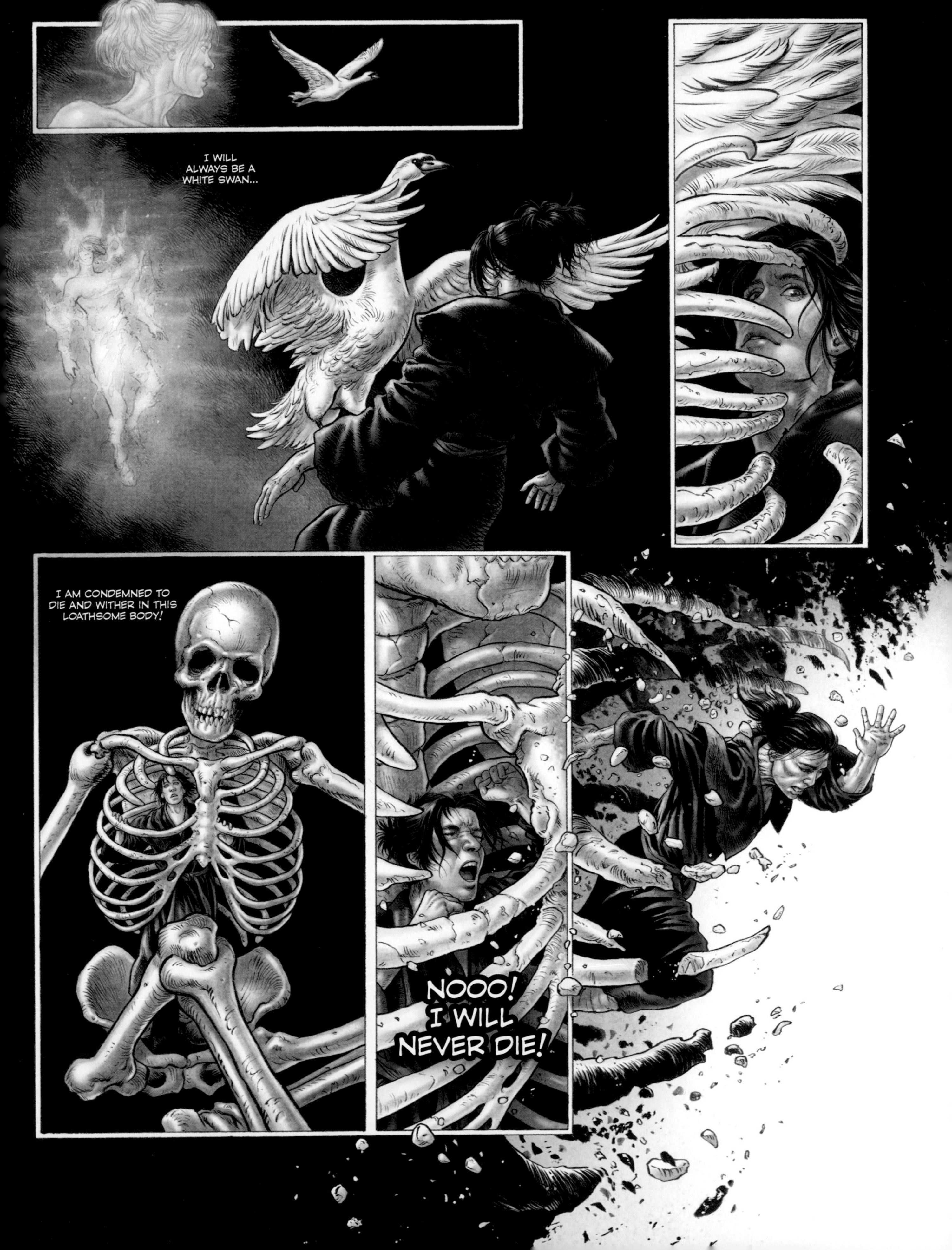
I WILL ALWAYS BE A WHITE SWAN...
I AM CONDEMNED TO DIE AND WITHER IN THIS LOATHSOME BODY!
NOOO! I WILL NEVER DIE!

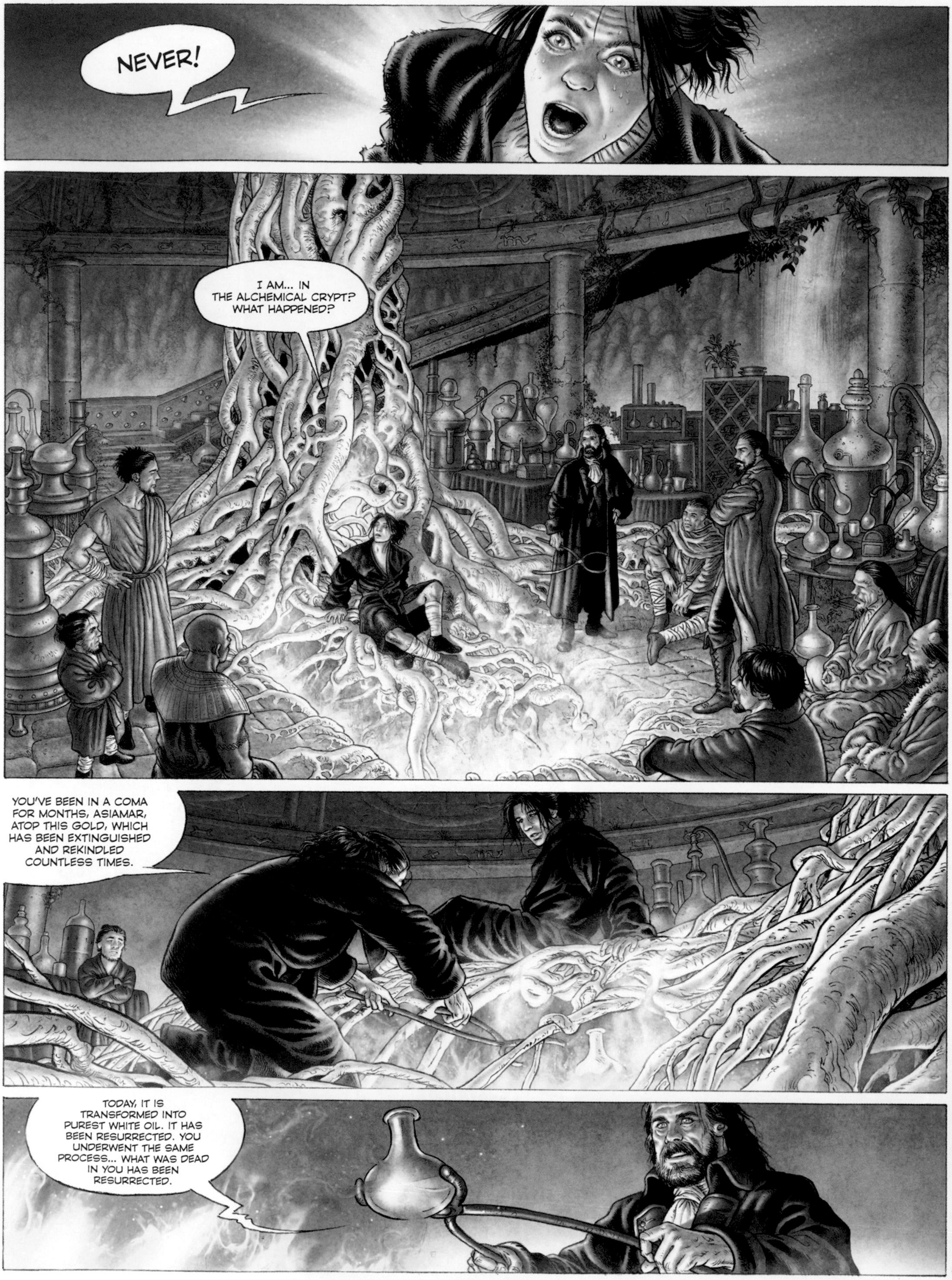
NEVER!
I AM... IN THE ALCHEMICAL CRYPT? WHAT HAPPENED?
YOU'VE BEEN IN A COMA FOR MONTHS, ASIAMAR, ATOP THIS GOLD, WHICH HAS BEEN EXTINGUISHED AND REKINDLED COUNTLESS TIMES.
TODAY, IT IS TRANSFORMED INTO PUREST WHITE OIL. IT HAS BEEN RESURRECTED. YOU UNDERWENT THE SAME PROCESS... WHAT WAS DEAD IN YOU HAS BEEN RESURRECTED.

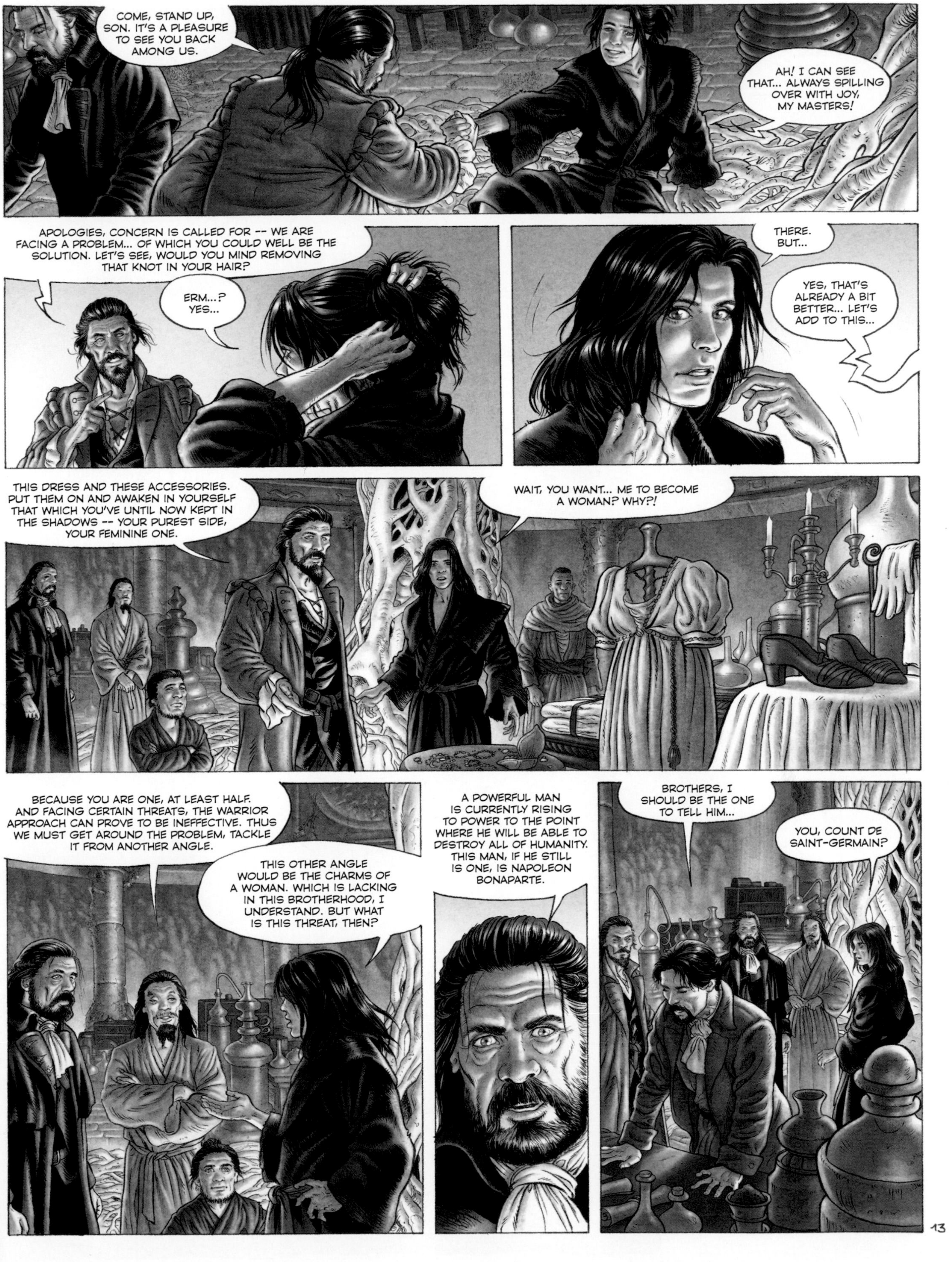
COME, STAND UP, SON. IT'S A PLEASURE TO SEE YOU BACK AMONG US.
AH! I CAN SEE THAT... ALWAYS SPILLING OVER WITH JOY, MY MASTERS!
APOLOGIES, CONCERN IS CALLED FOR -- WE ARE FACING A PROBLEM... OF WHICH YOU COULD WELL BE THE SOLUTION. LET'S SEE, WOULD YOU MIND REMOVING THAT KNOT IN YOUR HAIR?
ERM...? YES...
THERE. BUT...
YES, THAT'S ALREADY A BIT BETTER... LET'S ADD TO THIS...
THIS DRESS AND THESE ACCESSORIES. PUT THEM ON AND AWAKEN IN YOURSELF THAT WHICH YOU'VE UNTIL NOW KEPT IN THE SHADOWS -- YOUR PUREST SIDE, YOUR FEMININE ONE.
WAIT, YOU WANT... ME TO BECOME A WOMAN? WHY?!
BECAUSE YOU ARE ONE, AT LEAST HALF. AND FACING CERTAIN THREATS, THE WARRIOR APPROACH CAN PROVE TO BE INEFFECTIVE. THUS WE MUST GET AROUND THE PROBLEM, TACKLE IT FROM ANOTHER ANGLE.
THIS OTHER ANGLE WOULD BE THE CHARMS OF A WOMAN. WHICH IS LACKING IN THIS BROTHERHOOD, I UNDERSTAND. BUT WHAT IS THIS THREAT, THEN?
A POWERFUL MAN IS CURRENTLY RISING TO POWER TO THE POINT WHERE HE WILL BE ABLE TO DESTROY ALL OF HUMANITY. THIS MAN, IF HE STILL IS ONE, IS NAPOLEON BONAPARTE.
BROTHERS, I SHOULD BE THE ONE TO TELL HIM...
YOU, COUNT DE SAINT-GERMAIN?

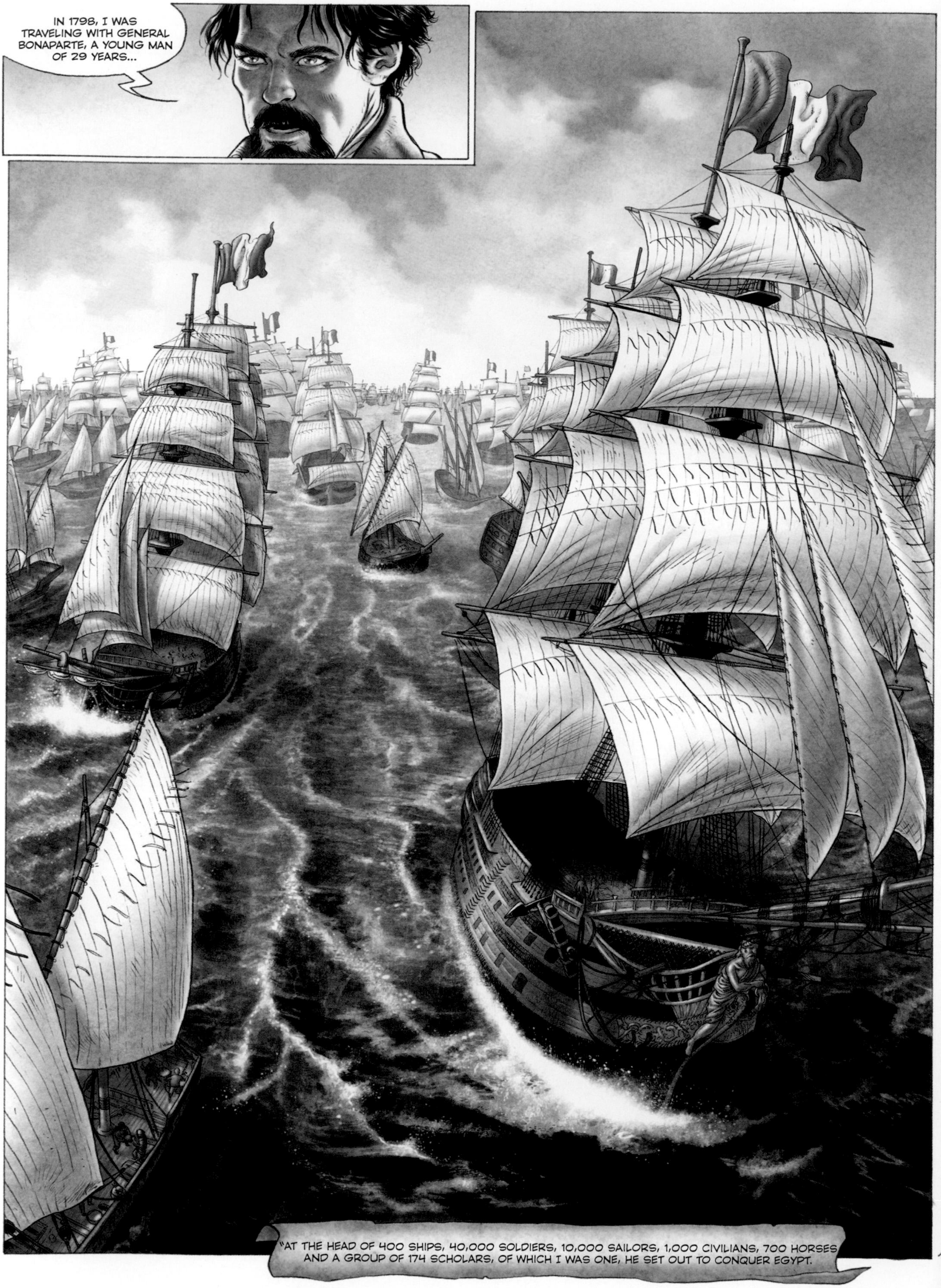
IN 1798, I WAS TRAVELING WITH GENERAL BONAPARTE, A YOUNG MAN OF 29 YEARS...
"AT THE HEAD OF 400 SHIPS, 40,000 SOLDIERS, 10,000 SAILORS, 1,000 CIVILIANS, 700 HORSES AND A GROUP OF 174 SCHOLARS, OF WHICH I WAS ONE, HE SET OUT TO CONQUER EGYPT.

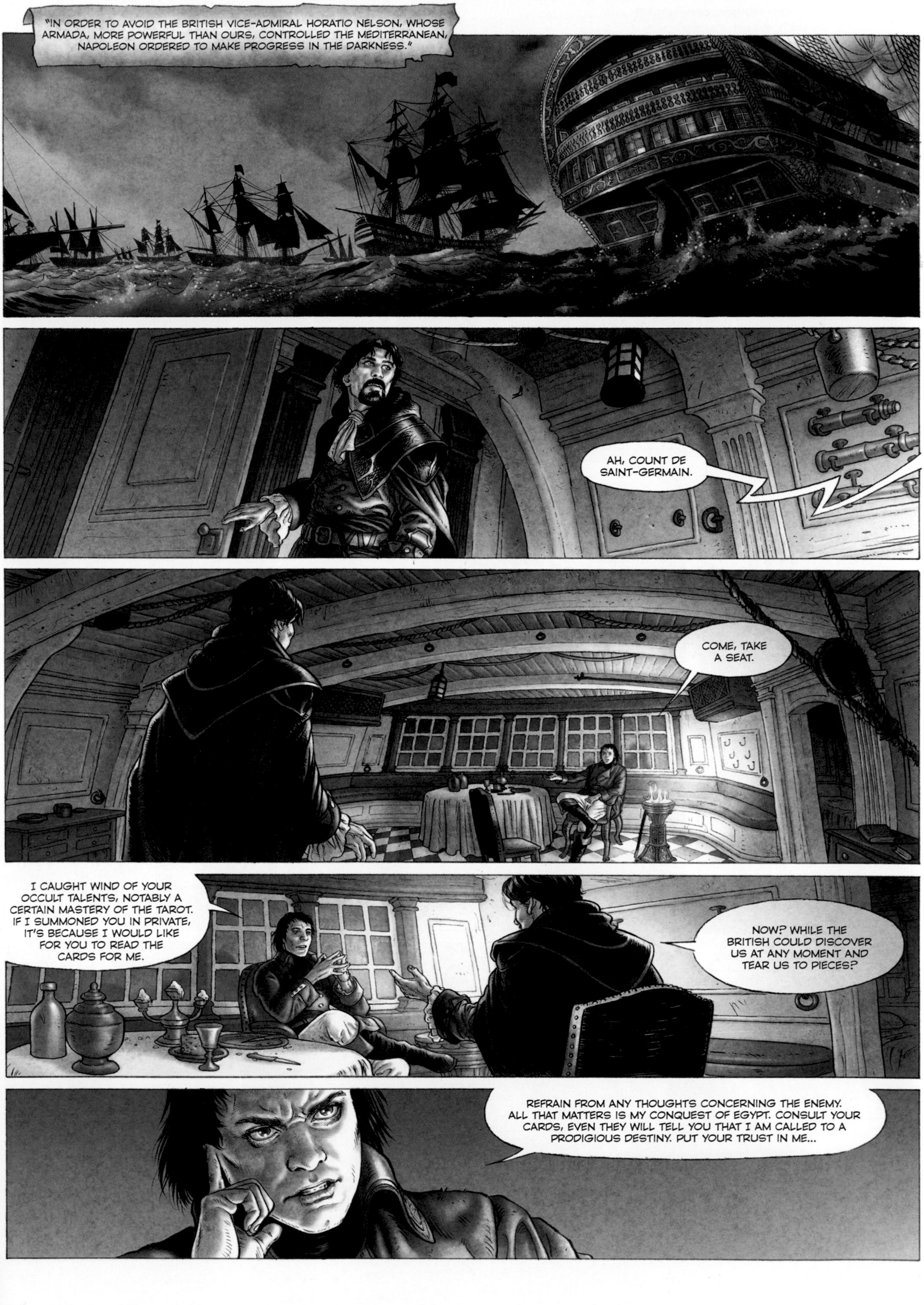
"IN ORDER TO AVOID THE BRITISH VICE-ADMIRAL HORATIO NELSON, WHOSE ARMADA, MORE POWERFUL THAN OURS, CONTROLLED THE MEDITERRANEAN, NAPOLEON ORDERED TO MAKE PROGRESS IN THE DARKNESS."
AH, COUNT DE SAINT-GERMAIN.
COME, TAKE A SEAT.
I CAUGHT WIND OF YOUR OCCULT TALENTS, NOTABLY A CERTAIN MASTERY OF THE TAROT. IF I SUMMONED YOU IN PRIVATE, IT'S BECAUSE I WOULD LIKE FOR YOU TO READ THE CARDS FOR ME.
NOW? WHILE THE BRITISH COULD DISCOVER US AT ANY MOMENT AND TEAR US TO PIECES?
REFRAIN FROM ANY THOUGHTS CONCERNING THE ENEMY. ALL THAT MATTERS IS MY CONQUEST OF EGYPT. CONSULT YOUR CARDS, EVEN THEY WILL TELL YOU THAT I AM CALLED TO A PRODIGIOUS DESTINY. PUT YOUR TRUST IN ME...

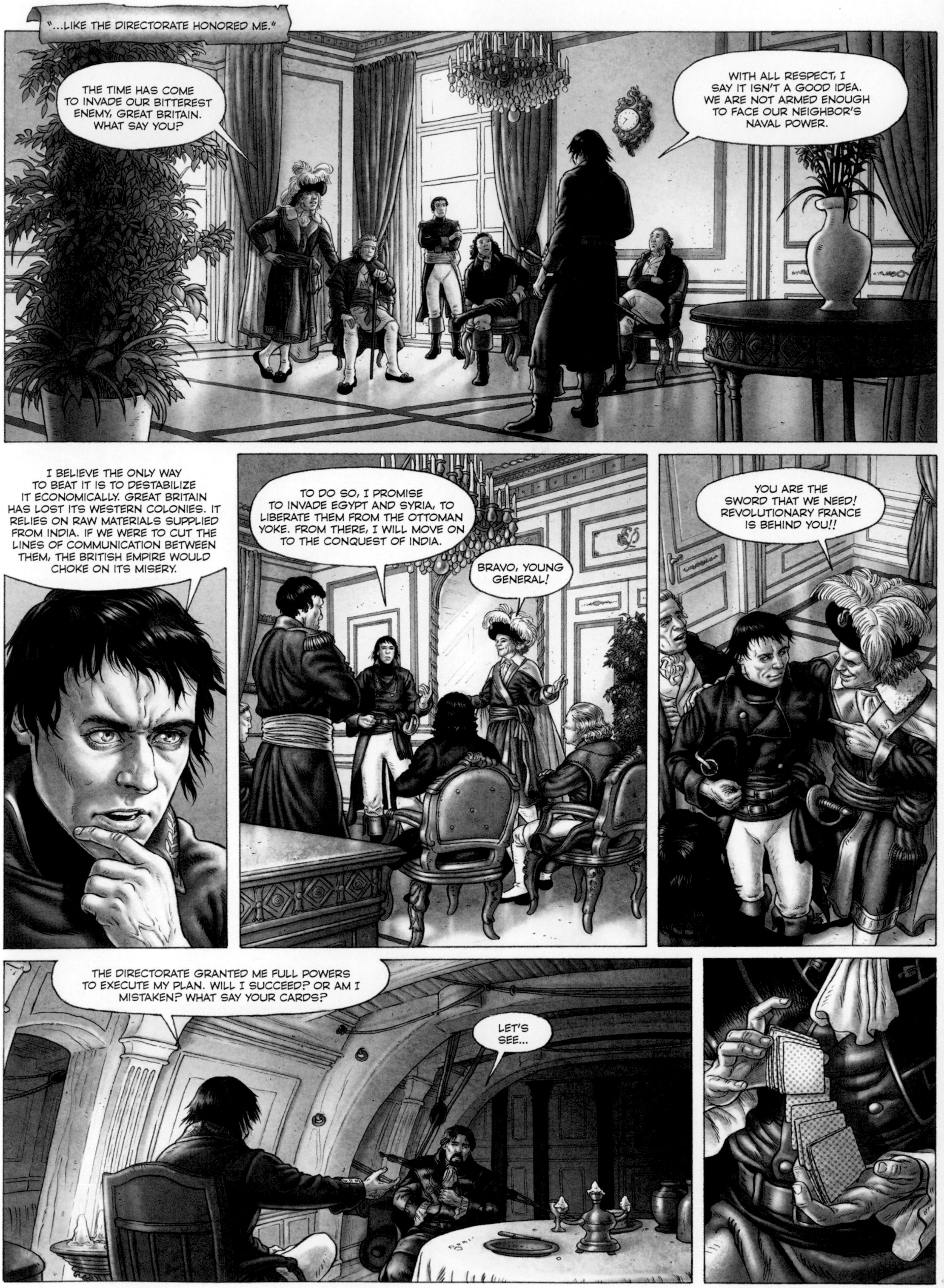
"...LIKE THE DIRECTORATE HONORED ME."
THE TIME HAS COME TO INVADE OUR BITTEREST ENEMY, GREAT BRITAIN. WHAT SAY YOU?
WITH ALL RESPECT, I SAY IT ISN'T A GOOD IDEA. WE ARE NOT ARMED ENOUGH TO FACE OUR NEIGHBOR'S NAVAL POWER.
I BELIEVE THE ONLY WAY TO BEAT IT IS TO DESTABILIZE IT ECONOMICALLY. GREAT BRITAIN HAS LOST ITS WESTERN COLONIES. IT RELIES ON RAW MATERIALS SUPPLIED FROM INDIA. IF WE WERE TO CUT THE LINES OF COMMUNICATION BETWEEN THEM, THE BRITISH EMPIRE WOULD CHOKE ON ITS MISERY.
TO DO SO, I PROMISE TO INVADE EGYPT AND SYRIA, TO LIBERATE THEM FROM THE OTTOMAN YOKE. FROM THERE, I WILL MOVE ON TO THE CONQUEST OF INDIA.
BRAVO, YOUNG GENERAL!
YOU ARE THE SWORD THAT WE NEED! REVOLUTIONARY FRANCE IS BEHIND YOU!!
THE DIRECTORATE GRANTED ME FULL POWERS TO EXECUTE MY PLAN. WILL I SUCCEED? OR AM I MISTAKEN? WHAT SAY YOUR CARDS?
LET'S SEE...

YOU ARE NOT MAKING A MISTAKE, MY GENERAL... BUT THE DEATH AND THE JUDGEMENT, THE EMPEROR AND THE WORLD SAY THAT YOUR CONQUEST OF EGYPT AND SYRIA TO IMPOVERISH GREAT BRITAIN IS NOT YOUR REAL OBJECTIVE...
LE JUGEMENT
L'EMPEREUR
LE MONDE
IF I ADD TO MY READING YOUR INTEREST IN ANCIENT EGYPTIAN RUINS AND TOMBS, I CAN DEDUCE FROM IT THAT... YOU ARE ON THE HUNT FOR SOMETHING LINKED TO RITES THAT GRANT ACCESS TO ETERNAL LIFE?!?
IT'S TRUE, I ADMIT IT! JESUS WAS DEAD AND THREE DAYS LATER HE WAS RESURRECTED. LIKE THE PHOENIX, LIKE THE GOD OSIRIS. WHY NOT ME? I HAVE NEVER KNOWN DEFEAT, I AM MARKED BY DESTINY SINCE I WAS BORN...
"MY MOTHER TOLD ME HOW, AT MY BIRTH, A SWARM OF BEES GATHERED AROUND THE WINDOW OF MY ROOM.
"THEY ENTERED AND BUZZED AROUND MY HEAD FOR A MOMENT, TRACING A CROWN IN THEIR FLIGHT. MY MOTHER SAW IT AS A WONDERFUL OMEN OF MY ROYAL DESTINY."
SO THAT'S IT?! YOU WANT TO BECOME KING OF THE WORLD?!!
NOT KING -- EMPEROR! AND THEN MORE! I WANT TO BE IMMORTAL, TO LIVE FOREVER, TO BECOME A GOD!

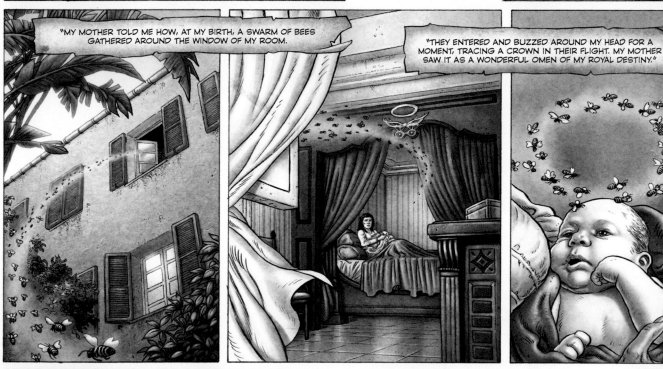

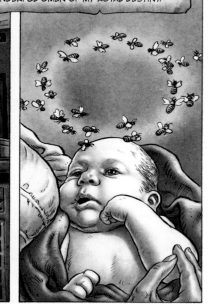

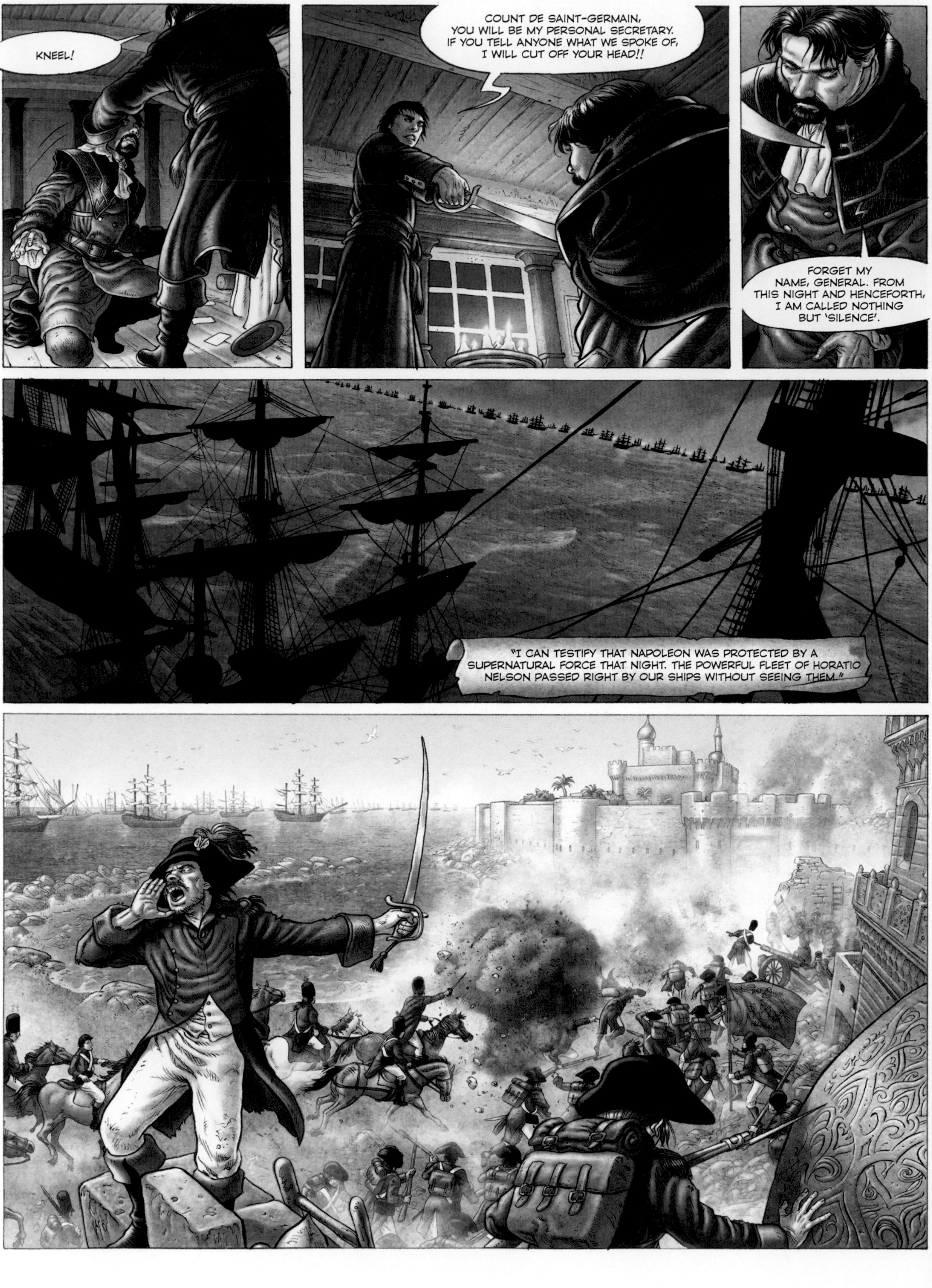
KNEEL!
COUNT DE SAINT-GERMAIN, YOU WILL BE MY PERSONAL SECRETARY. IF YOU TELL ANYONE WHAT WE SPOKE OF, I WILL CUT OFF YOUR HEAD!!
FORGET MY NAME, GENERAL. FROM THIS NIGHT AND HENCEFORTH, I AM CALLED NOTHING BUT 'SILENCE'.
"I CAN TESTIFY THAT NAPOLEON WAS PROTECTED BY A SUPERNATURAL FORCE THAT NIGHT. THE POWERFUL FLEET OF HORATIO NELSON PASSED RIGHT BY OUR SHIPS WITHOUT SEEING THEM."

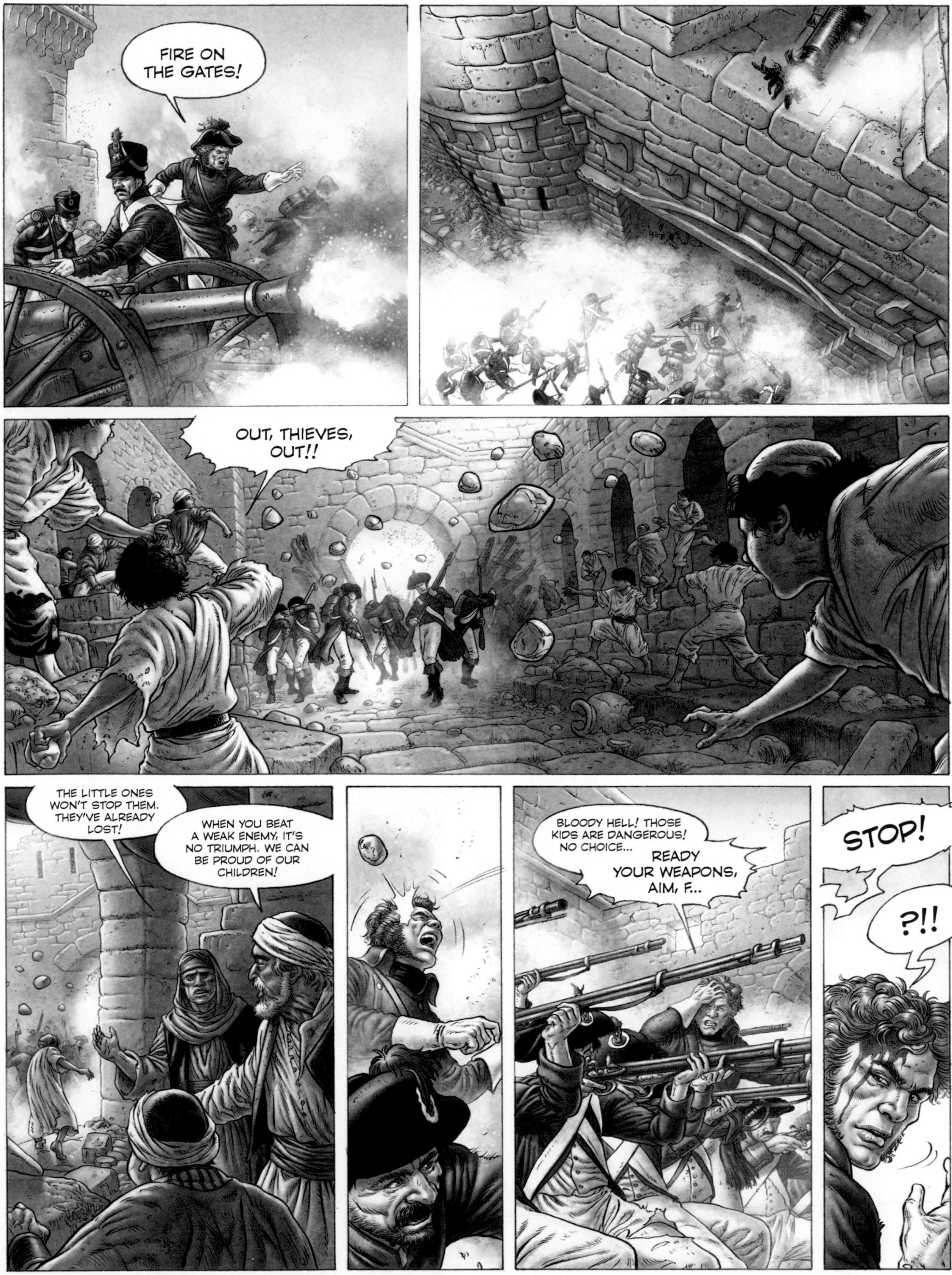
FIRE ON THE GATES!
OUT, THIEVES, OUT!!
THE LITTLE ONES WON'T STOP THEM. THEY'VE ALREADY LOST!
WHEN YOU BEAT A WEAK ENEMY, IT'S NO TRIUMPH. WE CAN BE PROUD OF OUR CHILDREN!
BLOODY HELL! THOSE KIDS ARE DANGEROUS! NO CHOICE...
READY YOUR WEAPONS, AIM, F...
STOP!
?!!

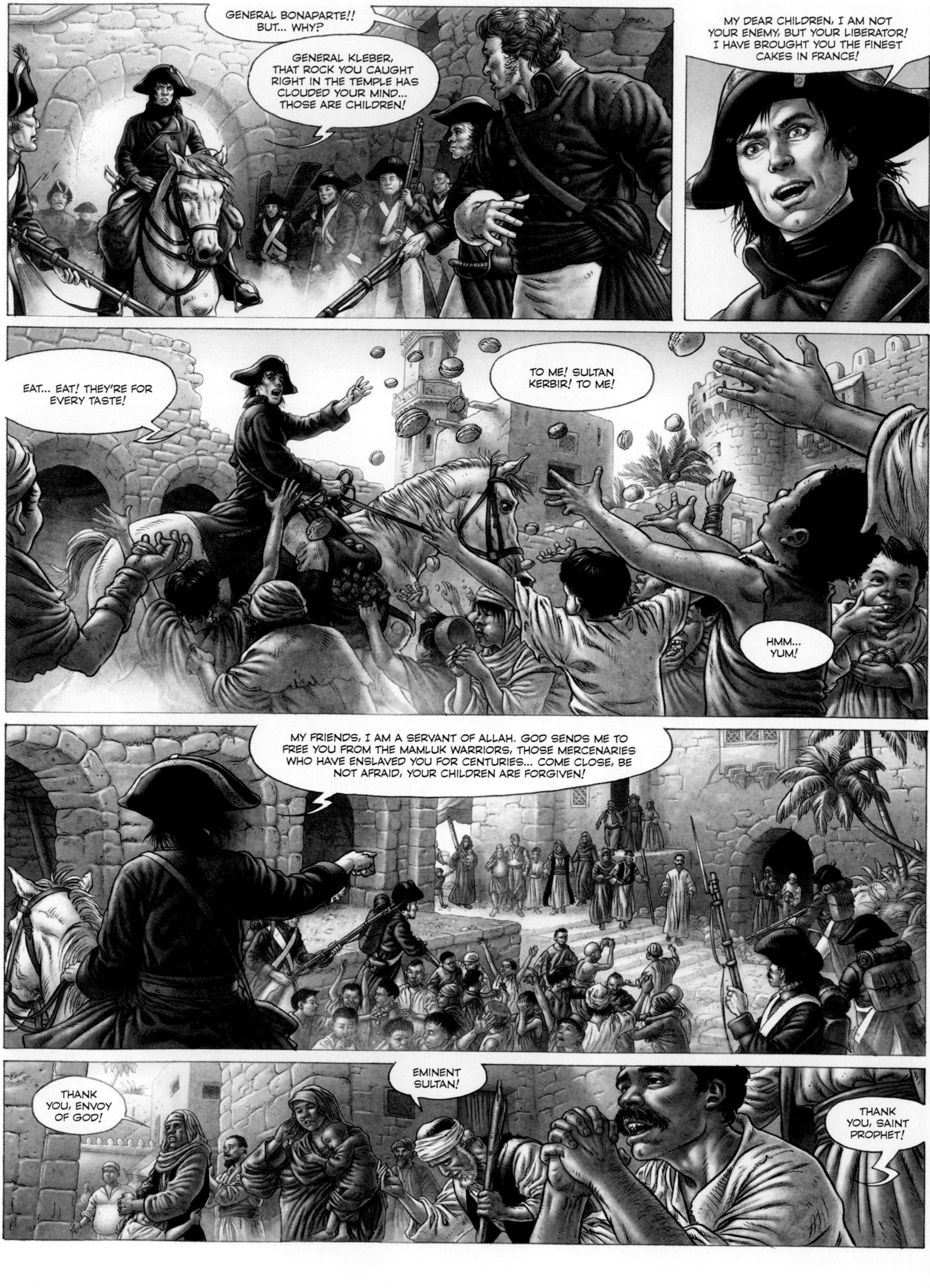
GENERAL BONAPARTE!! BUT... WHY?
GENERAL KLEBER, THAT ROCK YOU CAUGHT RIGHT IN THE TEMPLE HAS CLOUDED YOUR MIND... THOSE ARE CHILDREN!
MY DEAR CHILDREN, I AM NOT YOUR ENEMY, BUT YOUR LIBERATOR! I HAVE BROUGHT YOU THE FINEST CAKES IN FRANCE!
EAT... EAT! THEY'RE FOR EVERY TASTE!
TO ME! SULTAN KERBIR! TO ME!
HMM... YUM!
MY FRIENDS, I AM A SERVANT OF ALLAH. GOD SENDS ME TO FREE YOU FROM THE MAMLUK WARRIORS, THOSE MERCENARIES WHO HAVE ENSLAVED YOU FOR CENTURIES... COME CLOSE, BE NOT AFRAID, YOUR CHILDREN ARE FORGIVEN!
THANK YOU, ENVOY OF GOD!
EMINENT SULTAN!
THANK YOU, SAINT PROPHET!

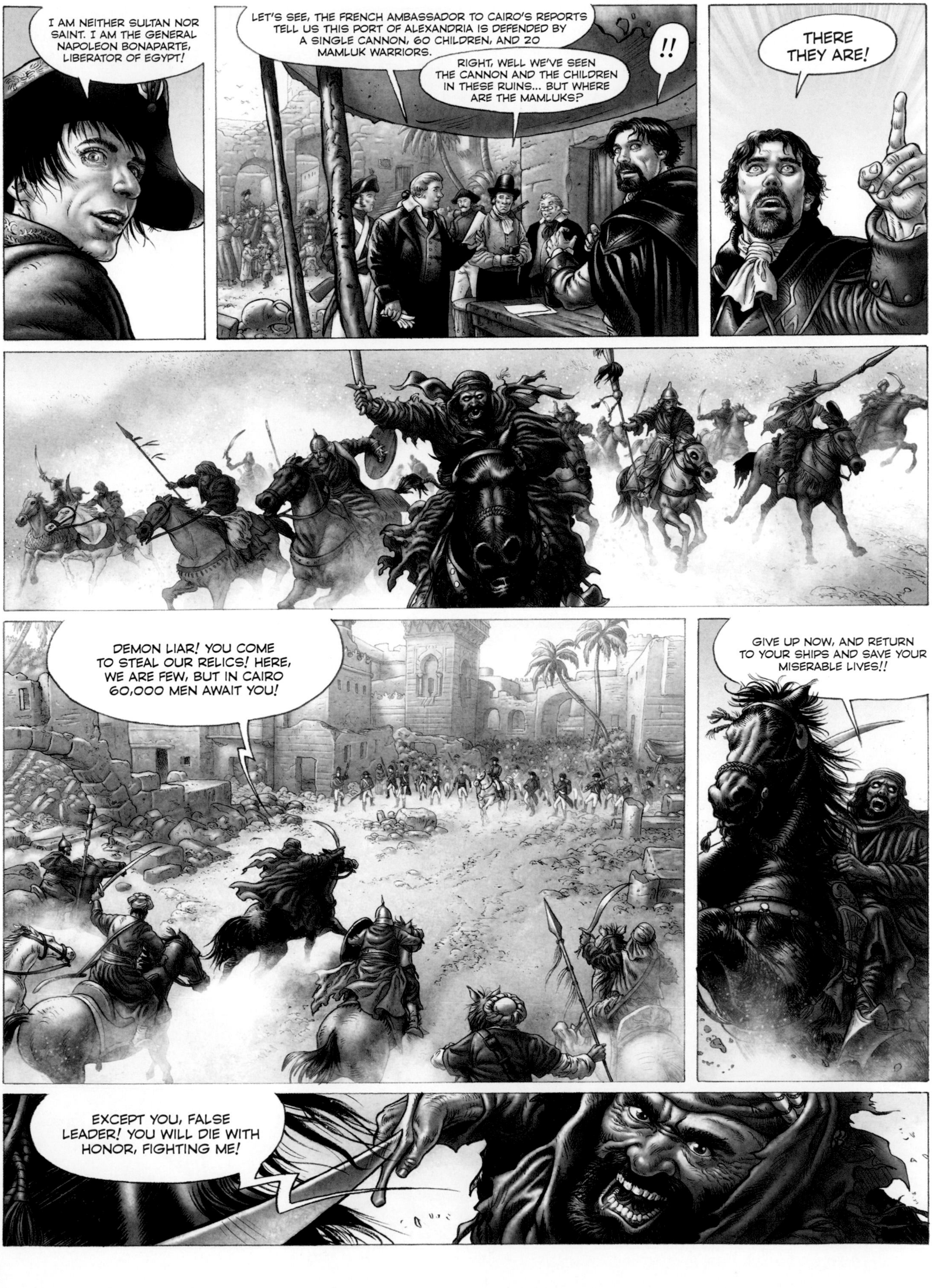
I AM NEITHER SULTAN NOR SAINT. I AM THE GENERAL NAPOLEON BONAPARTE, LIBERATOR OF EGYPT!
LET'S SEE, THE FRENCH AMBASSADOR TO CAIRO'S REPORTS TELL US THIS PORT OF ALEXANDRIA IS DEFENDED BY A SINGLE CANNON, 60 CHILDREN, AND 20 MAMLUK WARRIORS.
RIGHT, WELL WE'VE SEEN THE CANNON AND THE CHILDREN IN THESE RUINS... BUT WHERE ARE THE MAMLUKS?
!!
THERE THEY ARE!
DEMON LIAR! YOU COME TO STEAL OUR RELICS! HERE, WE ARE FEW, BUT IN CAIRO 60,000 MEN AWAIT YOU!
GIVE UP NOW, AND RETURN TO YOUR SHIPS AND SAVE YOUR MISERABLE LIVES!!
EXCEPT YOU, FALSE LEADER! YOU WILL DIE WITH HONOR, FIGHTING ME!

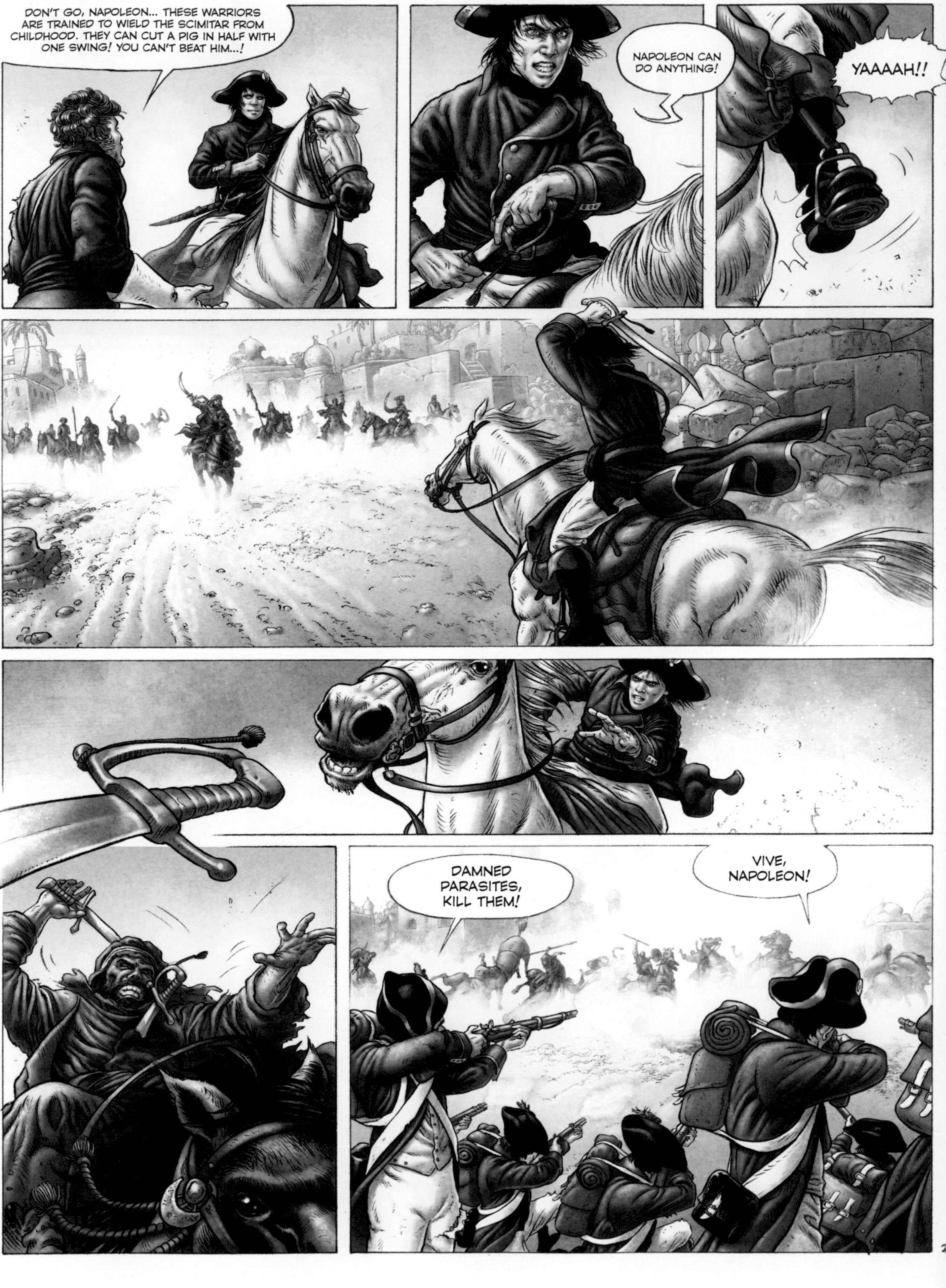
DON'T GO, NAPOLEON... THESE WARRIORS ARE TRAINED TO WIELD THE SCIMITAR FROM CHILDHOOD. THEY CAN CUT A PIG IN HALF WITH ONE SWING! YOU CAN'T BEAT HIM...!
NAPOLEON CAN DO ANYTHING!
YAAAAH!!
DAMNED PARASITES, KILL THEM!
VIVE, NAPOLEON!

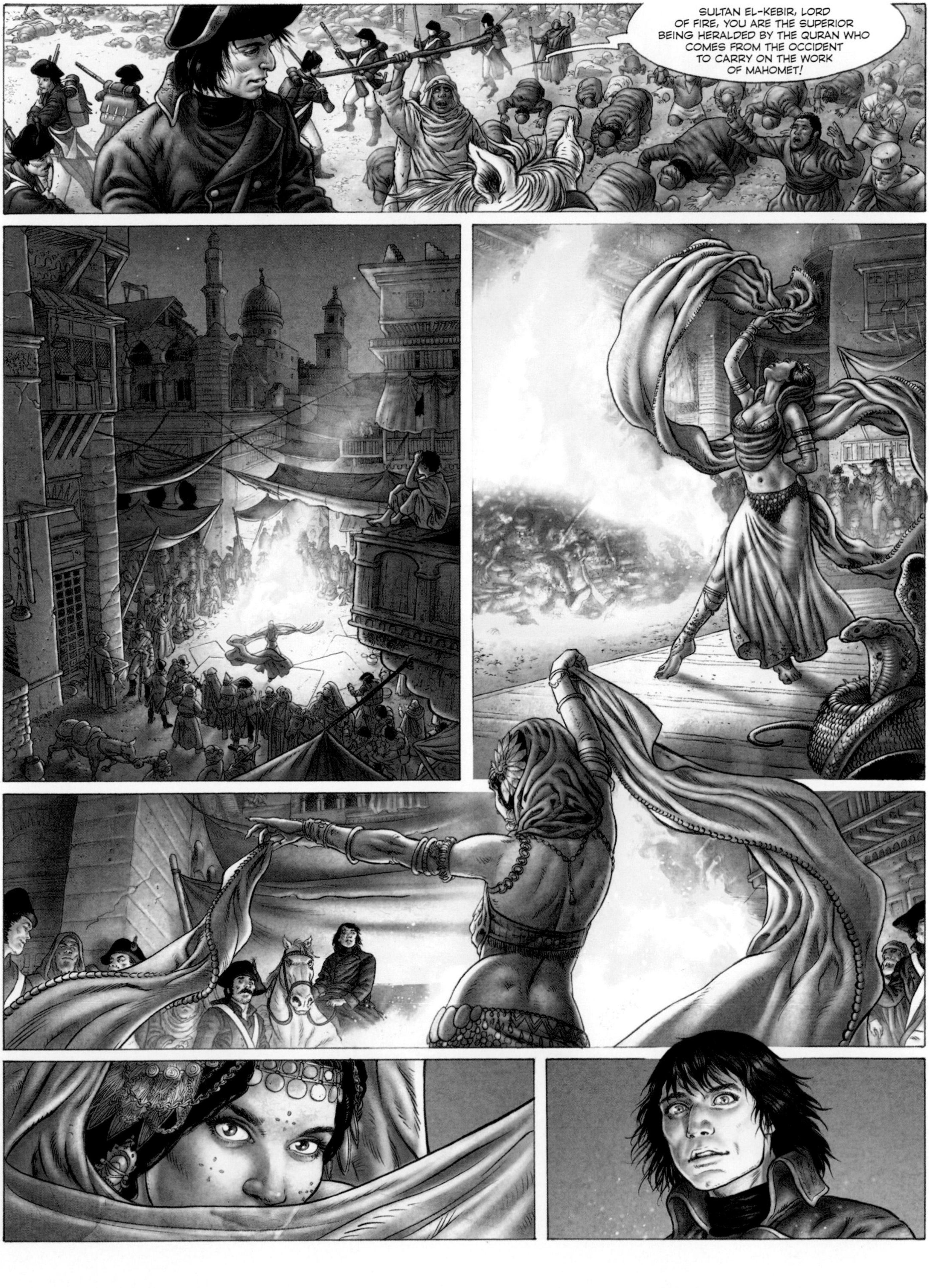
SULTAN EL-KEBIR, LORD OF FIRE, YOU ARE THE SUPERIOR BEING HERALDED BY THE QURAN WHO COMES FROM THE OCCIDENT TO CARRY ON THE WORK OF MAHOMET!

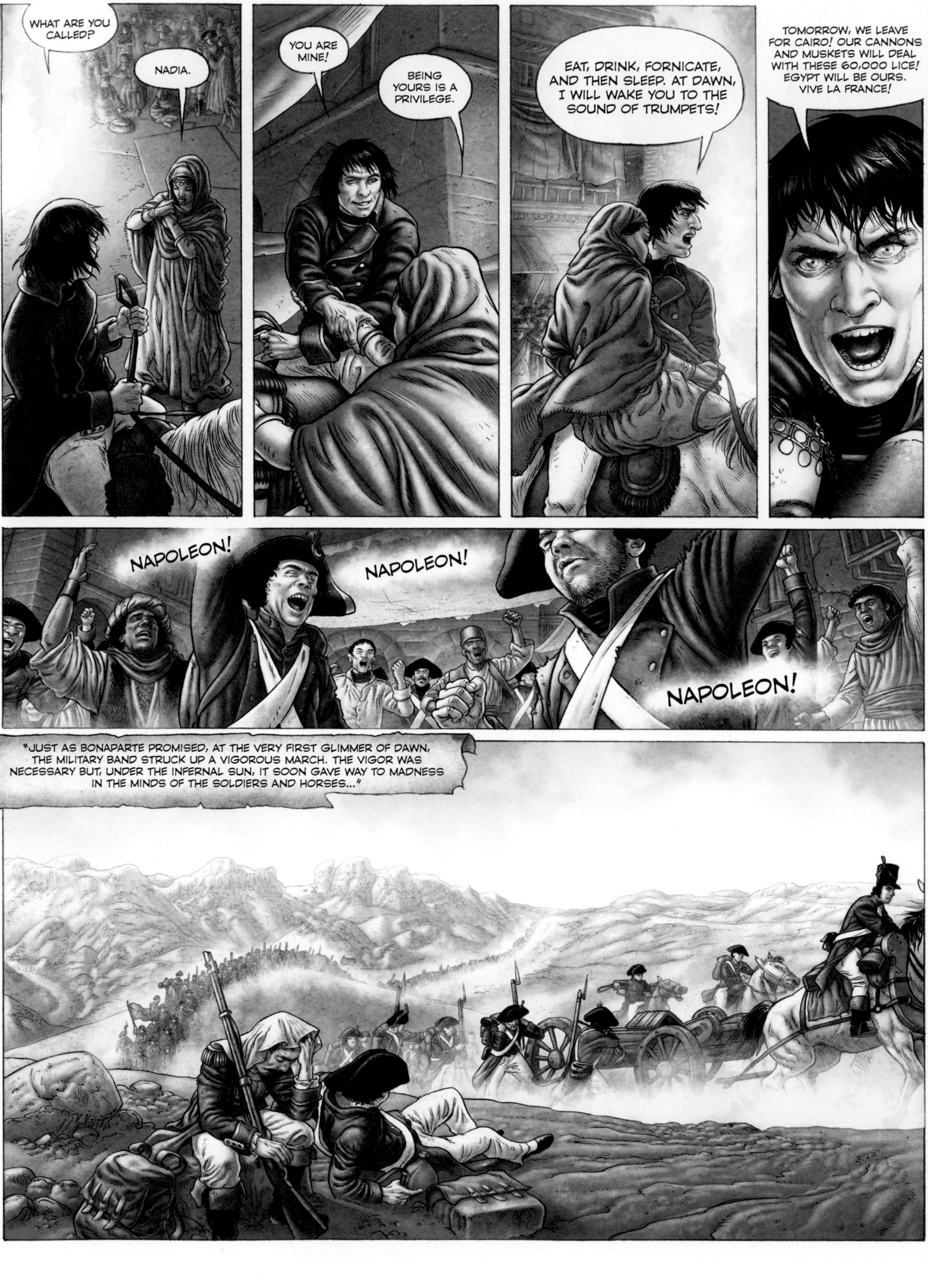
WHAT ARE YOU CALLED?
NADIA.
YOU ARE MINE!
BEING YOURS IS A PRIVILEGE.
EAT, DRINK, FORNICATE, AND THEN SLEEP. AT DAWN, I WILL WAKE YOU TO THE SOUND OF TRUMPETS!
TOMORROW, WE LEAVE FOR CAIRO! OUR CANNONS AND MUSKETS WILL DEAL WITH THESE 60,000 LICE! EGYPT WILL BE OURS. VIVE LA FRANCE!
NAPOLEON!
NAPOLEON!
NAPOLEON!
"JUST AS BONAPARTE PROMISED, AT THE VERY FIRST GLIMMER OF DAWN, THE MILITARY BAND STRUCK UP A VIGOROUS MARCH. THE VIGOR WAS NECESSARY BUT, UNDER THE INFERNAL SUN, IT SOON GAVE WAY TO MADNESS IN THE MINDS OF THE SOLDIERS AND HORSES..."

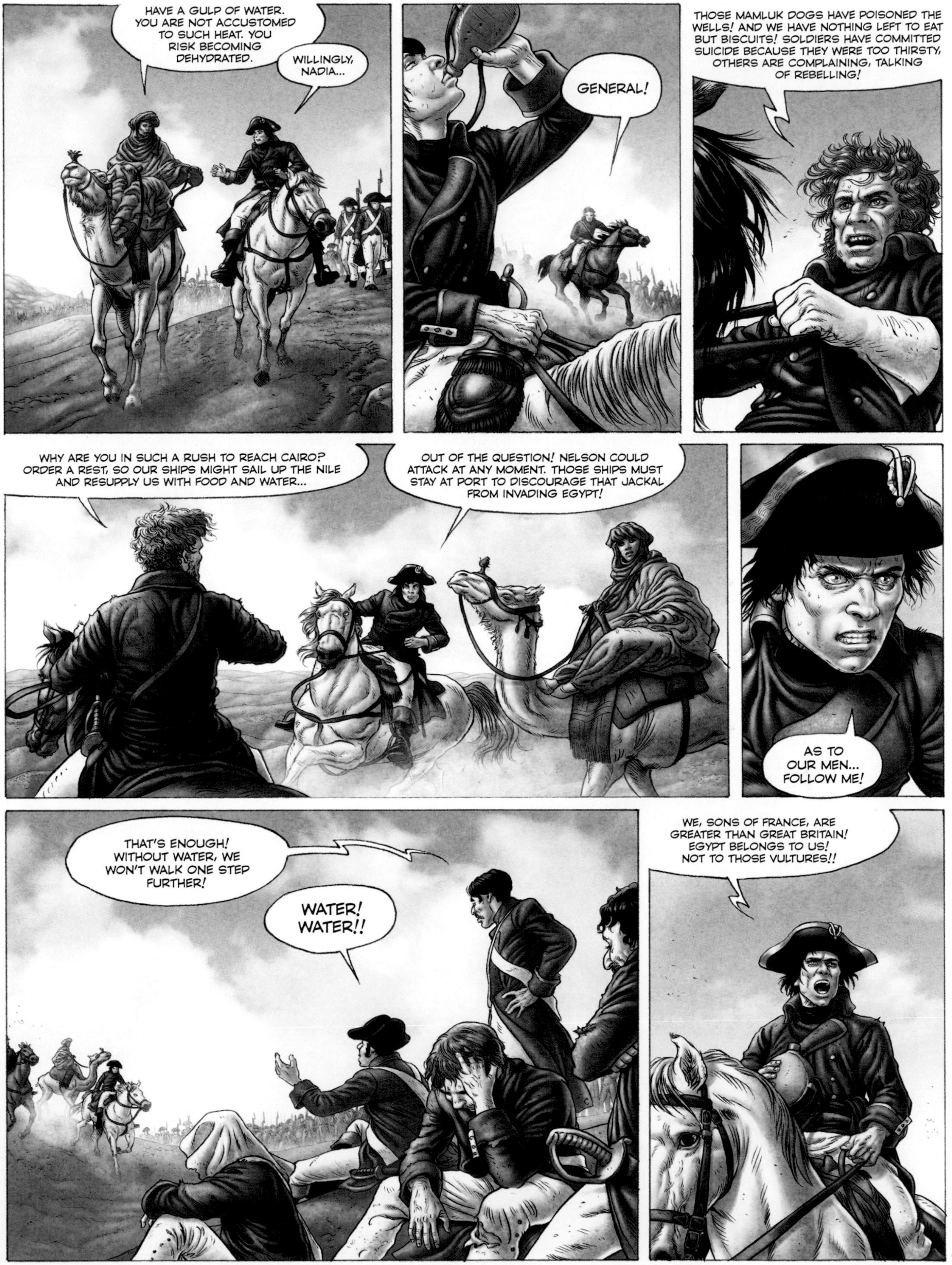
HAVE A GULP OF WATER. YOU ARE NOT ACCUSTOMED TO SUCH HEAT. YOU RISK BECOMING DEHYDRATED.
WILLINGLY, NADIA...
GENERAL!
THOSE MAMLUK DOGS HAVE POISONED THE WELLS! AND WE HAVE NOTHING LEFT TO EAT BUT BISCUITS! SOLDIERS HAVE COMMITTED SUICIDE BECAUSE THEY WERE TOO THIRSTY, OTHERS ARE COMPLAINING, TALKING OF REBELLING!
WHY ARE YOU IN SUCH A RUSH TO REACH CAIRO? ORDER A REST, SO OUR SHIPS MIGHT SAIL UP THE NILE AND RESUPPLY US WITH FOOD AND WATER...
OUT OF THE QUESTION! NELSON COULD ATTACK AT ANY MOMENT. THOSE SHIPS MUST STAY AT PORT TO DISCOURAGE THAT JACKAL FROM INVADING EGYPT!
AS TO OUR MEN... FOLLOW ME!
THAT'S ENOUGH! WITHOUT WATER, WE WON'T WALK ONE STEP FURTHER!
WATER! WATER!!
WE, SONS OF FRANCE, ARE GREATER THAN GREAT BRITAIN! EGYPT BELONGS TO US! NOT TO THOSE VULTURES!!

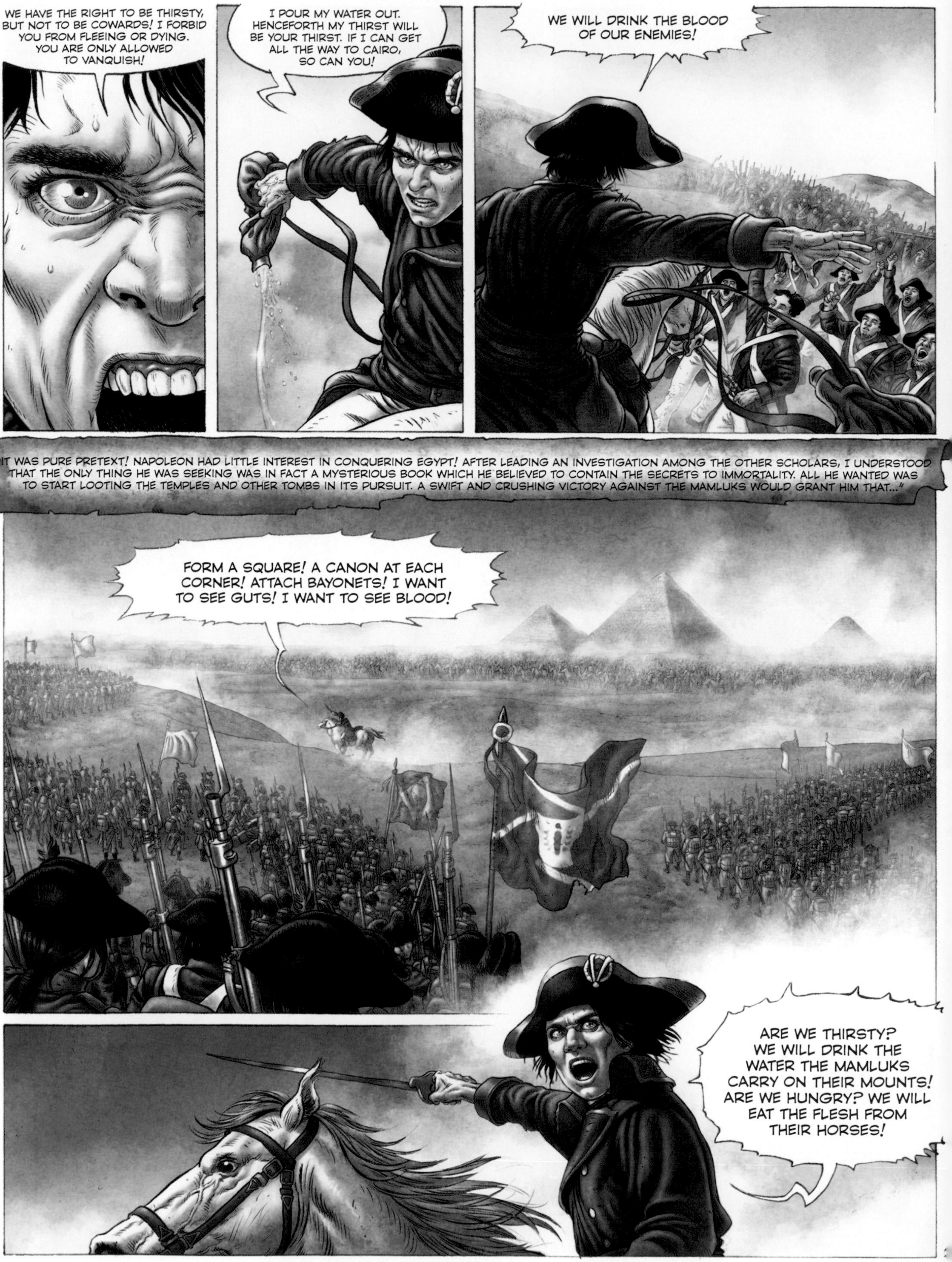
WE HAVE THE RIGHT TO BE THIRSTY, BUT NOT TO BE COWARDS! I FORBID YOU FROM FLEEING OR DYING. YOU ARE ONLY ALLOWED TO VANQUISH!
I POUR MY WATER OUT. HENCEFORTH MY THIRST WILL BE YOUR THIRST. IF I CAN GET ALL THE WAY TO CAIRO, SO CAN YOU!
WE WILL DRINK THE BLOOD OF OUR ENEMIES!
"IT WAS PURE PRETEXT! NAPOLEON HAD LITTLE INTEREST IN CONQUERING EGYPT! AFTER LEADING AN INVESTIGATION AMONG THE OTHER SCHOLARS, I UNDERSTOOD THAT THE ONLY THING HE WAS SEEKING WAS IN FACT A MYSTERIOUS BOOK WHICH HE BELIEVED TO CONTAIN THE SECRETS TO IMMORTALITY. ALL HE WANTED WAS TO START LOOTING THE TEMPLES AND OTHER TOMBS IN ITS PURSUIT. A SWIFT AND CRUSHING VICTORY AGAINST THE MAMLUKS WOULD GRANT HIM THAT..."
FORM A SQUARE! A CANON AT EACH CORNER! ATTACH BAYONETS! I WANT TO SEE GUTS! I WANT TO SEE BLOOD!
ARE WE THIRSTY? WE WILL DRINK THE WATER THE MAMLUKS CARRY ON THEIR MOUNTS! ARE WE HUNGRY? WE WILL EAT THE FLESH FROM THEIR HORSES!

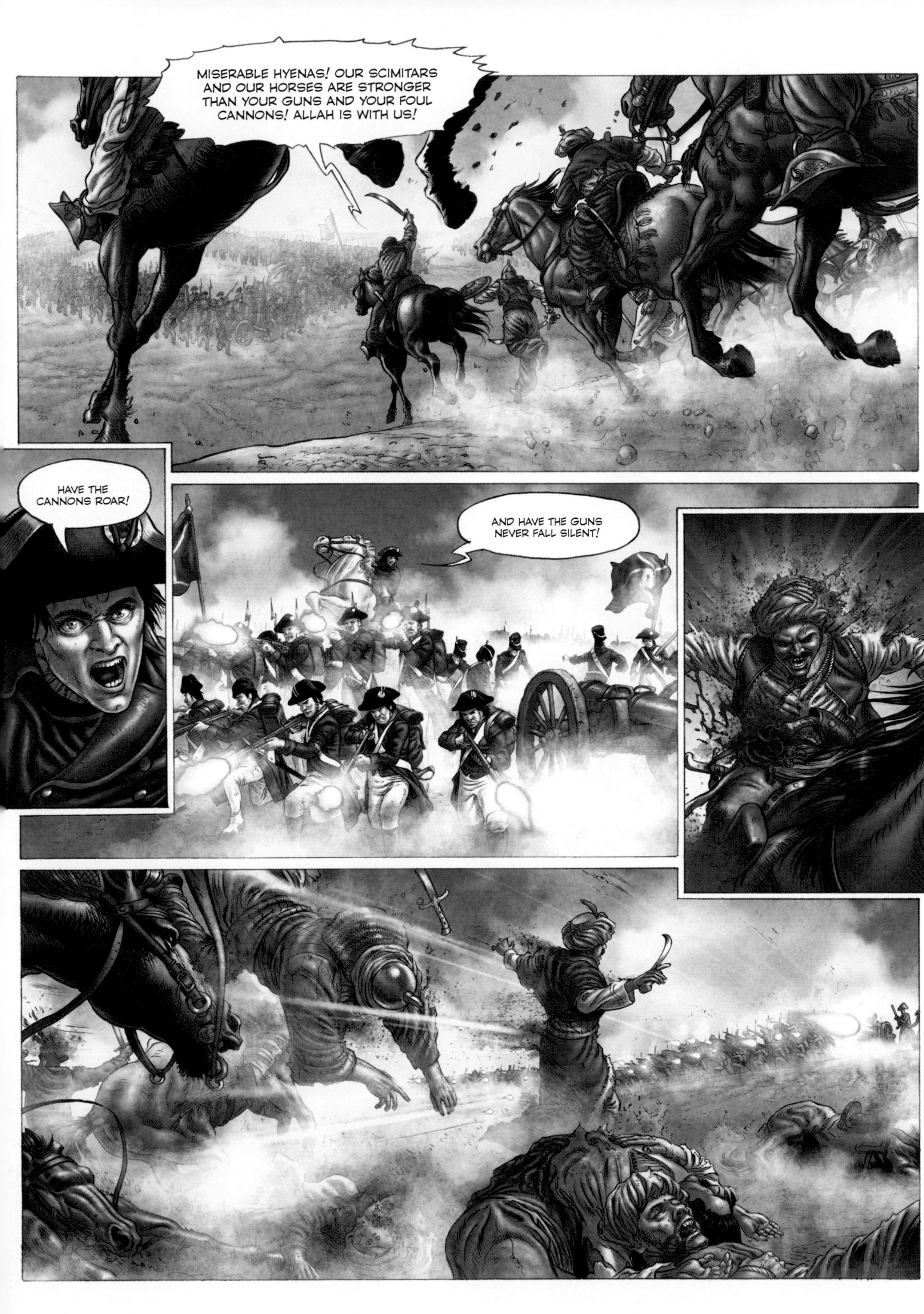
MISERABLE HYENAS! OUR SCIMITARS AND OUR HORSES ARE STRONGER THAN YOUR GUNS AND YOUR FOUL CANNONS! ALLAH IS WITH US!
HAVE THE CANNONS ROAR!
AND HAVE THE GUNS NEVER FALL SILENT!

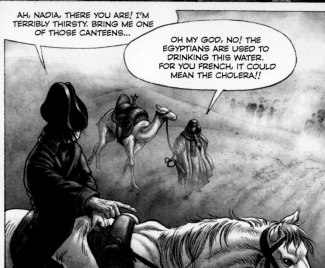

AH, NADIA, THERE YOU ARE! I'M TERRIBLY THIRSTY. BRING ME ONE OF THOSE CANTEENS...

OH MY GOD, NO! THE EGYPTIANS ARE USED TO DRINKING THIS WATER. FOR YOU FRENCH, IT COULD MEAN THE CHOLERA!!

I... I KNOW A FOUNTAIN OF PUREST WATER VERY CLOSE TO HERE.

LET'S GO, QUICKLY. TAKE ME TO THIS BLESSED SPRING!

CLOUDS OF SICKENING DUST, THE BURNING SAND, A BARREN SPHYNX -- THERE'S NO WATER HERE. YOU'RE MAD!!

2

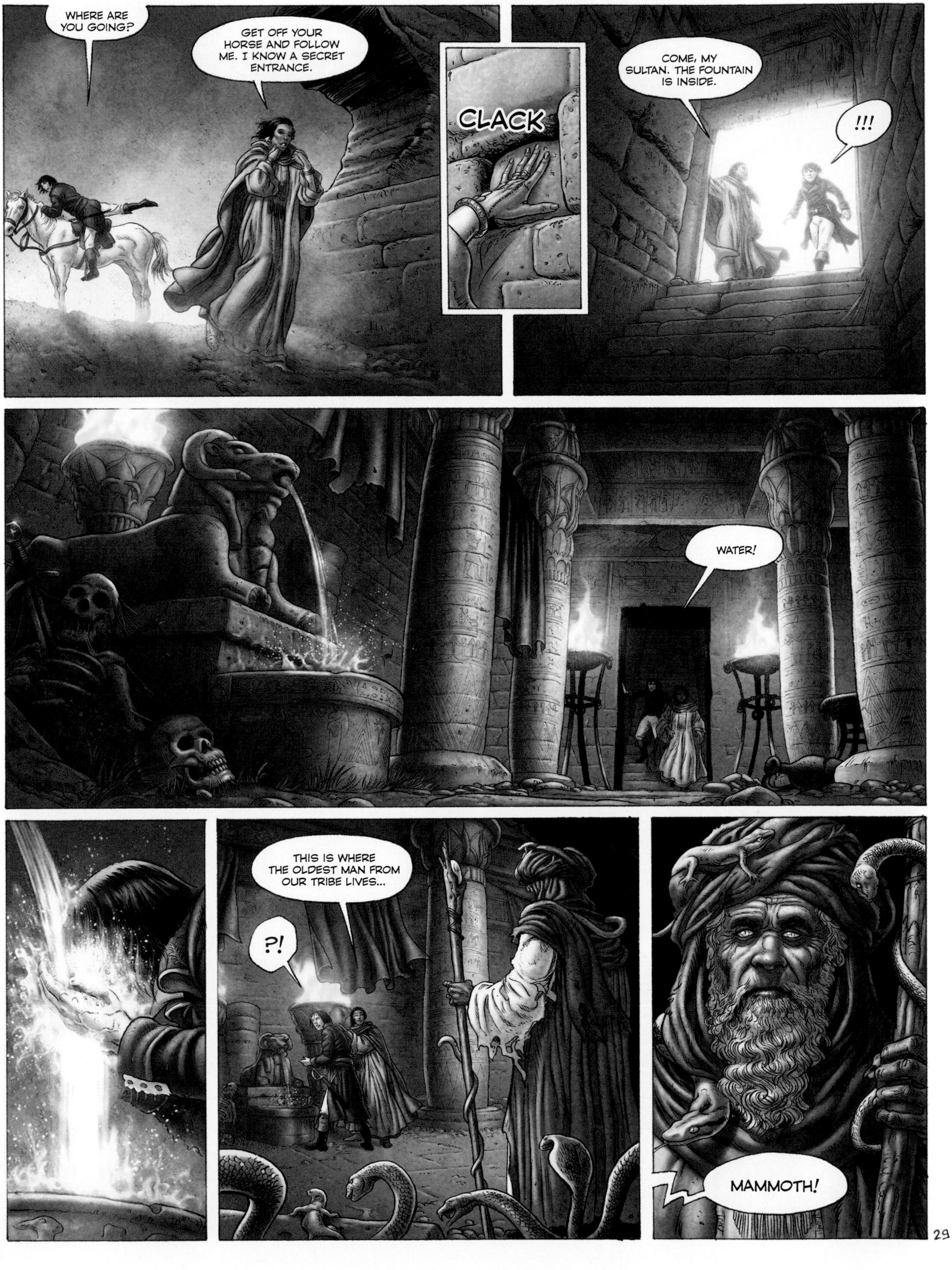

WHERE ARE YOU GOING?
GET OFF YOUR HORSE AND FOLLOW ME. I KNOW A SECRET ENTRANCE.
CLACK
COME, MY SULTAN. THE FOUNTAIN IS INSIDE.
!!!
WATER!
THIS IS WHERE THE OLDEST MAN FROM OUR TRIBE LIVES...
?!
MAMMOTH!

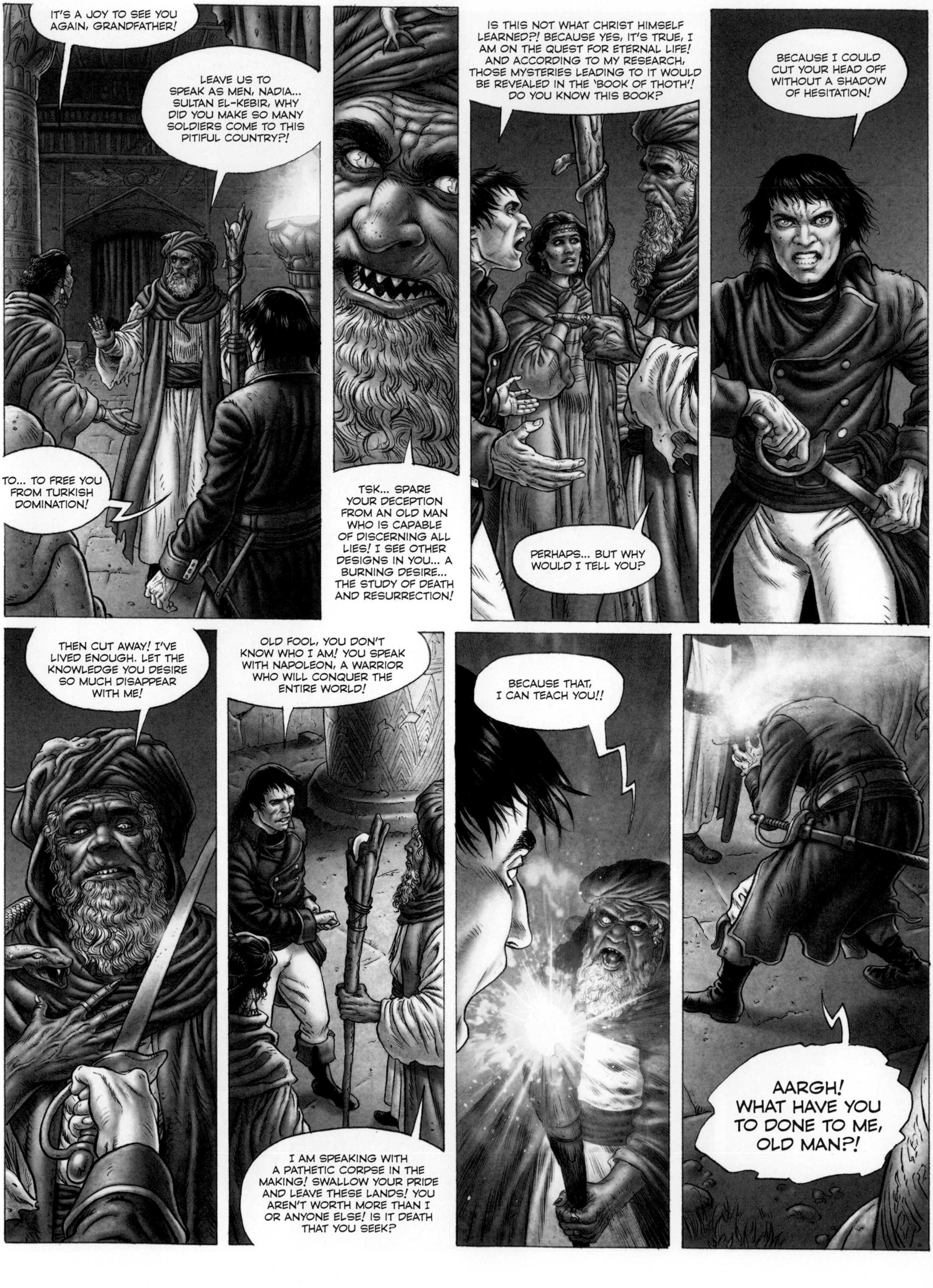
IT'S A JOY TO SEE YOU AGAIN, GRANDFATHER!
LEAVE US TO SPEAK AS MEN, NADIA... SULTAN EL-KEBIR, WHY DID YOU MAKE SO MANY SOLDIERS COME TO THIS PITIFUL COUNTRY?!
TO... TO FREE YOU FROM TURKISH DOMINATION!
TSK... SPARE YOUR DECEPTION FROM AN OLD MAN WHO IS CAPABLE OF DISCERNING ALL LIES! I SEE OTHER DESIGNS IN YOU... A BURNING DESIRE... THE STUDY OF DEATH AND RESURRECTION!
IS THIS NOT WHAT CHRIST HIMSELF LEARNED?! BECAUSE YES, IT'S TRUE, I AM ON THE QUEST FOR ETERNAL LIFE! AND ACCORDING TO MY RESEARCH, THOSE MYSTERIES LEADING TO IT WOULD BE REVEALED IN THE 'BOOK OF THOTH'! DO YOU KNOW THIS BOOK?
PERHAPS... BUT WHY WOULD I TELL YOU?
BECAUSE I COULD CUT YOUR HEAD OFF WITHOUT A SHADOW OF HESITATION!
THEN CUT AWAY! I'VE LIVED ENOUGH. LET THE KNOWLEDGE YOU DESIRE SO MUCH DISAPPEAR WITH ME!
OLD FOOL, YOU DON'T KNOW WHO I AM! YOU SPEAK WITH NAPOLEON, A WARRIOR WHO WILL CONQUER THE ENTIRE WORLD!
I AM SPEAKING WITH A PATHETIC CORPSE IN THE MAKING! SWALLOW YOUR PRIDE AND LEAVE THESE LANDS! YOU AREN'T WORTH MORE THAN I OR ANYONE ELSE! IS IT DEATH THAT YOU SEEK?
BECAUSE THAT, I CAN TEACH YOU!!
AARGH! WHAT HAVE YOU TO DONE TO ME, OLD MAN?!

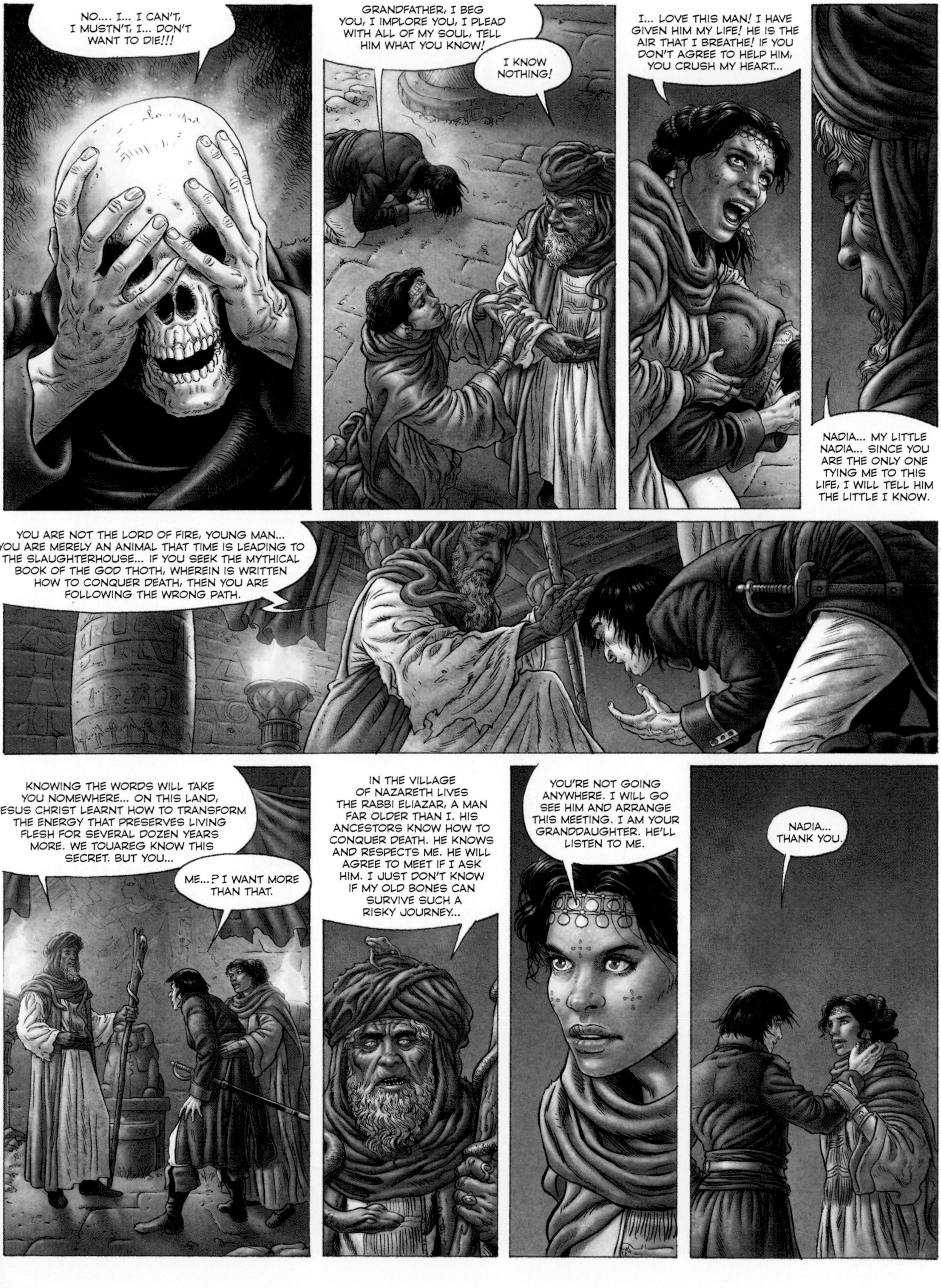
NO.... I... I CAN'T, I MUSTN'T, I... DON'T WANT TO DIE!!!
GRANDFATHER, I BEG YOU, I IMPLORE YOU, I PLEAD WITH ALL OF MY SOUL, TELL HIM WHAT YOU KNOW!
I KNOW NOTHING!
I... LOVE THIS MAN! I HAVE GIVEN HIM MY LIFE! HE IS THE AIR THAT I BREATHE! IF YOU DON'T AGREE TO HELP HIM, YOU CRUSH MY HEART...
NADIA... MY LITTLE NADIA... SINCE YOU ARE THE ONLY ONE TYING ME TO THIS LIFE, I WILL TELL HIM THE LITTLE I KNOW.
YOU ARE NOT THE LORD OF FIRE, YOUNG MAN... YOU ARE MERELY AN ANIMAL THAT TIME IS LEADING TO THE SLAUGHTERHOUSE... IF YOU SEEK THE MYTHICAL BOOK OF THE GOD THOTH, WHEREIN IS WRITTEN HOW TO CONQUER DEATH, THEN YOU ARE FOLLOWING THE WRONG PATH.
KNOWING THE WORDS WILL TAKE YOU NOWHERE... ON THIS LAND, JESUS CHRIST LEARNT HOW TO TRANSFORM THE ENERGY THAT PRESERVES LIVING FLESH FOR SEVERAL DOZEN YEARS MORE. WE TOUAREG KNOW THIS SECRET. BUT YOU...
ME...? I WANT MORE THAN THAT.
IN THE VILLAGE OF NAZARETH LIVES THE RABBI ELIAZAR, A MAN FAR OLDER THAN I. HIS ANCESTORS KNOW HOW TO CONQUER DEATH. HE KNOWS AND RESPECTS ME. HE WILL AGREE TO MEET IF I ASK HIM. I JUST DON'T KNOW IF MY OLD BONES CAN SURVIVE SUCH A RISKY JOURNEY...
YOU'RE NOT GOING ANYWHERE. I WILL GO SEE HIM AND ARRANGE THIS MEETING. I AM YOUR GRANDDAUGHTER. HE'LL LISTEN TO ME.
NADIA... THANK YOU.

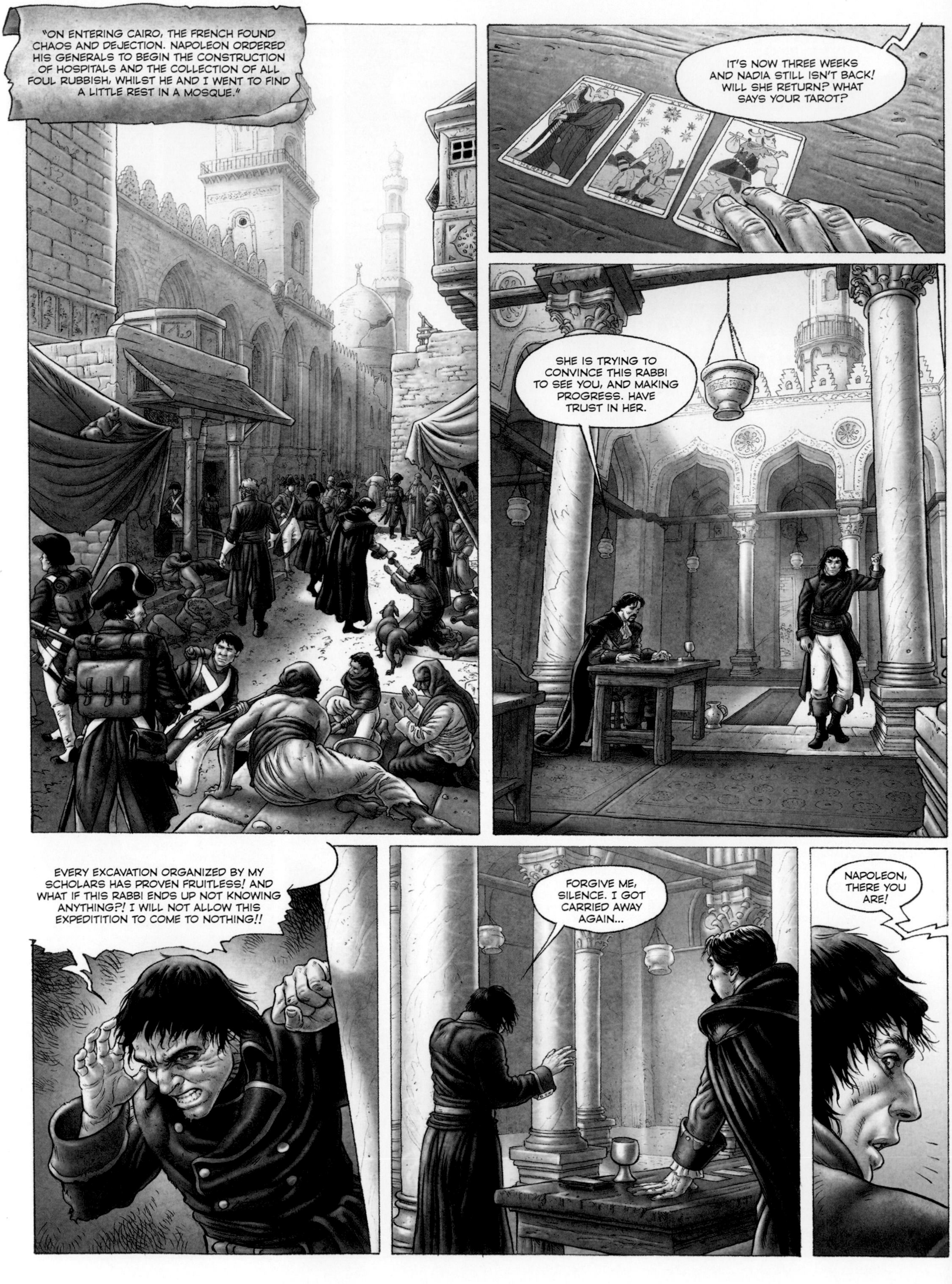
"ON ENTERING CAIRO, THE FRENCH FOUND CHAOS AND DEJECTION. NAPOLEON ORDERED HIS GENERALS TO BEGIN THE CONSTRUCTION OF HOSPITALS AND THE COLLECTION OF ALL FOUL RUBBISH, WHILST HE AND I WENT TO FIND A LITTLE REST IN A MOSQUE."
IT'S NOW THREE WEEKS AND NADIA STILL ISN'T BACK! WILL SHE RETURN? WHAT SAYS YOUR TAROT?
SHE IS TRYING TO CONVINCE THIS RABBI TO SEE YOU, AND MAKING PROGRESS. HAVE TRUST IN HER.
EVERY EXCAVATION ORGANIZED BY MY SCHOLARS HAS PROVEN FRUITLESS! AND WHAT IF THIS RABBI ENDS UP NOT KNOWING ANYTHING?! I WILL NOT ALLOW THIS EXPEDITITION TO COME TO NOTHING!!
FORGIVE ME, SILENCE. I GOT CARRIED AWAY AGAIN...
NAPOLEON, THERE YOU ARE!

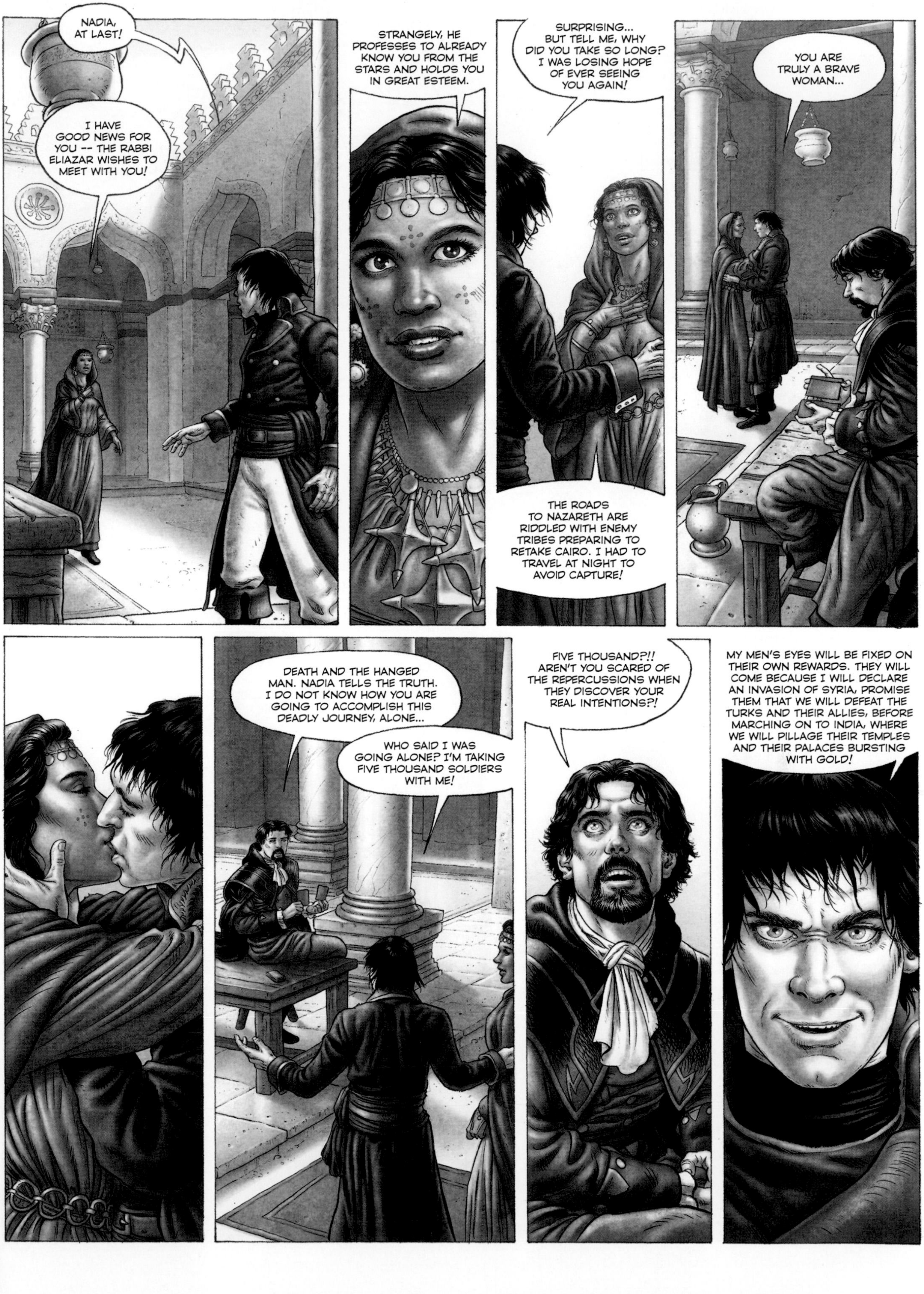
NADIA, AT LAST!
I HAVE GOOD NEWS FOR YOU -- THE RABBI ELIAZAR WISHES TO MEET WITH YOU!
STRANGELY, HE PROFESSES TO ALREADY KNOW YOU FROM THE STARS AND HOLDS YOU IN GREAT ESTEEM.
SURPRISING... BUT TELL ME, WHY DID YOU TAKE SO LONG? I WAS LOSING HOPE OF EVER SEEING YOU AGAIN!
THE ROADS TO NAZARETH ARE RIDDLED WITH ENEMY TRIBES PREPARING TO RETAKE CAIRO. I HAD TO TRAVEL AT NIGHT TO AVOID CAPTURE!
YOU ARE TRULY A BRAVE WOMAN...
DEATH AND THE HANGED MAN. NADIA TELLS THE TRUTH. I DO NOT KNOW HOW YOU ARE GOING TO ACCOMPLISH THIS DEADLY JOURNEY, ALONE...
WHO SAID I WAS GOING ALONE? I'M TAKING FIVE THOUSAND SOLDIERS WITH ME!
FIVE THOUSAND?!! AREN'T YOU SCARED OF THE REPERCUSSIONS WHEN THEY DISCOVER YOUR REAL INTENTIONS?!
MY MEN'S EYES WILL BE FIXED ON THEIR OWN REWARDS. THEY WILL COME BECAUSE I WILL DECLARE AN INVASION OF SYRIA, PROMISE THEM THAT WE WILL DEFEAT THE TURKS AND THEIR ALLIES, BEFORE MARCHING ON TO INDIA, WHERE WE WILL PILLAGE THEIR TEMPLES AND THEIR PALACES BURSTING WITH GOLD!

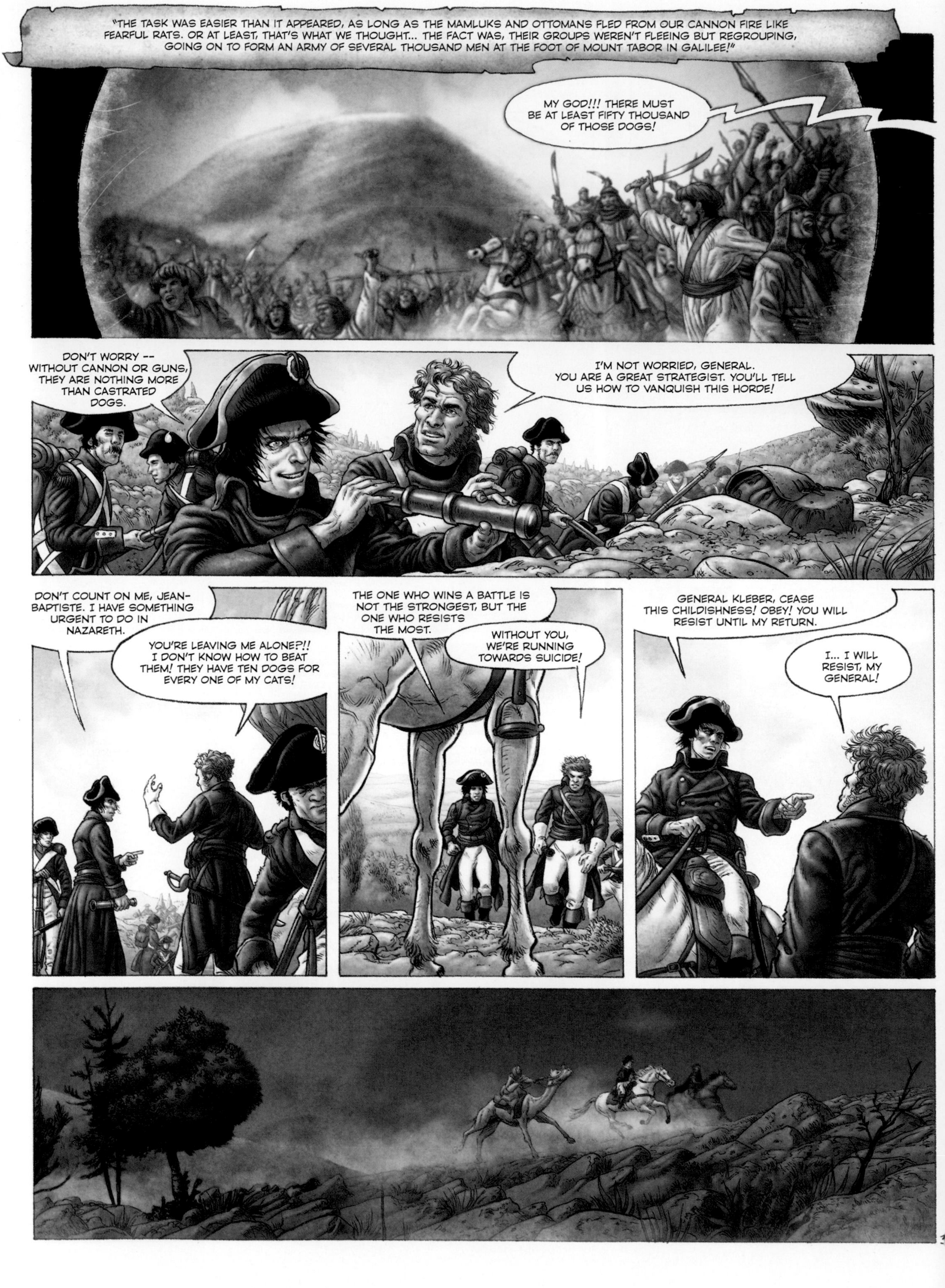
"THE TASK WAS EASIER THAN IT APPEARED, AS LONG AS THE MAMLUKS AND OTTOMANS FLED FROM OUR CANNON FIRE LIKE FEARFUL RATS. OR AT LEAST, THAT'S WHAT WE THOUGHT... THE FACT WAS, THEIR GROUPS WEREN'T FLEEING BUT REGROUPING, GOING ON TO FORM AN ARMY OF SEVERAL THOUSAND MEN AT THE FOOT OF MOUNT TABOR IN GALILEE!"
MY GOD!!! THERE MUST BE AT LEAST FIFTY THOUSAND OF THOSE DOGS!
DON'T WORRY -- WITHOUT CANNON OR GUNS, THEY ARE NOTHING MORE THAN CASTRATED DOGS.
I'M NOT WORRIED, GENERAL. YOU ARE A GREAT STRATEGIST. YOU'LL TELL US HOW TO VANQUISH THIS HORDE!
DON'T COUNT ON ME, JEAN-BAPTISTE. I HAVE SOMETHING URGENT TO DO IN NAZARETH.
YOU'RE LEAVING ME ALONE?!! I DON'T KNOW HOW TO BEAT THEM! THEY HAVE TEN DOGS FOR EVERY ONE OF MY CATS!
THE ONE WHO WINS A BATTLE IS NOT THE STRONGEST, BUT THE ONE WHO RESISTS THE MOST.
WITHOUT YOU, WE'RE RUNNING TOWARDS SUICIDE!
GENERAL KLEBER, CEASE THIS CHILDISHNESS! OBEY! YOU WILL RESIST UNTIL MY RETURN.
I... I WILL RESIST, MY GENERAL!

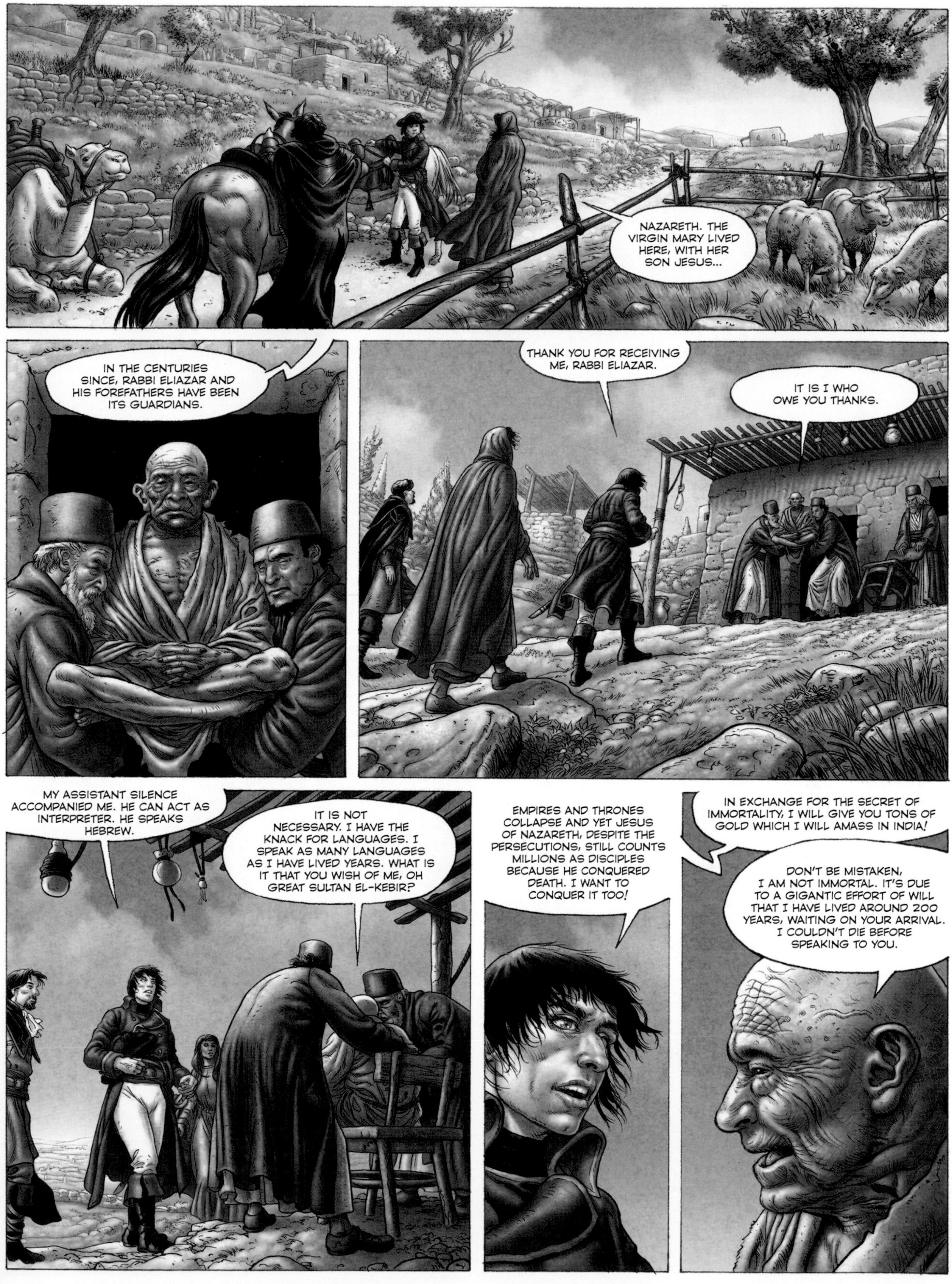
NAZARETH. THE VIRGIN MARY LIVED HERE, WITH HER SON JESUS...
IN THE CENTURIES SINCE, RABBI ELIAZAR AND HIS FOREFATHERS HAVE BEEN ITS GUARDIANS.
THANK YOU FOR RECEIVING ME, RABBI ELIAZAR.
IT IS I WHO OWE YOU THANKS.
MY ASSISTANT SILENCE ACCOMPANIED ME. HE CAN ACT AS INTERPRETER. HE SPEAKS HEBREW.
IT IS NOT NECESSARY. I HAVE THE KNACK FOR LANGUAGES. I SPEAK AS MANY LANGUAGES AS I HAVE LIVED YEARS. WHAT IS IT THAT YOU WISH OF ME, OH GREAT SULTAN EL-KEBIR?
EMPIRES AND THRONES COLLAPSE AND YET JESUS OF NAZARETH, DESPITE THE PERSECUTIONS, STILL COUNTS MILLIONS AS DISCIPLES BECAUSE HE CONQUERED DEATH. I WANT TO CONQUER IT TOO!
IN EXCHANGE FOR THE SECRET OF IMMORTALITY, I WILL GIVE YOU TONS OF GOLD WHICH I WILL AMASS IN INDIA!
DON'T BE MISTAKEN, I AM NOT IMMORTAL. IT'S DUE TO A GIGANTIC EFFORT OF WILL THAT I HAVE LIVED AROUND 200 YEARS, WAITING ON YOUR ARRIVAL. I COULDN'T DIE BEFORE SPEAKING TO YOU.

YOU WERE WAITING FOR ME? I FIND THAT HARD TO BELIEVE...

BELIEVE IT! ON THE HOLY TORAH, YOUR ARRIVAL WAS PREDICTED. YOU ARE GOING TO RETURN TO EGYPT ITS ANCIENT SPLENDOR, AND TO THE HEBREW PEOPLE THEIR HOLY LANDS. LISTEN TO ME WELL...

THERE IS NO SECRET MADE OF WORDS. IMMORTALITY IS INJECTED BY A SUPERHUMAN BEING INTO WEAK MEN WHO HAVE THE CAPACITY TO ACQUIRE IT...

A SUPERHUMAN BEING? WHO?

THE PYRAMID OF CHEOPS.

EXCUSE ME??! A PILE OF ROCKS IS NOT A LIVING BEING!

YOU ARE MISTAKEN. THE PLANETS ARE SPHERES OF STONE AND EARTH AND YET THEY ARE ALIVE. THAT PYRAMID WAS BUILT BY THOSE WHO THE EGYPTIANS ONCE CONSIDERED GODS. NO ONE KNOWS WHAT THEY TRULY WERE.

I AM STRUGGLING TO FOLLOW... BUT I HAVE THE FEELING YOU AREN'T LYING TO ME. WHAT... WHAT MUST I DO?

YOU MUST SLEEP A WHOLE NIGHT IN THE KING'S CHAMBER, AT THE CENTER OF THE PYRAMID. IF YOU ARE TRULY THE AVATAR I BELIEVE YOU TO BE, LIKE THE CHRIST, YOU WILL ACCESS ETERNAL LIFE.

AND... IF I AM NOT THE ONE YOU CLAIM?

YOU WILL BE DISINTEGRATED.

!!!

IT IS UP TO YOU TO DECIDE WHETHER TO RISK IT OR NOT. BUT KNOW THAT YOU WILL ONLY HAVE THIS ONE AND ONLY CHANCE -- IN FOUR DAYS, WHEN ALL THE PLANETS OF OUR SOLAR SYSTEM ARE ALIGNED. A PHENOMENON WHICH OCCURS ONLY EVERY SEVERAL CENTURIES.

MERCURY, VENUS, MARS, JUPITER, SATURN, URANUS, NEPTUNE, AND PLUTO WILL CAST A SINGLE BEAM THAT THE PYRAMID WILL ABSORB AND INJECT INTO YOUR BODY. YOU WILL DIE FOR THREE HOURS AND THEN BE RESURRECTED, YOUR MIND ALTERED. LIKE IT WAS WITH JESUS.

I HAVE COMPLETED MY MISSION, SULTAN KEL-KEBIR. I HAVE PASSED ON THE GREAT SECRET. I MAY NOW LEAVE IN PEACE...

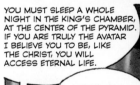

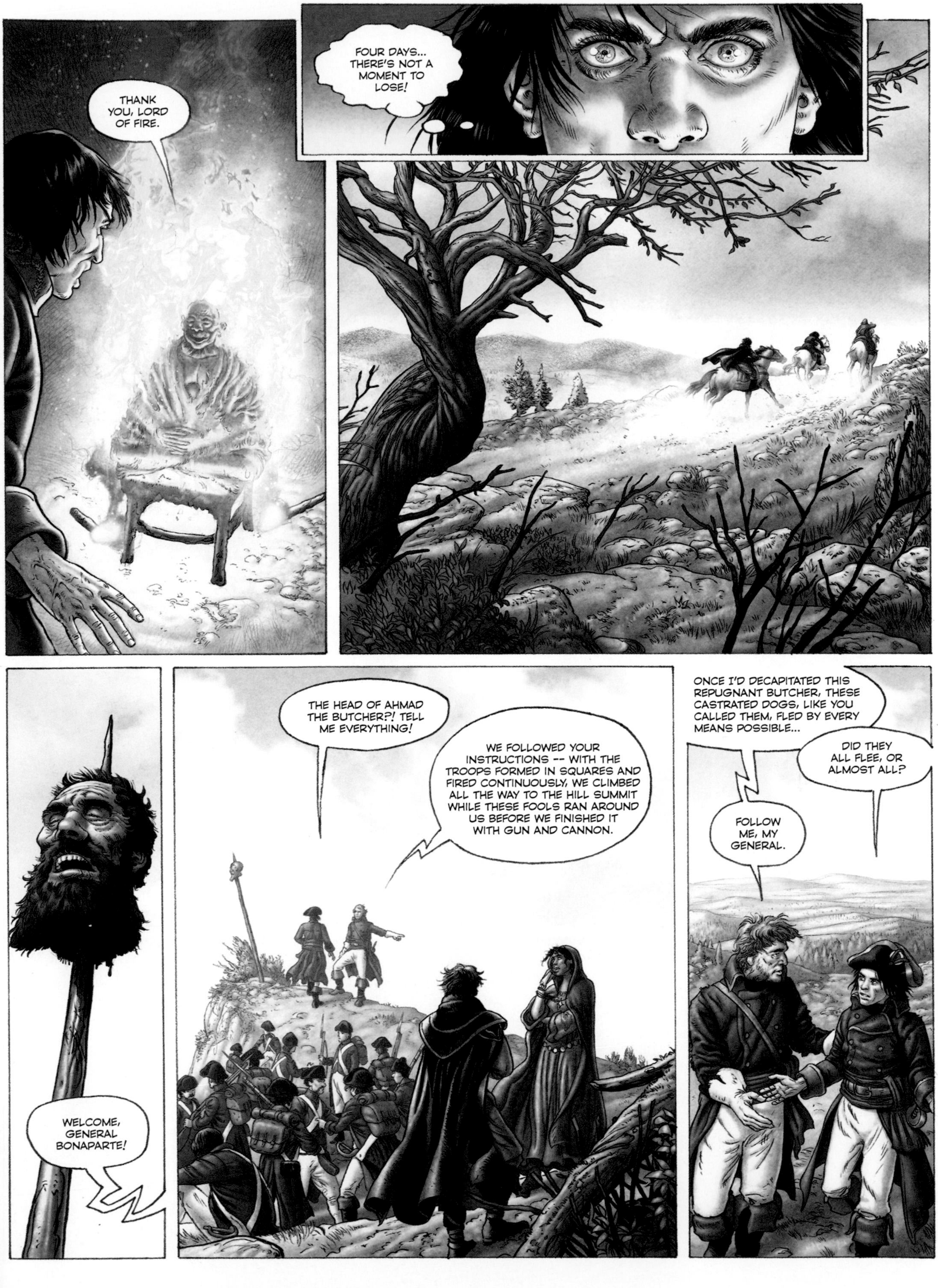
THANK YOU, LORD OF FIRE.
FOUR DAYS... THERE'S NOT A MOMENT TO LOSE!
WELCOME, GENERAL BONAPARTE!
THE HEAD OF AHMAD THE BUTCHER?! TELL ME EVERYTHING!
WE FOLLOWED YOUR INSTRUCTIONS -- WITH THE TROOPS FORMED IN SQUARES AND FIRED CONTINUOUSLY, WE CLIMBED ALL THE WAY TO THE HILL SUMMIT WHILE THESE FOOLS RAN AROUND US BEFORE WE FINISHED IT WITH GUN AND CANNON.
ONCE I'D DECAPITATED THIS REPUGNANT BUTCHER, THESE CASTRATED DOGS, LIKE YOU CALLED THEM, FLED BY EVERY MEANS POSSIBLE...
DID THEY ALL FLEE, OR ALMOST ALL?
FOLLOW ME, MY GENERAL.

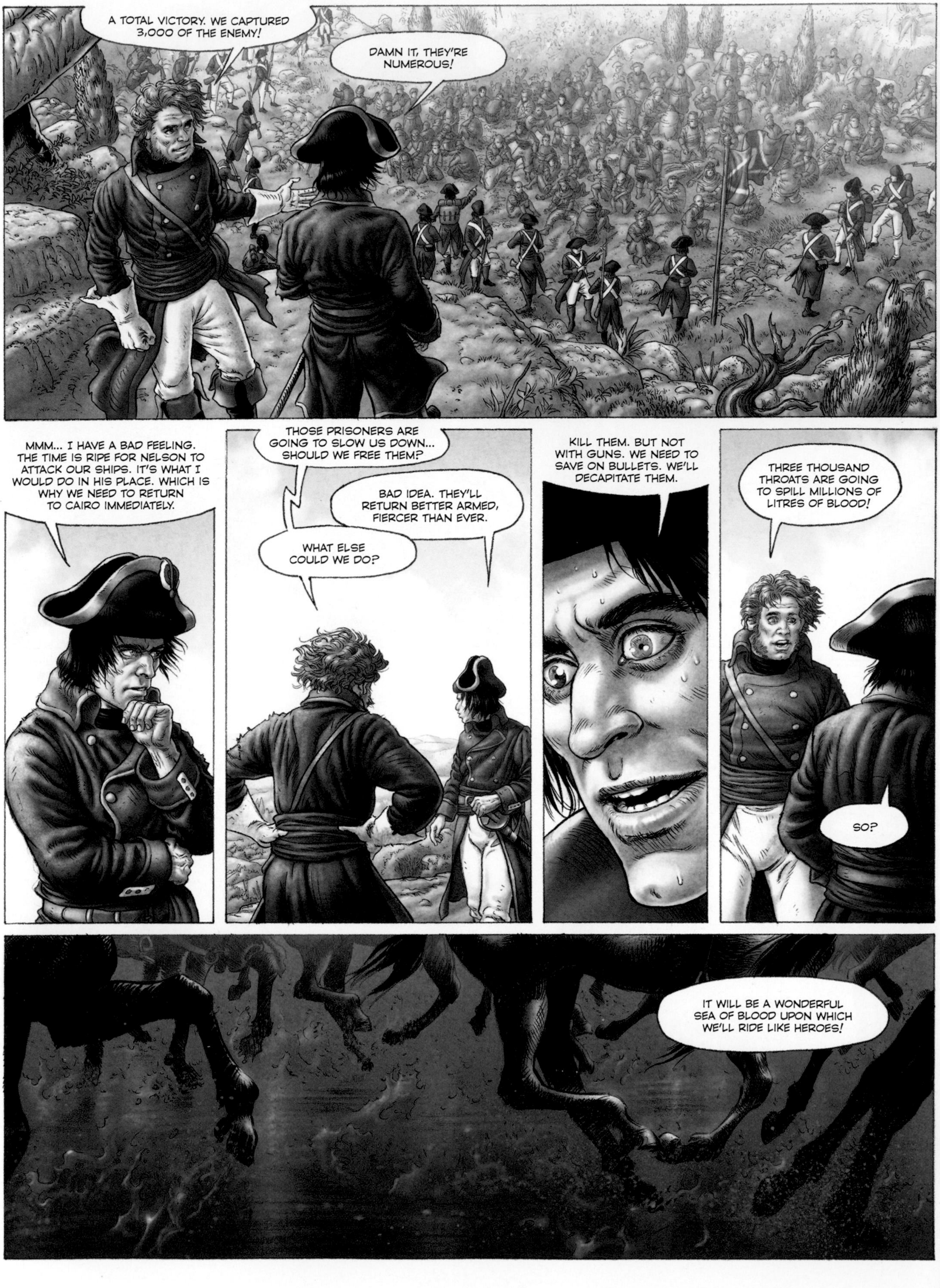
A TOTAL VICTORY. WE CAPTURED 3,000 OF THE ENEMY!
DAMN IT, THEY'RE NUMEROUS!
MMM... I HAVE A BAD FEELING. THE TIME IS RIPE FOR NELSON TO ATTACK OUR SHIPS. IT'S WHAT I WOULD DO IN HIS PLACE. WHICH IS WHY WE NEED TO RETURN TO CAIRO IMMEDIATELY.
THOSE PRISONERS ARE GOING TO SLOW US DOWN... SHOULD WE FREE THEM?
BAD IDEA. THEY'LL RETURN BETTER ARMED, FIERCER THAN EVER.
WHAT ELSE COULD WE DO?
KILL THEM. BUT NOT WITH GUNS. WE NEED TO SAVE ON BULLETS. WE'LL DECAPITATE THEM.
THREE THOUSAND THROATS ARE GOING TO SPILL MILLIONS OF LITRES OF BLOOD!
SO?
IT WILL BE A WONDERFUL SEA OF BLOOD UPON WHICH WE'LL RIDE LIKE HEROES!

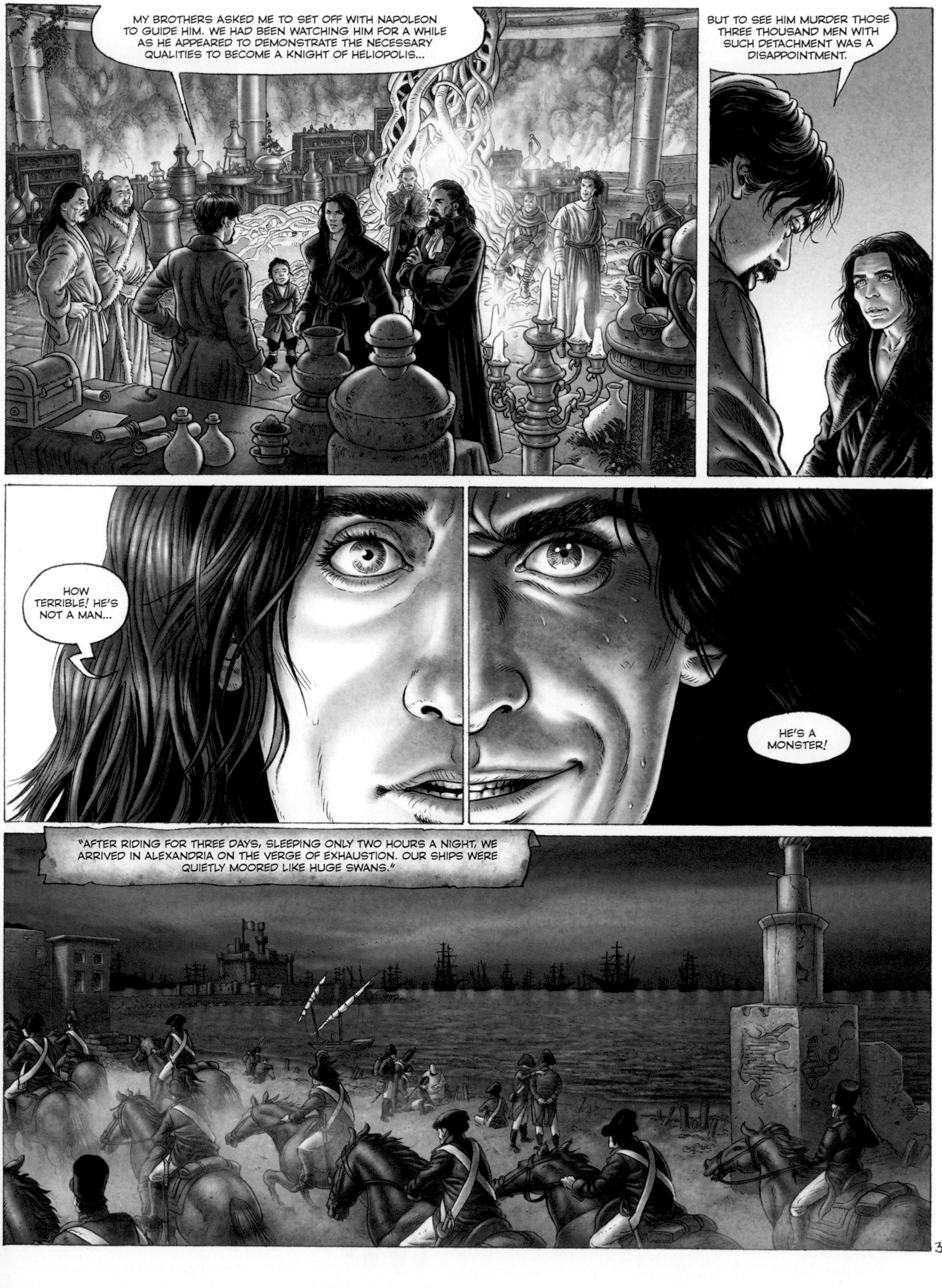
MY BROTHERS ASKED ME TO SET OFF WITH NAPOLEON TO GUIDE HIM. WE HAD BEEN WATCHING HIM FOR A WHILE AS HE APPEARED TO DEMONSTRATE THE NECESSARY QUALITIES TO BECOME A KNIGHT OF HELIOPOLIS...
BUT TO SEE HIM MURDER THOSE THREE THOUSAND MEN WITH SUCH DETACHMENT WAS A DISAPPOINTMENT.
HOW TERRIBLE! HE'S NOT A MAN...
HE'S A MONSTER!
"AFTER RIDING FOR THREE DAYS, SLEEPING ONLY TWO HOURS A NIGHT, WE ARRIVED IN ALEXANDRIA ON THE VERGE OF EXHAUSTION. OUR SHIPS WERE QUIETLY MOORED LIKE HUGE SWANS."

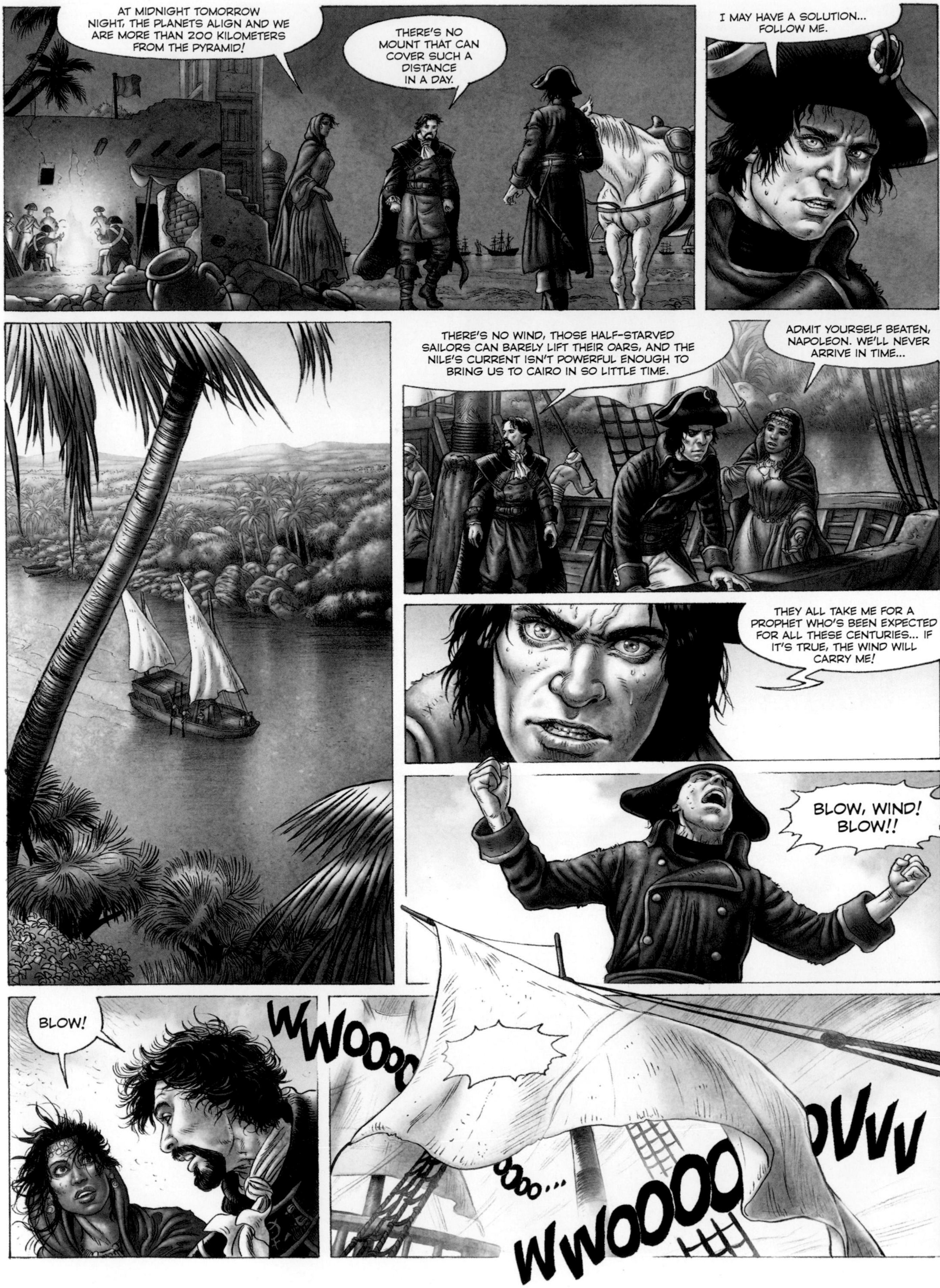
AT MIDNIGHT TOMORROW NIGHT, THE PLANETS ALIGN AND WE ARE MORE THAN 200 KILOMETERS FROM THE PYRAMID!
THERE'S NO MOUNT THAT CAN COVER SUCH A DISTANCE IN A DAY.
I MAY HAVE A SOLUTION... FOLLOW ME.
THERE'S NO WIND, THOSE HALF-STARVED SAILORS CAN BARELY LIFT THEIR OARS, AND THE NILE'S CURRENT ISN'T POWERFUL ENOUGH TO BRING US TO CAIRO IN SO LITTLE TIME.
ADMIT YOURSELF BEATEN, NAPOLEON. WE'LL NEVER ARRIVE IN TIME...
THEY ALL TAKE ME FOR A PROPHET WHO'S BEEN EXPECTED FOR ALL THESE CENTURIES... IF IT'S TRUE, THE WIND WILL CARRY ME!
BLOW, WIND! BLOW!!
BLOW!
WWOOOO
OOOO...
WWOOOO
OUVVV

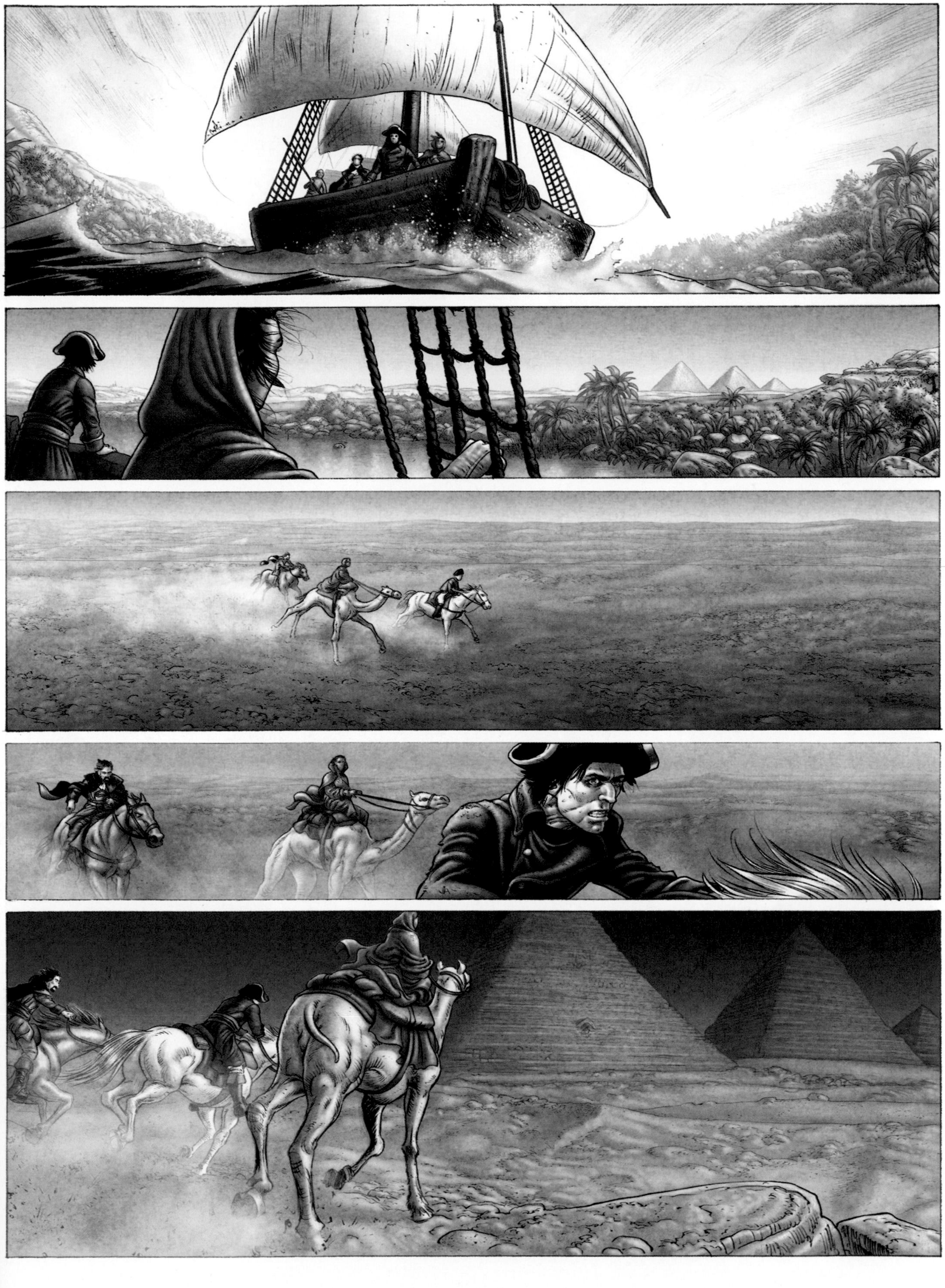

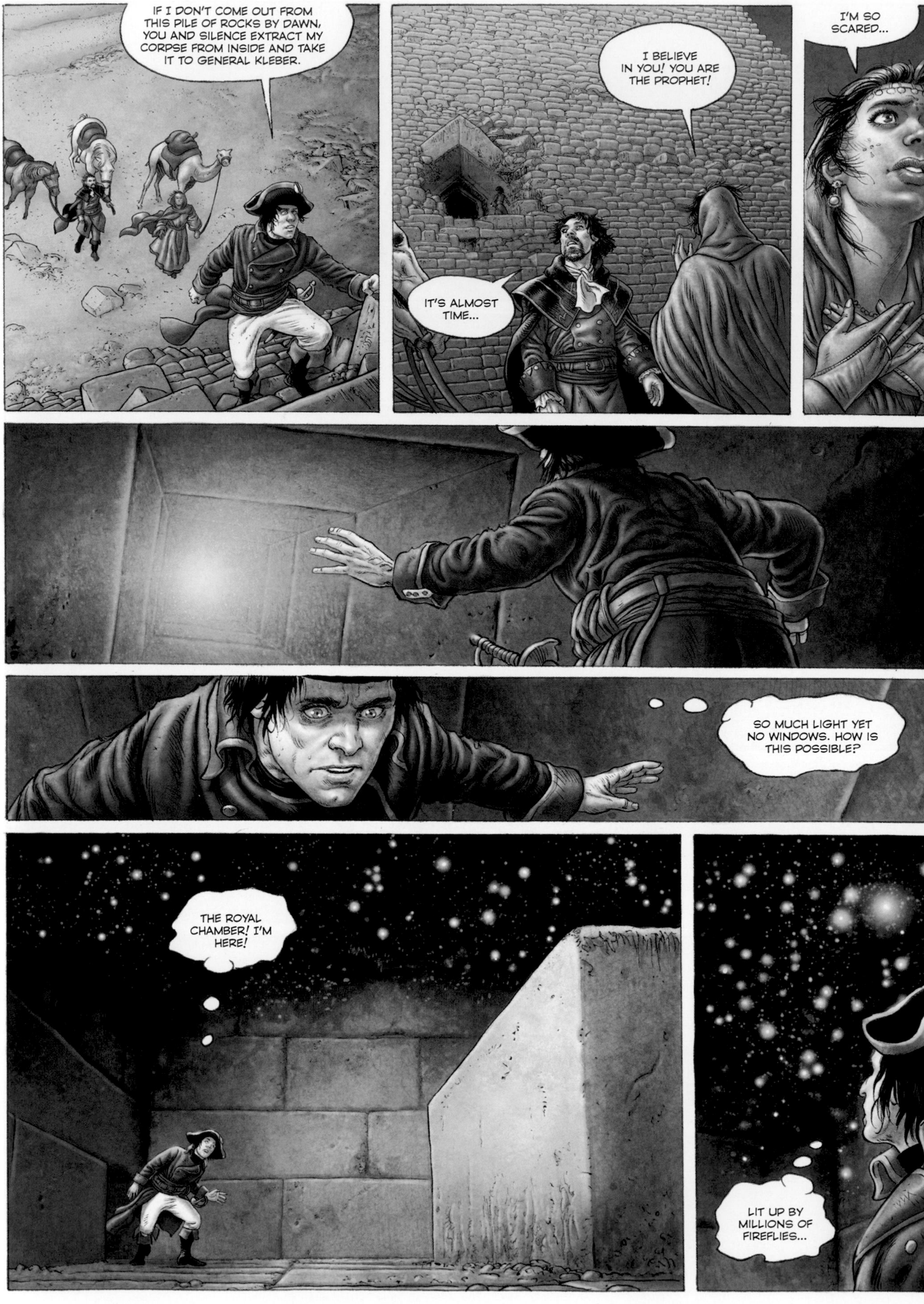
IF I DON'T COME OUT FROM THIS PILE OF ROCKS BY DAWN, YOU AND SILENCE EXTRACT MY CORPSE FROM INSIDE AND TAKE IT TO GENERAL KLEBER.
I BELIEVE IN YOU! YOU ARE THE PROPHET!
IT'S ALMOST TIME...
I'M SO SCARED...
SO MUCH LIGHT YET NO WINDOWS. HOW IS THIS POSSIBLE?
THE ROYAL CHAMBER! I'M HERE!
LIT UP BY MILLIONS OF FIREFLIES...

THAT ENORMOUS SARCOPHAGUS MUST HAVE BEEN BUILT FOR A GIGANTIC KING! THEY WEREN'T EXPECTING SOMEONE... OF MY SIZE...

QUITE THE OPPOSITE, IT'S A SMALL COFFIN! MAYBE TOO SMALL?

NO... IF I GO IN NAKED, IT'LL BE EXACTLY MY SIZE...

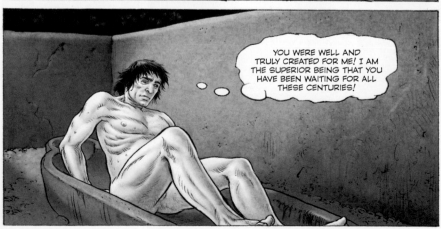

YOU WERE WELL AND TRULY CREATED FOR ME! I AM THE SUPERIOR BEING THAT YOU HAVE BEEN WAITING FOR ALL THESE CENTURIES!

!!!

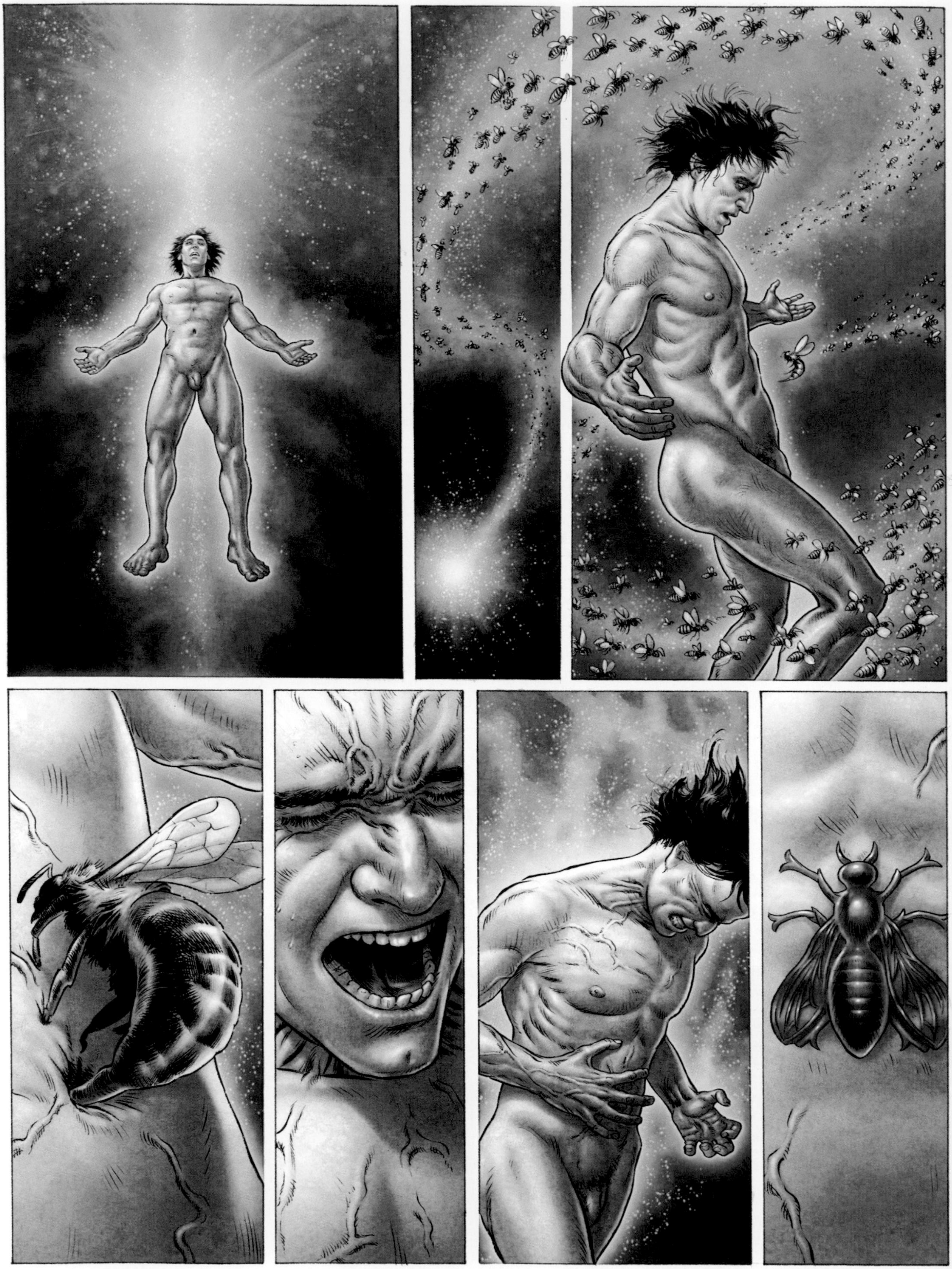

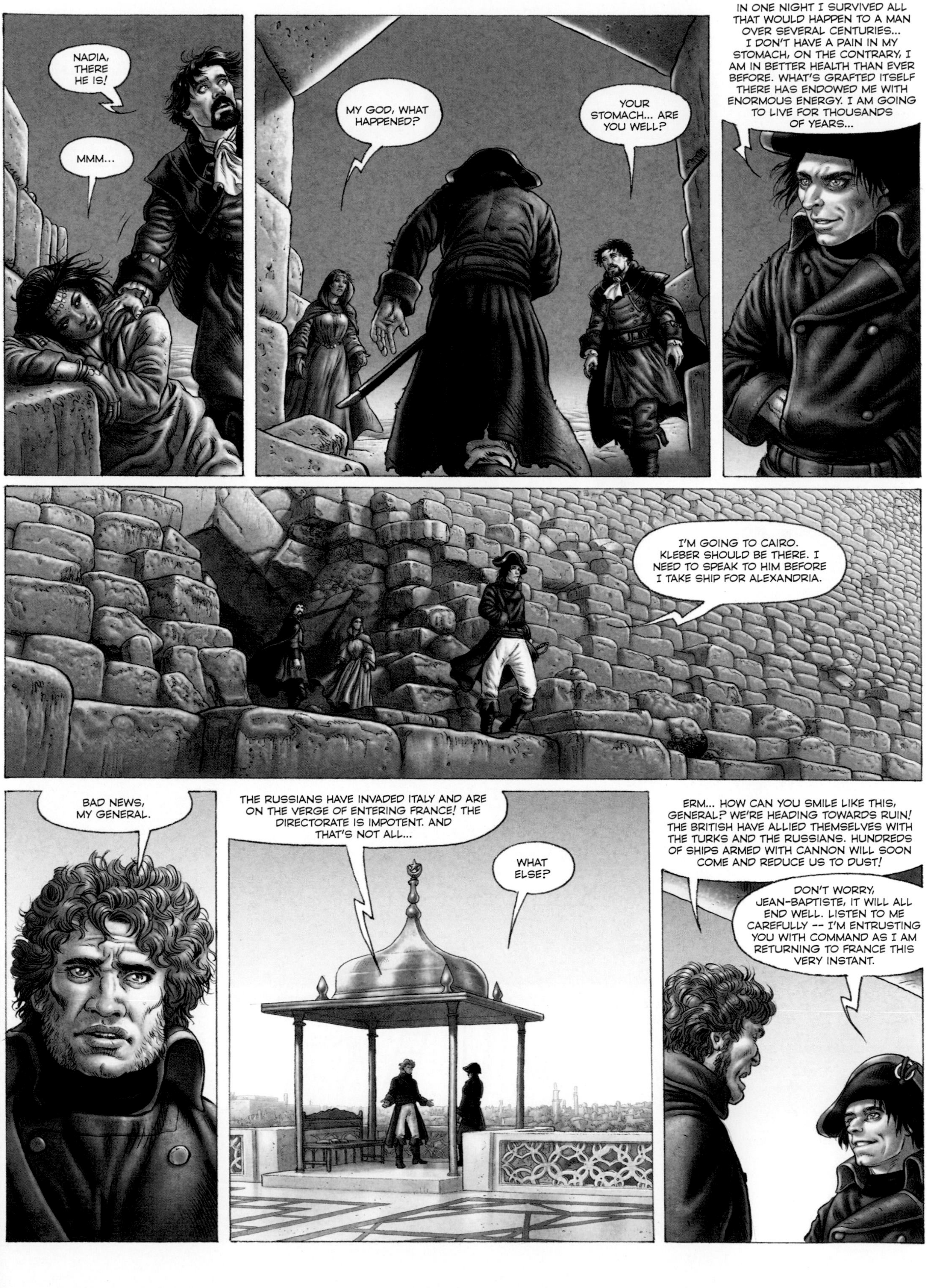
NADIA, THERE HE IS!
MMM...
MY GOD, WHAT HAPPENED?
YOUR STOMACH... ARE YOU WELL?
IN ONE NIGHT I SURVIVED ALL THAT WOULD HAPPEN TO A MAN OVER SEVERAL CENTURIES... I DON'T HAVE A PAIN IN MY STOMACH, ON THE CONTRARY, I AM IN BETTER HEALTH THAN EVER BEFORE. WHAT'S GRAFTED ITSELF THERE HAS ENDOWED ME WITH ENORMOUS ENERGY. I AM GOING TO LIVE FOR THOUSANDS OF YEARS...
I'M GOING TO CAIRO. KLEBER SHOULD BE THERE. I NEED TO SPEAK TO HIM BEFORE I TAKE SHIP FOR ALEXANDRIA.
BAD NEWS, MY GENERAL.
THE RUSSIANS HAVE INVADED ITALY AND ARE ON THE VERGE OF ENTERING FRANCE! THE DIRECTORATE IS IMPOTENT. AND THAT'S NOT ALL...
WHAT ELSE?
ERM... HOW CAN YOU SMILE LIKE THIS, GENERAL? WE'RE HEADING TOWARDS RUIN! THE BRITISH HAVE ALLIED THEMSELVES WITH THE TURKS AND THE RUSSIANS. HUNDREDS OF SHIPS ARMED WITH CANNON WILL SOON COME AND REDUCE US TO DUST!
DON'T WORRY, JEAN-BAPTISTE, IT WILL ALL END WELL. LISTEN TO ME CAREFULLY -- I'M ENTRUSTING YOU WITH COMMAND AS I AM RETURNING TO FRANCE THIS VERY INSTANT.

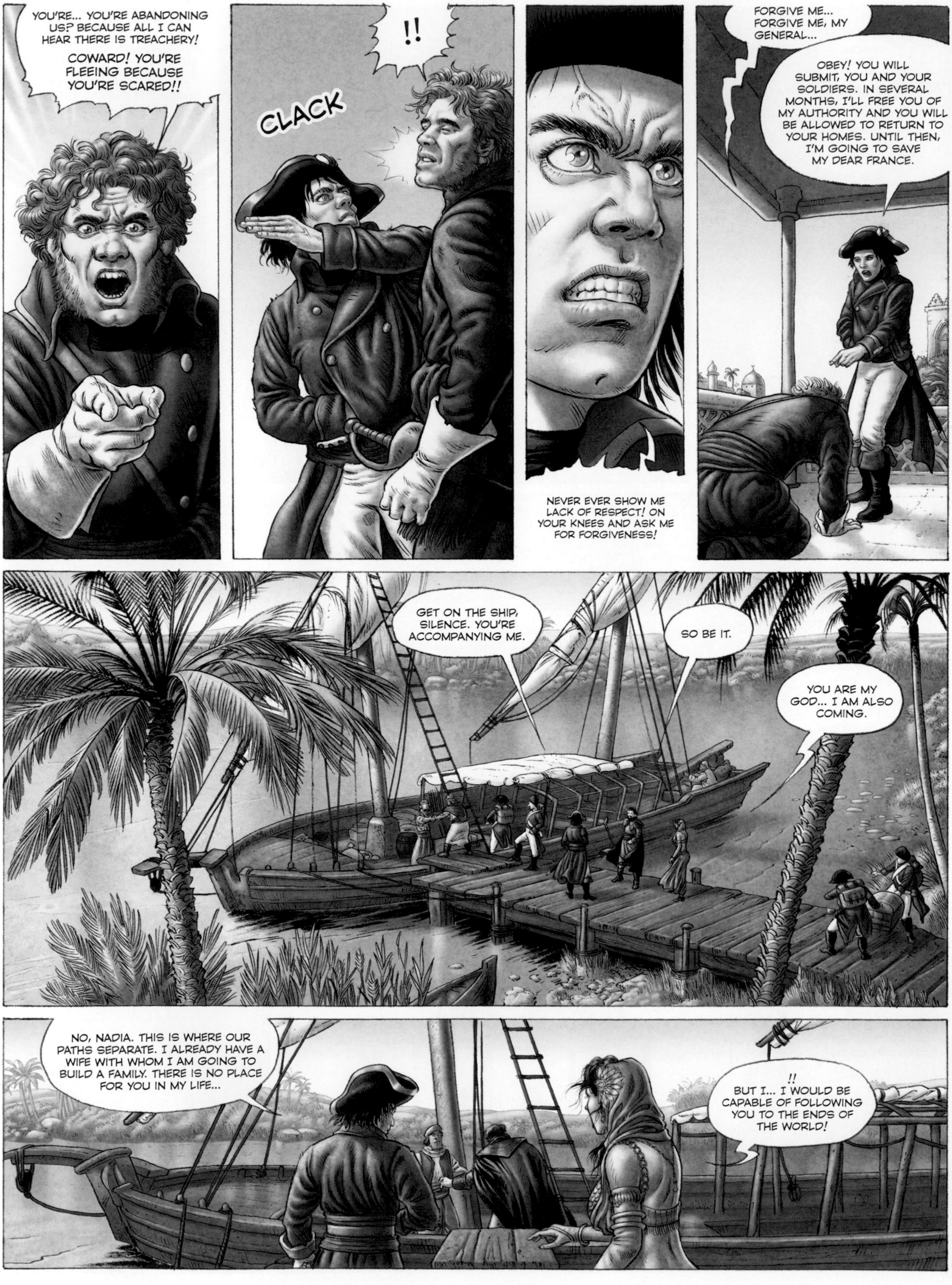
YOU'RE... YOU'RE ABANDONING US? BECAUSE ALL I CAN HEAR THERE IS TREACHERY!
COWARD! YOU'RE FLEEING BECAUSE YOU'RE SCARED!!
!!
CLACK
NEVER EVER SHOW ME LACK OF RESPECT! ON YOUR KNEES AND ASK ME FOR FORGIVENESS!
FORGIVE ME... FORGIVE ME, MY GENERAL...
OBEY! YOU WILL SUBMIT, YOU AND YOUR SOLDIERS. IN SEVERAL MONTHS, I'LL FREE YOU OF MY AUTHORITY AND YOU WILL BE ALLOWED TO RETURN TO YOUR HOMES. UNTIL THEN, I'M GOING TO SAVE MY DEAR FRANCE.
GET ON THE SHIP, SILENCE. YOU'RE ACCOMPANYING ME.
SO BE IT.
YOU ARE MY GOD... I AM ALSO COMING.
NO, NADIA. THIS IS WHERE OUR PATHS SEPARATE. I ALREADY HAVE A WIFE WITH WHOM I AM GOING TO BUILD A FAMILY. THERE IS NO PLACE FOR YOU IN MY LIFE...
!!
BUT I... I WOULD BE CAPABLE OF FOLLOWING YOU TO THE ENDS OF THE WORLD!

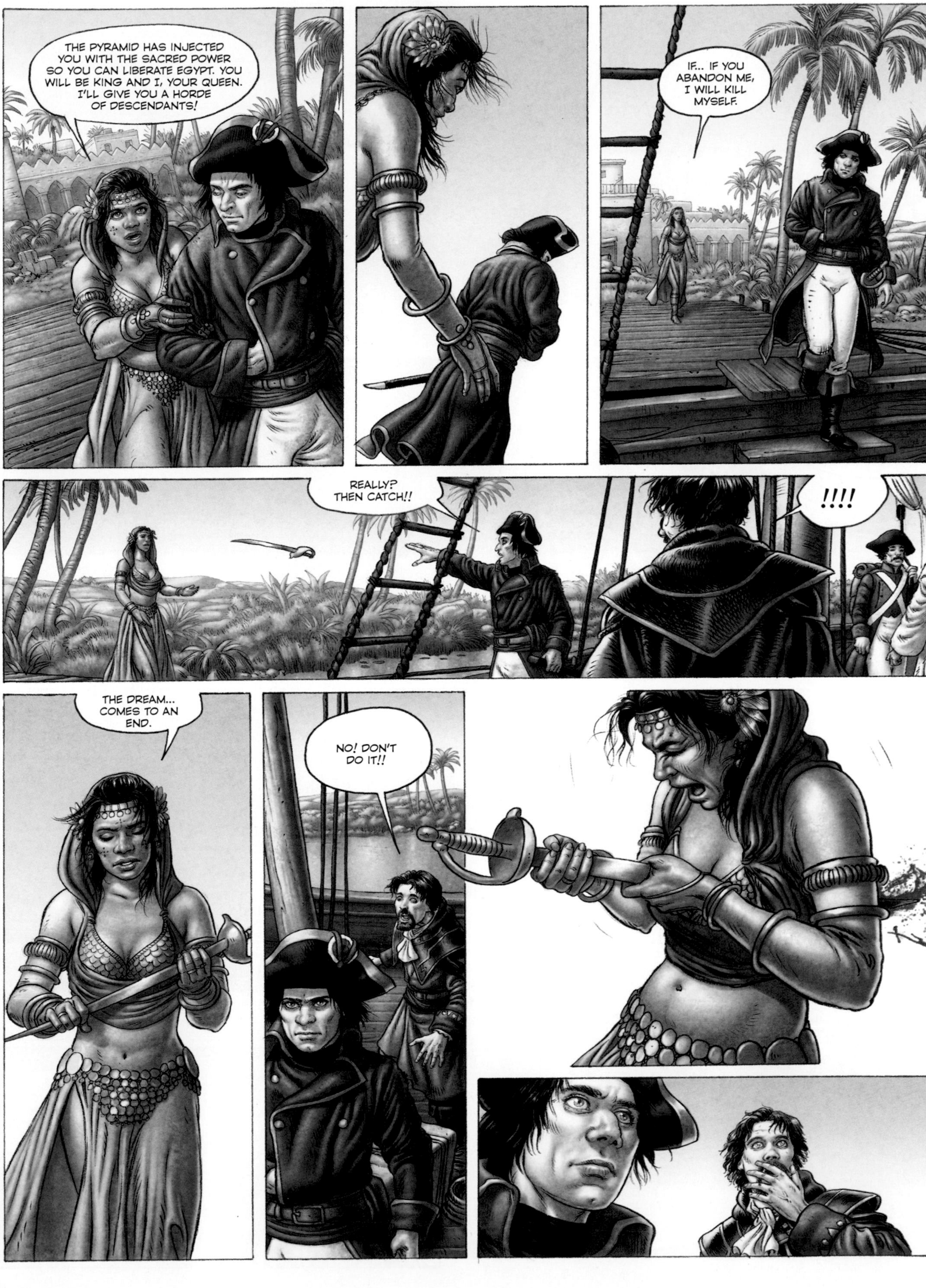
THE PYRAMID HAS INJECTED YOU WITH THE SACRED POWER SO YOU CAN LIBERATE EGYPT. YOU WILL BE KING AND I, YOUR QUEEN. I'LL GIVE YOU A HORDE OF DESCENDANTS!
IF... IF YOU ABANDON ME, I WILL KILL MYSELF.
REALLY? THEN CATCH!!
!!!!
THE DREAM... COMES TO AN END.
NO! DON'T DO IT!!

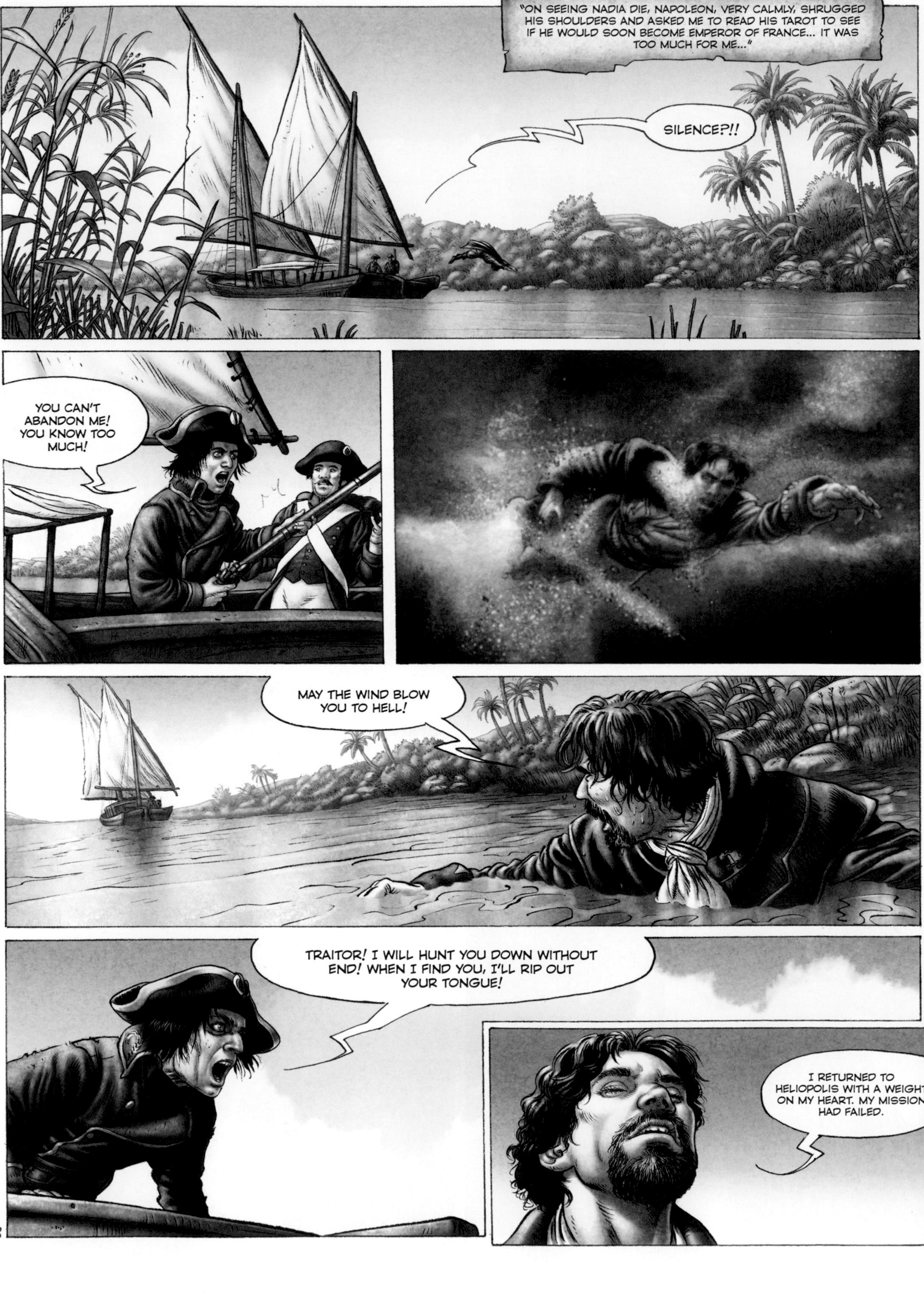
"ON SEEING NADIA DIE, NAPOLEON, VERY CALMLY, SHRUGGED HIS SHOULDERS AND ASKED ME TO READ HIS TAROT TO SEE IF HE WOULD SOON BECOME EMPEROR OF FRANCE... IT WAS TOO MUCH FOR ME..."
SILENCE?!!
YOU CAN'T ABANDON ME! YOU KNOW TOO MUCH!
MAY THE WIND BLOW YOU TO HELL!
TRAITOR! I WILL HUNT YOU DOWN WITHOUT END! WHEN I FIND YOU, I'LL RIP OUT YOUR TONGUE!
I RETURNED TO HELIOPOLIS WITH A WEIGHT ON MY HEART. MY MISSION HAD FAILED.

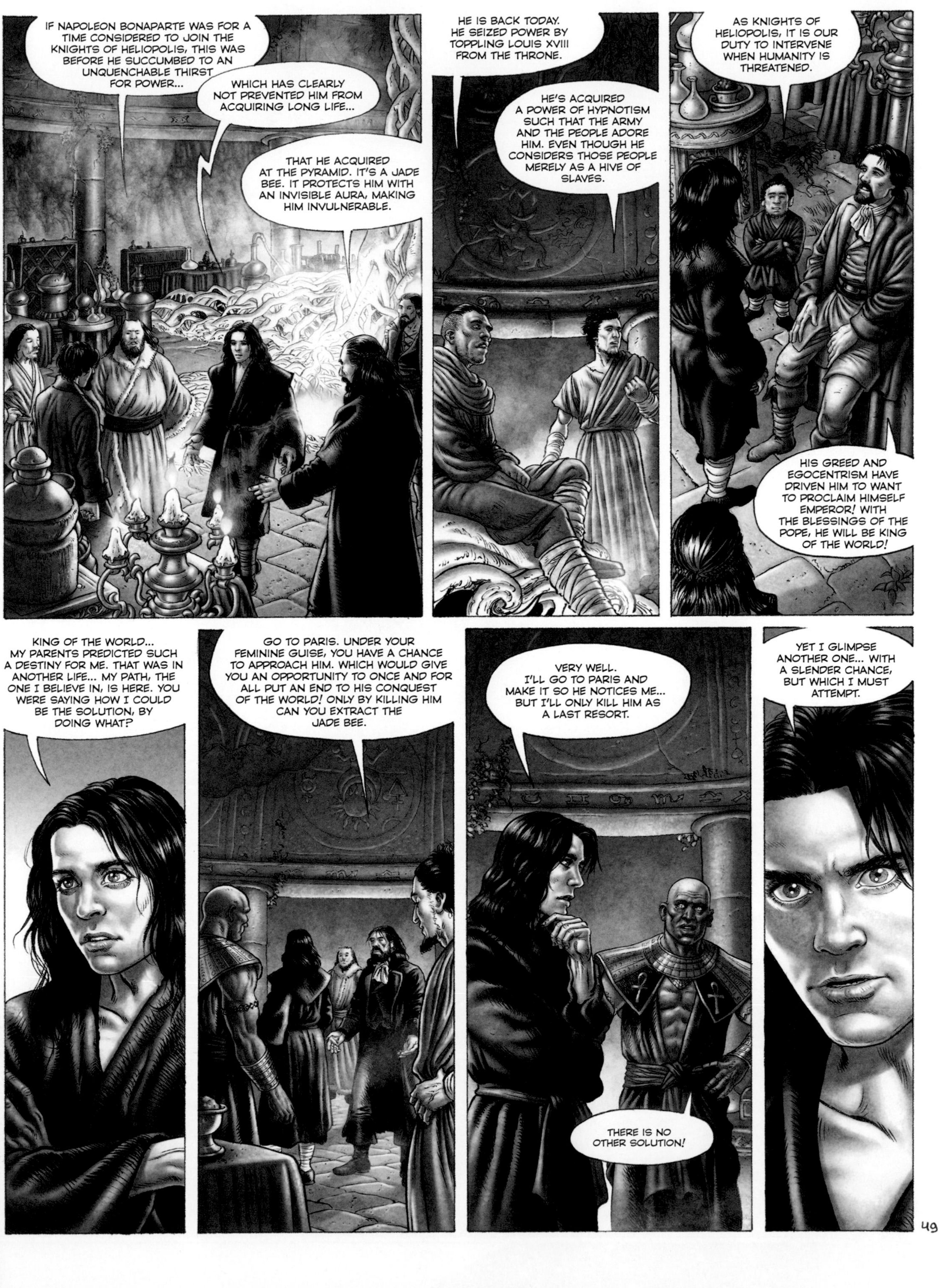
IF NAPOLEON BONAPARTE WAS FOR A TIME CONSIDERED TO JOIN THE KNIGHTS OF HELIOPOLIS, THIS WAS BEFORE HE SUCCUMBED TO AN UNQUENCHABLE THIRST FOR POWER...
WHICH HAS CLEARLY NOT PREVENTED HIM FROM ACQUIRING LONG LIFE...
THAT HE ACQUIRED AT THE PYRAMID. IT'S A JADE BEE. IT PROTECTS HIM WITH AN INVISIBLE AURA, MAKING HIM INVULNERABLE.
HE IS BACK TODAY. HE SEIZED POWER BY TOPPLING LOUIS XVIII FROM THE THRONE.
HE'S ACQUIRED A POWER OF HYPNOTISM SUCH THAT THE ARMY AND THE PEOPLE ADORE HIM. EVEN THOUGH HE CONSIDERS THOSE PEOPLE MERELY AS A HIVE OF SLAVES.
AS KNIGHTS OF HELIOPOLIS, IT IS OUR DUTY TO INTERVENE WHEN HUMANITY IS THREATENED.
HIS GREED AND EGOCENTRISM HAVE DRIVEN HIM TO WANT TO PROCLAIM HIMSELF EMPEROR! WITH THE BLESSINGS OF THE POPE, HE WILL BE KING OF THE WORLD!
KING OF THE WORLD... MY PARENTS PREDICTED SUCH A DESTINY FOR ME. THAT WAS IN ANOTHER LIFE... MY PATH, THE ONE I BELIEVE IN, IS HERE. YOU WERE SAYING HOW I COULD BE THE SOLUTION, BY DOING WHAT?
GO TO PARIS. UNDER YOUR FEMININE GUISE, YOU HAVE A CHANCE TO APPROACH HIM. WHICH WOULD GIVE YOU AN OPPORTUNITY TO ONCE AND FOR ALL PUT AN END TO HIS CONQUEST OF THE WORLD! ONLY BY KILLING HIM CAN YOU EXTRACT THE JADE BEE.
VERY WELL. I'LL GO TO PARIS AND MAKE IT SO HE NOTICES ME... BUT I'LL ONLY KILL HIM AS A LAST RESORT.
THERE IS NO OTHER SOLUTION!
YET I GLIMPSE ANOTHER ONE... WITH A SLENDER CHANCE, BUT WHICH I MUST ATTEMPT.

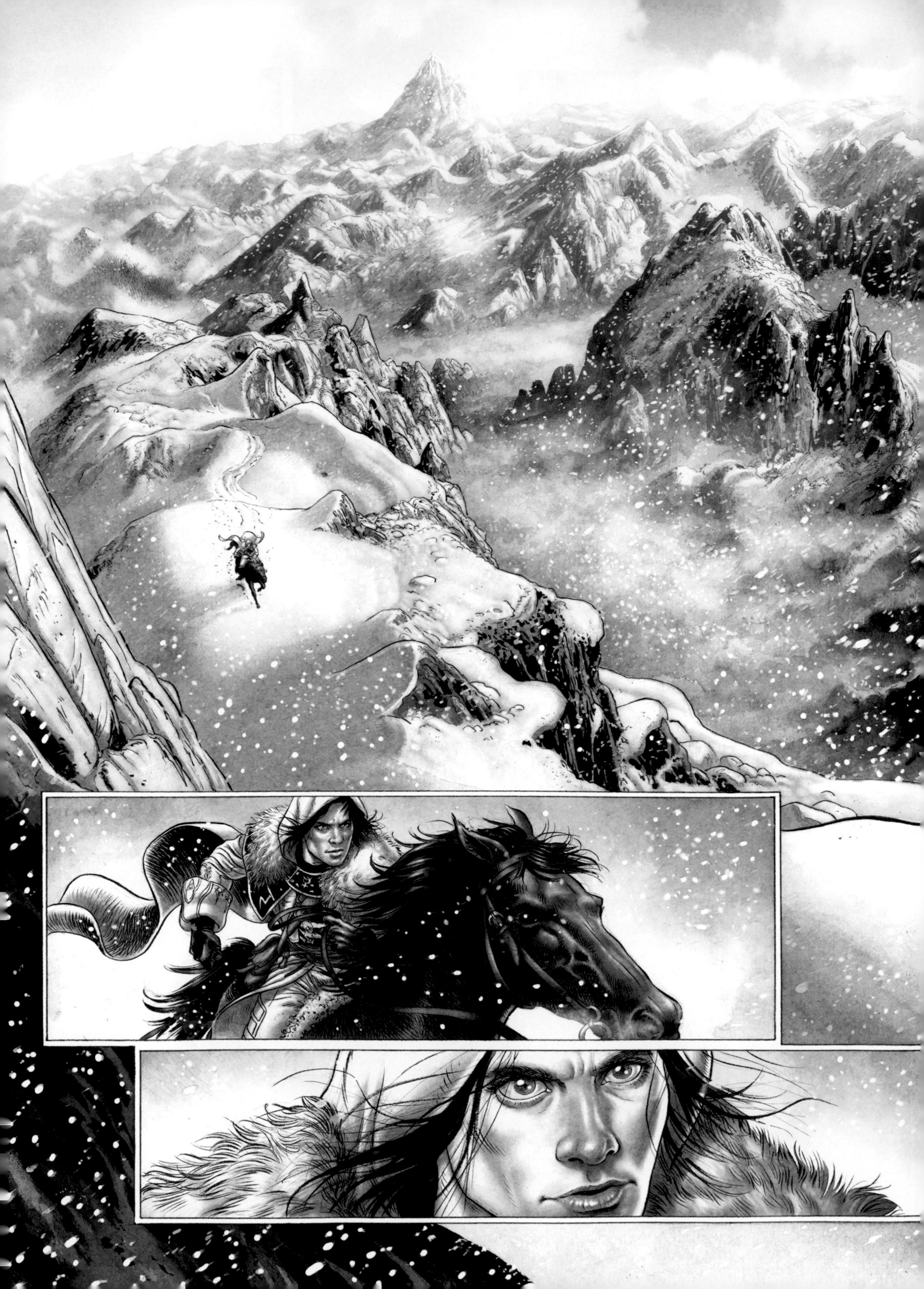

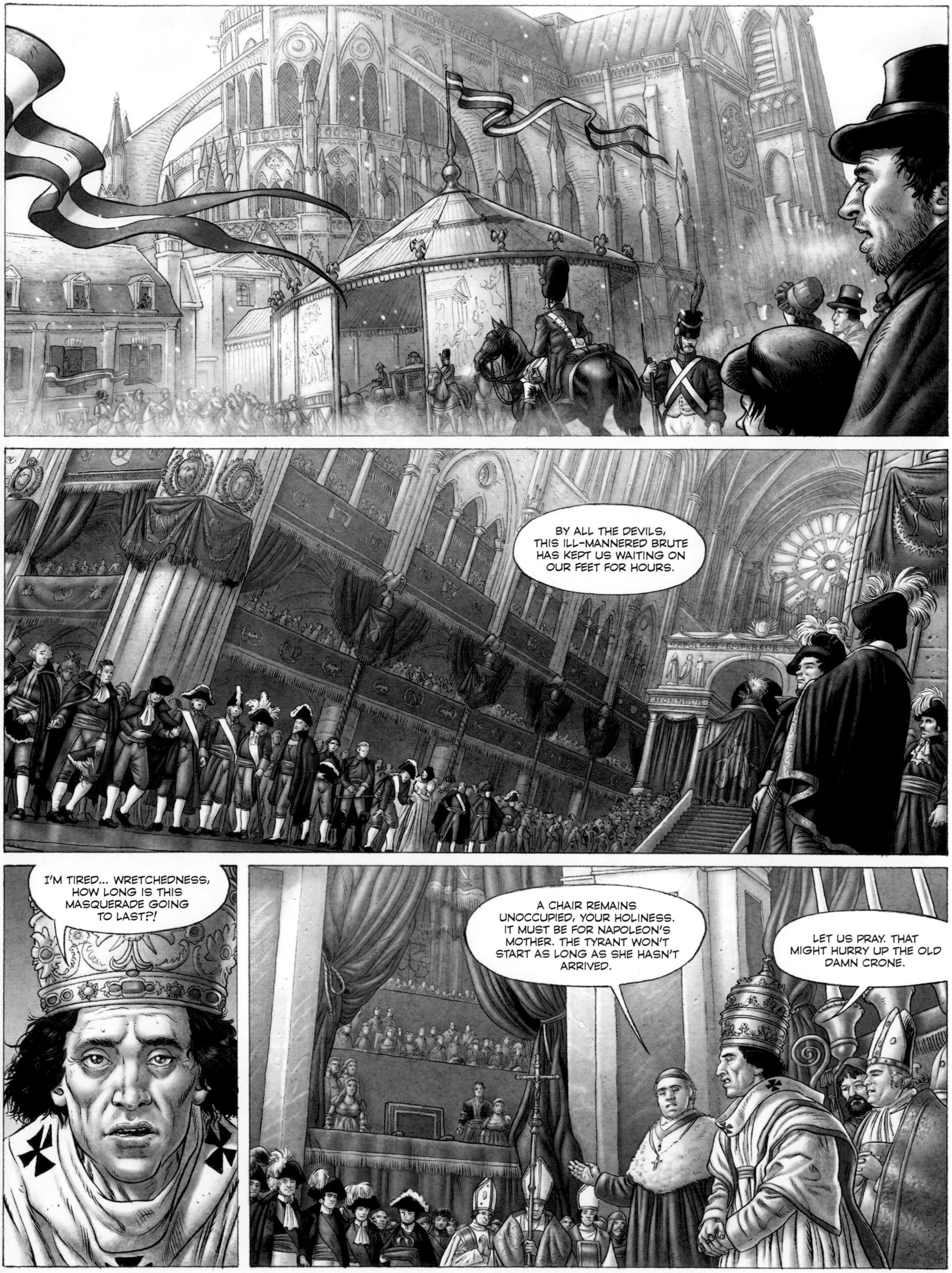

BY ALL THE DEVILS, THIS ILL-MANNERED BRUTE HAS KEPT US WAITING ON OUR FEET FOR HOURS.
I'M TIRED... WRETCHEDNESS, HOW LONG IS THIS MASQUERADE GOING TO LAST?!
A CHAIR REMAINS UNOCCUPIED, YOUR HOLINESS. IT MUST BE FOR NAPOLEON'S MOTHER. THE TYRANT WON'T START AS LONG AS SHE HASN'T ARRIVED.
LET US PRAY. THAT MIGHT HURRY UP THE OLD DAMN CRONE.

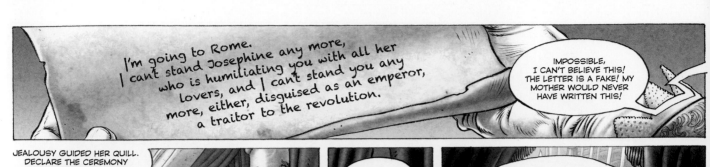

I'm going to Rome. I can't stand Josephine any more, who is humiliating you with all her lovers, and I can't stand you any more, either, disguised as an emperor, a traitor to the revolution.

IMPOSSIBLE, I CAN'T BELIEVE THIS! THE LETTER IS A FAKE! MY MOTHER WOULD NEVER HAVE WRITTEN THIS!

JEALOUSY GUIDED HER QUILL. DECLARE THE CEREMONY BEGUN, NAPOLEON. HER ABSENCE HAS NO IMPORTANCE!

NO! HER ABSENCE WOULD BLEMISH APPEARANCES! SUCH AN ACT WOULD BE PERCEIVED AS A LACK OF FAITH IN ME BY MY MOTHER. THAT PIUS VII AND THOSE OTHER ARISTOCRAT VULTURES WOULDN'T MISS THE CHANCE OF LAUGHING AT ME!

Y... YOUR EXCELLENCY!

WHAT NOW?!

THEY'VE JUST ANNOUNCED THE ARRIVAL OF MARIA-LETIZIA BONAPARTE, 'MADAME MOTHER'!

SHE'S HERE! AT LAST, JOSEPHINE, MOTHER CHANGED HER MIND. LET'S GO!

NAPOLEON CROWNED HIMSELF! HE'S MORE POWERFUL THAN THE POPE OR ANYONE ELSE IN THE WORLD!

GLORY TO NAPOLEON.

VIVE THE EMPEROR!

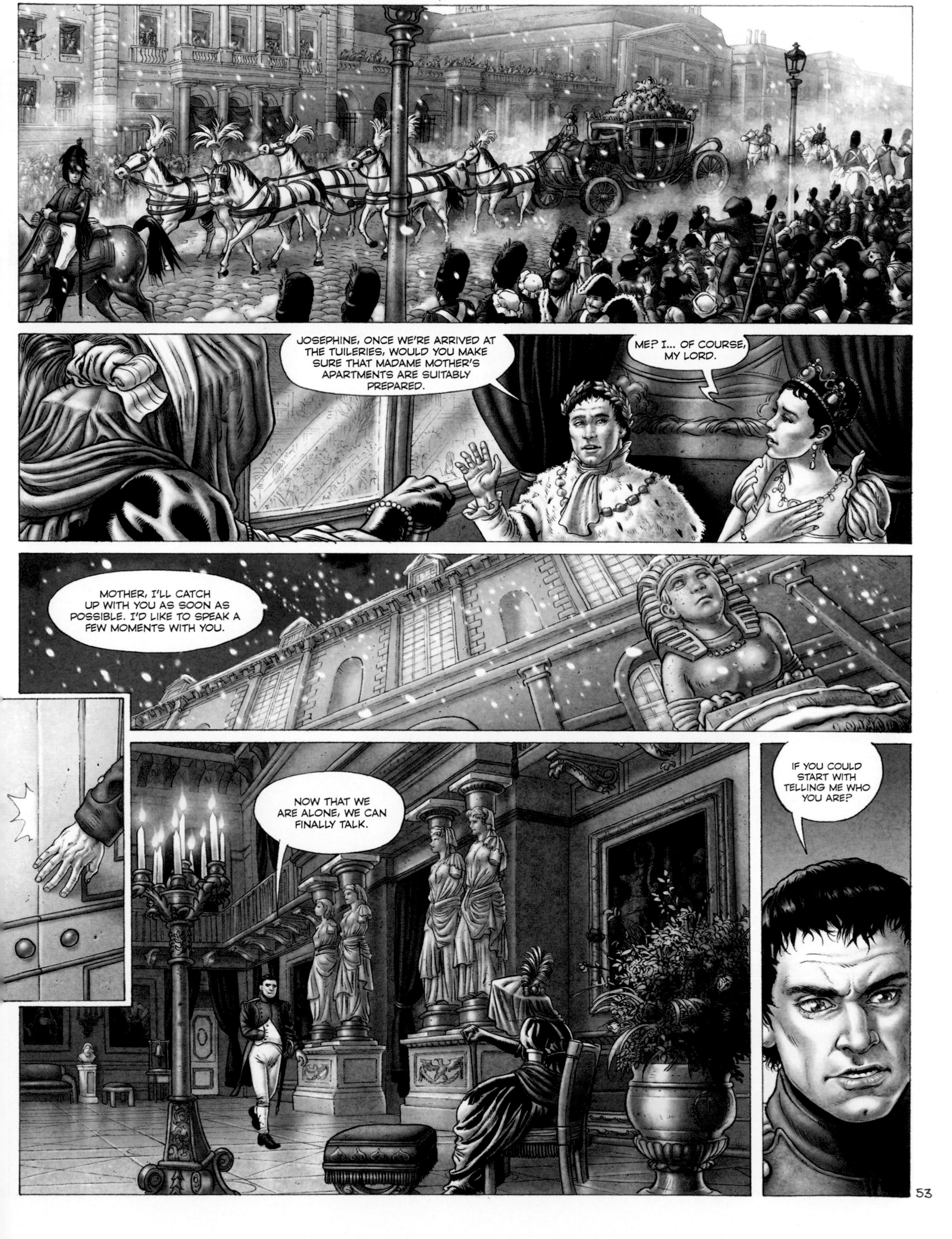

JOSEPHINE, ONCE WE'RE ARRIVED AT THE TUILERIES, WOULD YOU MAKE SURE THAT MADAME MOTHER'S APARTMENTS ARE SUITABLY PREPARED.
ME? I... OF COURSE, MY LORD.
MOTHER, I'LL CATCH UP WITH YOU AS SOON AS POSSIBLE. I'D LIKE TO SPEAK A FEW MOMENTS WITH YOU.
NOW THAT WE ARE ALONE, WE CAN FINALLY TALK.
IF YOU COULD START WITH TELLING ME WHO YOU ARE?

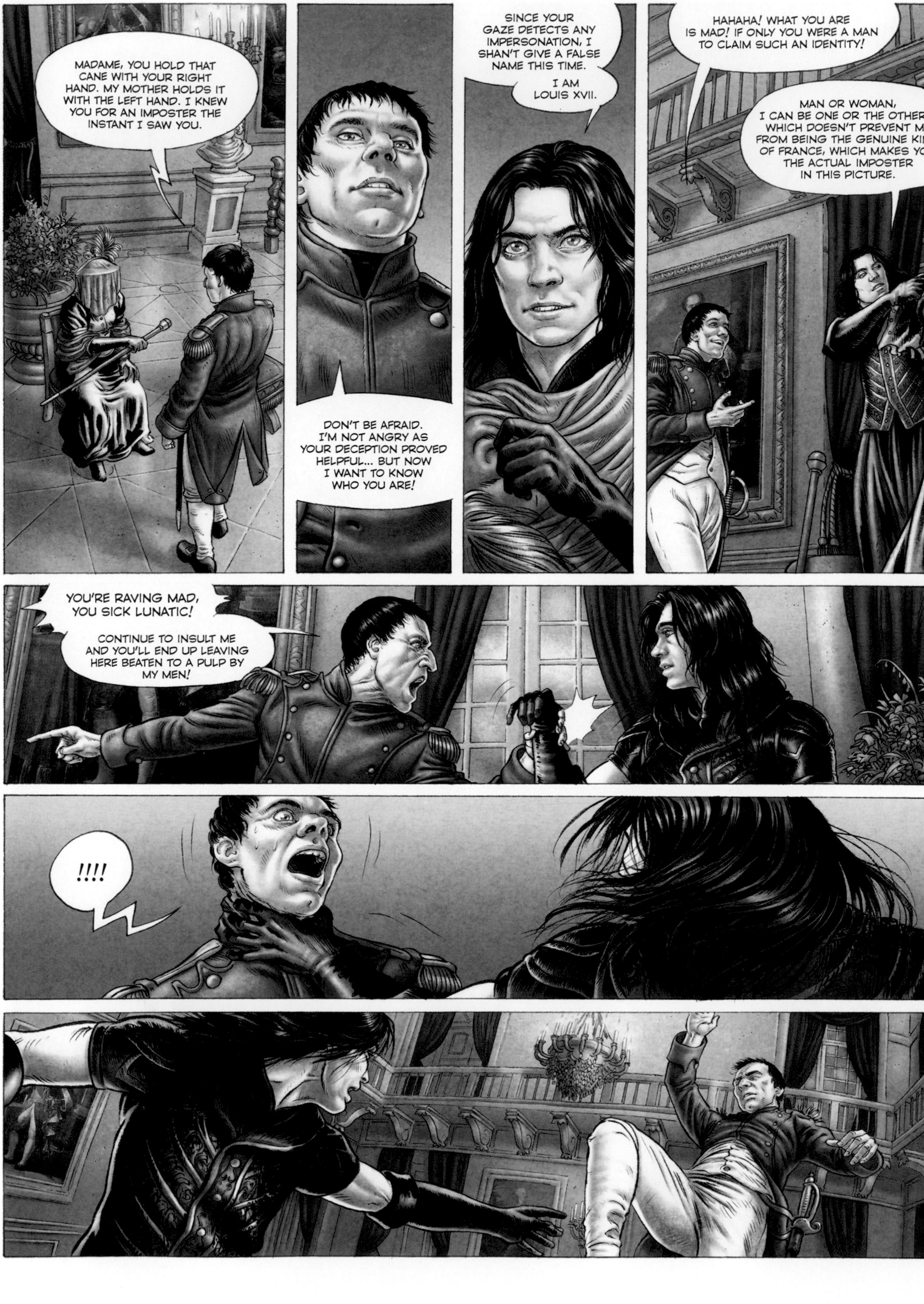
MADAME, YOU HOLD THAT CANE WITH YOUR RIGHT HAND. MY MOTHER HOLDS IT WITH THE LEFT HAND. I KNEW YOU FOR AN IMPOSTER THE INSTANT I SAW YOU.
DON'T BE AFRAID. I'M NOT ANGRY AS YOUR DECEPTION PROVED HELPFUL... BUT NOW I WANT TO KNOW WHO YOU ARE!
SINCE YOUR GAZE DETECTS ANY IMPERSONATION, I SHAN'T GIVE A FALSE NAME THIS TIME.
I AM LOUIS XVII.
HAHAHA! WHAT YOU ARE IS MAD! IF ONLY YOU WERE A MAN TO CLAIM SUCH AN IDENTITY!
MAN OR WOMAN, I CAN BE ONE OR THE OTHER... WHICH DOESN'T PREVENT ME FROM BEING THE GENUINE KING OF FRANCE, WHICH MAKES YOU THE ACTUAL IMPOSTER IN THIS PICTURE.
YOU'RE RAVING MAD, YOU SICK LUNATIC!
CONTINUE TO INSULT ME AND YOU'LL END UP LEAVING HERE BEATEN TO A PULP BY MY MEN!
!!!!

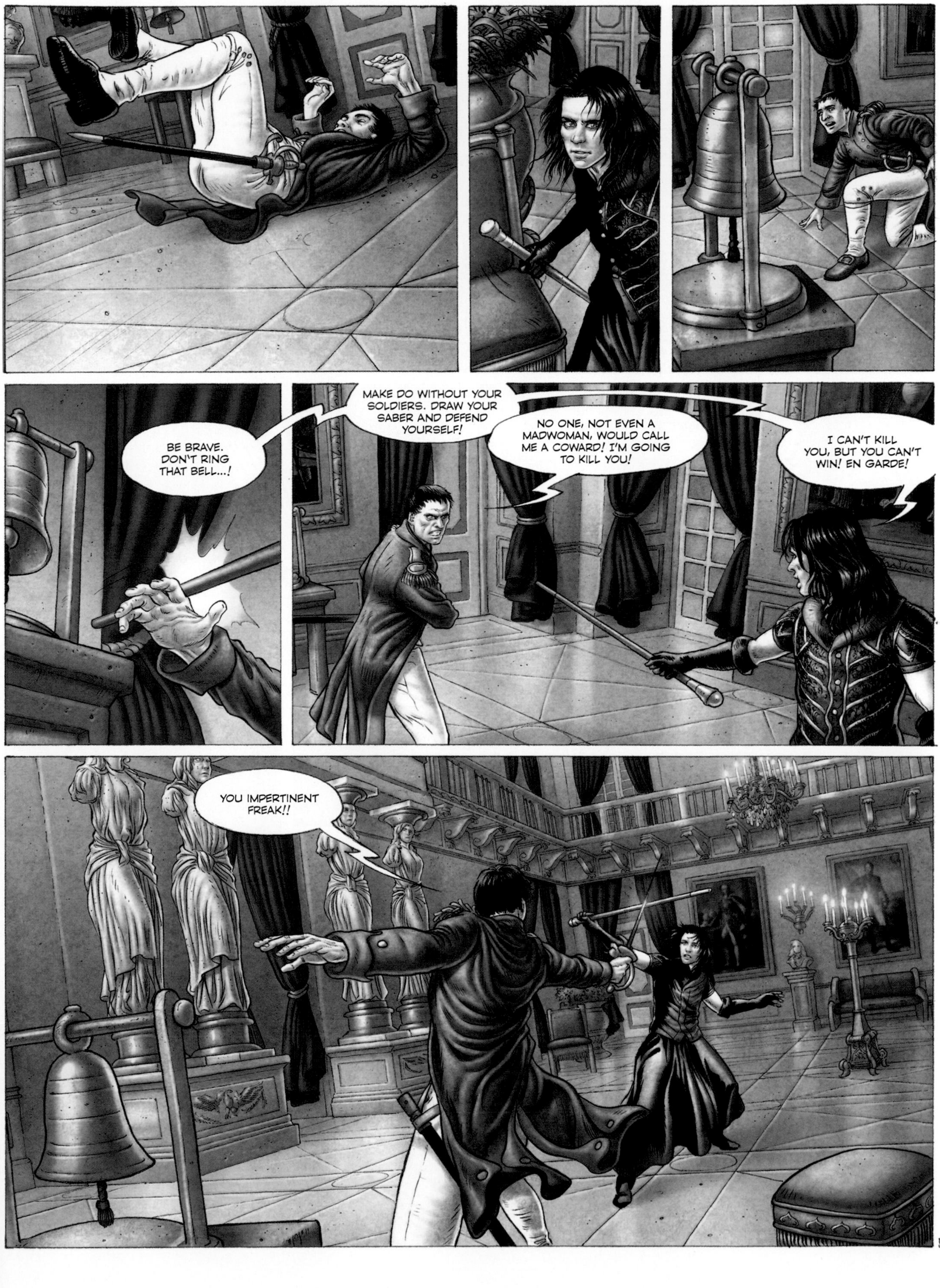

BE BRAVE. DON'T RING THAT BELL...!
MAKE DO WITHOUT YOUR SOLDIERS. DRAW YOUR SABER AND DEFEND YOURSELF!
NO ONE, NOT EVEN A MADWOMAN, WOULD CALL ME A COWARD! I'M GOING TO KILL YOU!
I CAN'T KILL YOU, BUT YOU CAN'T WIN! EN GARDE!
YOU IMPERTINENT FREAK!!

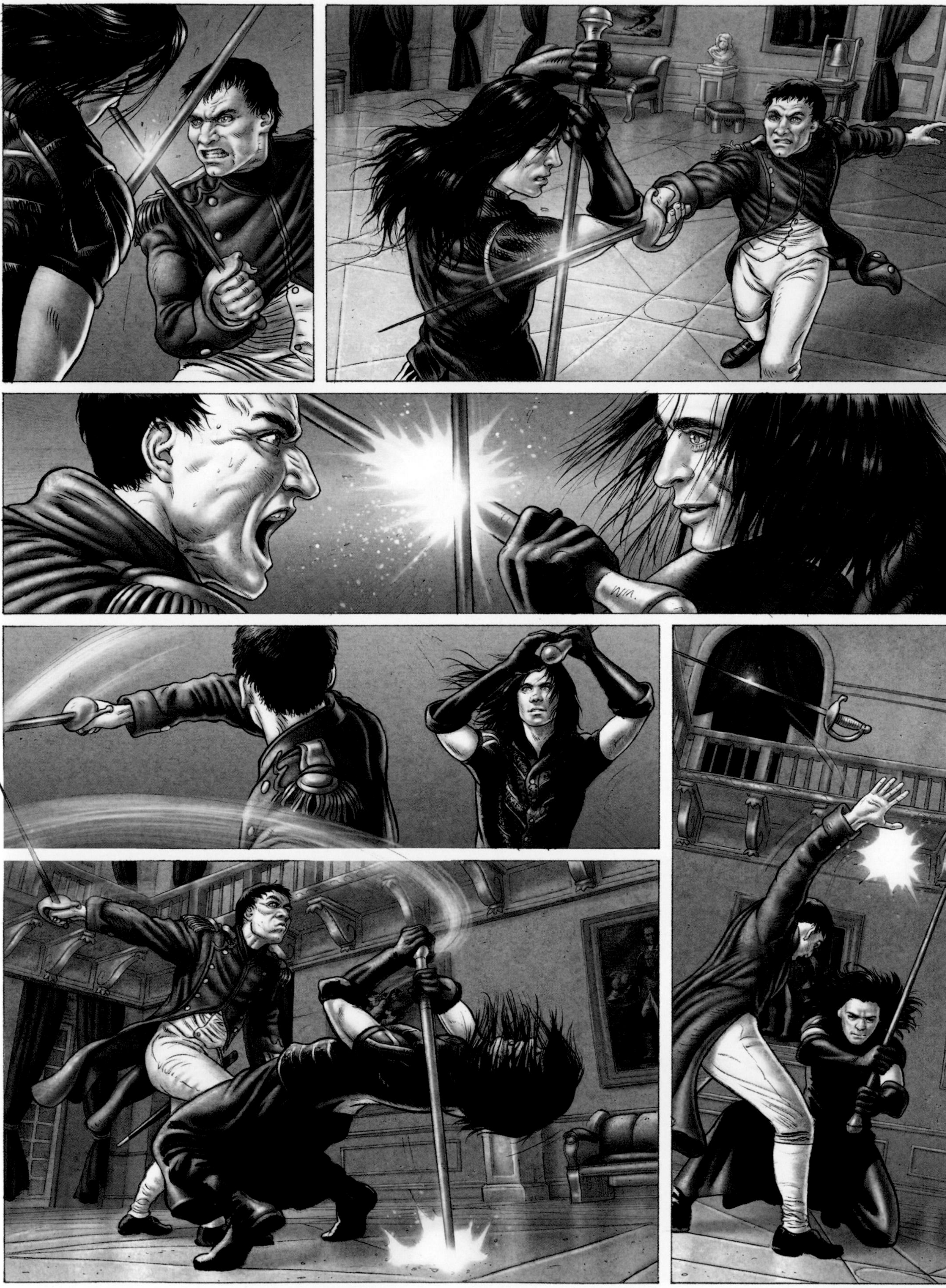

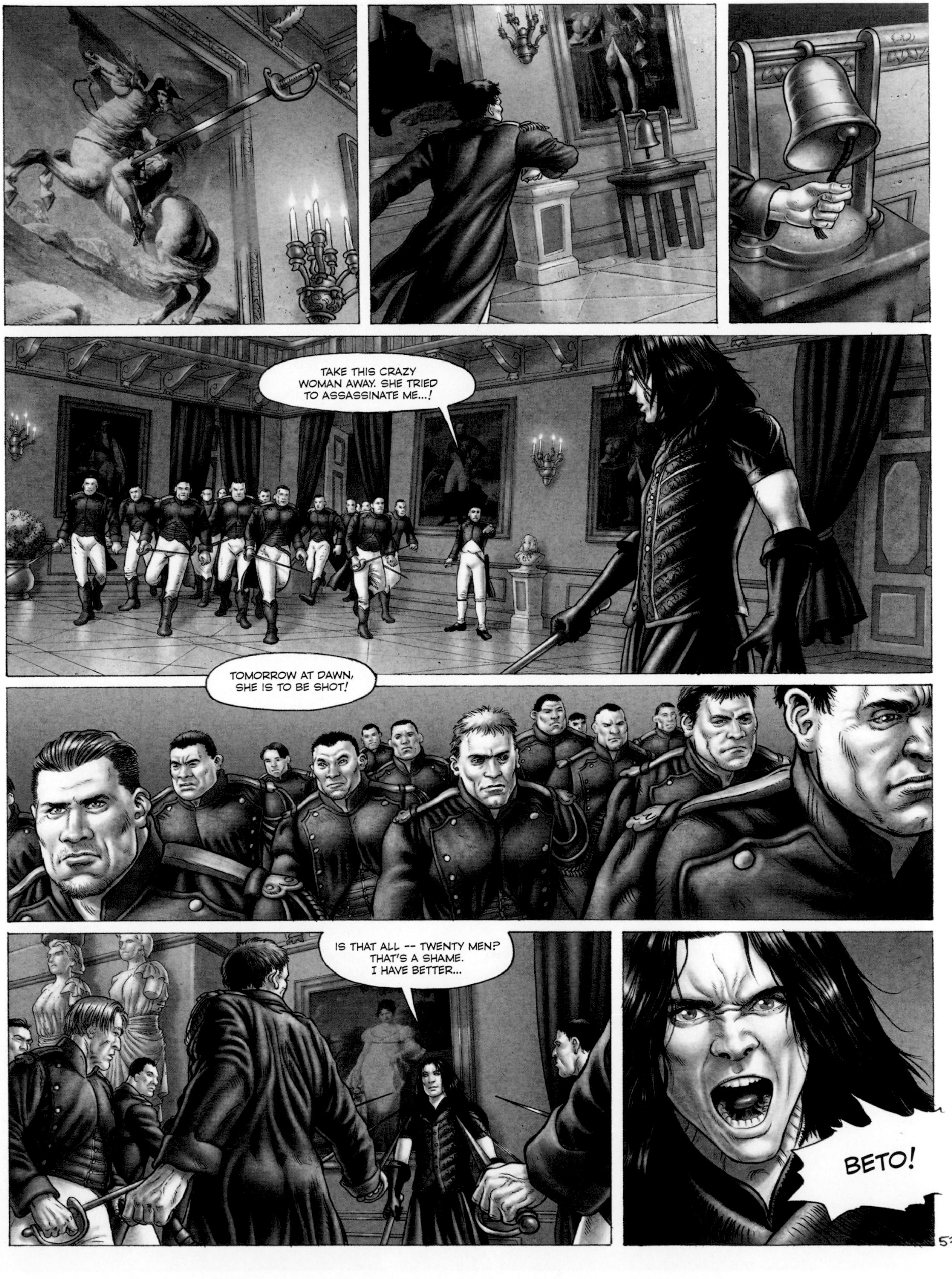
TAKE THIS CRAZY WOMAN AWAY. SHE TRIED TO ASSASSINATE ME...!
TOMORROW AT DAWN, SHE IS TO BE SHOT!
IS THAT ALL -- TWENTY MEN? THAT'S A SHAME. I HAVE BETTER...
BETO!

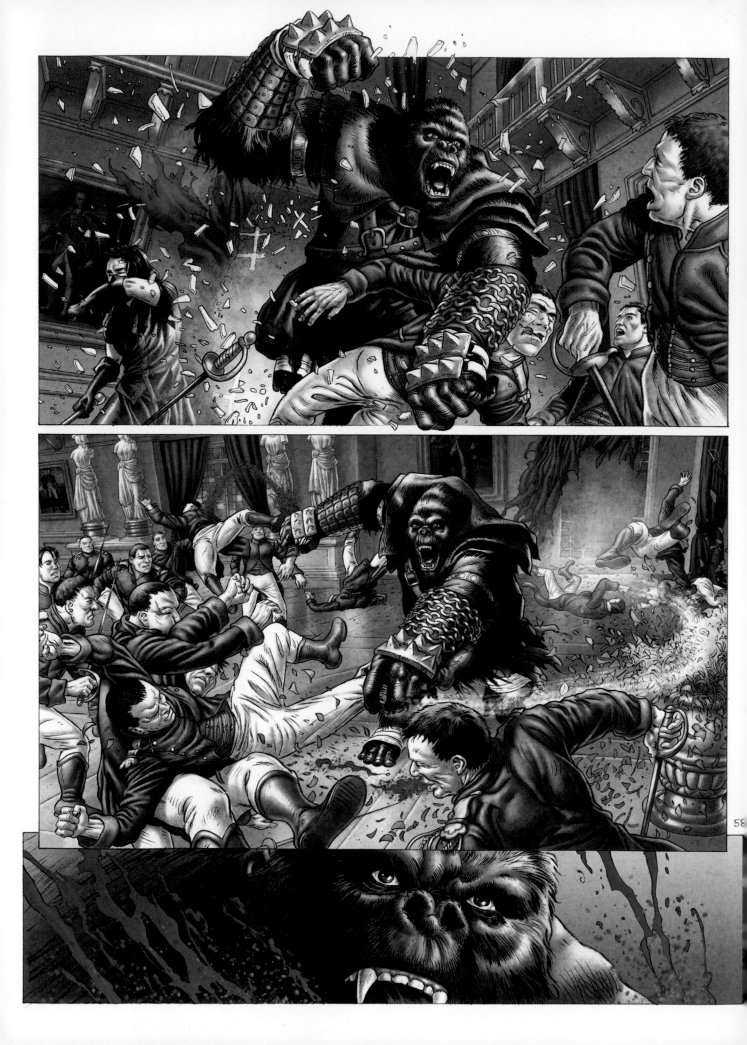

58

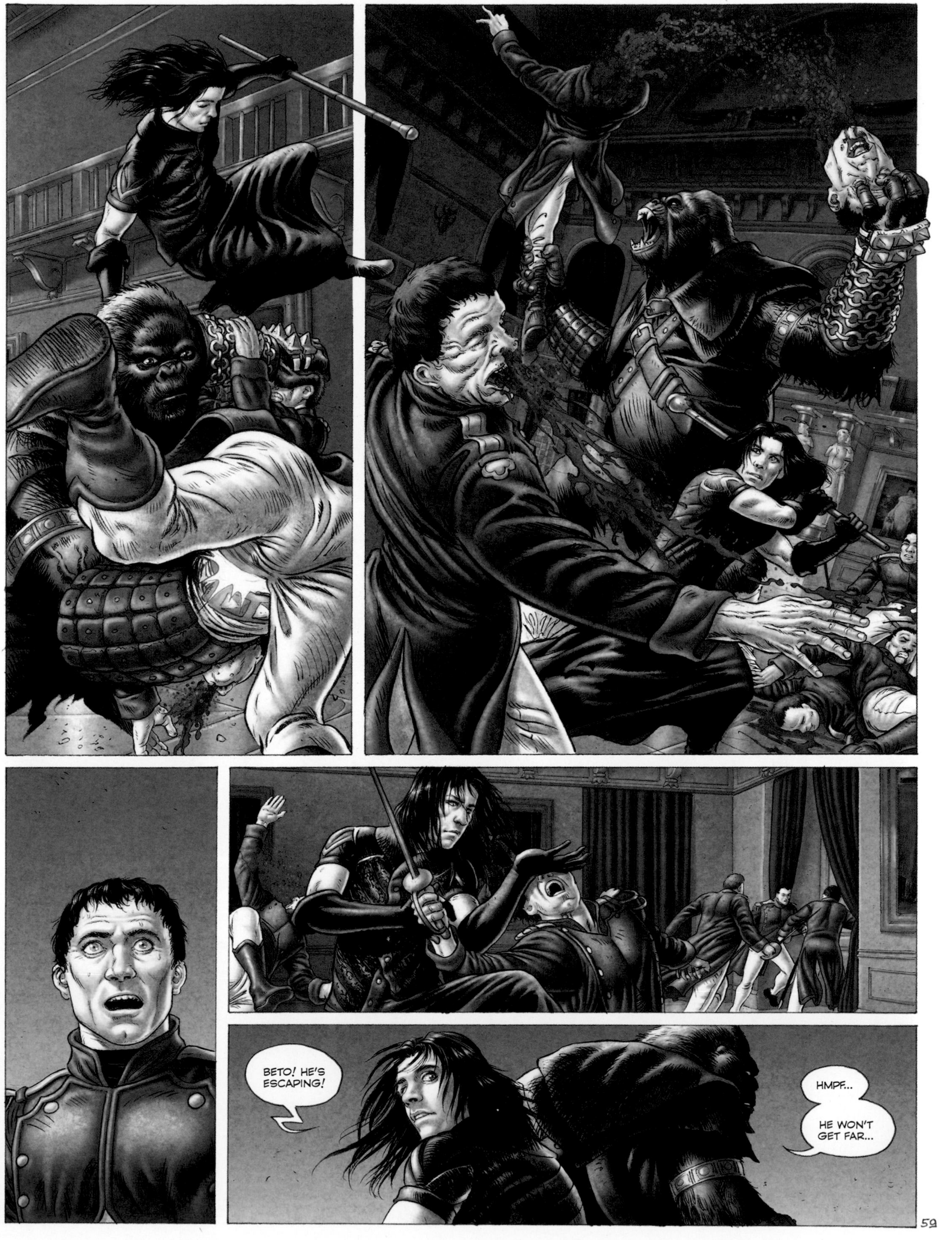
BETO! HE'S ESCAPING!
HMPF...
HE WON'T GET FAR...

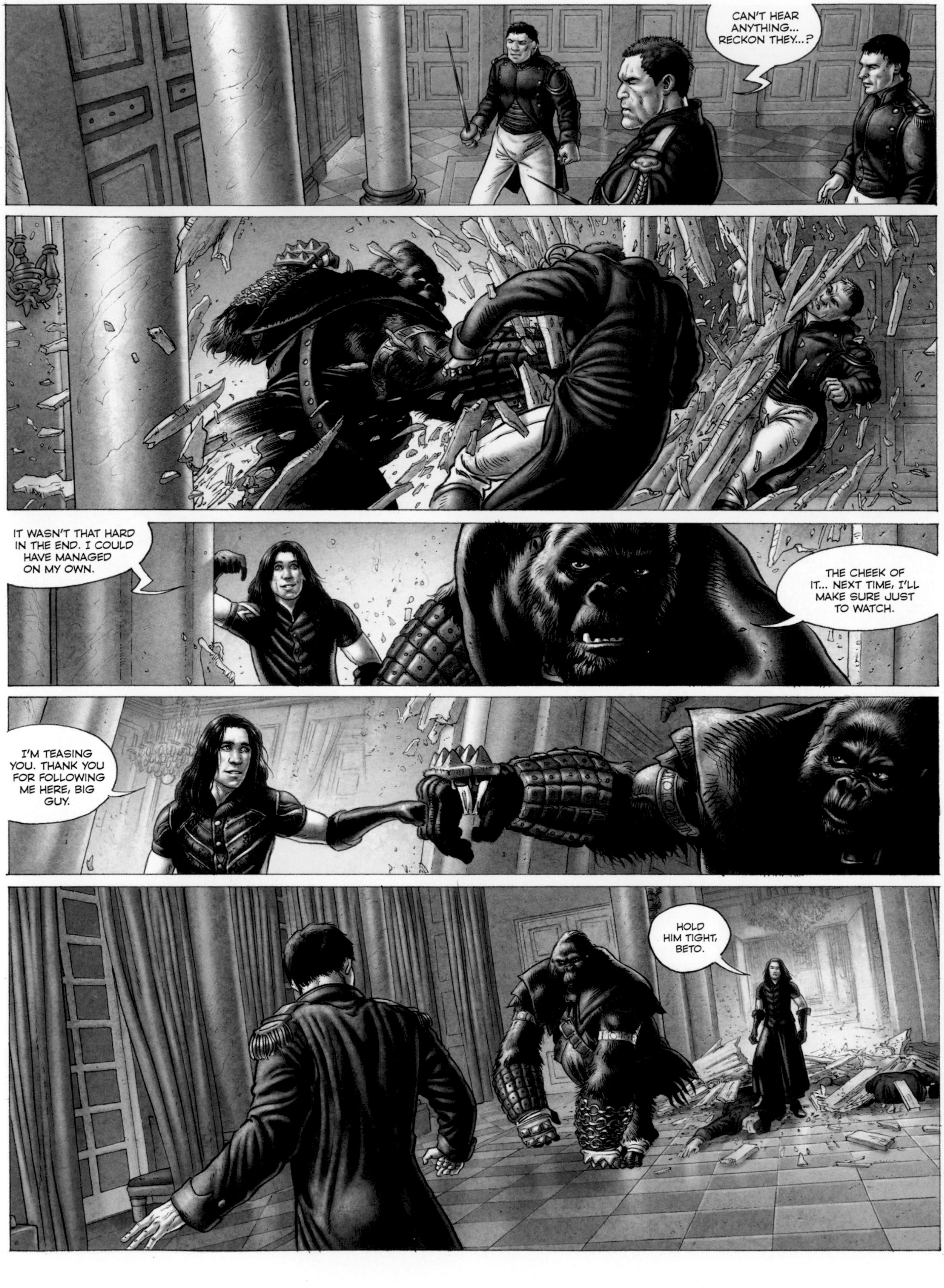
CAN'T HEAR ANYTHING... RECKON THEY...?
IT WASN'T THAT HARD IN THE END. I COULD HAVE MANAGED ON MY OWN.
THE CHEEK OF IT... NEXT TIME, I'LL MAKE SURE JUST TO WATCH.
I'M TEASING YOU. THANK YOU FOR FOLLOWING ME HERE, BIG GUY.
HOLD HIM TIGHT, BETO.

THANKS TO 'SILENCE', WHOM YOU CALL THE COUNT DE SAINT-GERMAIN, I KNOW THE REAL REASON YOU WERE IN EGYPT. YOU OBTAINED A BEE FROM THE GREAT PYRAMID, WHICH PROTECTS YOU. NOTHING AND NO ONE CAN KILL YOU.

YOU KNOW SILENCE? WHO ARE YOU?!

I ALREADY TOLD YOU AND I WASN'T LYING. I AM THE ONE WHO WAS MEANT TO BECOME KING OF FRANCE. AT PRESENT, I AM A MEMBER OF A GROUP OF ALCHEMISTS, THE KNIGHTS OF HELIOPOLIS, WHO HOLD THE SECRET TO LONG LIFE.

LONG... HOW?

IF YOU ARE STRONGER THAN YOUR THIRST FOR POWER, THAN YOUR NEED TO BECOME A GOD, YOU ALSO COULD LIVE FOR 300 CENTURIES -- AND NOT BY MASSACRING MILLIONS OF PEOPLE, BUT BY HELPING HUMANITY TO KNOW JOY AND ABUNDANCE.

AWAKEN YOUR CONSCIOUSNESS INSTEAD OF CONTINUING IN YOUR BESTIAL COMBAT. OTHERWISE, WE WILL FIND A WAY TO KILL YOU.

YOU ARE KING OF THE WORLD AS WAS DESTINED FOR MYSELF. I AM THE KNIGHT YOU WERE MEANT TO BE. YOU AND I, WE ARE IRREVERSIBLY LINKED, DRAWN TO EACH AS THOUGH ALTER-EGOS. WE WERE DESTINED TO MEET. I KNOW THAT YOU SENSE THIS AS WELL, DEEP INSIDE YOU.

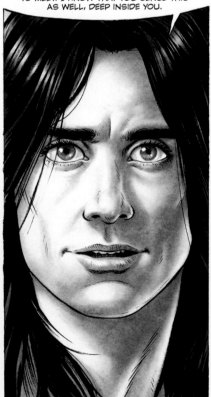

JOIN ME AND I COULD BECOME THE IDEAL BEING TO COMPLETE YOU -- THE QUEEN BEE THAT YOUR SOUL NEEDS...

61

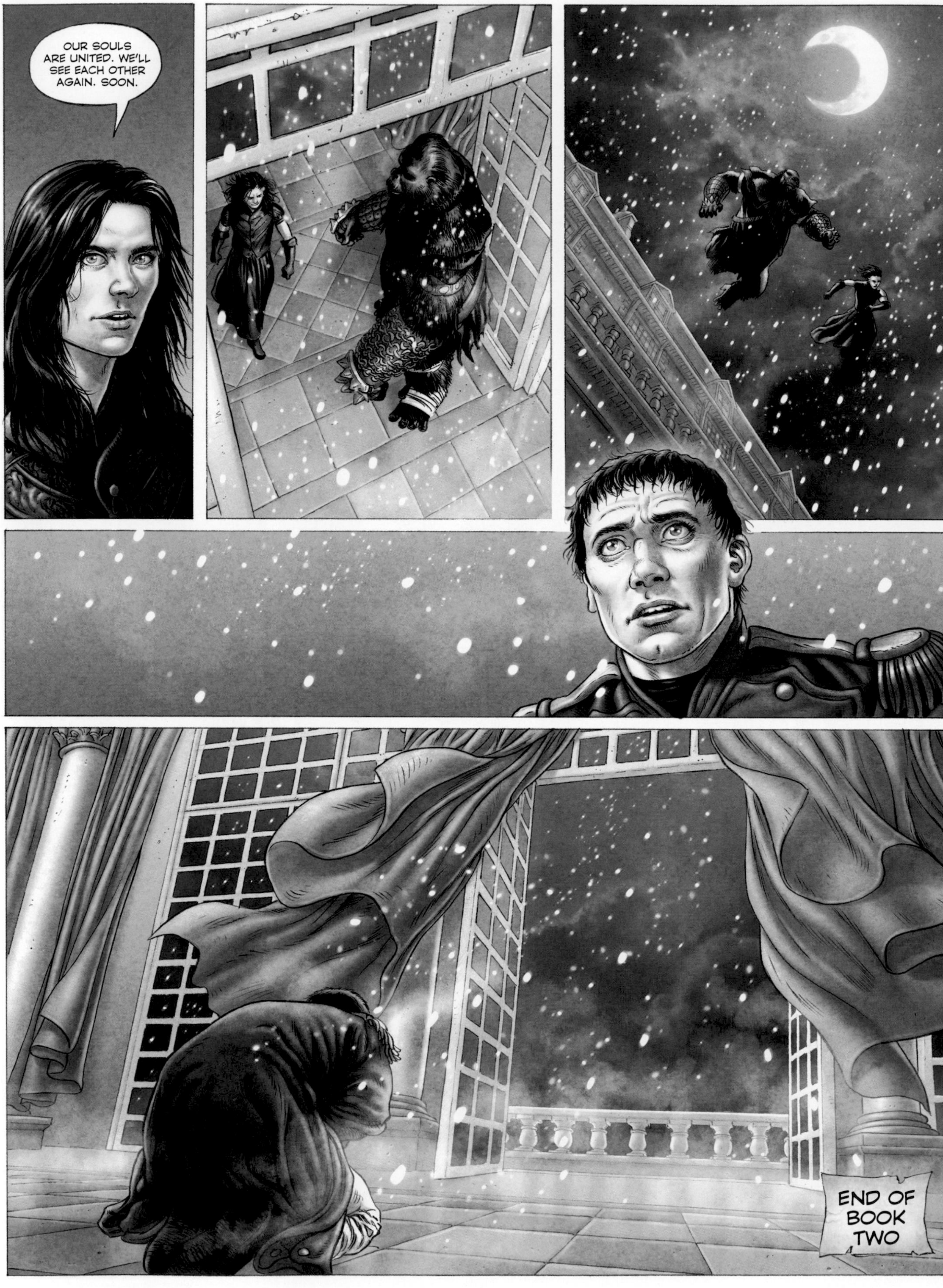
OUR SOULS ARE UNITED. WE'LL SEE EACH OTHER AGAIN. SOON.
END OF BOOK TWO

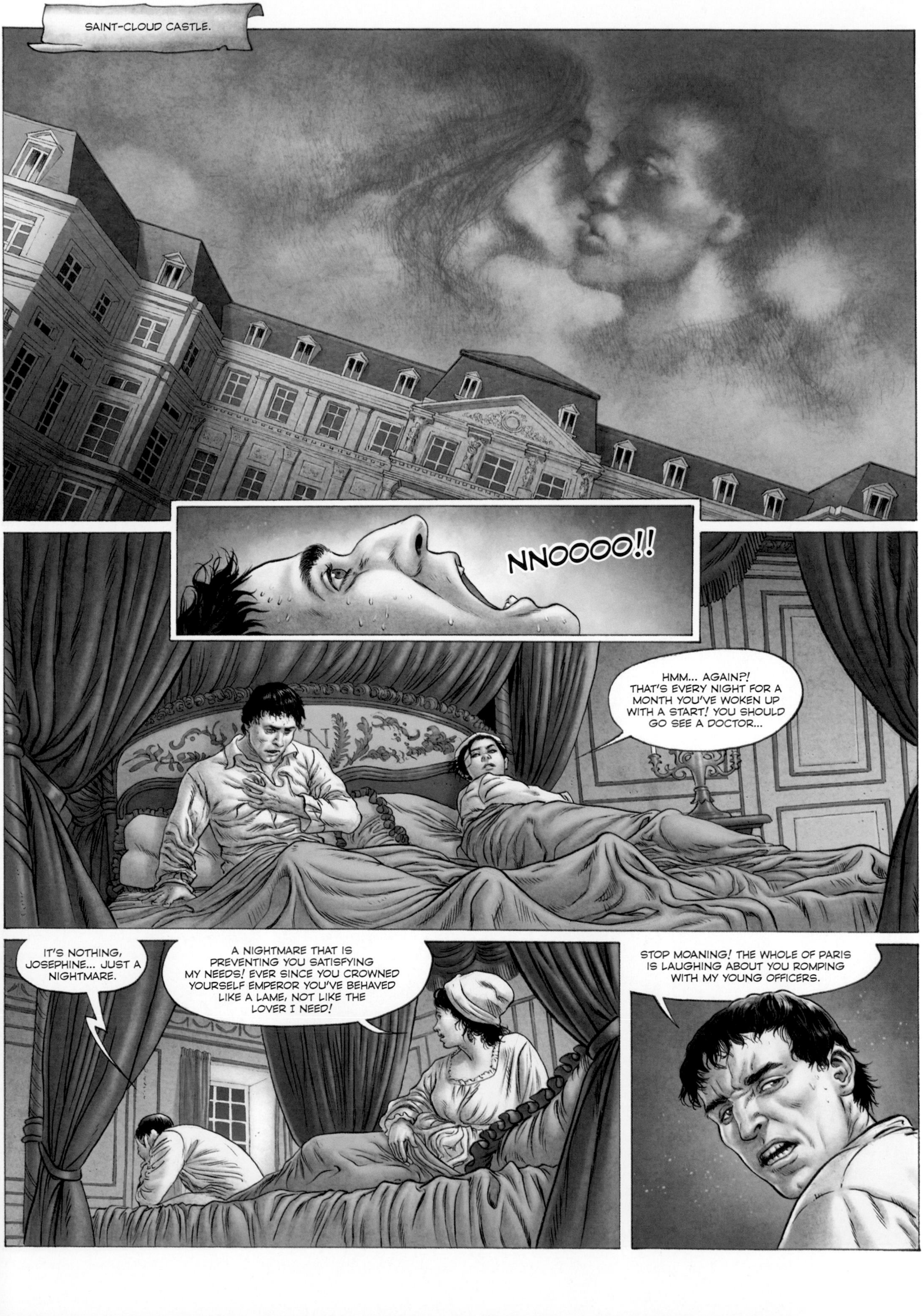
SAINT-CLOUD CASTLE.
NNOOOO!!
HMM... AGAIN?! THAT'S EVERY NIGHT FOR A MONTH YOU'VE WOKEN UP WITH A START! YOU SHOULD GO SEE A DOCTOR...
IT'S NOTHING, JOSEPHINE... JUST A NIGHTMARE.
A NIGHTMARE THAT IS PREVENTING YOU SATISFYING MY NEEDS! EVER SINCE YOU CROWNED YOURSELF EMPEROR YOU'VE BEHAVED LIKE A LAME, NOT LIKE THE LOVER I NEED!
STOP MOANING! THE WHOLE OF PARIS IS LAUGHING ABOUT YOU ROMPING WITH MY YOUNG OFFICERS.

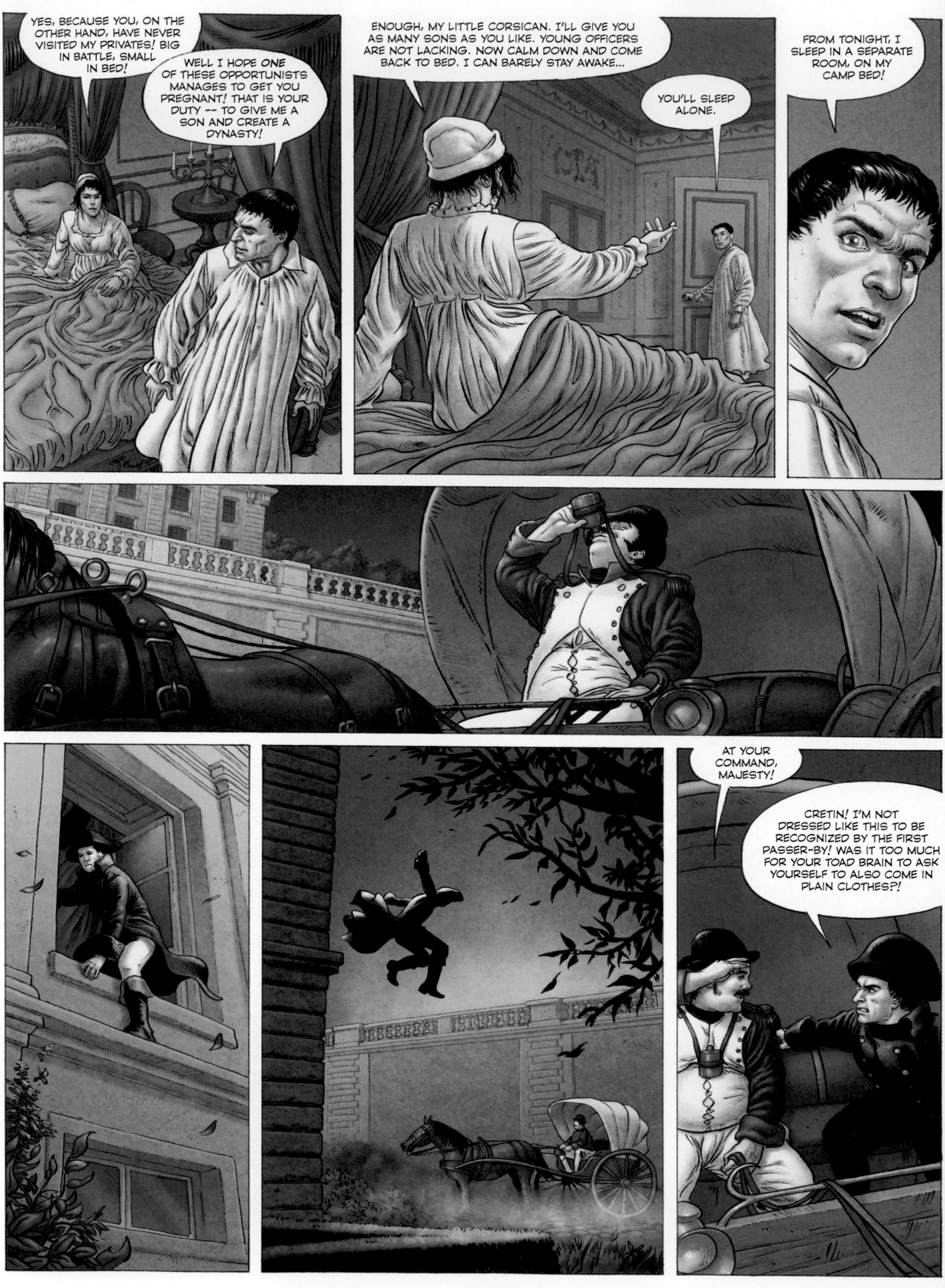
YES, BECAUSE YOU, ON THE OTHER HAND, HAVE NEVER VISITED MY PRIVATES! BIG IN BATTLE, SMALL IN BED!
WELL I HOPE ONE OF THESE OPPORTUNISTS MANAGES TO GET YOU PREGNANT! THAT IS YOUR DUTY -- TO GIVE ME A SON AND CREATE A DYNASTY!
ENOUGH, MY LITTLE CORSICAN. I'LL GIVE YOU AS MANY SONS AS YOU LIKE. YOUNG OFFICERS ARE NOT LACKING. NOW CALM DOWN AND COME BACK TO BED. I CAN BARELY STAY AWAKE...
YOU'LL SLEEP ALONE.
FROM TONIGHT, I SLEEP IN A SEPARATE ROOM, ON MY CAMP BED!
AT YOUR COMMAND, MAJESTY!
CRETIN! I'M NOT DRESSED LIKE THIS TO BE RECOGNIZED BY THE FIRST PASSER-BY! WAS IT TOO MUCH FOR YOUR TOAD BRAIN TO ASK YOURSELF TO ALSO COME IN PLAIN CLOTHES?!

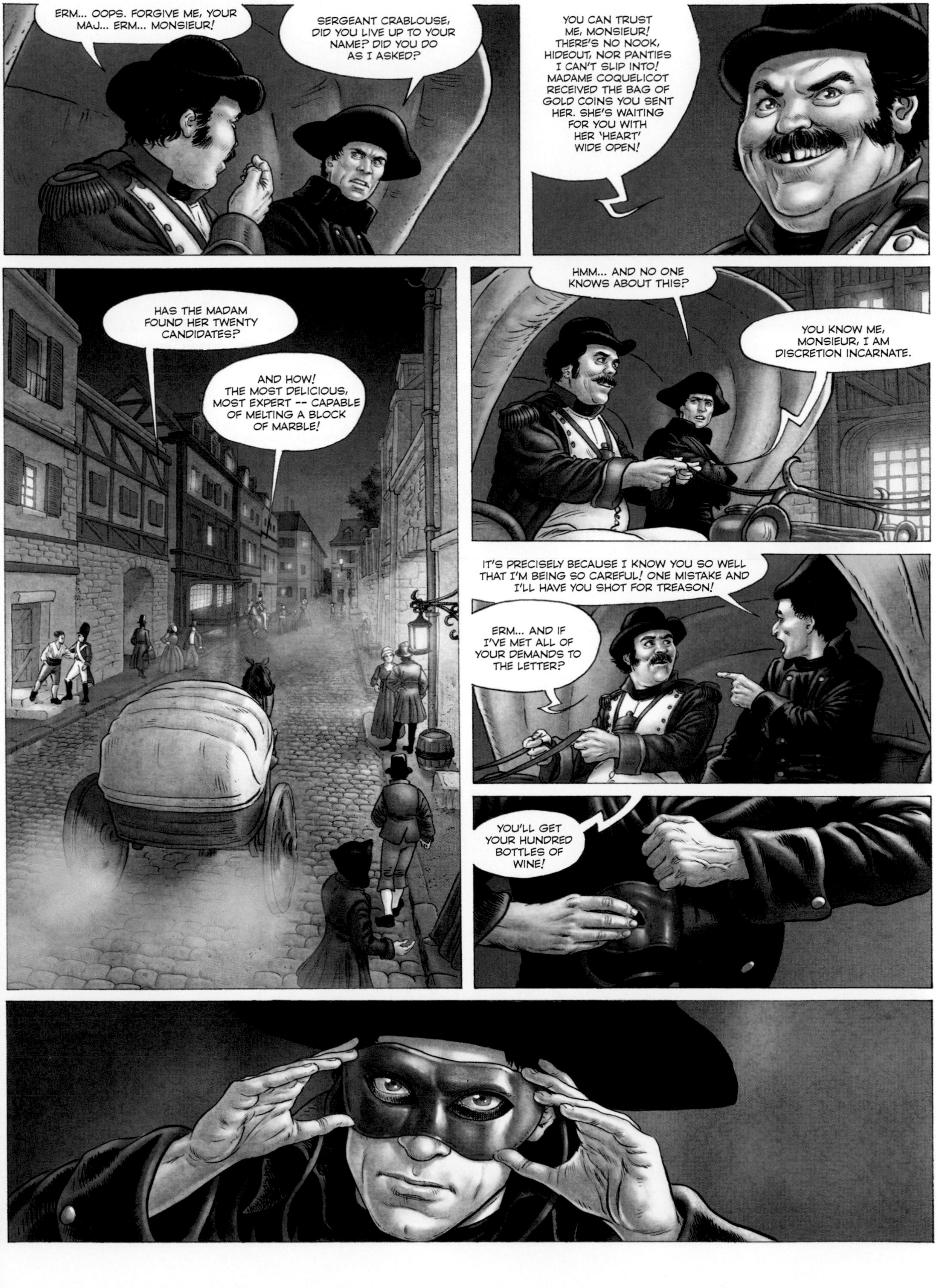
ERM... OOPS. FORGIVE ME, YOUR MAJ... ERM... MONSIEUR!
SERGEANT CRABLOUSE, DID YOU LIVE UP TO YOUR NAME? DID YOU DO AS I ASKED?
YOU CAN TRUST ME, MONSIEUR! THERE'S NO NOOK, HIDEOUT, NOR PANTIES I CAN'T SLIP INTO! MADAME COQUELICOT RECEIVED THE BAG OF GOLD COINS YOU SENT HER. SHE'S WAITING FOR YOU WITH HER 'HEART' WIDE OPEN!
HAS THE MADAM FOUND HER TWENTY CANDIDATES?
AND HOW! THE MOST DELICIOUS, MOST EXPERT -- CAPABLE OF MELTING A BLOCK OF MARBLE!
HMM... AND NO ONE KNOWS ABOUT THIS?
YOU KNOW ME, MONSIEUR, I AM DISCRETION INCARNATE.
IT'S PRECISELY BECAUSE I KNOW YOU SO WELL THAT I'M BEING SO CAREFUL! ONE MISTAKE AND I'LL HAVE YOU SHOT FOR TREASON!
ERM... AND IF I'VE MET ALL OF YOUR DEMANDS TO THE LETTER?
YOU'LL GET YOUR HUNDRED BOTTLES OF WINE!

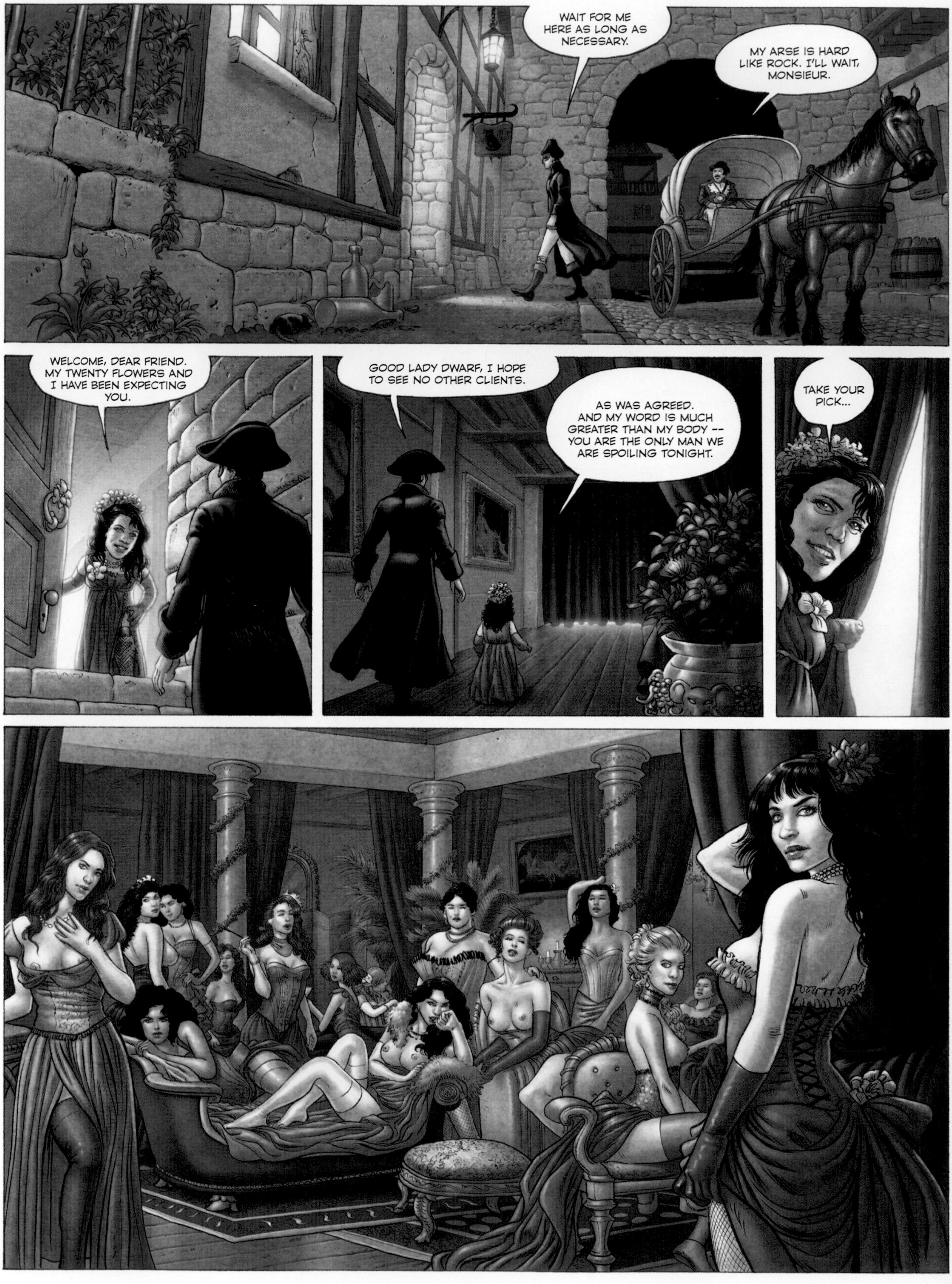
WAIT FOR ME HERE AS LONG AS NECESSARY.
MY ARSE IS HARD LIKE ROCK. I'LL WAIT, MONSIEUR.
WELCOME, DEAR FRIEND. MY TWENTY FLOWERS AND I HAVE BEEN EXPECTING YOU.
GOOD LADY DWARF, I HOPE TO SEE NO OTHER CLIENTS.
AS WAS AGREED. AND MY WORD IS MUCH GREATER THAN MY BODY -- YOU ARE THE ONLY MAN WE ARE SPOILING TONIGHT.
TAKE YOUR PICK...

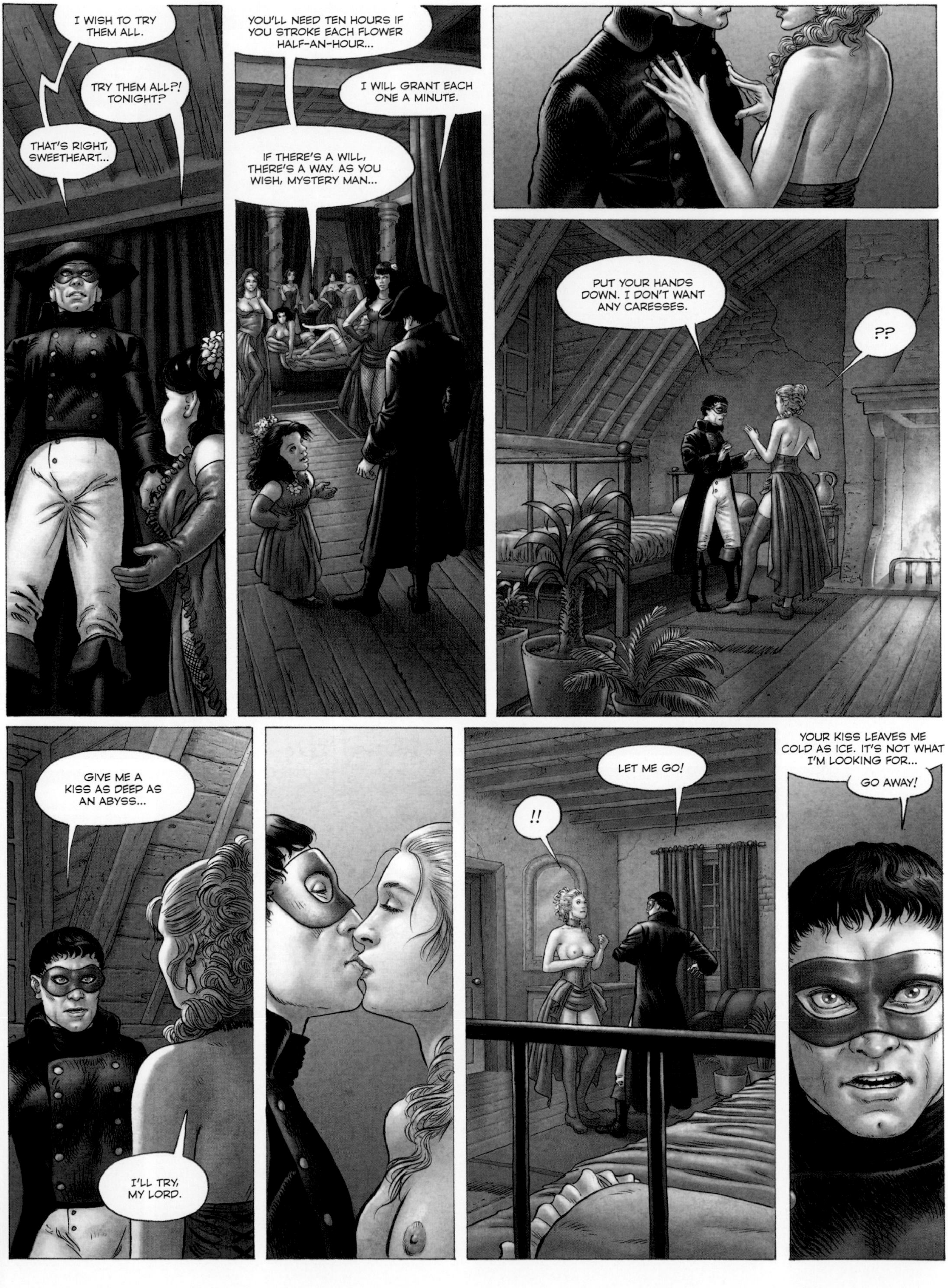

I WISH TO TRY THEM ALL.
TRY THEM ALL?! TONIGHT?
THAT'S RIGHT, SWEETHEART...
YOU'LL NEED TEN HOURS IF YOU STROKE EACH FLOWER HALF-AN-HOUR...
I WILL GRANT EACH ONE A MINUTE.
IF THERE'S A WILL, THERE'S A WAY. AS YOU WISH, MYSTERY MAN...
PUT YOUR HANDS DOWN. I DON'T WANT ANY CARESSES.
??
GIVE ME A KISS AS DEEP AS AN ABYSS...
I'LL TRY, MY LORD.
LET ME GO!
!!
YOUR KISS LEAVES ME COLD AS ICE. IT'S NOT WHAT I'M LOOKING FOR...
GO AWAY!

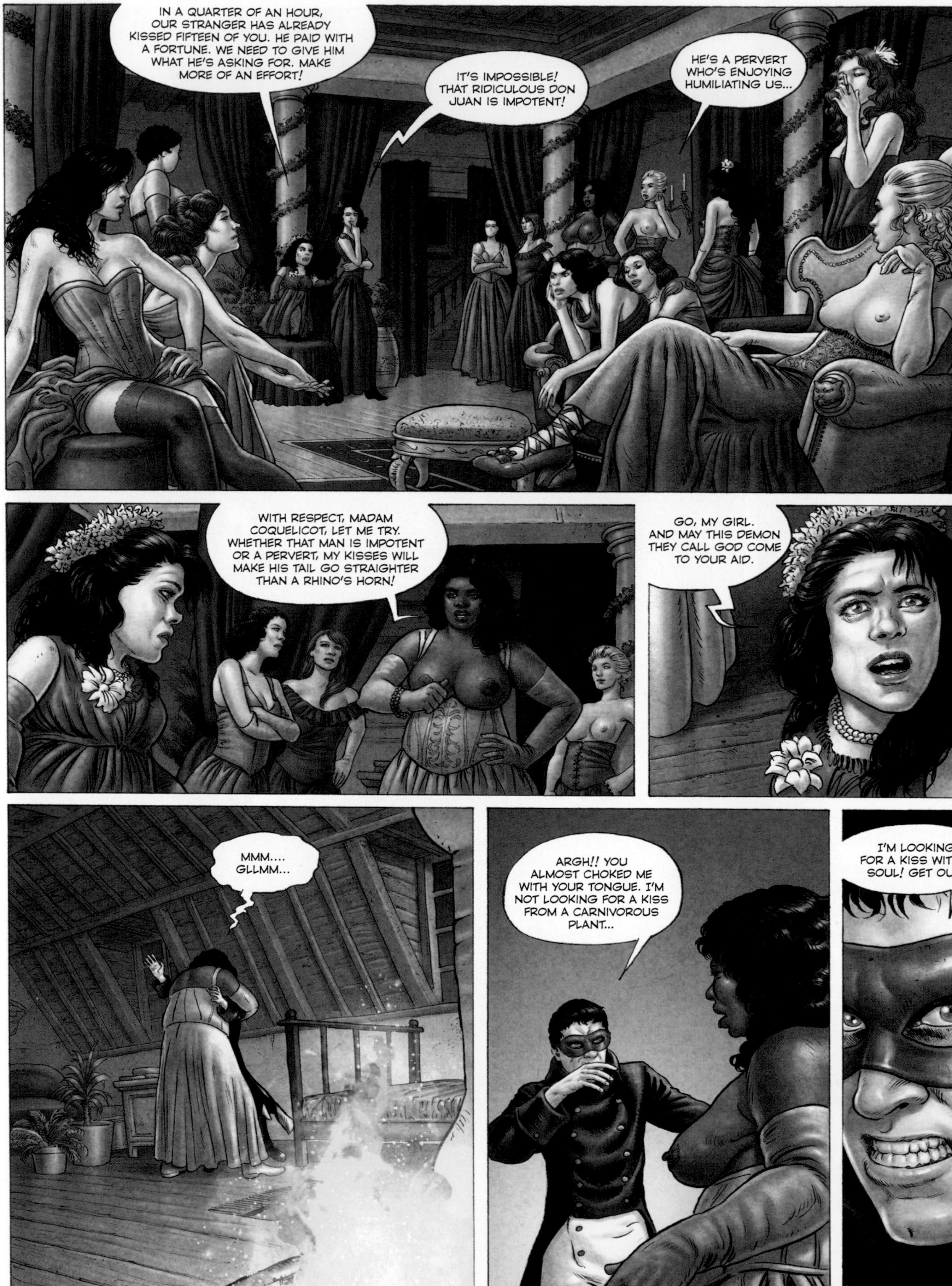
IN A QUARTER OF AN HOUR, OUR STRANGER HAS ALREADY KISSED FIFTEEN OF YOU. HE PAID WITH A FORTUNE. WE NEED TO GIVE HIM WHAT HE'S ASKING FOR. MAKE MORE OF AN EFFORT!
IT'S IMPOSSIBLE! THAT RIDICULOUS DON JUAN IS IMPOTENT!
HE'S A PERVERT WHO'S ENJOYING HUMILIATING US...
WITH RESPECT, MADAM COQUELICOT, LET ME TRY. WHETHER THAT MAN IS IMPOTENT OR A PERVERT, MY KISSES WILL MAKE HIS TAIL GO STRAIGHTER THAN A RHINO'S HORN!
GO, MY GIRL. AND MAY THIS DEMON THEY CALL GOD COME TO YOUR AID.
MMM.... GLLMM...
ARGH!! YOU ALMOST CHOKED ME WITH YOUR TONGUE. I'M NOT LOOKING FOR A KISS FROM A CARNIVOROUS PLANT...
I'M LOOKING FOR A KISS WITH A SOUL! GET OUT!

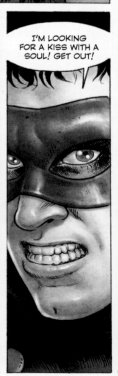

CLACK

?!!

NOTHING! NOTHING! NOTHING!

GET ME AWAY FROM THIS HELL, CRABLOUSE!

FORGIVE ME, MONSIEUR, BUT IT DOESN'T LOOK LIKE YOU FOUND WHAT YOU WERE LOOKING FOR.

I'D NEED TO KISS MY OWN MIND TO FIND WHAT I'M LOOKING FOR.

ERM... I DON'T UNDERSTAND, MONSIEUR...

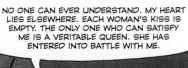

NO ONE CAN EVER UNDERSTAND. MY HEART LIES ELSEWHERE. EACH WOMAN'S KISS IS EMPTY. THE ONLY ONE WHO CAN SATISFY ME IS A VERITABLE QUEEN. SHE HAS ENTERED INTO BATTLE WITH ME.

WHAT ARE YOU GOING TO DO?

THE ONLY BATTLES WON BY FLEEING ARE THOSE WAGED AGAINST WOMEN. I WILL FORGET THIS QUEEN BY CONQUERING THE WORLD...

VIVE LA FRANCE!

OH SHUT UP, YOU HYPOCRITE. DON'T EVEN THINK OF GOSSIPING ABOUT ANY OF THIS DECEIT! AND IF YOU REPEAT A SINGLE THING OF WHAT I SAID, I'LL HAVE YOU SKINNED ALIVE AND FED TO THE DOGS!

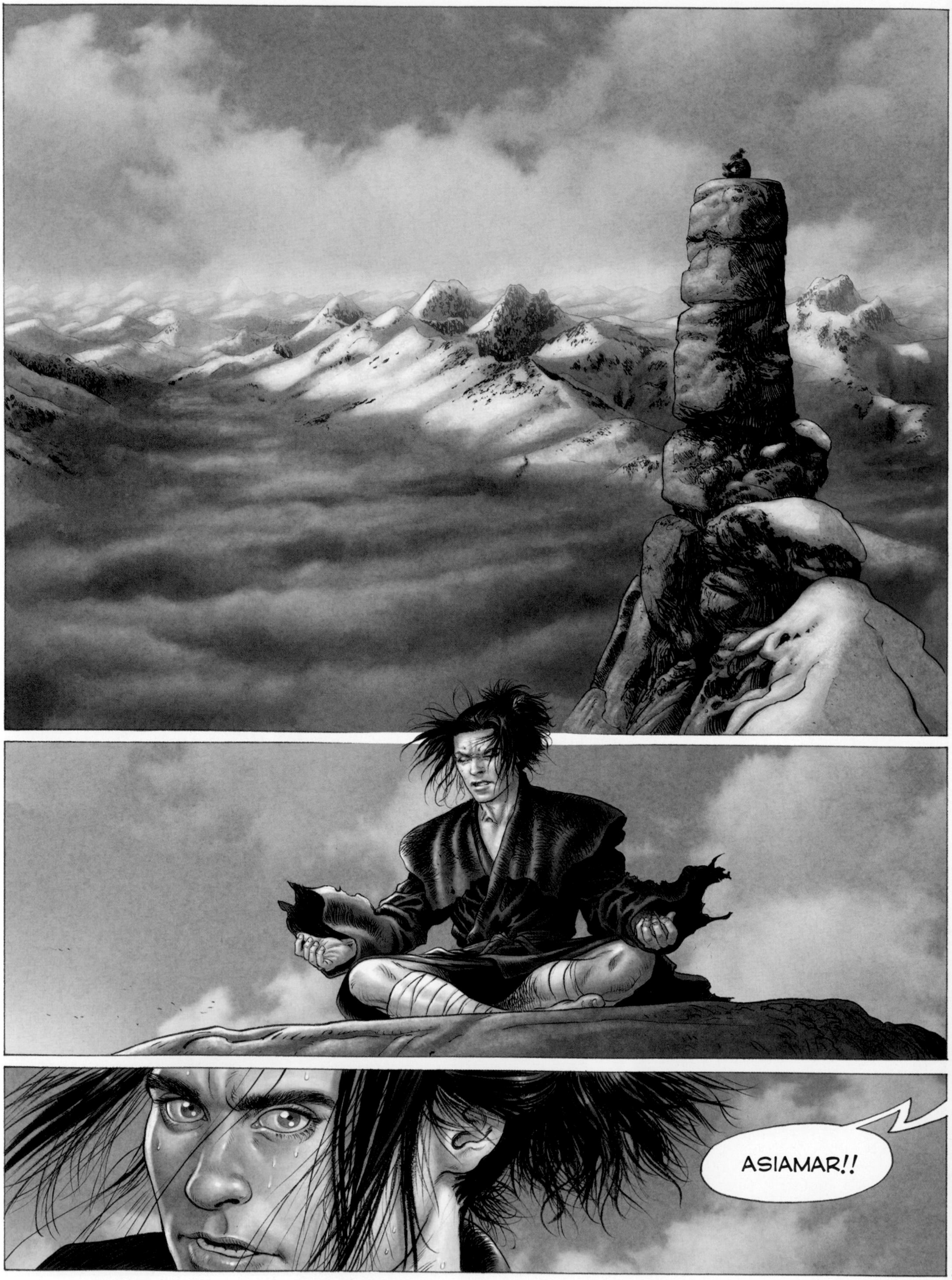
ASIAMAR!!

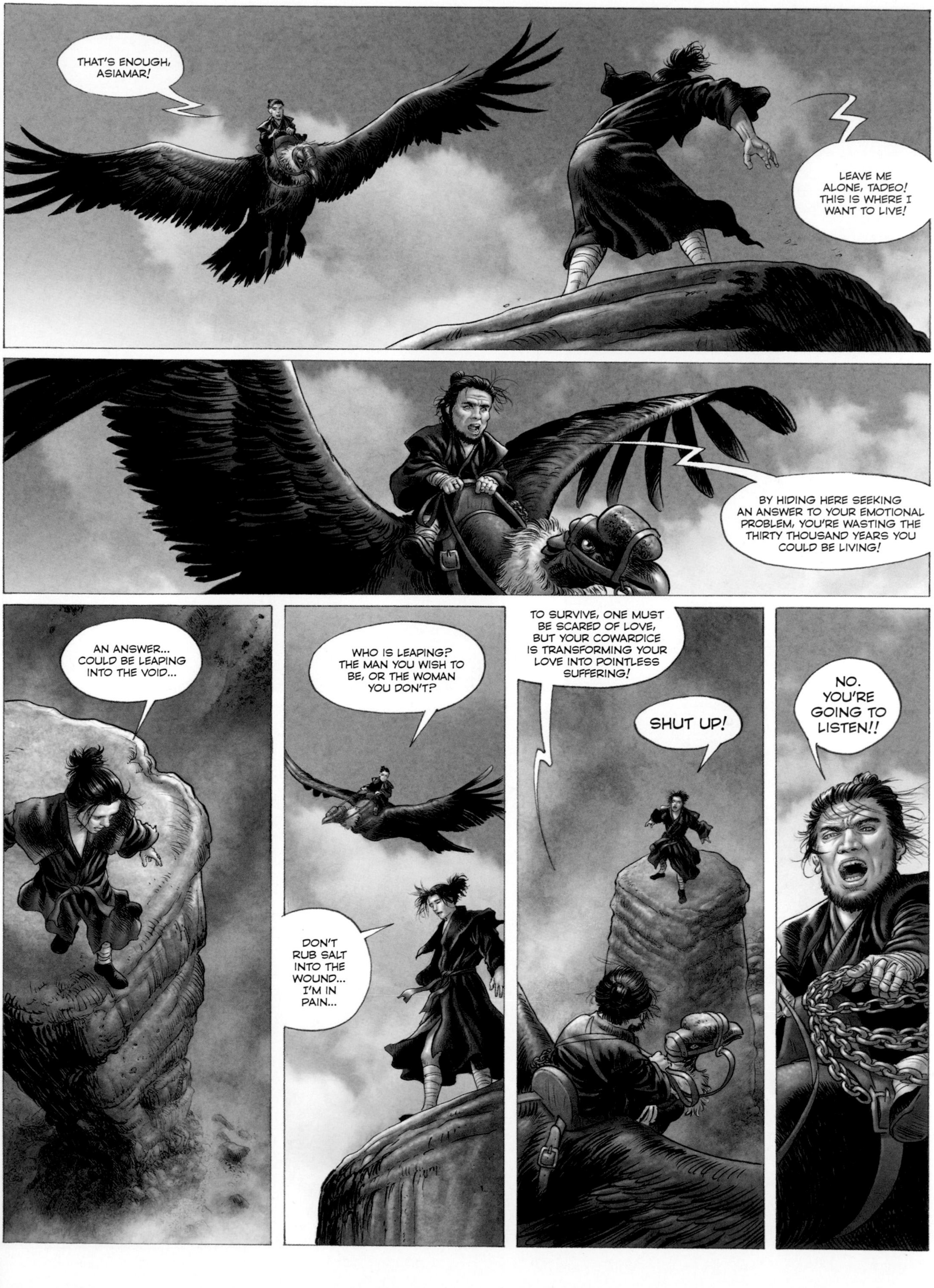

THAT'S ENOUGH, ASIAMAR!
LEAVE ME ALONE, TADEO! THIS IS WHERE I WANT TO LIVE!
BY HIDING HERE SEEKING AN ANSWER TO YOUR EMOTIONAL PROBLEM, YOU'RE WASTING THE THIRTY THOUSAND YEARS YOU COULD BE LIVING!
AN ANSWER... COULD BE LEAPING INTO THE VOID...
WHO IS LEAPING? THE MAN YOU WISH TO BE, OR THE WOMAN YOU DON'T?
DON'T RUB SALT INTO THE WOUND... I'M IN PAIN...
TO SURVIVE, ONE MUST BE SCARED OF LOVE, BUT YOUR COWARDICE IS TRANSFORMING YOUR LOVE INTO POINTLESS SUFFERING!
SHUT UP!
NO. YOU'RE GOING TO LISTEN!!

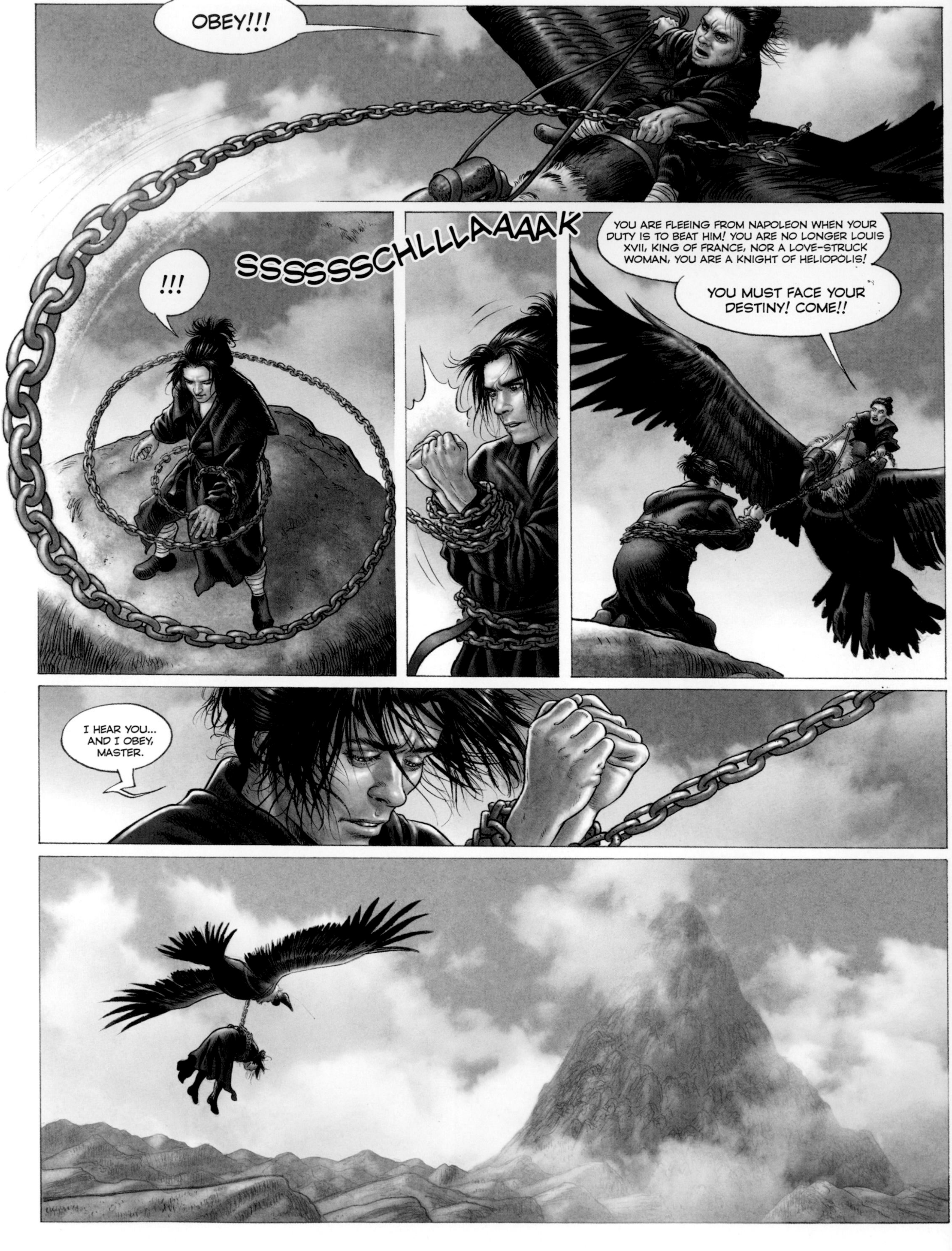
OBEY!!!
!!!
SSSSSSCHLLLAAAAK
YOU ARE FLEEING FROM NAPOLEON WHEN YOUR DUTY IS TO BEAT HIM! YOU ARE NO LONGER LOUIS XVII, KING OF FRANCE, NOR A LOVE-STRUCK WOMAN, YOU ARE A KNIGHT OF HELIOPOLIS!
YOU MUST FACE YOUR DESTINY! COME!!
I HEAR YOU... AND I OBEY, MASTER.

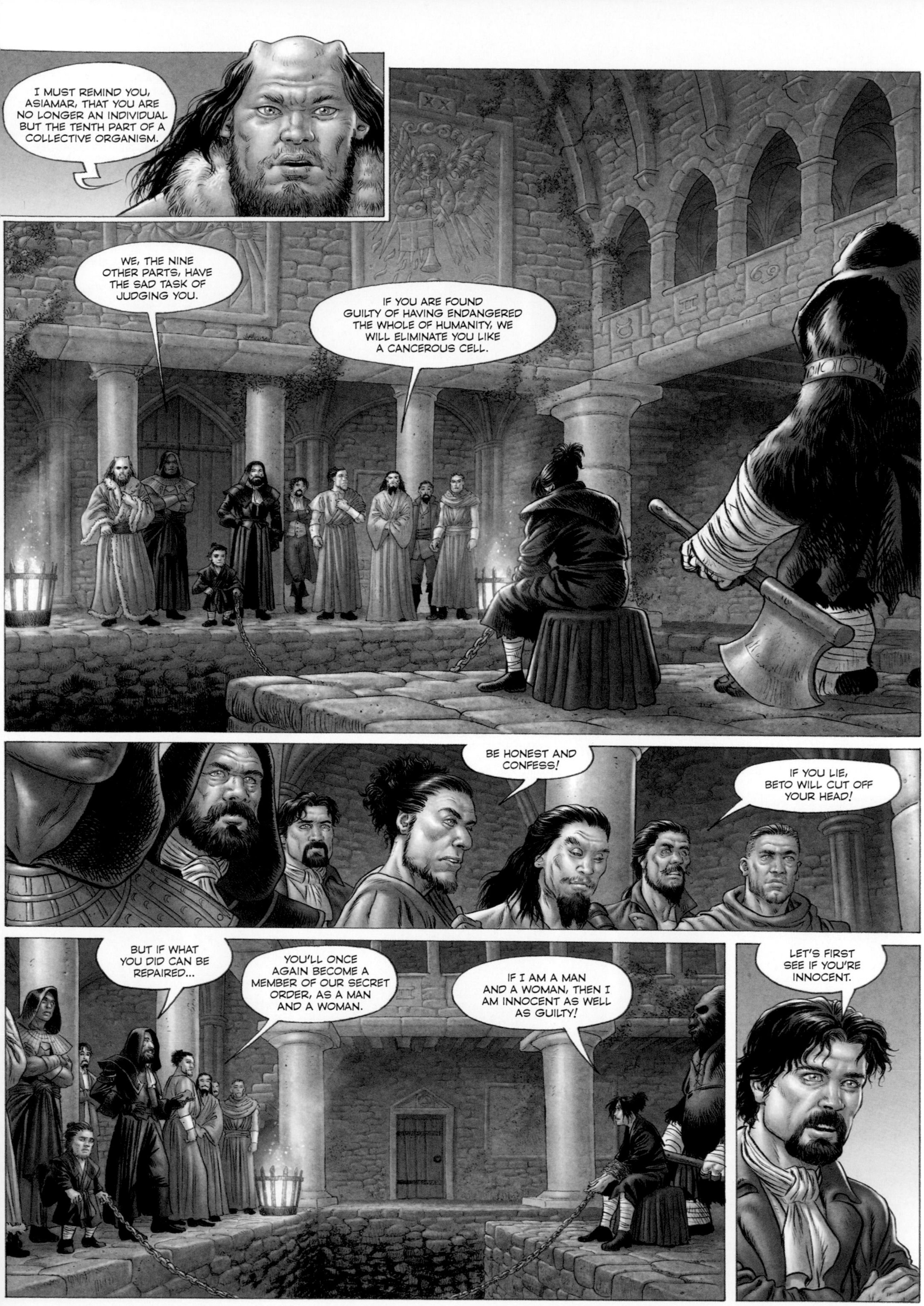
I MUST REMIND YOU, ASIAMAR, THAT YOU ARE NO LONGER AN INDIVIDUAL BUT THE TENTH PART OF A COLLECTIVE ORGANISM.
WE, THE NINE OTHER PARTS, HAVE THE SAD TASK OF JUDGING YOU.
IF YOU ARE FOUND GUILTY OF HAVING ENDANGERED THE WHOLE OF HUMANITY, WE WILL ELIMINATE YOU LIKE A CANCEROUS CELL.
BE HONEST AND CONFESS!
IF YOU LIE, BETO WILL CUT OFF YOUR HEAD!
BUT IF WHAT YOU DID CAN BE REPAIRED...
YOU'LL ONCE AGAIN BECOME A MEMBER OF OUR SECRET ORDER, AS A MAN AND A WOMAN.
IF I AM A MAN AND A WOMAN, THEN I AM INNOCENT AS WELL AS GUILTY!
LET'S FIRST SEE IF YOU'RE INNOCENT.

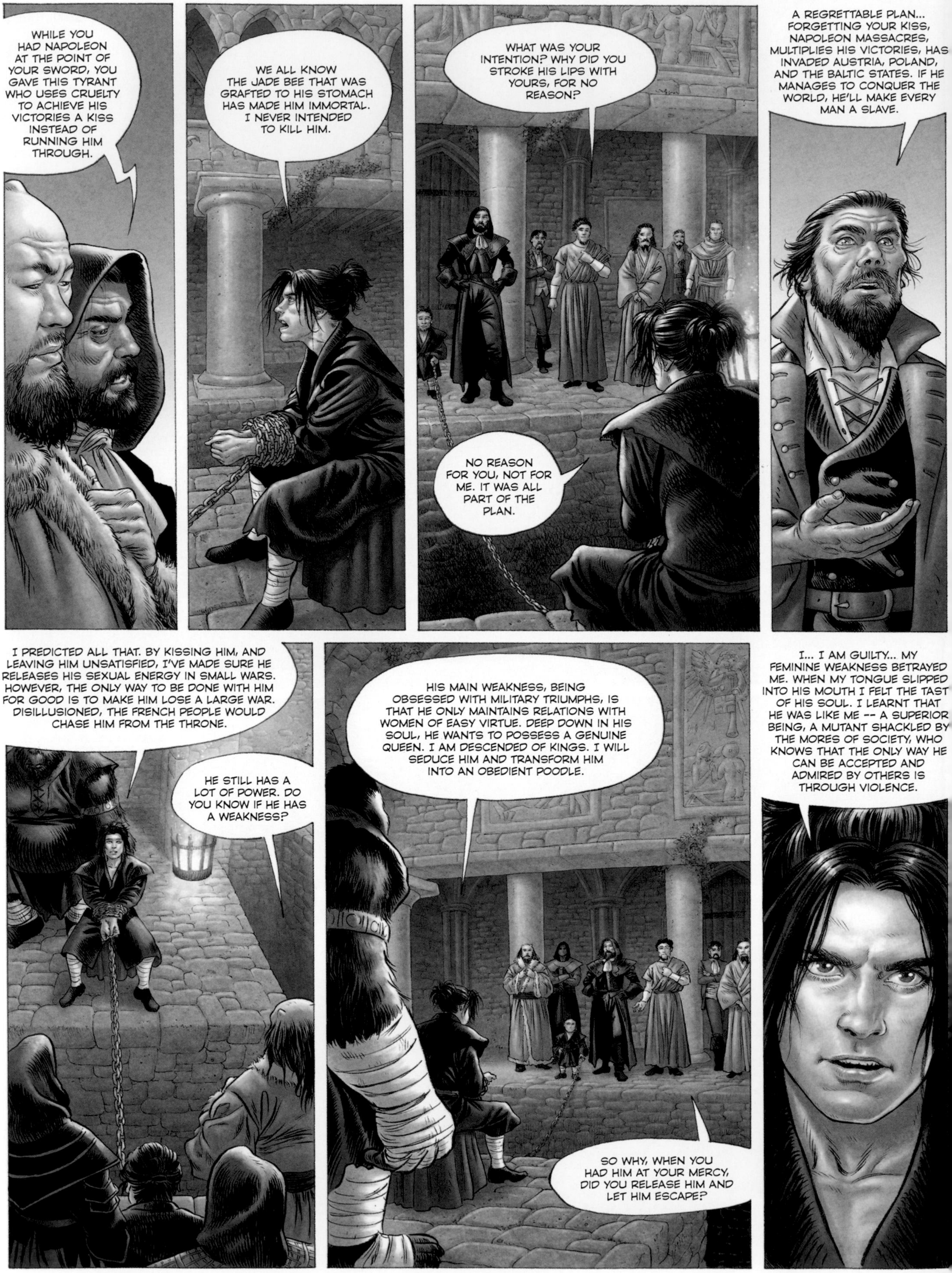
WHILE YOU HAD NAPOLEON AT THE POINT OF YOUR SWORD, YOU GAVE THIS TYRANT WHO USES CRUELTY TO ACHIEVE HIS VICTORIES A KISS INSTEAD OF RUNNING HIM THROUGH.
WE ALL KNOW THE JADE BEE THAT WAS GRAFTED TO HIS STOMACH HAS MADE HIM IMMORTAL. I NEVER INTENDED TO KILL HIM.
WHAT WAS YOUR INTENTION? WHY DID YOU STROKE HIS LIPS WITH YOURS, FOR NO REASON?
NO REASON FOR YOU, NOT FOR ME. IT WAS ALL PART OF THE PLAN.
A REGRETTABLE PLAN... FORGETTING YOUR KISS, NAPOLEON MASSACRES, MULTIPLIES HIS VICTORIES, HAS INVADED AUSTRIA, POLAND, AND THE BALTIC STATES. IF HE MANAGES TO CONQUER THE WORLD, HE'LL MAKE EVERY MAN A SLAVE.
I PREDICTED ALL THAT. BY KISSING HIM, AND LEAVING HIM UNSATISFIED, I'VE MADE SURE HE RELEASES HIS SEXUAL ENERGY IN SMALL WARS. HOWEVER, THE ONLY WAY TO BE DONE WITH HIM FOR GOOD IS TO MAKE HIM LOSE A LARGE WAR. DISILLUSIONED, THE FRENCH PEOPLE WOULD CHASE HIM FROM THE THRONE.
HE STILL HAS A LOT OF POWER. DO YOU KNOW IF HE HAS A WEAKNESS?
HIS MAIN WEAKNESS, BEING OBSESSED WITH MILITARY TRIUMPHS, IS THAT HE ONLY MAINTAINS RELATIONS WITH WOMEN OF EASY VIRTUE. DEEP DOWN IN HIS SOUL, HE WANTS TO POSSESS A GENUINE QUEEN. I AM DESCENDED OF KINGS. I WILL SEDUCE HIM AND TRANSFORM HIM INTO AN OBEDIENT POODLE.
SO WHY, WHEN YOU HAD HIM AT YOUR MERCY, DID YOU RELEASE HIM AND LET HIM ESCAPE?
I... I AM GUILTY... MY FEMININE WEAKNESS BETRAYED ME. WHEN MY TONGUE SLIPPED INTO HIS MOUTH I FELT THE TAST OF HIS SOUL. I LEARNT THAT HE WAS LIKE ME -- A SUPERIOR BEING, A MUTANT SHACKLED BY THE MORES OF SOCIETY, WHO KNOWS THAT THE ONLY WAY HE CAN BE ACCEPTED AND ADMIRED BY OTHERS IS THROUGH VIOLENCE.

WHAT DO YOU INTEND TO DO WITH THIS CRIMINAL EMPEROR?

I COULD AWAKEN HIM TO HIS EXTRAORDINARY SPIRITUAL TALENT, SO DESTROYING ANY DREAMS OF GLORY AND POWER. IN ONE WORD -- HEAL HIM. IF... I SUCCEED IN THIS, NAPOLEON WOULD EARN THE RIGHT TO BECOME A KNIGHT OF HELIOPOLIS.

AH, I SEE... DEEP DOWN, YOU WANT TO BE A STRONG MAN, BUT YOU'RE NOTHING BUT A WEAK, LOVESICK WOMAN. OUR WHITE QUEEN HAS MET HER RED KING! HAHAHA!

IT'S TRUE.... MY FEMININE SIDE IS IN LOVE.... BUT IF YOU HELP ME TO MAKE THE RIDICULOUS QUEEN THAT I AM STRONGER, I PROMISE TO INVADE HIS MIND AND MAKE HIM COMMIT MISTAKES THAT LEAD TO HIS DOWNFALL.

DO YOU THINK YOU'LL BE ABLE TO UPROOT THE POISONOUS MUSHROOM THAT IS ROMANTIC LOVE FROM YOUR HEART?

WITH NIGREDO, I OVERCAME MY MENTAL CHAOS, MY EMOTIONAL ARMOR, MY ANIMAL COWARDICE, AND THE SHADOWS WHICH DARKENED MY SOUL. WITH ALBEDO, I WAS ABLE TO REACH SPIRITUAL PURITY, THE LUMINOUS VIRTUE OF BEAUTY AND GOODNESS. WHAT AM I LACKING?

YOU'VE KNOWN ONLY FEMININE GOODNESS. YOU MUST LEARN FEMININE CRUELTY.

FREE HIM.

SSSSSSSCCCCHHHLLLLLLLAAAKKKKKK

13

ASIAMAR, IF YOU ARE ABLE TO FIND ABSOLUTE CRUELTY, WE WILL GIVE YOU A NEW CHANCE.

I'LL FIND IT!A

HALLELUJAH!

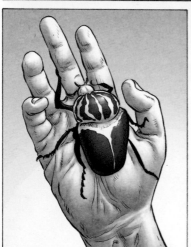

YOU HAVE DRUNK THE VISCERA OF THE HOLY SCARAB. DON'T WASTE YOUR TIME TRYING TO FIND OUT IF WHAT'S HAPPENING TO YOU IS REAL OR IMAGINARY BUT READY YOURSELF FOR THE EXPERIENCE, BODY AND SOUL, FOR IT HAS THE POTENTIAL TO SHATTER YOU INTO PIECES.

BODY AND SOUL. BECAUSE I KNOW THAT WHOEVER LIES AT THE END OF THIS PATH IS THE REAL ME.

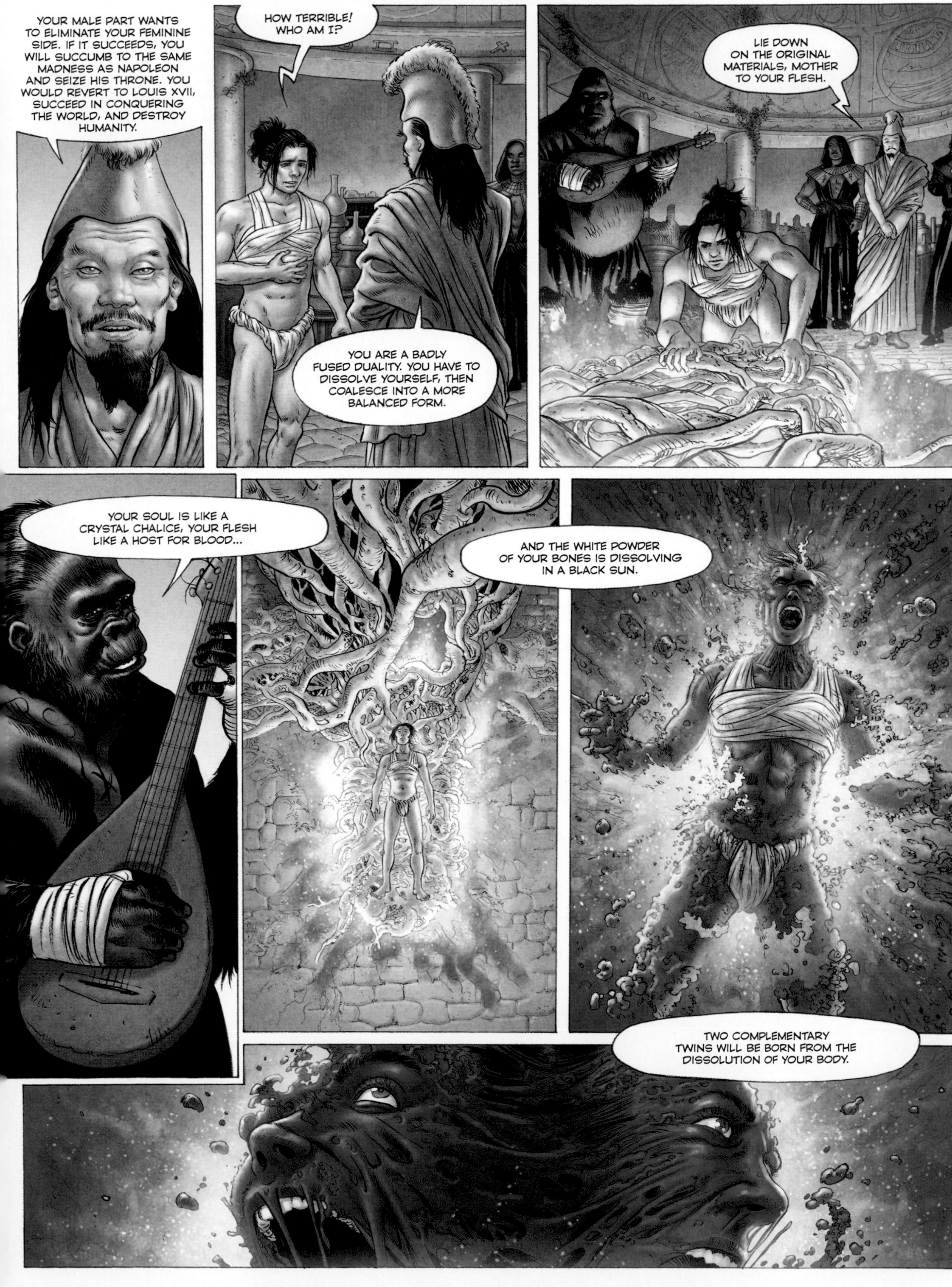
YOUR MALE PART WANTS TO ELIMINATE YOUR FEMININE SIDE. IF IT SUCCEEDS, YOU WILL SUCCUMB TO THE SAME MADNESS AS NAPOLEON AND SEIZE HIS THRONE. YOU WOULD REVERT TO LOUIS XVII, SUCCEED IN CONQUERING THE WORLD, AND DESTROY HUMANITY.
HOW TERRIBLE! WHO AM I?
YOU ARE A BADLY FUSED DUALITY. YOU HAVE TO DISSOLVE YOURSELF, THEN COALESCE INTO A MORE BALANCED FORM.
LIE DOWN ON THE ORIGINAL MATERIALS, MOTHER TO YOUR FLESH.
YOUR SOUL IS LIKE A CRYSTAL CHALICE, YOUR FLESH LIKE A HOST FOR BLOOD...
AND THE WHITE POWDER OF YOUR BONES IS DISSOLVING IN A BLACK SUN.
TWO COMPLEMENTARY TWINS WILL BE BORN FROM THE DISSOLUTION OF YOUR BODY.

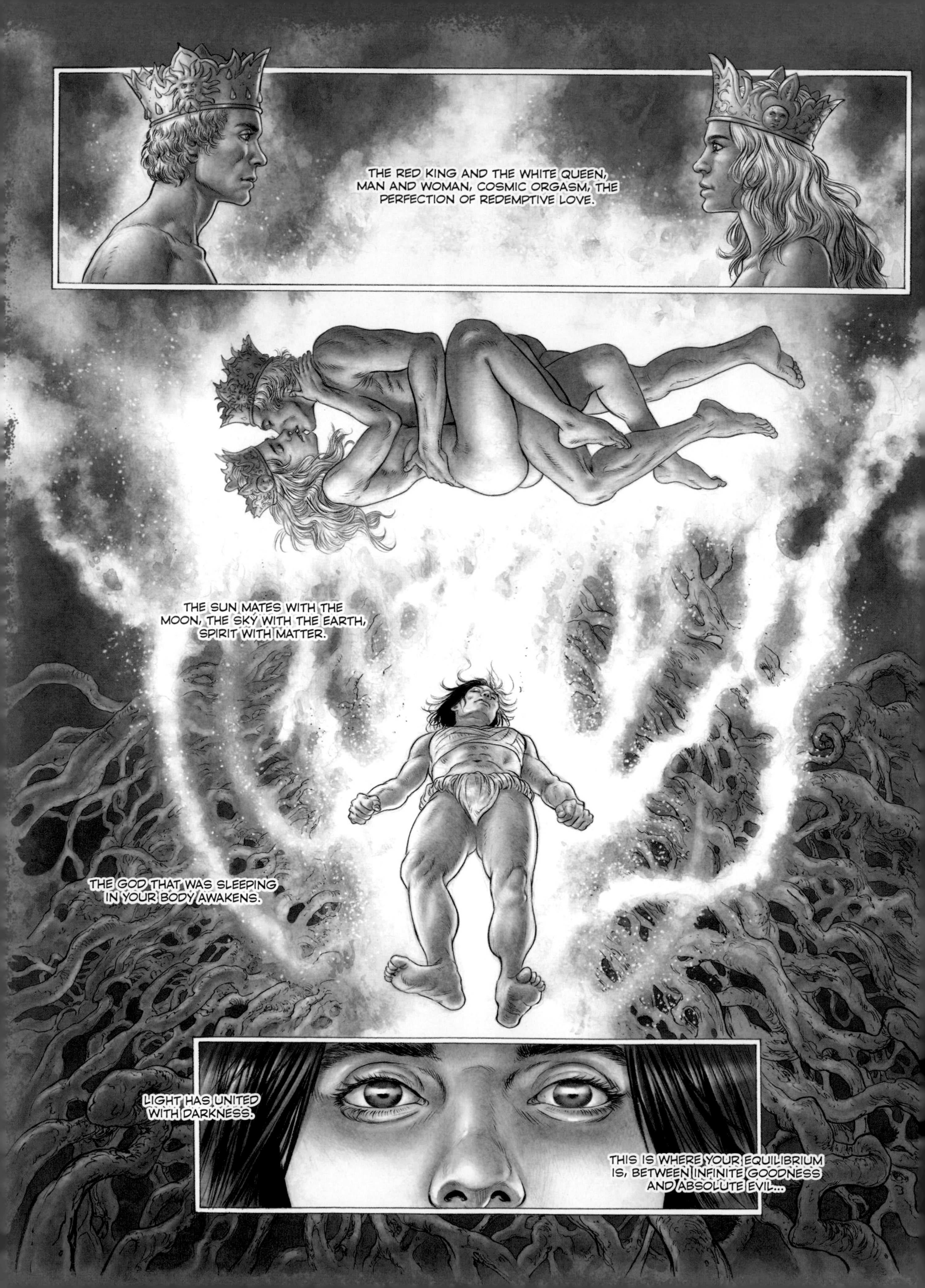
THE RED KING AND THE WHITE QUEEN, MAN AND WOMAN, COSMIC ORGASM, THE PERFECTION OF REDEMPTIVE LOVE.
THE SUN MATES WITH THE MOON, THE SKY WITH THE EARTH, SPIRIT WITH MATTER.
THE GOD THAT WAS SLEEPING IN YOUR BODY AWAKENS.
LIGHT HAS UNITED WITH DARKNESS.
THIS IS WHERE YOUR EQUILIBRIUM IS, BETWEEN INFINITE GOODNESS AND ABSOLUTE EVIL...

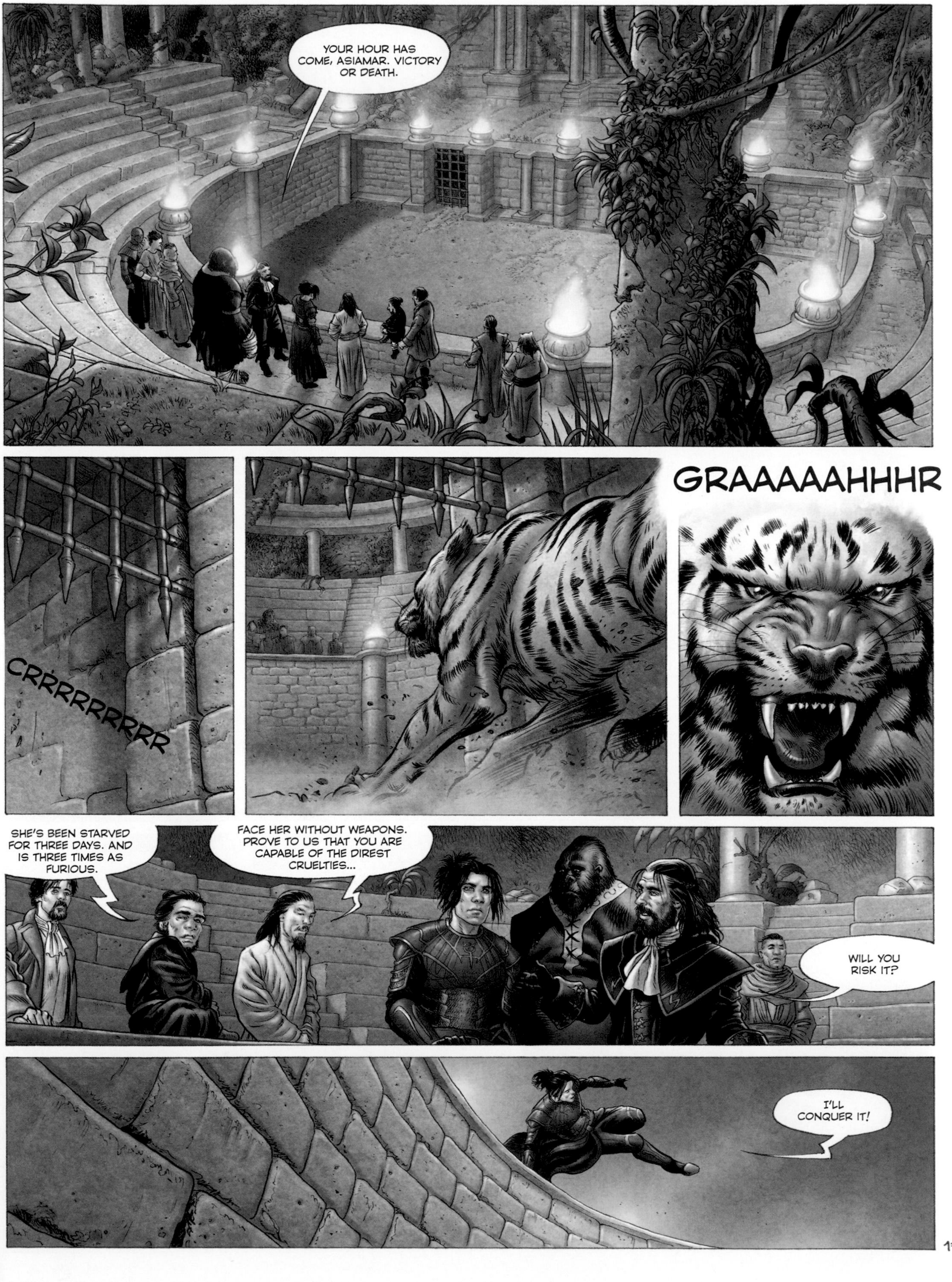
YOUR HOUR HAS COME, ASIAMAR. VICTORY OR DEATH.
CRRRRRRRRRR
GRAAAAAHHHR
SHE'S BEEN STARVED FOR THREE DAYS. AND IS THREE TIMES AS FURIOUS.
FACE HER WITHOUT WEAPONS. PROVE TO US THAT YOU ARE CAPABLE OF THE DIREST CRUELTIES...
WILL YOU RISK IT?
I'LL CONQUER IT!

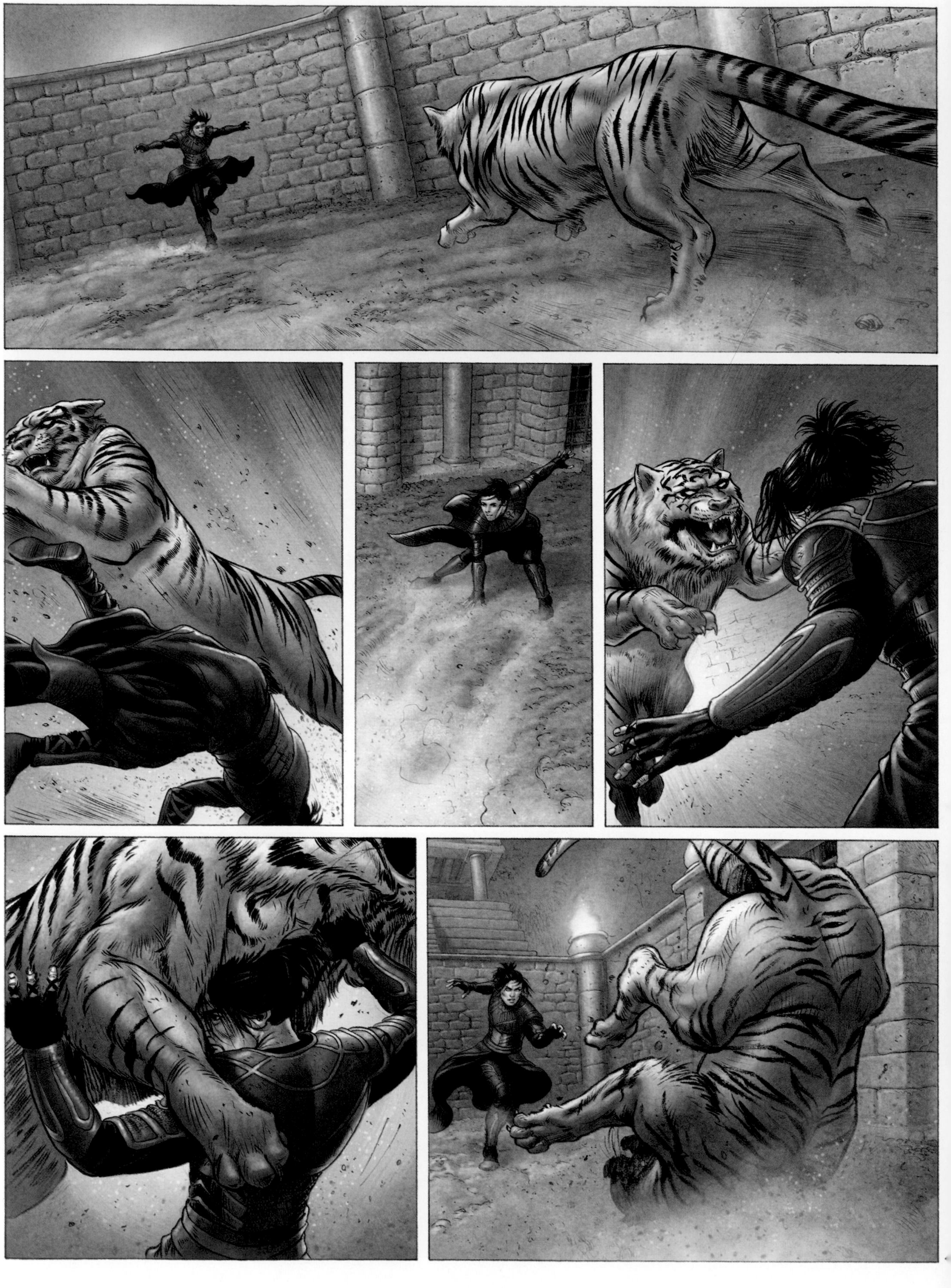

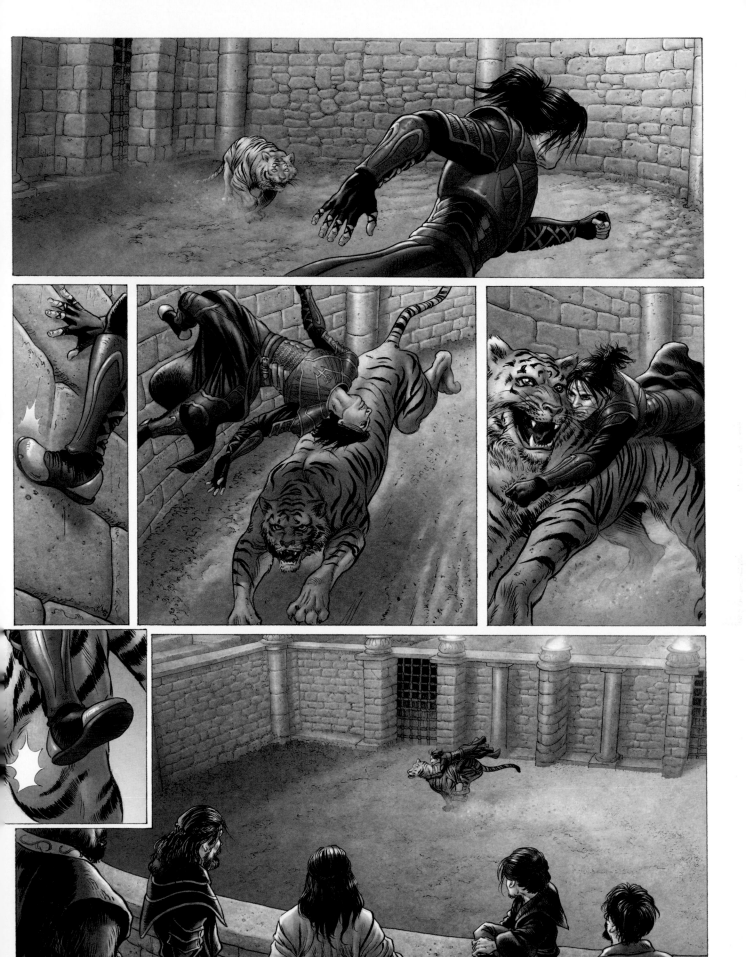

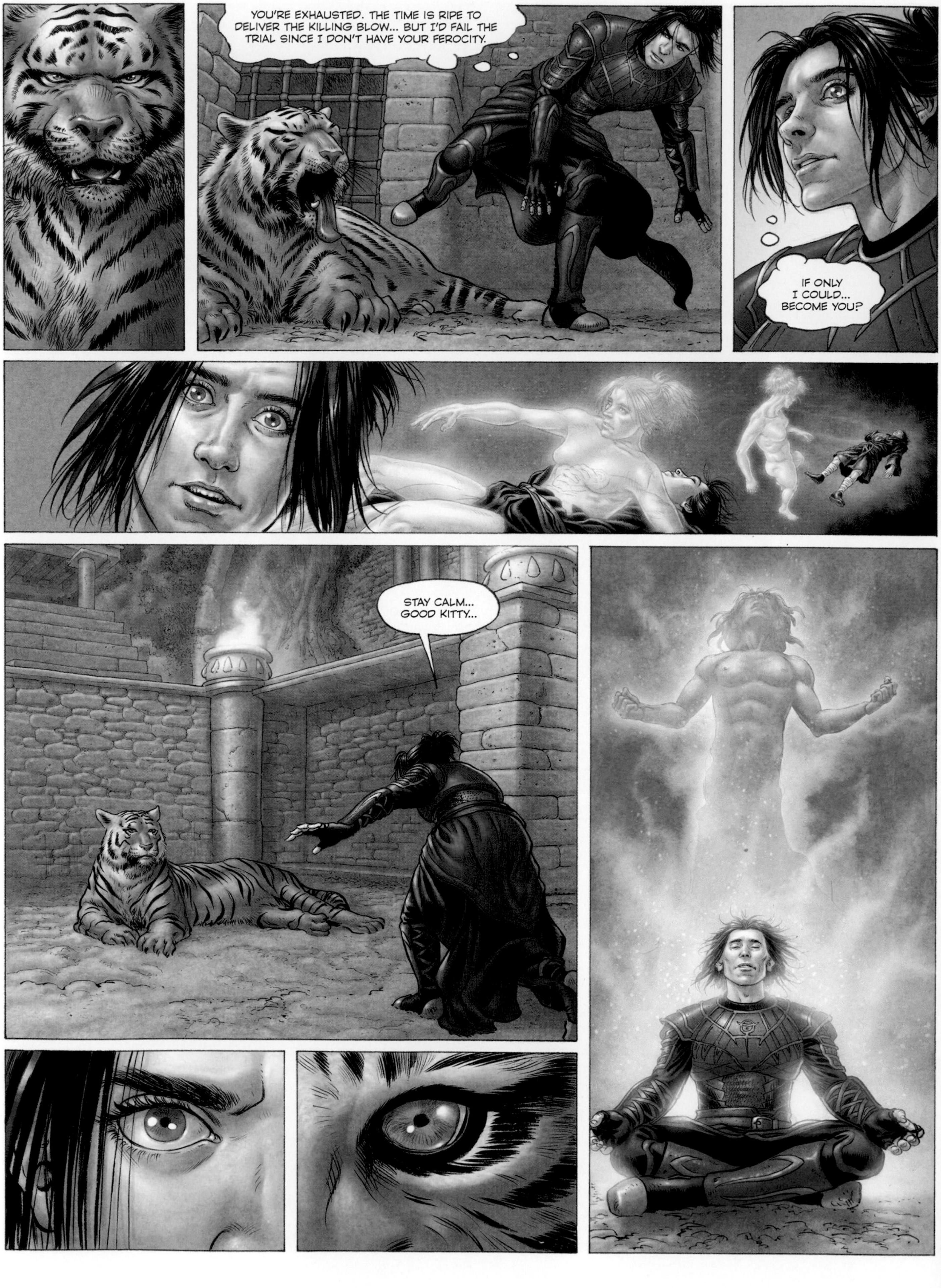
YOU'RE EXHAUSTED. THE TIME IS RIPE TO DELIVER THE KILLING BLOW... BUT I'D FAIL THE TRIAL SINCE I DON'T HAVE YOUR FEROCITY.
IF ONLY I COULD... BECOME YOU?
STAY CALM... GOOD KITTY...

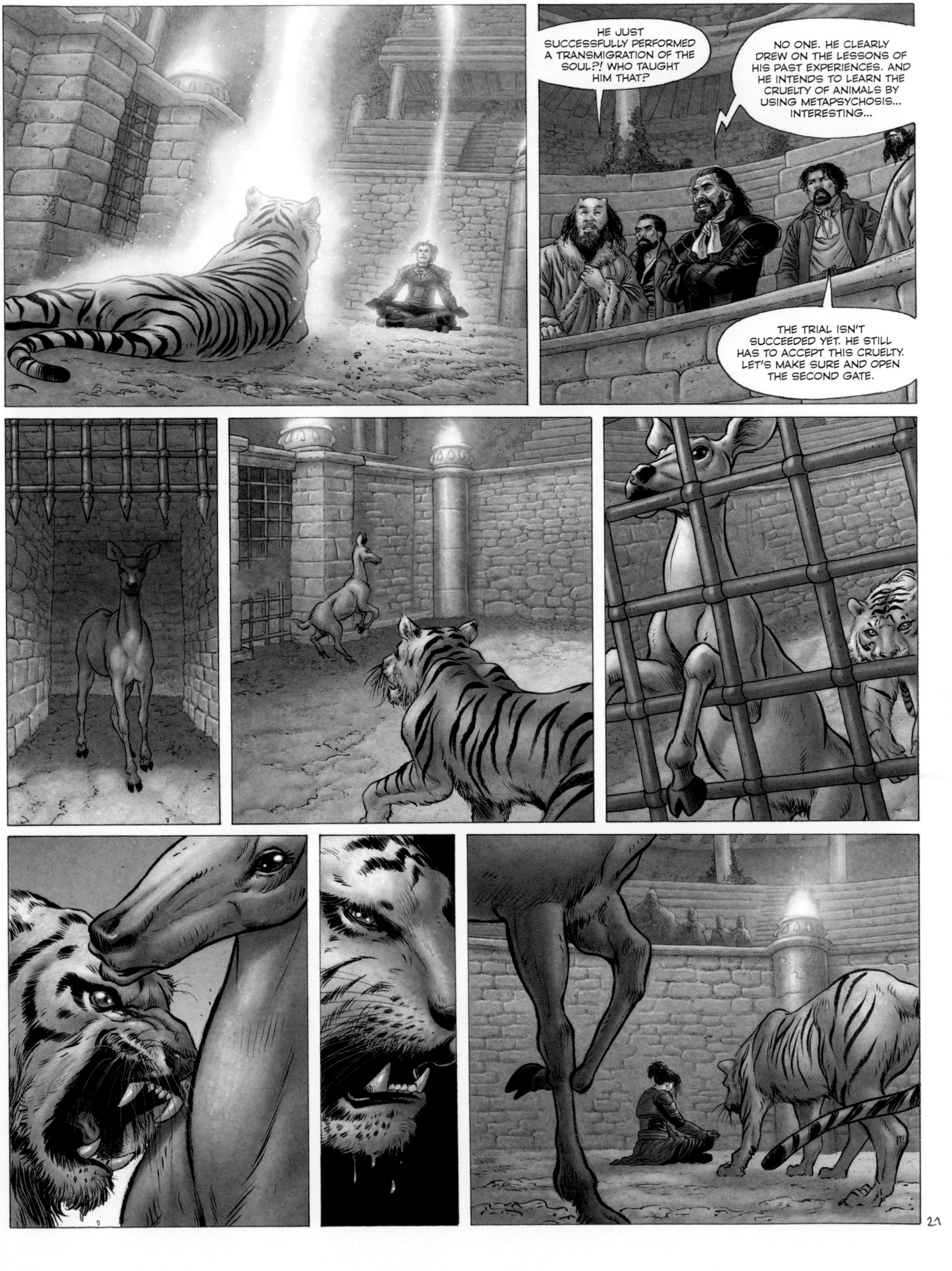
HE JUST SUCCESSFULLY PERFORMED A TRANSMIGRATION OF THE SOUL?! WHO TAUGHT HIM THAT?
NO ONE. HE CLEARLY DREW ON THE LESSONS OF HIS PAST EXPERIENCES. AND HE INTENDS TO LEARN THE CRUELTY OF ANIMALS BY USING METAPSYCHOSIS... INTERESTING...
THE TRIAL ISN'T SUCCEEDED YET. HE STILL HAS TO ACCEPT THIS CRUELTY. LET'S MAKE SURE AND OPEN THE SECOND GATE.

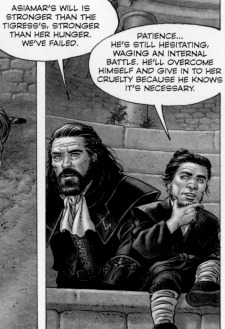

ASIAMAR'S WILL IS STRONGER THAN THE TIGRESS'S, STRONGER THAN HER HUNGER. WE'VE FAILED.

PATIENCE... HE'S STILL HESITATING, WAGING AN INTERNAL BATTLE. HE'LL OVERCOME HIMSELF AND GIVE IN TO HER CRUELTY BECAUSE HE KNOWS IT'S NECESSARY.

HE ALSO KNOWS WE'RE RUNNING OUT OF TIME. IF ASIAMAR DOES NOTHING IN THE NEXT TEN SECONDS, I'LL INTERRUPT THE EXPERIMENT, EXPEL HIM FROM THE TIGRESS, AND PUT HIM IN A CELL FOR THE REST OF HIS DAYS.

ONE... TWO... THREE... FOUR...

FIVE...

SIX...

SEVAN...

EIGAHT...

IT'S A BATTLE OF WILLS.

ASIAMAR IS GOING TO GIVE IN TO THE TIGRESS!

NINE.

HIS GOODNESS WILL TRIUMPH. HE WON'T DO IT.

TEN!

2

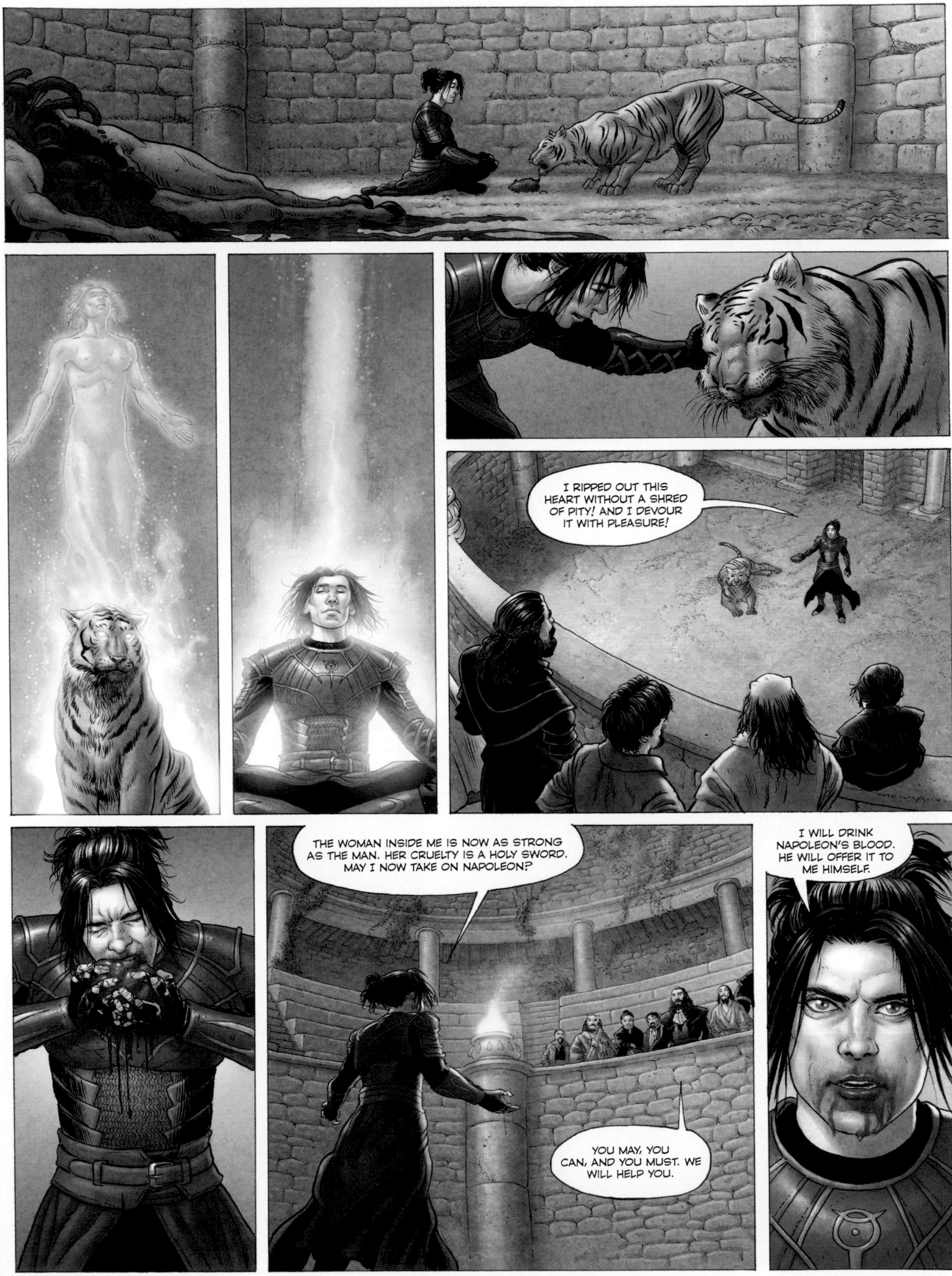

I RIPPED OUT THIS HEART WITHOUT A SHRED OF PITY! AND I DEVOUR IT WITH PLEASURE!
THE WOMAN INSIDE ME IS NOW AS STRONG AS THE MAN. HER CRUELTY IS A HOLY SWORD. MAY I NOW TAKE ON NAPOLEON?
YOU MAY, YOU CAN, AND YOU MUST. WE WILL HELP YOU.
I WILL DRINK NAPOLEON'S BLOOD. HE WILL OFFER IT TO ME HIMSELF.

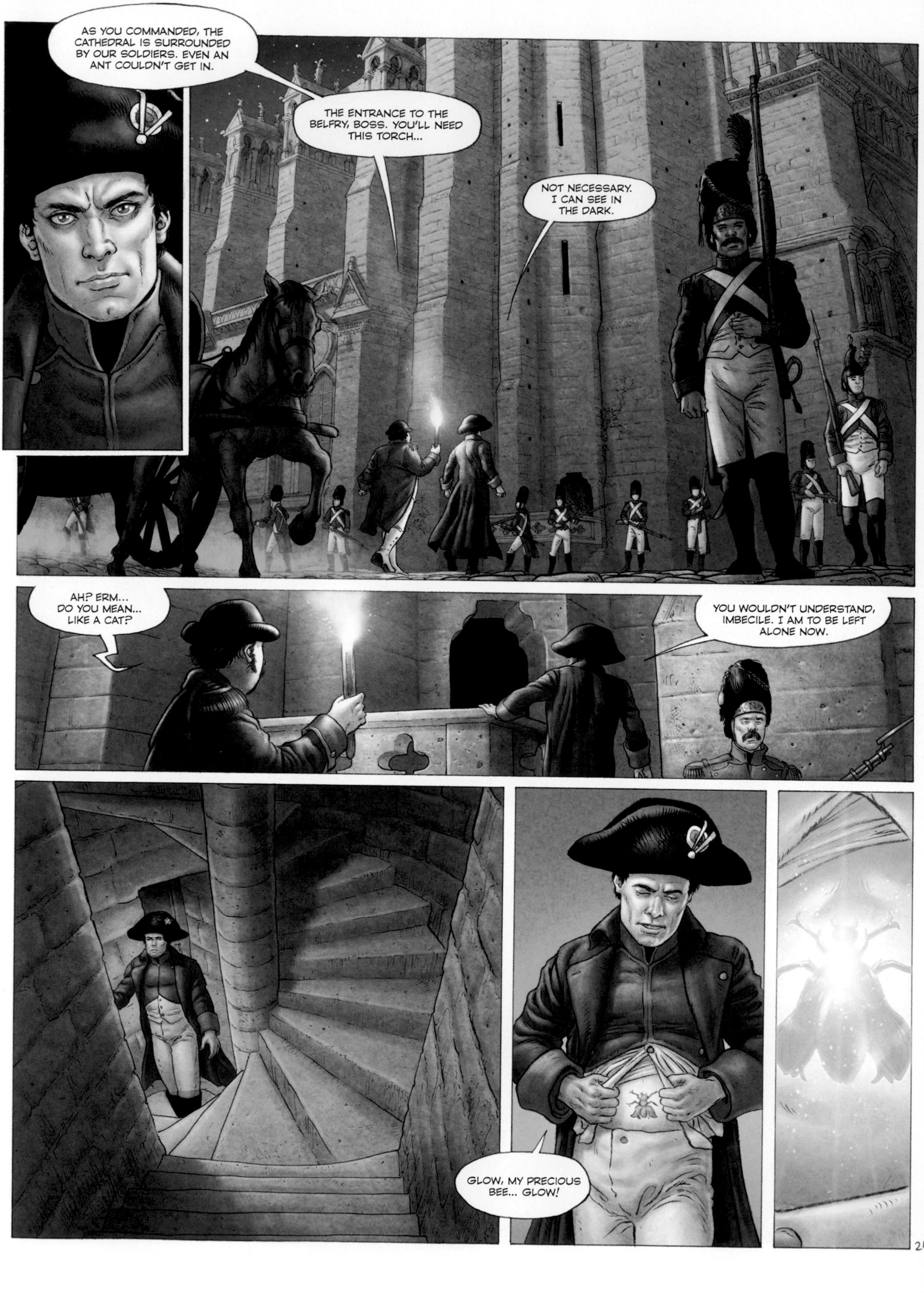
AS YOU COMMANDED, THE CATHEDRAL IS SURROUNDED BY OUR SOLDIERS. EVEN AN ANT COULDN'T GET IN.
THE ENTRANCE TO THE BELFRY, BOSS. YOU'LL NEED THIS TORCH...
NOT NECESSARY. I CAN SEE IN THE DARK.
AH? ERM... DO YOU MEAN... LIKE A CAT?
YOU WOULDN'T UNDERSTAND, IMBECILE. I AM TO BE LEFT ALONE NOW.
GLOW, MY PRECIOUS BEE... GLOW!

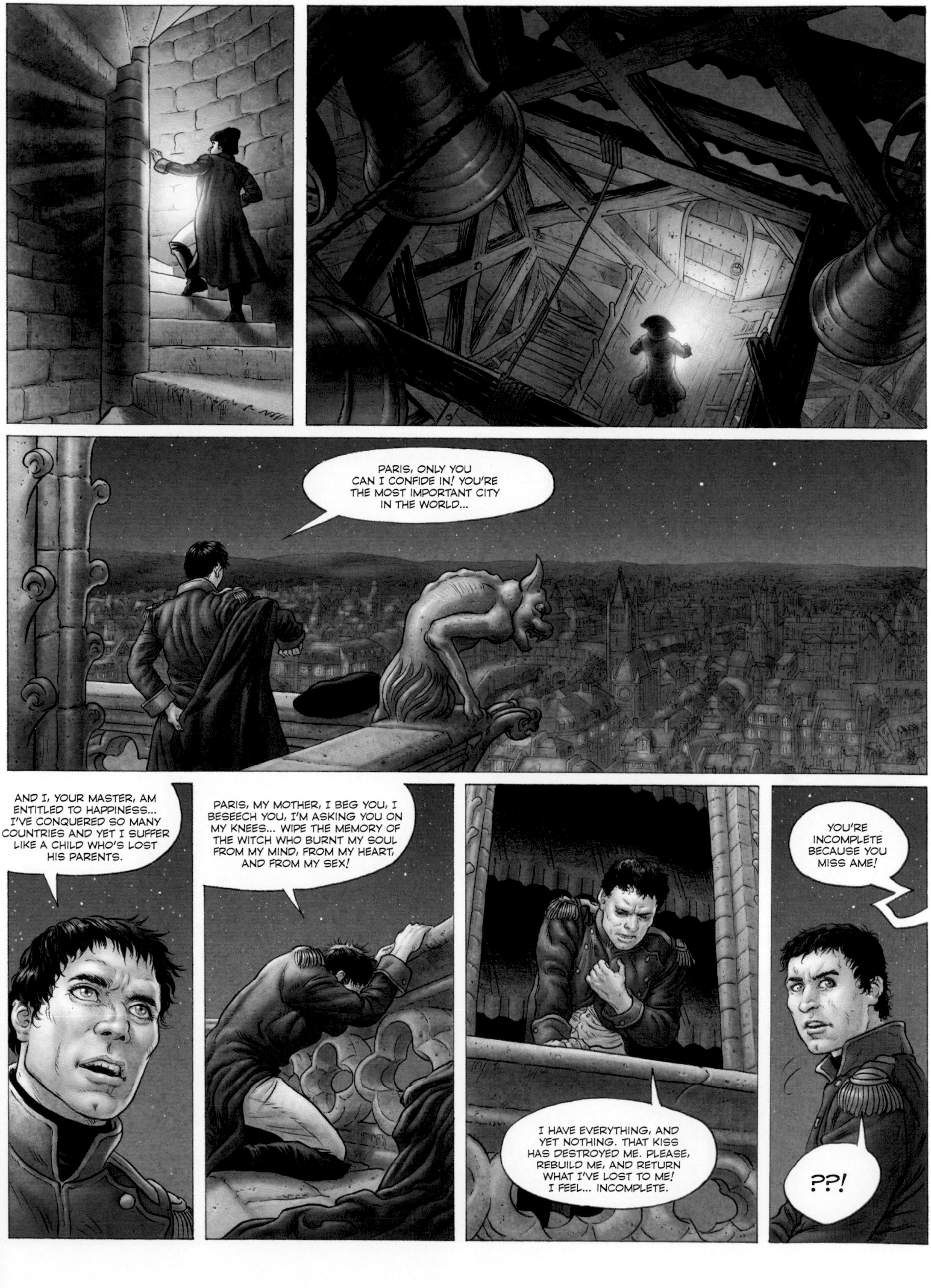
PARIS, ONLY YOU CAN I CONFIDE IN! YOU'RE THE MOST IMPORTANT CITY IN THE WORLD...
AND I, YOUR MASTER, AM ENTITLED TO HAPPINESS... I'VE CONQUERED SO MANY COUNTRIES AND YET I SUFFER LIKE A CHILD WHO'S LOST HIS PARENTS.
PARIS, MY MOTHER, I BEG YOU, I BESEECH YOU, I'M ASKING YOU ON MY KNEES... WIPE THE MEMORY OF THE WITCH WHO BURNT MY SOUL FROM MY MIND, FROM MY HEART, AND FROM MY SEX!
I HAVE EVERYTHING, AND YET NOTHING. THAT KISS HAS DESTROYED ME. PLEASE, REBUILD ME, AND RETURN WHAT I'VE LOST TO ME! I FEEL... INCOMPLETE.
YOU'RE INCOMPLETE BECAUSE YOU MISS AME!
??!

YOU?! IMPOSSIBLE... HOW DID YOU GET IN? MY FINEST SOLDIERS ARE PREVENTING ANYONE FROM SNEAKING INTO THE CATHEDRAL! YOU'RE A HALLUCINATION!

WOULD A HALLUCINATION RIP OFF THIS PIECE OF ROCK?

WOULD A HALLUCINATION RING THAT BELL?

DOOOoONNGG

IF YOU'RE NOT A COWARD, LET ME GIVE YOU ANOTHER KISS.

DON'T COME CLOSER, WITCH!

DON'T INSULT ME. YOU OWE ME RESPECT! I AM NAPOLEON BONAPARTE, EMPEROR OF FRANCE, ALMOST OF ALL EUROPE, AND SOON MASTER OF THE WORLD!

SHOULD I BE IMPRESSED? I AM THE LEGITIMATE QUEEN OF THE FRENCH, OF A LINE OF KINGS DESCENDED FROM A SON OF MARIE-MAGDALENE AND JESUS CHRIST.

ARE YOU A WOMAN OR A DEMON?

WHAT AM I? I AM THE BEING THAT NEEDS YOUR SOUL TO BE COMPLETE. TO KISS ME IS TO LOOK IN A MIRROR. COME HERE AND ONCE AGAIN FEEL THE LINK THAT UNITES US.

YOU'RE TRYING TO GET TO ME. NOTHING AND NOBODY CAN. YOU WON'T TAKE HOLD OF EITHER MY MIND OR MY BODY.

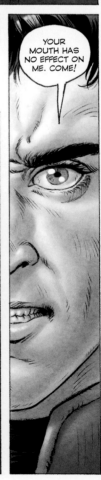

YOUR MOUTH HAS NO EFFECT ON ME. COME!

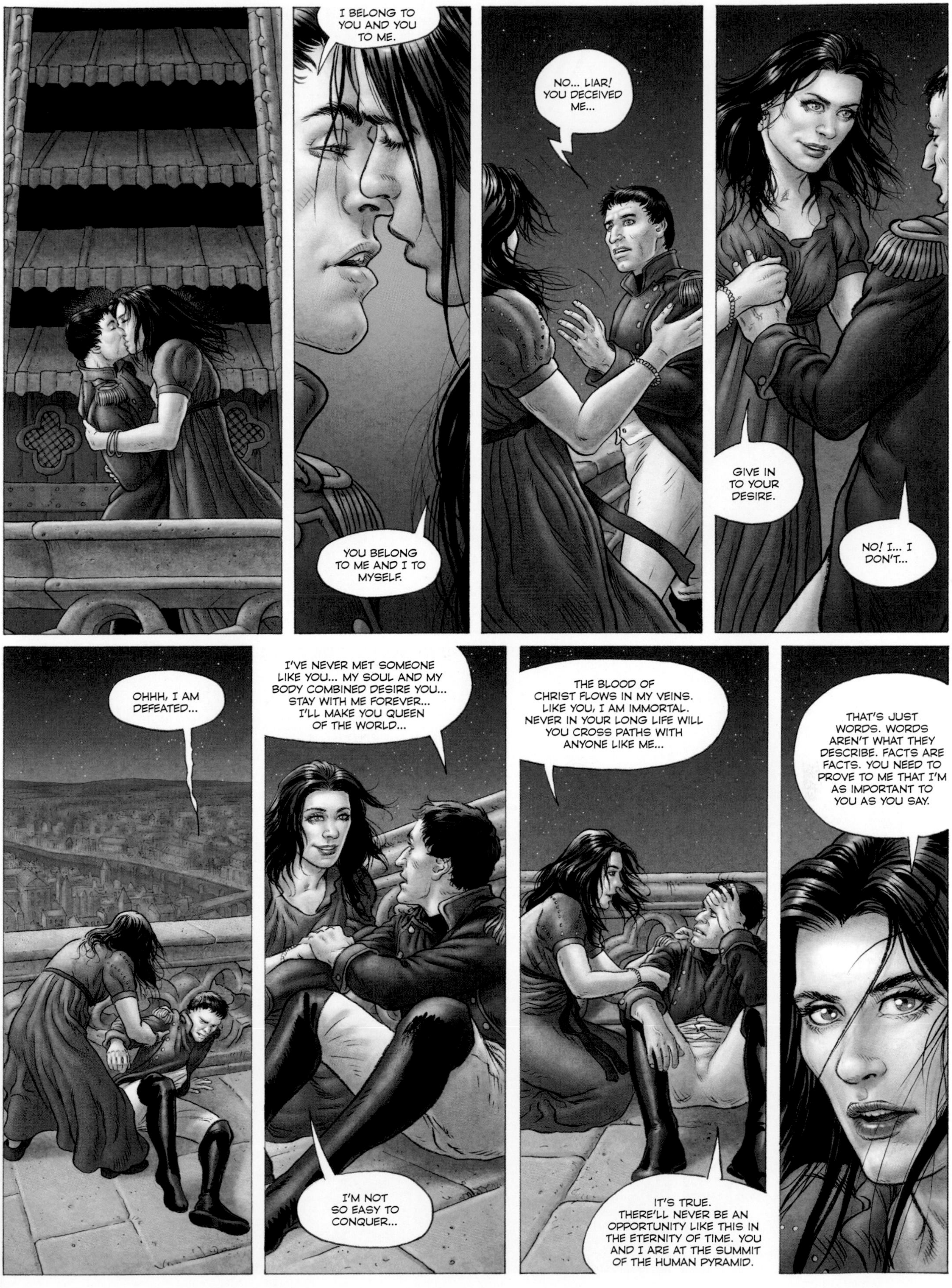
I BELONG TO YOU AND YOU TO ME.
YOU BELONG TO ME AND I TO MYSELF.
NO... LIAR! YOU DECEIVED ME...
GIVE IN TO YOUR DESIRE.
NO! I... I DON'T...
OHHH, I AM DEFEATED...
I'VE NEVER MET SOMEONE LIKE YOU... MY SOUL AND MY BODY COMBINED DESIRE YOU... STAY WITH ME FOREVER... I'LL MAKE YOU QUEEN OF THE WORLD...
I'M NOT SO EASY TO CONQUER...
THE BLOOD OF CHRIST FLOWS IN MY VEINS. LIKE YOU, I AM IMMORTAL. NEVER IN YOUR LONG LIFE WILL YOU CROSS PATHS WITH ANYONE LIKE ME...
IT'S TRUE. THERE'LL NEVER BE AN OPPORTUNITY LIKE THIS IN THE ETERNITY OF TIME. YOU AND I ARE AT THE SUMMIT OF THE HUMAN PYRAMID.
THAT'S JUST WORDS. WORDS AREN'T WHAT THEY DESCRIBE. FACTS ARE FACTS. YOU NEED TO PROVE TO ME THAT I'M AS IMPORTANT TO YOU AS YOU SAY.

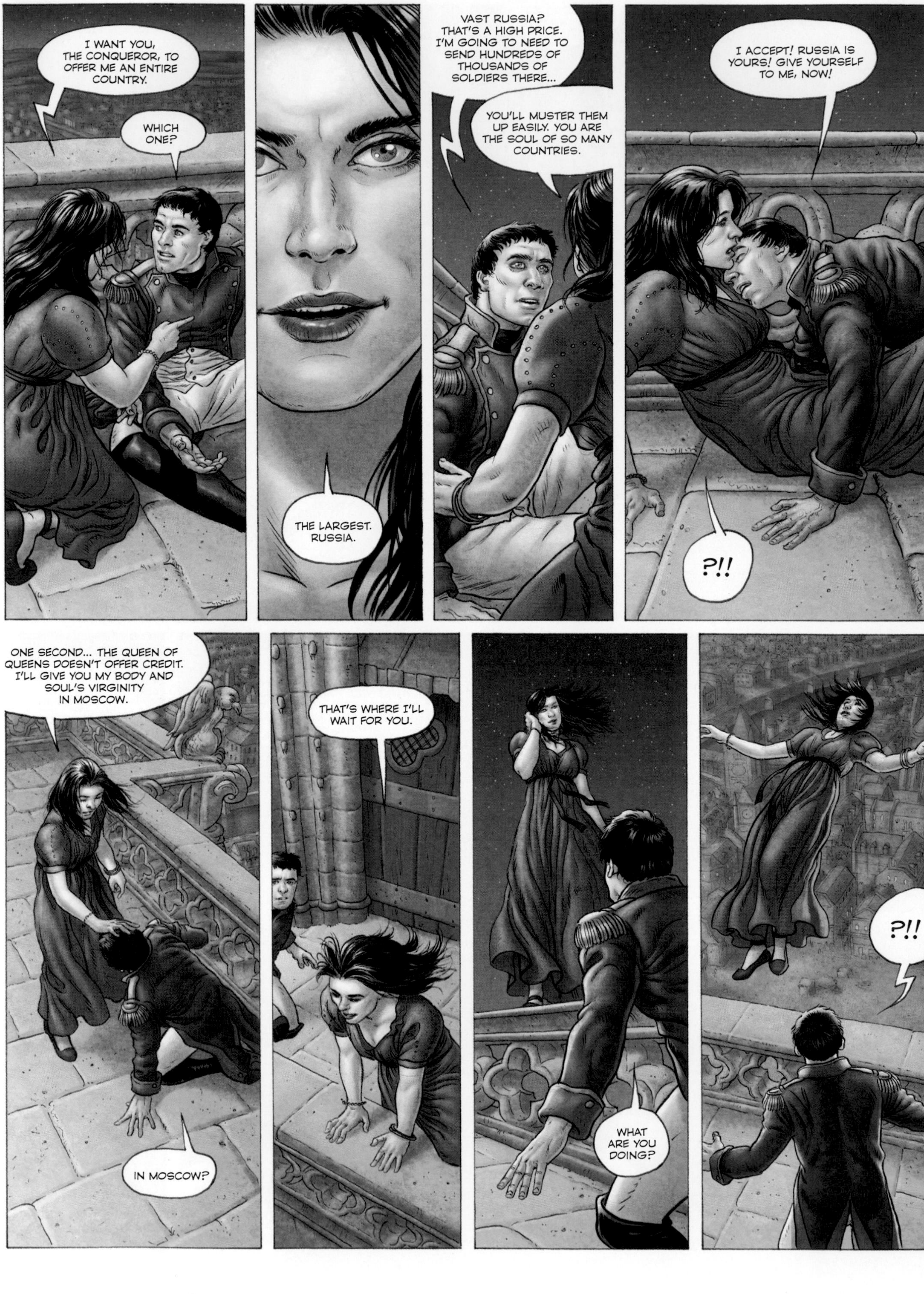
I WANT YOU, THE CONQUEROR, TO OFFER ME AN ENTIRE COUNTRY.
WHICH ONE?
THE LARGEST. RUSSIA.
VAST RUSSIA? THAT'S A HIGH PRICE. I'M GOING TO NEED TO SEND HUNDREDS OF THOUSANDS OF SOLDIERS THERE...
YOU'LL MUSTER THEM UP EASILY. YOU ARE THE SOUL OF SO MANY COUNTRIES.
I ACCEPT! RUSSIA IS YOURS! GIVE YOURSELF TO ME, NOW!
?!!
ONE SECOND... THE QUEEN OF QUEENS DOESN'T OFFER CREDIT. I'LL GIVE YOU MY BODY AND SOUL'S VIRGINITY IN MOSCOW.
IN MOSCOW?
THAT'S WHERE I'LL WAIT FOR YOU.
WHAT ARE YOU DOING?
?!!

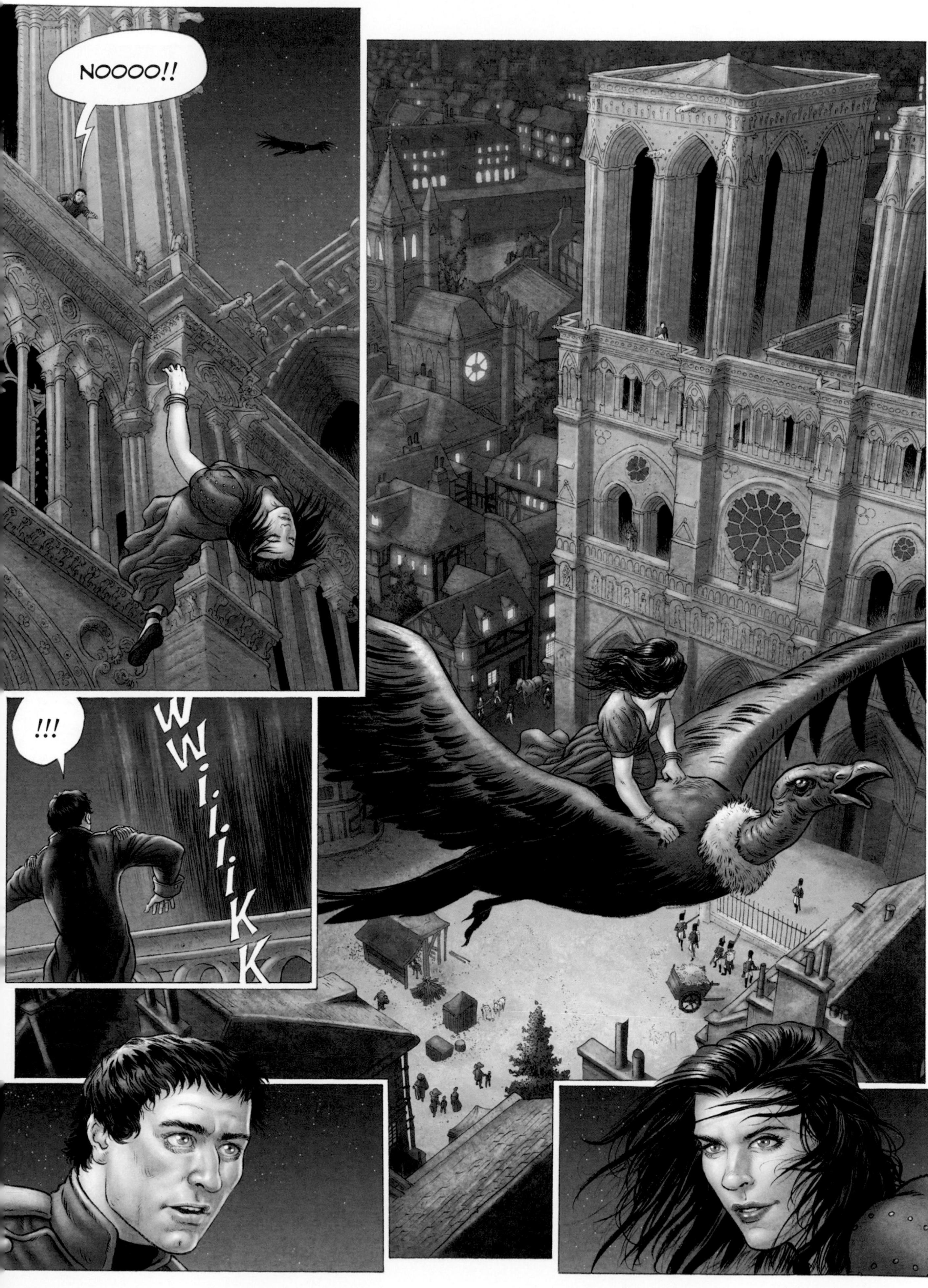
NOOOO!!
!!!
WWIIIIKK

MASTER! TWO CARRIER SWANS HAVE ARRIVED!

AT LAST, NEWS FROM OUR BROTHERS!

FULCANELLI, IN PARIS, TELLS US: "NAPOLEON HAS RAISED AN ARMY COMPRISED OF FRENCH SOLDIERS, PLUS TROOPS COME FROM SPAIN, ITALY, PRUSSIA, AUSTRIA, WESTPHALIA, BAVARIA, WURTTEMBERG, SAXONY...

"600,000 MEN, LIKE A MASSIVE BEAST, DRUNK ON BLOOD, EN ROUTE TO RUSSIA."

ASIAMAR'S KISS MADE AN IMPRESSION!

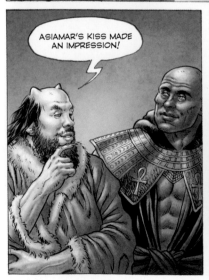

THIS ONE IS FROM NOSTRADAMUS, IN MOSCOW...

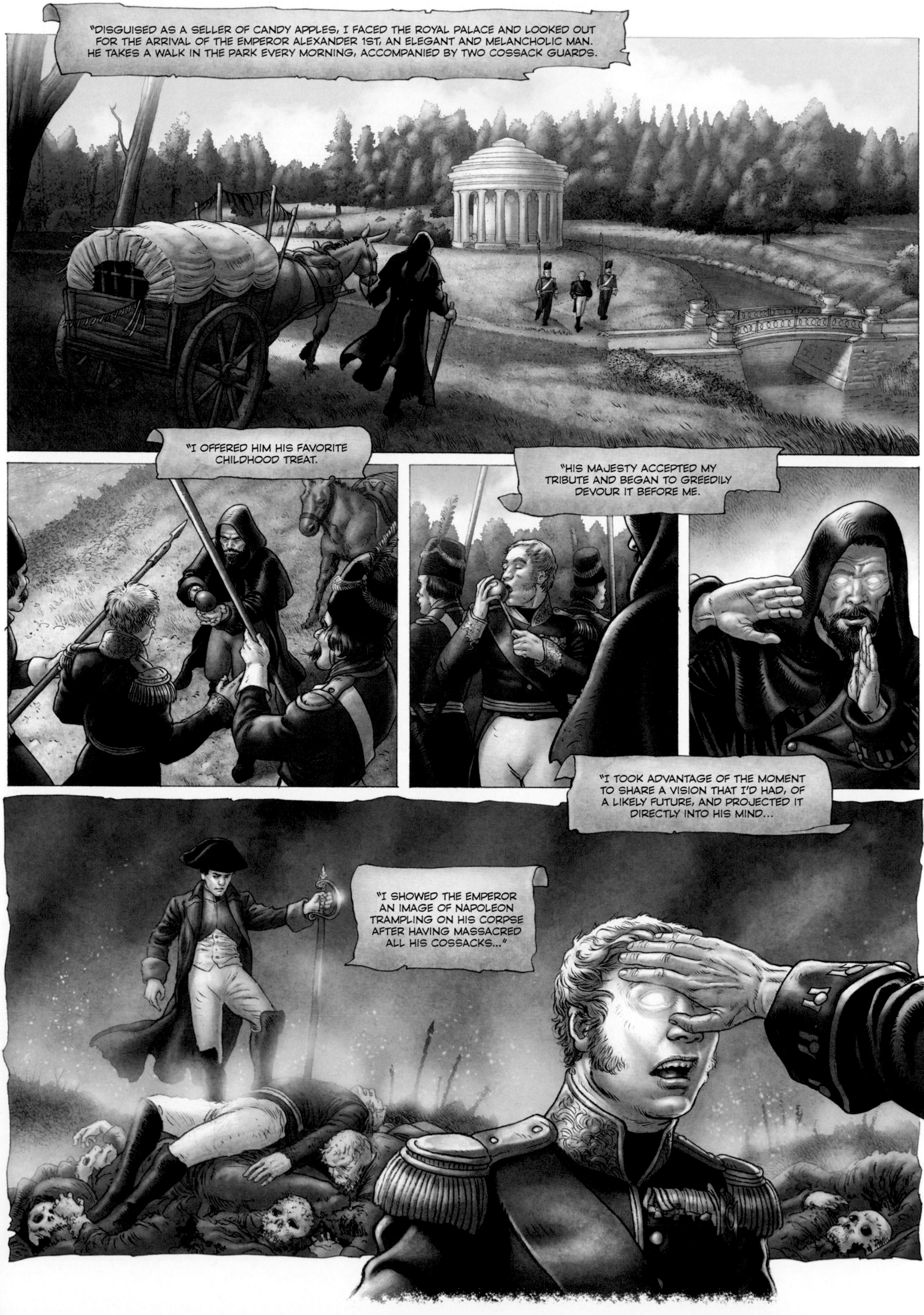
"DISGUISED AS A SELLER OF CANDY APPLES, I FACED THE ROYAL PALACE AND LOOKED OUT FOR THE ARRIVAL OF THE EMPEROR ALEXANDER 1ST, AN ELEGANT AND MELANCHOLIC MAN. HE TAKES A WALK IN THE PARK EVERY MORNING, ACCOMPANIED BY TWO COSSACK GUARDS.
"I OFFERED HIM HIS FAVORITE CHILDHOOD TREAT.
"HIS MAJESTY ACCEPTED MY TRIBUTE AND BEGAN TO GREEDILY DEVOUR IT BEFORE ME.
"I TOOK ADVANTAGE OF THE MOMENT TO SHARE A VISION THAT I'D HAD, OF A LIKELY FUTURE, AND PROJECTED IT DIRECTLY INTO HIS MIND...
"I SHOWED THE EMPEROR AN IMAGE OF NAPOLEON TRAMPLING ON HIS CORPSE AFTER HAVING MASSACRED ALL HIS COSSACKS..."

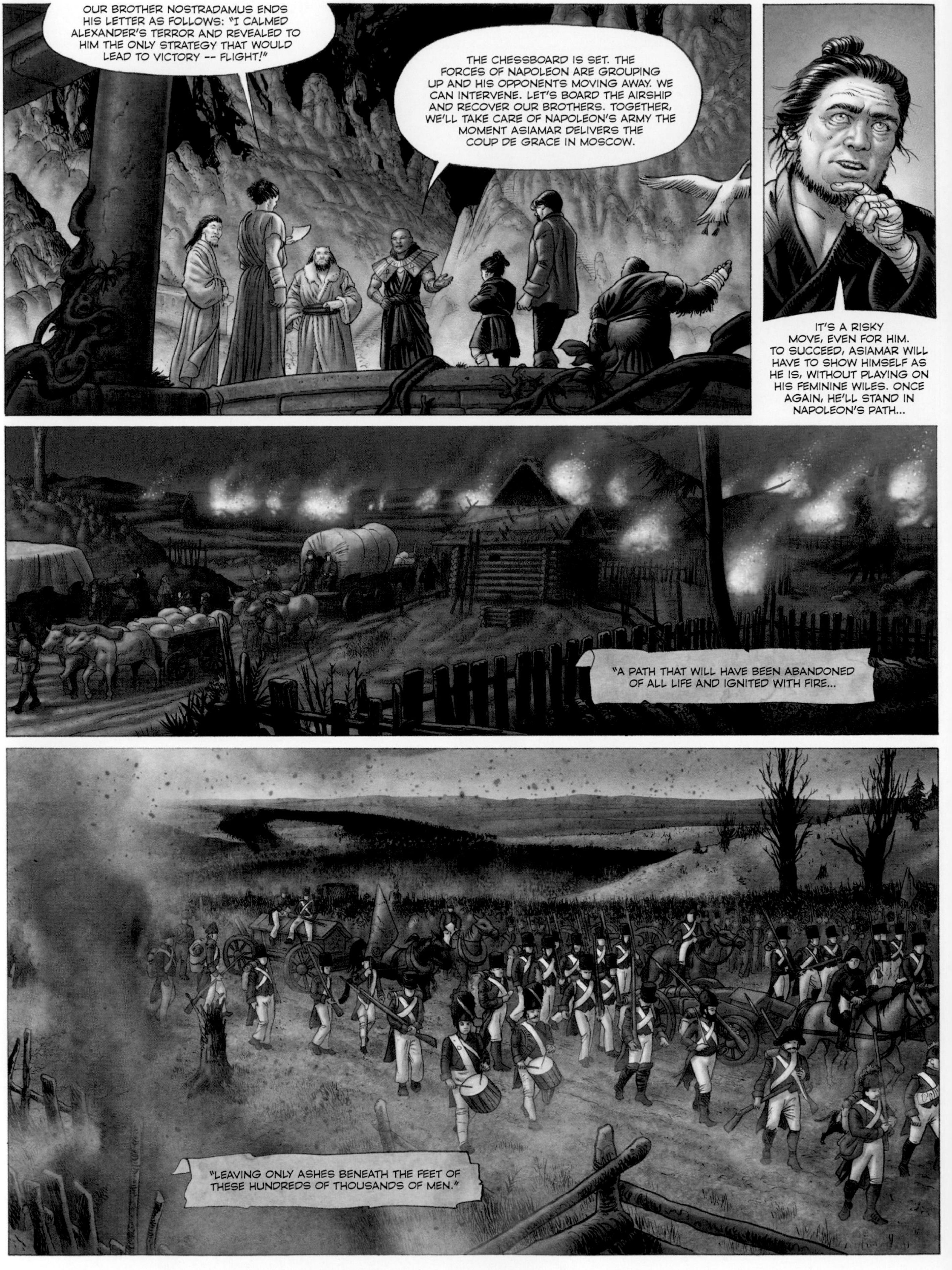
OUR BROTHER NOSTRADAMUS ENDS HIS LETTER AS FOLLOWS: "I CALMED ALEXANDER'S TERROR AND REVEALED TO HIM THE ONLY STRATEGY THAT WOULD LEAD TO VICTORY -- FLIGHT!"
THE CHESSBOARD IS SET. THE FORCES OF NAPOLEON ARE GROUPING UP AND HIS OPPONENTS MOVING AWAY. WE CAN INTERVENE. LET'S BOARD THE AIRSHIP AND RECOVER OUR BROTHERS. TOGETHER, WE'LL TAKE CARE OF NAPOLEON'S ARMY THE MOMENT ASIAMAR DELIVERS THE COUP DE GRACE IN MOSCOW.
IT'S A RISKY MOVE, EVEN FOR HIM. TO SUCCEED, ASIAMAR WILL HAVE TO SHOW HIMSELF AS HE IS, WITHOUT PLAYING ON HIS FEMININE WILES. ONCE AGAIN, HE'LL STAND IN NAPOLEON'S PATH...
"A PATH THAT WILL HAVE BEEN ABANDONED OF ALL LIFE AND IGNITED WITH FIRE...
"LEAVING ONLY ASHES BENEATH THE FEET OF THESE HUNDREDS OF THOUSANDS OF MEN."

BOSS, OPEN UP, IT'S CRABLOUSE.

TOC TOC

ARE YOU HERE FOR YOUR WINE? TAKE IT AND GO. I HAVEN'T GOT THE HEART TO LISTEN TO YOUR IDIOT GOSSIP TODAY.

AH! I'M JUST LIKE YOU. GOSSIP'S LIKE CHEAP PLONK AND DOESN'T GO DOWN WELL WITH ME! NONE OF THAT AT MY DOOR! NO, I'VE ONLY COME HERE TO LET YOU KNOW WHAT'S BEING MURMURED, WHAT'S BEING WHISPERED AROUND YOU.

OUR WONDERFUL ARMY, IMPATIENT TO SPILL BLOOD AS I AM TO SPILL THIS WINE, IS DOING NOTHING EXCEPT MARCHING THROUGH A DESERTED LAND. THE SOLDIERS ONLY HAVE THE WIND AND QUIET TO SHOOT AT! MY INSTINCTS TELL ME WE ARE WALKING INTO A TRAP AND SHOULD HEAD BACK!

YOU CANNOT HOLD DEAR TO YOUR LIFE IF YOU DARE SPEAK TO ME LIKE THAT, YOU DISRESPECTFUL TOAD! I AND I ALONE KNOWS WHAT NEEDS TO BE DONE!

AN ABSOLUTE TREASURE AWAITS IN MOSCOW, WORTH MORE THAN ALL THE GOLD IN THE WORLD!

YOUR HIGHNESS, WITH ALL RESPECT, CAN YOU TELL ME WHAT NEEDS TO BE DONE?

NOTHING. ABSOLUTELY NOTHING. WIND AND QUIET SUITS ME. I DON'T WANT ANYTHING TO DELAY MY ARRIVAL IN MOSCOW.

GO GET DRUNK. I DON'T WANT TO SEE YOUR WINO FACE UNTIL WE'VE ARRIVED! OH, AND... TURN AROUND.

HUM... ERM... OF COURSE, BOSS!

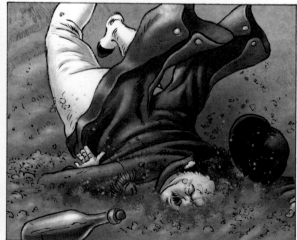

33

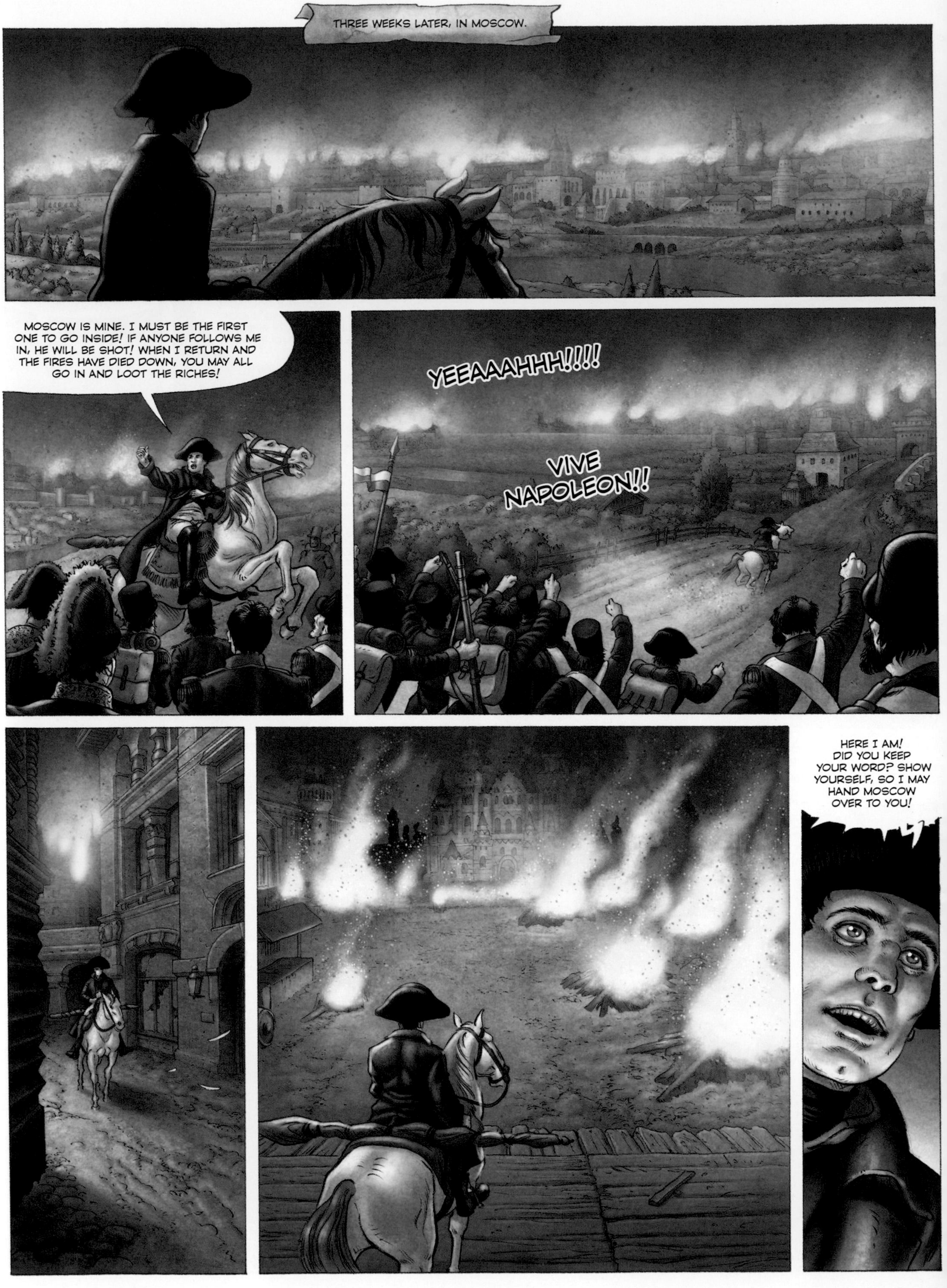
THREE WEEKS LATER, IN MOSCOW.
MOSCOW IS MINE. I MUST BE THE FIRST ONE TO GO INSIDE! IF ANYONE FOLLOWS ME IN, HE WILL BE SHOT! WHEN I RETURN AND THE FIRES HAVE DIED DOWN, YOU MAY ALL GO IN AND LOOT THE RICHES!
YEEAAAHHH!!!!
VIVE NAPOLEON!!
HERE I AM! DID YOU KEEP YOUR WORD? SHOW YOURSELF, SO I MAY HAND MOSCOW OVER TO YOU!

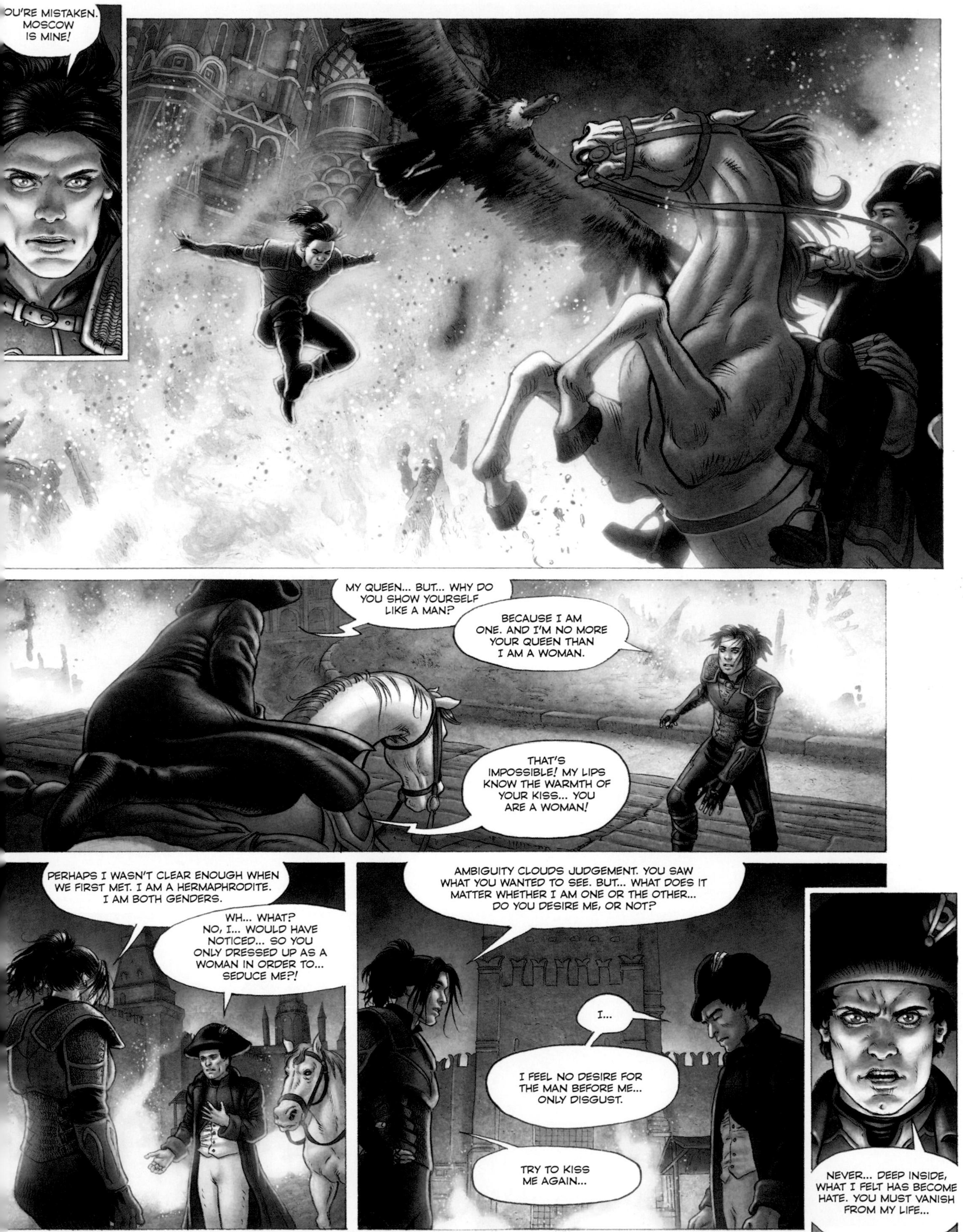

OU'RE MISTAKEN. MOSCOW IS MINE!
MY QUEEN... BUT... WHY DO YOU SHOW YOURSELF LIKE A MAN?
BECAUSE I AM ONE. AND I'M NO MORE YOUR QUEEN THAN I AM A WOMAN.
THAT'S IMPOSSIBLE! MY LIPS KNOW THE WARMTH OF YOUR KISS... YOU ARE A WOMAN!
PERHAPS I WASN'T CLEAR ENOUGH WHEN WE FIRST MET. I AM A HERMAPHRODITE. I AM BOTH GENDERS.
WH... WHAT? NO, I... WOULD HAVE NOTICED... SO YOU ONLY DRESSED UP AS A WOMAN IN ORDER TO... SEDUCE ME?!
AMBIGUITY CLOUDS JUDGEMENT. YOU SAW WHAT YOU WANTED TO SEE. BUT... WHAT DOES IT MATTER WHETHER I AM ONE OR THE OTHER... DO YOU DESIRE ME, OR NOT?
I...
I FEEL NO DESIRE FOR THE MAN BEFORE ME... ONLY DISGUST.
TRY TO KISS ME AGAIN...
NEVER... DEEP INSIDE, WHAT I FELT HAS BECOME HATE. YOU MUST VANISH FROM MY LIFE...

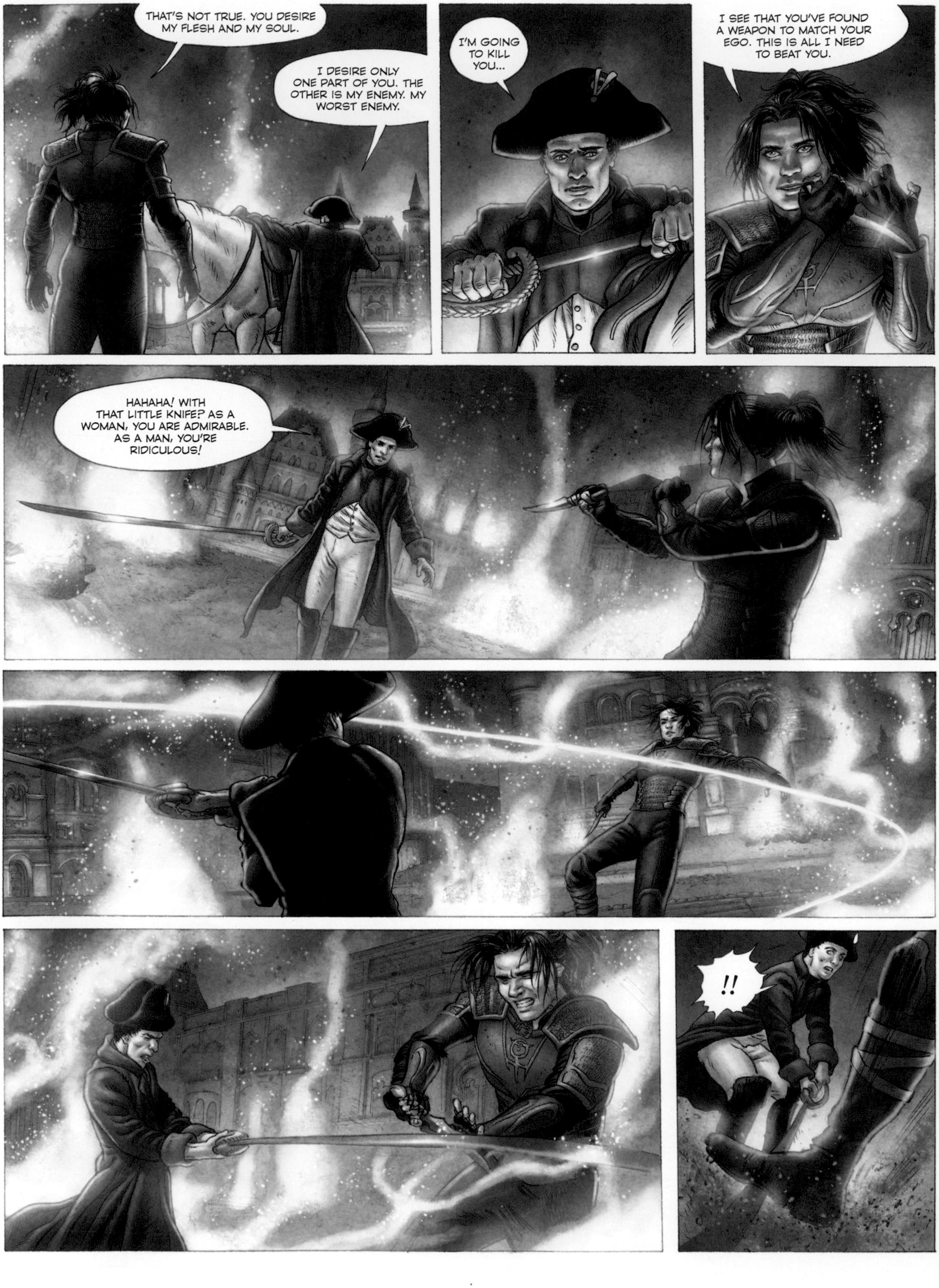
THAT'S NOT TRUE. YOU DESIRE MY FLESH AND MY SOUL.
I DESIRE ONLY ONE PART OF YOU. THE OTHER IS MY ENEMY. MY WORST ENEMY.
I'M GOING TO KILL YOU...
I SEE THAT YOU'VE FOUND A WEAPON TO MATCH YOUR EGO. THIS IS ALL I NEED TO BEAT YOU.
HAHAHA! WITH THAT LITTLE KNIFE? AS A WOMAN, YOU ARE ADMIRABLE. AS A MAN, YOU'RE RIDICULOUS!
!!

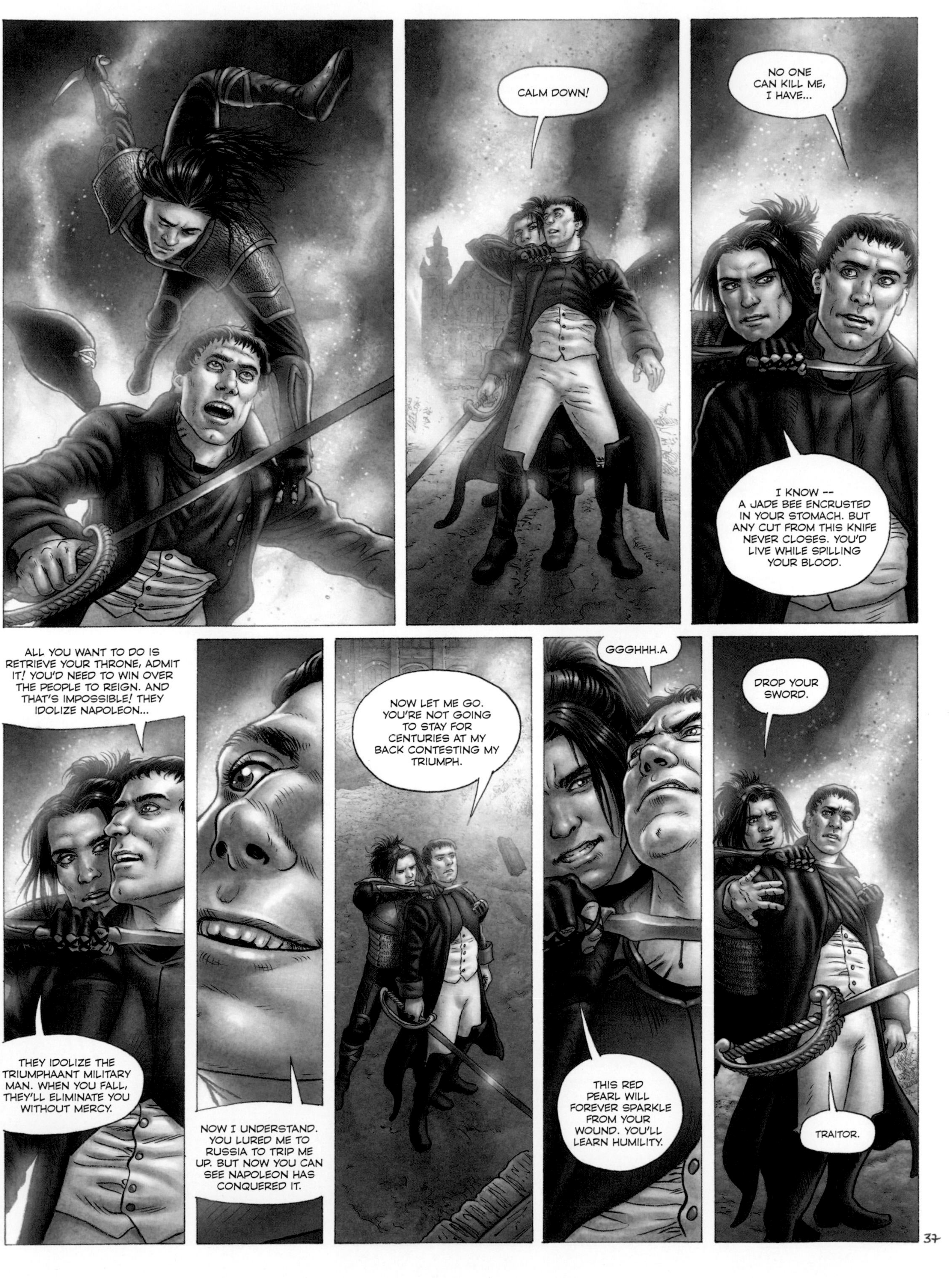
CALM DOWN!
NO ONE CAN KILL ME, I HAVE...
I KNOW -- A JADE BEE ENCRUSTED IN YOUR STOMACH. BUT ANY CUT FROM THIS KNIFE NEVER CLOSES. YOU'D LIVE WHILE SPILLING YOUR BLOOD.
ALL YOU WANT TO DO IS RETRIEVE YOUR THRONE, ADMIT IT! YOU'D NEED TO WIN OVER THE PEOPLE TO REIGN. AND THAT'S IMPOSSIBLE! THEY IDOLIZE NAPOLEON...
THEY IDOLIZE THE TRIUMPHAANT MILITARY MAN. WHEN YOU FALL, THEY'LL ELIMINATE YOU WITHOUT MERCY.
NOW I UNDERSTAND. YOU LURED ME TO RUSSIA TO TRIP ME UP. BUT NOW YOU CAN SEE NAPOLEON HAS CONQUERED IT.
NOW LET ME GO. YOU'RE NOT GOING TO STAY FOR CENTURIES AT MY BACK CONTESTING MY TRIUMPH.
GGGHHH.A
THIS RED PEARL WILL FOREVER SPARKLE FROM YOUR WOUND. YOU'LL LEARN HUMILITY.
DROP YOUR SWORD.
TRAITOR.

YOU'RE THE TRAITOR. YOU BETRAYED YOURSELF. YOU ARE AN ULTIMATE BEING AND ALLOWED YOURSELF TO BE CONSUMED BY DESIRE FOR POWER. WE, THE KNIGHTS OF HELIOPOLIS, WILL TEACH YOU DEFEAT.

ON MY RETURN, THE PEOPLE WILL LOVE ME. THE WORLD OVER WILL REVERE A NEW GOD. ME!

I'LL HUNT YOU DOWN AND FIND YOU, YOU AND YOUR ALCHEMISTS. I WILL SLIT YOUR THROATS IN YOUR LAIR LIKE RATS.

DON'T FORGET THAT I HAVE THE POWER TO EXTERMINATE YOU...

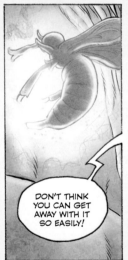

DON'T THINK YOU CAN GET AWAY WITH IT SO EASILY!

PIERCE HIM, MY BEE! KILL HIM!!!

!!!

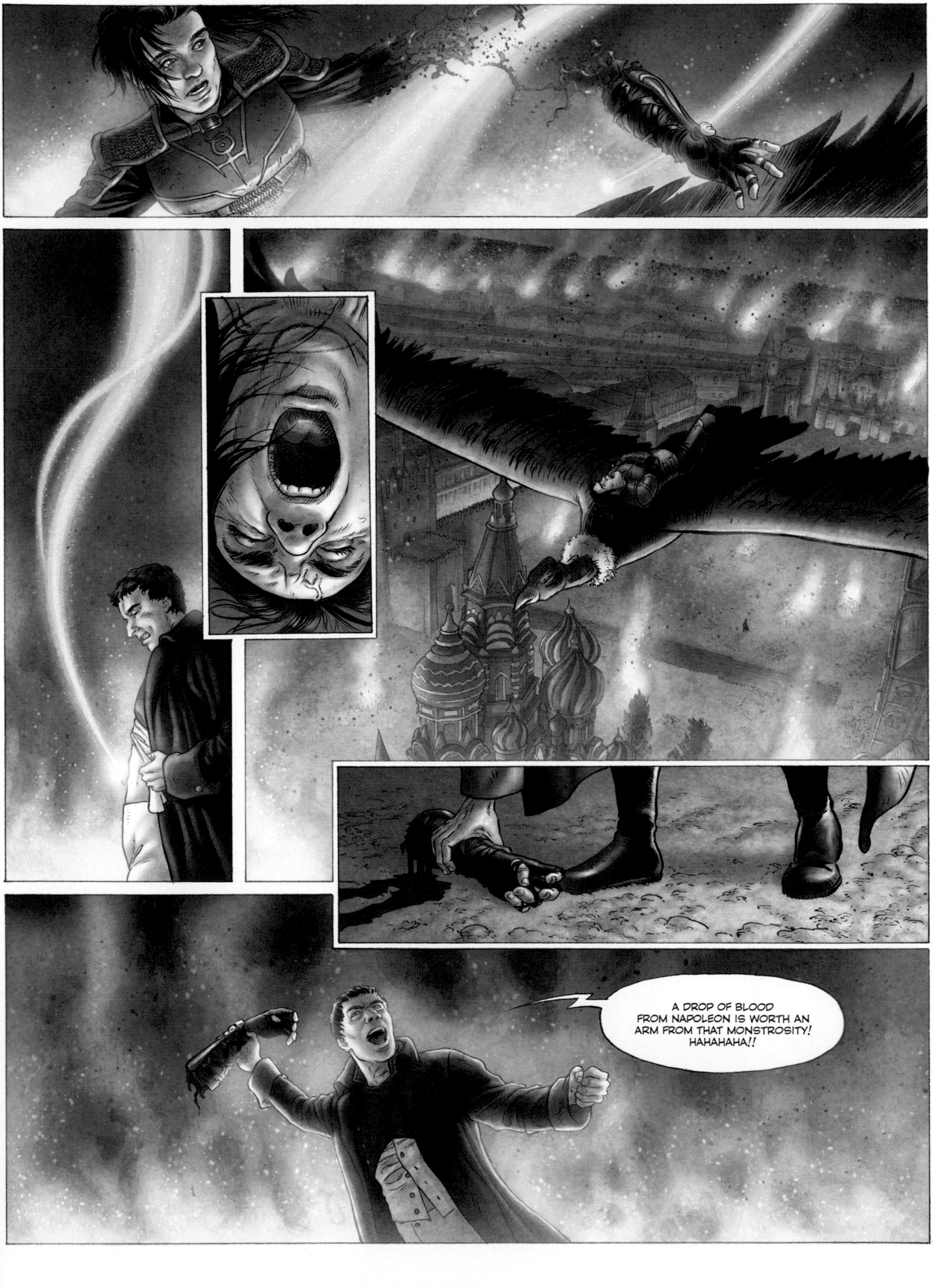
A DROP OF BLOOD FROM NAPOLEON IS WORTH AN ARM FROM THAT MONSTROSITY! HAHAHAHA!!

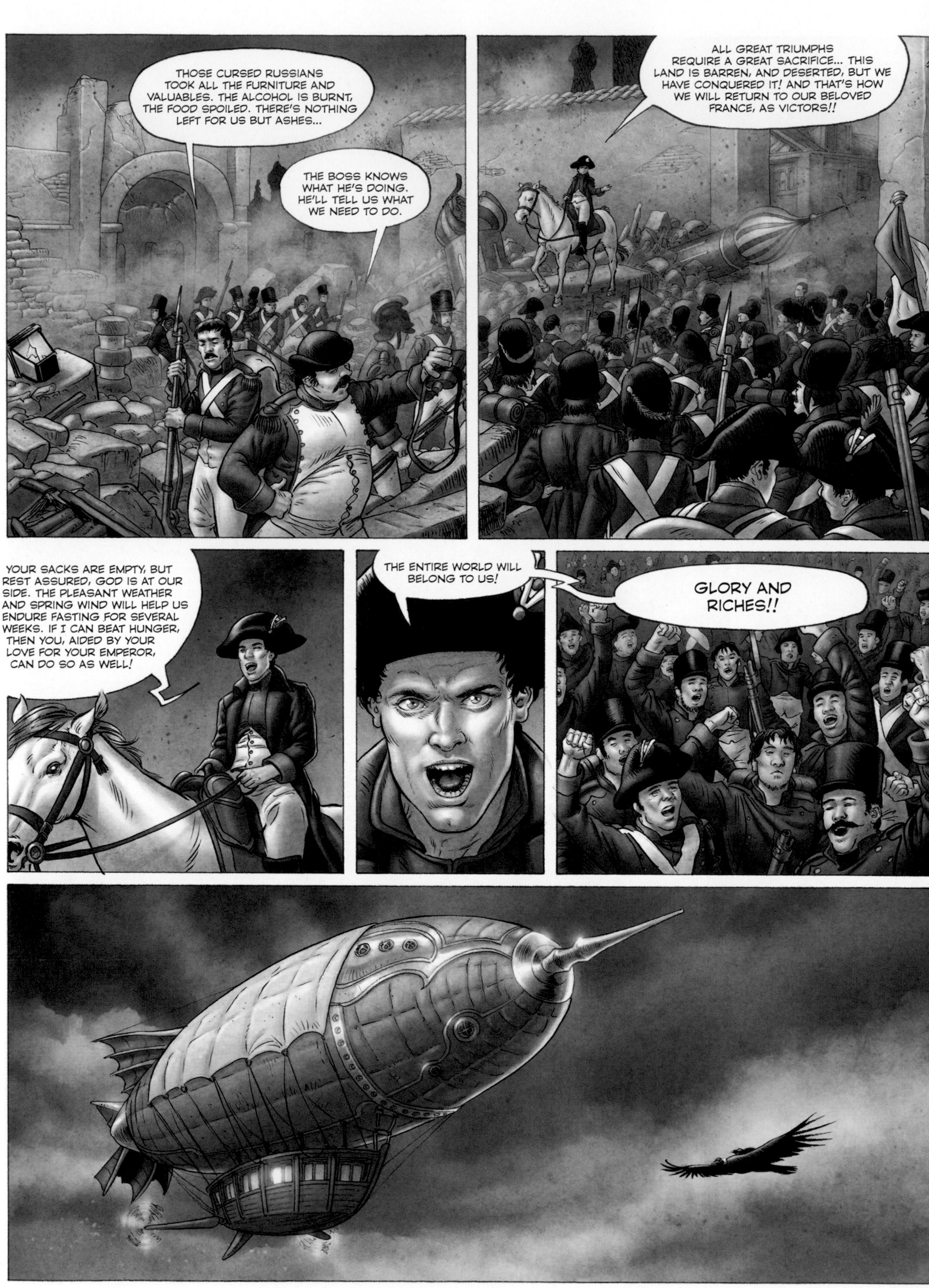
THOSE CURSED RUSSIANS TOOK ALL THE FURNITURE AND VALUABLES. THE ALCOHOL IS BURNT, THE FOOD SPOILED. THERE'S NOTHING LEFT FOR US BUT ASHES...
THE BOSS KNOWS WHAT HE'S DOING. HE'LL TELL US WHAT WE NEED TO DO.
ALL GREAT TRIUMPHS REQUIRE A GREAT SACRIFICE... THIS LAND IS BARREN, AND DESERTED, BUT WE HAVE CONQUERED IT! AND THAT'S HOW WE WILL RETURN TO OUR BELOVED FRANCE, AS VICTORS!!
YOUR SACKS ARE EMPTY, BUT REST ASSURED, GOD IS AT OUR SIDE. THE PLEASANT WEATHER AND SPRING WIND WILL HELP US ENDURE FASTING FOR SEVERAL WEEKS. IF I CAN BEAT HUNGER, THEN YOU, AIDED BY YOUR LOVE FOR YOUR EMPEROR, CAN DO SO AS WELL!
THE ENTIRE WORLD WILL BELONG TO US!
GLORY AND RICHES!!

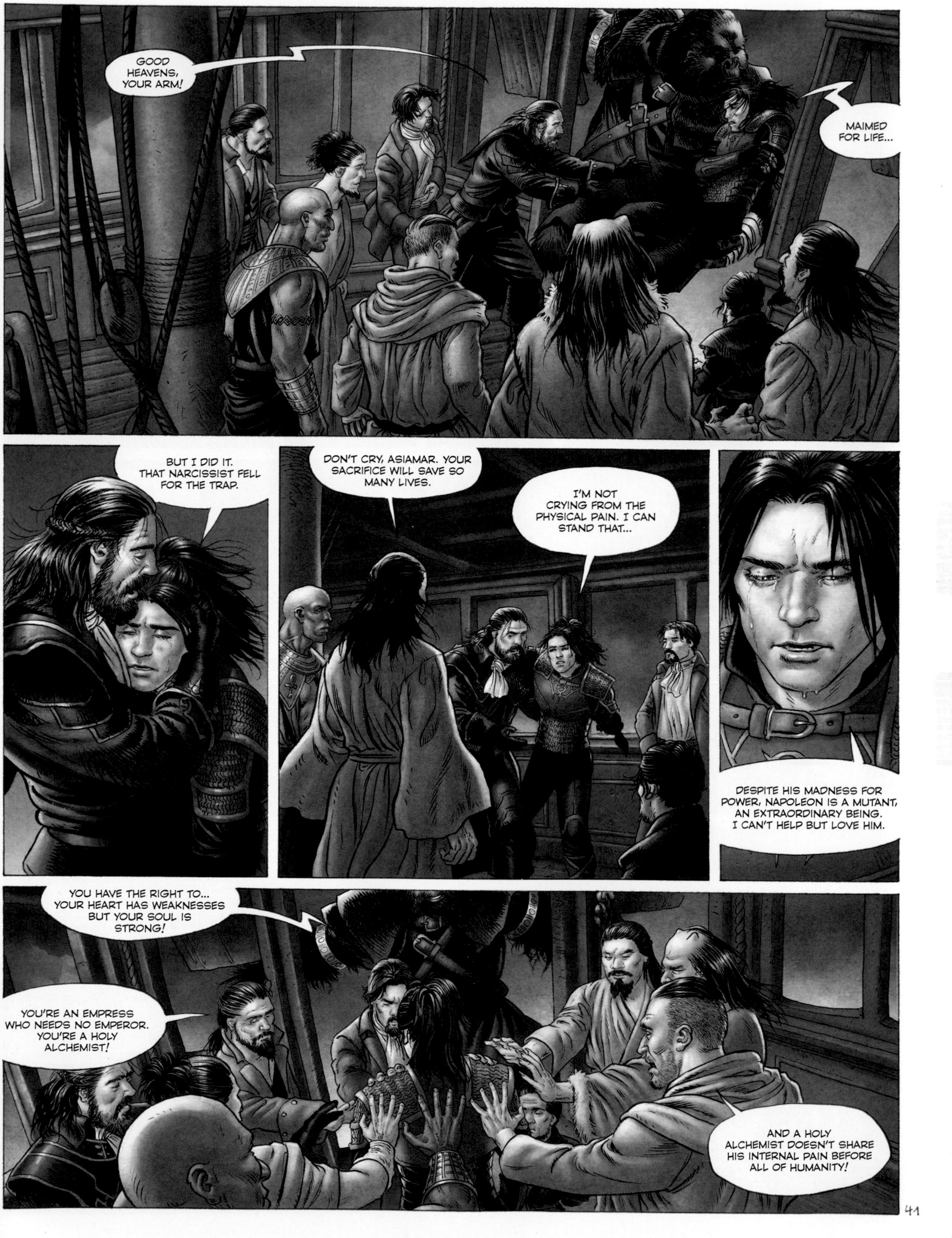
GOOD HEAVENS, YOUR ARM!
MAIMED FOR LIFE...
BUT I DID IT. THAT NARCISSIST FELL FOR THE TRAP.
DON'T CRY, ASIAMAR. YOUR SACRIFICE WILL SAVE SO MANY LIVES.
I'M NOT CRYING FROM THE PHYSICAL PAIN. I CAN STAND THAT...
DESPITE HIS MADNESS FOR POWER, NAPOLEON IS A MUTANT, AN EXTRAORDINARY BEING. I CAN'T HELP BUT LOVE HIM.
YOU HAVE THE RIGHT TO... YOUR HEART HAS WEAKNESSES BUT YOUR SOUL IS STRONG!
YOU'RE AN EMPRESS WHO NEEDS NO EMPEROR. YOU'RE A HOLY ALCHEMIST!
AND A HOLY ALCHEMIST DOESN'T SHARE HIS INTERNAL PAIN BEFORE ALL OF HUMANITY!

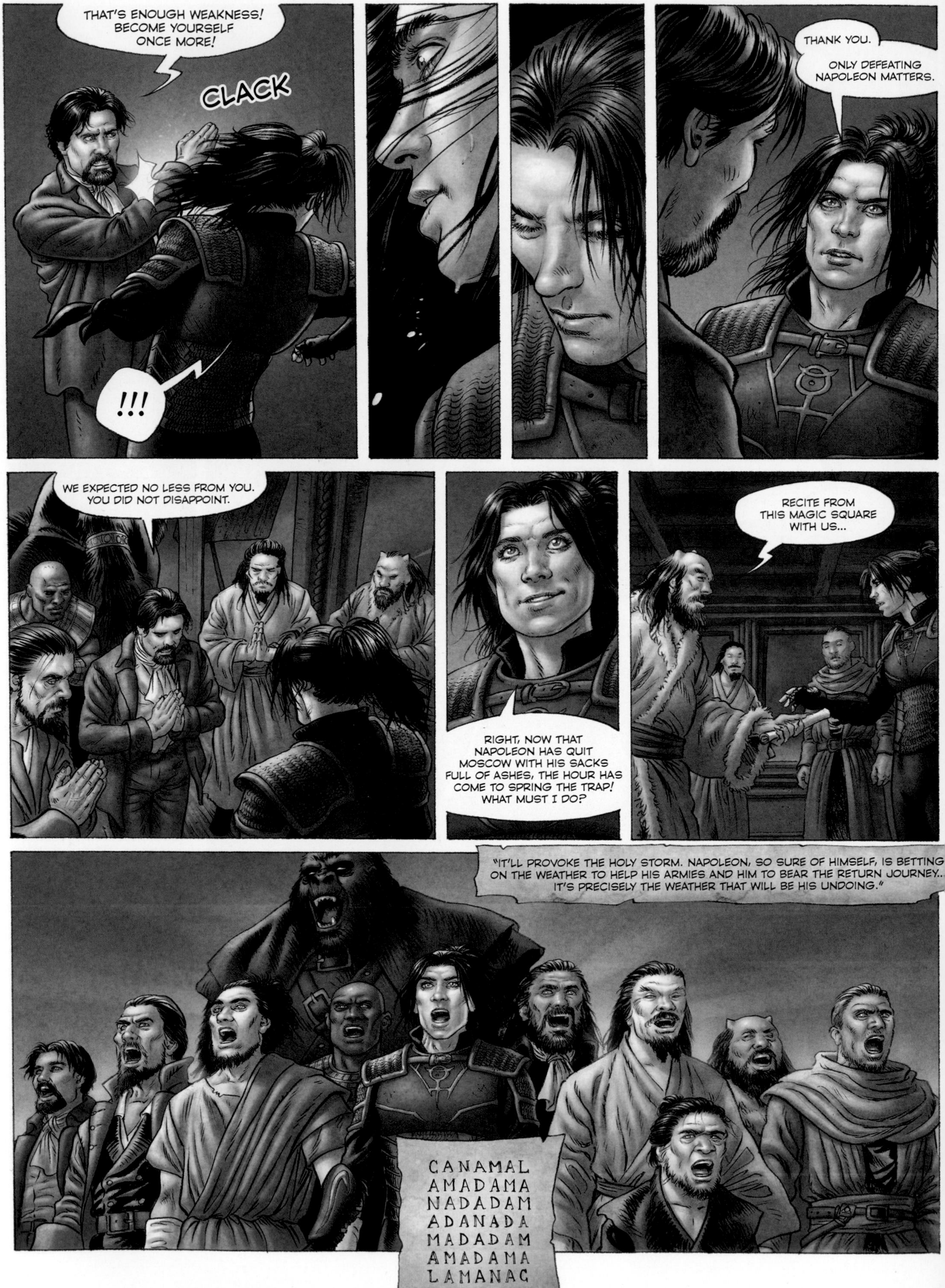

THAT'S ENOUGH WEAKNESS! BECOME YOURSELF ONCE MORE!
CLACK
!!!
THANK YOU.
ONLY DEFEATING NAPOLEON MATTERS.
WE EXPECTED NO LESS FROM YOU. YOU DID NOT DISAPPOINT.
RIGHT, NOW THAT NAPOLEON HAS QUIT MOSCOW WITH HIS SACKS FULL OF ASHES, THE HOUR HAS COME TO SPRING THE TRAP! WHAT MUST I DO?
RECITE FROM THIS MAGIC SQUARE WITH US...
"IT'LL PROVOKE THE HOLY STORM. NAPOLEON, SO SURE OF HIMSELF, IS BETTING ON THE WEATHER TO HELP HIS ARMIES AND HIM TO BEAR THE RETURN JOURNEY... IT'S PRECISELY THE WEATHER THAT WILL BE HIS UNDOING."
CANAMAL
AMADAMA
NADADAM
ADANADA
MADADAM
AMADAMA
LAMANAC

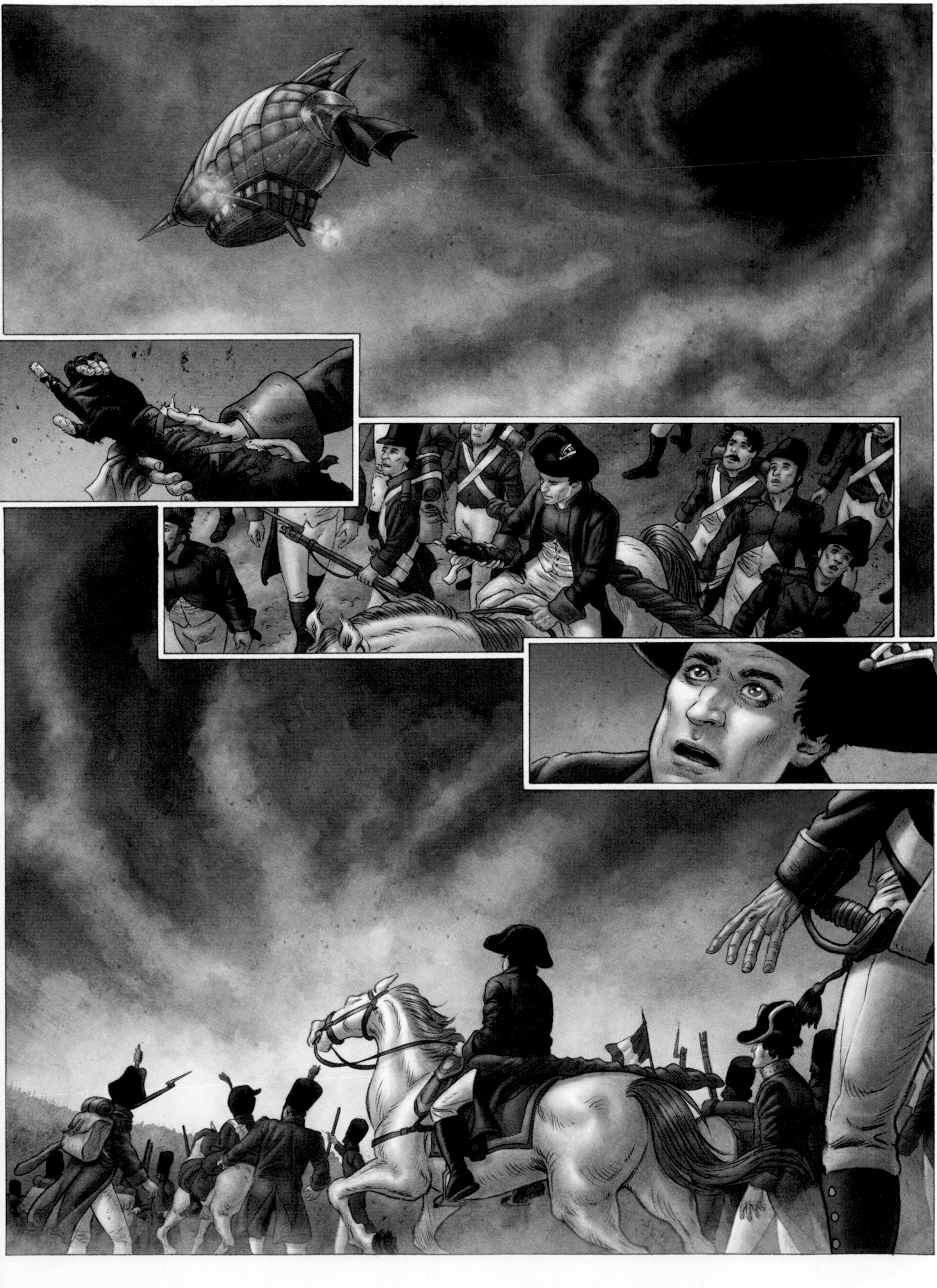

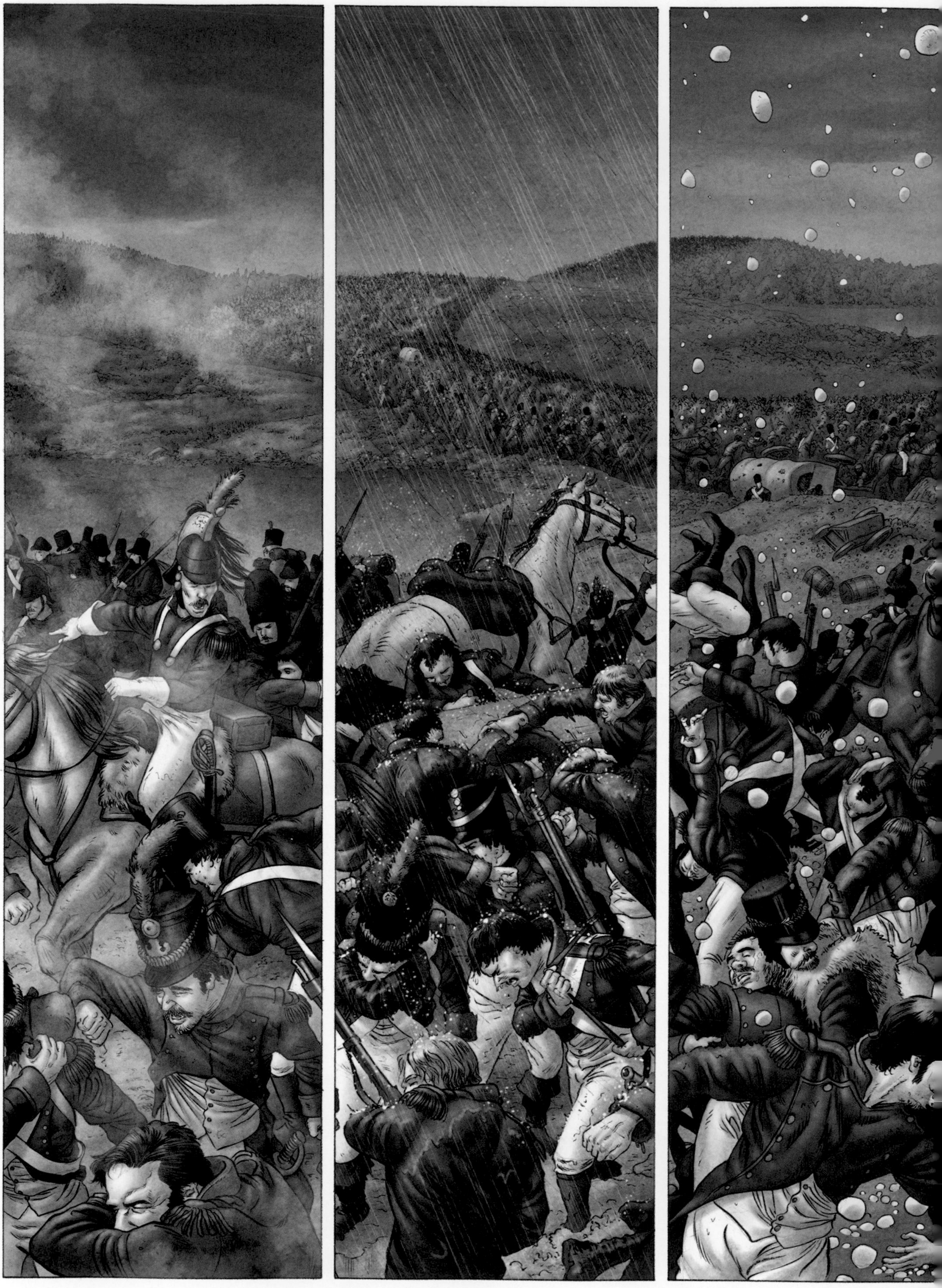

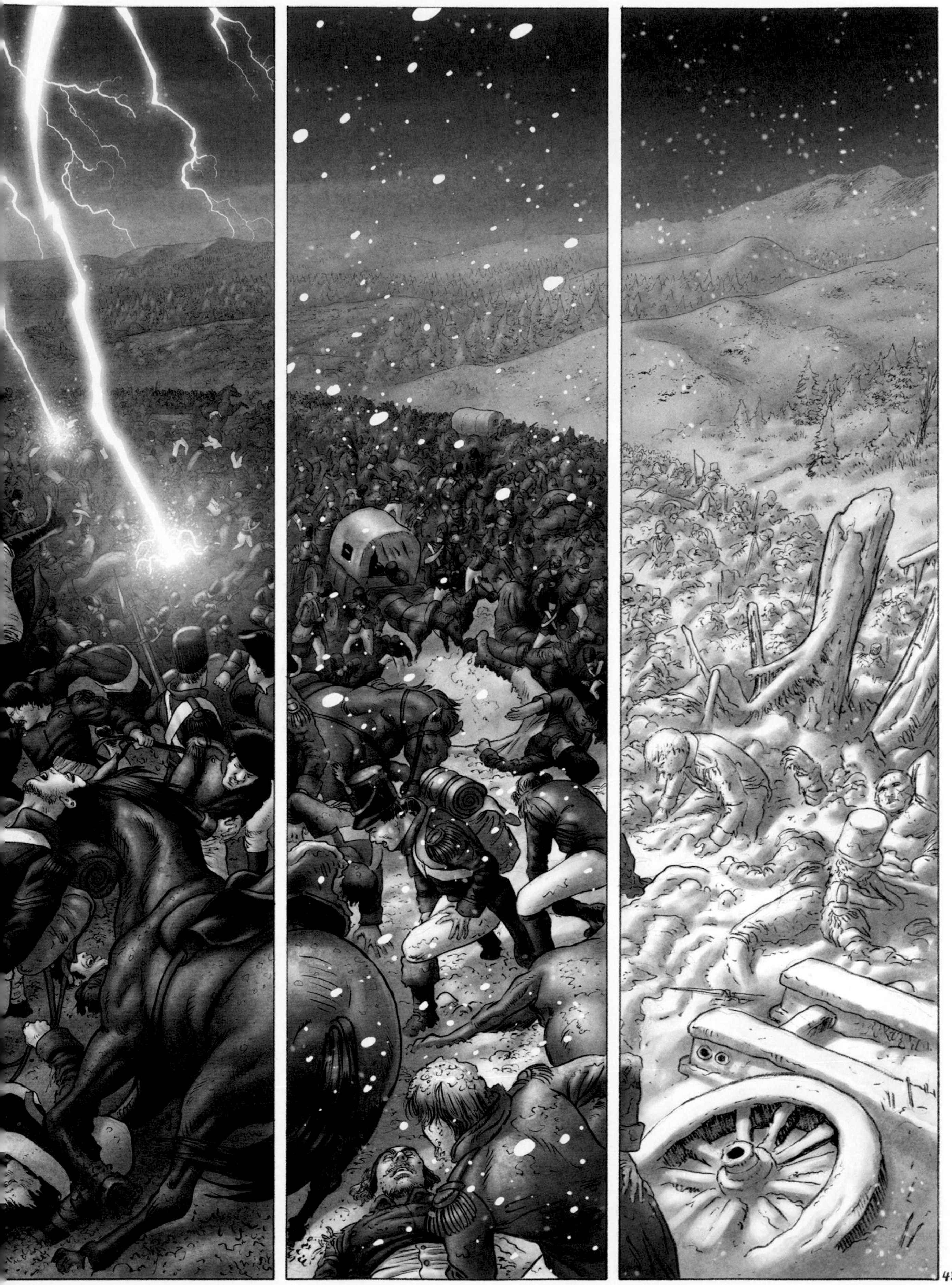

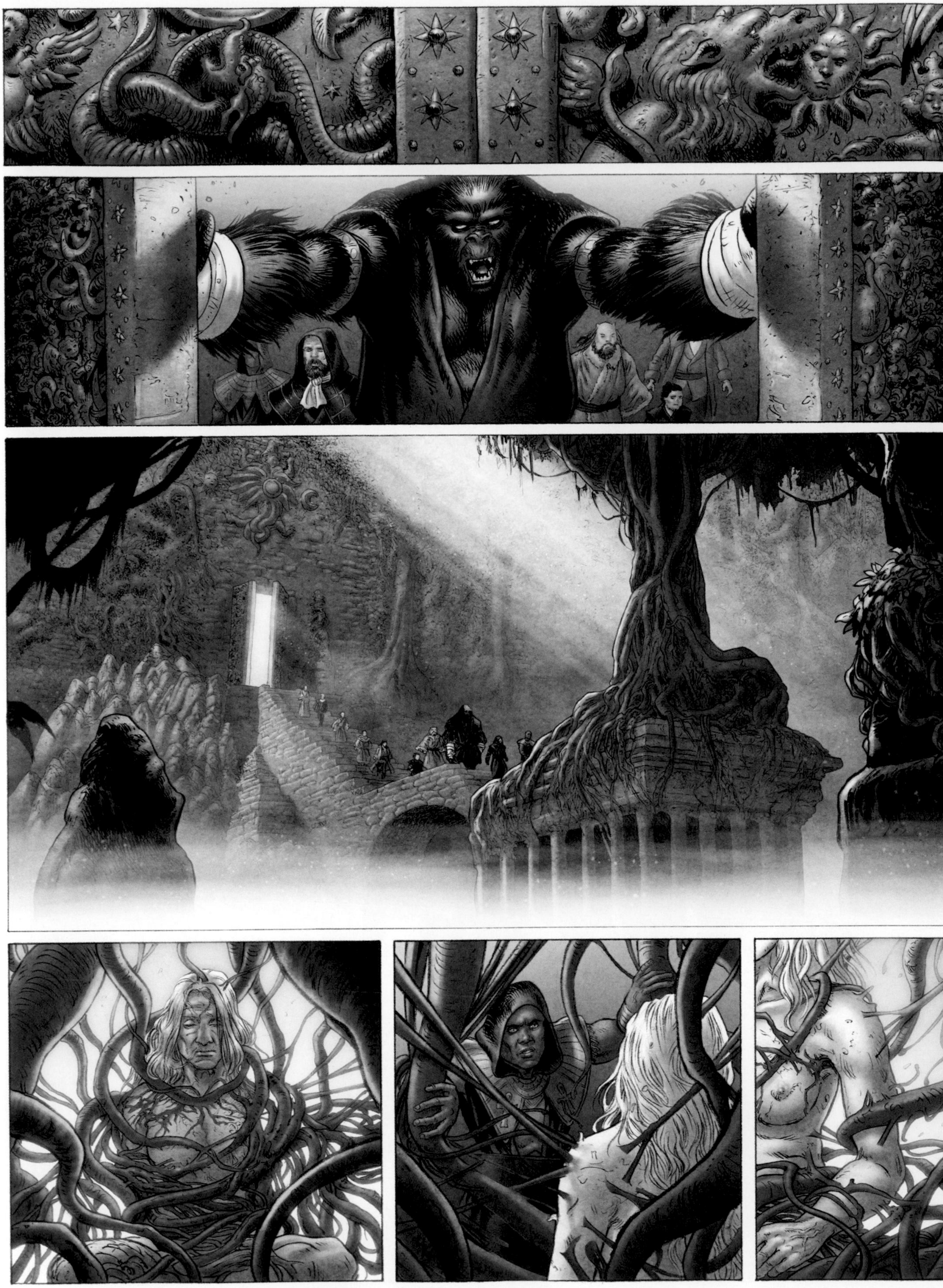

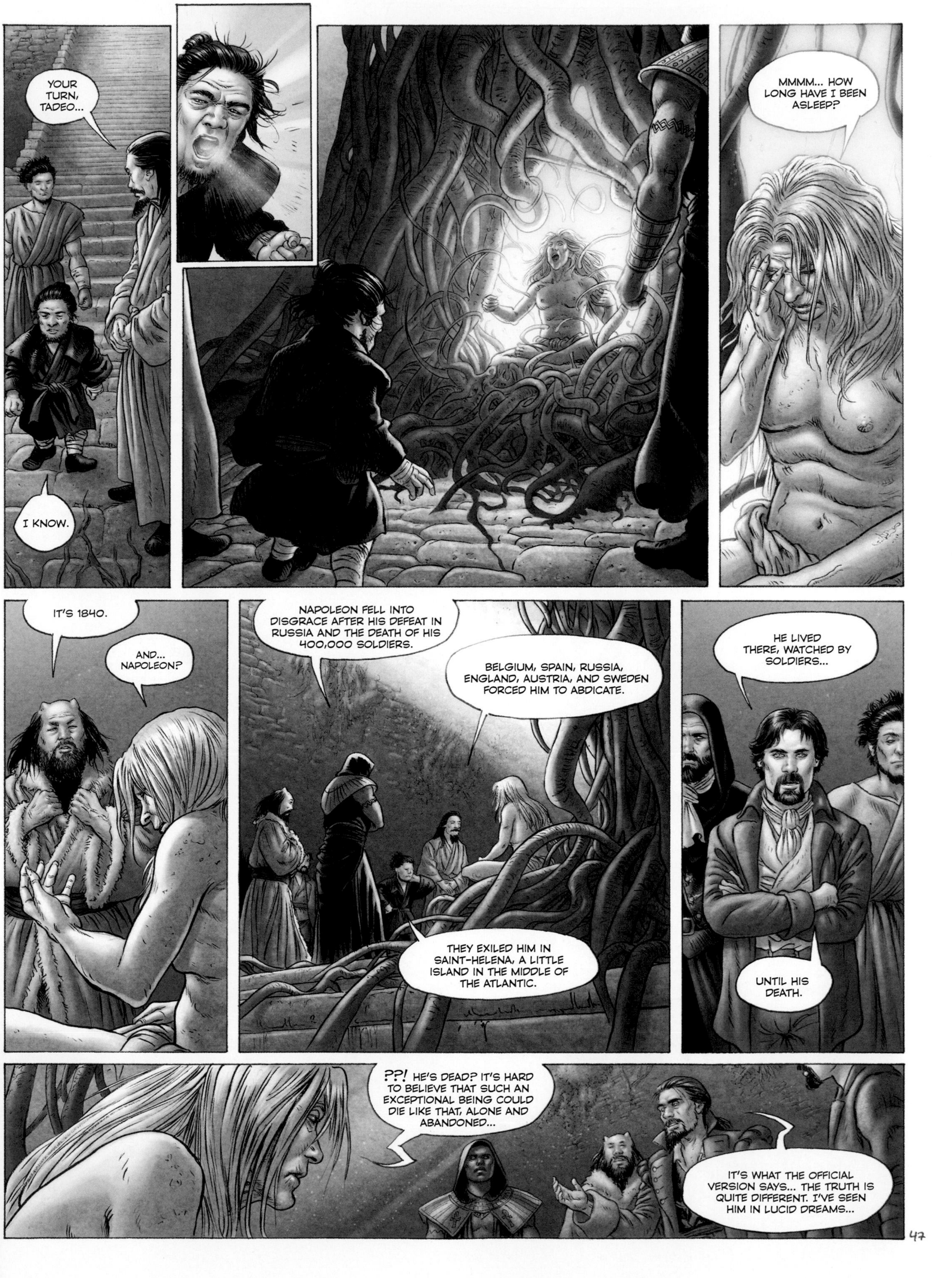
YOUR TURN, TADEO...
I KNOW.
MMMM... HOW LONG HAVE I BEEN ASLEEP?
IT'S 1840.
AND... NAPOLEON?
NAPOLEON FELL INTO DISGRACE AFTER HIS DEFEAT IN RUSSIA AND THE DEATH OF HIS 400,000 SOLDIERS.
BELGIUM, SPAIN, RUSSIA, ENGLAND, AUSTRIA, AND SWEDEN FORCED HIM TO ABDICATE.
THEY EXILED HIM IN SAINT-HELENA, A LITTLE ISLAND IN THE MIDDLE OF THE ATLANTIC.
HE LIVED THERE, WATCHED BY SOLDIERS...
UNTIL HIS DEATH.
??! HE'S DEAD? IT'S HARD TO BELIEVE THAT SUCH AN EXCEPTIONAL BEING COULD DIE LIKE THAT, ALONE AND ABANDONED...
IT'S WHAT THE OFFICIAL VERSION SAYS... THE TRUTH IS QUITE DIFFERENT. I'VE SEEN HIM IN LUCID DREAMS...

"NAPOLEON LIVED THERE IN A HUT RIDDLED WITH RATS FOR SIX YEARS UNDER THE SUPERVISION OF THE ISLAND'S GOVERNOR, WITH HIS ONLY COMPANION, SERGEANT CRABLOUSE..."

HUDSON LOWE.

MISTER BONAPARTE, WHAT UNBEARABLE HEAT, DON'T YOU THINK? ALLOW ME TO OFFER SOMETHING TO DRINK...

HAVE A GULP OF THIS NECTAR.

WITH DELIGHT, GOVERNOR LOWE.

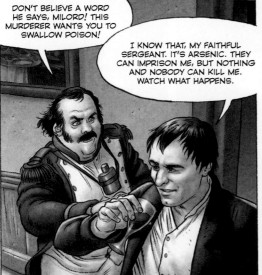

DON'T BELIEVE A WORD HE SAYS, MILORD! THIS MURDERER WANTS YOU TO SWALLOW POISON!

I KNOW THAT, MY FAITHFUL SERGEANT. IT'S ARSENIC. THEY CAN IMPRISON ME, BUT NOTHING AND NOBODY CAN KILL ME. WATCH WHAT HAPPENS.

THE ENGLISH AUTHORITIES HAVE CONDEMNED YOU TO DEATH FOR REPRESENTING A LASTING DANGER. WE'LL BE RID OF YOUR DISGUSTING LIFE IN EXACTLY FIVE SECONDS, BONAPARTE. ONE, TWO...

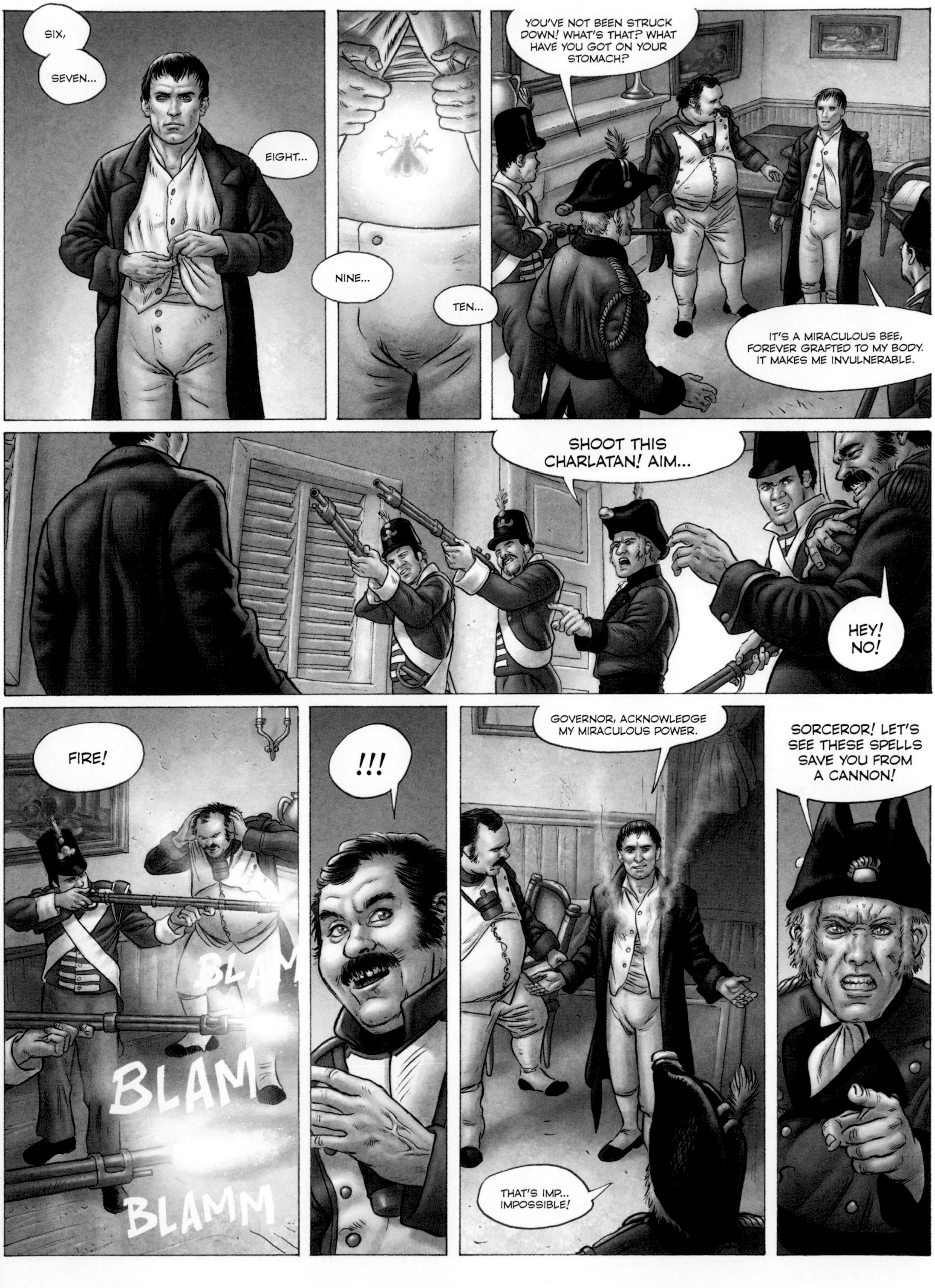

SIX,
SEVEN...
EIGHT...
NINE...
TEN...
YOU'VE NOT BEEN STRUCK DOWN! WHAT'S THAT? WHAT HAVE YOU GOT ON YOUR STOMACH?
IT'S A MIRACULOUS BEE, FOREVER GRAFTED TO MY BODY. IT MAKES ME INVULNERABLE.
SHOOT THIS CHARLATAN! AIM...
HEY! NO!
FIRE!
BLAM
BLAM
BLAMM
!!!
GOVERNOR, ACKNOWLEDGE MY MIRACULOUS POWER.
THAT'S IMP... IMPOSSIBLE!
SORCEROR! LET'S SEE THESE SPELLS SAVE YOU FROM A CANNON!

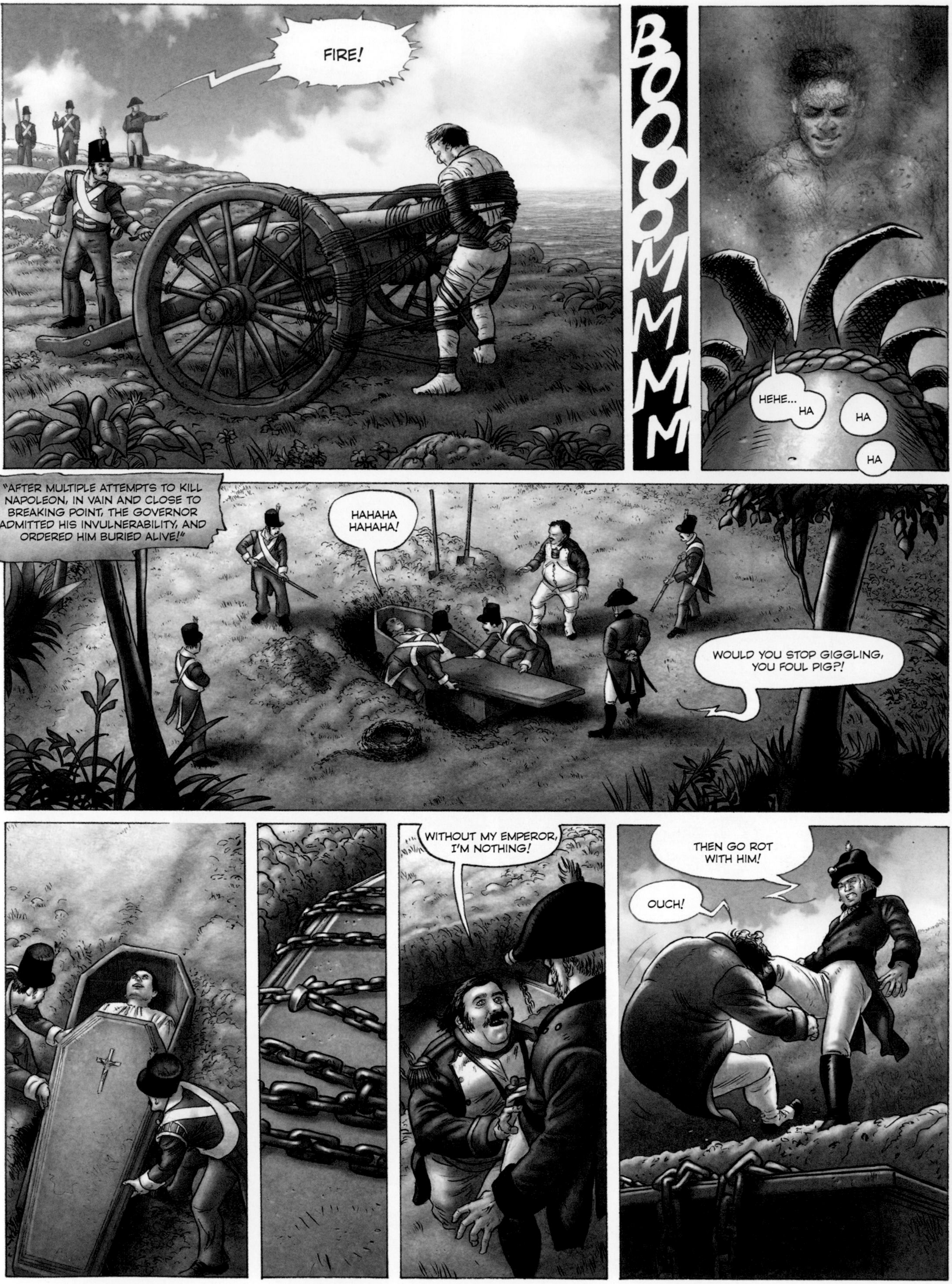
FIRE!
BOOOOOMMMM
HEHE... HA
HA
HA
"AFTER MULTIPLE ATTEMPTS TO KILL NAPOLEON, IN VAIN AND CLOSE TO BREAKING POINT, THE GOVERNOR ADMITTED HIS INVULNERABILITY, AND ORDERED HIM BURIED ALIVE!"
HAHAHA HAHAHA!
WOULD YOU STOP GIGGLING, YOU FOUL PIG?!
WITHOUT MY EMPEROR, I'M NOTHING!
THEN GO ROT WITH HIM!
OUCH!

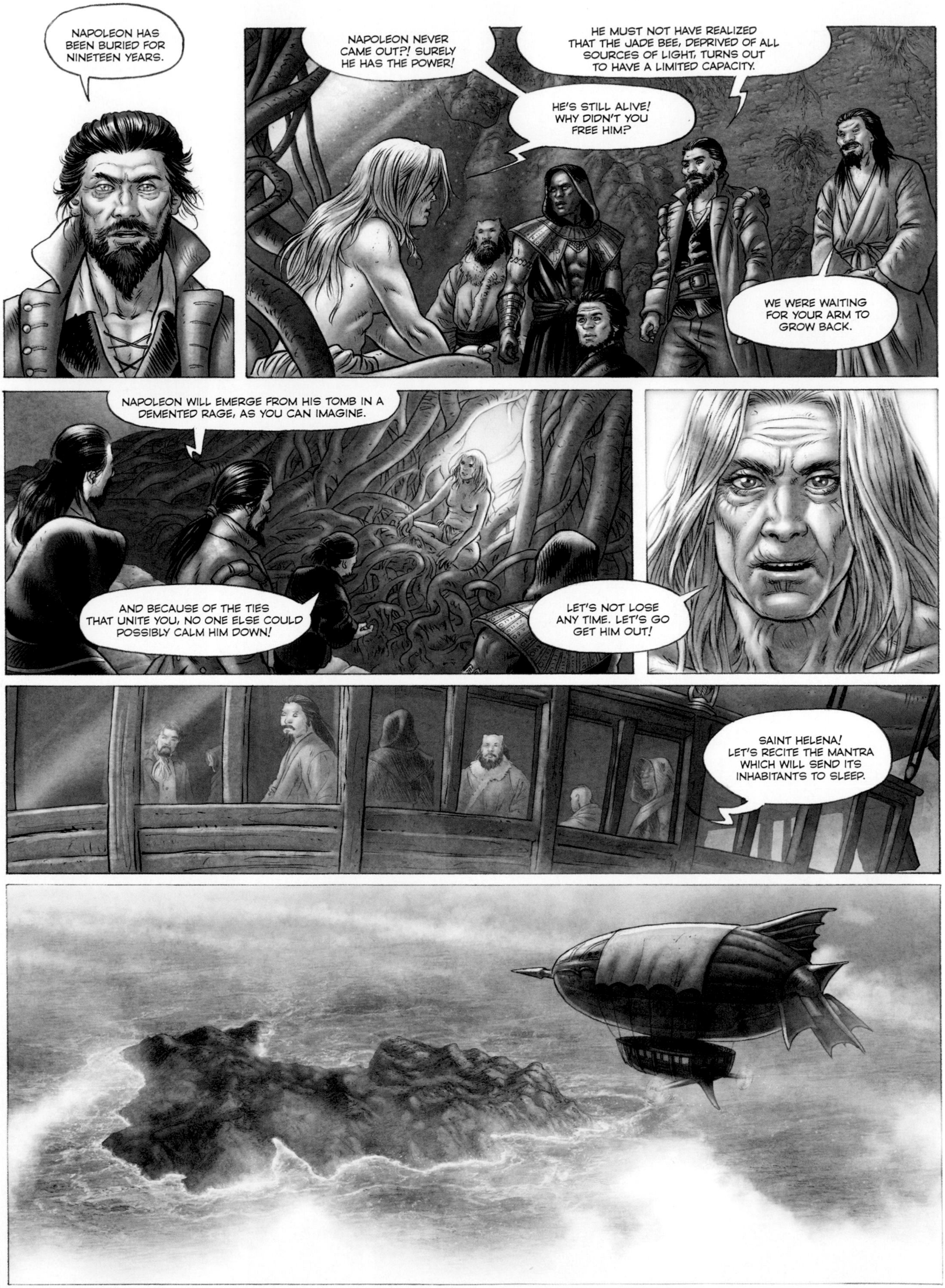
NAPOLEON HAS BEEN BURIED FOR NINETEEN YEARS.
NAPOLEON NEVER CAME OUT?! SURELY HE HAS THE POWER!
HE MUST NOT HAVE REALIZED THAT THE JADE BEE, DEPRIVED OF ALL SOURCES OF LIGHT, TURNS OUT TO HAVE A LIMITED CAPACITY.
HE'S STILL ALIVE! WHY DIDN'T YOU FREE HIM?
WE WERE WAITING FOR YOUR ARM TO GROW BACK.
NAPOLEON WILL EMERGE FROM HIS TOMB IN A DEMENTED RAGE, AS YOU CAN IMAGINE.
AND BECAUSE OF THE TIES THAT UNITE YOU, NO ONE ELSE COULD POSSIBLY CALM HIM DOWN!
LET'S NOT LOSE ANY TIME. LET'S GO GET HIM OUT!
SAINT HELENA! LET'S RECITE THE MANTRA WHICH WILL SEND ITS INHABITANTS TO SLEEP.

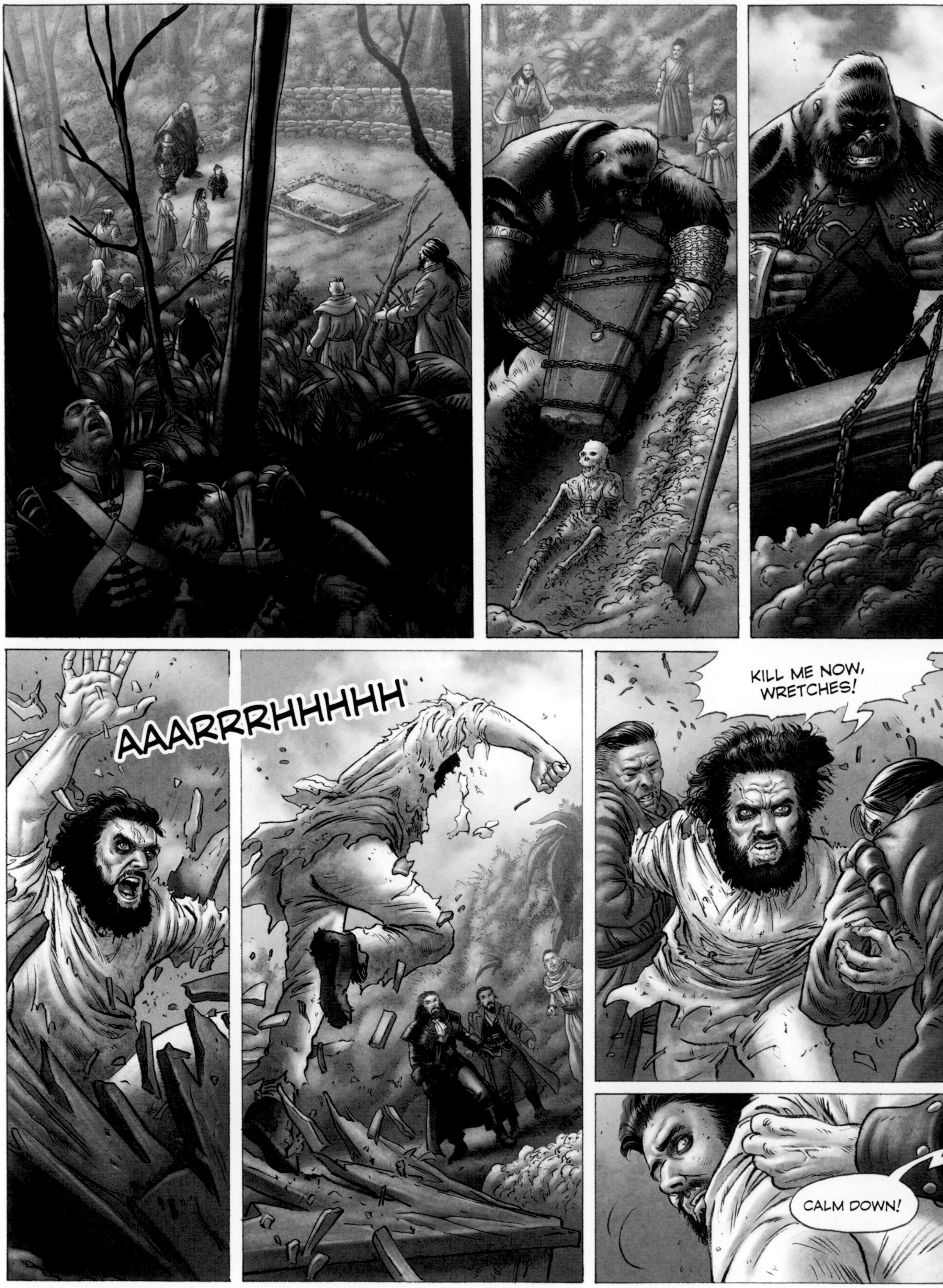
AAARRRHHHHH
KILL ME NOW, WRETCHES!
CALM DOWN!

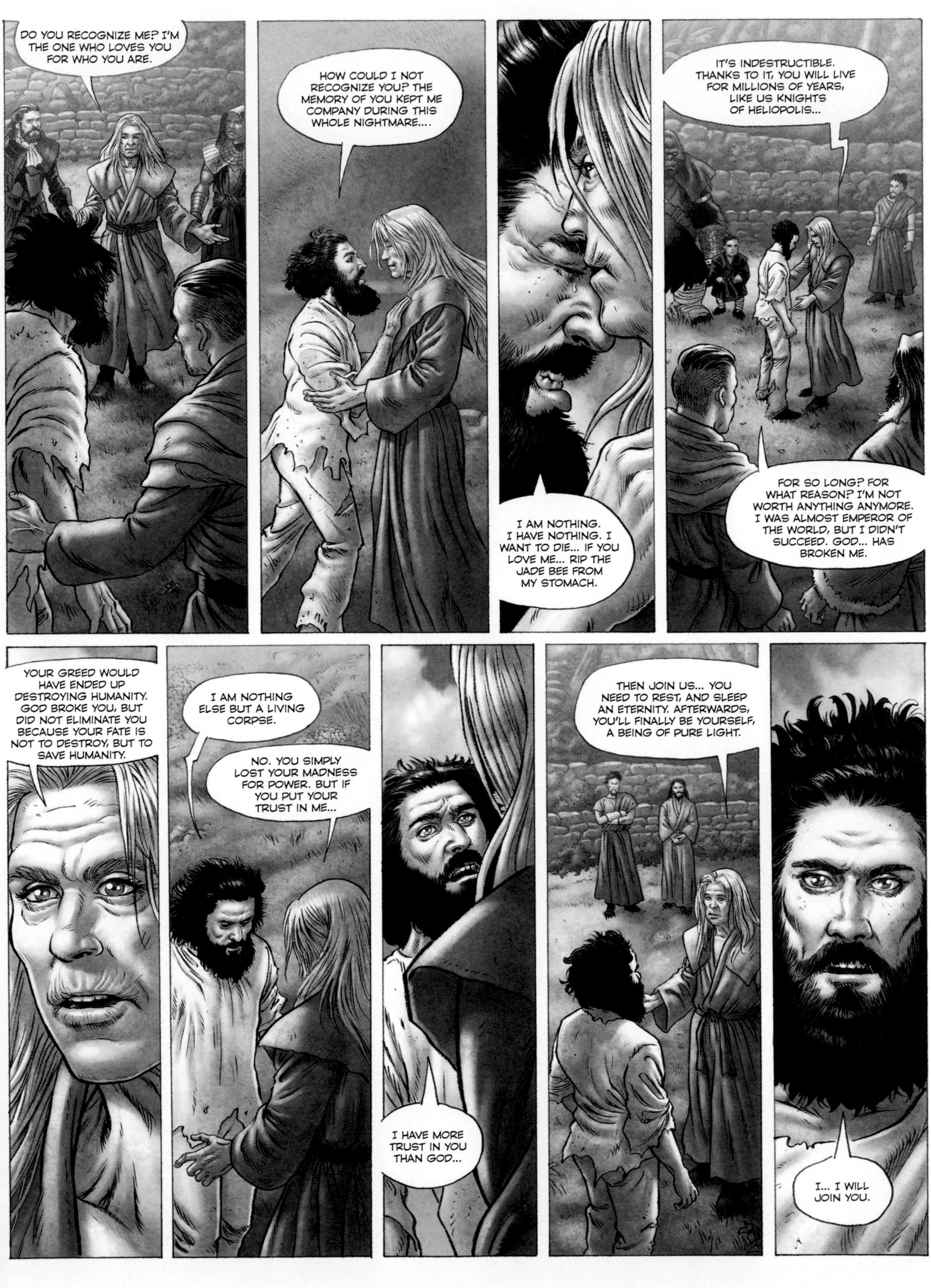

DO YOU RECOGNIZE ME? I'M THE ONE WHO LOVES YOU FOR WHO YOU ARE.
HOW COULD I NOT RECOGNIZE YOU? THE MEMORY OF YOU KEPT ME COMPANY DURING THIS WHOLE NIGHTMARE....
I AM NOTHING. I HAVE NOTHING. I WANT TO DIE... IF YOU LOVE ME... RIP THE JADE BEE FROM MY STOMACH.
IT'S INDESTRUCTIBLE. THANKS TO IT, YOU WILL LIVE FOR MILLIONS OF YEARS, LIKE US KNIGHTS OF HELIOPOLIS...
FOR SO LONG? FOR WHAT REASON? I'M NOT WORTH ANYTHING ANYMORE. I WAS ALMOST EMPEROR OF THE WORLD, BUT I DIDN'T SUCCEED. GOD... HAS BROKEN ME.
YOUR GREED WOULD HAVE ENDED UP DESTROYING HUMANITY. GOD BROKE YOU, BUT DID NOT ELIMINATE YOU BECAUSE YOUR FATE IS NOT TO DESTROY, BUT TO SAVE HUMANITY.
I AM NOTHING ELSE BUT A LIVING CORPSE.
NO. YOU SIMPLY LOST YOUR MADNESS FOR POWER. BUT IF YOU PUT YOUR TRUST IN ME...
I HAVE MORE TRUST IN YOU THAN GOD...
THEN JOIN US... YOU NEED TO REST, AND SLEEP AN ETERNITY. AFTERWARDS, YOU'LL FINALLY BE YOURSELF, A BEING OF PURE LIGHT.
I... I WILL JOIN YOU.

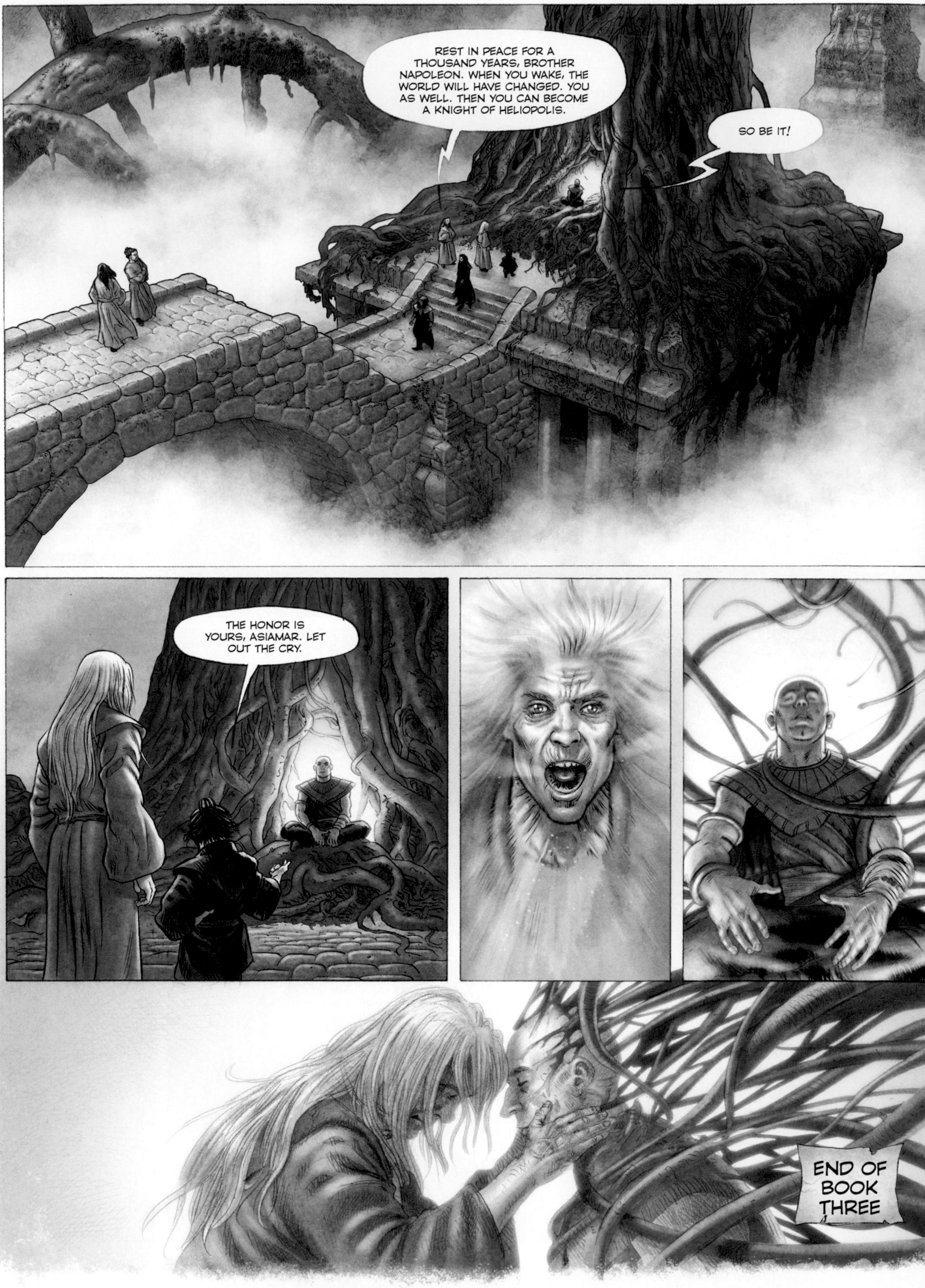
REST IN PEACE FOR A THOUSAND YEARS, BROTHER NAPOLEON. WHEN YOU WAKE, THE WORLD WILL HAVE CHANGED. YOU AS WELL. THEN YOU CAN BECOME A KNIGHT OF HELIOPOLIS.
SO BE IT!
THE HONOR IS YOURS, ASIAMAR. LET OUT THE CRY.
END OF BOOK THREE

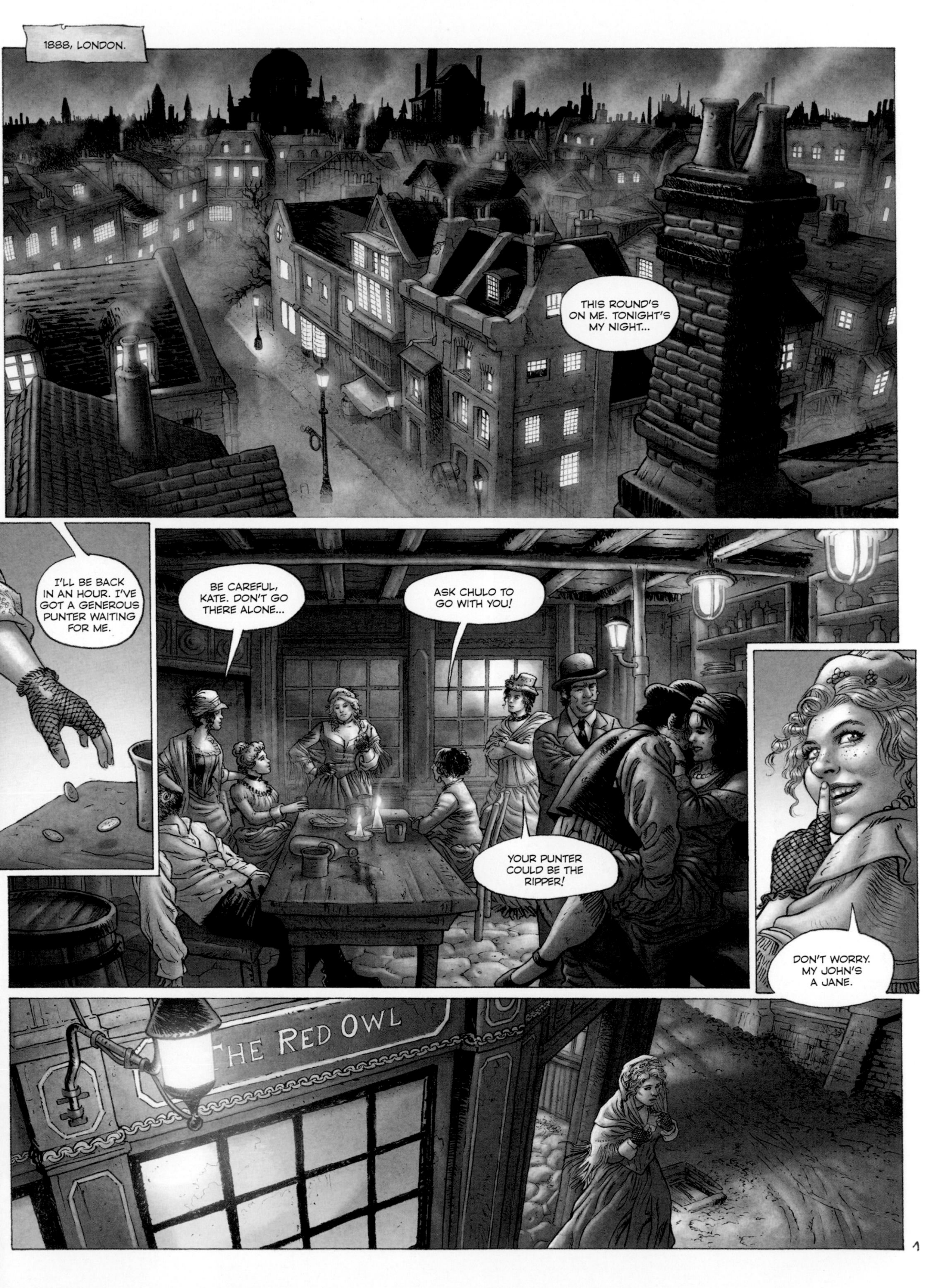
1888, LONDON.
THIS ROUND'S ON ME. TONIGHT'S MY NIGHT...
I'LL BE BACK IN AN HOUR. I'VE GOT A GENEROUS PUNTER WAITING FOR ME.
BE CAREFUL, KATE. DON'T GO THERE ALONE...
ASK CHULO TO GO WITH YOU!
YOUR PUNTER COULD BE THE RIPPER!
DON'T WORRY. MY JOHN'S A JANE.
THE RED OWL

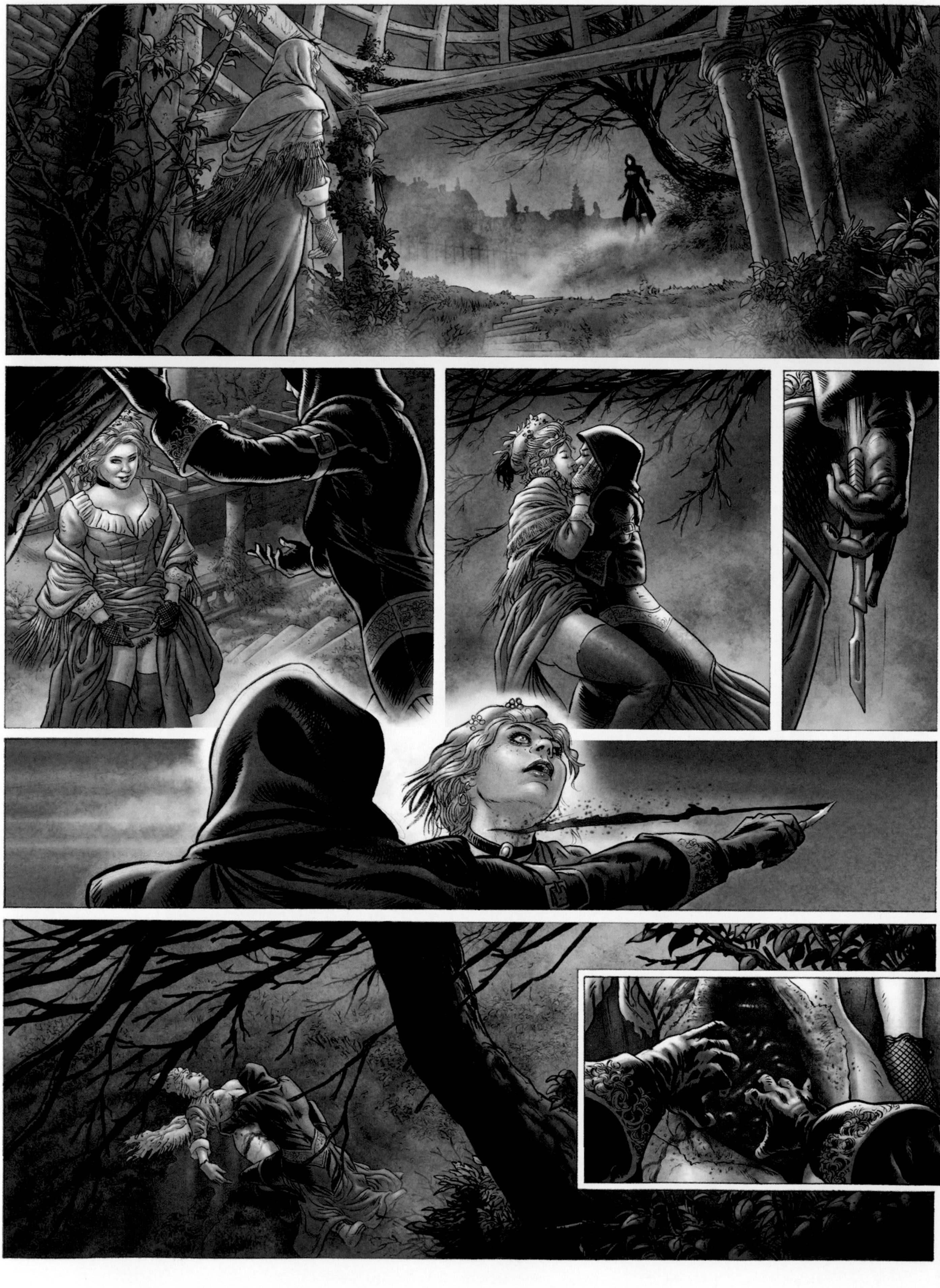

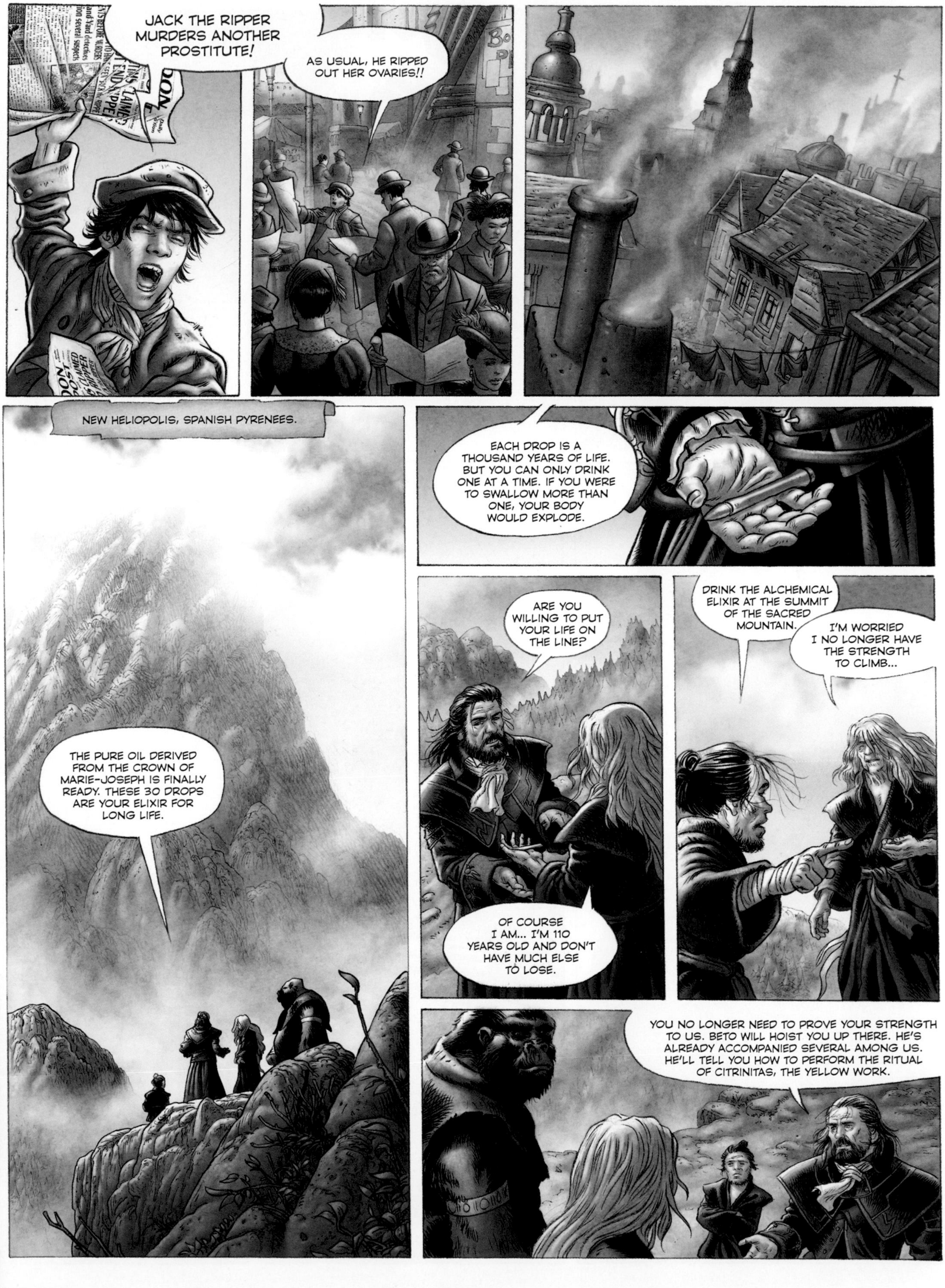
JACK THE RIPPER MURDERS ANOTHER PROSTITUTE!
AS USUAL, HE RIPPED OUT HER OVARIES!!
NEW HELIOPOLIS, SPANISH PYRENEES.
THE PURE OIL DERIVED FROM THE CROWN OF MARIE-JOSEPH IS FINALLY READY. THESE 30 DROPS ARE YOUR ELIXIR FOR LONG LIFE.
EACH DROP IS A THOUSAND YEARS OF LIFE. BUT YOU CAN ONLY DRINK ONE AT A TIME. IF YOU WERE TO SWALLOW MORE THAN ONE, YOUR BODY WOULD EXPLODE.
ARE YOU WILLING TO PUT YOUR LIFE ON THE LINE?
OF COURSE I AM... I'M 110 YEARS OLD AND DON'T HAVE MUCH ELSE TO LOSE.
DRINK THE ALCHEMICAL ELIXIR AT THE SUMMIT OF THE SACRED MOUNTAIN.
I'M WORRIED I NO LONGER HAVE THE STRENGTH TO CLIMB...
YOU NO LONGER NEED TO PROVE YOUR STRENGTH TO US. BETO WILL HOIST YOU UP THERE. HE'S ALREADY ACCOMPANIED SEVERAL AMONG US. HE'LL TELL YOU HOW TO PERFORM THE RITUAL OF CITRINITAS, THE YELLOW WORK.

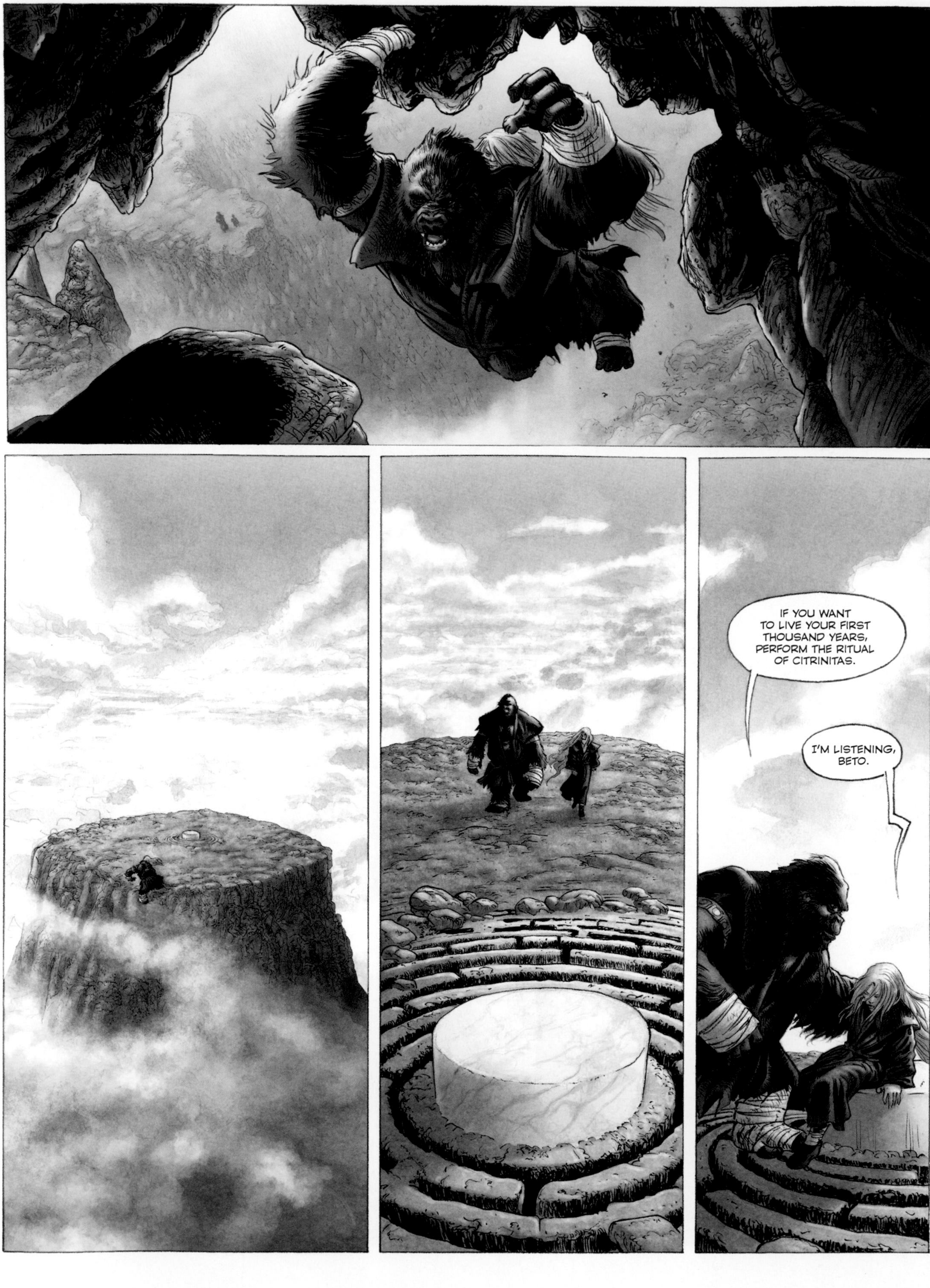
IF YOU WANT TO LIVE YOUR FIRST THOUSAND YEARS, PERFORM THE RITUAL OF CITRINITAS.
I'M LISTENING, BETO.

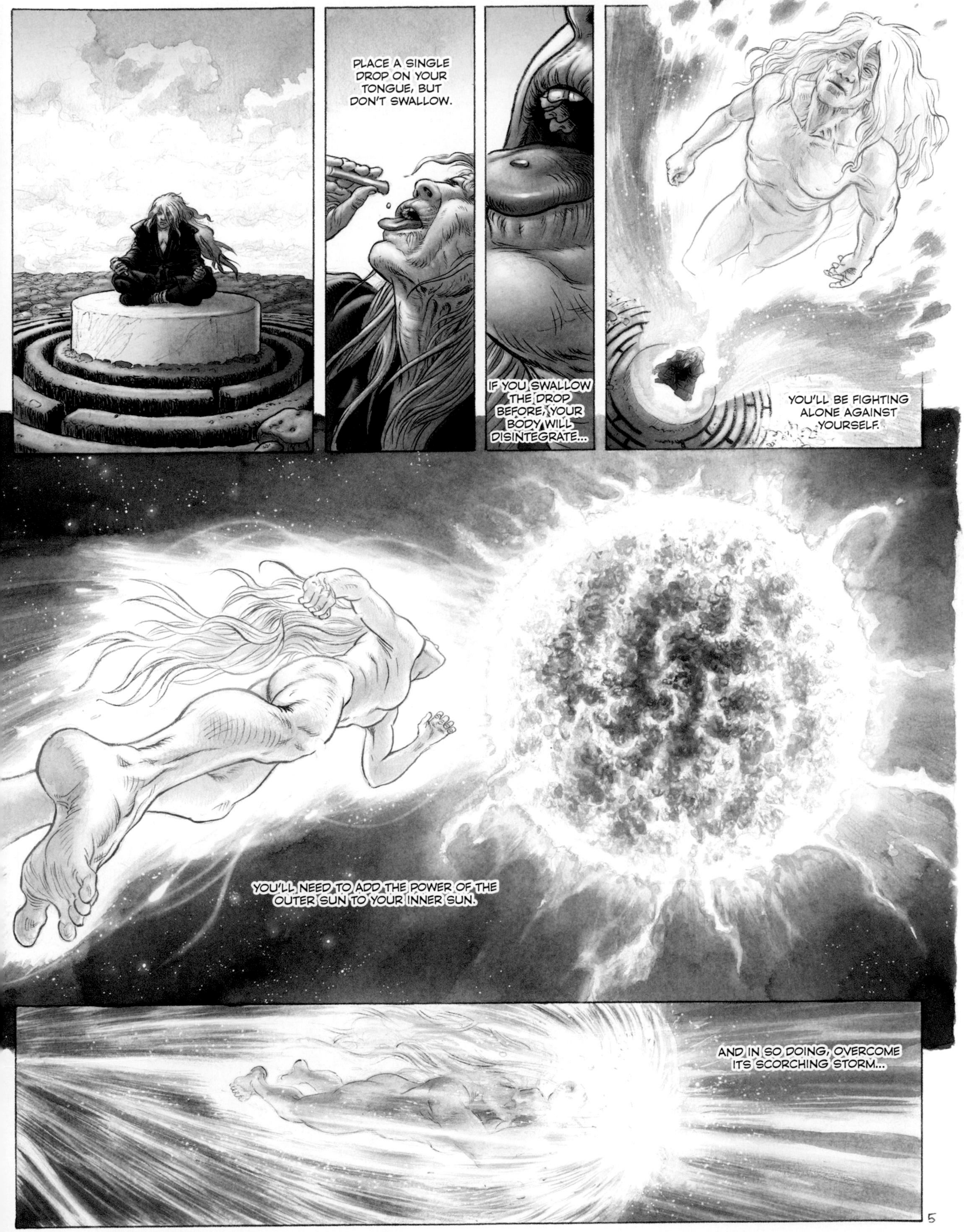
PLACE A SINGLE DROP ON YOUR TONGUE, BUT DON'T SWALLOW.
IF YOU SWALLOW THE DROP BEFORE, YOUR BODY WILL DISINTEGRATE...
YOU'LL BE FIGHTING ALONE AGAINST YOURSELF.
YOU'LL NEED TO ADD THE POWER OF THE OUTER SUN TO YOUR INNER SUN.
AND IN SO DOING, OVERCOME ITS SCORCHING STORM...

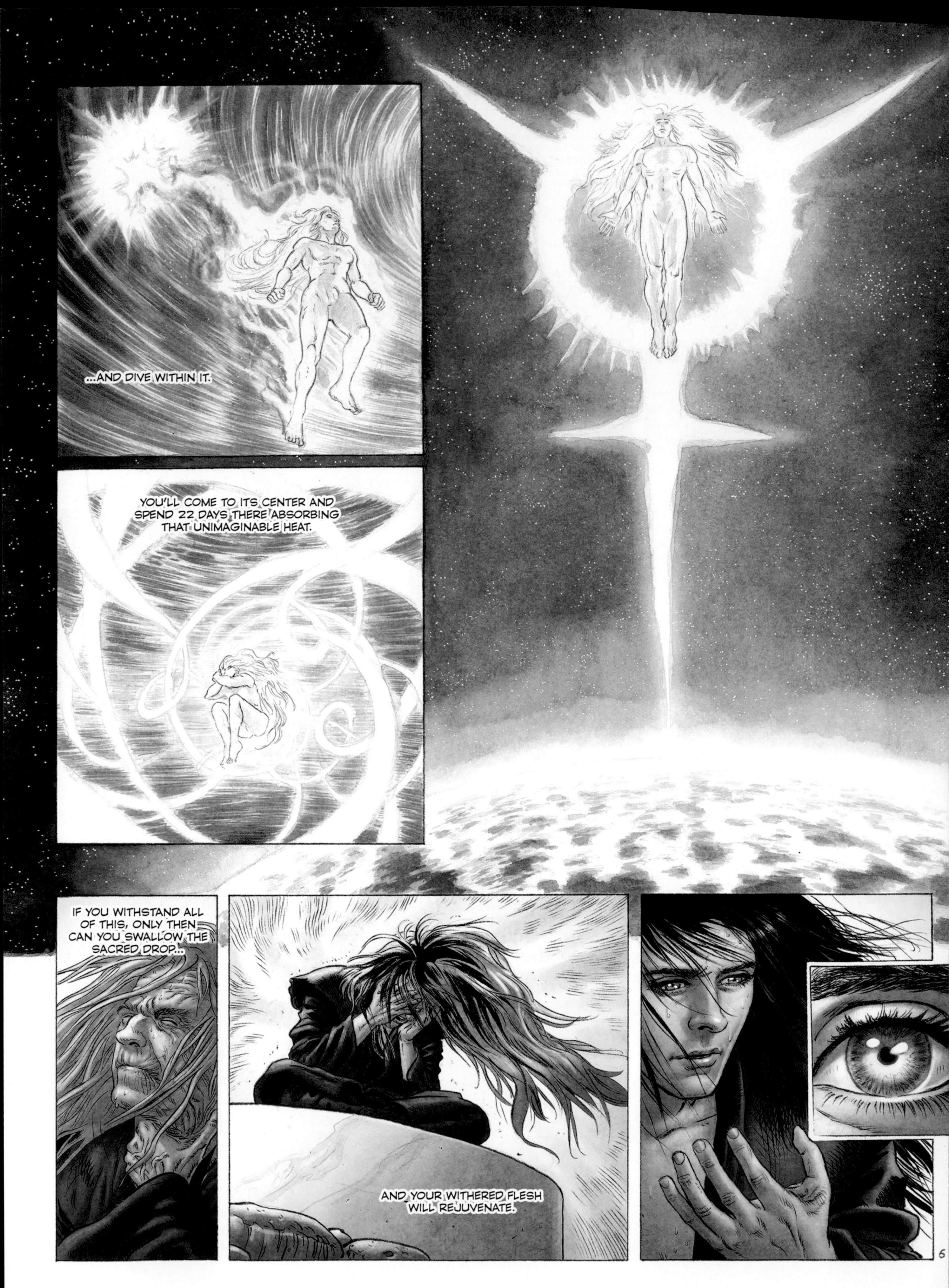
...AND DIVE WITHIN IT.
YOU'LL COME TO ITS CENTER AND SPEND 22 DAYS THERE ABSORBING THAT UNIMAGINABLE HEAT.
IF YOU WITHSTAND ALL OF THIS, ONLY THEN CAN YOU SWALLOW THE SACRED DROP...
AND YOUR WITHERED FLESH WILL REJUVENATE.

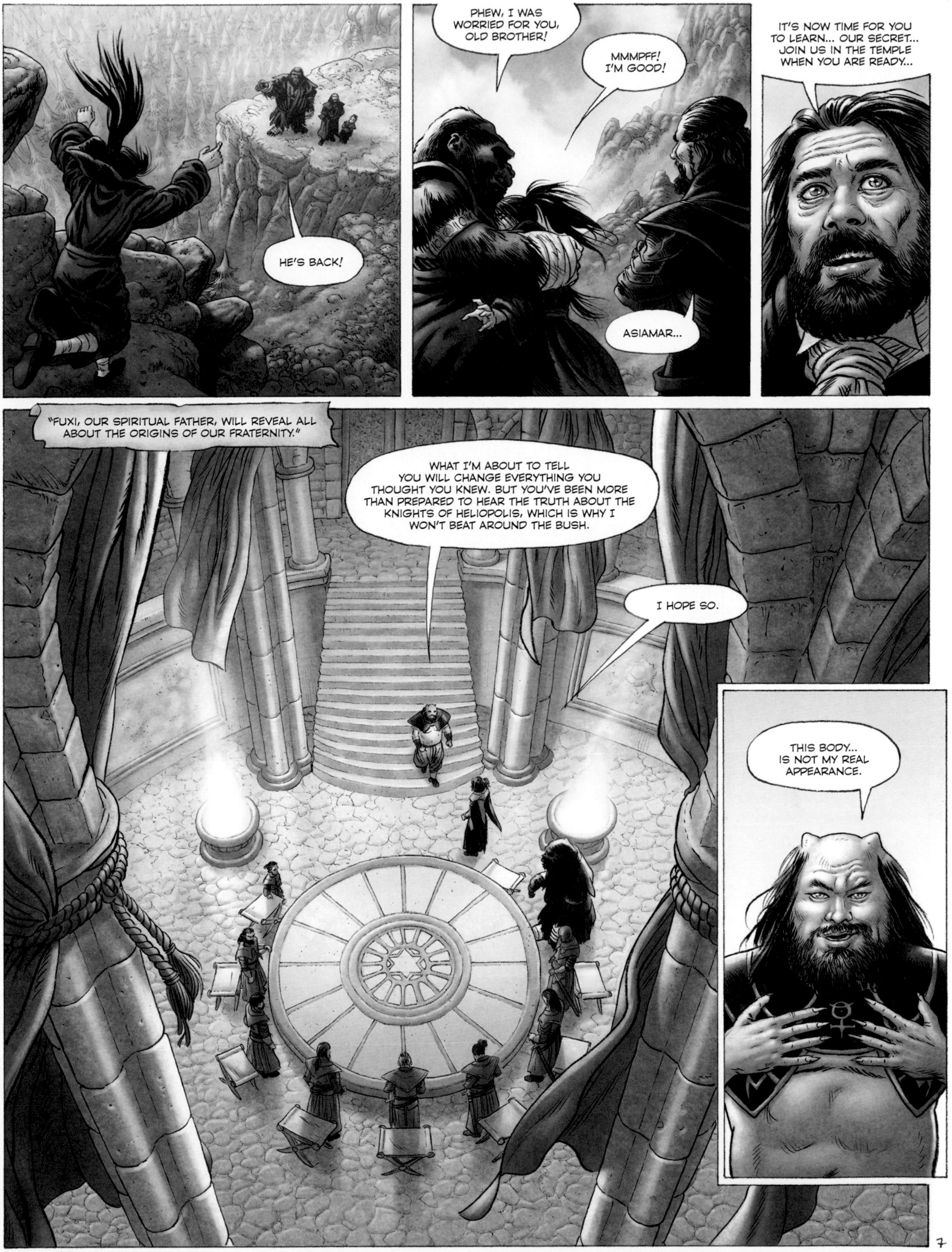
HE'S BACK!
PHEW, I WAS WORRIED FOR YOU, OLD BROTHER!
MMMPFF! I'M GOOD!
ASIAMAR...
IT'S NOW TIME FOR YOU TO LEARN... OUR SECRET... JOIN US IN THE TEMPLE WHEN YOU ARE READY...
"FUXI, OUR SPIRITUAL FATHER, WILL REVEAL ALL ABOUT THE ORIGINS OF OUR FRATERNITY."
WHAT I'M ABOUT TO TELL YOU WILL CHANGE EVERYTHING YOU THOUGHT YOU KNEW. BUT YOU'VE BEEN MORE THAN PREPARED TO HEAR THE TRUTH ABOUT THE KNIGHTS OF HELIOPOLIS, WHICH IS WHY I WON'T BEAT AROUND THE BUSH.
I HOPE SO.
THIS BODY... IS NOT MY REAL APPEARANCE.

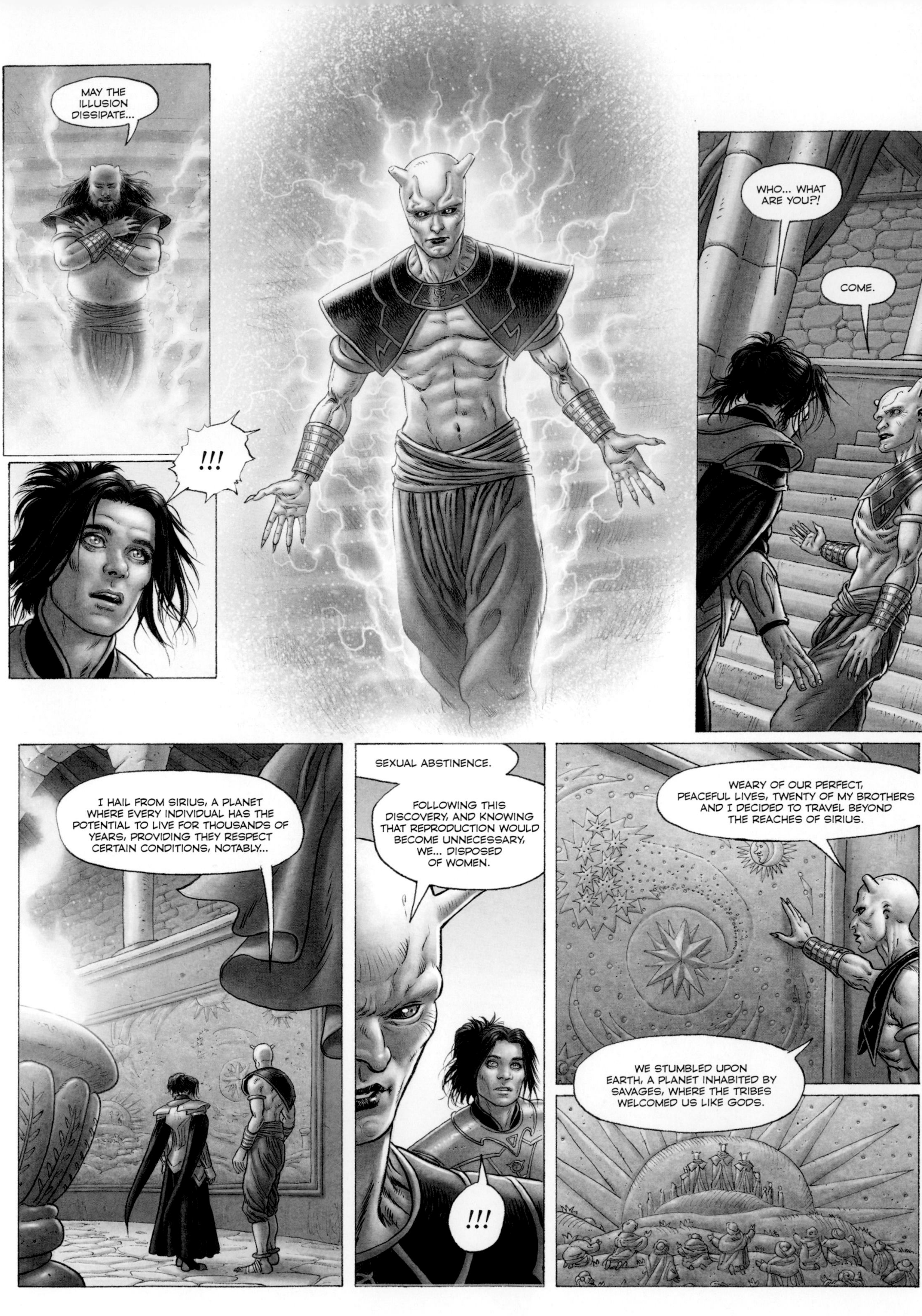

MAY THE ILLUSION DISSIPATE...
!!!
WHO... WHAT ARE YOU?!
COME.
I HAIL FROM SIRIUS, A PLANET WHERE EVERY INDIVIDUAL HAS THE POTENTIAL TO LIVE FOR THOUSANDS OF YEARS, PROVIDING THEY RESPECT CERTAIN CONDITIONS, NOTABLY...
SEXUAL ABSTINENCE.
FOLLOWING THIS DISCOVERY, AND KNOWING THAT REPRODUCTION WOULD BECOME UNNECESSARY, WE... DISPOSED OF WOMEN.
!!!
WEARY OF OUR PERFECT, PEACEFUL LIVES, TWENTY OF MY BROTHERS AND I DECIDED TO TRAVEL BEYOND THE REACHES OF SIRIUS.
WE STUMBLED UPON EARTH, A PLANET INHABITED BY SAVAGES, WHERE THE TRIBES WELCOMED US LIKE GODS.

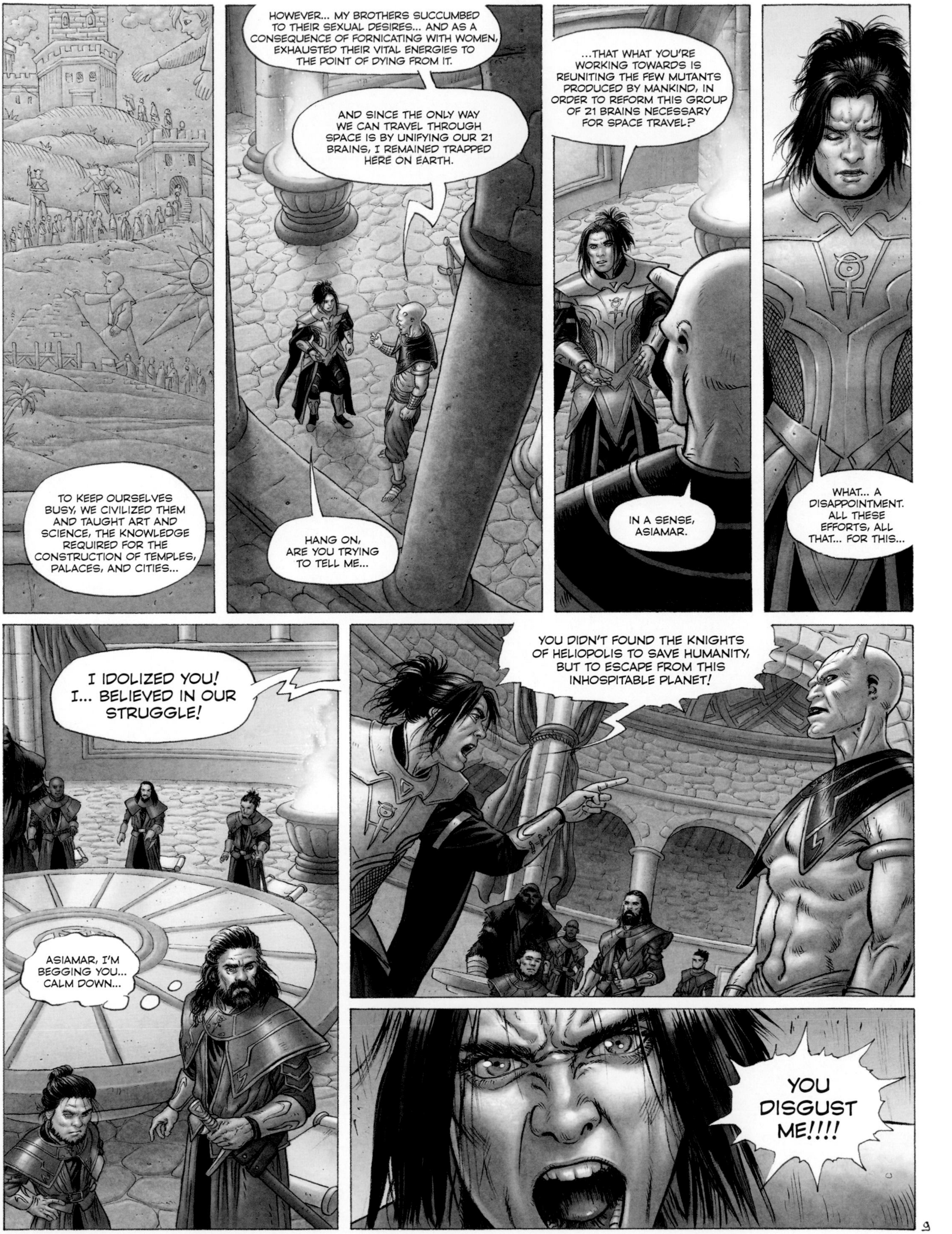
TO KEEP OURSELVES BUSY, WE CIVILIZED THEM AND TAUGHT ART AND SCIENCE, THE KNOWLEDGE REQUIRED FOR THE CONSTRUCTION OF TEMPLES, PALACES, AND CITIES...
HOWEVER... MY BROTHERS SUCCUMBED TO THEIR SEXUAL DESIRES... AND AS A CONSEQUENCE OF FORNICATING WITH WOMEN, EXHAUSTED THEIR VITAL ENERGIES TO THE POINT OF DYING FROM IT.
AND SINCE THE ONLY WAY WE CAN TRAVEL THROUGH SPACE IS BY UNIFYING OUR 21 BRAINS, I REMAINED TRAPPED HERE ON EARTH.
HANG ON, ARE YOU TRYING TO TELL ME...
...THAT WHAT YOU'RE WORKING TOWARDS IS REUNITING THE FEW MUTANTS PRODUCED BY MANKIND, IN ORDER TO REFORM THIS GROUP OF 21 BRAINS NECESSARY FOR SPACE TRAVEL?
IN A SENSE, ASIAMAR.
WHAT... A DISAPPOINTMENT. ALL THESE EFFORTS, ALL THAT... FOR THIS...
I IDOLIZED YOU! I... BELIEVED IN OUR STRUGGLE!
ASIAMAR, I'M BEGGING YOU... CALM DOWN...
YOU DIDN'T FOUND THE KNIGHTS OF HELIOPOLIS TO SAVE HUMANITY, BUT TO ESCAPE FROM THIS INHOSPITABLE PLANET!
YOU DISGUST ME!!!!

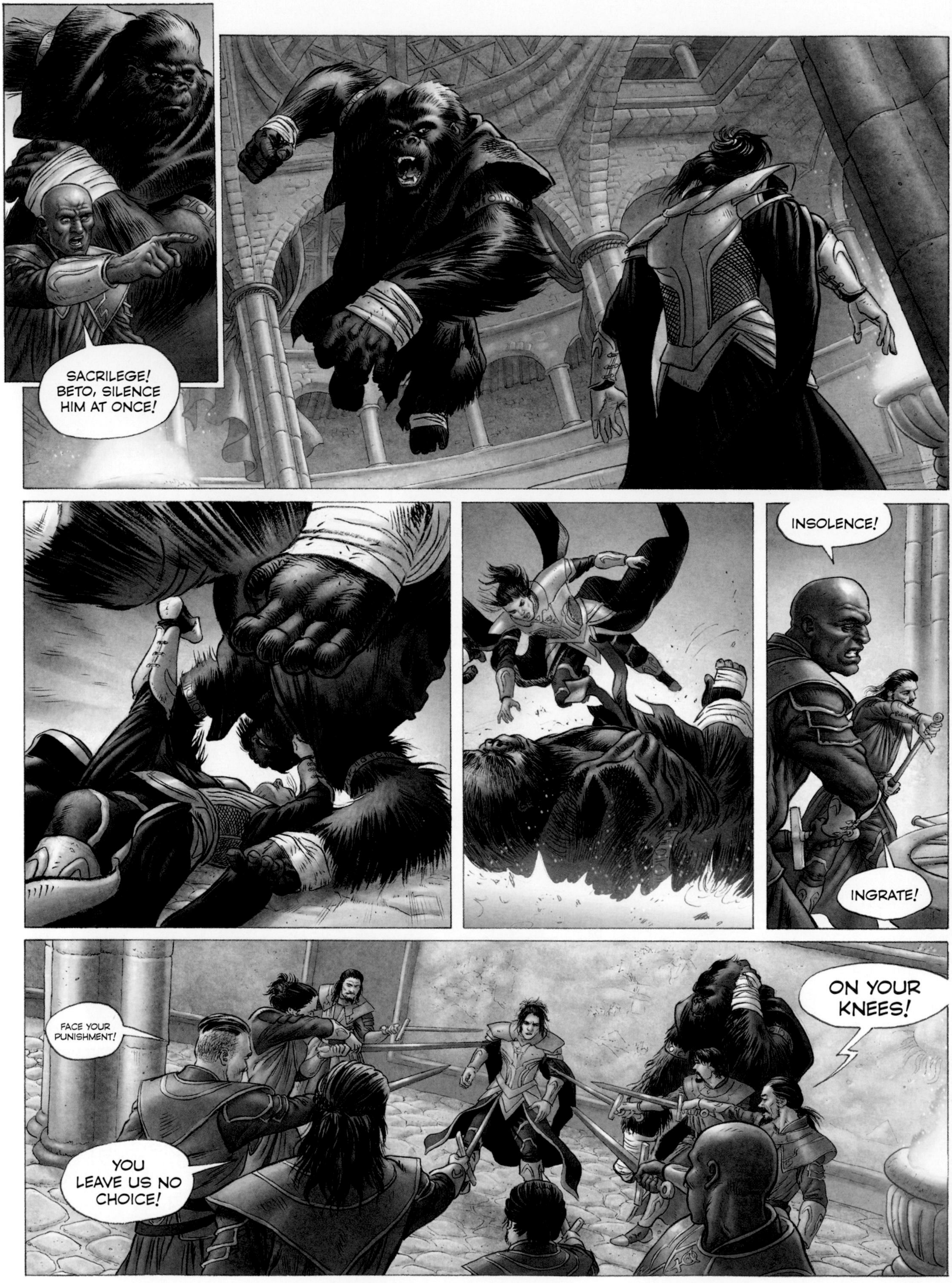
SACRILEGE! BETO, SILENCE HIM AT ONCE!
INSOLENCE!
INGRATE!
FACE YOUR PUNISHMENT!
ON YOUR KNEES!
YOU LEAVE US NO CHOICE!

SINCE YOU SHOW YOURSELF UNABLE TO ACCEPT THIS TRUTH, WE WILL CUT OFF YOUR HEAD...
WORTHY OF AN HEIR TO LOUIS XVI!
CALM DOWN, MY CHILDREN...
ASIAMAR EXPRESSED IN ALL HONESTY HOW HE FELT.
THIS SINCERITY IS ADMIRABLE.
MY DEAR ASIAMAR, YOU MISUNDERSTOOD MY WORDS. BEFORE WE LEFT EARTH, WE WOULD SAVE THE HUMAN RACE FROM SELF-DESTRUCTION.
MY... HEART BELIEVES YOU, FUXI. YOU'VE FORGIVEN MY INSOLENCE, PERHAPS, BUT MY LIFE NO LONGER HAS ANY MEANING. IF WOMEN ARE POISON TO THE KNIGHTS OF HELIOPOLIS, THEN WHY I AM STILL AT YOUR SIDE.
YOUR FEMALE HALF WILL PLAY A VITAL ROLE IN FULFILLING OUR PLAN...

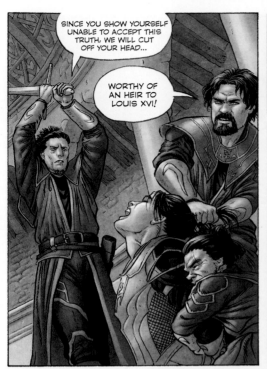

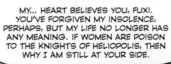

FOR REASONS I'LL LATER EXPLAIN, JACK THE RIPPER, A DANGEROUS MUTANT AND WOMAN-KILLER, HAS THE POWER TO ANNIHILATE US, YOUR BROTHER ALCHEMISTS AND I.

SINCE YOUR HEART BELIEVES ME, AND QUESTIONS ME NO MORE, THEN DO AS I ASK. GO TO LONDON AND DRAW THIS MONSTER OUT, SOMETHING WE MEN ARE UNABLE TO DO. AT THE RISK OF GETTING DISEMBOWELED, CUT OFF HIS HEAD AND BRING ME HIS BRAIN.

SO BE IT, MASTER.

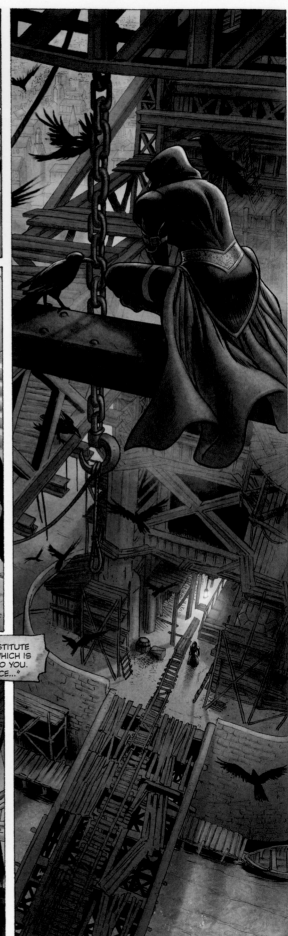

"ONCE IN LONDON, DISGUISE YOURSELF AS A PROSTITUTE AND WANDER THE STREETS NEAR TOWER BRIDGE, WHICH IS WHERE I BELIEVE HE IS HIDING. LET HIM TO COME TO YOU. AND BE CAREFUL -- DON'T TRUST HIS APPEARANCE..."

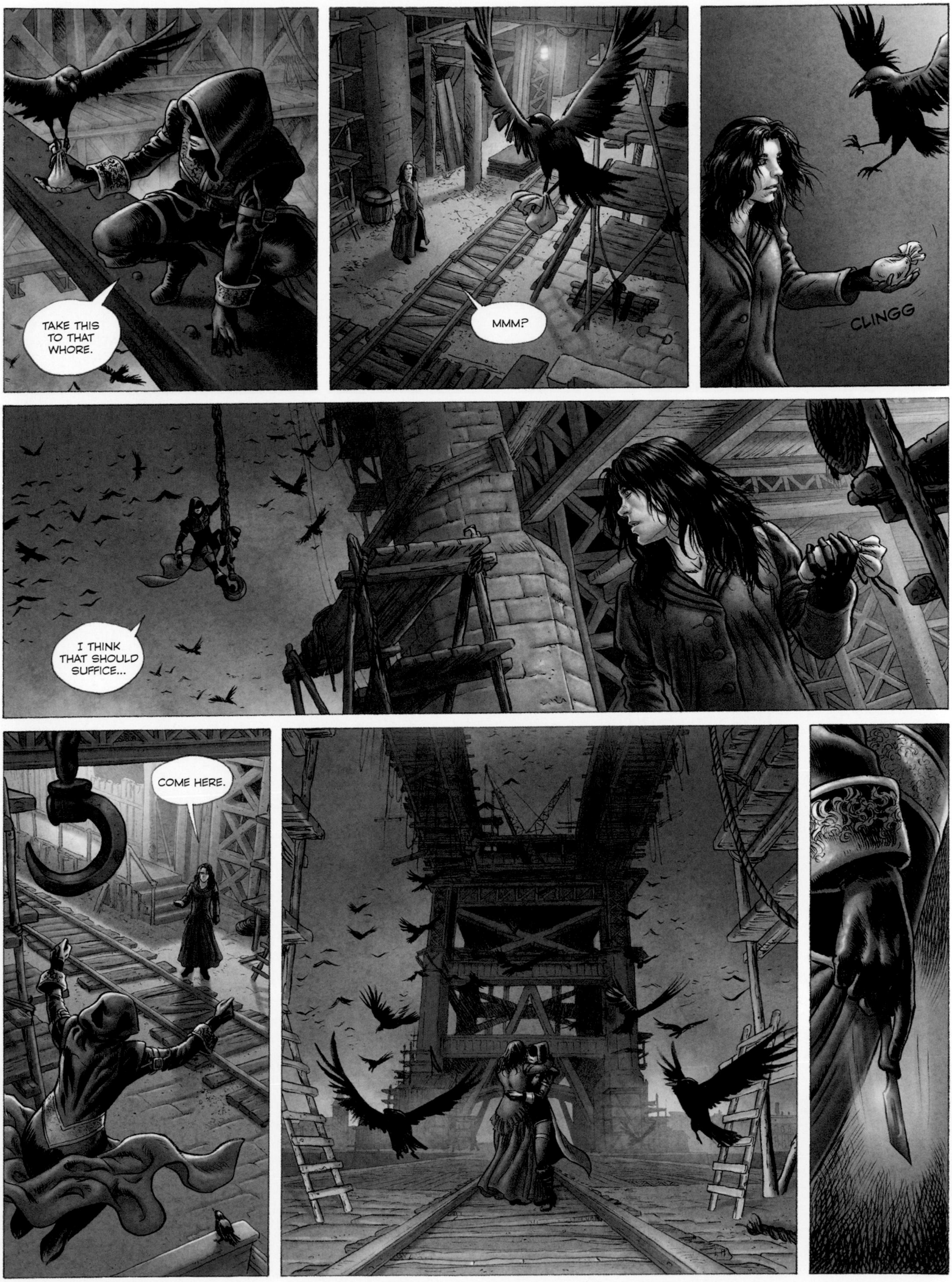
TAKE THIS TO THAT WHORE.
MMM?
CLINGG
I THINK THAT SHOULD SUFFICE...
COME HERE.

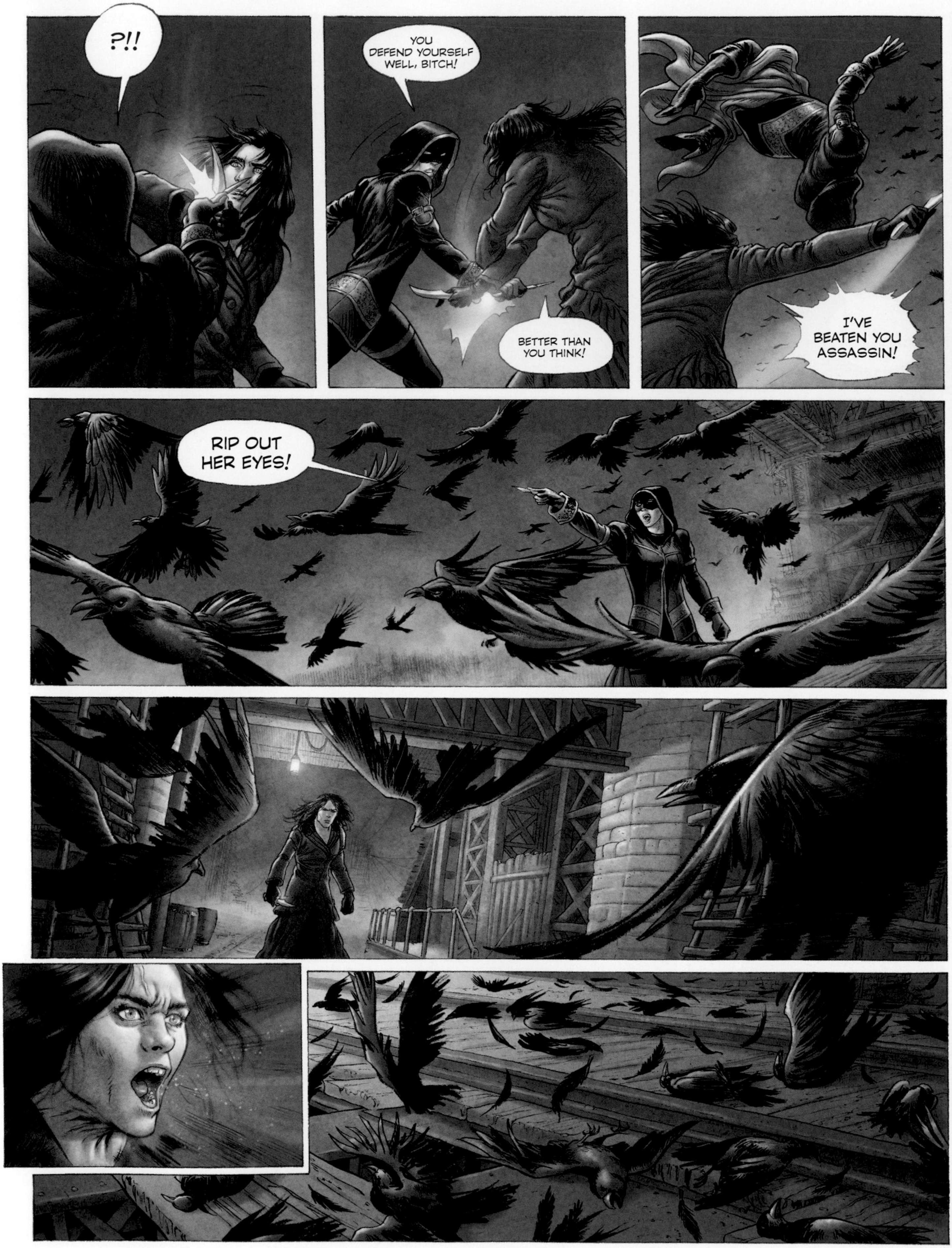
?!!
YOU DEFEND YOURSELF WELL, BITCH!
BETTER THAN YOU THINK!
I'VE BEATEN YOU ASSASSIN!
RIP OUT HER EYES!

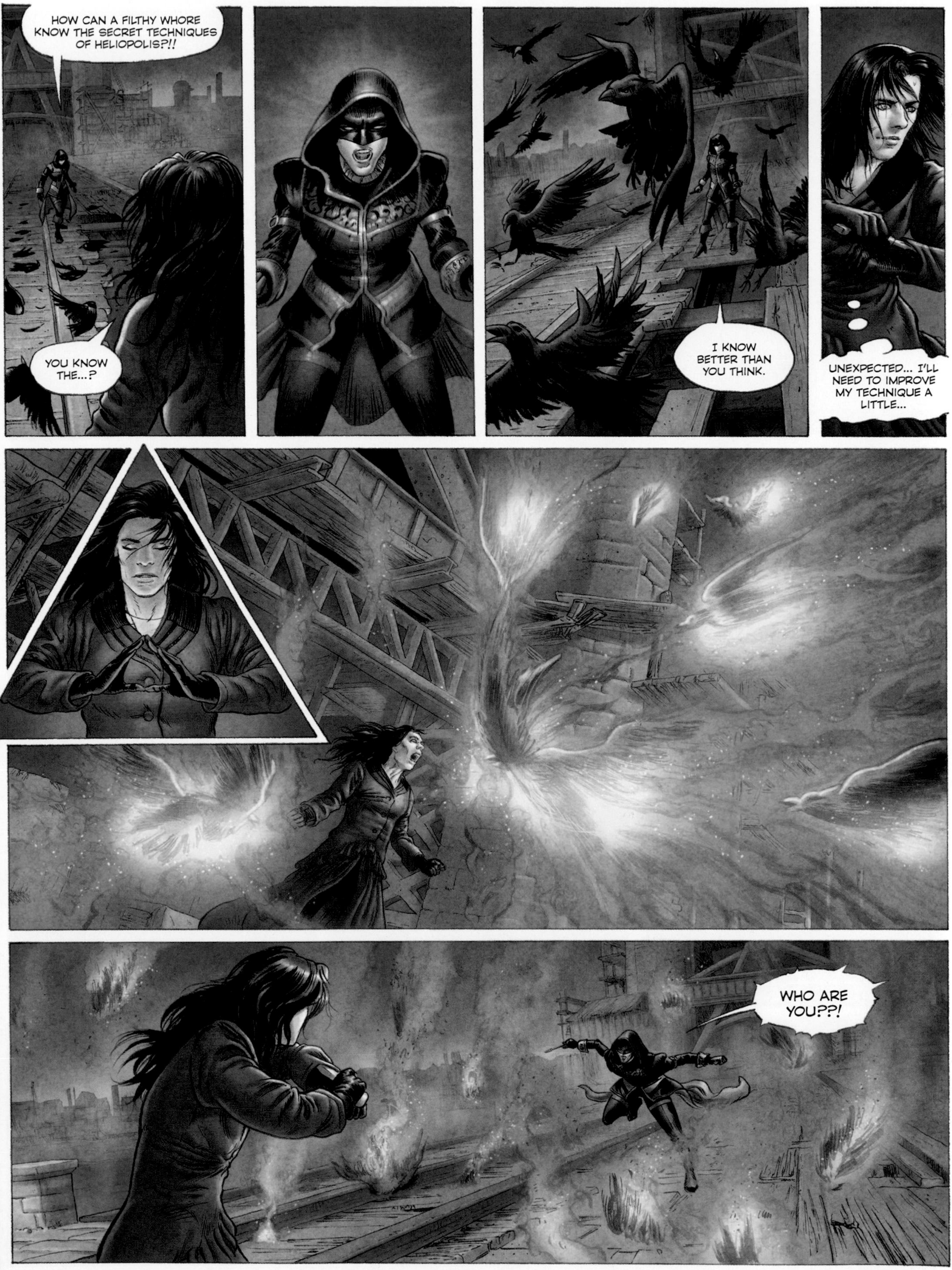
HOW CAN A FILTHY WHORE KNOW THE SECRET TECHNIQUES OF HELIOPOLIS?!!
YOU KNOW THE...?
I KNOW BETTER THAN YOU THINK.
UNEXPECTED... I'LL NEED TO IMPROVE MY TECHNIQUE A LITTLE...
WHO ARE YOU??!

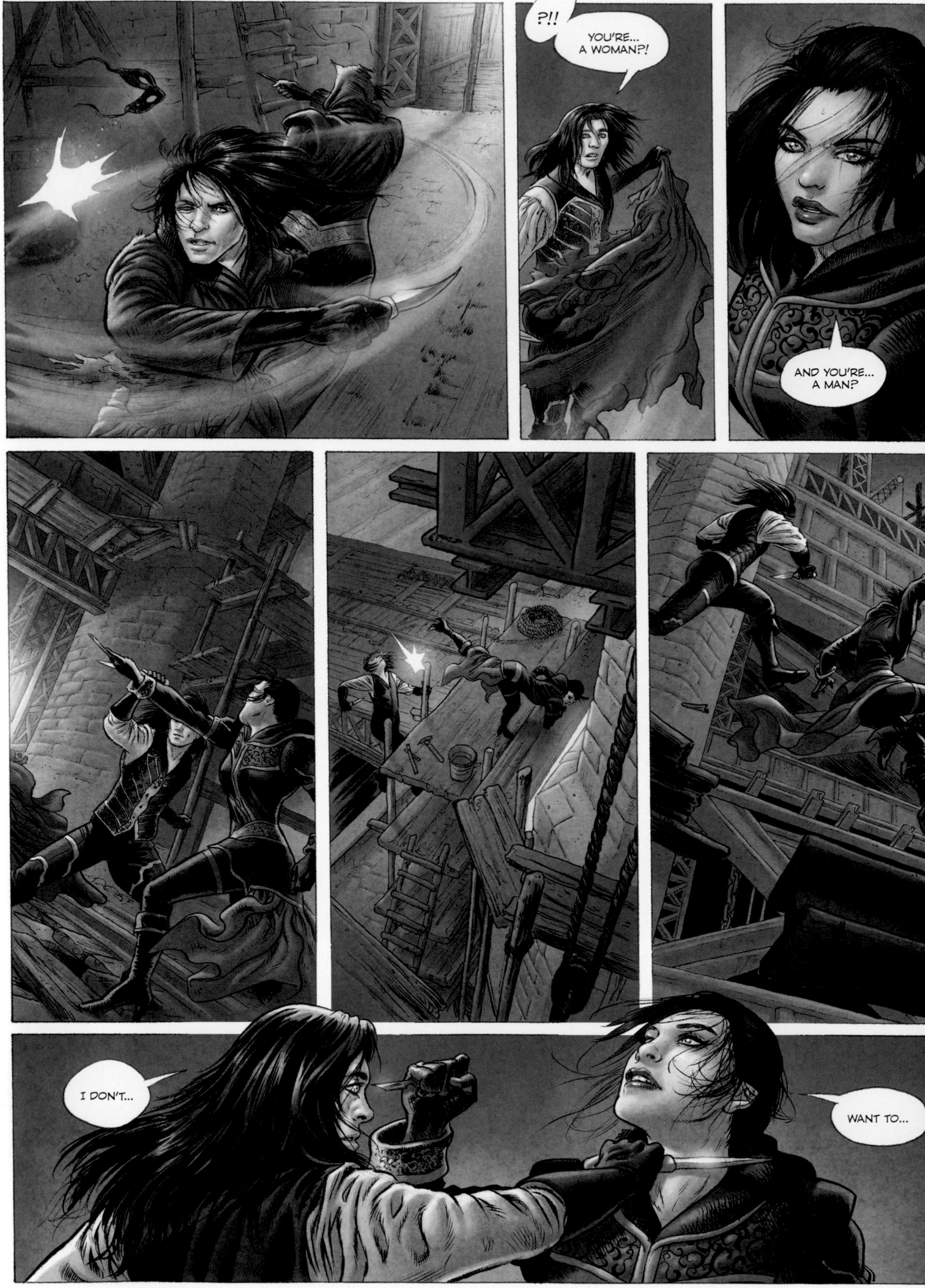
?!!
YOU'RE... A WOMAN?!
AND YOU'RE... A MAN?
I DON'T...
WANT TO...

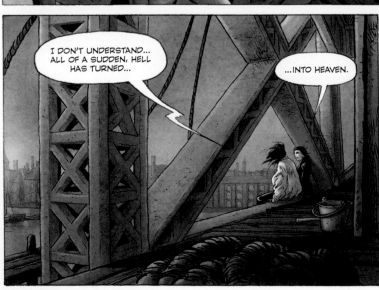

I DON'T UNDERSTAND... ALL OF A SUDDEN, HELL HAS TURNED...

...INTO HEAVEN.

YOU ARE... MY FIRST MAN.

AND YOU MY FIRST WOMAN.

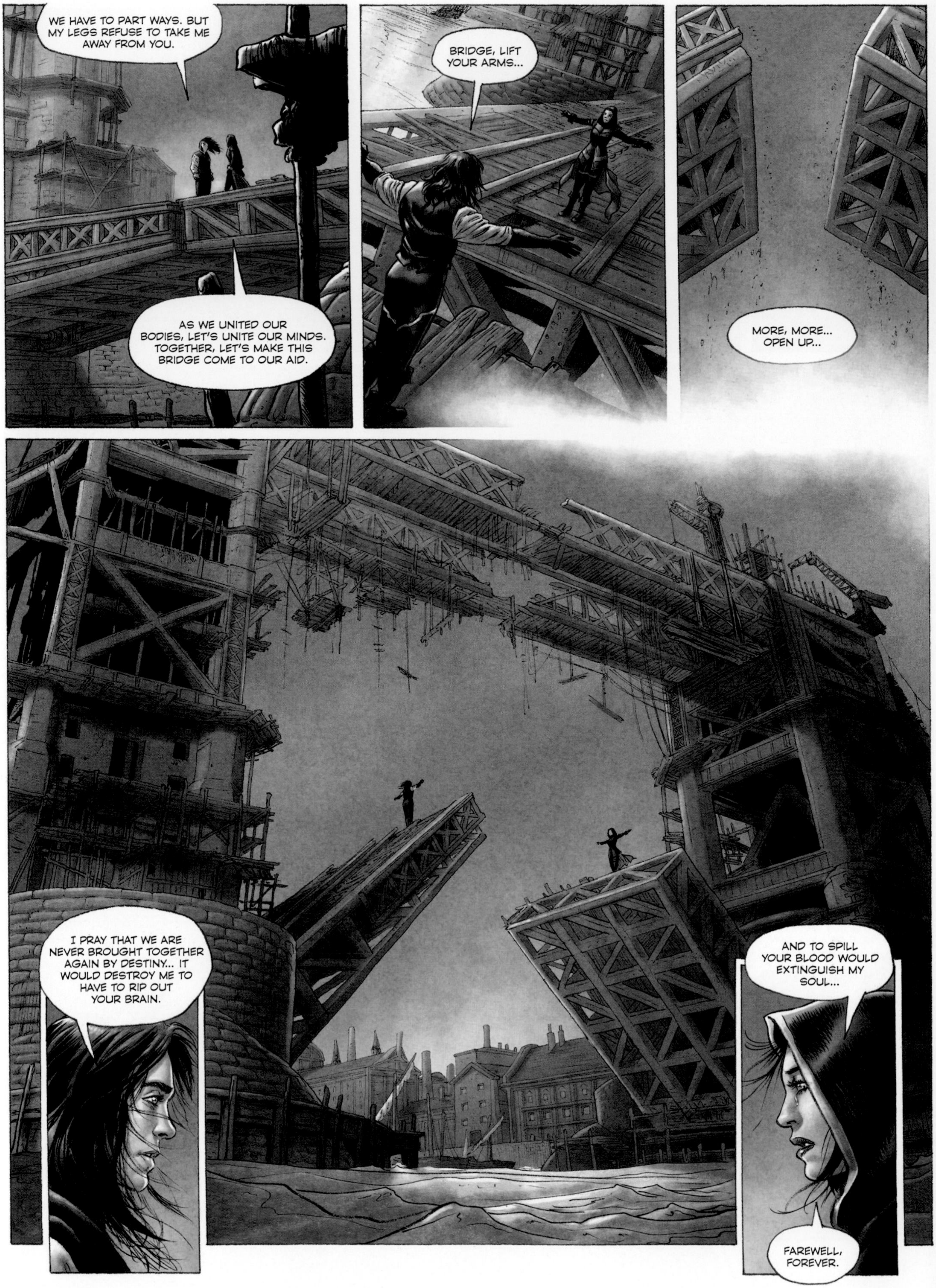
WE HAVE TO PART WAYS. BUT MY LEGS REFUSE TO TAKE ME AWAY FROM YOU.
AS WE UNITED OUR BODIES, LET'S UNITE OUR MINDS. TOGETHER, LET'S MAKE THIS BRIDGE COME TO OUR AID.
BRIDGE, LIFT YOUR ARMS...
MORE, MORE... OPEN UP...
I PRAY THAT WE ARE NEVER BROUGHT TOGETHER AGAIN BY DESTINY... IT WOULD DESTROY ME TO HAVE TO RIP OUT YOUR BRAIN.
AND TO SPILL YOUR BLOOD WOULD EXTINGUISH MY SOUL...
FAREWELL, FOREVER.

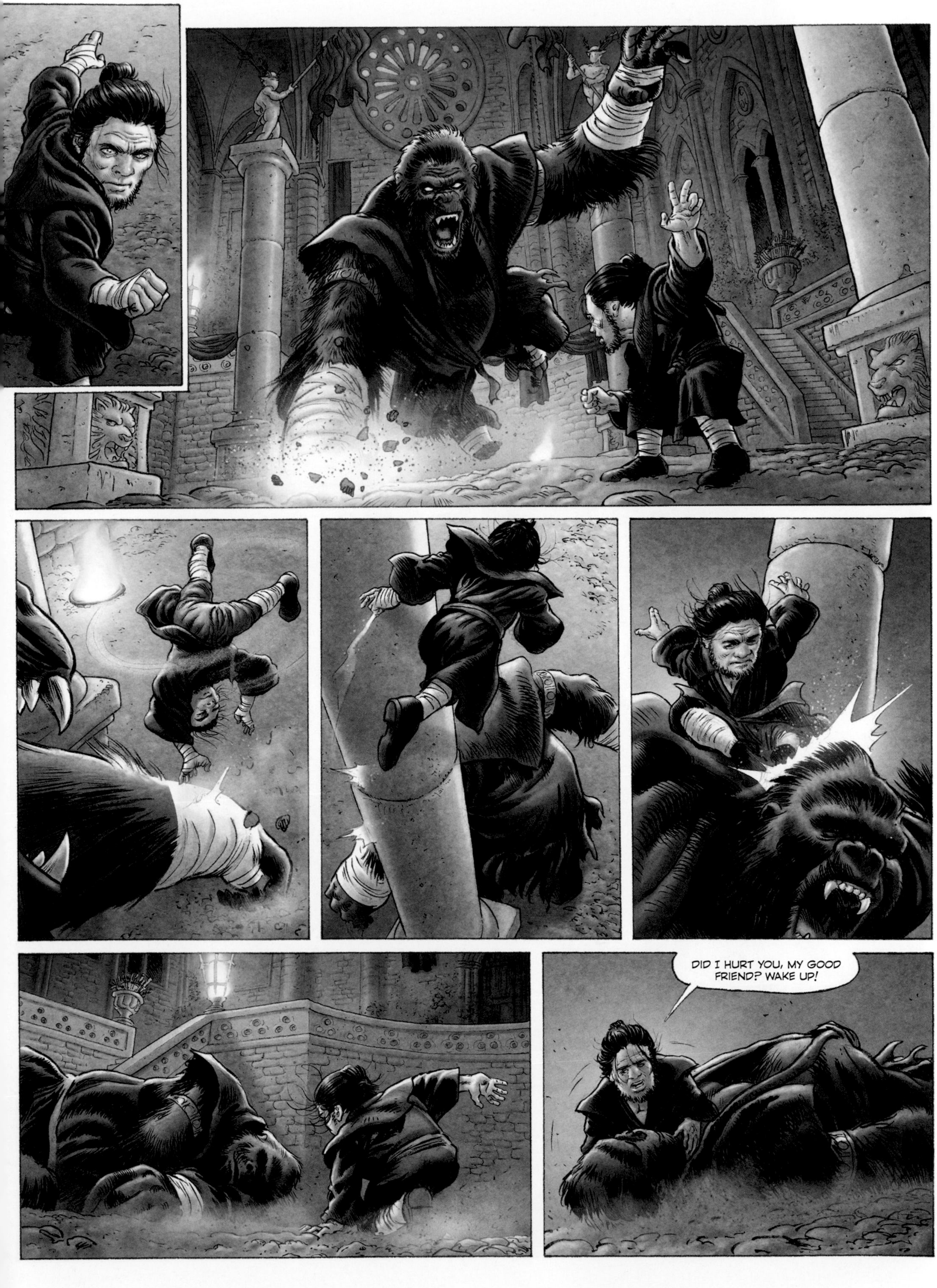
DID I HURT YOU, MY GOOD FRIEND? WAKE UP!

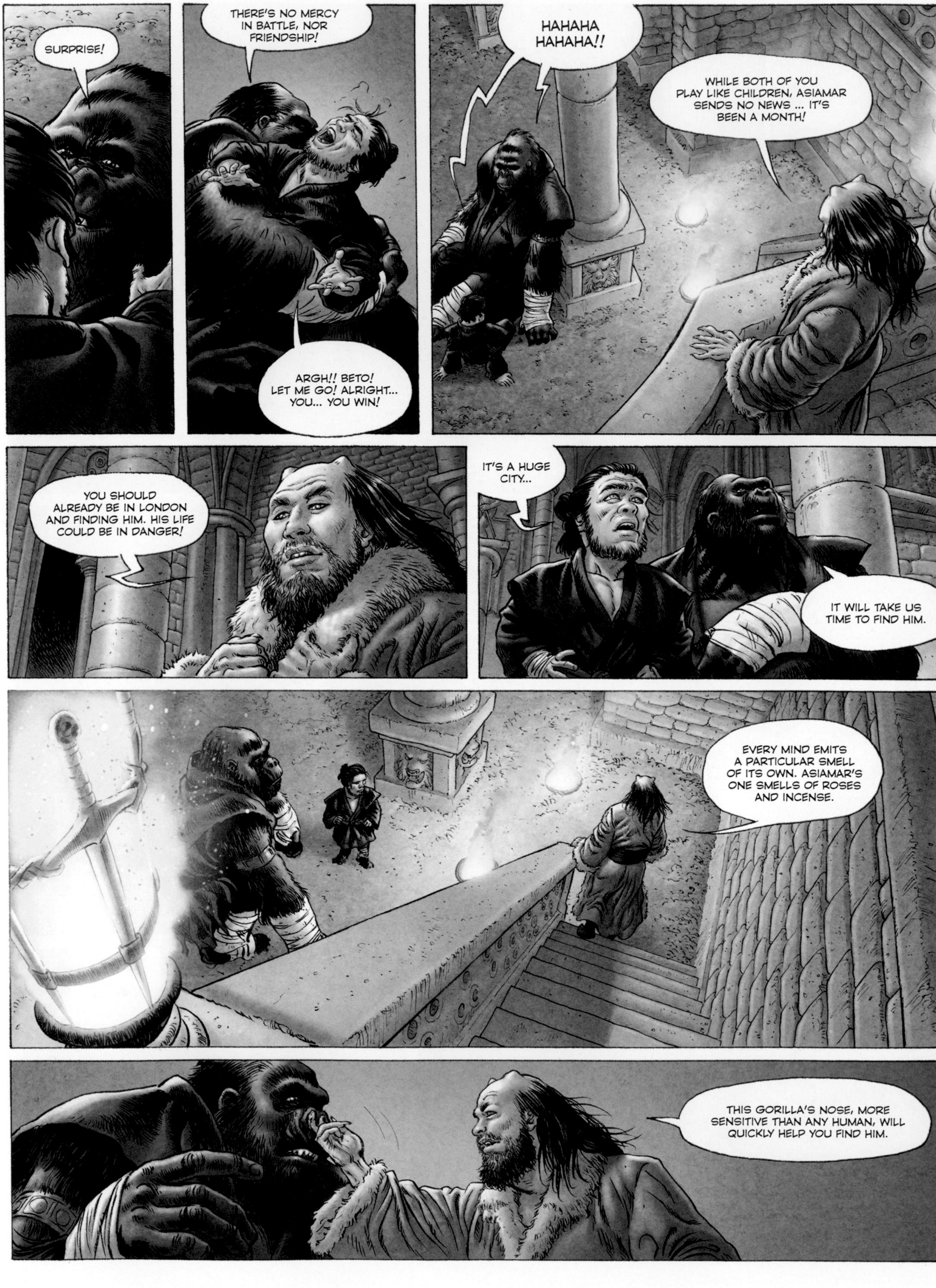
SURPRISE!
THERE'S NO MERCY IN BATTLE, NOR FRIENDSHIP!
ARGH!! BETO! LET ME GO! ALRIGHT... YOU... YOU WIN!
HAHAHA HAHAHA!!
WHILE BOTH OF YOU PLAY LIKE CHILDREN, ASIAMAR SENDS NO NEWS ... IT'S BEEN A MONTH!
YOU SHOULD ALREADY BE IN LONDON AND FINDING HIM. HIS LIFE COULD BE IN DANGER!
IT'S A HUGE CITY...
IT WILL TAKE US TIME TO FIND HIM.
EVERY MIND EMITS A PARTICULAR SMELL OF ITS OWN. ASIAMAR'S ONE SMELLS OF ROSES AND INCENSE.
THIS GORILLA'S NOSE, MORE SENSITIVE THAN ANY HUMAN, WILL QUICKLY HELP YOU FIND HIM.

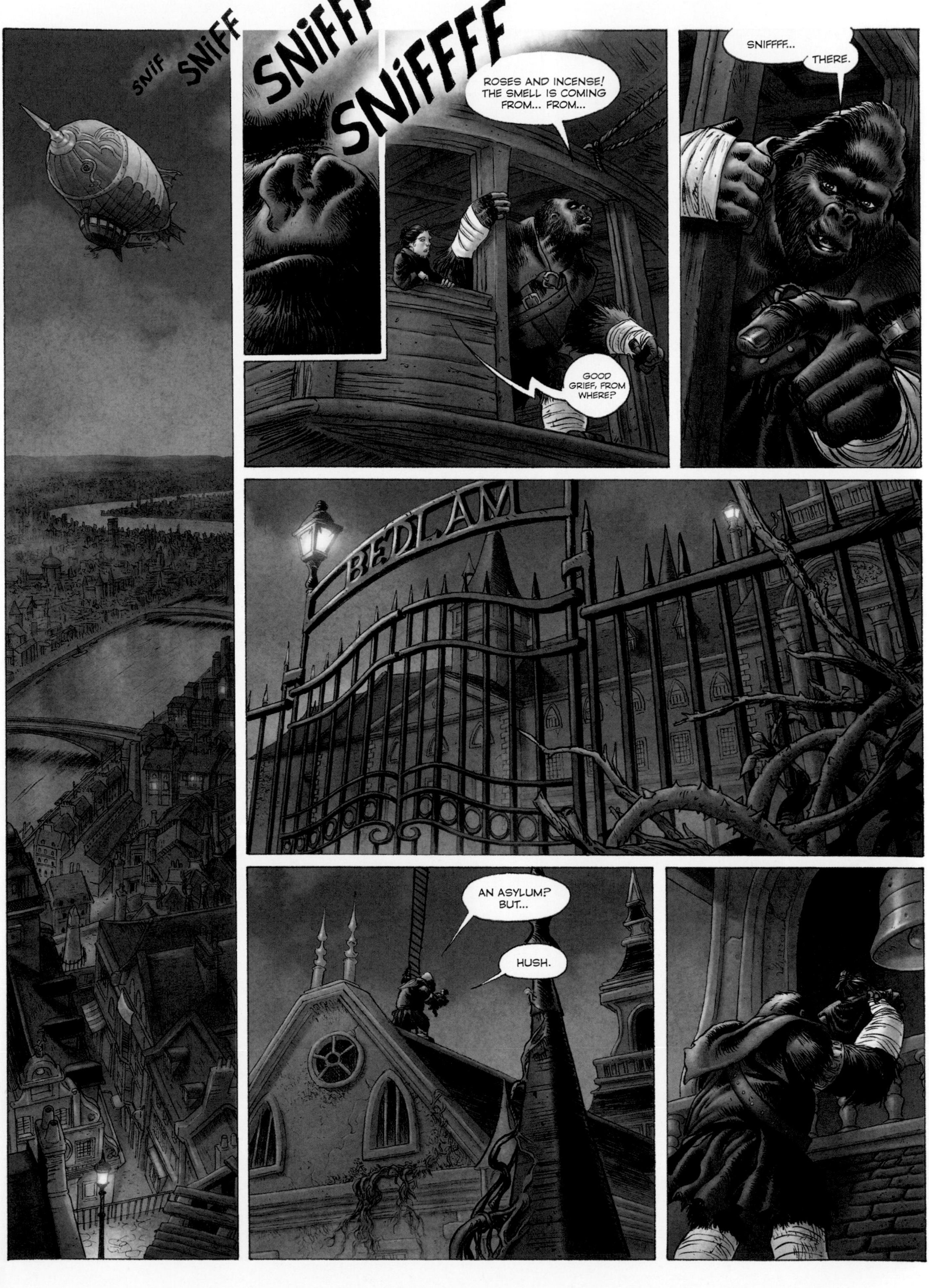
SNIF
SNIFF
SNIFFF
SNIFFFF
ROSES AND INCENSE! THE SMELL IS COMING FROM... FROM...
GOOD GRIEF, FROM WHERE?
SNIFFFF...
THERE.
BEDLAM
AN ASYLUM? BUT...
HUSH.

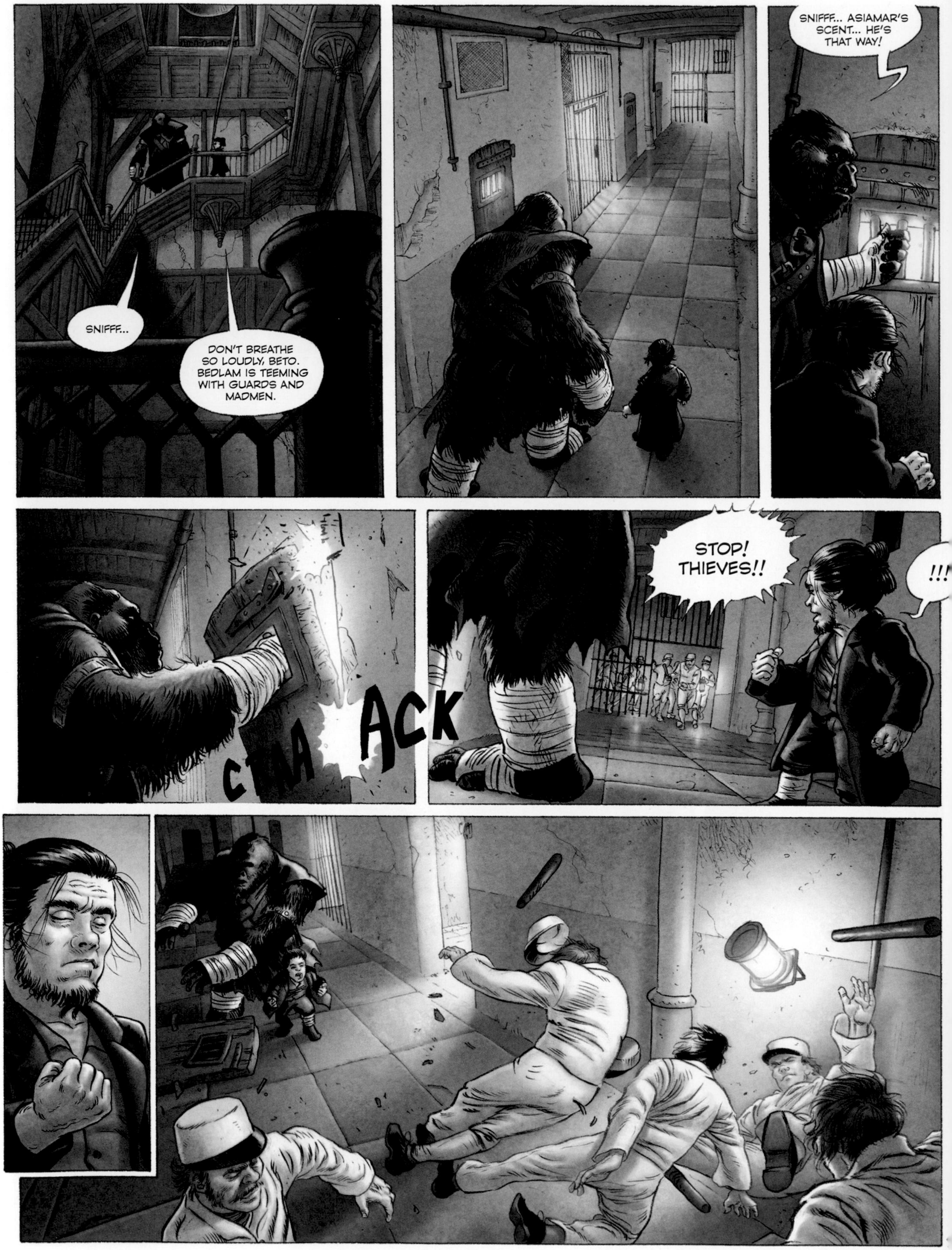
SNIFFF...
DON'T BREATHE SO LOUDLY, BETO. BEDLAM IS TEEMING WITH GUARDS AND MADMEN.
SNIFFF... ASIAMAR'S SCENT... HE'S THAT WAY!
CRAACK
STOP! THIEVES!!
!!!

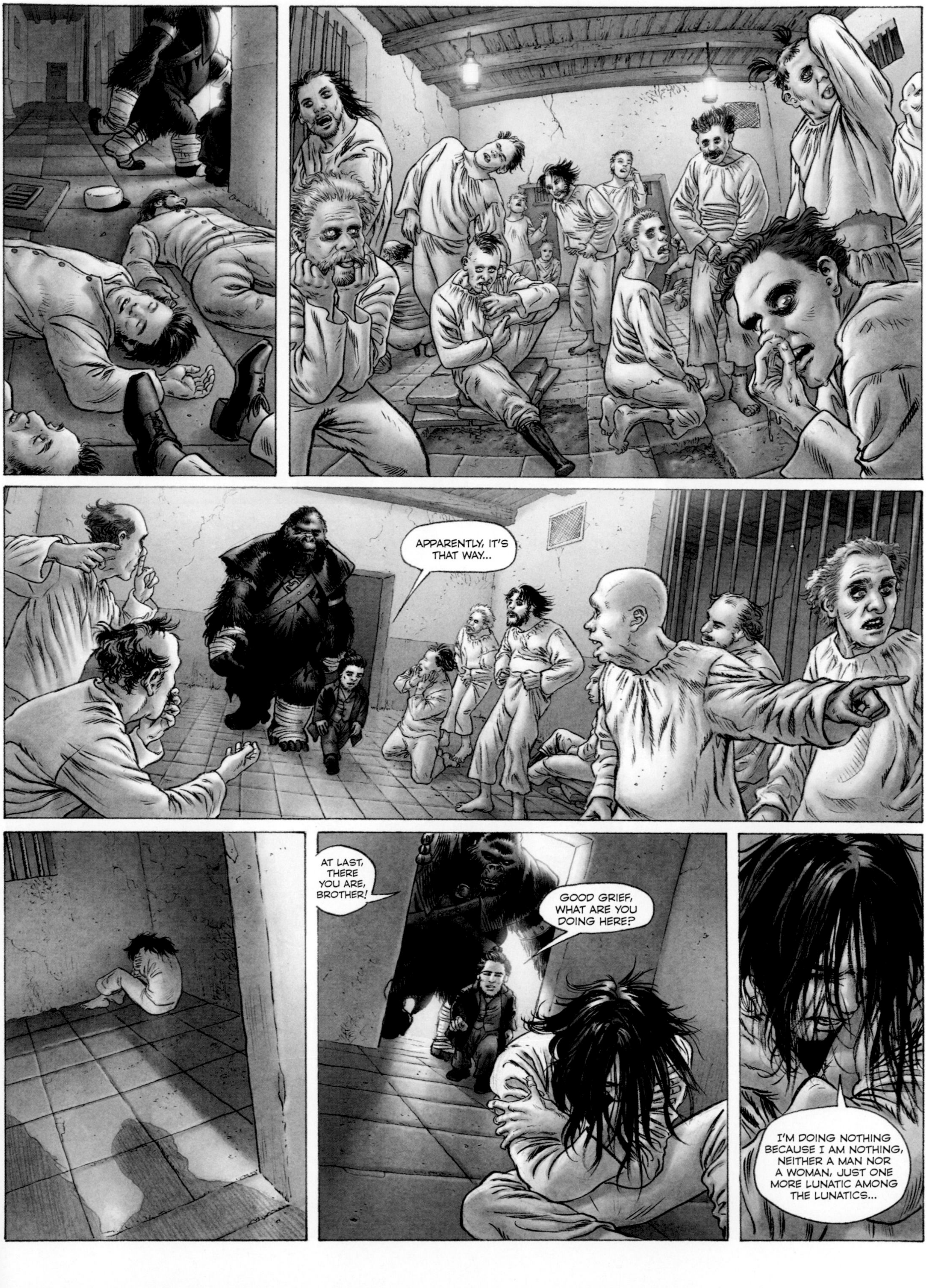
APPARENTLY, IT'S THAT WAY...
AT LAST, THERE YOU ARE, BROTHER!
GOOD GRIEF, WHAT ARE YOU DOING HERE?
I'M DOING NOTHING BECAUSE I AM NOTHING, NEITHER A MAN NOR A WOMAN, JUST ONE MORE LUNATIC AMONG THE LUNATICS...

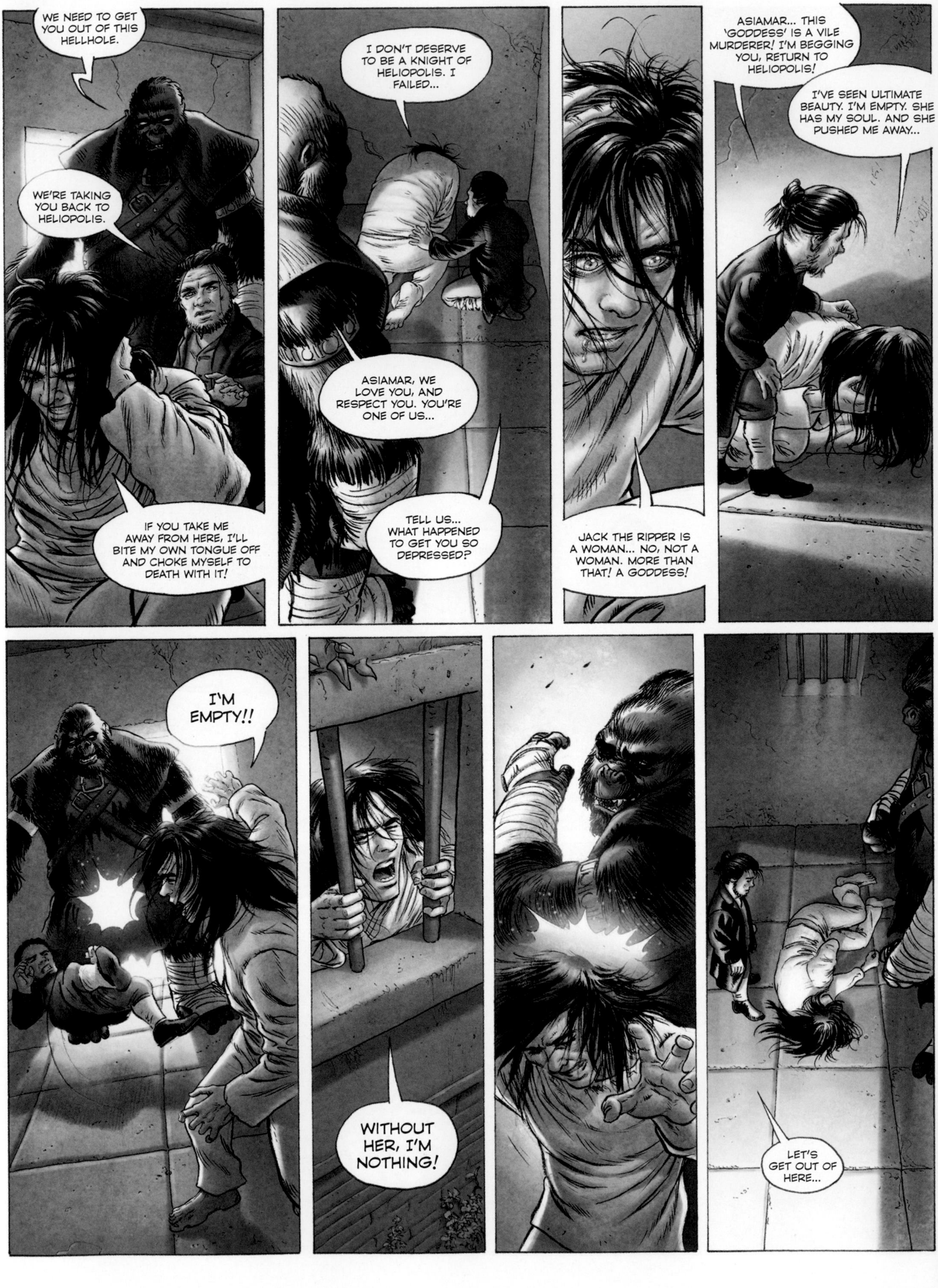
WE NEED TO GET YOU OUT OF THIS HELLHOLE.
WE'RE TAKING YOU BACK TO HELIOPOLIS.
IF YOU TAKE ME AWAY FROM HERE, I'LL BITE MY OWN TONGUE OFF AND CHOKE MYSELF TO DEATH WITH IT!
I DON'T DESERVE TO BE A KNIGHT OF HELIOPOLIS. I FAILED...
ASIAMAR, WE LOVE YOU, AND RESPECT YOU. YOU'RE ONE OF US...
TELL US... WHAT HAPPENED TO GET YOU SO DEPRESSED?
JACK THE RIPPER IS A WOMAN... NO, NOT A WOMAN. MORE THAN THAT! A GODDESS!
ASIAMAR... THIS 'GODDESS' IS A VILE MURDERER! I'M BEGGING YOU, RETURN TO HELIOPOLIS!
I'VE SEEN ULTIMATE BEAUTY. I'M EMPTY. SHE HAS MY SOUL. AND SHE PUSHED ME AWAY...
I'M EMPTY!!
WITHOUT HER, I'M NOTHING!
LET'S GET OUT OF HERE...

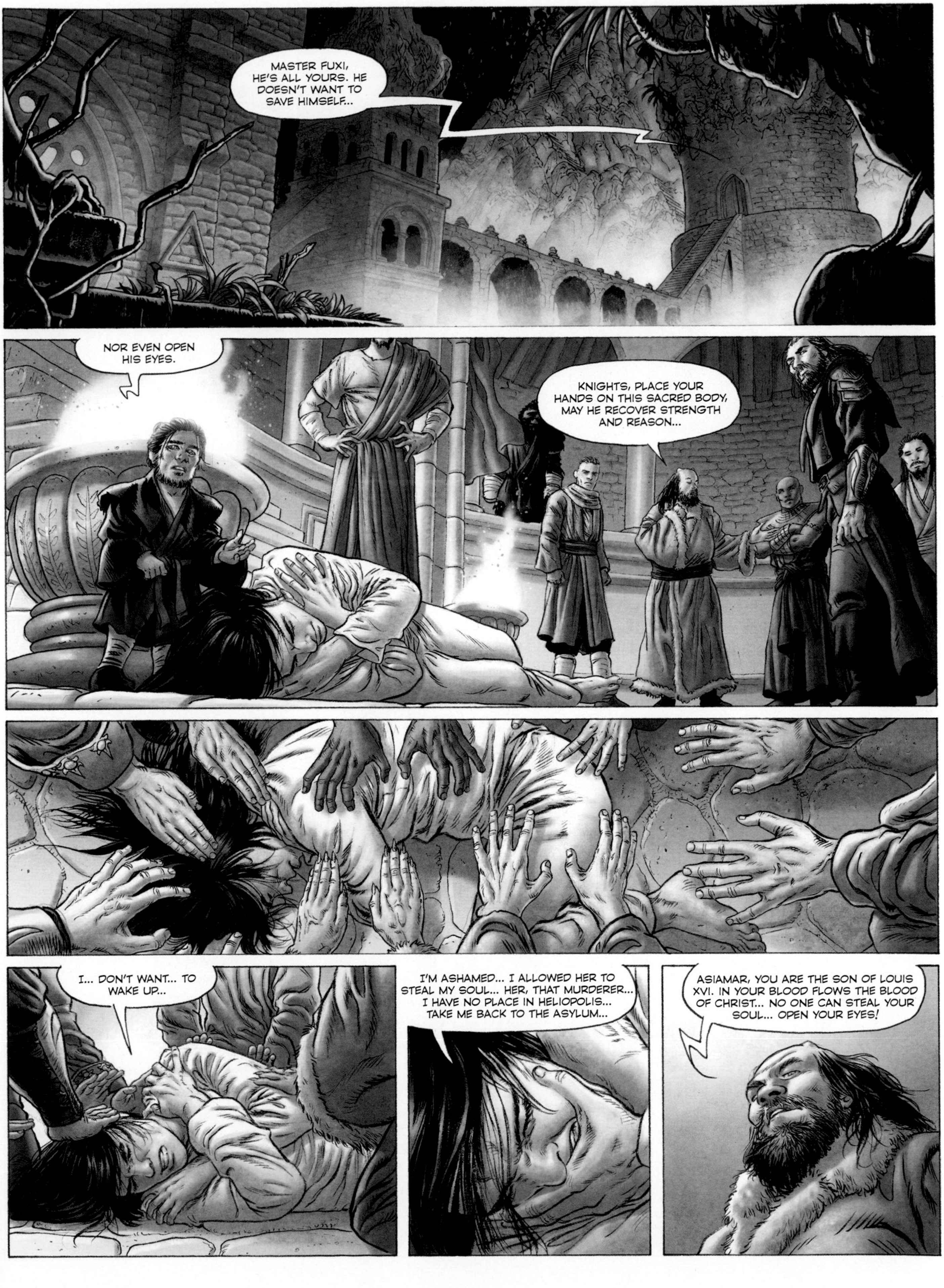
MASTER FUXI, HE'S ALL YOURS. HE DOESN'T WANT TO SAVE HIMSELF...
NOR EVEN OPEN HIS EYES.
KNIGHTS, PLACE YOUR HANDS ON THIS SACRED BODY, MAY HE RECOVER STRENGTH AND REASON...
I... DON'T WANT... TO WAKE UP...
I'M ASHAMED... I ALLOWED HER TO STEAL MY SOUL... HER, THAT MURDERER... I HAVE NO PLACE IN HELIOPOLIS... TAKE ME BACK TO THE ASYLUM...
ASIAMAR, YOU ARE THE SON OF LOUIS XVI. IN YOUR BLOOD FLOWS THE BLOOD OF CHRIST... NO ONE CAN STEAL YOUR SOUL... OPEN YOUR EYES!

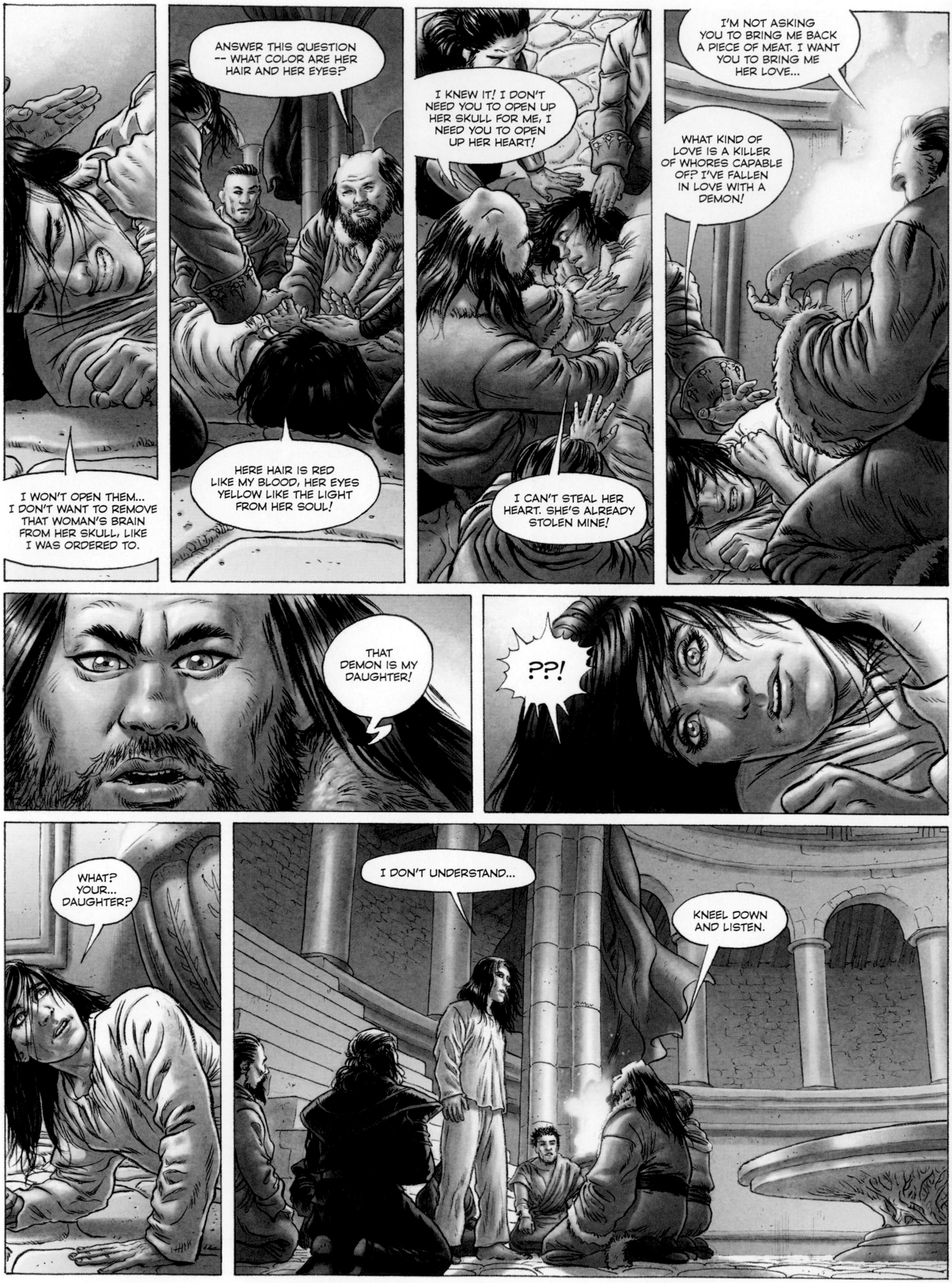

I WON'T OPEN THEM... I DON'T WANT TO REMOVE THAT WOMAN'S BRAIN FROM HER SKULL, LIKE I WAS ORDERED TO.
ANSWER THIS QUESTION -- WHAT COLOR ARE HER HAIR AND HER EYES?
HERE HAIR IS RED LIKE MY BLOOD, HER EYES YELLOW LIKE THE LIGHT FROM HER SOUL!
I KNEW IT! I DON'T NEED YOU TO OPEN UP HER SKULL FOR ME, I NEED YOU TO OPEN UP HER HEART!
I CAN'T STEAL HER HEART. SHE'S ALREADY STOLEN MINE!
I'M NOT ASKING YOU TO BRING ME BACK A PIECE OF MEAT. I WANT YOU TO BRING ME HER LOVE...
WHAT KIND OF LOVE IS A KILLER OF WHORES CAPABLE OF? I'VE FALLEN IN LOVE WITH A DEMON!
THAT DEMON IS MY DAUGHTER!
??!
WHAT? YOUR... DAUGHTER?
I DON'T UNDERSTAND...
KNEEL DOWN AND LISTEN.

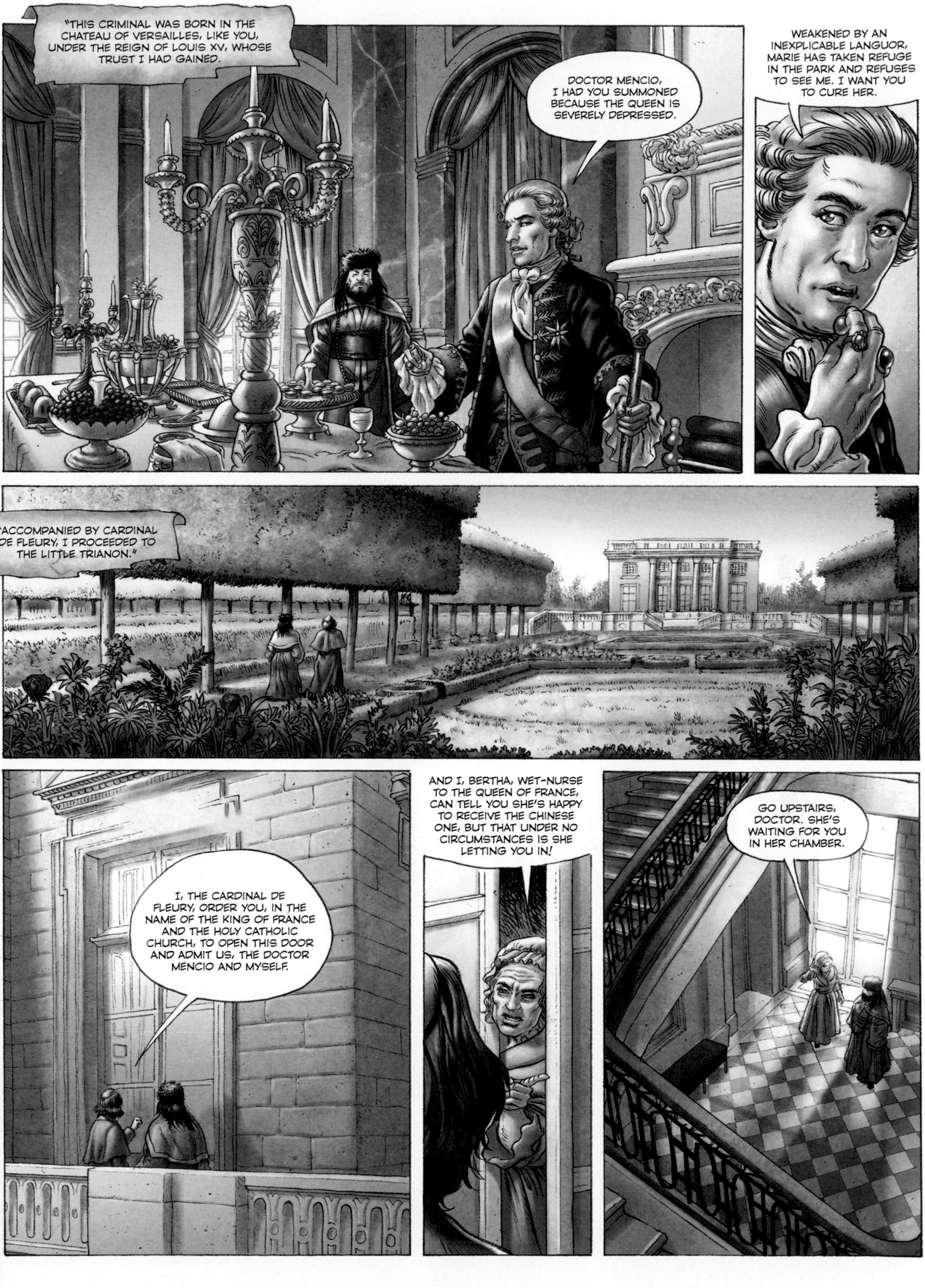
"THIS CRIMINAL WAS BORN IN THE CHATEAU OF VERSAILLES, LIKE YOU, UNDER THE REIGN OF LOUIS XV, WHOSE TRUST I HAD GAINED.
DOCTOR MENCIO, I HAD YOU SUMMONED BECAUSE THE QUEEN IS SEVERELY DEPRESSED.
WEAKENED BY AN INEXPLICABLE LANGUOR, MARIE HAS TAKEN REFUGE IN THE PARK AND REFUSES TO SEE ME. I WANT YOU TO CURE HER.
"ACCOMPANIED BY CARDINAL DE FLEURY, I PROCEEDED TO THE LITTLE TRIANON."
I, THE CARDINAL DE FLEURY, ORDER YOU, IN THE NAME OF THE KING OF FRANCE AND THE HOLY CATHOLIC CHURCH, TO OPEN THIS DOOR AND ADMIT US, THE DOCTOR MENCIO AND MYSELF.
AND I, BERTHA, WET-NURSE TO THE QUEEN OF FRANCE, CAN TELL YOU SHE'S HAPPY TO RECEIVE THE CHINESE ONE, BUT THAT UNDER NO CIRCUMSTANCES IS SHE LETTING YOU IN!
GO UPSTAIRS, DOCTOR. SHE'S WAITING FOR YOU IN HER CHAMBER.

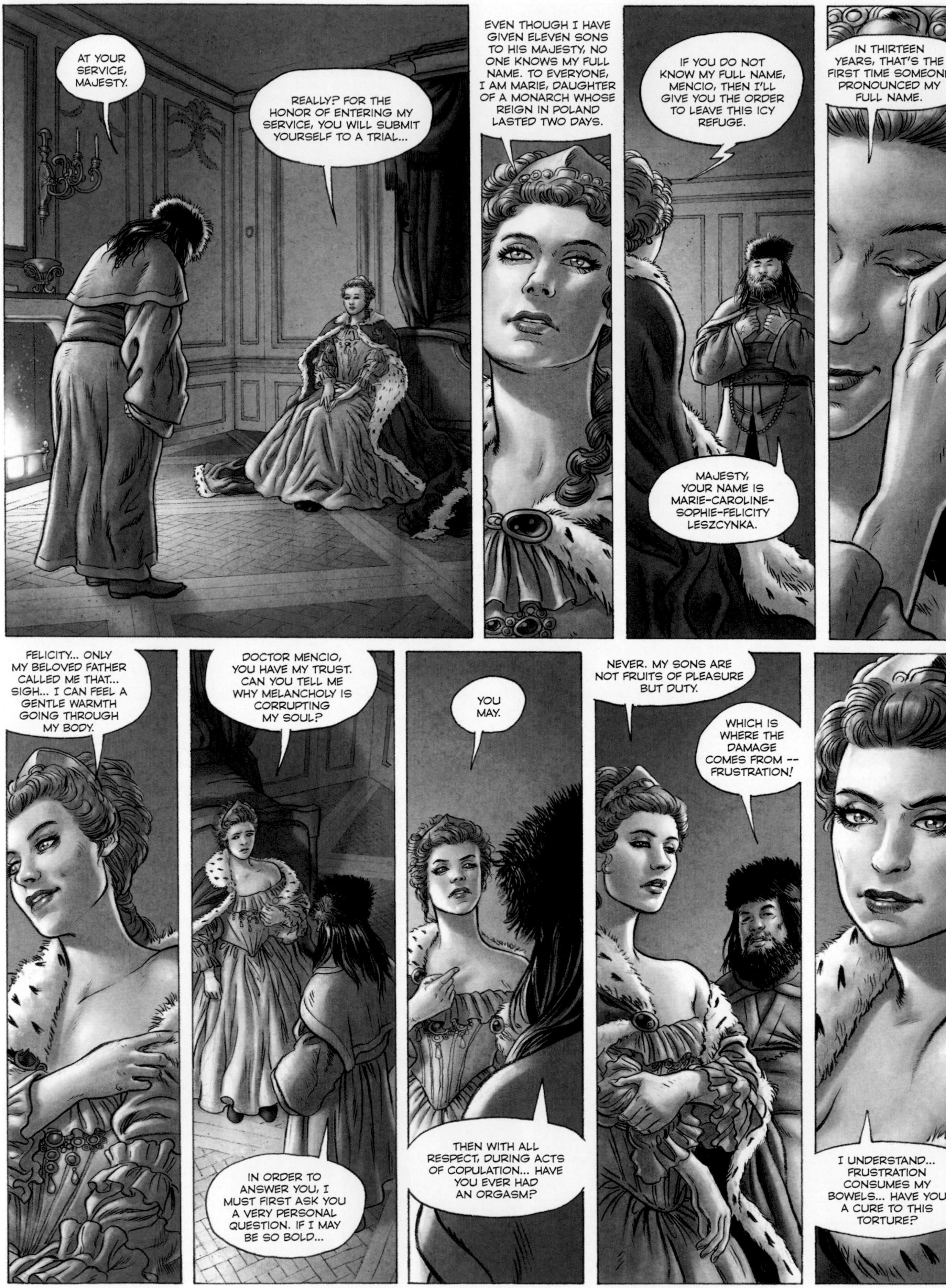
AT YOUR SERVICE, MAJESTY.
REALLY? FOR THE HONOR OF ENTERING MY SERVICE, YOU WILL SUBMIT YOURSELF TO A TRIAL...
EVEN THOUGH I HAVE GIVEN ELEVEN SONS TO HIS MAJESTY, NO ONE KNOWS MY FULL NAME. TO EVERYONE, I AM MARIE, DAUGHTER OF A MONARCH WHOSE REIGN IN POLAND LASTED TWO DAYS.
IF YOU DO NOT KNOW MY FULL NAME, MENCIO, THEN I'LL GIVE YOU THE ORDER TO LEAVE THIS ICY REFUGE.
MAJESTY, YOUR NAME IS MARIE-CAROLINE-SOPHIE-FELICITY LESZCYNKA.
IN THIRTEEN YEARS, THAT'S THE FIRST TIME SOMEONE PRONOUNCED MY FULL NAME.
FELICITY... ONLY MY BELOVED FATHER CALLED ME THAT... SIGH... I CAN FEEL A GENTLE WARMTH GOING THROUGH MY BODY.
DOCTOR MENCIO, YOU HAVE MY TRUST. CAN YOU TELL ME WHY MELANCHOLY IS CORRUPTING MY SOUL?
IN ORDER TO ANSWER YOU, I MUST FIRST ASK YOU A VERY PERSONAL QUESTION. IF I MAY BE SO BOLD...
YOU MAY.
THEN WITH ALL RESPECT, DURING ACTS OF COPULATION... HAVE YOU EVER HAD AN ORGASM?
NEVER. MY SONS ARE NOT FRUITS OF PLEASURE BUT DUTY.
WHICH IS WHERE THE DAMAGE COMES FROM -- FRUSTRATION!
I UNDERSTAND... FRUSTRATION CONSUMES MY BOWELS... HAVE YOU A CURE TO THIS TORTURE?

I HAVE A CURE, BUT I ADMIT THAT IT EMBARRASSES ME...

I ORDER YOU TO CARRY ON! SPEAK!

I AM THE CURE. I HAVE LEARNED, FROM MY SACRED SCIENCE, HOW TO GIVE A WOMAN EVERY ORGASM NECESSARY.

MARIE-CAROLINE-SOPHIE-FELICITY LESZCYNKA, OFFER YOUR BODY TO ME WITHOUT RESISTANCE.

DOCTOR, DO NOT DISAPPOINT ME!

"I DID NOT DISAPPOINT. THE QUEEN ORDERED ME TO VISIT HER EVERY DAY FOR THREE MONTHS... AFTER WHICH SHE INFORMED ME THAT SHE WAS EXPECTANT WITH CHILD.

"NO CLOTHES COULD CONCEAL HER CONDITION. I TOLD THE KING SHE NEEDED REST AND THAT SHE SHOULD STAY CONFINED IN THE TRIANON FOR SEVERAL MONTHS."

IT'S ALREADY COMING OUT, MAJESTY!

KEEP PUSHING WITH ALL YOUR STRENGTH...

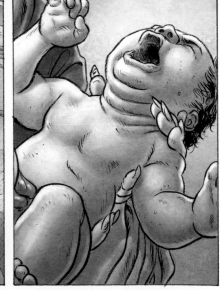

29

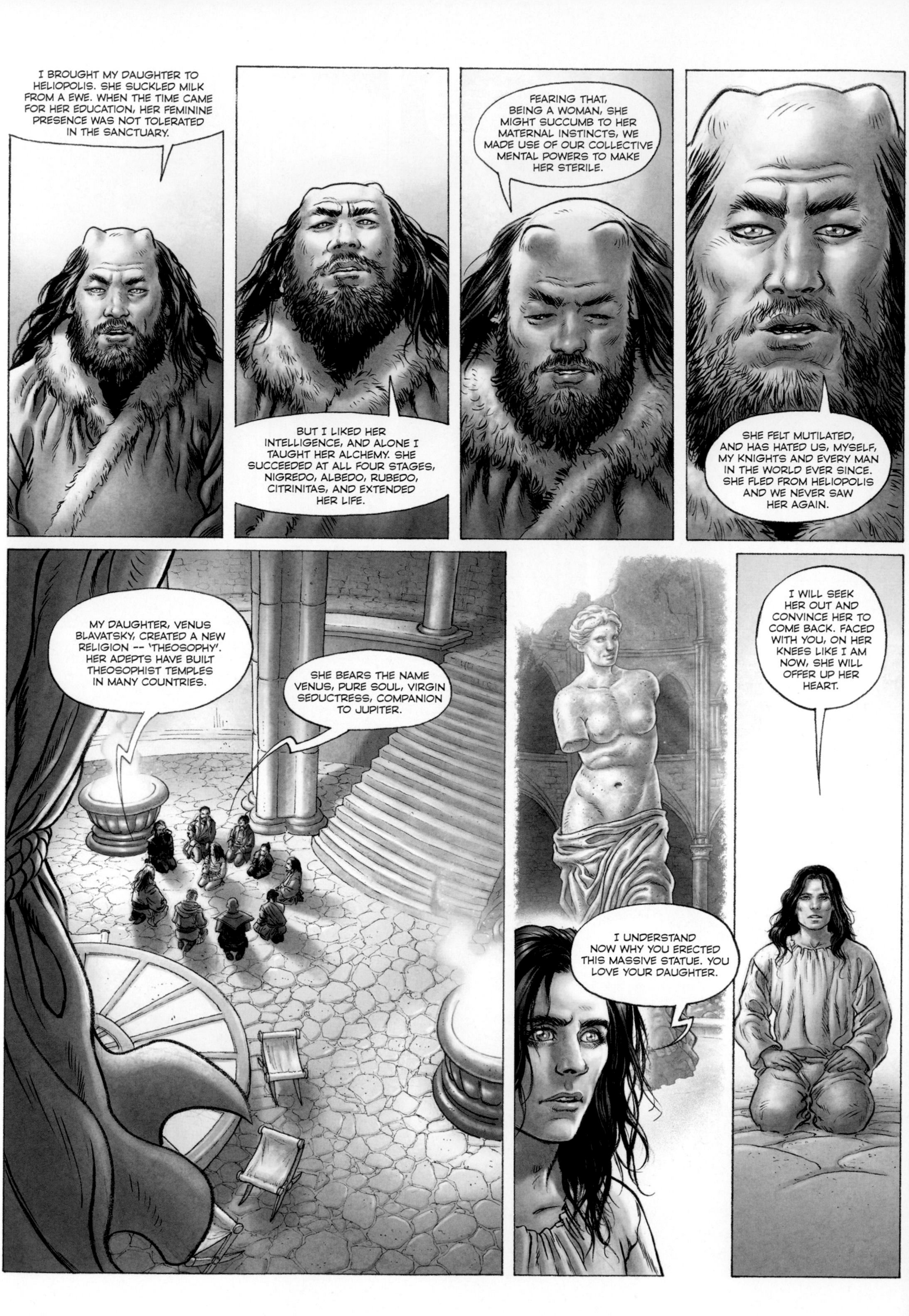
I BROUGHT MY DAUGHTER TO HELIOPOLIS. SHE SUCKLED MILK FROM A EWE. WHEN THE TIME CAME FOR HER EDUCATION, HER FEMININE PRESENCE WAS NOT TOLERATED IN THE SANCTUARY.
BUT I LIKED HER INTELLIGENCE, AND ALONE I TAUGHT HER ALCHEMY. SHE SUCCEEDED AT ALL FOUR STAGES, NIGREDO, ALBEDO, RUBEDO, CITRINITAS, AND EXTENDED HER LIFE.
FEARING THAT, BEING A WOMAN, SHE MIGHT SUCCUMB TO HER MATERNAL INSTINCTS, WE MADE USE OF OUR COLLECTIVE MENTAL POWERS TO MAKE HER STERILE.
SHE FELT MUTILATED, AND HAS HATED US, MYSELF, MY KNIGHTS AND EVERY MAN IN THE WORLD EVER SINCE. SHE FLED FROM HELIOPOLIS AND WE NEVER SAW HER AGAIN.
MY DAUGHTER, VENUS BLAVATSKY, CREATED A NEW RELIGION -- 'THEOSOPHY'. HER ADEPTS HAVE BUILT THEOSOPHIST TEMPLES IN MANY COUNTRIES.
SHE BEARS THE NAME VENUS, PURE SOUL, VIRGIN SEDUCTRESS, COMPANION TO JUPITER.
I UNDERSTAND NOW WHY YOU ERECTED THIS MASSIVE STATUE. YOU LOVE YOUR DAUGHTER.
I WILL SEEK HER OUT AND CONVINCE HER TO COME BACK. FACED WITH YOU, ON HER KNEES LIKE I AM NOW, SHE WILL OFFER UP HER HEART.

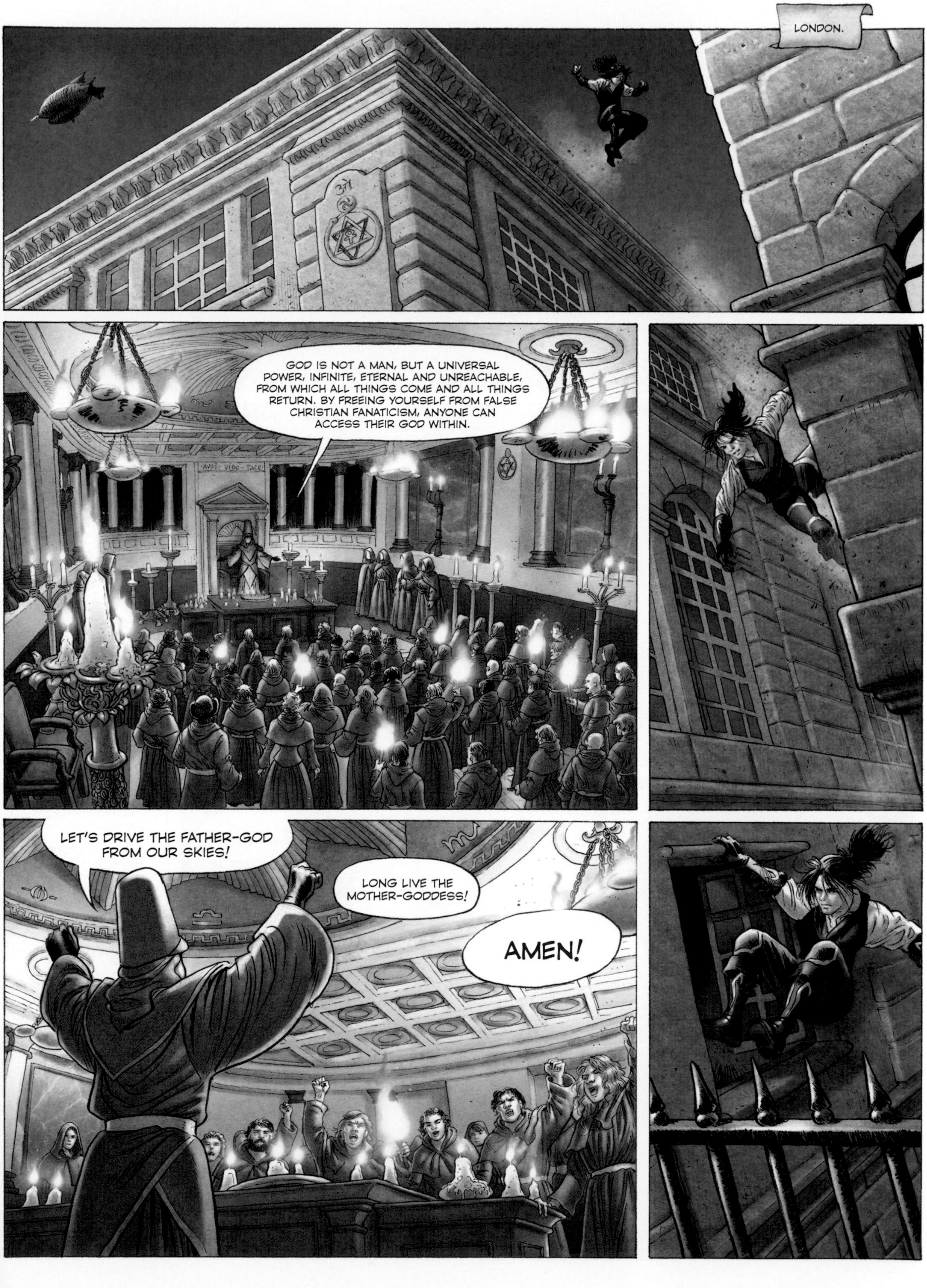
LONDON.
GOD IS NOT A MAN, BUT A UNIVERSAL POWER, INFINITE, ETERNAL AND UNREACHABLE, FROM WHICH ALL THINGS COME AND ALL THINGS RETURN. BY FREEING YOURSELF FROM FALSE CHRISTIAN FANATICISM, ANYONE CAN ACCESS THEIR GOD WITHIN.
LET'S DRIVE THE FATHER-GOD FROM OUR SKIES!
LONG LIVE THE MOTHER-GODDESS!
AMEN!

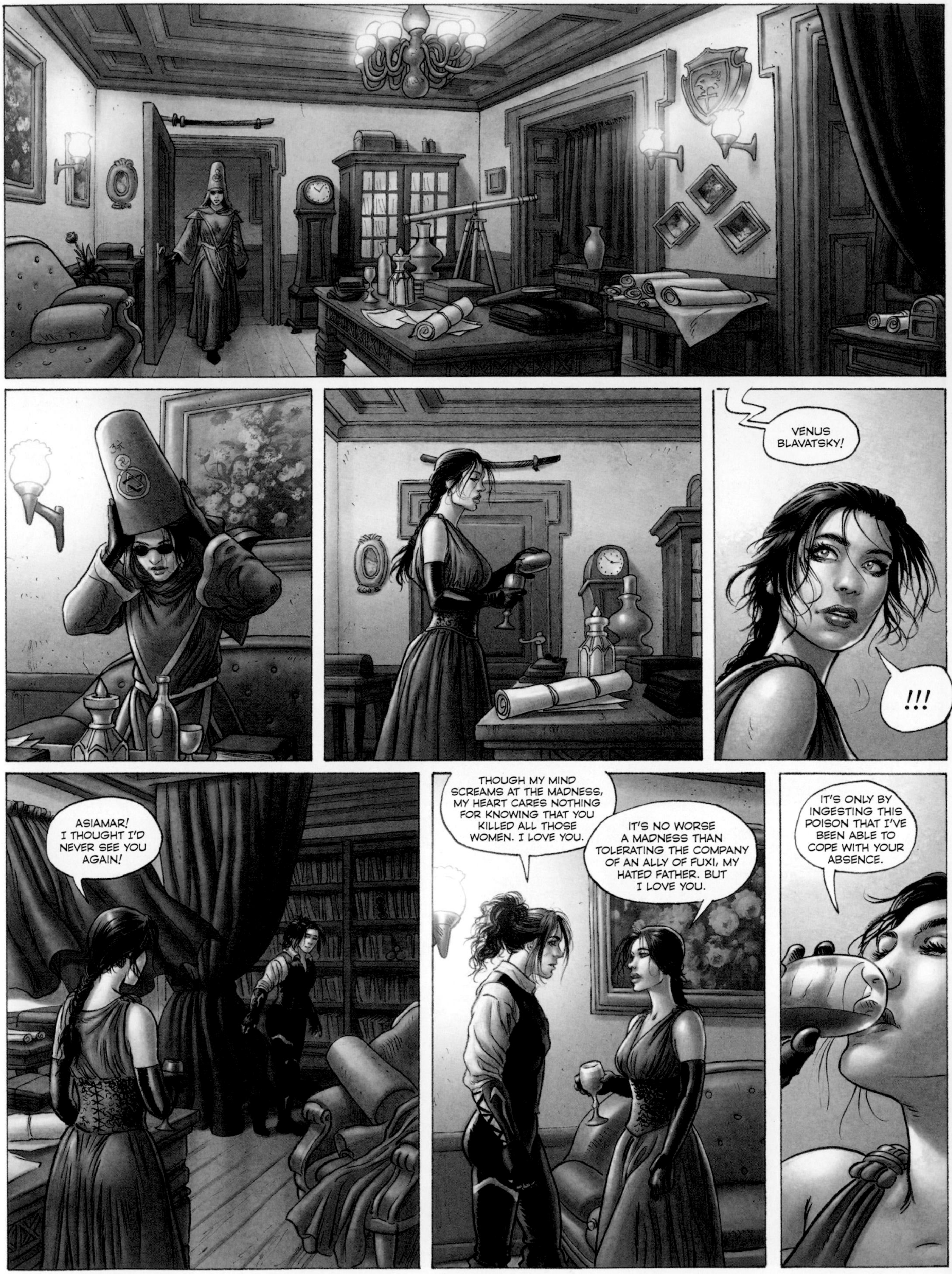
VENUS BLAVATSKY!
!!!
ASIAMAR! I THOUGHT I'D NEVER SEE YOU AGAIN!
THOUGH MY MIND SCREAMS AT THE MADNESS, MY HEART CARES NOTHING FOR KNOWING THAT YOU KILLED ALL THOSE WOMEN. I LOVE YOU.
IT'S NO WORSE A MADNESS THAN TOLERATING THE COMPANY OF AN ALLY OF FUXI, MY HATED FATHER. BUT I LOVE YOU.
IT'S ONLY BY INGESTING THIS POISON THAT I'VE BEEN ABLE TO COPE WITH YOUR ABSENCE.

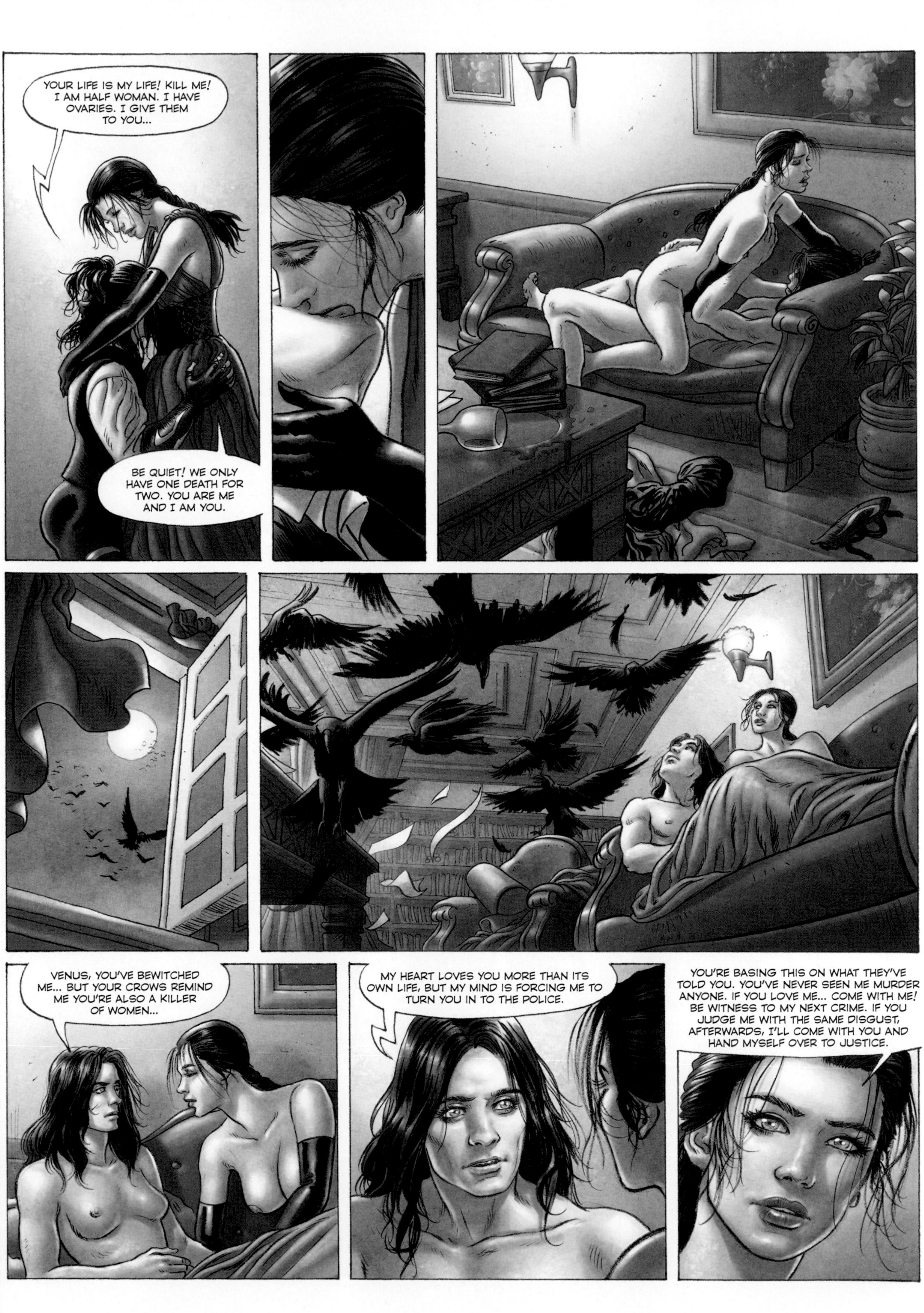
YOUR LIFE IS MY LIFE! KILL ME! I AM HALF WOMAN. I HAVE OVARIES. I GIVE THEM TO YOU...
BE QUIET! WE ONLY HAVE ONE DEATH FOR TWO. YOU ARE ME AND I AM YOU.
VENUS, YOU'VE BEWITCHED ME... BUT YOUR CROWS REMIND ME YOU'RE ALSO A KILLER OF WOMEN...
MY HEART LOVES YOU MORE THAN ITS OWN LIFE, BUT MY MIND IS FORCING ME TO TURN YOU IN TO THE POLICE.
YOU'RE BASING THIS ON WHAT THEY'VE TOLD YOU. YOU'VE NEVER SEEN ME MURDER ANYONE. IF YOU LOVE ME... COME WITH ME! BE WITNESS TO MY NEXT CRIME. IF YOU JUDGE ME WITH THE SAME DISGUST, AFTERWARDS, I'LL COME WITH YOU AND HAND MYSELF OVER TO JUSTICE.

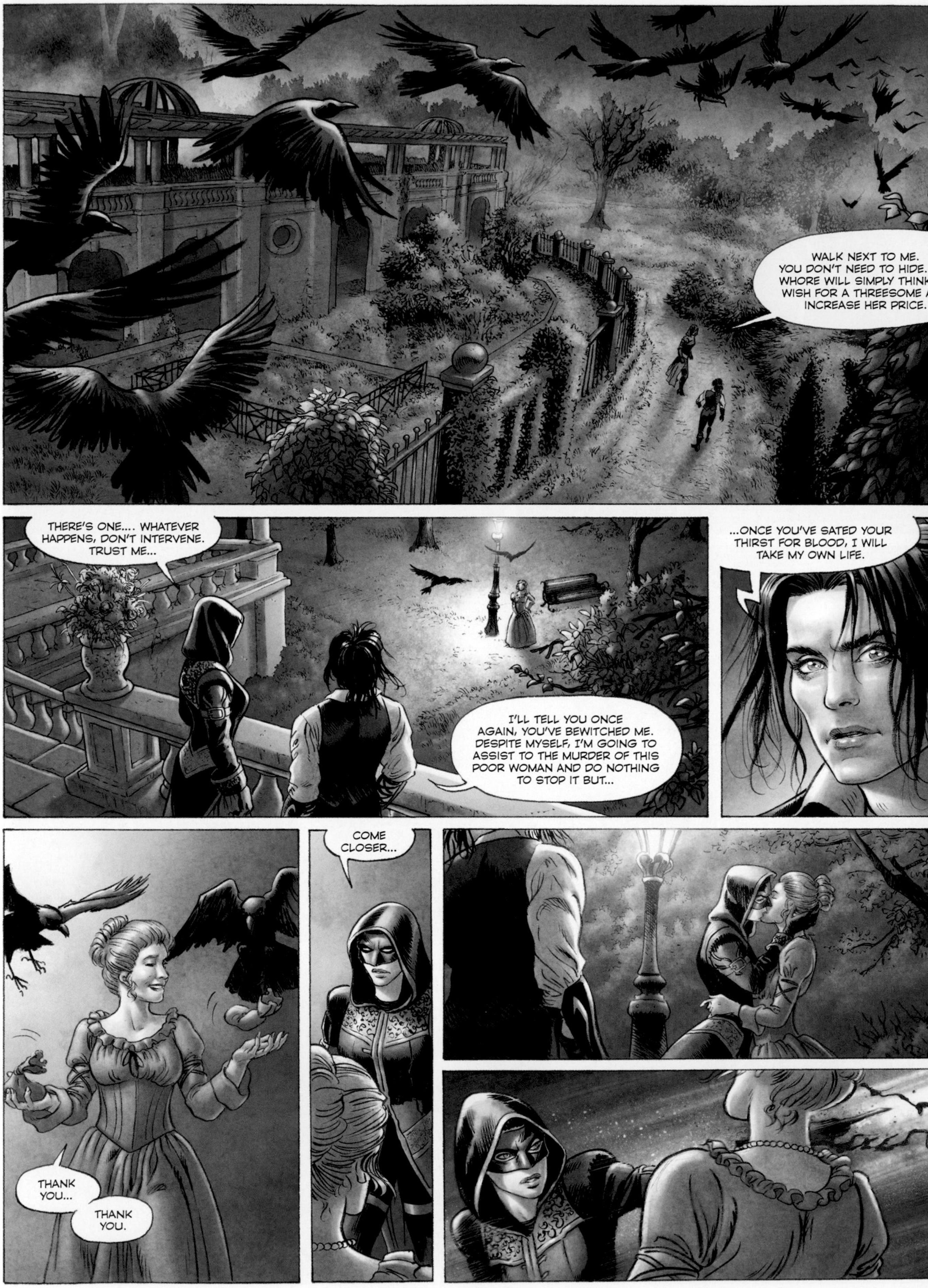

WALK NEXT TO ME. YOU DON'T NEED TO HIDE. THE WHORE WILL SIMPLY THINK WE WISH FOR A THREESOME AND INCREASE HER PRICE.
THERE'S ONE.... WHATEVER HAPPENS, DON'T INTERVENE. TRUST ME...
I'LL TELL YOU ONCE AGAIN, YOU'VE BEWITCHED ME. DESPITE MYSELF, I'M GOING TO ASSIST TO THE MURDER OF THIS POOR WOMAN AND DO NOTHING TO STOP IT BUT...
...ONCE YOU'VE SATED YOUR THIRST FOR BLOOD, I WILL TAKE MY OWN LIFE.
THANK YOU...
THANK YOU.
COME CLOSER...

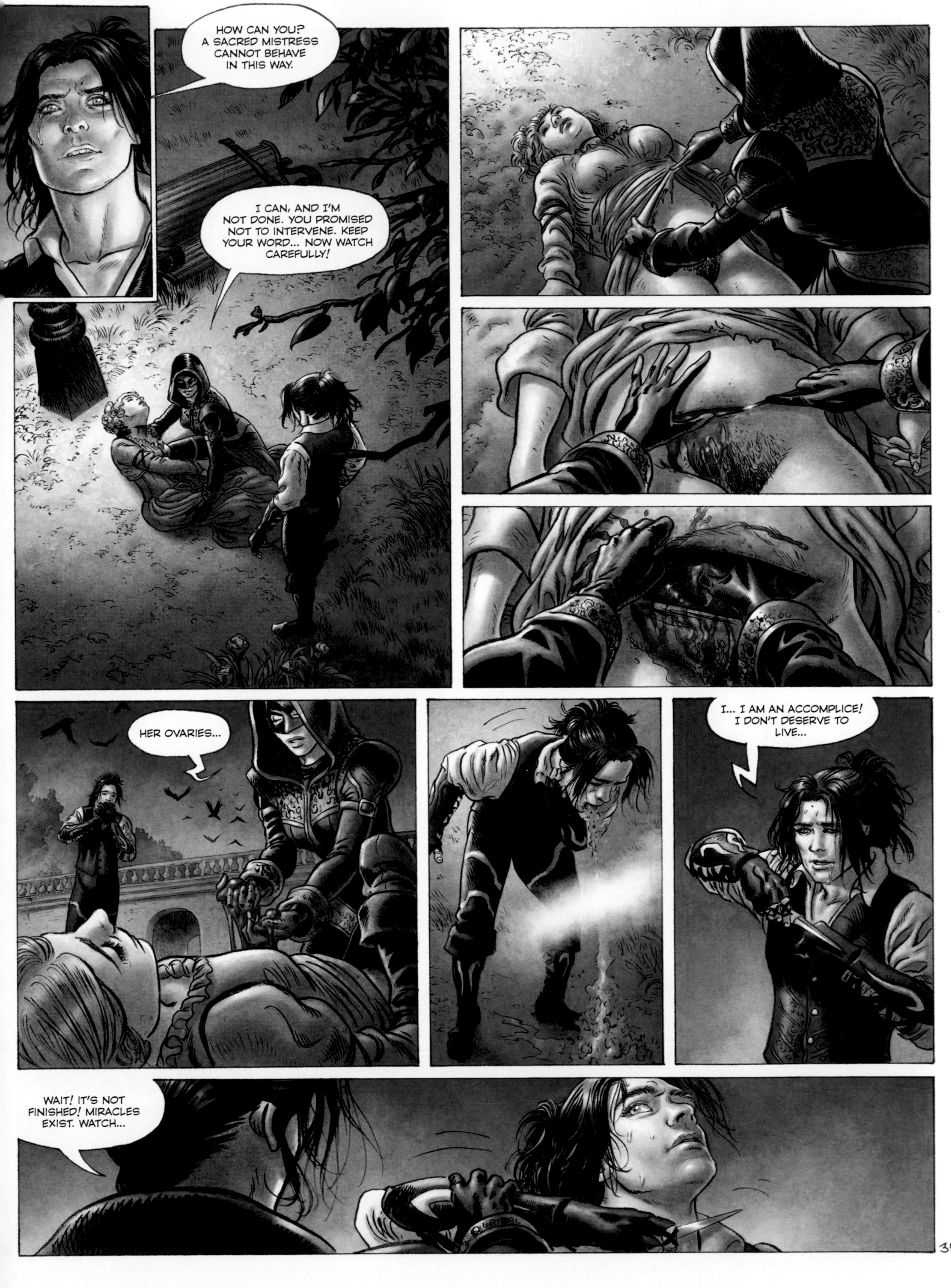

HOW CAN YOU? A SACRED MISTRESS CANNOT BEHAVE IN THIS WAY.
I CAN, AND I'M NOT DONE. YOU PROMISED NOT TO INTERVENE. KEEP YOUR WORD... NOW WATCH CAREFULLY!
HER OVARIES...
I... I AM AN ACCOMPLICE! I DON'T DESERVE TO LIVE...
WAIT! IT'S NOT FINISHED! MIRACLES EXIST. WATCH...

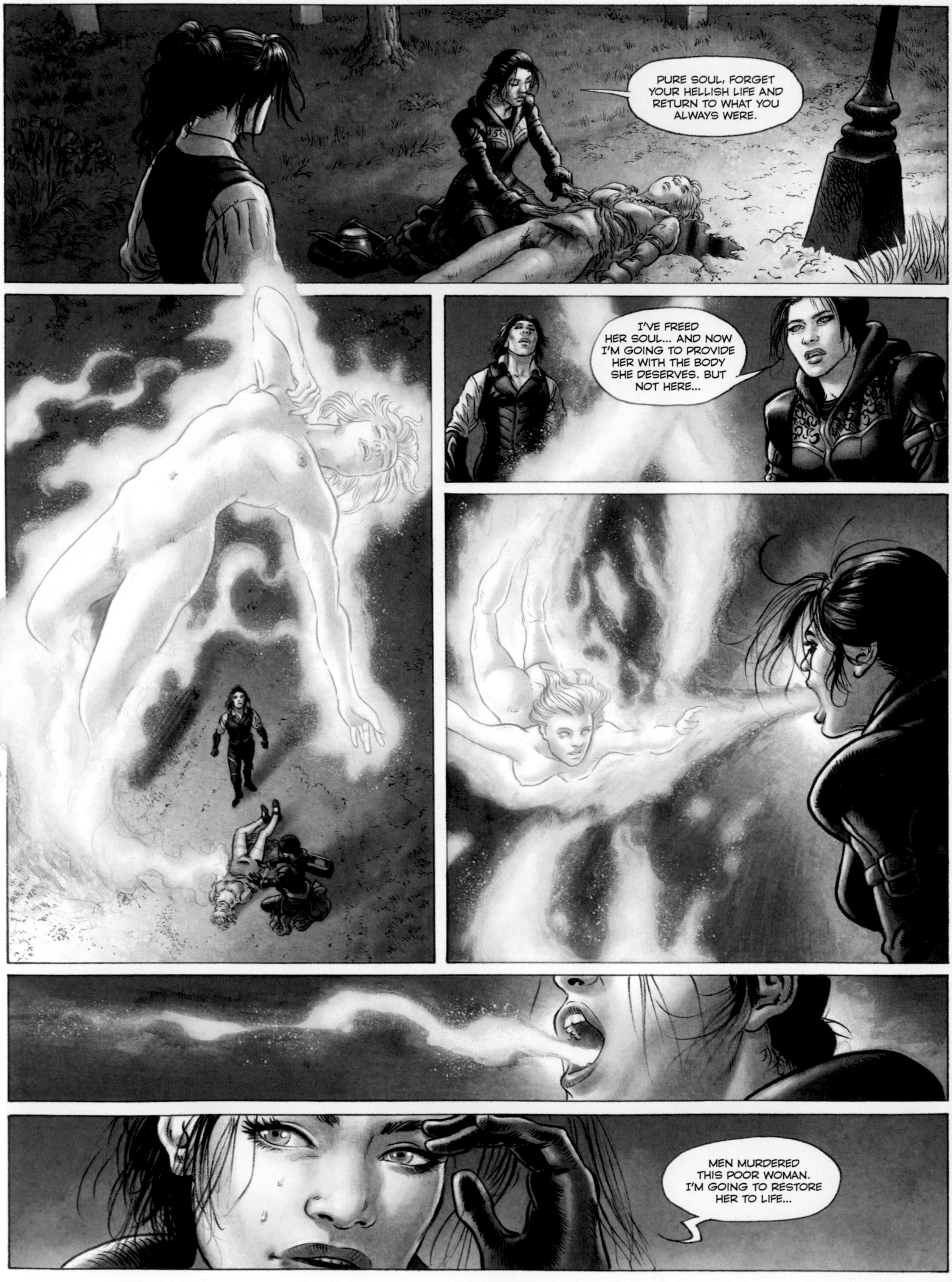

PURE SOUL, FORGET YOUR HELLISH LIFE AND RETURN TO WHAT YOU ALWAYS WERE.
I'VE FREED HER SOUL... AND NOW I'M GOING TO PROVIDE HER WITH THE BODY SHE DESERVES. BUT NOT HERE...
MEN MURDERED THIS POOR WOMAN. I'M GOING TO RESTORE HER TO LIFE...

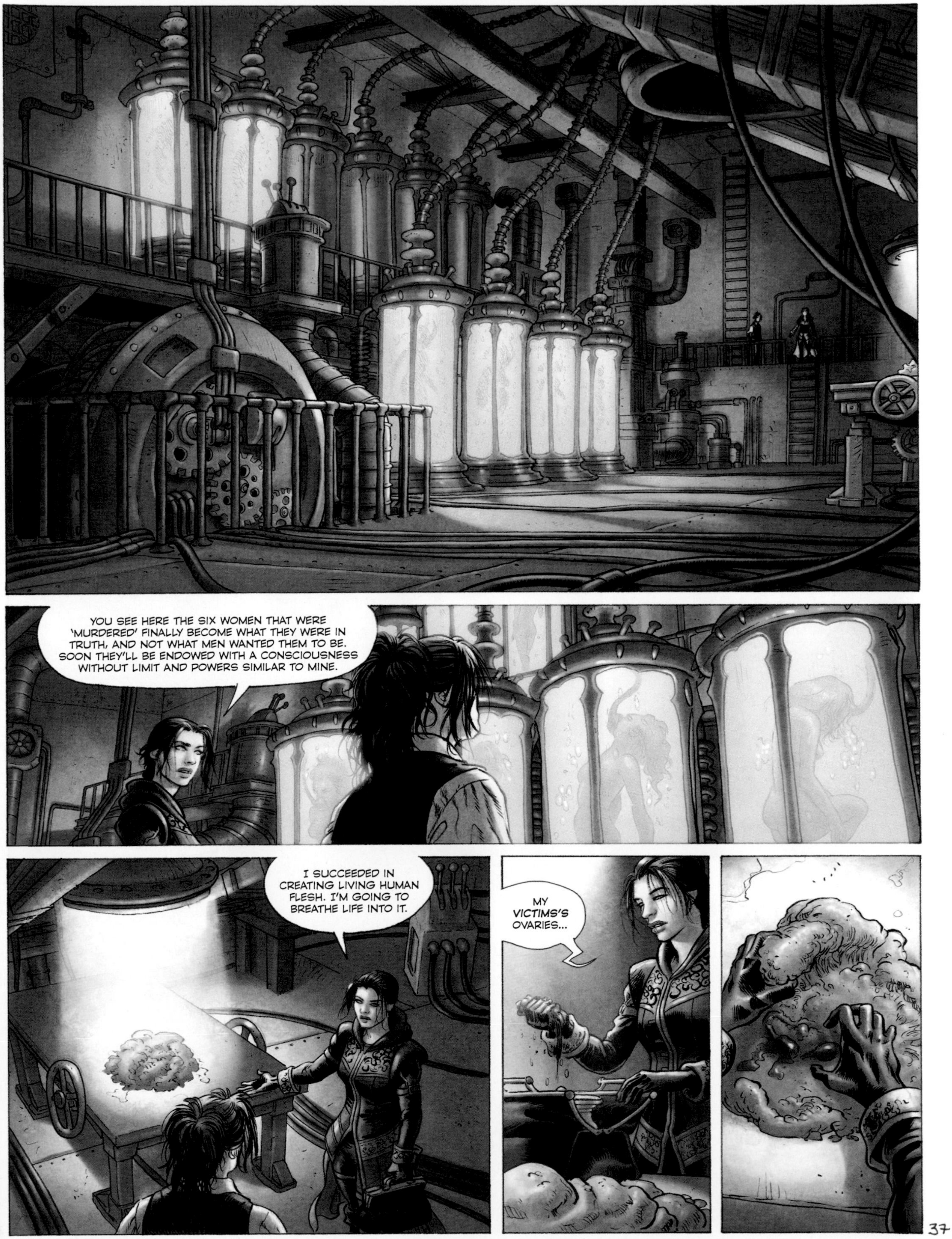
YOU SEE HERE THE SIX WOMEN THAT WERE 'MURDERED' FINALLY BECOME WHAT THEY WERE IN TRUTH, AND NOT WHAT MEN WANTED THEM TO BE. SOON THEY'LL BE ENDOWED WITH A CONSCIOUSNESS WITHOUT LIMIT AND POWERS SIMILAR TO MINE.
I SUCCEEDED IN CREATING LIVING HUMAN FLESH. I'M GOING TO BREATHE LIFE INTO IT.
MY VICTIMS'S OVARIES...

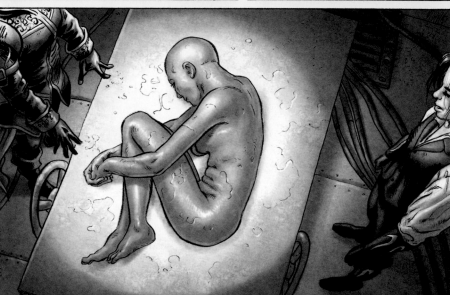

THAT'S THE SEVENTH WHORE I'VE RESURRECTED INTO HER GLORIOUS FORM. I STILL NEED TO KILL THREE MORE, AND BRING THEM BACK TO LIFE.

THREE MORE CRIMES? WHY?

THEY'RE NOT CRIMES BUT GESTATIONS. LISTEN TO ME CAREFULLY, KNIGHT OF HELIOPOLIS.

3

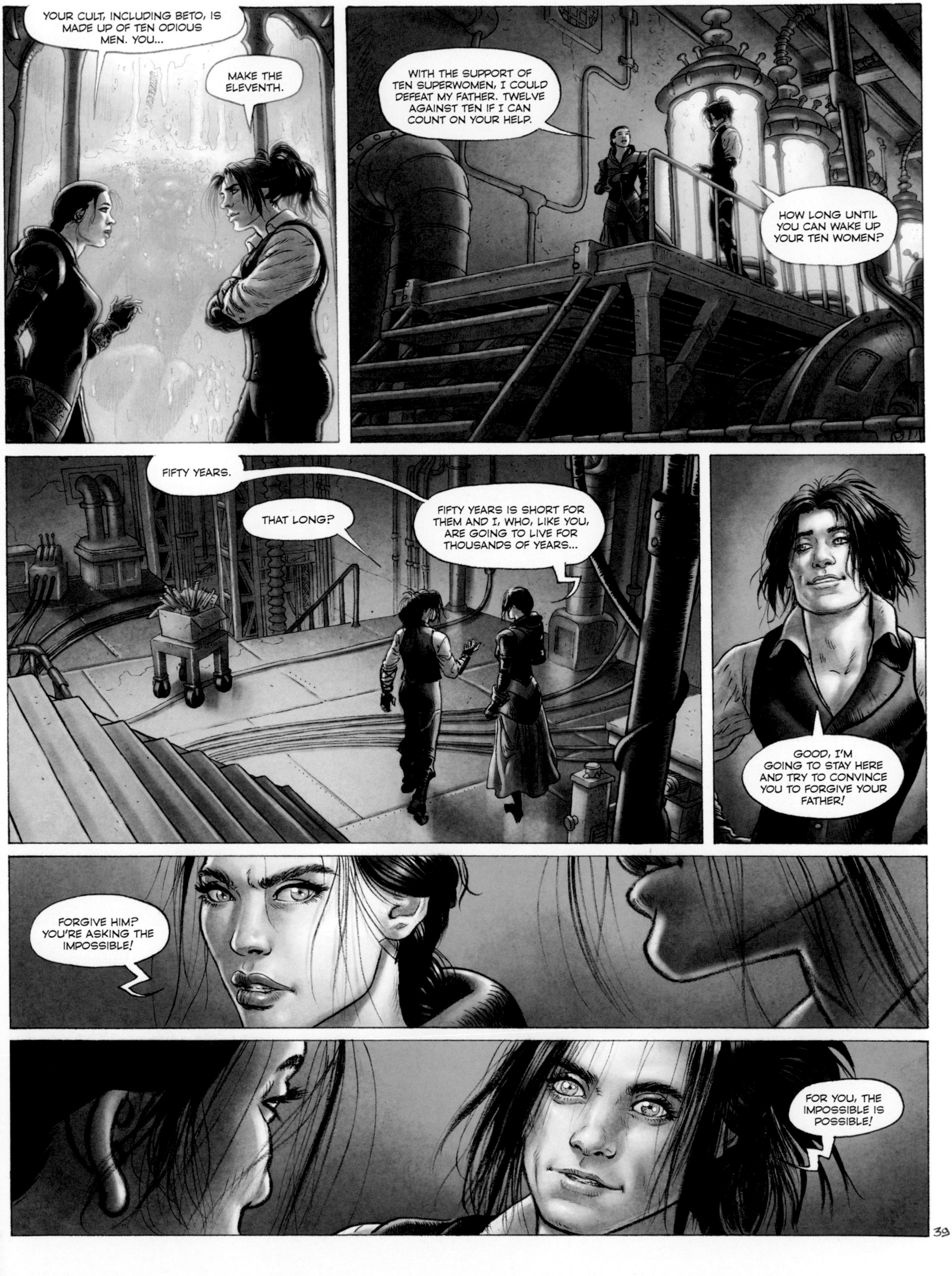
YOUR CULT, INCLUDING BETO, IS MADE UP OF TEN ODIOUS MEN. YOU...
MAKE THE ELEVENTH.
WITH THE SUPPORT OF TEN SUPERWOMEN, I COULD DEFEAT MY FATHER. TWELVE AGAINST TEN IF I CAN COUNT ON YOUR HELP.
HOW LONG UNTIL YOU CAN WAKE UP YOUR TEN WOMEN?
FIFTY YEARS.
THAT LONG?
FIFTY YEARS IS SHORT FOR THEM AND I, WHO, LIKE YOU, ARE GOING TO LIVE FOR THOUSANDS OF YEARS...
GOOD, I'M GOING TO STAY HERE AND TRY TO CONVINCE YOU TO FORGIVE YOUR FATHER!
FORGIVE HIM? YOU'RE ASKING THE IMPOSSIBLE!
FOR YOU, THE IMPOSSIBLE IS POSSIBLE!

LONDON, 1941.

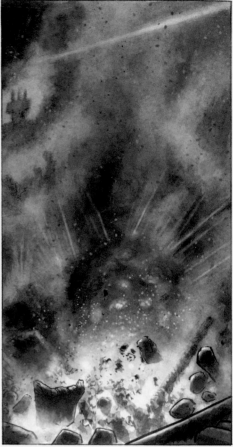

YOU WOKE ME UP, ASIAMAR... WHERE ARE YOU GOING?

AS USUAL THESE DAYS, TO DEAL WITH THE WOUNDED IN THE RUBBLE...

NOT TODAY, THERE'S MORE IMPORTANT THINGS TO DO THAN RESCUING THE DYING -- AND THAT'S HELPING ME. WE HAVE AN IMPORTANT RENDEZVOUS.

THE NAZIS HAVE BOMBED THE CITY EVERY NIGHT FOR TWO MONTHS. TEN OF THOUSANDS DEAD AND HOMES DESTROYED, I MUST...

MY TEN DAUGHTERS AWAKE TODAY, AFTER 50 YEARS OF GESTATION! FORGET THE WOUNDED. YOU'RE COMING WITH ME TO THE LABORATORY!

4

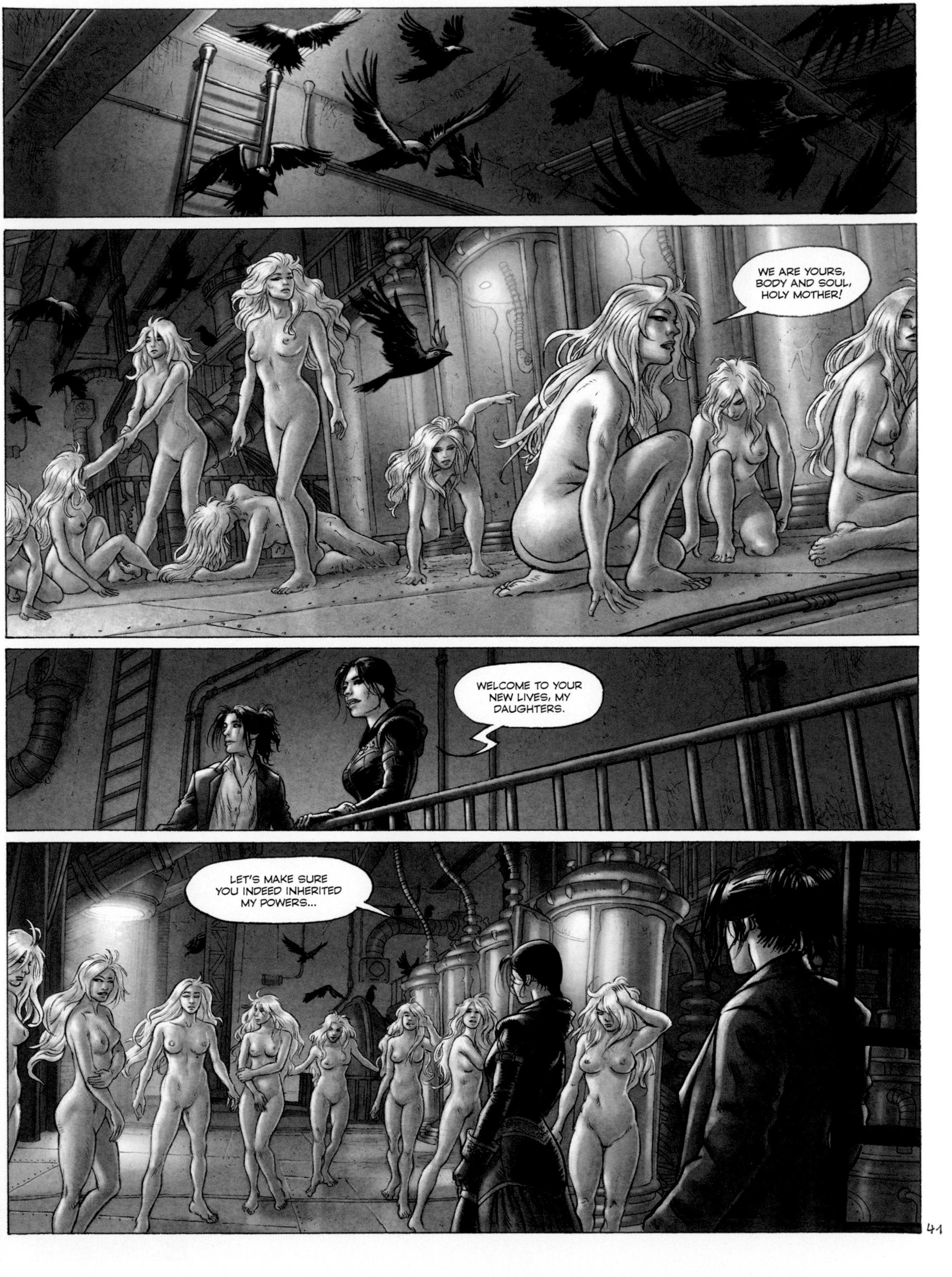
WE ARE YOURS, BODY AND SOUL, HOLY MOTHER!
WELCOME TO YOUR NEW LIVES, MY DAUGHTERS.
LET'S MAKE SURE YOU INDEED INHERITED MY POWERS...

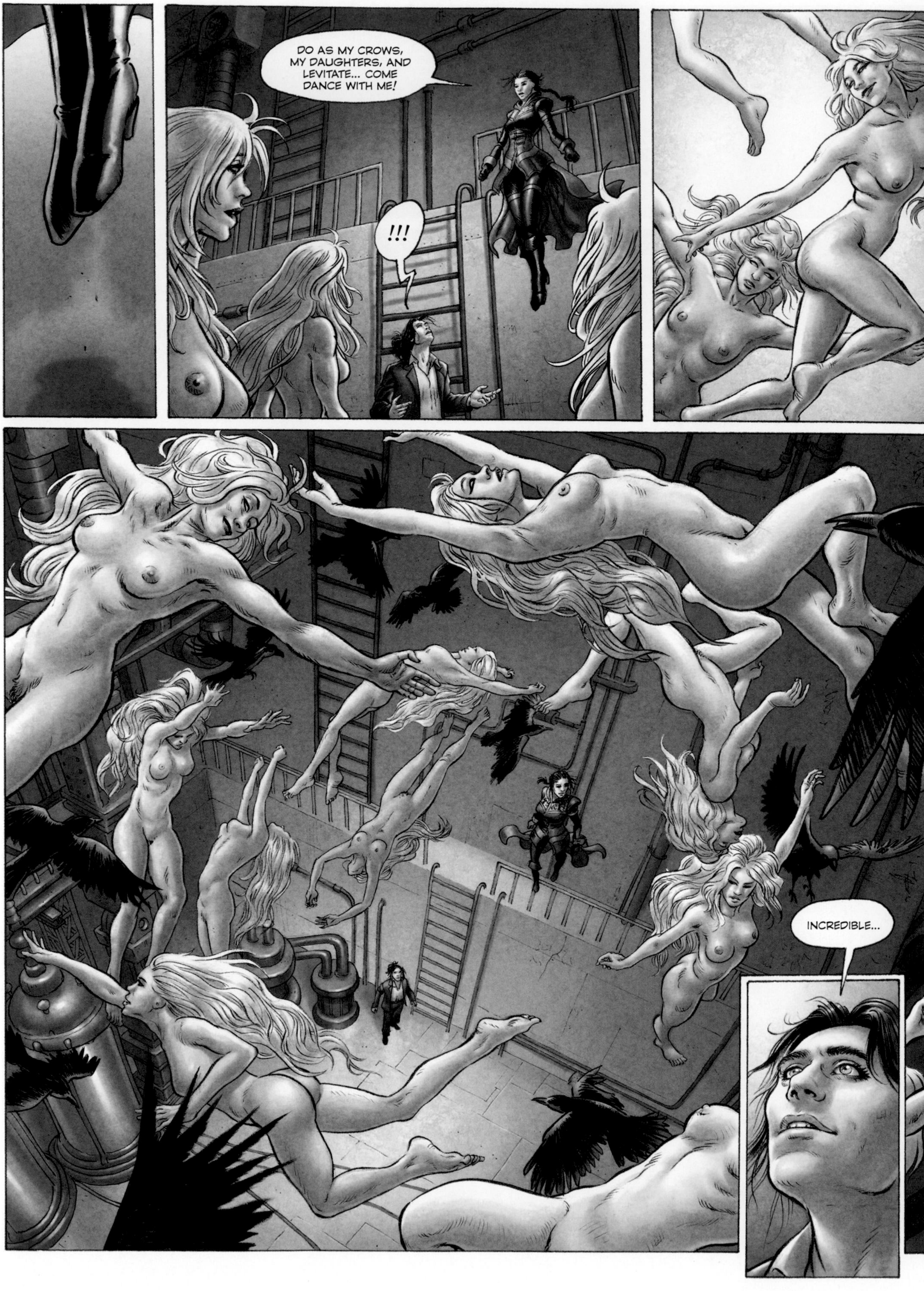
DO AS MY CROWS, MY DAUGHTERS, AND LEVITATE... COME DANCE WITH ME!
!!!
INCREDIBLE...

COME, ASIAMAR!

ERM... I DON'T...

MY LOVE, FOR FIFTY YEARS YOU HAVE DRANK OF MY SALIVA. A PART OF ME FLOWS IN YOU, WITH THE BLOOD IN YOUR VEINS. WHAT I CAN DO, YOU CAN ALSO... COME!

YOU'VE CONVINCED ME. I WILL GO TO HELIOPOLIS. I MUST FACE MY FATHER!

YOU HAVE A GENEROUS SOUL. YOU'LL FORGIVE HIM!

ASIAMAR, I MUST FACE MY FATHER, NOT TO TAKE HIM IN MY ARMS BUT KILL HIM...

LET'S GO!

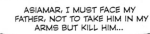

IT'S CERTAIN. YOU POSSESS THE SAME POWERS AS YOUR FATHER...

...BUT HE HAS LIVED MANY MORE LIVES THAN YOU... HE'LL WIN NOT THROUGH STRENGTH BUT THANKS TO HIS VAST EXPERIENCE.

DON'T WORRY. I'VE DEVELOPED MY OWN POTENTIAL, LIKE YOU... I'VE ACQUIRED A POWER HE DOESN'T HAVE.

43

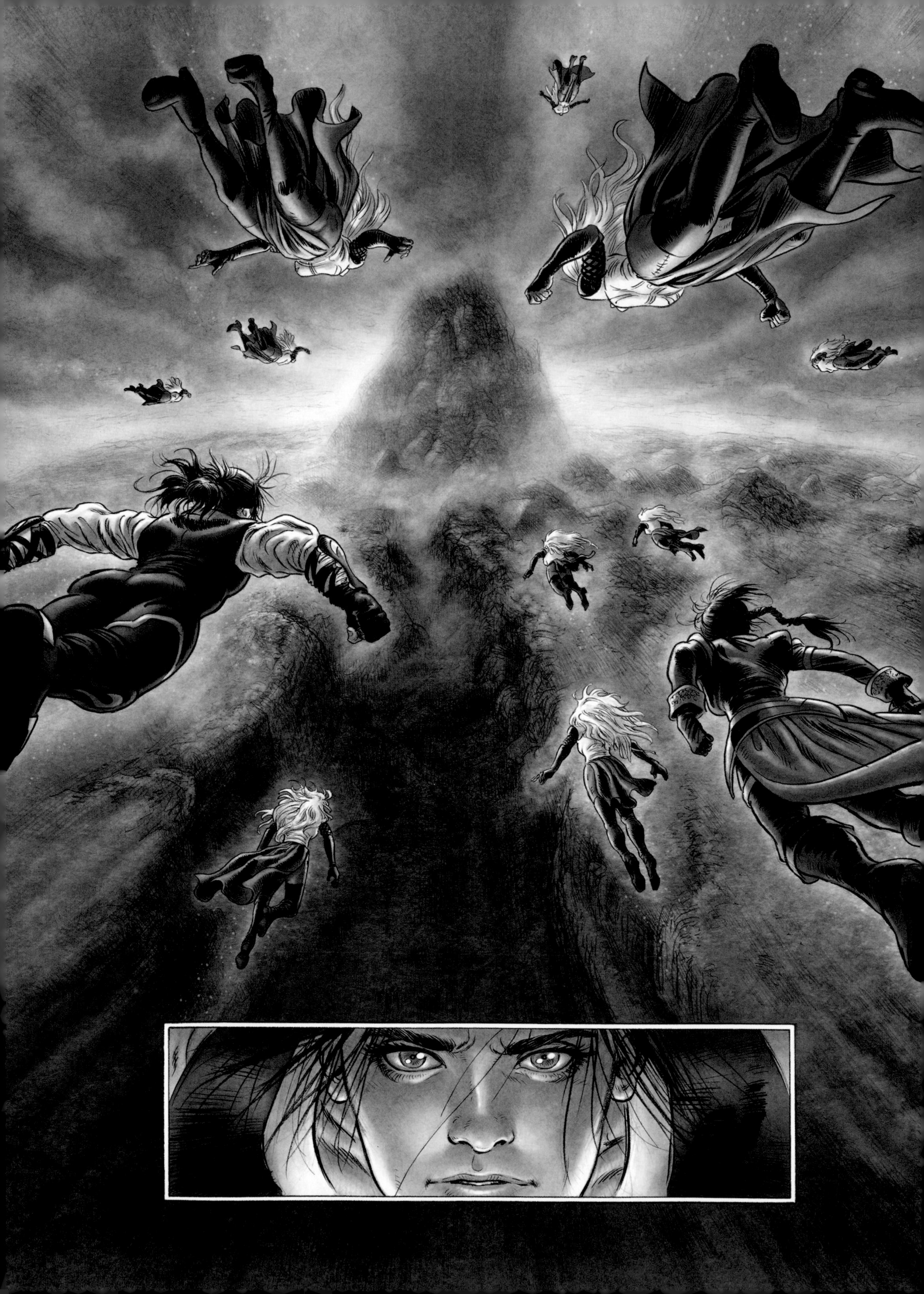

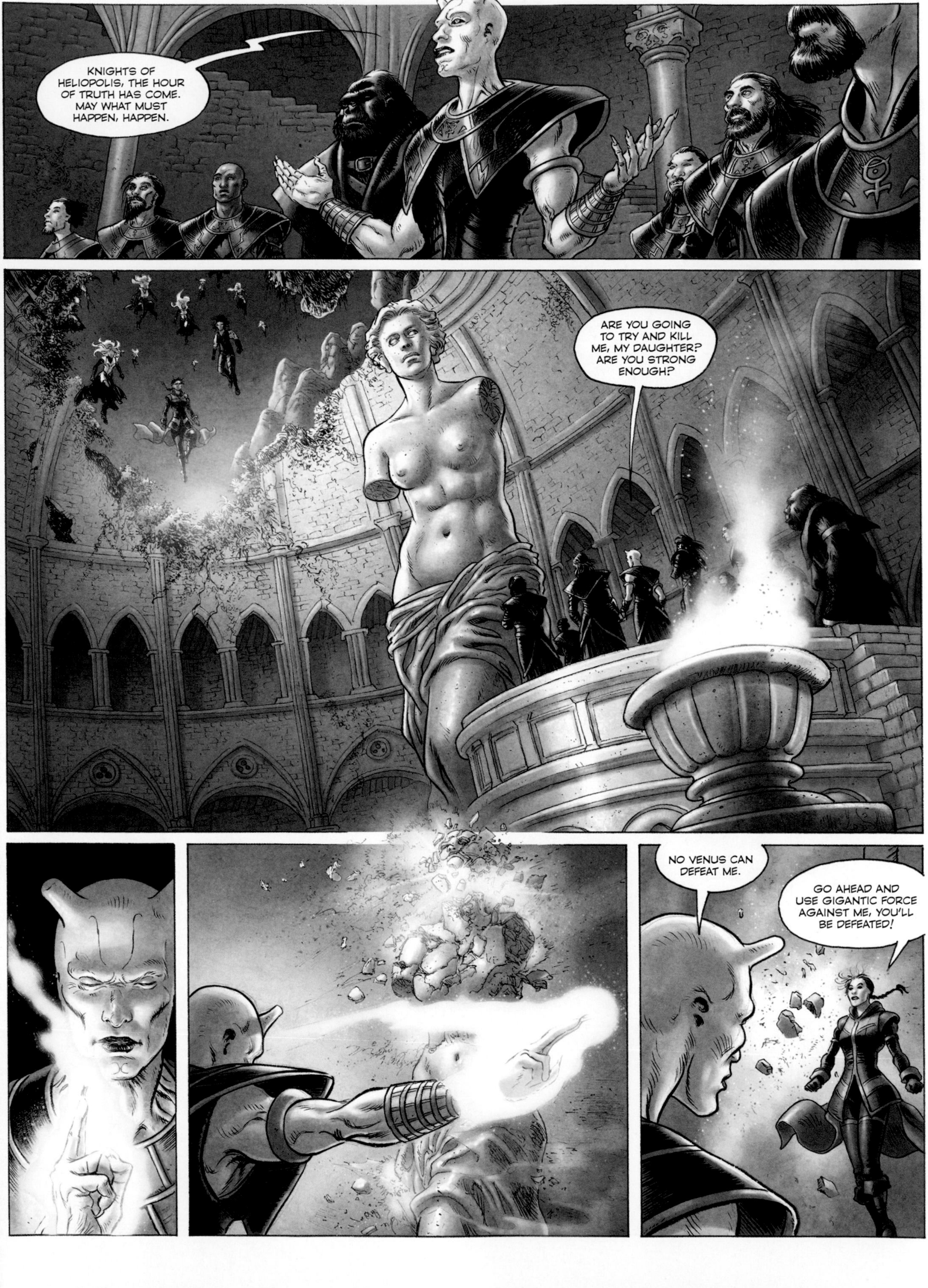
KNIGHTS OF HELIOPOLIS, THE HOUR OF TRUTH HAS COME. MAY WHAT MUST HAPPEN, HAPPEN.
ARE YOU GOING TO TRY AND KILL ME, MY DAUGHTER? ARE YOU STRONG ENOUGH?
NO VENUS CAN DEFEAT ME.
GO AHEAD AND USE GIGANTIC FORCE AGAINST ME, YOU'LL BE DEFEATED!

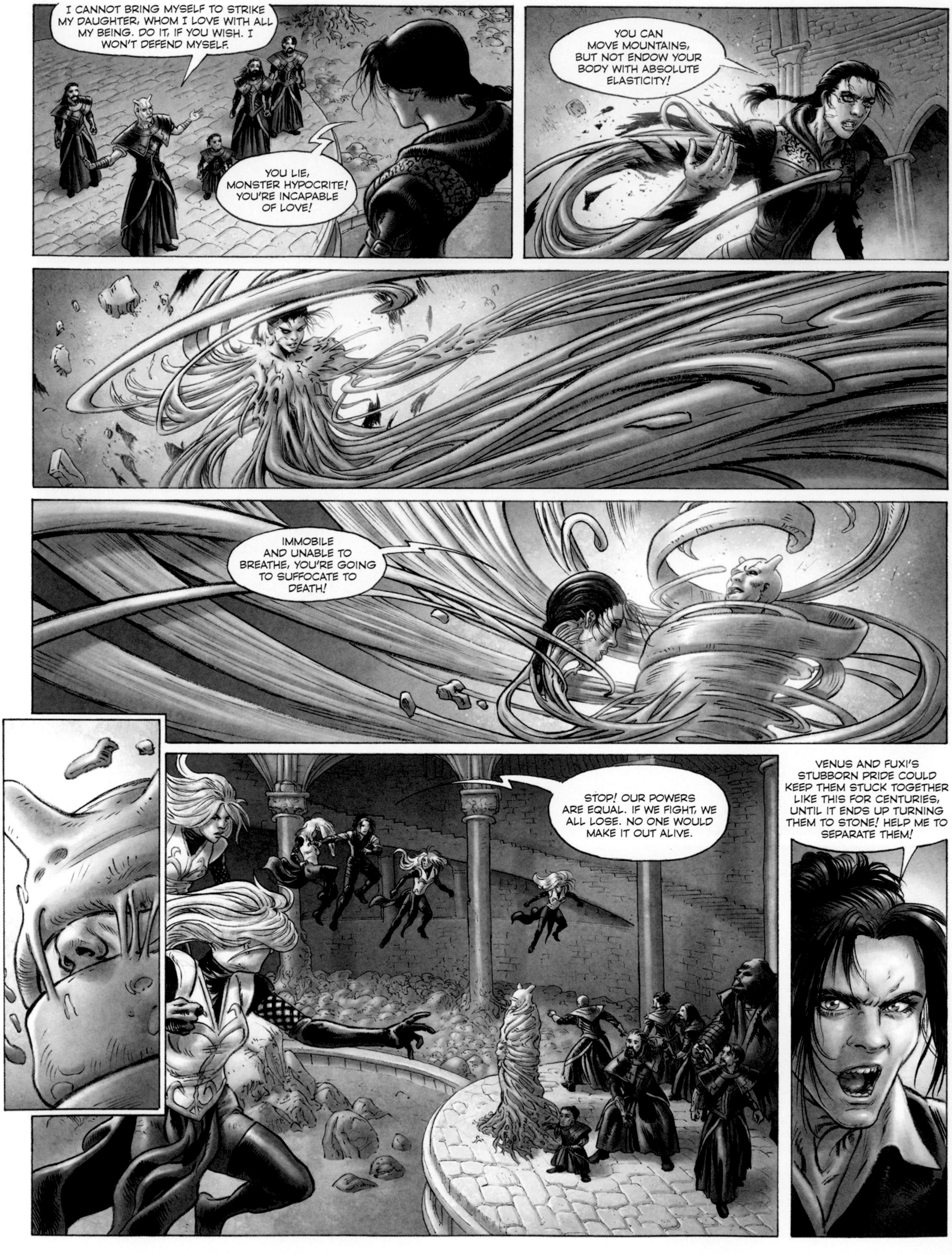
I CANNOT BRING MYSELF TO STRIKE MY DAUGHTER, WHOM I LOVE WITH ALL MY BEING. DO IT, IF YOU WISH. I WON'T DEFEND MYSELF.
YOU LIE, MONSTER HYPOCRITE! YOU'RE INCAPABLE OF LOVE!
YOU CAN MOVE MOUNTAINS, BUT NOT ENDOW YOUR BODY WITH ABSOLUTE ELASTICITY!
IMMOBILE AND UNABLE TO BREATHE, YOU'RE GOING TO SUFFOCATE TO DEATH!
STOP! OUR POWERS ARE EQUAL. IF WE FIGHT, WE ALL LOSE. NO ONE WOULD MAKE IT OUT ALIVE.
VENUS AND FUXI'S STUBBORN PRIDE COULD KEEP THEM STUCK TOGETHER LIKE THIS FOR CENTURIES, UNTIL IT ENDS UP TURNING THEM TO STONE! HELP ME TO SEPARATE THEM!

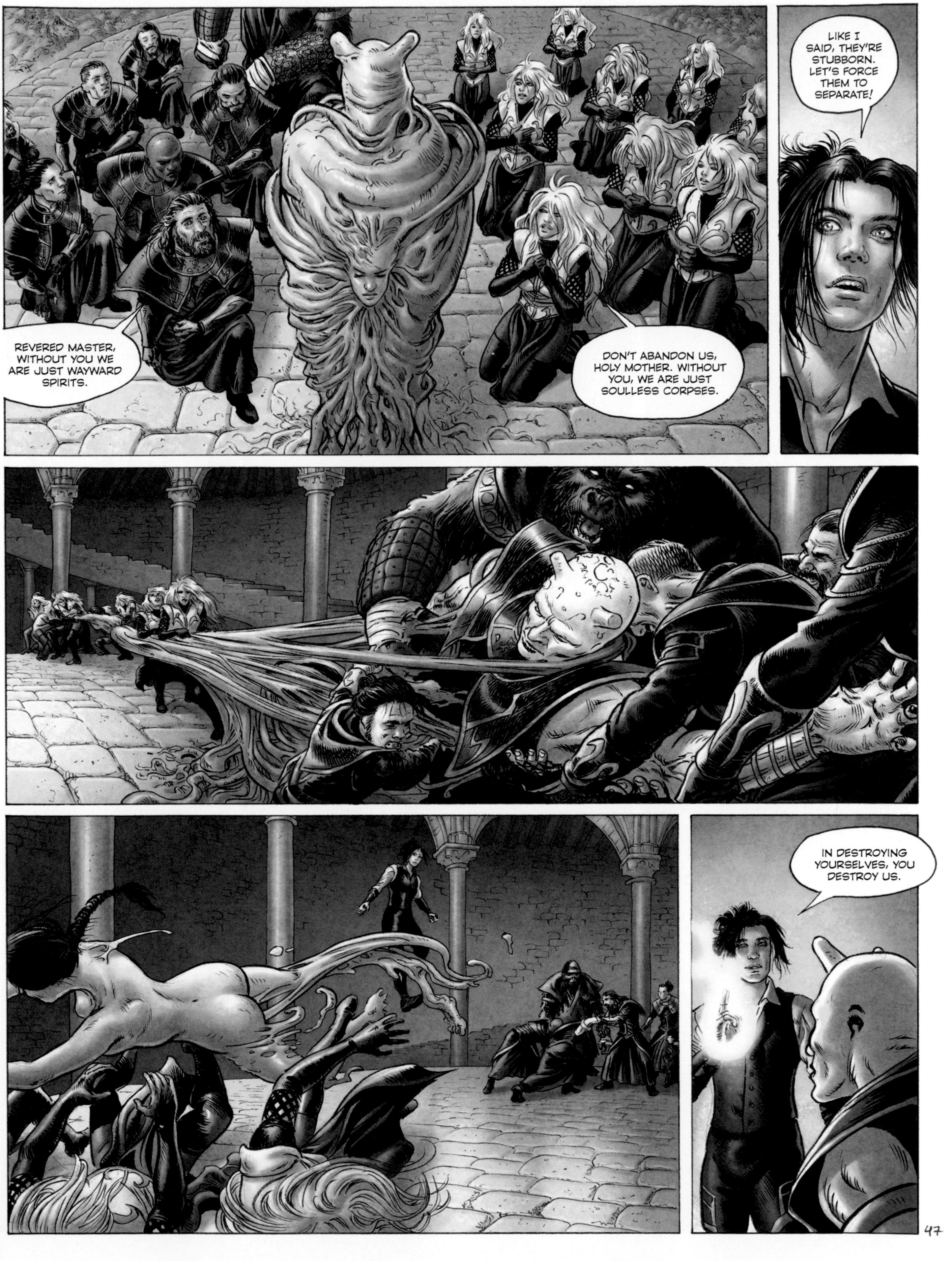
REVERED MASTER, WITHOUT YOU WE ARE JUST WAYWARD SPIRITS.
DON'T ABANDON US, HOLY MOTHER. WITHOUT YOU, WE ARE JUST SOULLESS CORPSES.
LIKE I SAID, THEY'RE STUBBORN. LET'S FORCE THEM TO SEPARATE!
IN DESTROYING YOURSELVES, YOU DESTROY US.

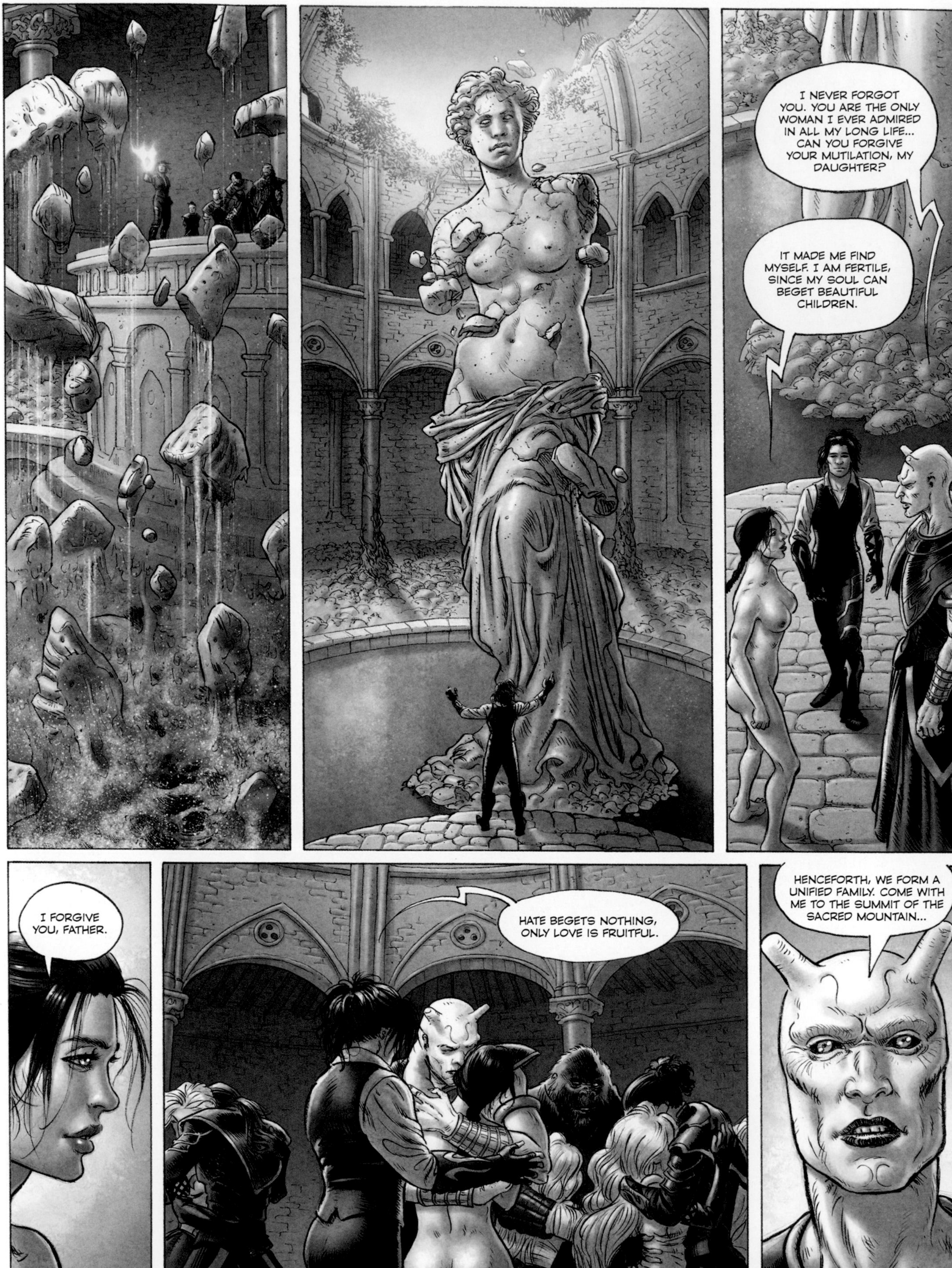
I NEVER FORGOT YOU. YOU ARE THE ONLY WOMAN I EVER ADMIRED IN ALL MY LONG LIFE... CAN YOU FORGIVE YOUR MUTILATION, MY DAUGHTER?
IT MADE ME FIND MYSELF. I AM FERTILE, SINCE MY SOUL CAN BEGET BEAUTIFUL CHILDREN.
I FORGIVE YOU, FATHER.
HATE BEGETS NOTHING, ONLY LOVE IS FRUITFUL.
HENCEFORTH, WE FORM A UNIFIED FAMILY. COME WITH ME TO THE SUMMIT OF THE SACRED MOUNTAIN...

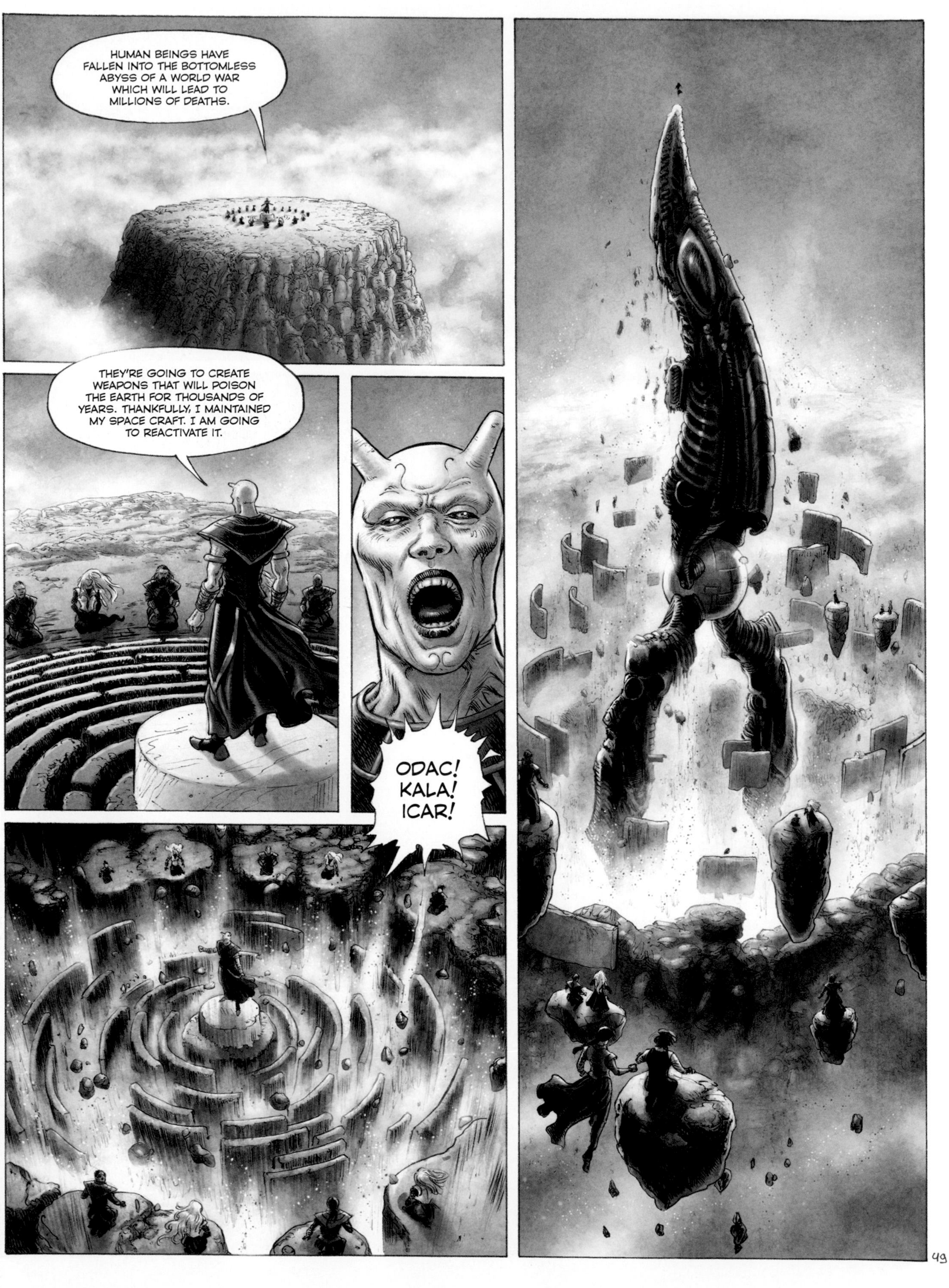
HUMAN BEINGS HAVE FALLEN INTO THE BOTTOMLESS ABYSS OF A WORLD WAR WHICH WILL LEAD TO MILLIONS OF DEATHS.
THEY'RE GOING TO CREATE WEAPONS THAT WILL POISON THE EARTH FOR THOUSANDS OF YEARS. THANKFULLY, I MAINTAINED MY SPACE CRAFT. I AM GOING TO REACTIVATE IT.
ODAC! KALA! ICAR!

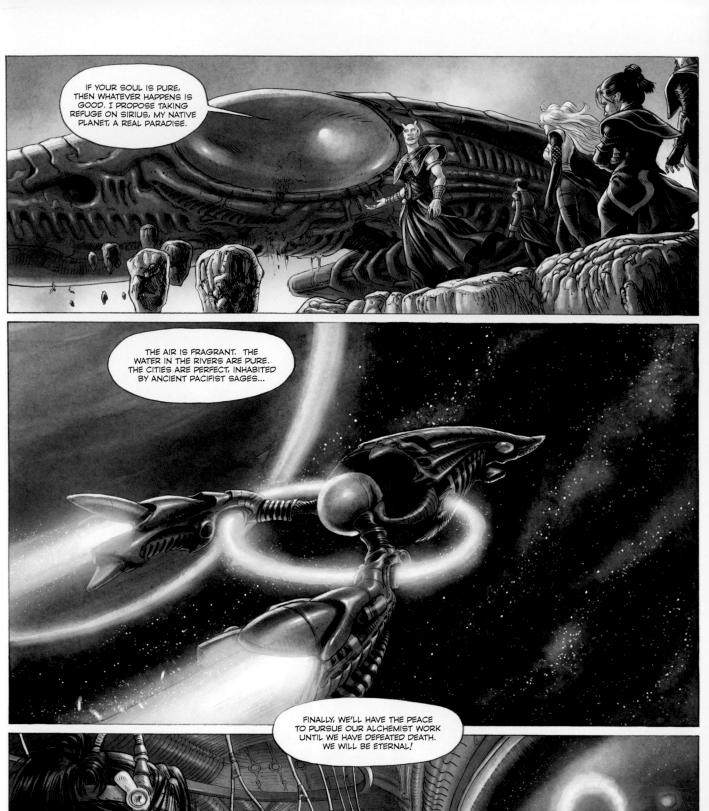

IF YOUR SOUL IS PURE, THEN WHATEVER HAPPENS IS GOOD. I PROPOSE TAKING REFUGE ON SIRIUS, MY NATIVE PLANET, A REAL PARADISE.

THE AIR IS FRAGRANT. THE WATER IN THE RIVERS ARE PURE. THE CITIES ARE PERFECT, INHABITED BY ANCIENT PACIFIST SAGES...

FINALLY, WE'LL HAVE THE PEACE TO PURSUE OUR ALCHEMIST WORK UNTIL WE HAVE DEFEATED DEATH. WE WILL BE ETERNAL!

THAT'S THE MASSIVE SUN AROUND WHICH SIRIUS SPINS.

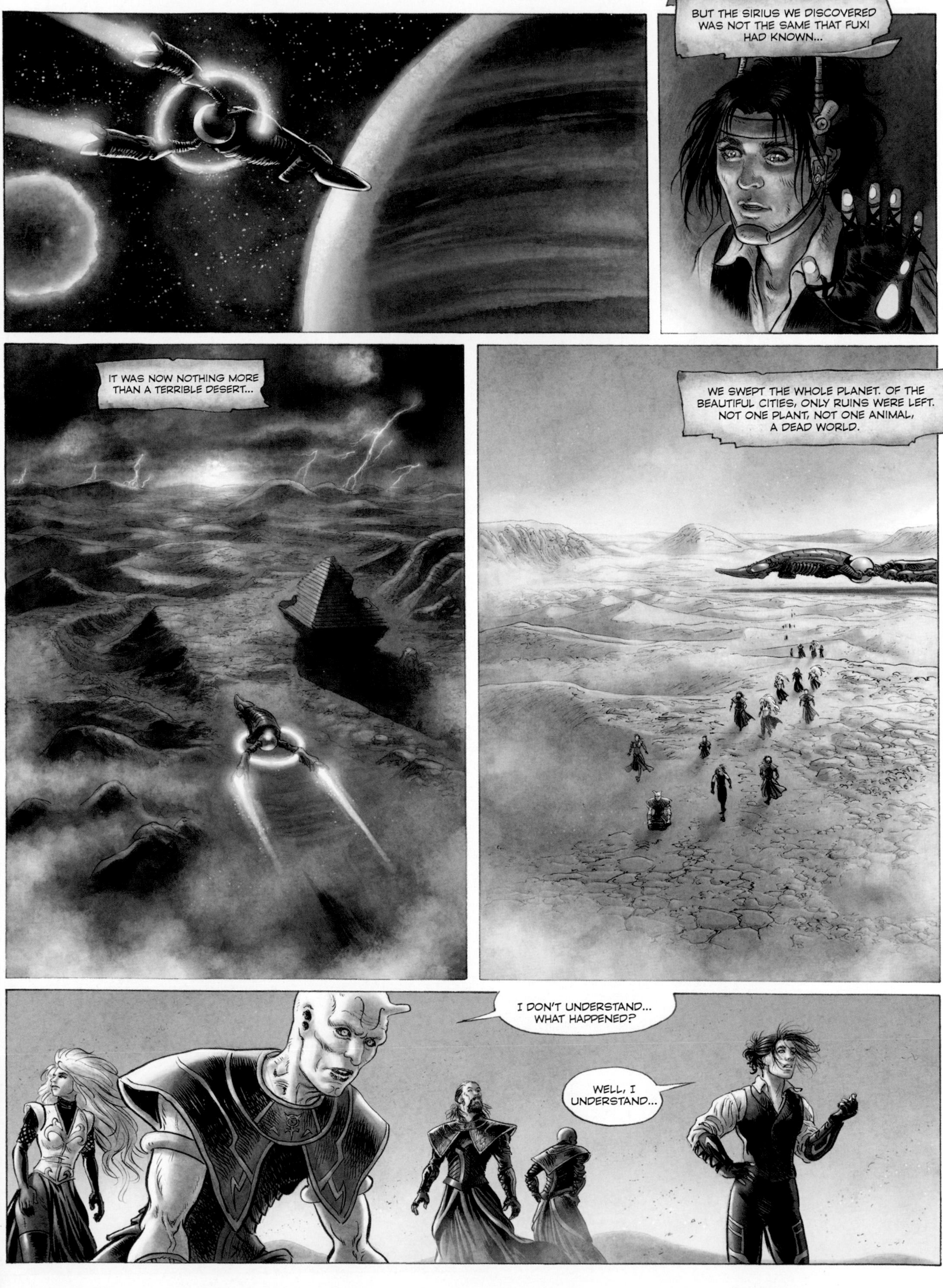
BUT THE SIRIUS WE DISCOVERED WAS NOT THE SAME THAT FUXI HAD KNOWN...
IT WAS NOW NOTHING MORE THAN A TERRIBLE DESERT...
WE SWEPT THE WHOLE PLANET. OF THE BEAUTIFUL CITIES, ONLY RUINS WERE LEFT. NOT ONE PLANT, NOT ONE ANIMAL, A DEAD WORLD.
I DON'T UNDERSTAND... WHAT HAPPENED?
WELL, I UNDERSTAND...

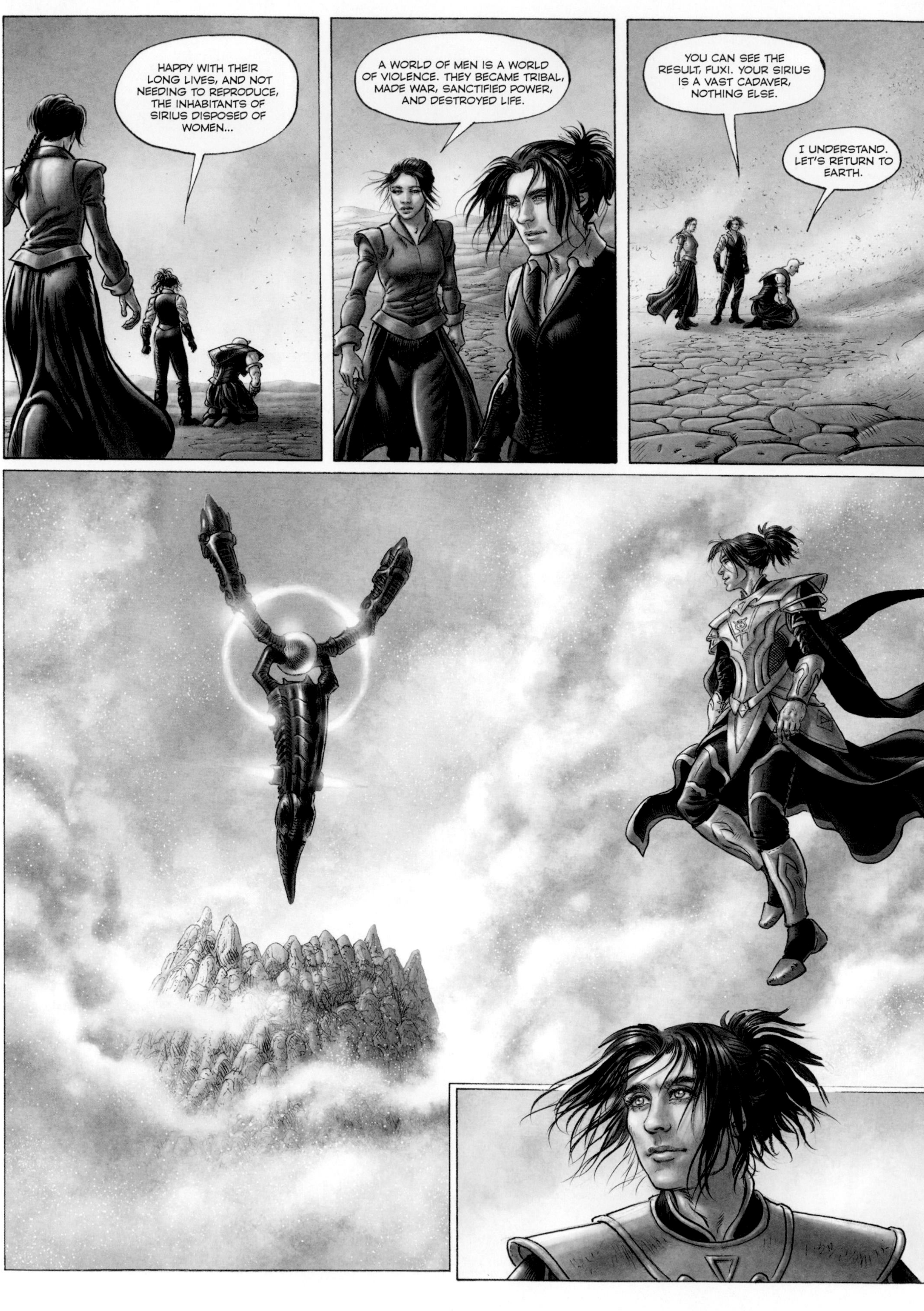
HAPPY WITH THEIR LONG LIVES, AND NOT NEEDING TO REPRODUCE, THE INHABITANTS OF SIRIUS DISPOSED OF WOMEN...
A WORLD OF MEN IS A WORLD OF VIOLENCE. THEY BECAME TRIBAL, MADE WAR, SANCTIFIED POWER, AND DESTROYED LIFE.
YOU CAN SEE THE RESULT, FUXI. YOUR SIRIUS IS A VAST CADAVER, NOTHING ELSE.
I UNDERSTAND. LET'S RETURN TO EARTH.

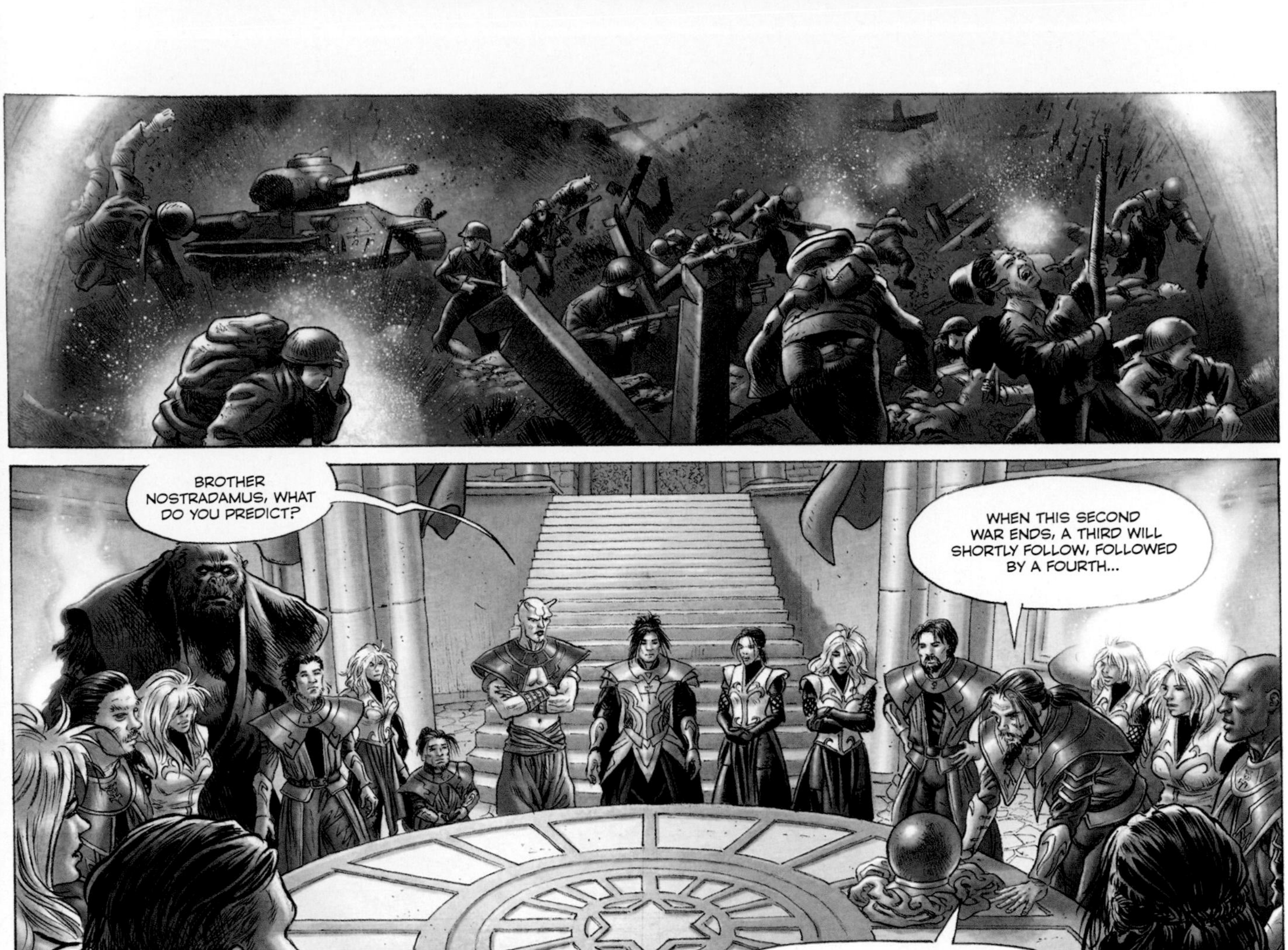
BROTHER NOSTRADAMUS, WHAT DO YOU PREDICT?
WHEN THIS SECOND WAR ENDS, A THIRD WILL SHORTLY FOLLOW, FOLLOWED BY A FOURTH...
AND POSSIBLY A FIFTH.... IN WHICH MEN CONTINUE TO KILL EACH OTHER UNTIL IT LEADS TO EXTERMINATION.
BROTHERS AND SISTERS, IF WE FAIL TO ACT AT THE HEART OF WORLD POWER, THEN EARTH, LIKE SIRIUS...
...WILL TURN INTO A STERILE ORB.

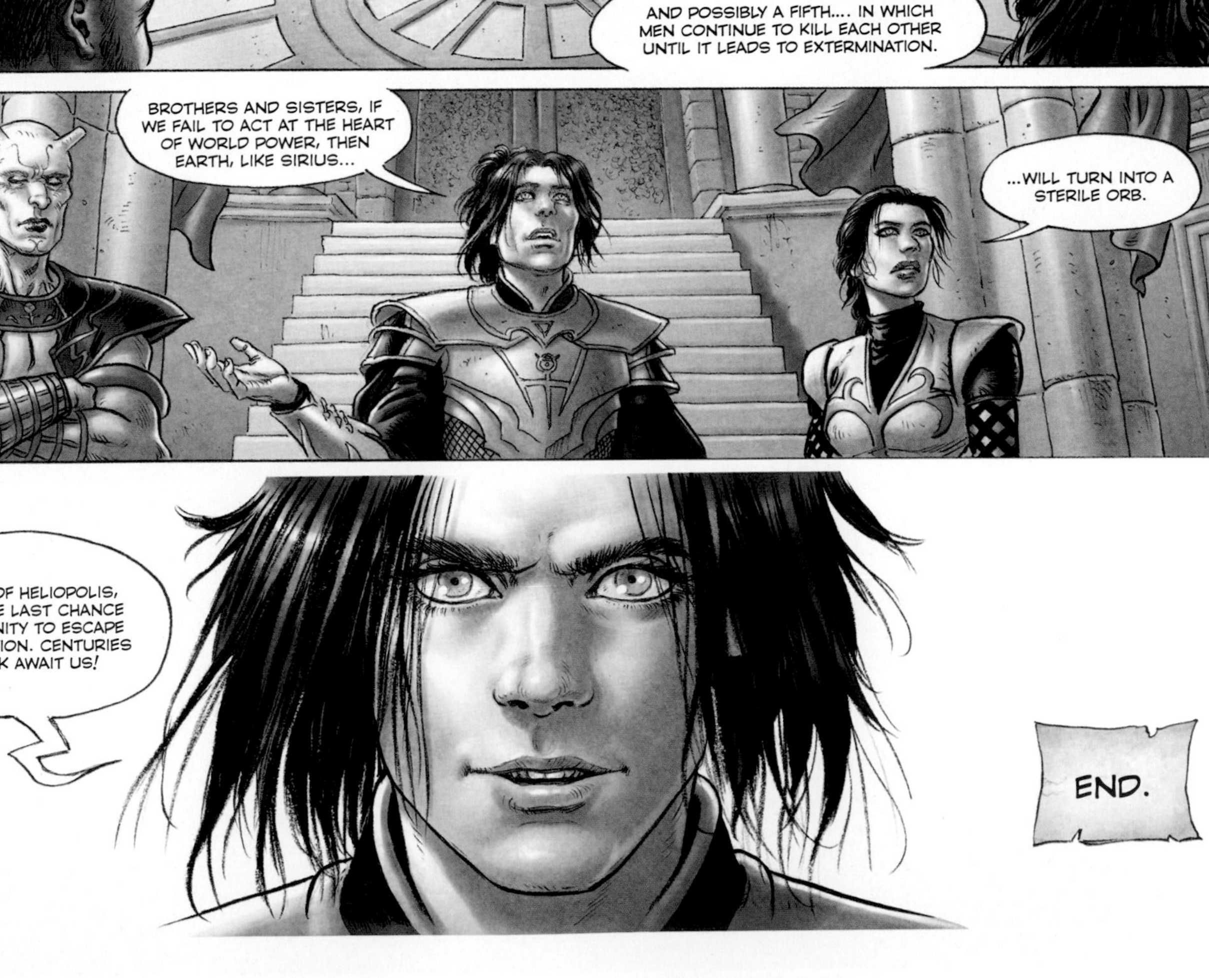
KNIGHTS OF HELIOPOLIS, WE ARE THE LAST CHANCE FOR HUMANITY TO ESCAPE EXTERMINATION. CENTURIES OF WORK AWAIT US!
END.

KNIGHTS OF HELIOPOLIS

COVER GALLERY

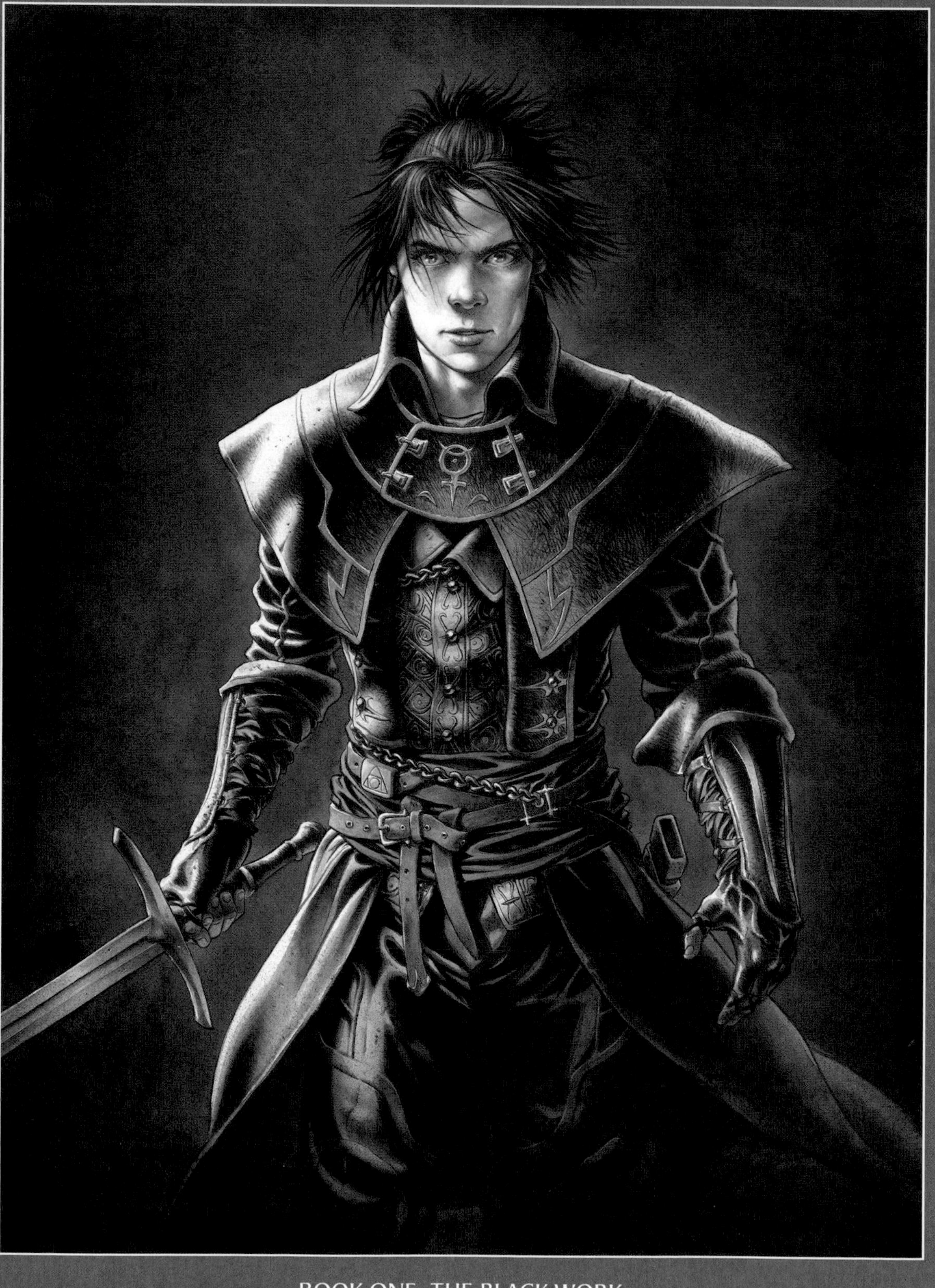

BOOK ONE: THE BLACK WORK
ARTIST - JÉRÉMY

KNIGHTS OF HELIOPOLIS

COVER GALLERY

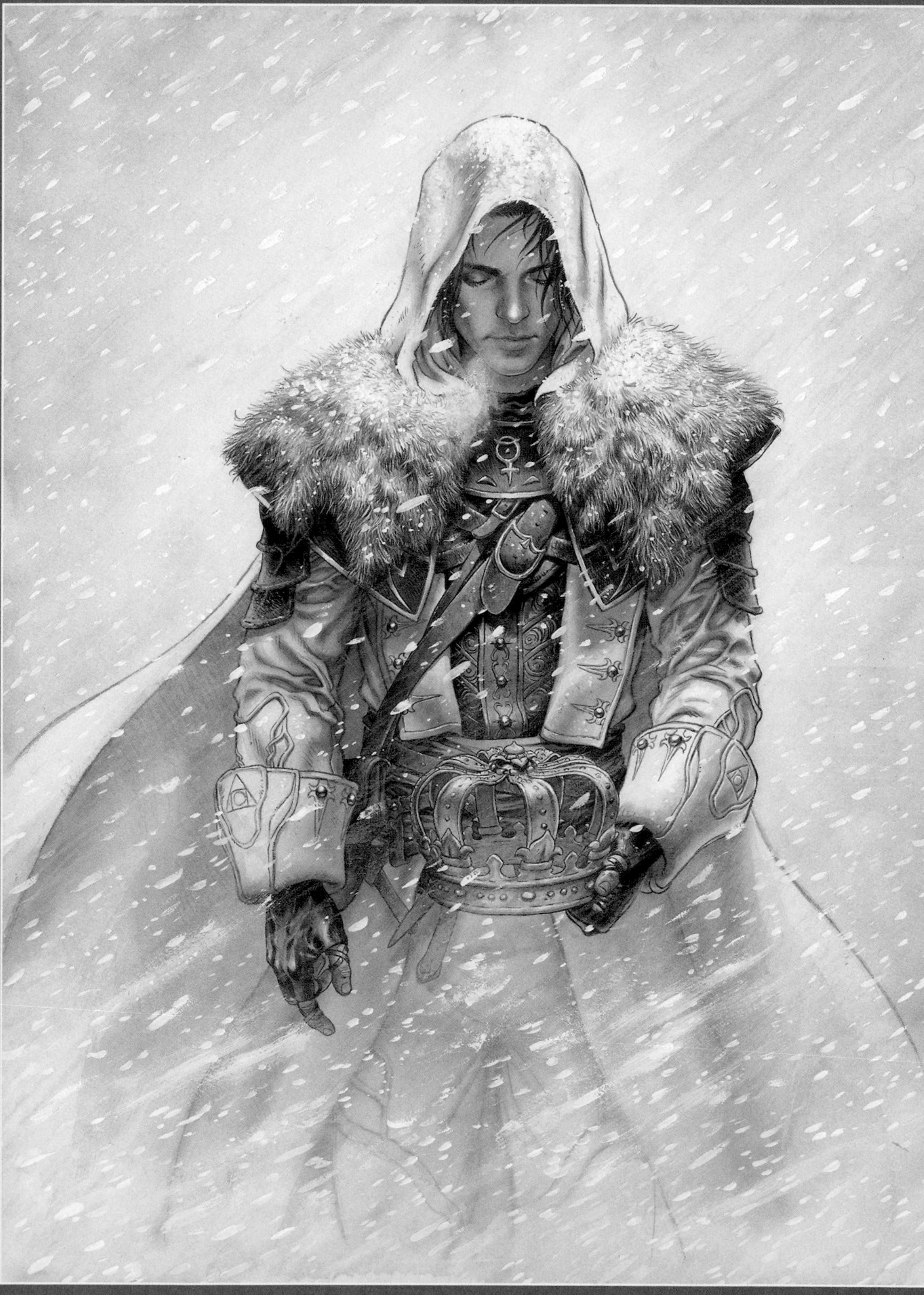

BOOK TWO: THE WHITE WORK
ARTIST - JÉRÉMY

KNIGHTS OF HELIOPOLIS

COVER GALLERY

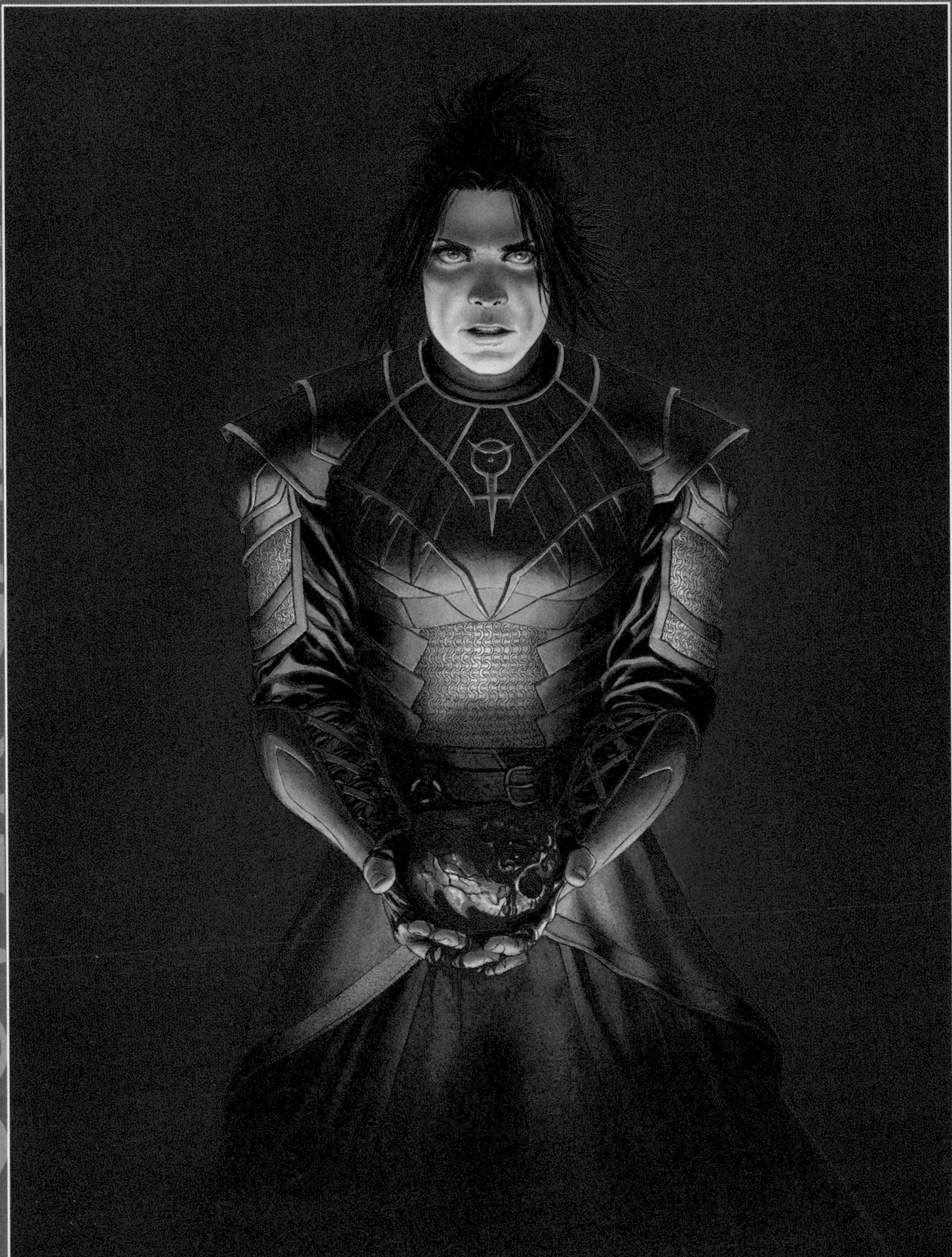

BOOK THREE: THE RED WORK
ARTIST - JÉRÉMY

KNIGHTS OF HELIOPOLIS

COVER GALLERY

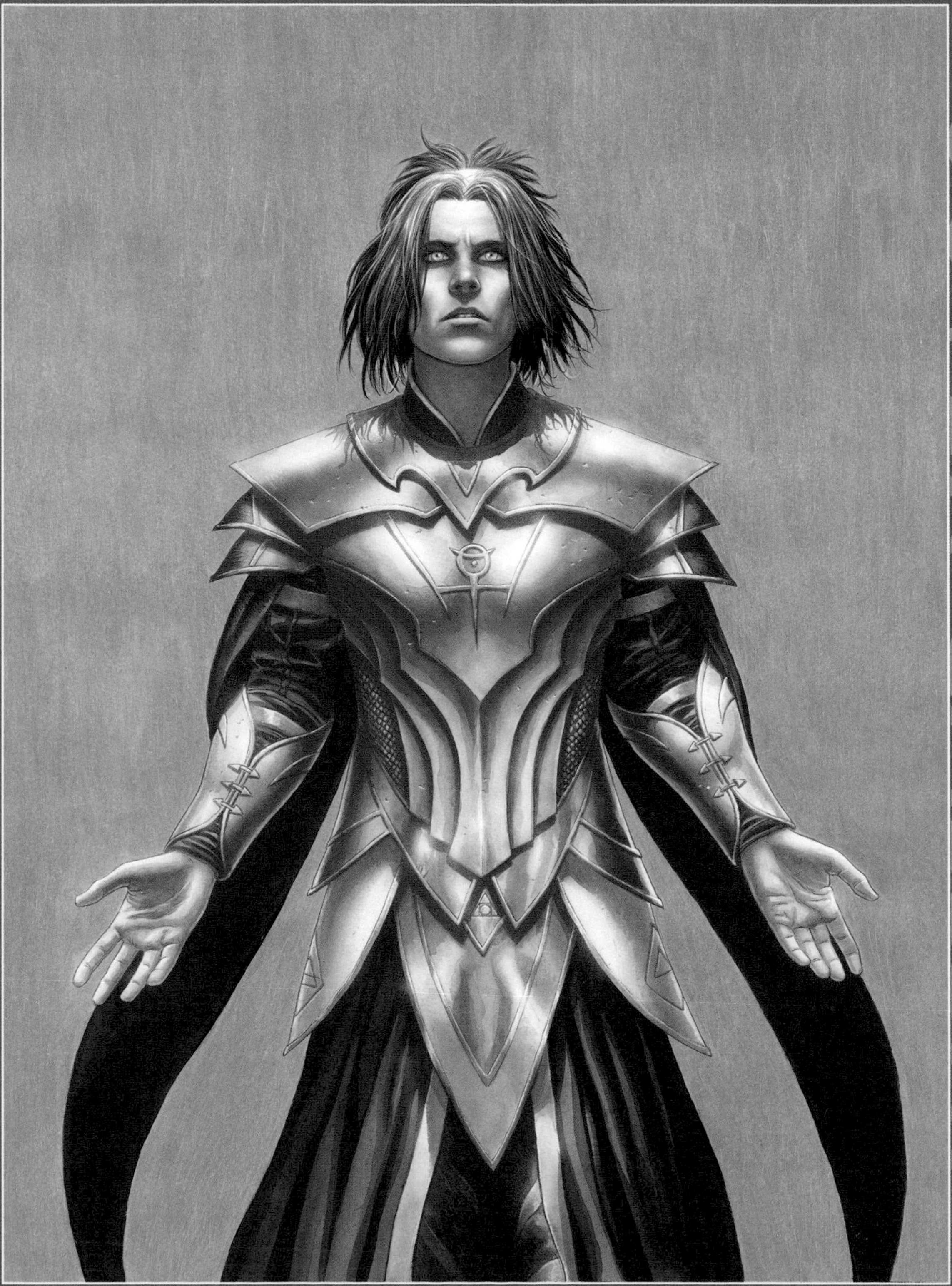

BOOK FOUR: THE YELLOW WORK
ARTIST - JÉRÉMY

KNIGHTS
OF HELIOPOLIS

BIOS

WRITER

Alejandro Jodorowsky is a French-Chilean film-maker, playwright, actor, author, musician, comics writer and spiritual guru. He is best known for his controversial avant-garde films – including his first feature, Fando y Lis, which was banned in Mexico, and El Topo in 1970, often regarded as the first ever classic midnight cult movie. He has established himself as a notable comic writer with The Incal, the seminal work of the comic book medium, created in conjunction with the late Moebius, often cited as the greatest comic ever written. Other works include Technopriests and Metabarons. Jodorowsky is also involved in psychological therapy using his own personal system called Psychomagic or Psychoshamanism, which is derived from his interest in alchemy, tarot, Zen Buddhism and shamanism.

ARTIST

Jérémy, born in 1984, started alongside Philippe Delaby as a colorist at just 17 years old. While working on coloring projects, he took the time to produce a comic strip about pirates, Barracuda, written by Jean Dufaux. On the death of his master Philippe Delaby, Jérémy agreed to complete the 21 remaining plates from volume 4 of the second cycle of La Complainte des landes perdus. After completing the Barracuda series with a sixth volume, he began Knights of Heliopolis, with Alejandro Jodorowsky writing the script.

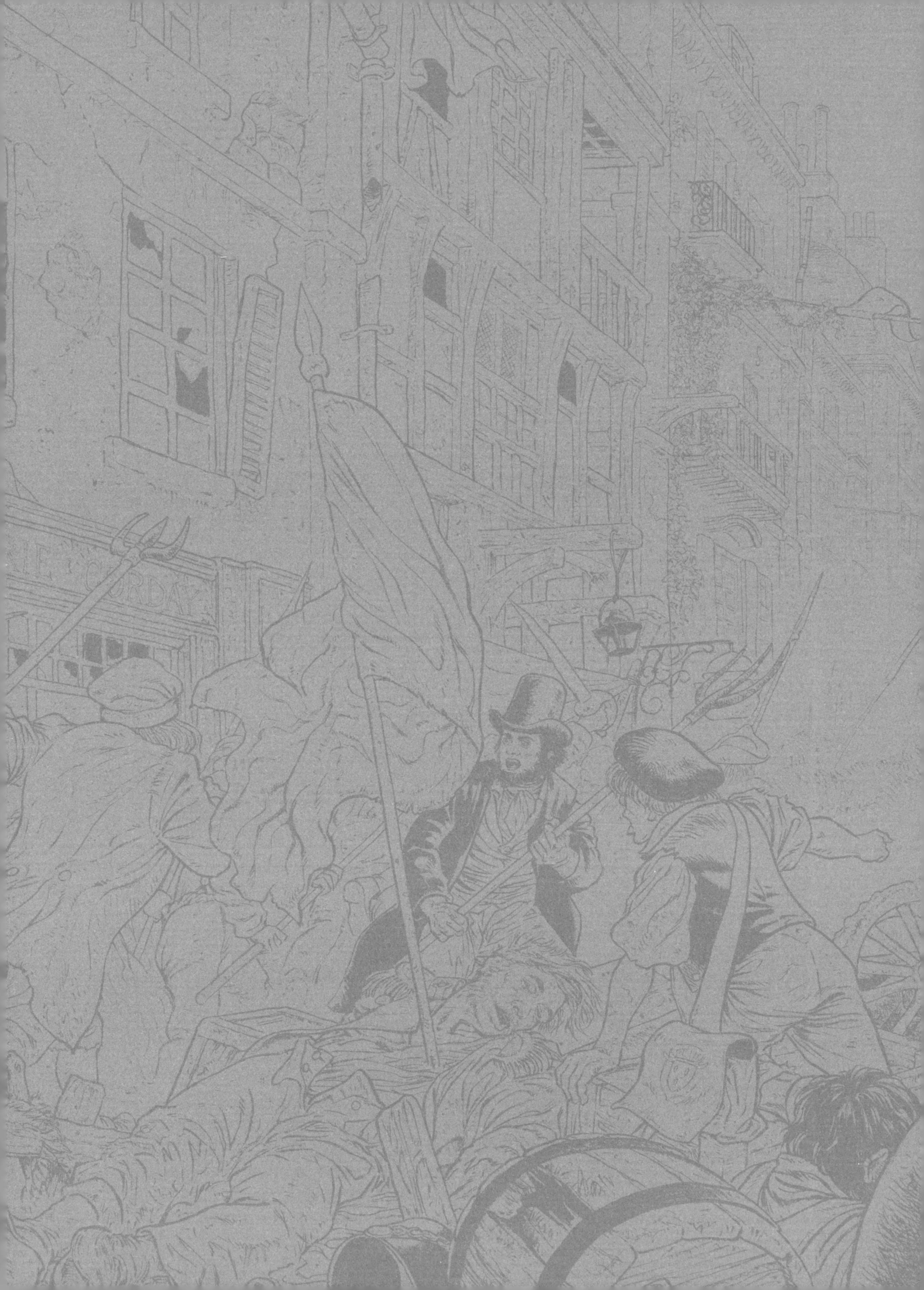

SHAQUILLE O'NEAL

Basketball Sensation

BY BILL GUTMAN

MILLBROOK SPORTS WORLD
THE MILLBROOK PRESS
BROOKFIELD, CONNECTICUT

Library of Congress Cataloging-in-Publication Data
Gutman, Bill.
Shaquille O'Neal : basketball sensation / by Bill Gutman.
p. cm.—(Millbrook sports world.)
Includes bibliographical references and index.
Summary: The story of basketball's superstar center
Shaquille O'Neal.
ISBN 1-56294-460-6
1. O'Neal, Shaquille—Juvenile literature. 2. Basketball
players—United States—Biography—Juvenile literature.
[1. O'Neal, Shaquille. 2. Basketball players. 3. Afro-
Americans—Biography.] I. Title. II. Series.
GV884.054G88 1994
796.323'092—dc20 [B] 93-38971 CIP AC

Photographs courtesy of: Allsport USA: cover inset (Tom Smart), pp. 34, 38 (Jonathan Daniel), 44 (Tim DeFrisco), 46 (Jonathan Daniel); John McDonough/Sports Illustrated: cover, p. 40; AP/Wide World: pp. 3, 7, 21, 29, 30, 33, 37; Barry Gossage: p. 4; U.S. Army: p. 11 (J. Paul Bruton); University of Texas, Institute of Texan Cultures, San Antonio Express-News Collection: pp. 13, 16; Brad Messina, LSU Sports Information: pp. 18–19, 22, 25, 26, 43.

Published by The Millbrook Press
2 Old New Milford Road
Brookfield, Connecticut 06804

Printed in the United States of America
5 4 3 2 1

SHAQUILLE O'NEAL

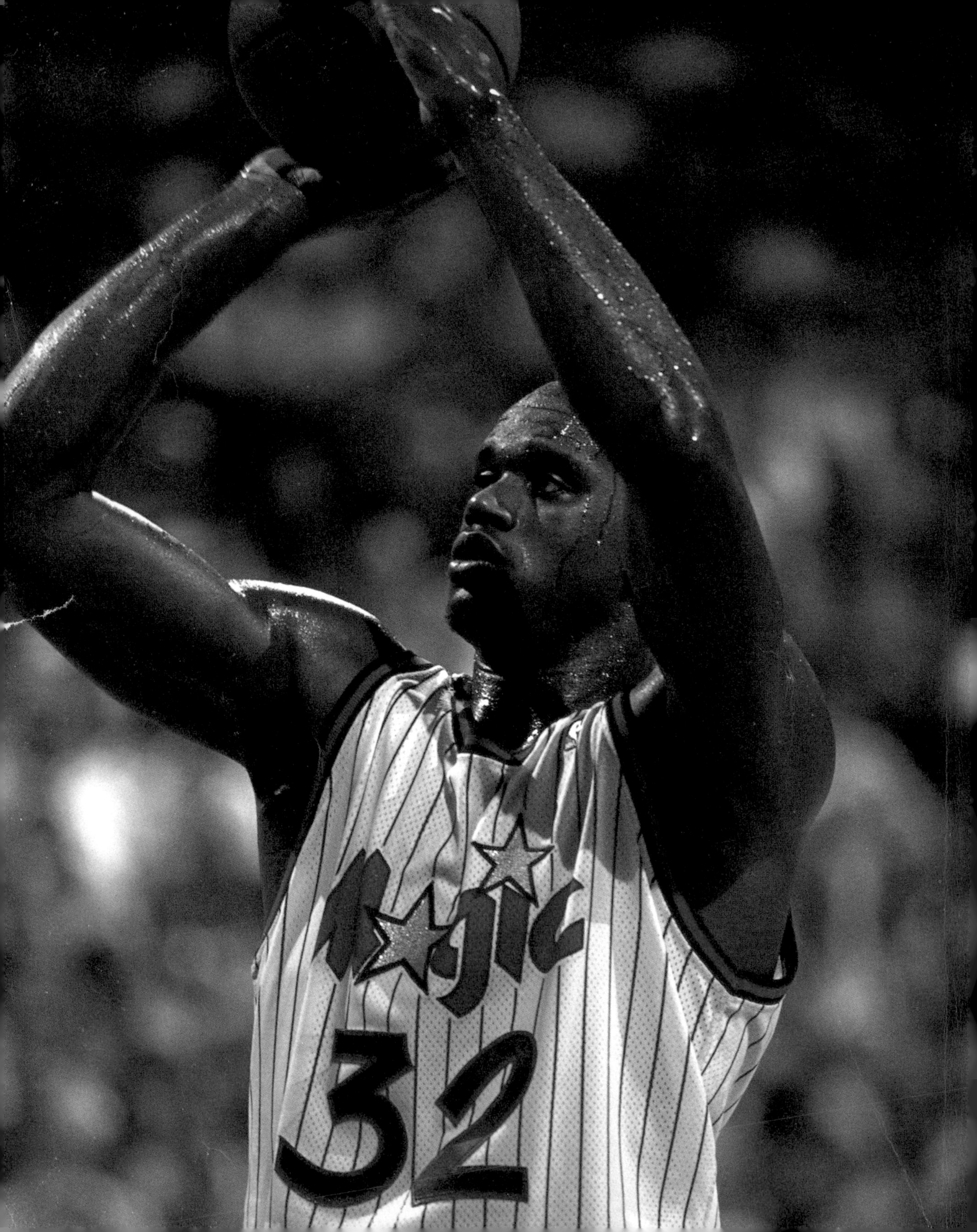
32

It was almost the mid-point of the 1992–1993 National Basketball Association (NBA) season, and things couldn't have been better for Shaquille O'Neal. O'Neal was the 7-foot-1-inch (238-centimeter) rookie center for the Orlando Magic. He was already being called the next great superstar center in the NBA. Yet "the Shaq," as he was known, was just 20 years old and the youngest player in the league.

Shaquille had been playing very well all year. Now he had learned that the fans had voted him the starting center for the East in the upcoming mid-season All-Star Game. So he was a happy man when his team arrived in Phoenix to play the Suns. The Suns had the best record in the NBA, which meant it wouldn't be an easy game for the Magic. In addition, the game would be shown on national television. And when Shaquille O'Neal was on TV, millions of people watched.

The game was less than three minutes old when it happened. Shaq got the ball in close to the basket. Although a rookie, he was already being called the most powerful player in the league. When he went up for his trademark slam dunk, it was said he just "exploded" into the air. Sure enough, he went up to jam.

No Phoenix player challenged him as he blasted the ball through the net. Then he hung on the rim briefly before letting go. Many players do this when they dunk. But Shaquille O'Neal weighed 300 pounds (136 kilograms). The sellout crowd at America West Arena gasped in disbelief. The rim and backboard began to slowly sag to the court.

The force of Shaq's dunk had snapped a steel hook that held the base of the backboard to the concrete under the floor. When it snapped, the welding broke loose. Then the entire stanchion gave way, and it all came down. It would take 37 minutes to get it set up again so the game could continue. During that time, everyone watching marveled at the power of Shaquille O'Neal.

"It just couldn't withstand the strength of his 300 pounds," said Arena manager Bob Machen. "Charles Barkley (the Suns' star forward) dunks pretty well here, and nothing like this has ever happened before."

As for Shaq, he was also surprised by the result of his dunk. "I've hit them a lot harder than that before," he said, meaning the rim. "When it started coming down, I started running the other way."

Although Phoenix won the game, Shaquille O'Neal was once again the talk of the basketball world. He was the most exciting rookie to come into the NBA since Michael Jordan eight years earlier. Like Jordan, the Shaq could be seen everywhere. His quick smile made him perfect for

As an NBA rookie in 1992–1993, Shaquille saw two backboards collapse after his thunderous dunks. This photograph was taken at the Meadowlands in New Jersey in a game against the Nets. Shaq had to duck to keep from being hit by the 24-second clock.

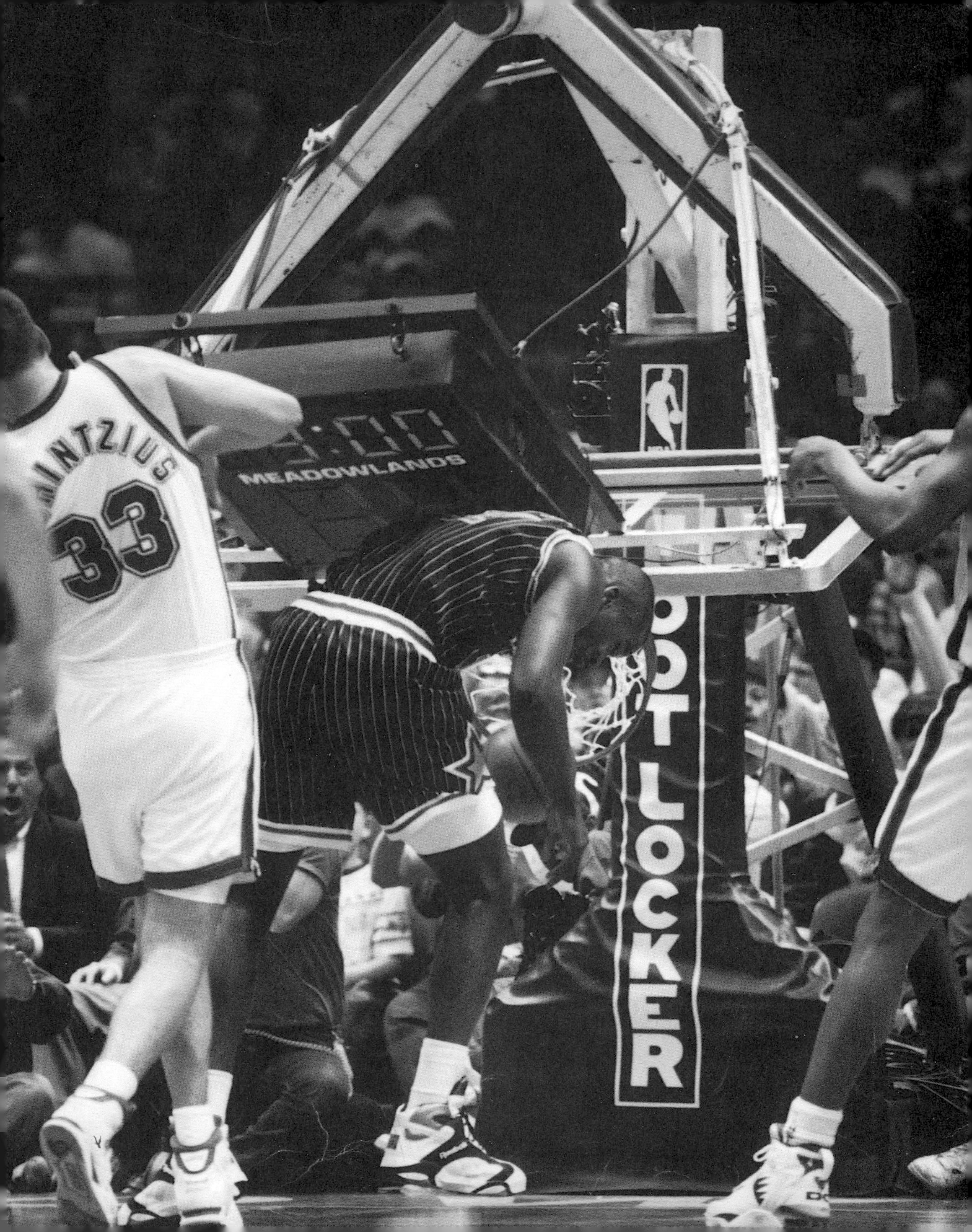
INTZIUS
33
MEADOWLANDS
LOCKER

commercials. He had his own basketball shoe, he sang rap music with the group Fu Schnickens, and he was up among the NBA leaders in scoring, rebounding, and blocked shots.

And nobody else could slam dunk like the Shaq. Just ask the fans in Phoenix.

THE EARLY YEARS

Shaquille O'Neal had a different kind of childhood from most. He was what is known as an ''army brat.'' That doesn't mean he was a bad kid. It means his father's career was the army, and the rest of the family went with him to different army bases around the United States and in Europe. They never lived in one place for very long.

In a sense, that was a good thing because Shaquille was born in a very rough place. Newark, New Jersey, is a large city that had been hit hard by street riots in 1967. When Shaquille was born on March 6, 1972, there was a great deal of poverty in the inner city of Newark. That meant there was also crime and drugs. The streets were a hard place to grow up.

Shaquille was born before his parents, Lucille O'Neal and Philip Harrison, could marry. His father wanted to take his family out of Newark. He felt the best way was to join the army. But before he and Lucille could marry, he was sent overseas. Lucille O'Neal had her baby without him. As soon as Philip Harrison returned, they were married.

It was Lucille O'Neal who named her infant son. ''I wanted my children to have unique names,'' she said. ''To me, just having a name that means something makes you special.''

She began looking through a book of Arabic names. She finally chose Shaquille Rashaun. It's a name that means "Little Warrior" in Arabic. Lucille O'Neal had no way of knowing then that her son would be far from little. Even though Lucille O'Neal soon became Lucille Harrison, Shaquille kept his mother's maiden name as a special tribute to her.

The Harrisons eventually had three more children, two girls and a boy. Mrs. Harrison continued to find special names for them. Shaquille's sisters are named LaTeefah and Ayesha, and his brother is named Jamal.

It took several years for Philip Harrison to get his family out of Newark. Shaquille was about six years old when they left for good. At first he didn't want to go. He wanted to live with his grandmother. But his father said they had to stay together as a family. That was the rule.

Going from place to place was not easy for Shaquille. The family traveled to Germany, then back to the United States. They would live in one place for a year or two, then move again. That was hard for a youngster growing up.

"The worst part was the traveling," Shaquille said. "I would meet people, become friends with them, then have to leave. When I came to a new place I was tested and teased a lot. I remember kids teasing me about my name and about my size. I got in a lot of fights in those years and it sometimes took me awhile to make new friends."

But there was very little chance of Shaquille becoming a problem kid—not with Sergeant Philip Harrison around. Shaquille's father was 6 feet 5 inches (195 centimeters) tall and weighed more than 250 pounds (113 kilograms). Being in the army, he believed in discipline. Shaquille always answered his questions with a crisp "Yes, sir" or "No, sir."

When the family moved back to Germany for the second time, Shaquille was ready to enter junior high school. He was already well over 6 feet (180 centimeters) tall and had started to play basketball. But when he began getting in fights at school again, his father stepped in.

"I almost got thrown out of school," Shaquille admitted. "Now I look back and say thank goodness I had two parents who loved me enough to stay on my case."

It was about that time that Philip Harrison gave his son some good advice. What he told Shaquille would always stay with him.

"I told Shaquille that the world has too many followers," Sergeant Harrison said. "What he needed to be was a leader. I told him there was no half-steppin' in his life."

Shaquille thought about what his father said for a long time. The more he thought about it, the more he knew what he wanted to be—and it wasn't a follower.

ON TO HIGH SCHOOL

Shaquille was 13 years old when he heard there would be a basketball clinic held at the army base in Germany. The visitor running the clinic was Dale Brown, head basketball coach at Louisiana State University. When Coach Brown first saw Shaquille O'Neal, he thought he was one of the soldiers.

"What rank are you?" he asked Shaquille.

"I don't have a rank, sir," Shaquille said. "I'm just 13."

Coach Brown thought the boy was a soldier because Shaquille was already 6 feet 6 (197 centimeters) and wore a size 16 (15T) shoe. The coach met Shaquille's father and said that he would keep in touch. Basketball coaches remember kids who are that big at age 13.

Two years later the family returned to the United States for good. They moved to Fort Sam Houston in San Antonio, Texas. Shaquille was 15 and would be starting his junior year at Robert G. Cole High School, a school for the children of army personnel.

An aerial view of Fort Sam Houston, where Shaquille's father was stationed with the Fifth Army.

Shaquille was now 6 feet 8 (202 centimeters) and weighed nearly 240 pounds (109 kilograms). He had learned most of his basketball skills from his father. Sergeant Harrison had been a good schoolyard player when he was younger. He taught his son many of the fundamentals of the sport.

Even then, Shaquille had a great deal of natural talent. Despite his huge size he could run like a deer, jump very well, and was very quick. He had all the qualities needed to be a star. That's what Cole High's head coach, Dave Madura, thought when he first saw him. He knew right away that he would build his team around the big guy.

STAR OF THE TEAM

Shaquille quickly showed that he had the makings of a great player. He was the star of the team and led Cole High to a 32–1 record for the season. They lost their only game in the playoffs when Shaquille got four fouls in the first quarter and had to spend a lot of time on the bench.

The next year, the coach felt the team had a good chance to win the state championship. He brought in an assistant coach named Herb More to help work with Shaquille. More had once played at Cole. At 6 feet 6 (197 centimeters), he was the only one tall enough to go against Shaquille in practice.

"The first thing I noticed about him was that he was a great person," said Coach More. "He was very bright and very polite. It was 'Yes, Sir' and 'No, Sir.' He was a natural leader and very popular with the other kids at Cole. He fit right in with them and never acted as if he was above them."

Just as Shaquille's senior year was beginning, he and his family had to wrestle with a big decision. They knew that a large number of colleges would want Shaquille after he'd finished his last year at Cole High. Colleges "recruit" all the top high school athletes. Recruiting can be very difficult for a high schooler. Some recruiters don't always tell the truth. And some bother the family at all hours of the day and night. Shaquille O'Neal and his parents didn't want that.

The family had stayed in touch with Dale Brown ever since the Louisiana State University coach had come to Germany years before. Shaquille visited the LSU campus during the first week of school. He visited a couple of other schools as well, but had already made up his mind.

Shaquille was already showing his rim-grabbing style as a high school basketball player at Cole High School in San Antonio, Texas.

By November of his senior year at Cole High, Shaquille had decided. He signed a letter of intent to go to LSU the following fall. So he had chosen which college he would attend even before he started his final high school basketball season.

PLAYING TO THE FINISH

In practice, Herb More played against Shaquille. The coach fouled him often because he knew that's what many of Shaq's opponents would do. But Shaquille did more than just play in close to the basket. The coaches wanted all their players to be able to do everything on the court.

"Shaquille was fully capable of getting a rebound and then dribbling the ball the length of the court," Herb More said. "He could go all the way for a slam, throw a no-look pass, or pull up and take a 15-foot (4.6-meter) jumper. He did all of that in our games at one time or another."

It was no surprise when Shaquille got off to a great start. He was averaging more than 30 points and 20 rebounds a game. High school games were just 32 minutes long. In addition, Cole was often so far ahead that Shaquille would sit down for a quarter or more so everyone could play. That's how good he had become.

Coach More was right about one thing. Many defenses double- and triple-teamed Shaquille. They fouled him all the time, and because he was so big the refs didn't always call it. When Shaquille got the ball in close early in the season, he would turn and bank in a short layup. But the more the defenders fouled him, the more he missed these short shots.

"We were playing a tournament game up in Marble Falls," Herb More remembered. "The other team was holding Shaquille every time he went up, just hanging all over him. The referees weren't calling anything. So we all started yelling to him, 'Go up and just slam the sucker.'"

The next time Shaquille got the ball underneath, he went up hard and just slam-dunked the ball. From that point on, he would dunk every chance he had. More and more opponents just got out of his way. He was so strong and went up to the basket so hard, that they just didn't want to get hurt.

With Shaquille playing at the top of his form, Cole High remained unbeaten. Wherever the team went, large crowds came out just to see the big guy play. There was one game in which he slam-dunked so hard he bent the rim in several places. In another, a teammate missed a shot and Shaquille streaked under the basket. He caught the rebound low in his left hand and in one motion brought the ball up and slam-dunked it home.

The opposing coach said that Shaquille's rebound and slam was "NBA material or nothing is."

When the state tournament began, Cole still hadn't lost. Now the team wanted to win the championship. In one playoff game, Coach More said Shaquille had nearly 12 assists and in the first half alone blocked about 10 shots. He didn't have to always score big to lead his team to victory. But in another he scored a career high 47 points as Cole cruised into the semi-finals.

Then they defeated Hearne High, 69–56, and were in the final against Clarksville. Once again Shaquille was the best player on the floor. Cole

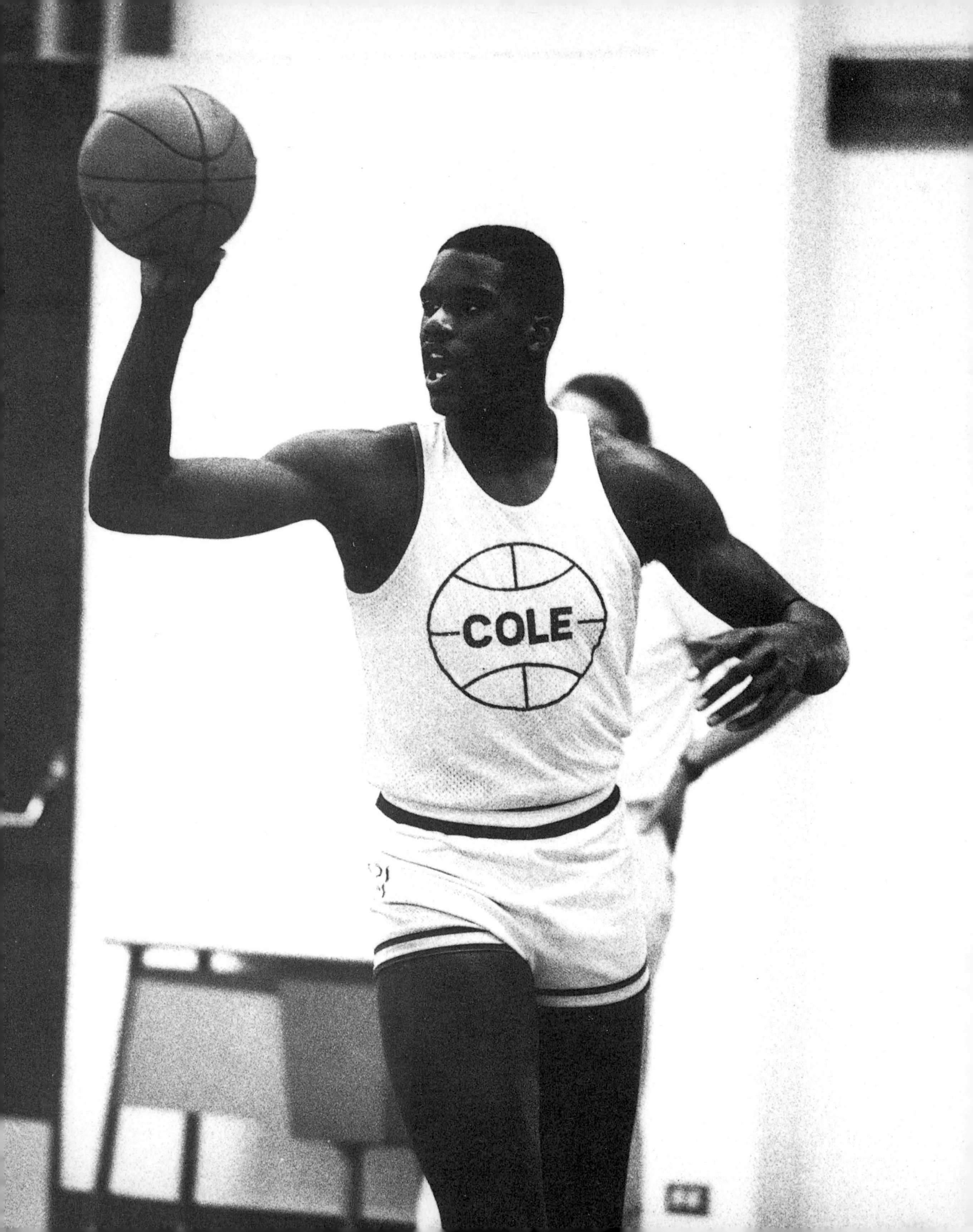
COLE

won the game, 66–60, as Shaquille scored 19 points and grabbed 26 rebounds. The team completed a 36–0 season and were state champs.

When it ended, Shaquille had averaged 32.1 points and 22 rebounds a game. He was not only a high school All-American, but had also grown to 7 feet (213 centimeters) tall.

Shaquille O'Neal graduated from Cole High School in June 1989. Before the year ended, he would already be on his way to becoming a college basketball legend.

OPENING EYES AT LSU

When Shaquille entered LSU in the fall of 1989, his first goal was to get an education. Basketball was second. Even Philip Harrison said that his son would complete his four years and leave with a degree.

"We want Shaquille to get an education so he doesn't need basketball," said Sergeant Harrison.

That was sound thinking. No one can count on making a career of sports. A college star can't be sure he will be a star in the pros. Sometimes a star college player might suffer a serious injury that can shorten or end his career. So it's always a good idea for even a great athlete to also aim for a college degree.

LSU expected to have a very good ball club in 1989–1990. The Tigers had a 6-foot-1 (200-centimeter) sophomore guard named Chris Jack-

*By the time Shaquille graduated from
high school in 1989, he was a star athlete—
and 7 feet (213 centimeters) tall!*

son. He was a great shooter who had a chance to be an All-American. They also had a 7-foot (213-centimeter) center named Stanley Roberts. He, too, was a sophomore, though he hadn't played the year before. Shaquille was now 7 feet 1 inch (238 centimeters) and 295 pounds (134 kilograms). The question was: Which big man would play?

"I saw tremendous skills in both players," said LSU assistant coach Craig Carse. "Stanley was more skilled offensively, while Shaquille was a great athlete who could run, could pull down rims, and played a hard, intimidating game."

Many experts thought the LSU Tigers would be one of the three best teams in the country. That was a lot of pressure to put on young athletes who hadn't played together before. In the early games, Roberts started at center and Shaquille came in off the bench. Jackson was the top scorer. In the first three games he scored 37, 32, and 27 points.

Shaquille (right) and Stanley Roberts, LSU's 7-foot (213-centimeter) centers, hold guard Chris Jackson aloft before a practice session. The three players formed the heart of the Tiger team in 1989–1990, Shaq's freshman year.

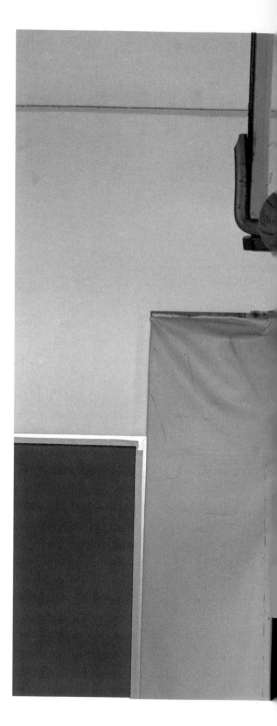

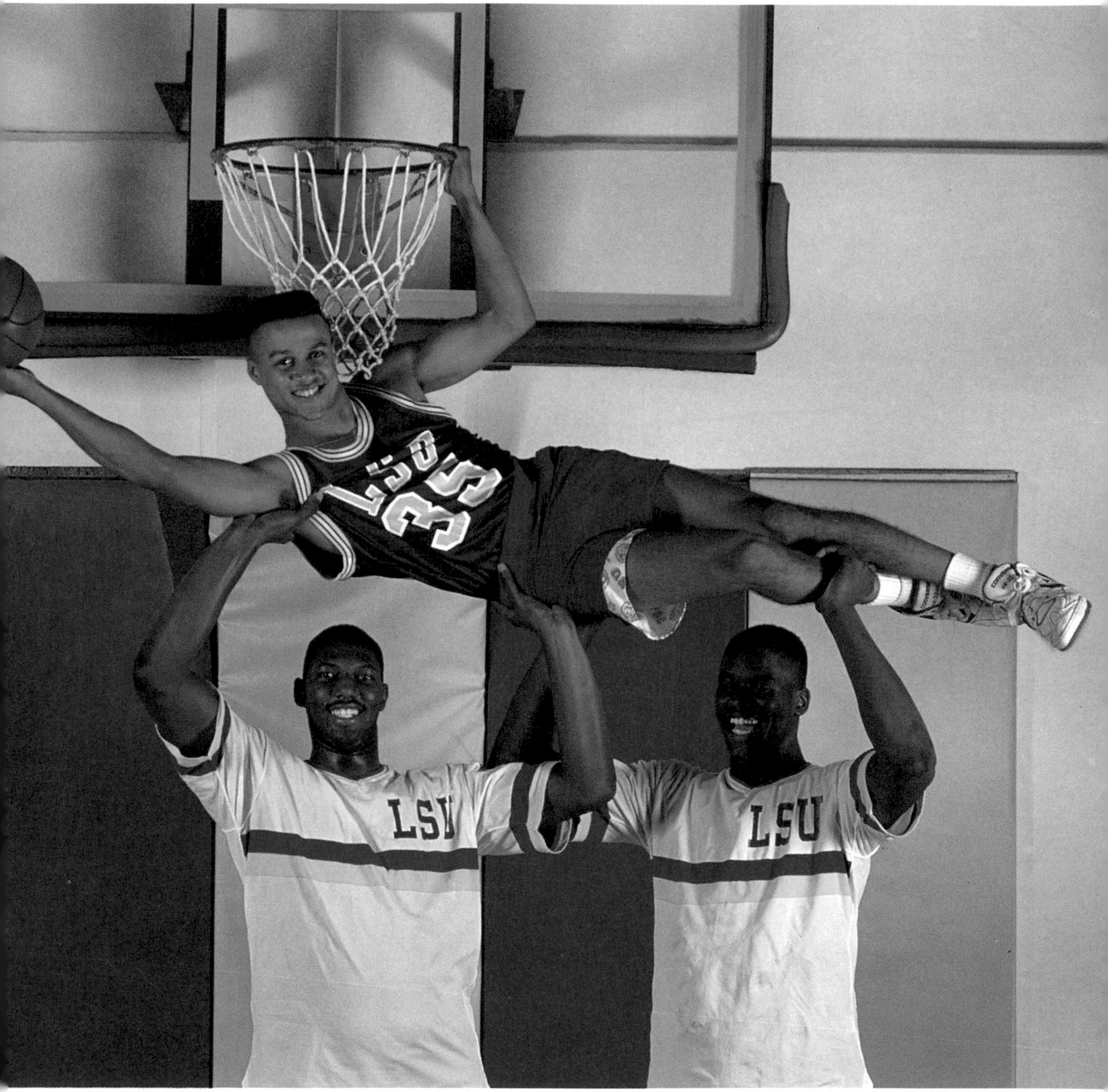
LSU
35
LSU
LSU

In the fourth game, Shaquille began playing more. He led the team with 17 rebounds as LSU won easily. After that, he began starting alongside Roberts. In a big game against Texas, Shaquille had 19 rebounds as LSU won, 124–113. Coach Carse remembered one play Shaquille made that opened a lot of eyes.

"One of the Texas players took a shot from close in and Shaquille went up and blocked it," the coach recalled. "He was up so high that it looked as if his armpit was up over the rim. One of our guys got the ball and Shaquille sprinted downcourt. He cut to the hoop and took a pass which he kind of cuffed in his hand and in one motion just went over everybody and dunked it down. It really showed what he was all about."

There were more highlights. Against Nevada-Las Vegas, Shaquille had 17 points and 14 rebounds as LSU won, 107–105. And against Loyola-Marymount, he had 24 rebounds and blocked an amazing 12 shots. But there were also nine games in which he fouled out. Part of that was due to his inexperience.

The Tigers finished the season at 23–9. Shaquille played in all 32 games and averaged 13.9 points and 12 rebounds. He led the Southeastern Conference in rebounds and set a conference record with 115 blocked shots.

He was on his way.

THE SHAQNIFICENT

It had been a very good freshman year for Shaquille. Besides basketball, he had worked hard in his classes. His 3.0 grade point average (out of a possible 4.0) was the best on the team. After the season ended he lifted weights and kept practicing.

When he came back for his sophomore year he weighed 300 pounds (136 kilograms). He could also jump 8 inches (20 centimeters) higher than he could as a freshman. Coach Carse couldn't believe how strong he was.

"He's a true 300 pounds," the coach said. "He's all muscle without an ounce of fat on him."

There were also some changes on the LSU team. Chris Jackson had left to play in the NBA, and Stanley Roberts had failed to keep his grades up. (He would end up playing in Spain.) So now the Tigers built their team around Shaquille. By this time many people were calling the big guy by a new nickname. At first it was spelled "Shack." But Shaquille himself had coined the name. He wanted it spelled "Shaq," and that's how it has stayed.

In fact, Shaquille loved to make up new phrases using his nickname. He

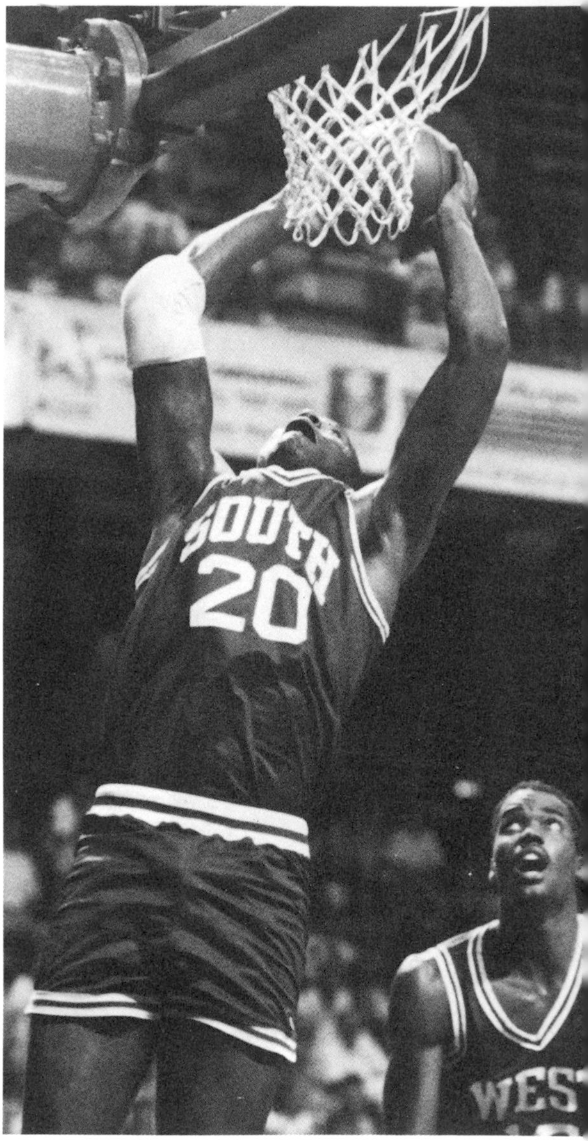
SOUTH
20
WEST

After a great freshman year at LSU, Shaq (20) dazzled the fans at the Olympic Festival in Minneapolis. He had a triple double (26 points, 10 rebounds, and 10 blocks) as the South beat the West, 112–110.

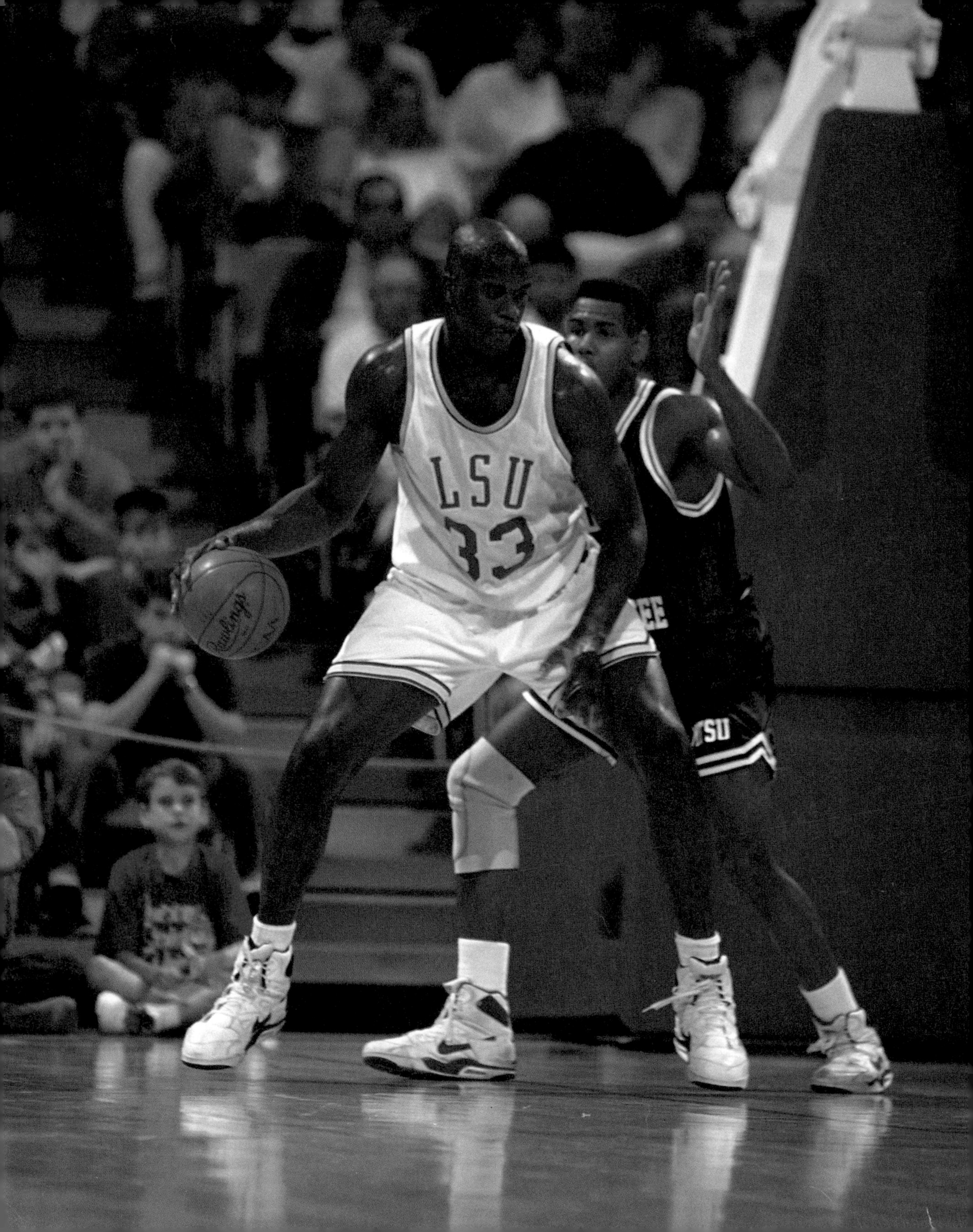
LSU
33

called a victory dance he did the "Shaq-de-Shaq" and wore a baseball cap that read "I am the Shaqnificent."

Once the 1990–1991 season started it was easy to see that Shaquille was an even better player than he had been before. In a game against number two-ranked Arizona, Shaq scored 29 points in just 28 minutes. He also had 14 rebounds and 6 blocks. Arizona had a great frontcourt, but Shaq dominated them. After the game, Shaquille said playing that well meant a lot to him.

"I'd heard stuff from out there that I was just another player," he said. "They said I was too young. I wanted to show I could play with anybody."

He would show that again and again. Teams tried to find new ways to stop him, but they just couldn't. Georgia Coach Hugh Durham spoke for many when he said, "Trying to stop Shaquille is a joke. No matter what you do, he can muscle you out of the lane. He just may be unguardable."

Jamal Mashburn of Kentucky, himself one of the finest players in the country, said "Shaq belongs in a higher league," after he scored 33 points and grabbed 16 rebounds as LSU topped the Wildcats.

Shaq finished his sophomore season scoring 27.6 points a game, and his 14.7 rebound average was the best in the country. He also set a na-

Shaq was looking more and more like a man playing against boys. In many LSU games, he was the biggest, tallest, and strongest player on the court. His skills were getting better, too—so much so that he was named a consensus All-American his sophomore year.

tional record for sophomores with an average of 5.0 blocks a game. The only disappointment was that the Tigers lost to Connecticut in the NCAA playoffs, 79–62. The team finished the year with a 20–10 record.

After the season, Shaquille was named to all the major All-American teams. He was also chosen Player of the Year by the Associated Press, United Press International, and *Sports Illustrated* magazine. There were other awards as well. Although he was barely 19 years old, almost every coach in the NBA wanted him. In fact, some thought he would leave LSU and jump into the pro ranks right away.

If Shaq had decided to leave LSU he probably would have been the number one pick of the NBA draft. He also would have received a contract worth millions of dollars. For awhile, he felt that by turning pro he could help give his family a better life. But his father told him that money alone wasn't a good enough reason for Shaq to leave school.

POPULAR AND FEARED

Shaquille returned to LSU for the 1991–1992 school year. He was a business major and still doing well with his studies. In addition, he was probably the most popular athlete in the state. When a couple in Geismar, Louisiana, named their baby Shaquille O'Neal Long, Shaq surprised them by going to their home and having his picture taken with them.

On the court, he looked as good as ever. After the team split its first six games, the Tigers got hot and won 11 of the next 12, giving them a 14–4 record. Shaq, of course, was still the most feared player in the college ranks.

Shaq and kids were always a perfect fit. Wherever he went, kids would flock around him, and Shaq seemed to enjoy every minute of it.

But there was a problem. It was what his opponents were doing to him defensively. In many games, their tactics were turning very rough and sometimes even dirty.

"Shaq wasn't able to play his game that year," said Craig Carse. "They [his opponents] were trying everything possible. They were double- and triple-teaming him. Sometimes they brought a player off the bench

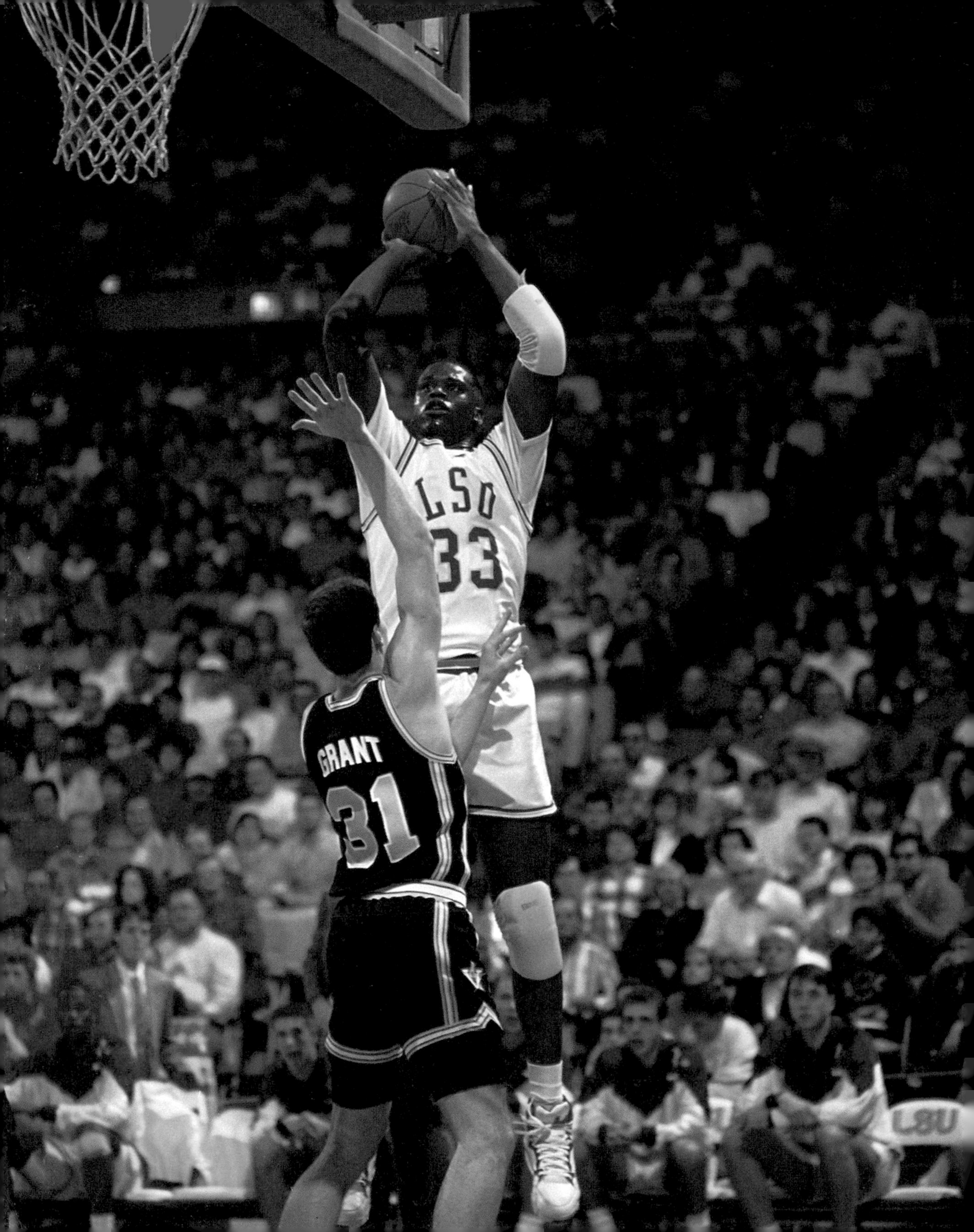
LSU
33
GRANT
31
LSU

just to foul him or talk trash to him, anything to rile him. It got to the point where even the officiating wasn't working well.''

Despite these tactics, Shaquille had some big games. He scored 43 points against Northern Arizona and was over 30 several times. He also went over the 20-rebound mark in a number of games.

LSU returned to the NCAA tournament, but lost to Indiana in the second round, 89–79. Shaq had 36 points and 12 rebounds, and had played great basketball. However, the team had been eliminated once again. The Tigers finished the year at 21–10. As for Shaq, he averaged 24.1 points a game. He also finished second in rebounding with 14.0 a game, and led the country with 157 blocks.

TIME TO TURN PRO

Shaquille was a consensus All-American again and won a number of other awards. The big question, though, was whether he would come back to LSU for his senior year. He didn't keep people waiting for long. On April 3, right after the end of the NCAA tournament, there was a press conference on the LSU campus.

Shaquille stepped to the microphone and announced that he would pass up his senior year at LSU. Instead, he would turn pro and put his name in the National Basketball Association draft. This time, he said the

In 1991–1992, Shaq dominated the college scene. Here he shows almost perfect form as he goes up for another hoop.

reason wasn't just money. It was the way defenses were playing him, the rough and dirty tactics. College basketball, for him, was no longer fun.

"I played my heart out," he said. "I remember one game when I was doing my spin move and guys were coming under me, trying to push my legs out. I was taught at a young age that if you're not having fun at something, then it's time to go.

"This time my father agreed. I also promised that I'd try to find a way to return and complete my degree."

The NBA draft was held on June 24, 1992. The team with the first pick was the Orlando Magic. The Magic had been an expansion team in 1989–1990. They had never won many games. In 1990–1991, the team had a poor 21–61 record. So it was no surprise when they made Shaquille O'Neal their choice, the number one pick in the entire draft.

TAKING THE NBA BY STORM

The two biggest attractions in Orlando, Florida, were Disney World and Sea World. That was before Shaquille O'Neal came along. Now, everyone wanted a glimpse of this huge, 20-year-old youngster. Shaq came to town with a friendly smile and a good attitude.

"I'm not promising a championship the first year," he said. "Things take time. But I'll learn the ropes, get my feet wet, and become a good player."

The James J. Corbett Memorial Award was just one of the post-season prizes Shaquille won during his LSU career. He received this one in April 1992 at the Louisiana Superdome. It was given to him as the outstanding college athlete in Louisiana.

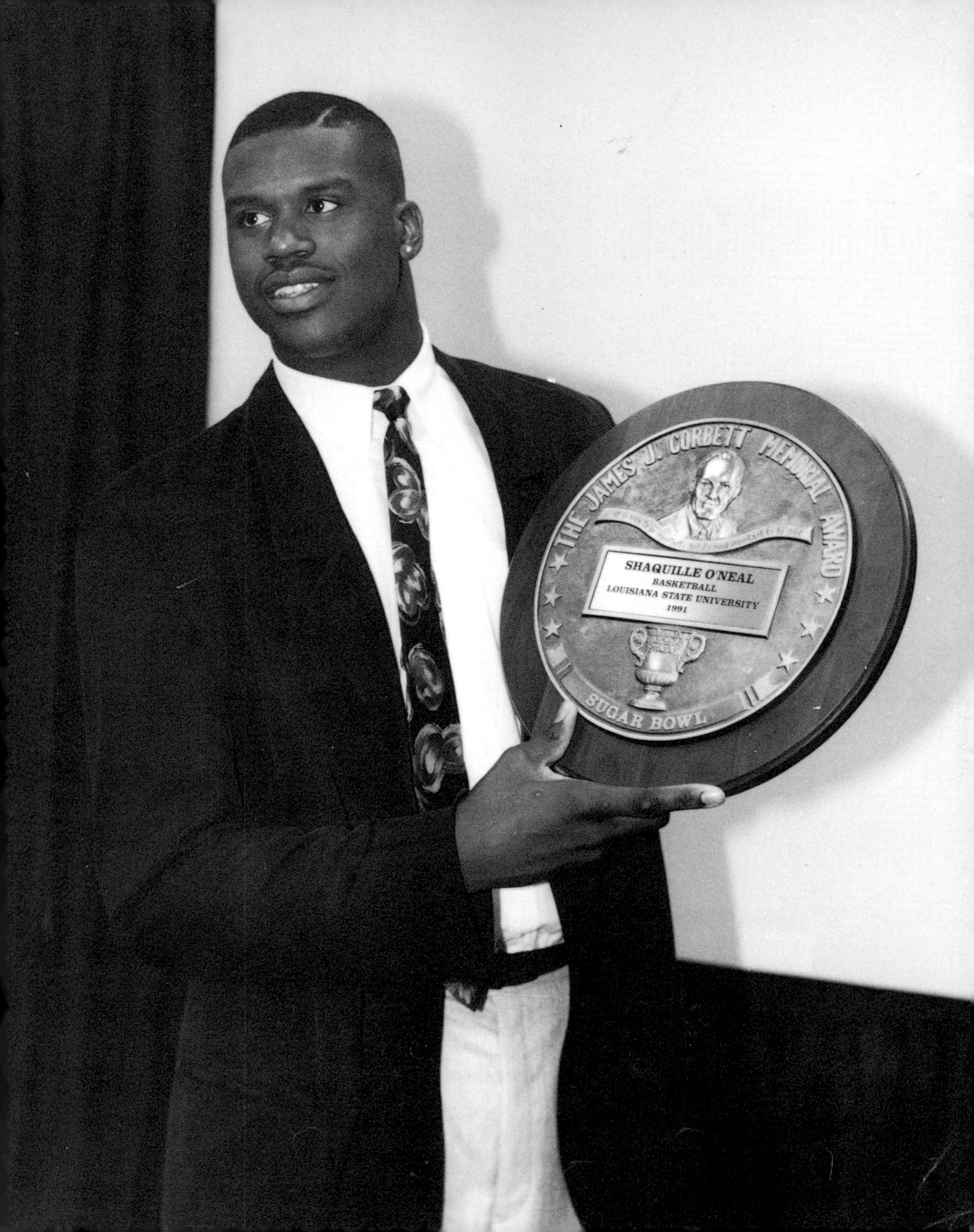
THE JAMES J. CORBETT MEMORIAL AWARD
SHAQUILLE O'NEAL
BASKETBALL
LOUISIANA STATE UNIVERSITY
1991
SUGAR BOWL

The first thing was agreeing to a contract. Shaq and his family were represented by agent/lawyer Leonard Armato. Armato worked very closely with the Magic, and they got the deal signed quickly. The contract was huge. Shaq would earn nearly $40 million over seven years. It was the largest contract ever given a rookie in any sport.

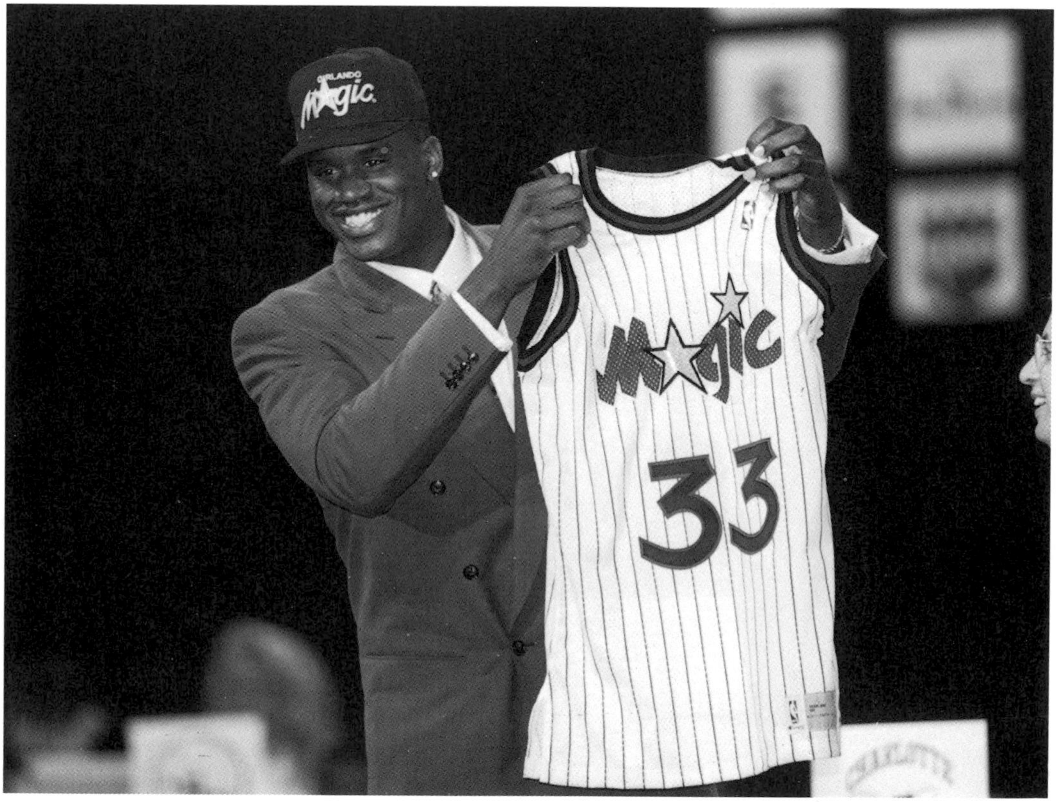
Magic
Magic
33

In June 1992, Shaquille became the NBA's top draft pick. He soon signed a seven-year, $40 million contract with the Orlando Magic. At age 20, he was the youngest player in the league.

Now he had to produce. Shaq knew that everyone would be watching him. People would expect a lot. Many people were already saying that he would be the next great center in the NBA. They said he would follow in a line that included George Mikan in the 1940s and 1950s, Bill Russell and Wilt Chamberlain in the 1950s and 1960s, and Kareem Abdul-Jabbar in the 1970s and 1980s.

"Very few people come into the league and dominate right away," Shaquille said. "I'm not rushing into anything. What will be, will be."

Many felt that Shaq would dominate. One of those who did was the superstar Earvin "Magic" Johnson. "Shaq will be great and I mean *great,*" said Magic. "The guy is a monster, a true prime time player."

The three best centers in the NBA coming into the 1992 season were David Robinson of the San Antonio Spurs, Patrick Ewing of the New York Knicks, and Hakeem Olajuwon of the Houston Rockets. Greg Kite, the backup center with the Magic, had played against all three. After he practiced with Shaquille, he quickly formed an opinion.

"Ewing has a lot of strength," said Kite, "and Robinson is really quick. But nobody combines the strength and quickness that Shaquille has."

Soon the season began and all the guesswork ended. The Magic still didn't have a lot of really good players, but they had a few. Scott Skiles was a tough little point guard who could run the offense. Nick Anderson was a shooting guard who scored big on some nights. And forward Dennis Scott was one of the best three-point shooters in the league. They joined with Shaq to form the heart of the team.

The Magic opened the season on November 6, 1992, against the Miami Heat. Miami had a tough, 6-foot-10-inch (200-centimeter) center in Rony Seikaly. Seikaly was a good player, but Shaq seemed much bigger and stronger. Seikaly couldn't move the rookie around the court at all.

Shaq played just 32 minutes in his first game before fouling out in the fourth quarter. But he scored 12 points and grabbed 18 rebounds as the Magic won, 110–100. That was the bottom line—Orlando came away with a "W."

In his first week as a pro, Shaq took the NBA by storm. In fact, he was more like a tornado. He had 22 points and 15 rebounds as the Magic beat Washington. Against Charlotte he had 35 points and 13 rebounds. Two nights later against Washington again he scored 31 points, grabbed 21 rebounds, and blocked 4 shots. The Magic won three of their first four as Shaq became the first rookie in NBA history to be named Player of the Week in his very first week in the league.

He continued to play very well. Everyone who saw him for the first time couldn't believe his size, strength, and skill.

At the end of November, the Magic were the surprise team of the league with an 8–3 record. Shaq had played so well that he was named NBA Player of the Month. He had been even better than expected.

As was the case when he was in college, Shaq had to face all kinds of defenses in the NBA. It didn't matter if he was double-or triple-teamed —he still got his points and his rebounds, as in this game against the Phoenix Suns.

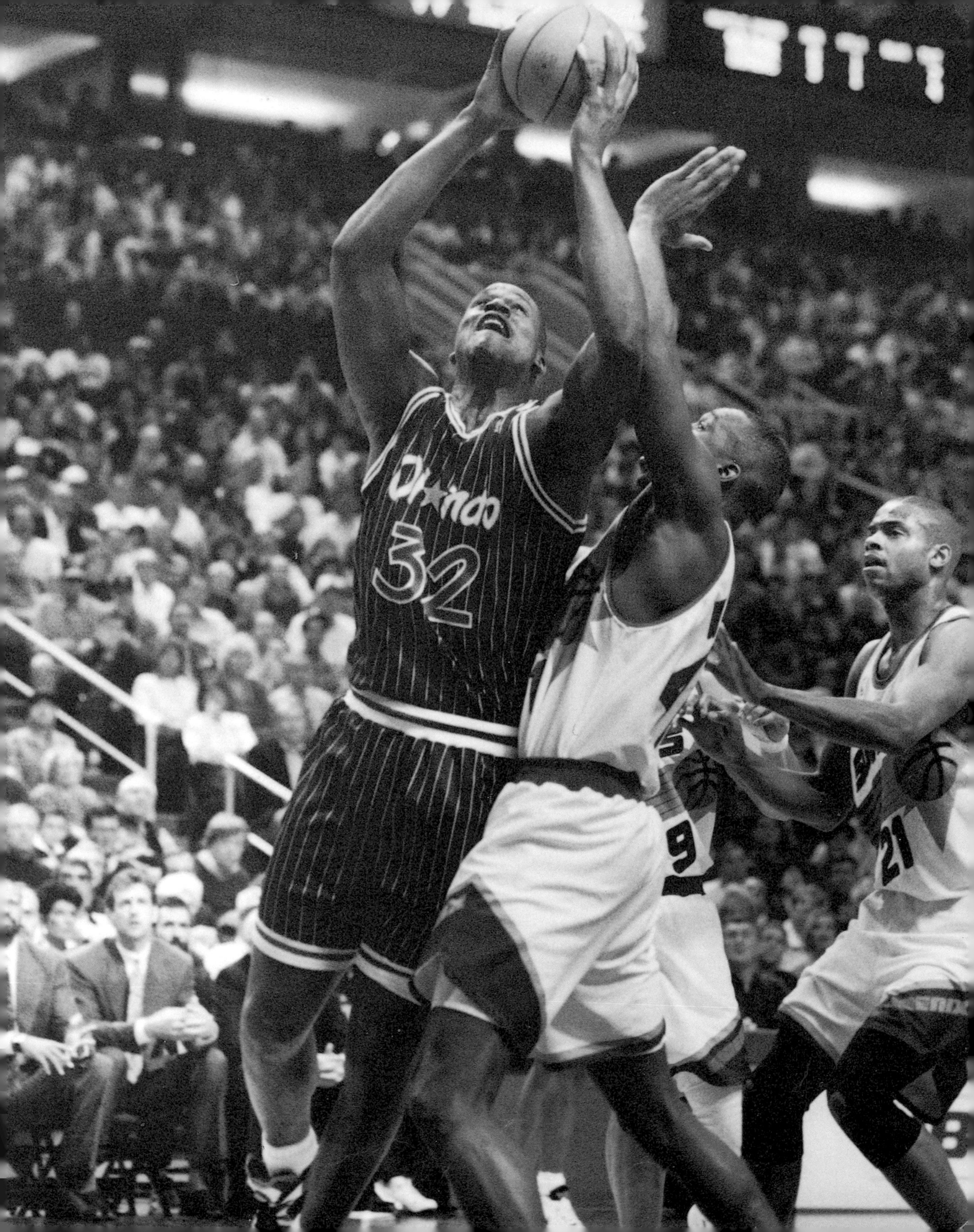
Orlando
32
9
21

A CARING PERSON

By this time, Shaq was doing more than just playing basketball. His out-going personality and quick smile made him a natural to appear in com-mercials. His love of rap music and video games helped to make him even more of a favorite with youngsters all over the country.

Many kids identified with Shaq because he spoke their language. Rap music was a big part of his life. Here he performs with the well-known rap group Fu Schnikens.

Soon Shaq was appearing in commercials for top-brand basketball shoes and soft drinks. He was also a spokesman for a sporting goods company and several other products. After being in the NBA for just two months, he was the league's most popular player after the magnificent Michael Jordan.

He did other things that surprised people, as well. At Thanksgiving time, Shaq held a dinner for about 300 homeless people. He paid for the food himself, then stayed and ate with those who came for the meal. With a wink of his eye, he called the dinner *Shaqsgiving*.

"Basketball is not everything in life," he said. "It doesn't make a difference if these people know me or not. As long as they can eat and they're happy."

At Christmas time, Shaq bought toys for needy children in the Orlando area. They weren't just little gifts. They were all good-quality, popular toys that youngsters wanted and enjoyed.

"I brought good gifts," he said. "I did it because I wanted to do it and was able to do it. Money doesn't make people change. People make people change, and I'm not going to let that happen."

One of the people impressed with Shaquille was Glenda Hood, the mayor of Orlando.

"Once you start talking to [Shaquille] you realize that there's a real person who is caring and committed," she said, "and wants to be part of the community."

No one said a bad word about Shaq. There were dozens of requests for interviews almost every day. Photographers wanted pictures of him.

Fans wanted autographs or just to shake his hand. All the Magic home games were sold out. On the road, fans came out by the thousands to see him play.

Shaq's best friend on the Magic was second-year forward Dennis Scott. The two young stars trusted each other.

"Shaq knows I don't want anything from him besides his friendship," said Scott. "I'm not going to let anyone mess up his head. I always tell it like it is. I don't give Shaq lip service. I think he appreciates the honesty."

SHAQ ATTAQ

As the season wore on, the Magic fell back to around the .500 mark. They just didn't have enough good players to become a top team. But they still had a chance for the playoffs. And they still had Shaquille O'Neal.

Shaq showed he could play with the big three—Robinson, Ewing, and Olajuwon. In fact, on occasion he outplayed them. With the midseason All-Star Game coming up, Shaquille was voted the starting center on the East team. He was the first rookie to be named a starter since Michael Jordan back in 1984.

By mid-season, Shaq had already made his mark as one of the top centers in the NBA. Here he goes over the Lakers' Sam Perkins for a short jumper. When he was named to start for the East in the NBA All-Star Game, he became the first rookie to earn that honor since Michael Jordan in 1984.

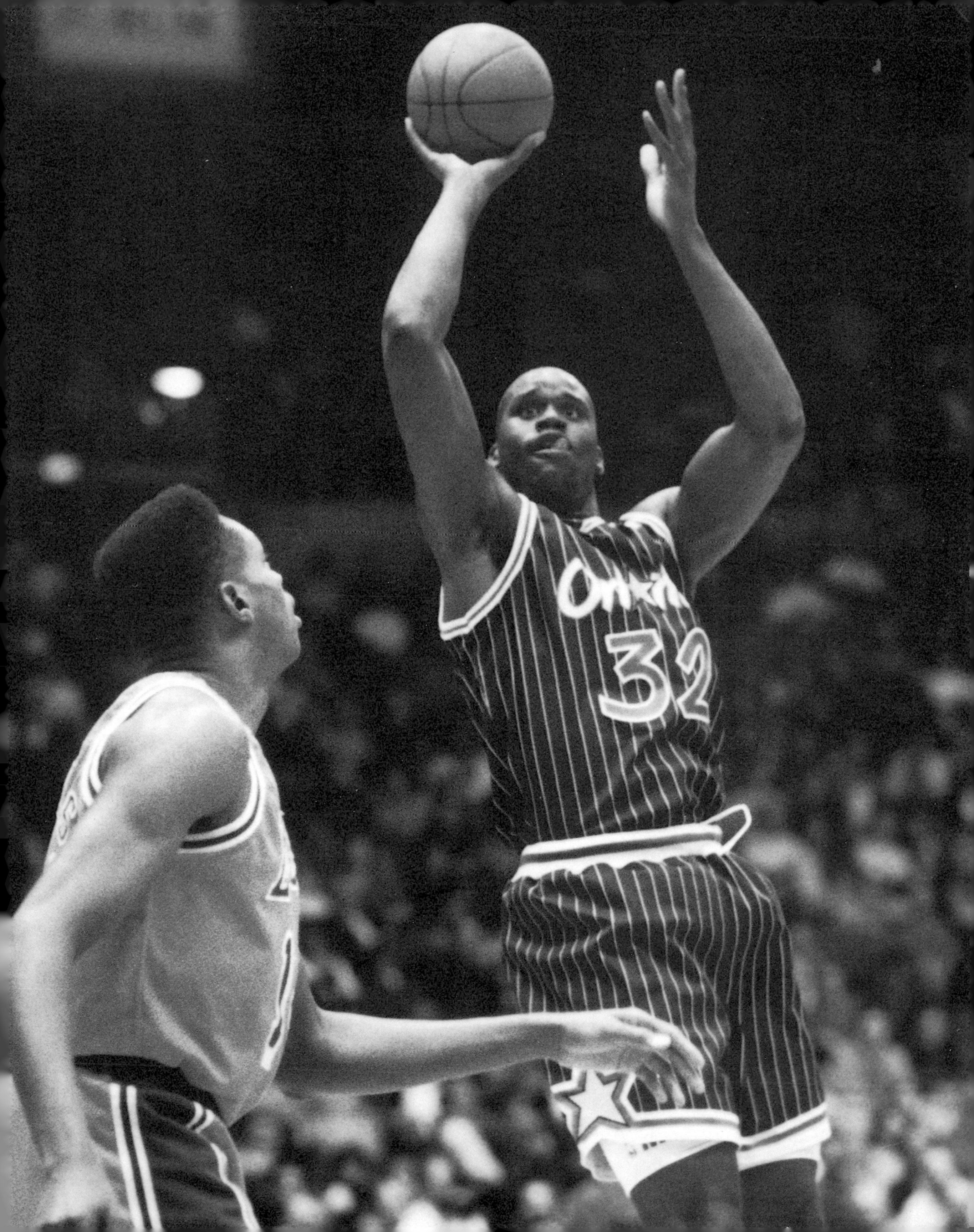
32

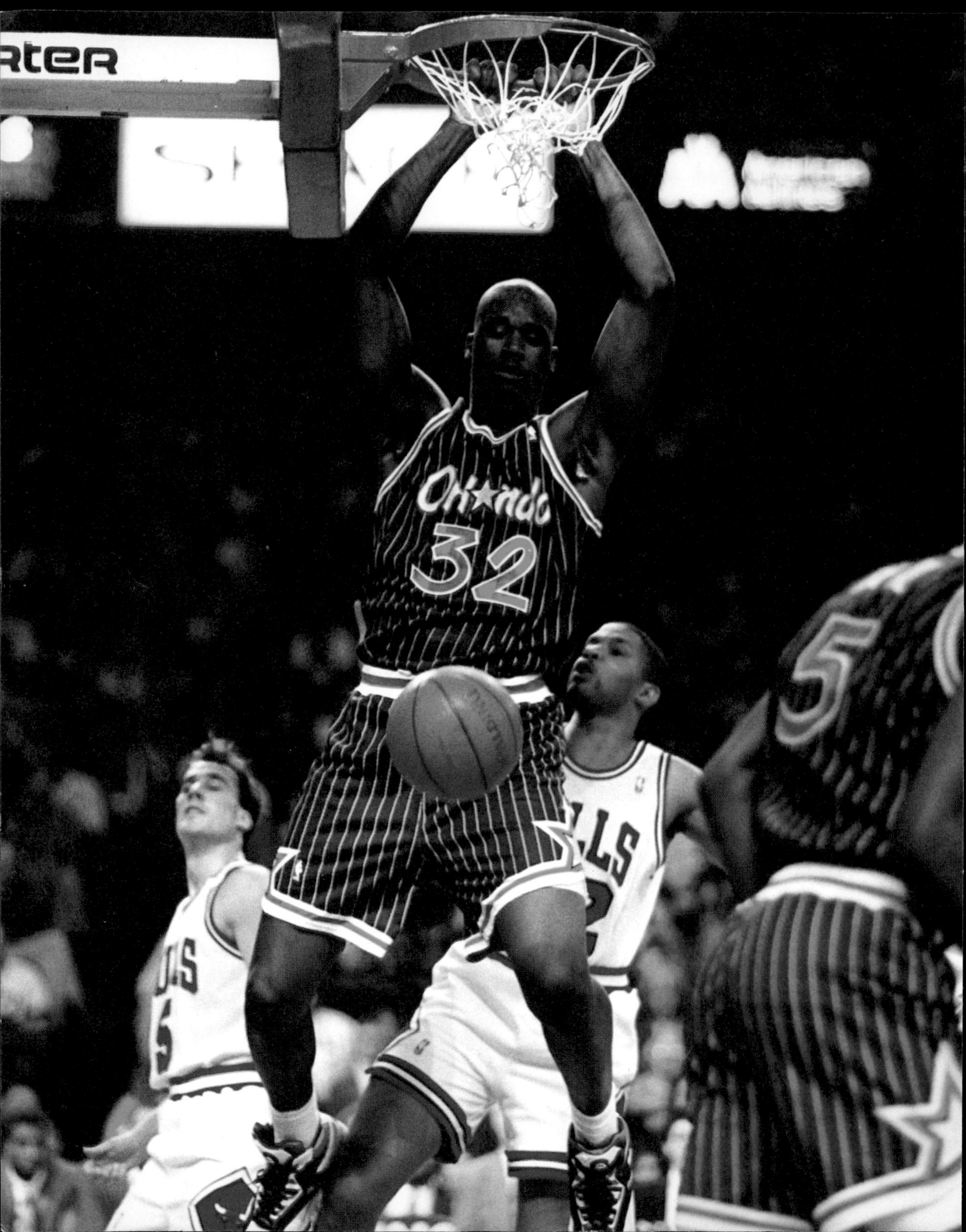

Orlando
32

There was a special excitement when Shaq's team met Jordan's. In one game in Chicago, Jordan led the Bulls with an incredible 64 points. But Shaq also played a great game, and it went into overtime. Orlando won the game in the OT as Shaq wound up with 29 points, 24 rebounds, and 5 blocked shots. After playing 50 minutes, he didn't even seem tired.

"Michael Jordan is the best player in the world," Shaq said, afterward. "Maybe if I continue to work hard, someday I'll be the greatest player in the world. That would be nice to say . . . someday."

At the halfway point of the season the Magic were 21–20. A year earlier, without Shaq, they were 10–31. It wasn't hard to see the difference he had made.

Before the All-Star Game there was an exciting triple-overtime contest against the Knicks. The Magic won it, 102–100, as Shaquille was the star in OT. He blocked several key Knick shots, scored the winning basket, and had a number of key rebounds. He finished with 21 points, 19 rebounds, and a team record 9 blocks.

"I'm pretty proud of myself," he said, after the game.

In the next game, against Detroit, he just couldn't be stopped. He hit 19 of 25 shots from the field and 8 of 16 from the free throw line for a career best 46 points. He also had 21 rebounds and 5 blocks. He was doing it at both ends of the floor.

There was always great excitement when Shaq and the Magic played against the Chicago Bulls. In one overtime game in Chicago, Shaq had 29 points and 24 rebounds as Orlando won in overtime.

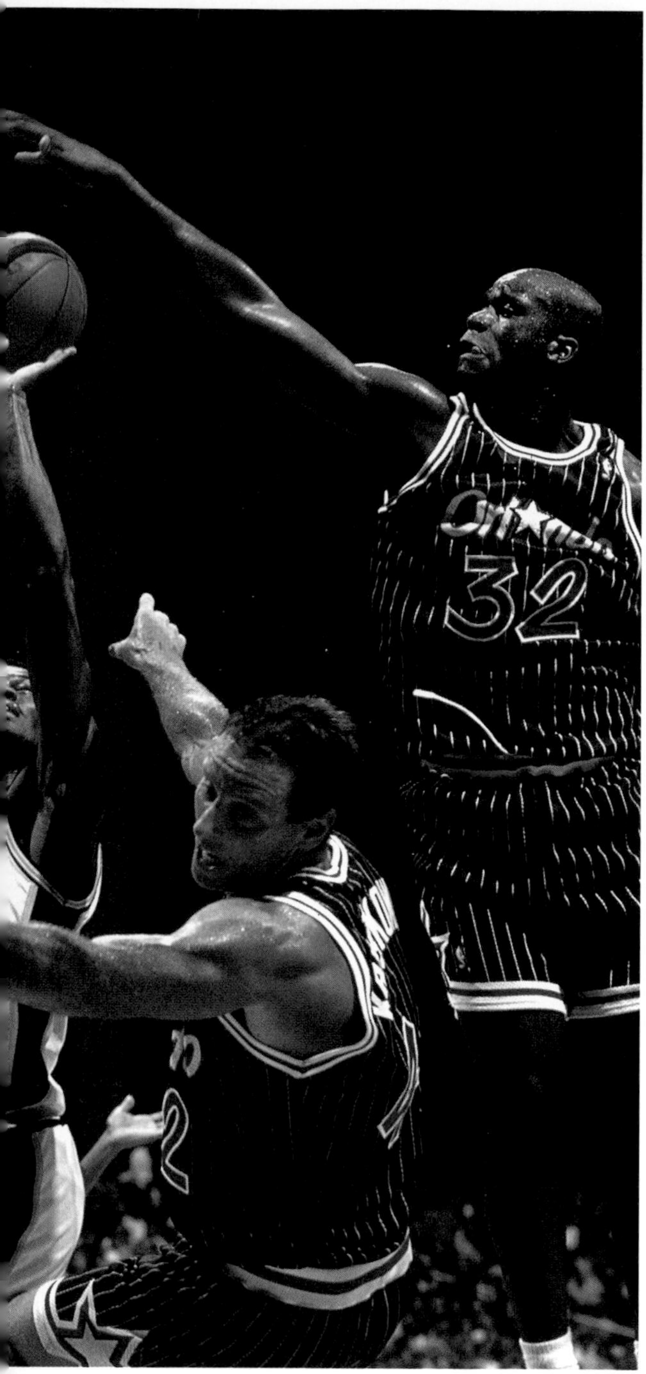
Orlando
32

At All-Star Weekend many former NBA stars came to play in an old-timers' or Legends' game. Most of them wanted to talk about the Shaq. Perhaps it was former great Connie Hawkins who spoke for most when he said, "Once [Shaq] really learns how to play the game, he is going to be the greatest player ever."

In the All-Star Game, Shaq had 14 points and 7 rebounds. But he only played 25 minutes in a game that went into overtime. Some felt that he should have played more, but, as usual, Shaq always seemed to say the right thing.

"I had fun and I wasn't upset," he said. "I'll tell you something else. Shaq will be back."

Everyone agreed with that. He would be an all-star for many years.

Because he was so quick for a big man, Shaq was also a great shot blocker. Anyone driving to the hoop against the Magic had to watch for him swooping in from above to swat the ball away. Here Shaq goes up to block a shot in a game against the San Antonio Spurs.

Now it was time to get back to the season. The Magic were 24–23 at the break. They still had a chance to make the playoffs. That was the most important thing now.

ROOKIE OF THE YEAR

Shaquille's numbers were down slightly in the second half of the season. But he continued to have some big nights as the team battled to make the playoffs. He didn't seem to get as tired as some rookies who can't cope with the long NBA season.

Off the court, he was the same giving person. At Easter, he visited the Arnold Palmer Hospital for Children and Women. He brought the youngsters special Easter baskets filled with candy and one of his basketball cards. Once again he was a gentle giant who brought gifts, a smile, and some happiness to a group of sick children.

Finally, the battle for the playoffs came down to the last weekend of the season. In the second-to-last game, Shaq showed his awesome power once more. Playing against the New Jersey Nets in the Meadowlands Arena, he went up for another of his thunderous slam dunks.

As he came down, the backboard came loose from its top supports and tumbled to the floor. Shaq had destroyed a backboard for the second time that season. No wonder his opponents got out of the way when he dunked.

The Magic won that game, then won the final game of the year, against Atlanta, 104–85. Shaq had 31 points and 18 rebounds in the finale. It gave the Magic a .500 record at 41–41.

Unfortunately, the team just missed the final playoff spot. Indiana was also 41–41, but had taken the season series from the Magic. So it was the Pacers that made the playoffs.

But Shaquille had a brilliant rookie season. He was eighth in the league in scoring with a 23.4 average, second in rebounding with 13.8 per game, and second in blocked shots with an average of 3.5 per game. He was also fourth in shooting percentage, hitting on 56.2 percent of his shots. Shortly after the season ended, he was named NBA Rookie of the Year.

"I'm very proud and happy to win this," Shaquille said. "It's been a long year, but I learned a lot and I'm already looking forward to next season."

The Magic were truly an up-and-coming team. If Dennis Scott hadn't been hurt for most of the year, the team might have won more games. Then, in June, the Magic picked point guard Anfernee Hardaway as their first draft choice. At 6 feet 7-inches (200 centimeters), the former Memphis State star was expected to team with Shaq to make the Magic even better.

Shaquille O'Neal celebrated his good fortune by buying a 7,000-square-foot (650-square-meter) home in a golf club community in Central Florida. His neighbors included successful people from many different fields. His house became famous for its full arcade-amusement center, including a full-size Terminator II game. He also had a stereo system installed that can make the walls shake.

"I like toys and I like my music," Shaq has said.

He has always been, after all, just a big kid at heart. In 1992–1993, he was the youngest player in the NBA, as well as one of the best. At the All-Star break of the 1993–1994 season, Shaquille was the top scorer in the entire league, averaging nearly 30 points a game. Early 1994 also marked the release of *Blue Chips,* a major motion picture starring Nick Nolte, with Shaq in a supporting role. He had completed the film before the start of the 1993–1994 season.

He has been perhaps the most powerful player ever to play basketball. As Miami Heat center Rony Seikaly put it, "When Shaq backs into you, it's like a house falling on you."

That's what's been called a real Shaq Attaq.

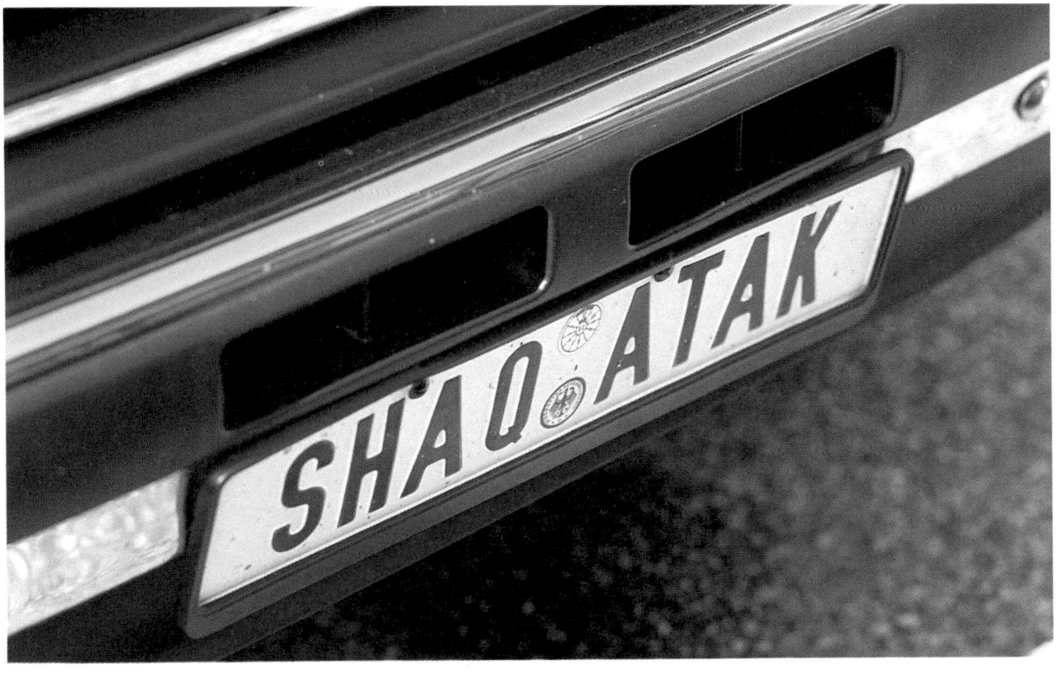
SHAQ ATAK

By now, everyone knew what a Shaq Attaq was, but just in case anyone forgot, Shaq's custom license plates were a constant reminder.

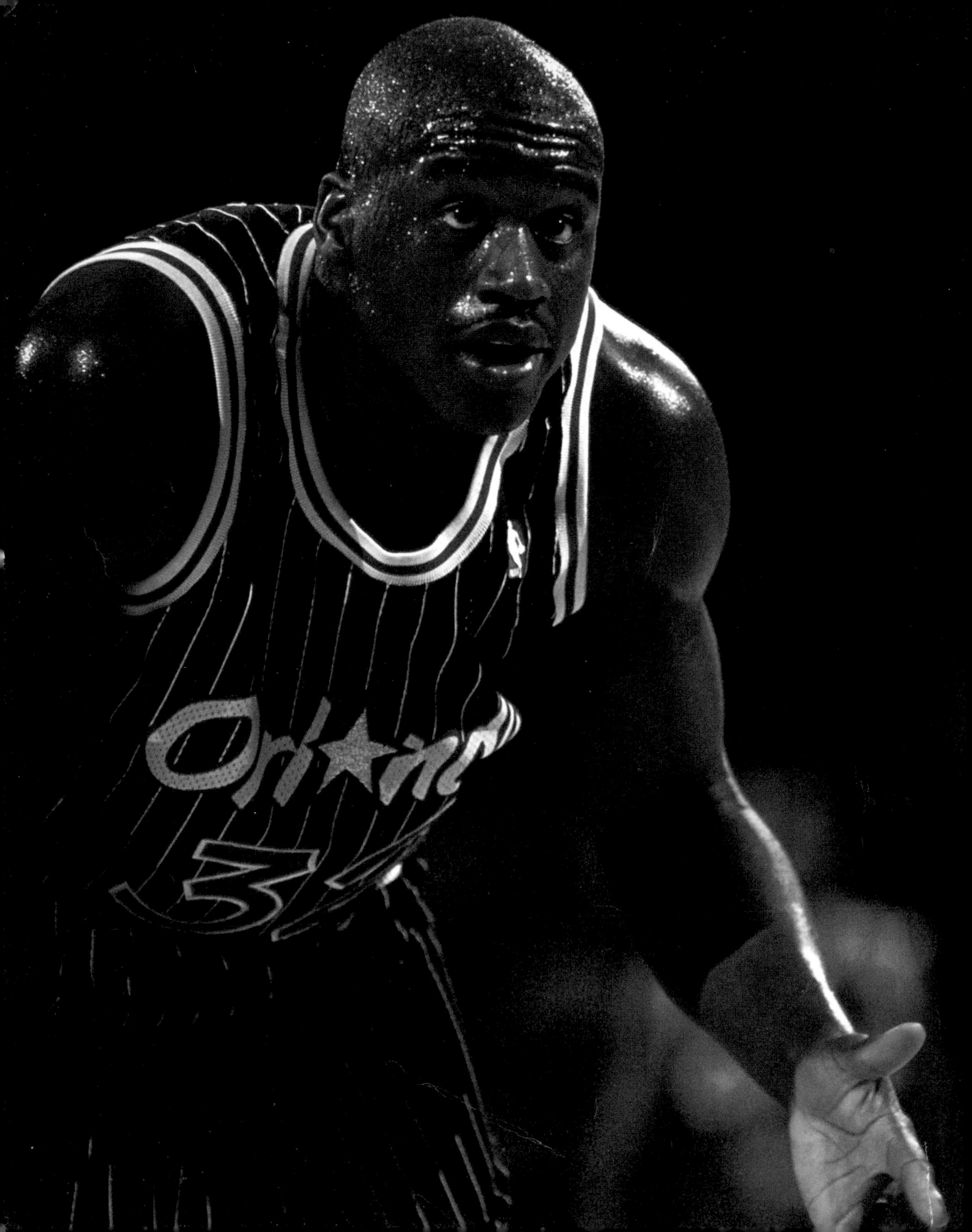

SHAQUILLE O'NEAL: HIGHLIGHTS

1972	Born on March 6 in Newark, New Jersey.
1988	As a junior at Cole High School in San Antonio, Texas, leads basketball team to a 32–1 record.
1989	Leads Cole High School to a 36–0 record and the state championship. Enters Louisiana State University.
1990	Averages 13.9 points per game and 12.0 rebounds per game as a freshman. Sets Southeastern Conference (SEC) record with 115 blocked shots. Scores 53 points against Arkansas State in December.
1991	Named National Player of the Year by the Associated Press, United Press International, and *Sports Illustrated.* Named to All-American first team. Named SEC Athlete of the Year. Named SEC Player of the Year. Leads nation in rebounding with 14.7 average. Sets SEC record with 140 blocked shots. Becomes first player to lead SEC in scoring, rebounding, field goal percentage, and blocked shots in the same year.
1992	Named to All-American first team. Named SEC Player of the Year. Is second nationally in rebounding with 14.0 average. Sets SEC record with 157 blocked shots. Signs with Orlando Magic of the National Basketball Association (NBA).
1993	Is named starting center for the East in the NBA All-Star Game. Leads Magic to 41–41 record, the best in the team's history. Is named Rookie of the Year. Averages 23.4 points (eighth in the NBA), 13.9 rebounds (second), and 3.53 blocked shots (second) per game.

FIND OUT MORE

Aaseng, Nathan. *Basketball's Playmakers*. Minneapolis, Minn.: Lerner, 1983.

Anderson, Dave. *The Story of Basketball*. New York: Morrow Junior Books, 1988.

Balzar, Howard. *Basketball Super Stars*. Fenton, Mo.: Marketcom, 1990.

Basketball: Superstars & Superstats. Racine, Wisc.: Western Publishing Company, 1991.

Sullivan, George. *All About Basketball*. New York: Putnam Publishing Group, 1991.

How to write to Shaquille O'Neal:
Shaquille O'Neal
c/o Orlando Magic
One Magic Place, Orlando Arena
Orlando, Florida 32801

INDEX

Page numbers in *italics* refer to illustrations.

Abdul-Jabbar, Kareem, 31
All-Star Game, 5, 36, 40
All-Star Weekend, 40
Anderson, Nick, 31
Arizona, University of, 23
Armato, Leonard, 30
Atlanta Hawks, 41

Barkley, Charles, 6
Blue Chips, 43
Brown, Dale, 10-11, 13

Carse, Craig, 18, 20, 21, 25
Chamberlain, Wilt, 31
Charlotte Hornets, 32
Chicago Bulls, *38,* 39
Commercials, 8, 34, 35

Detroit Pistons, 39
Durham, Hugh, 23

Ewing, Patrick, 31, 36

Fort Sam Houston, *11*
Fu Schnickens, 8, *34*

Hardaway, Anfernee, 42
Harrison, Ayesha, 9
Harrison, Jamal, 9

Harrison, LaTeefah, 9
Harrison, Lucille O'Neal, 8-9
Harrison, Philip, 8-12, 17
Hawkins, Connie, 40
Hood, Glenda, 35
Houston Rockets, 31

Indiana Pacers, 42

Jackson, Chris, 17-18, *18-19,* 21
James J. Corbett Memorial Award, *29*
Johnson, Earvin "Magic," 31
Jordan, Michael, 6, 35, 36, 39

Kentucky Wildcats, 23
Kite, Greg, 31

Los Angeles Lakers, *37*
Louisiana State University, 13-14, 17-18,
    18-19, 20-21, 23-25, 27-28

Machen, Bob, 6
Madura, Dave, 12
Mashburn, Jamal, 23
Miami Heat, 32
Mikan, George, 31
More, Herb, 12, 14-15

NBA draft, 27-28, *30*
NCAA playoffs, 24, 27
Nevada-Las Vegas, 20
Newark, New Jersey, 8

New Jersey Nets, 41
New York Knicks, 31, 39
Northern Arizona University, 27

Olajuwon, Hakeem, 31, 36
Olympic Festival, *21*
O'Neal, Shaquille, *16, 18-19, 22, 25, 26*
  All-Star Game, 5, 36, 40
  awards, *29*, 42
  birth of, 8
  character of, 12, 35-36, 41
  childhood of, 8-10
  in commercials, 8, 34, 35
  defenses against, 14-15, 25, 27, 28, *33*
  education of, 10, 17, 20-21, 24
  in high school, 11, 12, 14-15, 17
  at Louisiana State University, 13-14, 17-
    18, 20-21, 23-25, 27-28, *29*
  movie role and, 43
  naming, 8-9
  NBA draft, 27-28, *30*
  nickname, 21, 23
  Orlando Magic, 5-6, 28, 30-32, *33*, 36,
    37, 38, 39, *40*, 41-42
  physical appearance of, 10-12, *16*, 17,
    18, 21
  rap music and, 8, *34*
  Rookie of the Year, 42
  slam dunks, 5-6, 8, *13*, 15, 41

Orlando Magic, 5-6, 28, 30-32, *33*, 36, *37*,
  38, 39, *40*, 41-42

Perkins, Sam, *37*
Phoenix Suns, 5-6, *33*
Player of the Month, 32
Player of the Week, 32

Rap music, 8, *34*
Robert G. Cole High School, 11-15, 17
Roberts, Stanley, 18, *18-19*, 21
Robinson, Dave, 31, 36
Russell, Bill, 31

San Antonio Spurs, 31, *40*
Scott, Dennis, 31, 36, 42
Seikaly, Rony, 32, 43
Skiles, Scott, 31
Slam dunks, 5-6, 8, *13*, 15, 41
Southeastern Conference, 20

Tigers
  (*see* Louisiana State University)

University of Connecticut, 24
University of Indiana, 27
University of Texas, 20

Washington Bullets, 32

Sara Diepersloot

Fast and Fun
First Quilts

18 Projects for
Instant Gratification

Martingale®
& COMPANY

COTTAGE

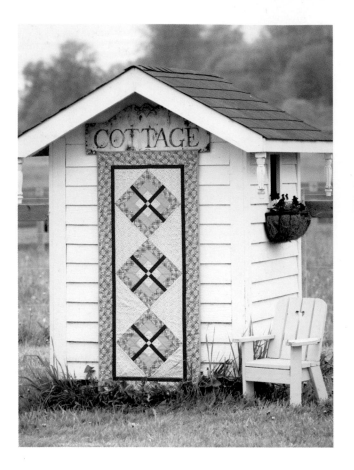

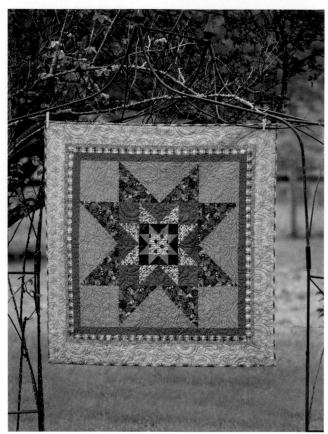

Fast and Fun First Quilts:
18 Projects for Instant Gratification

That Patchwork Place
Martingale & COMPANY

That Patchwork Place® is an imprint of Martingale & Company®.

Martingale & Company
19021 120th Ave. NE, Ste. 102
Bothell, WA 98011-9511 USA
www.martingale-pub.com

Printed in China
16 15 14 13 12 11 8 7 6 5 4 3 2 1

Library of Congress Cataloging-in-Publication Data is available upon request.

ISBN: 978-1-60468-064-5

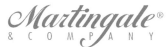

Dedication

To my amazing kids: Laura, Kimmie, Ryan, and David. Your creativity inspires me and you fill my days with laughter and fun. I love you all so much!

CREDITS

President & CEO: Tom Wierzbicki
Editor in Chief: Mary V. Green
Managing Editor: Karen Costello Soltys
Technical Editor: Ellen Pahl
Copy Editor: Sheila Chapman Ryan
Design Director: Stan Green
Production Manager: Regina Girard
Illustrators: Laurel Strand & Robin Strobel
Cover & Text Designer: Regina Girard
Photographer: Brent Kane

Special thanks to Tanya Mock and Rosemary and Cliff Bailey, all of Snohomish, Washington, for generously allowing us to photograph at their homes.

MISSION STATEMENT

Dedicated to providing quality products and service to inspire creativity.

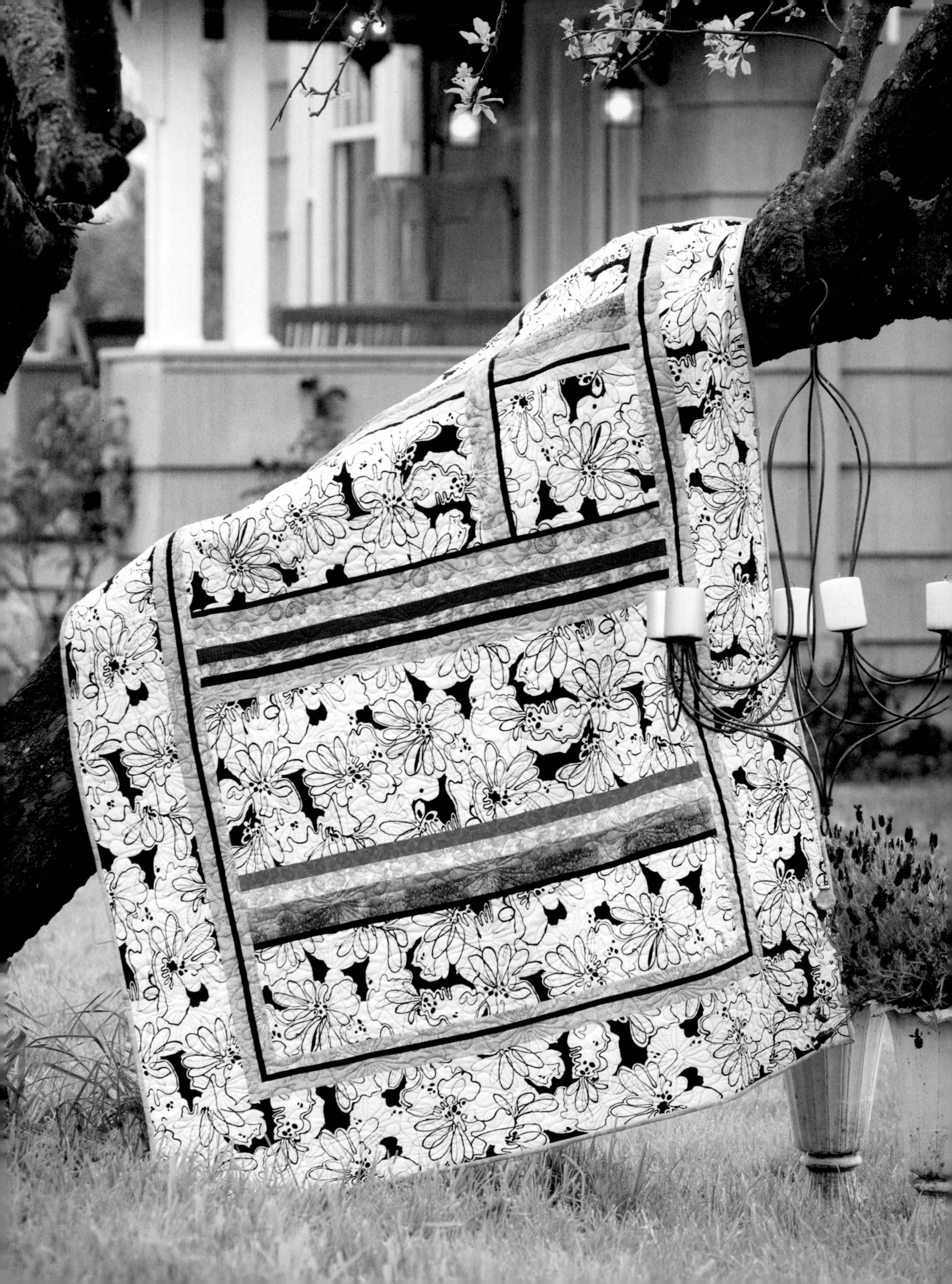

Contents

Introduction	7	Summer BBQ	46
		Seaside Table Runner	49
Cupcake Delight	8	Simple Strips	52
Be Mine	11	Harvest Star	56
Nest	15	Harvest Time	60
Cracked Up	18	Cozy Winter Night	64
Lime Punch	21	Winter Wonderland	67
Fresh Floral Table Runner	27	Snowmen's Forest	71
Summer Garden	31		
Campout	35	Quiltmaking Techniques	75
Summer Camp	39	Acknowledgments	79
Picnic Day	42	About the Author	79

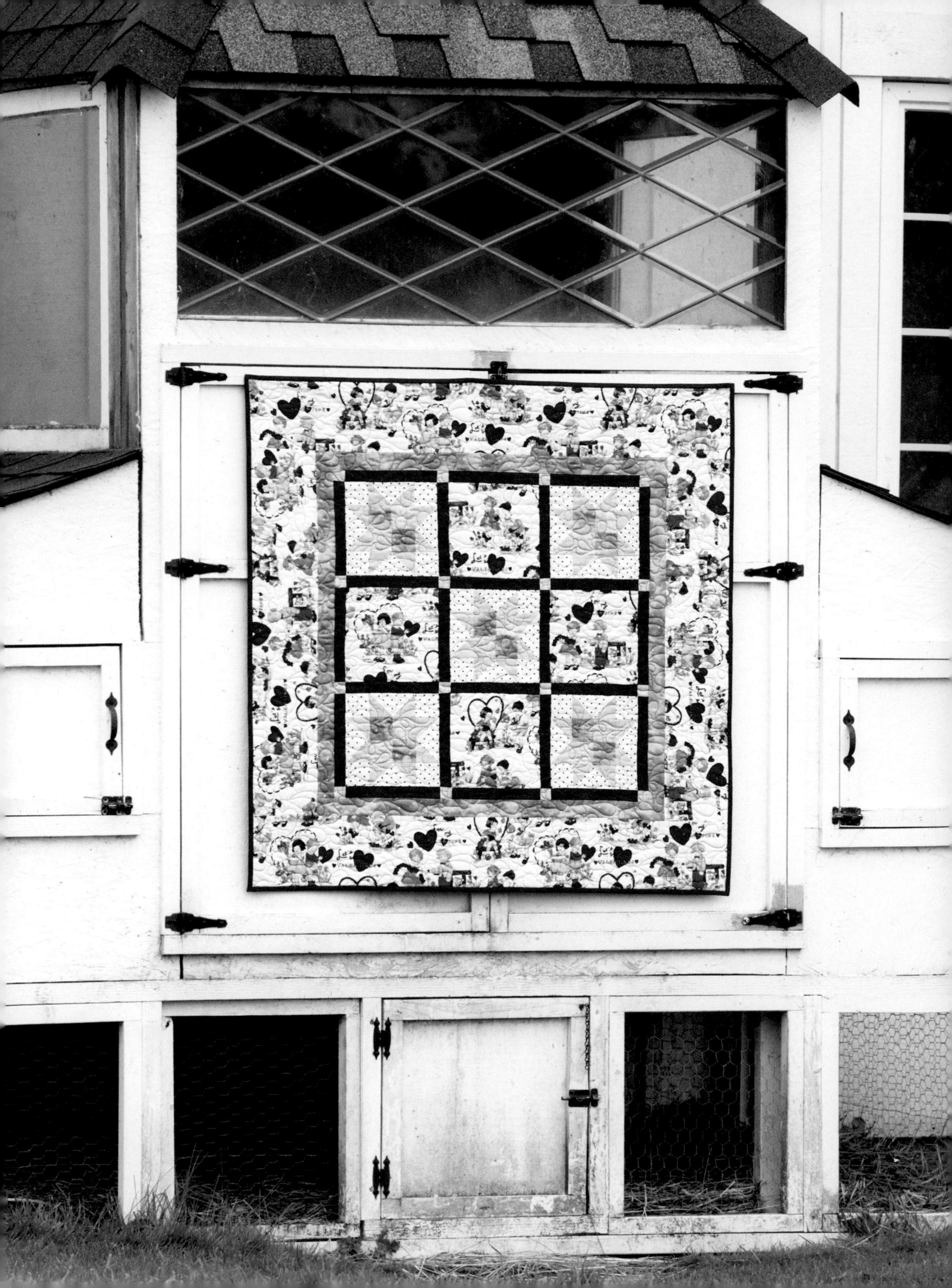

Introduction

One of my favorite pastimes is exploring quilt shops. Whenever I travel, I make time to visit any new shops I can find. I love to be inspired by fabric!

Usually my design process begins with the fabric. It seems that I'm often drawn to large-scale prints or fun novelty prints. It's not always easy to find a way to use these wonderful fabrics effectively. The designs in this book incorporate a lot of fabulous prints, providing ways to really showcase them.

All of the 18 quilts in this book are simple but stylish, quick projects using large pieces, strip piecing, and simple techniques. They're easy enough to make as your first quilt and beautiful enough for an experienced quilter who has collected some special fabrics. Those very fabrics are often the ones that sit on shelves the longest, awaiting the perfect quilt design.

Whether you're shopping for fabrics or using your stash, you'll undoubtedly be selecting different prints than the ones I chose when making the photographed quilts. Fabrics come and go, and most of the prints I've used will probably not be available to you. It doesn't matter because you'll want to make your own version anyway. To help you imagine what the quilt would look like in other fabrics, I've included a section called "Fabric Alternatives" with each quilt design. I chose some other fabrics, equally stunning or whimsical, and we've created quilt diagrams using those alternate fabrics. So, check those out for additional inspiration and ideas.

It's my hope that you'll be inspired and excited by my designs and the many wonderful fabrics available today. Visit your favorite quilt shop, or check your stash and spend some time being creative!

Cupcake Delight

This sweet quilt is a variation of the traditional checkerboard, but with rectangular shapes and three alternating prints. I love the bright fun colors in this quilt.

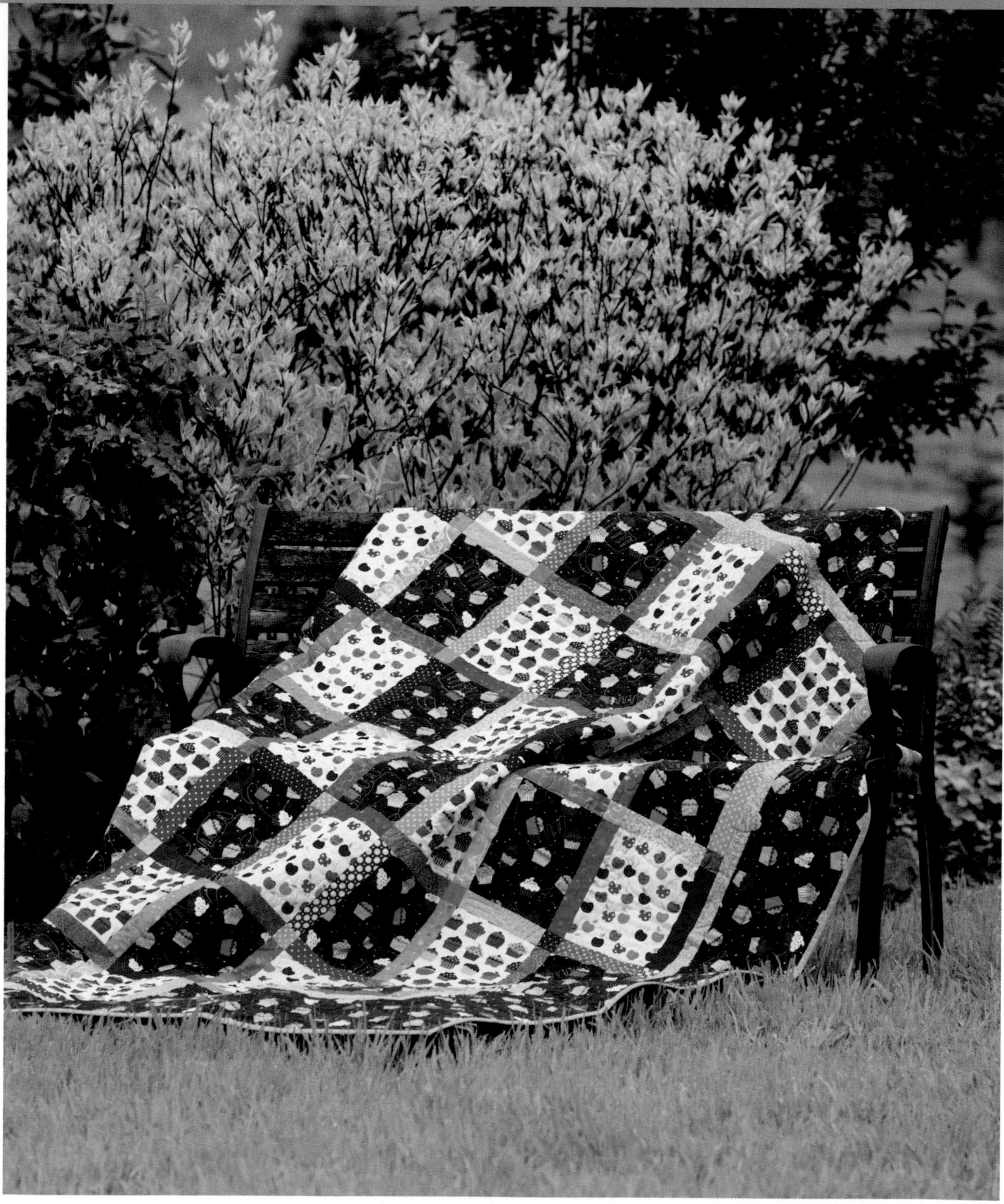

Finished quilt: 67½" x 81½"
Finished block: 6" x 8"

*Pieced by Sara Diepersloot;
quilted by Deborah Rasmussen*

MATERIALS

Yardage is based on 42"-wide fabric.

2⅞ yards of brown cupcake print for blocks and
   outer border

1¾ yards *total* of assorted bright prints for sashing

⅝ yard of white cherry print for blocks

⅝ yard of white cupcake print for blocks

⅜ yard of blue fabric for inner border

⅝ yard of green fabric for binding

5 yards of fabric for backing

76" x 90" piece of batting

CUTTING

From the assorted bright prints, cut:
56 pieces, 1¾" x 6½"
56 pieces, 1¾" x 8½"
64 squares, 1¾" x 1¾"

From the brown cupcake print, cut:
5 strips, 8½" x 42"; crosscut into 25 rectangles,
   6½" x 8½"
7 strips, 7" x 42"

From the white cherry print, cut:
2 strips, 8½" x 42"; crosscut into 12 rectangles,
   6½" x 8½"

From the white cupcake print, cut:
2 strips, 8½" x 42"; crosscut into 12 rectangles,
   6½" x 8½"

From the blue fabric, cut:
6 strips, 1½" x 42"*

From the green fabric, cut:
8 strips, 2¼" x 42"

**If your strips are less than 40½" wide after wash-
   ing and removing selvages, you'll need to cut an
   extra strip.*

ASSEMBLING THE QUILT TOP

1. Sew eight assorted bright 1¾" squares and
   seven assorted 1¾" x 6½" pieces together into
   a row. Press the seam allowances toward the
   squares. Make eight rows.

Make 8.

2. Join four brown cupcake rectangles, two white
   cupcake rectangles, and one white cherry print
   rectangle into a row, alternating them with the
   assorted bright 1¾" x 8½" sashing pieces. Press
   the seam allowances toward the rectangles.
   Make two rows. Make two rows with four
   brown cupcake print rectangles, two white
   cherry print rectangles, and one white cupcake
   print rectangle as shown on page 10. Repeat
   with three brown cupcake rectangles, two

cherry print, and two white cupcake print rect-angles. Make two rows and one row as shown.

Make 2.

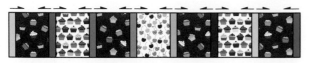

Make 2.

Make 2.

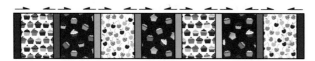

Make 1.

3. Sew the rows made in steps 1 and 2 together, alternating them as shown in the quilt diagram. Press the seam allowances in one direction.

4. Referring to "Adding Borders" on page 76, attach the blue inner and brown cupcake outer borders.

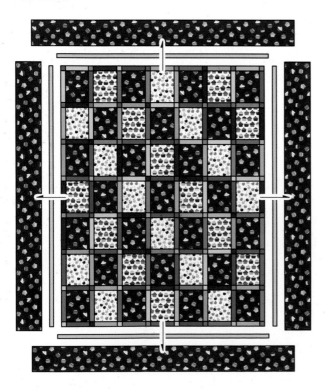

FINISHING THE QUILT

1. Layer the quilt top with batting and backing and quilt as desired.

   Quilting Note: This quilt has the cutest cupcake design stitched all over it. Yumm!

2. Referring to "Binding" on page 77, bind the edges of the quilt using the green strips.

Fabric Alternatives

Celebrate spring! The great cupcake print I used is bright and whimsical, but here's another idea. Replace the cupcakes with a colorful spring print and accent it with coordinating colors.

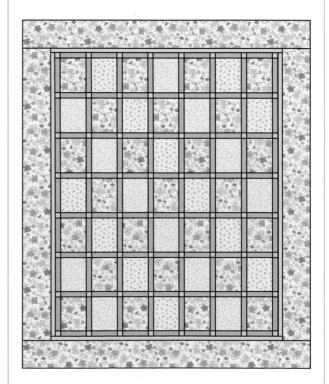

Be Mine

Show off those delightful seasonal prints in this quilt. It can serve as a perky wall hanging or table topper.

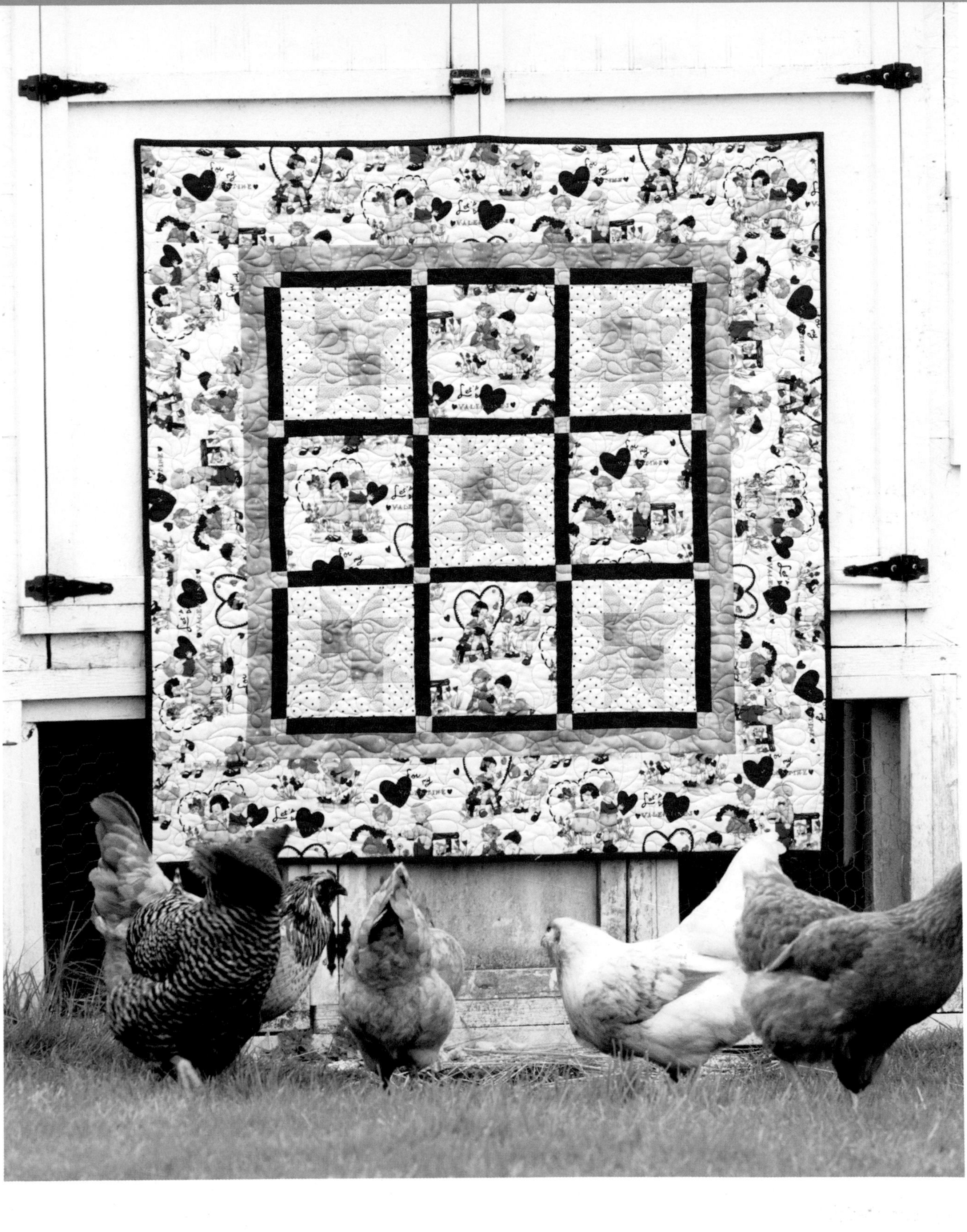

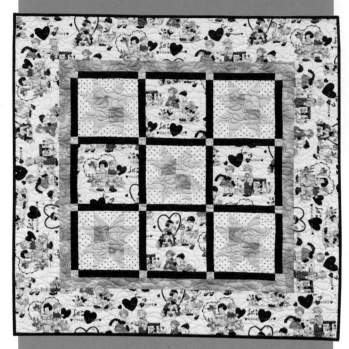

Finished quilt: 43½" x 43½"
Finished block: 8" x 8"

*Pieced by Sara Diepersloot;
quilted by Deborah Rasmussen*

MATERIALS

Yardage is based on 42"-wide fabric.

1⅓ yards of valentine print for blocks and outer border

⅔ yard of red print for sashing and binding

½ yard of white-and-red polka-dot print for blocks

⅜ yard of green print for blocks and inner border

⅓ yard of light blue print for blocks

¼ yard of lavender print for blocks and sashing squares

2⅞ yards of fabric for backing

52" x 52" piece of batting

CUTTING

From the green print, cut:
1 strip, 2½" x 42"
3 strips, 2" x 42"

From the lavender print, cut:
1 strip, 2½" x 42"
1 strip, 1½" x 42"; crosscut into 16 squares, 1½" x 1½"

From the light blue print, cut:
3 strips, 2½" x 42"; crosscut into 40 squares, 2½" x 2½"

From the white-and-red polka-dot print, cut:
5 strips, 2½" x 42"; crosscut into 20 rectangles, 2½" x 4½", and 20 squares, 2½" x 2½"

From the valentine print, cut:
1 strip, 8½" x 42"; crosscut into 4 squares, 8½" x 8½"
5 strips, 6½" x 42"

From the red print, cut:
6 strips, 1½" x 42"; crosscut into 24 pieces, 1½" x 8½"
5 strips, 2¼" x 42"

MAKING THE BLOCKS

1. Sew the green 2½" x 42" strip and the lavender 2½" x 42" strip together to make a strip set. Press the seam allowances toward the green. Crosscut the strip set into 10 segments, 2½" wide.

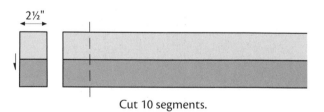

2½"

Cut 10 segments.

2. Sew two 2½" segments together to make a four-patch unit. Make five units.

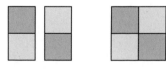

Make 5.

3. Draw a diagonal line from corner to corner on the wrong side of the light blue 2½" squares. Lay a square on one end of a polka-dot 2½" x 4½" rectangle, right sides together. Sew on the drawn line. Trim off the excess ¼" from the stitching line. Press the seam allowances toward the triangle. Repeat on the other end of the rectangle, orienting the diagonal line in the opposite direction. Make 20 of these star-point units.

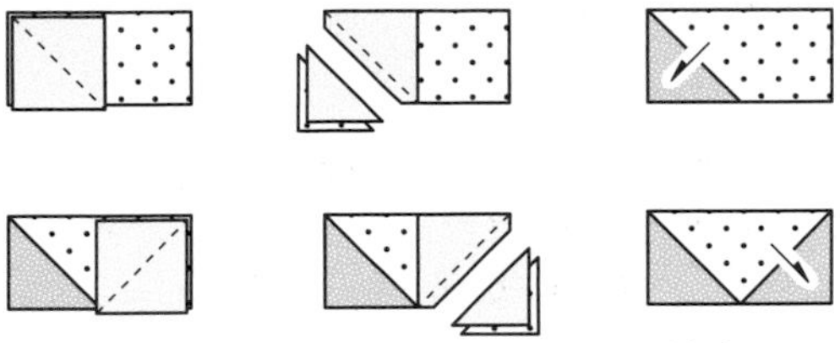

Make 20.

4. Arrange the polka-dot 2½" squares, the star-point units, and the four-patch units as shown. Join the units into rows, and then sew the rows together to make the block. Make five blocks.

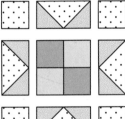 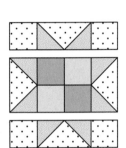

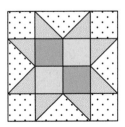

Make 5.

ASSEMBLING THE QUILT TOP

1. Sew three red print sashing pieces together with four lavender sashing squares. Press the seam allowances toward the sashing. Make four sashing rows.

Make 4.

2. Arrange the pieced blocks and setting squares in rows along with the red print sashing pieces as shown in the quilt diagram. Join into rows. Press the seam allowances toward the sashing pieces. Sew the rows together with the sashing rows. Press.

3. Referring to "Adding Borders" on page 76, attach the green inner border and valentine print outer borders.

FINISHING THE QUILT

1. Layer the quilt top with batting and backing and quilt as desired.

   Quilting Note: This sweet valentine quilt has a flowing heart design quilted in red thread for a more dramatic look.

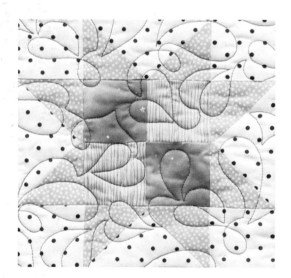

2. Referring to "Binding" on page 77, bind the edges of the quilt using the red strips.

Fabric Alternatives

This quilt would be excellent for a baby. Find a playful focus fabric, like this light blue with animals, and a few coordinating prints for the star blocks. You'll have a perfect quilt for your little one to cuddle up in.

Nest

I fell in love with this collection of fabrics (called It's a Hoot by Moda) and used it in these super-easy blocks that are pieced like a Half Log Cabin block. The large block pieces allow the fabrics to shine.

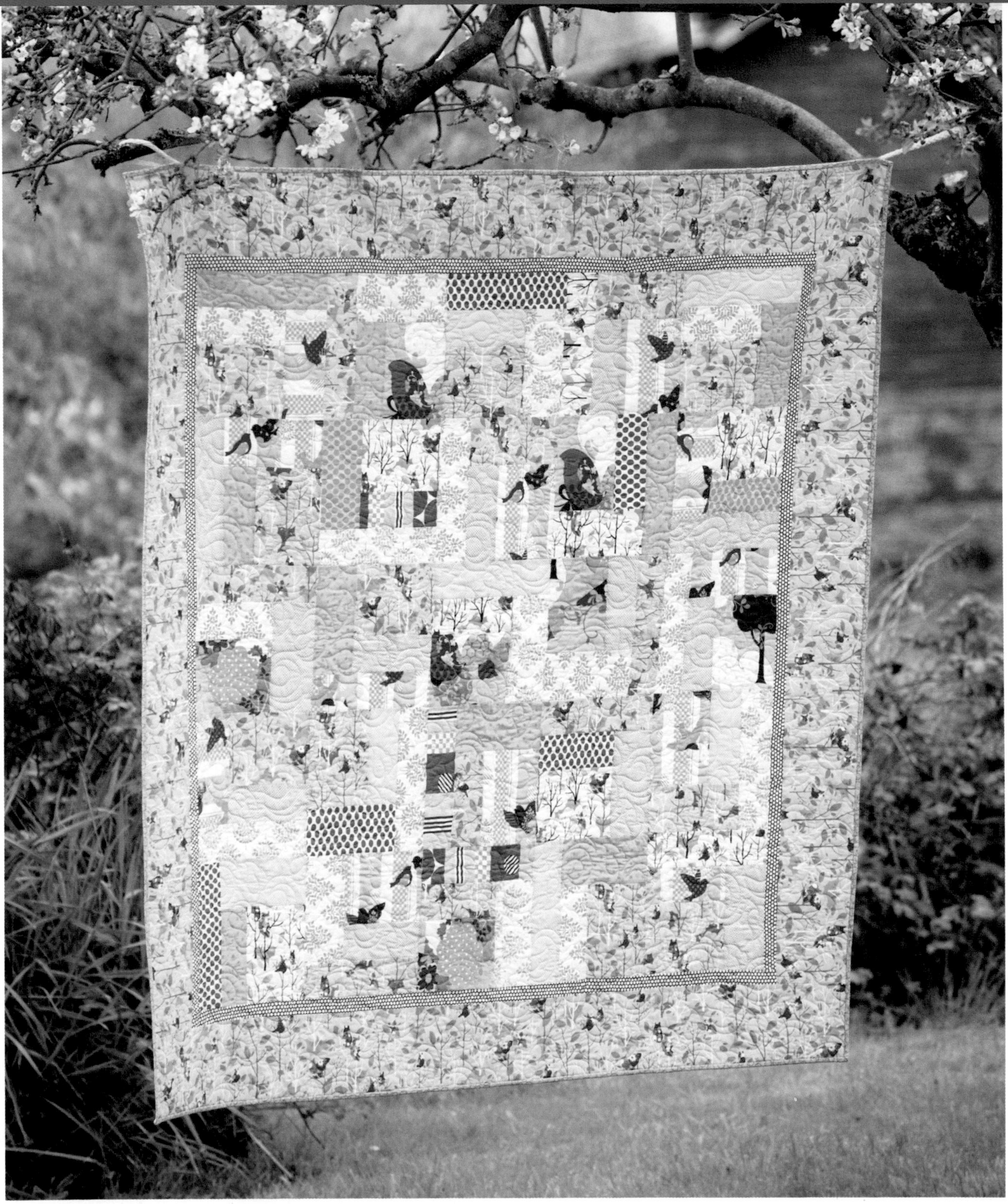

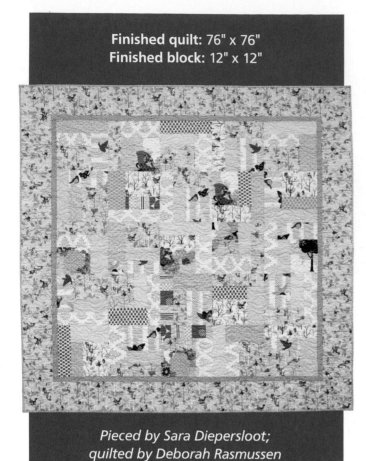

Finished quilt: 76" x 76"
Finished block: 12" x 12"

Pieced by Sara Diepersloot;
quilted by Deborah Rasmussen

MATERIALS

Yardage is based on 42"-wide fabric.

4 yards *total* of assorted prints for blocks*

2 yards of blue owl print for blocks and outer border

½ yard of pink polka-dot print for inner border

⅝ yard of pink print for binding

4¾ yards of fabric for backing

84" x 84" piece of batting

*I bought ½-yard cuts of about 12 fabrics. I ended up with some extra, but I had enough to fussy cut pieces for my blocks as desired.

CUTTING

From the assorted prints and blue owl print, cut *a total of:*

25 pieces, 6½" x 8½"

25 pieces, 3½" x 8½"

25 pieces, 3½" x 12½"

25 pieces, 4½" x 9½"

From the pink polka-dot print, cut:

7 strips, 1¾" x 42"

From the remainder of the blue owl print, cut:

7 strips, 7" x 42"

From the pink print, cut:

8 strips, 2¼" x 42"

MAKING THE BLOCKS

I like to cut my blocks out one at a time and decide which fabrics I want next to each other. I rotated the orientation of the blocks throughout the quilt, so you'll need to pay attention when using any directional fabrics. This is a great time for using a design wall.

1. Sew an assorted 3½" x 8½" rectangle to a 6½" x 8½" rectangle as shown. Press the seam allowances toward the smaller rectangle.

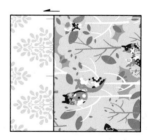

2. Sew a 4½" x 9½" rectangle to the top of the unit made in step 1. Press toward the rectangle just added.

3. Sew a 3½" x 12½" rectangle to the left side of the unit made in step 2. Press toward the rectangle just added.

4. Repeat steps 1–3 to make 25 blocks.

ASSEMBLING THE QUILT TOP

1. Arrange the blocks in five rows of five blocks each as shown in the quilt diagram, rotating the blocks as desired. Join the blocks into rows. Press the seam allowances in opposite directions from row to row. Sew the rows together. Press the seam allowances in one direction.

2. Referring to "Adding Borders" on page 76, attach the pink polka-dot inner and blue owl outer borders.

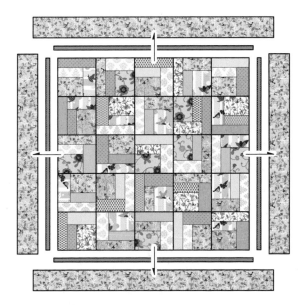

FINISHING THE QUILT

1. Layer the quilt top with batting and backing and quilt as desired.

Quilting Note: To echo the nature theme, this pretty quilt has a subtle swirling vine pattern in the quilting.

2. Referring to "Binding" on page 77, bind the edges of the quilt using the pink strips.

Fabric Alternatives

Try some fab florals! There are so many wonderful floral prints in quilt shops today, and most of them offer a large number of coordinates. Using all of the fabrics from one collection is a great option if you find choosing fabrics to be difficult. The fabrics I used in "Nest" are one example; here's another using a modern floral collection. Feel free to swap in any coordinated grouping of prints and solids or tone-on-tone prints that read as solid. This will provide a visual resting place among the eye-catching prints.

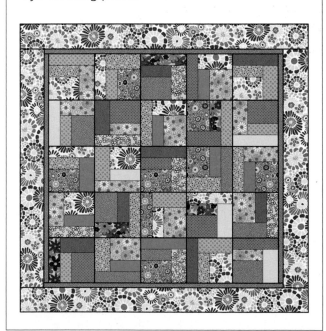

Cracked Up

This light-hearted print made me laugh and I knew I had to make something out of it. The simply pieced large blocks allow those cheery chickens and their eggs to take center stage.

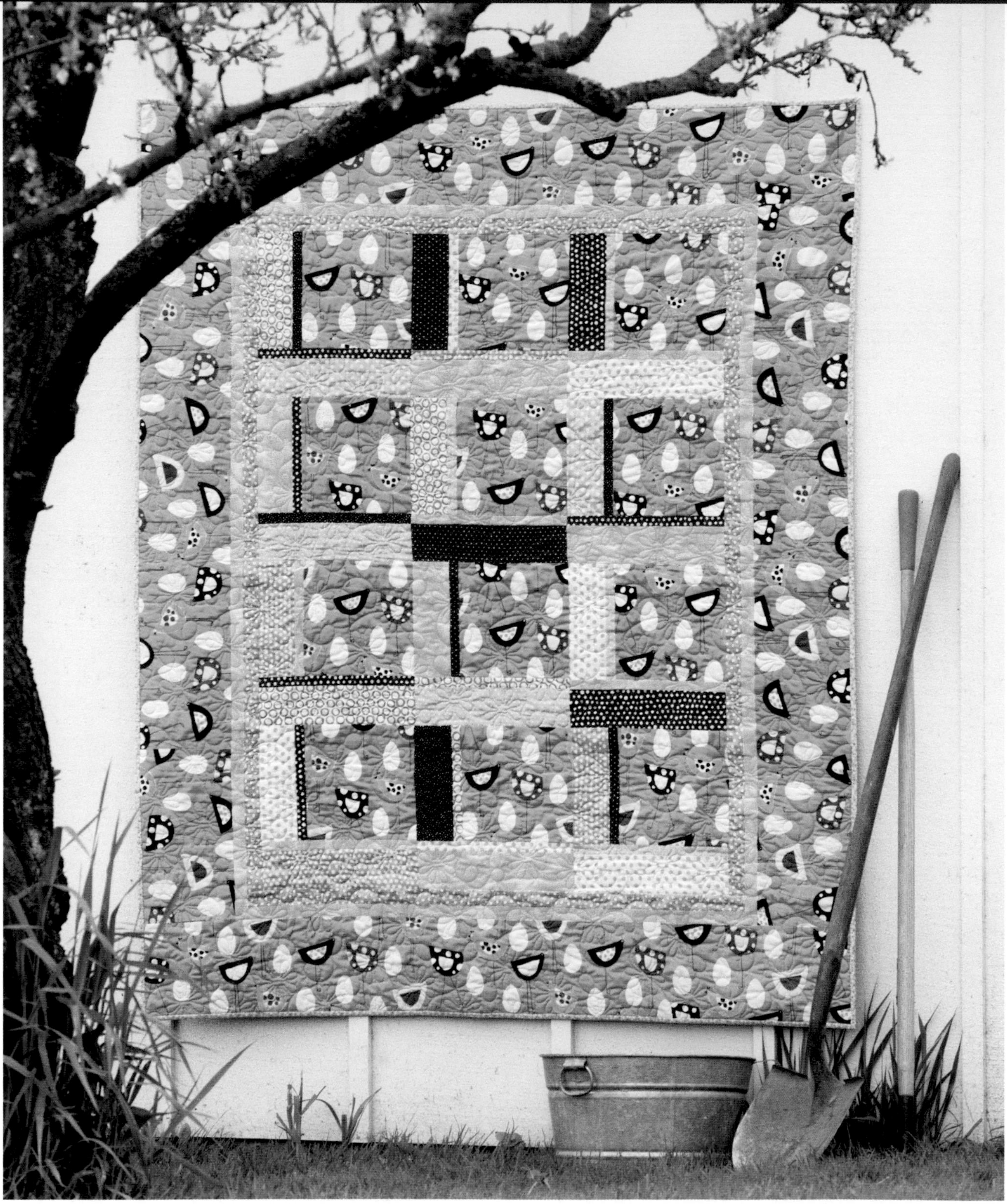

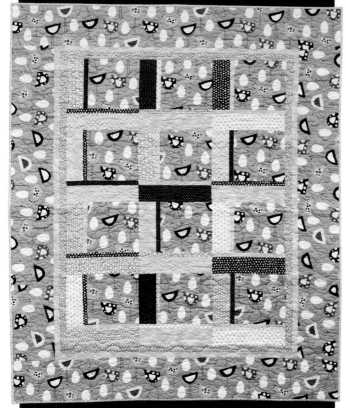

Finished quilt: 58" x 70½"
Finished block: 12½" x 12½"

*Pieced by Sara Diepersloot;
quilted by Deborah Rasmussen*

MATERIALS

Yardage is based on 42"-wide fabric.

⅜ yard *each* of 9 different green, yellow, and brown polka-dot prints for blocks

2½ yards of green chick print for blocks and outer border

⅞ yard of green-and-white dot print for inner border

⅓ yard of yellow dot print for middle border

⅝ yard of green dot print for binding

3¾ yards of fabric for backing

66" x 78" piece of batting

CUTTING

From the green chick print, cut:*
3 strips, 9¼" x 42"; crosscut into 12 squares, 9¼" x 9¼"

6 strips, 8" x 42"

From the 9 green, yellow, and brown polka-dot prints, cut *a total of*:
12 pieces, 1¼" x 9¼"
12 pieces, 3½" x 9¼"
12 pieces, 1¼" x 13"
12 pieces, 3½" x 13"

From the green-and-white dot print, cut:
5 strips, 1¾" x 42"

From the yellow dot print, cut:
5 strips, 1¾" x 42"

From the green dot print, cut:
7 strips, 2¼" x 42"

*This is one of those prints that I pieced to match for the outer border. See the tip on page 77 for additional information.

MAKING THE BLOCKS

1. Sew an assorted 1¼" x 9¼" piece to a green chick 9¼" square. Press the seam allowances toward the 1¼" piece. Add an assorted 3½" x 9¼" piece and press toward the piece just added.

2. Sew an assorted 1¼" x 13" piece to an assorted 3½" x 13" piece. Press.

3. Sew the units from steps 1 and 2 together to make the block. Press.

4. Repeat steps 1–3 to make a total of 12 blocks.

ASSEMBLING THE QUILT TOP

1. Arrange the blocks into four rows of three blocks each. Sew the blocks together into rows. Press the seam allowances in opposite directions from row to row. Join the rows together. Press the seam allowances in one direction.

2. Referring to "Adding Borders" on page 76, attach the green-and-white dot inner, yellow dot middle, and chick print outer borders.

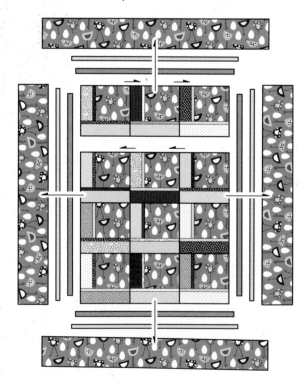

FINISHING THE QUILT

1. Layer the quilt top with batting and backing and quilt as desired.

   Quilting Note: This chicken quilt has a big, bold daisy pattern quilted across it.

2. Referring to "Binding" on page 77, bind the edges of the quilt using the green dot strips.

Fabric Alternatives

Give this silly quilt a completely different and sophisticated look with your favorite batik fabrics. This version features a floral batik with some pretty pink, green, and yellow prints. It would work equally well with a large-scale cabbage rose print.

Lime Punch

When I saw this bright citrus print, it just seemed to be calling out for pinwheels and polka dots. Of course, it called out my name first, and I just had to buy it.

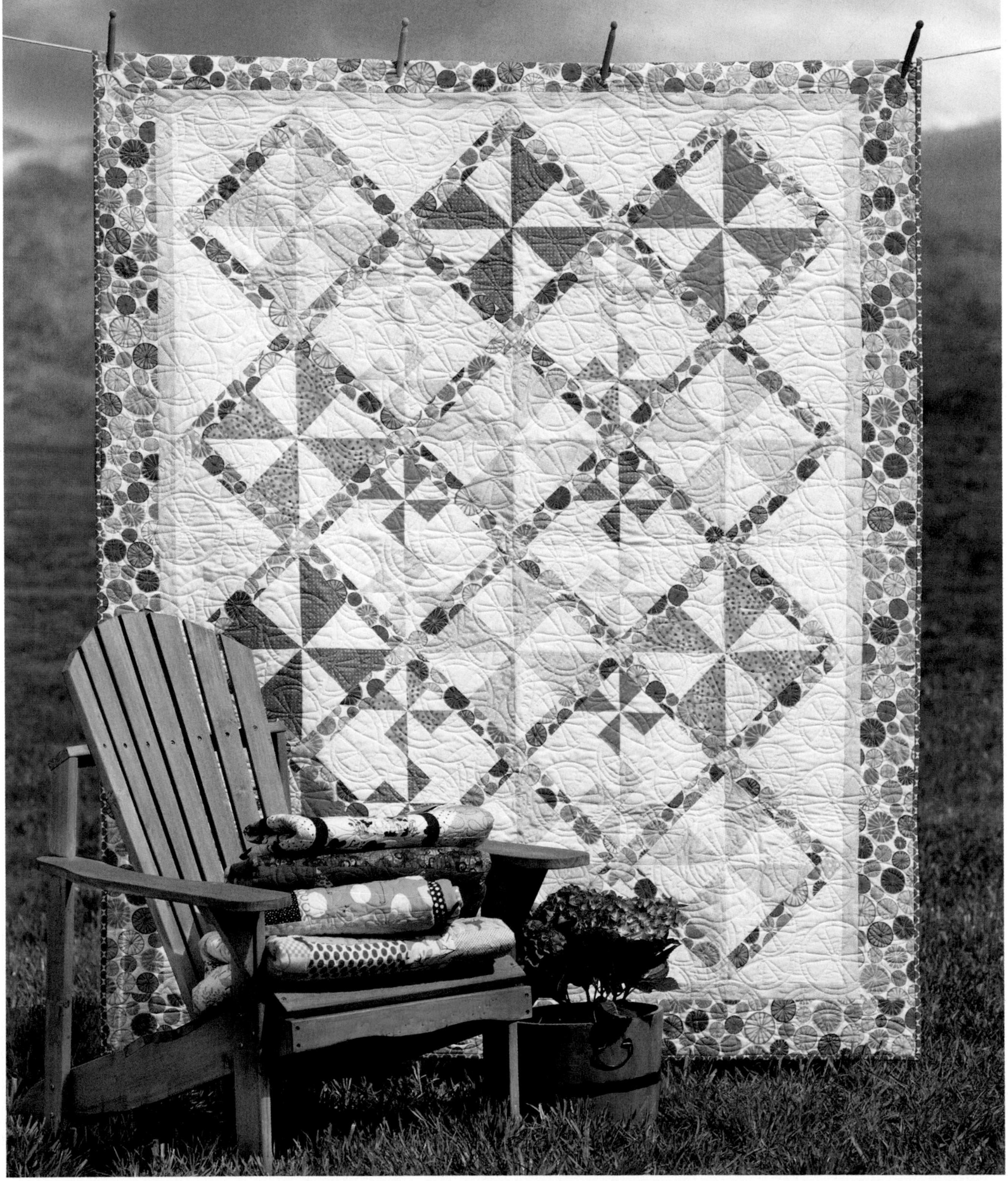

Finished quilt: 63" x 79¼"
Finished block: 10" x 10"

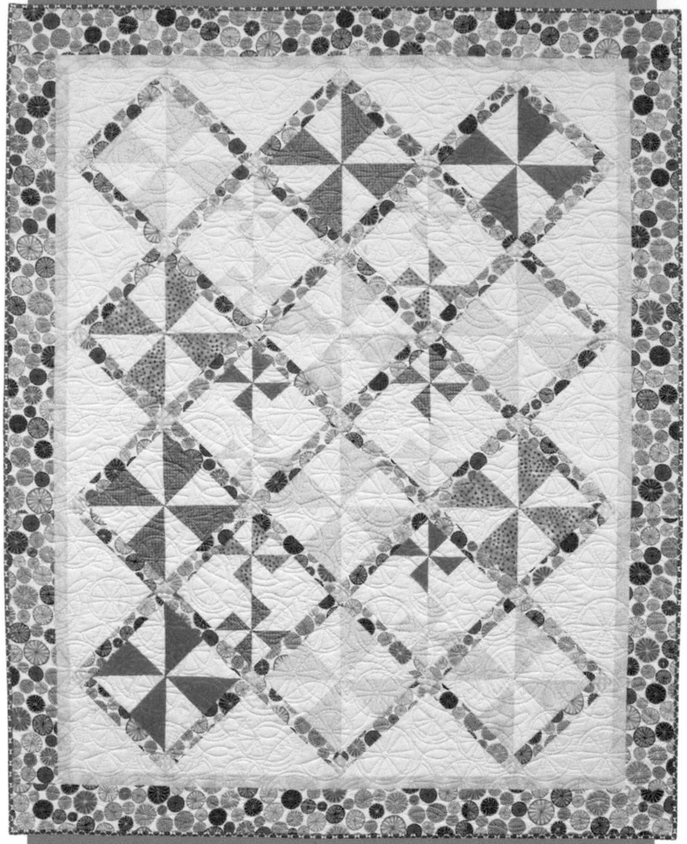

Pieced by Sara Diepersloot; quilted by Deborah Rasmussen

MATERIALS

Yardage is based on 42"-wide fabric.

2⅞ yards of white print for blocks and setting triangles

2⅛ yards of bright citrus print for sashing and outer border

¼ yard *each* of 6 assorted green 1, pink, yellow, orange, and blue polka-dot prints for blocks

½ yard of yellow dot print for inner border

¼ yard of green polka-dot print 2 for sashing squares

⅝ yard of pink dot print for binding

5 yards of fabric for backing

70" x 88" piece of batting

CUTTING

From the white print, cut:

3 strips, 3½" x 42"; crosscut into 24 squares, 3½" x 3½"

2 strips, 5½" x 42"; crosscut into 12 squares, 5½" x 5½"

4 strips, 6" x 42"; crosscut into 24 squares, 6" x 6"

2 squares, 10¾" x 10¾"; cut in half diagonally to make 4 corner setting triangles

3 squares, 18¼" x 18¼"; cut into quarters diagonally to make 12 side setting triangles (2 are extra)

From *each* of the 6 polka-dot prints, cut:

1 strip, 6" x 42"; crosscut into 4 squares, 6" x 6" (24 total), and 4 squares, 3½" x 3½" (24 total)

From the green polka-dot print 2, cut:

2 strips, 2" x 42"; crosscut into 31 squares, 2" x 2"

From the citrus print, cut:

16 strips, 2" x 42"; crosscut into 48 sashing pieces, 2" x 10½"

7 strips, 5" x 42"

From the yellow dot print, cut:

7 strips, 1¾" x 42"

From the pink dot print, cut:

8 strips, 2¼" x 42"

MAKING THE LARGE PINWHEEL BLOCKS

1. Draw a diagonal line from corner to corner on the wrong side of the white print 6" squares. Lay a square on an assorted polka-dot 6" square, right sides together. Sew ¼" away from the drawn line on *both* sides of the line. Cut directly on the drawn line. Press the seam allowances toward the polka-dot print. Make 48 half-square-triangle units.

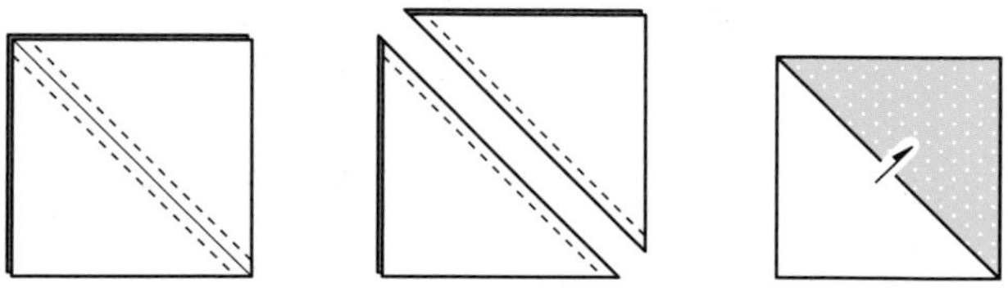

Make 48.

2. Square up each triangle unit to be 5½" x 5½". This is a very important step to ensure that your blocks line up and come out beautifully.

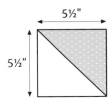

3. Sew four triangle units of the same color together to make a Large Pinwheel block as shown. Make 12 blocks.

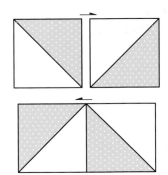

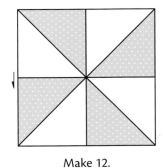

Make 12.

MAKING THE DOUBLE PINWHEEL BLOCKS

1. Draw a diagonal line from corner to corner on the wrong side of the white 3½" squares. Lay a white square on an assorted polka-dot 3½" square, right sides together. Sew ¼" away from the drawn line on *both* sides of the line. Cut on the drawn line. Press the seam allowances toward the polka-dot fabric. Make 48 half-square-triangle units.

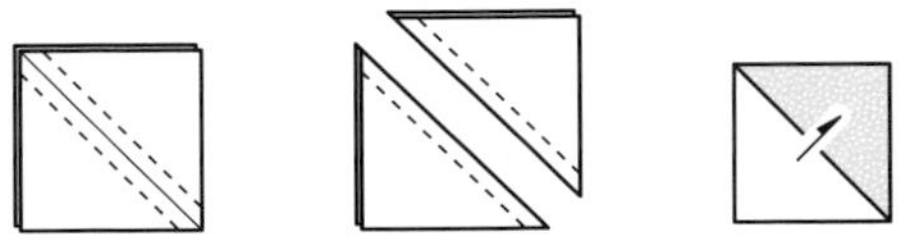

Make 48.

2. Square up each triangle unit to be 3" x 3".

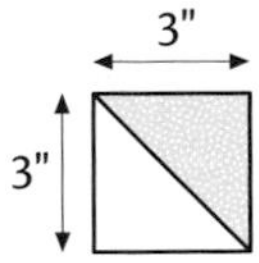

3. Sew four triangle units of the same color together to make a pinwheel unit as shown. Make 12 units.

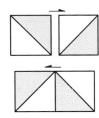 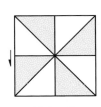

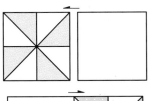

Make 12.

4. Sew two pinwheel units and two white 5½" squares together to make the Double Pinwheel blocks, following the color placement in the quilt diagram on page 26. Press the seam allowances toward the pinwheel units. Make six blocks.

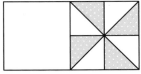

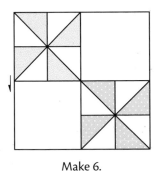

Make 6.

ASSEMBLING THE QUILT TOP

The blocks are assembled in diagonal rows with sashing strips and squares in between. Press all seam allowances toward the citrus print sashing strips. The side and corner setting triangles are added at the ends of the rows. They are cut oversized and will be trimmed after the quilt center is assembled.

1. Sew green dot 2" squares and citrus print 2" x 10½" sashing pieces together in rows as shown. Press.

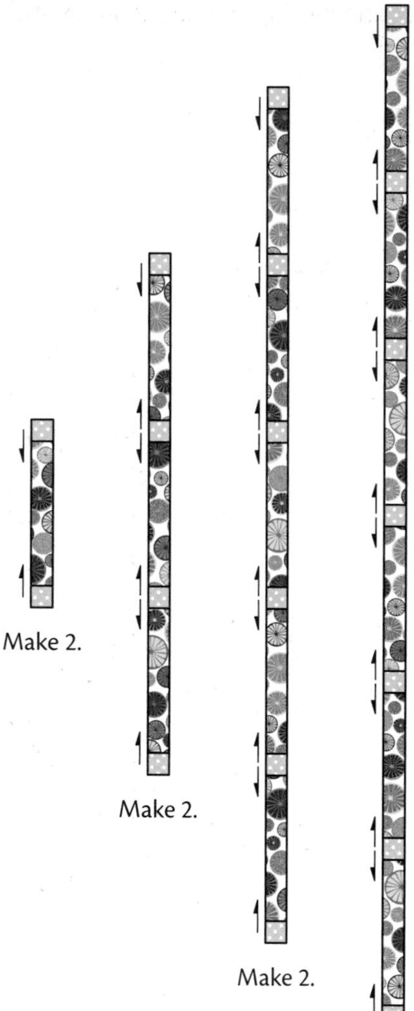

2. To make row 1, sew citrus print 2" x 10½" sashing pieces to opposite sides of one Large Pinwheel block. Press. Add a sashing unit with two green dot squares to the block, and then sew a side setting triangle cut from the 18¼" squares to each end of the row. Press.

3. To make row 2, sew four citrus print 2" x 10½" sashing pieces, two Large Pinwheel blocks, and one Double Pinwheel block together as shown. Press. Join a sashing unit with four green dot squares to the top of the row (left side in the illustration). Press. Sew a side setting triangle to each end of the row and press.

Make 2.

Make 2.

Make 2.

Make 1.

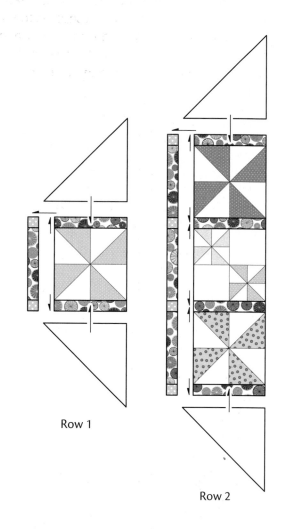

Row 1

Row 2

4. To make row 3, sew six citrus print 2" x 10½" sashing pieces and five blocks together into a row, alternating three Large Pinwheel blocks and two Double Pinwheel blocks. Press. Join to a sashing unit with six green dot squares. Press. Sew a side setting triangle to the left side of the row (bottom in the illustration) and press. Sew the sashing unit with seven green dot squares to the bottom of the row (right side in the illustration). Press.

5. To make row 4, sew six citrus print 2" x 10½" sashing pieces and five blocks together into a row, alternating three Large Pinwheel blocks and two Double Pinwheel blocks. Press. Sew a sashing unit with six green dot squares to the bottom of the row (right side in the illustration) and press. Sew a side setting triangle to the right side of the row (top in the illustration). Press.

6. To make row 5, sew four citrus print 2" x 10½" sashing pieces, two Large Pinwheel blocks, and one Double Pinwheel block together into a row. Press. Sew a sashing unit with four green dot squares to the bottom of the row (right side in the illustration) and press. Sew a side setting triangle to each end of the row. Press.

7. To make row 6, sew two citrus print 2" x 10½" sashing pieces and one Large Pinwheel block together into a row. Press. Sew a sashing unit with two green dot squares to the bottom of the row (right side in the illustration) and press. Sew a side setting triangle to each end of the row. Press.

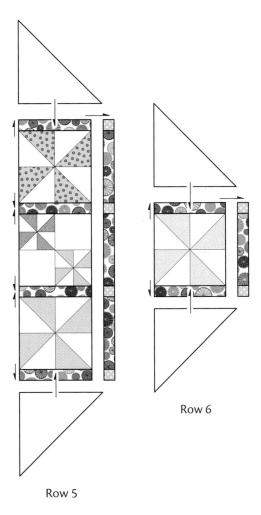

Row 5

Row 6

Row 3   Row 4

8. Sew the rows together. Press. Add a corner setting triangle cut from the white print 10¾" squares to each corner of the quilt. Press.

9. Referring to "Making Diagonally Set Quilts" on page 75, trim and square up your quilt top.

10. Referring to "Adding Borders" on page 76, attach the yellow dot inner and citrus print outer borders.

FINISHING THE QUILT

1. Layer the quilt top with batting and backing and quilt as desired.

Quilting Note: The citrus motif in the fabric is mimicked in the quilting on this bright quilt. Big lemons and limes dance across the quilt top.

2. Referring to "Binding" on page 77, bind the edges of the quilt using the pink dot strips.

Fabric Alternatives

The bright colors I used in this quilt speak of warm summer days. It would be just as merry in reds, greens, and gold with a Christmas print to keep you cozy during the holidays and those cold winter nights.

Fresh Floral Table Runner

This quick-to-make runner will brighten up any room. Here I've used a charming floral print in the outer portion of the pieced blocks and in the border.

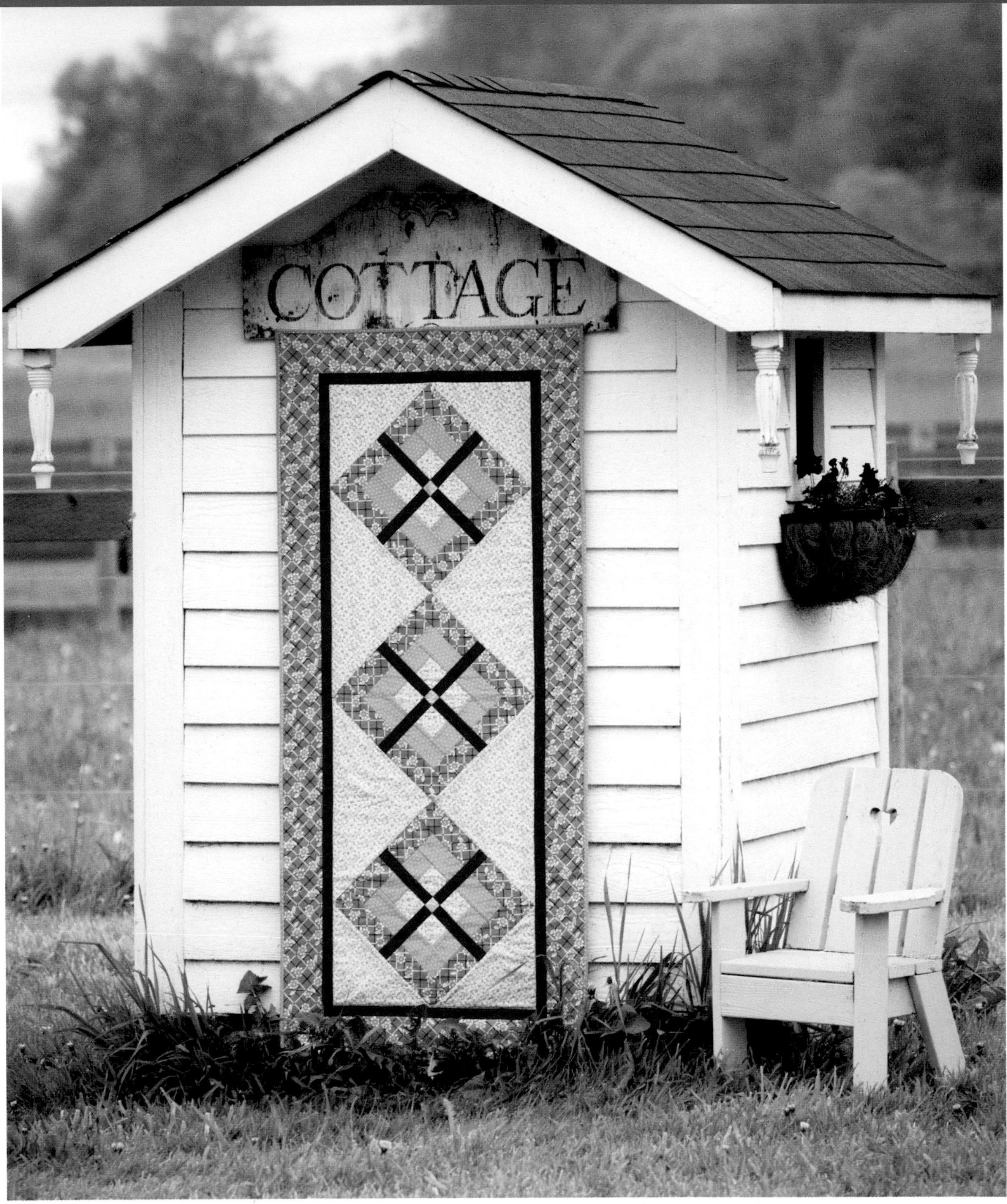
COTTAGE

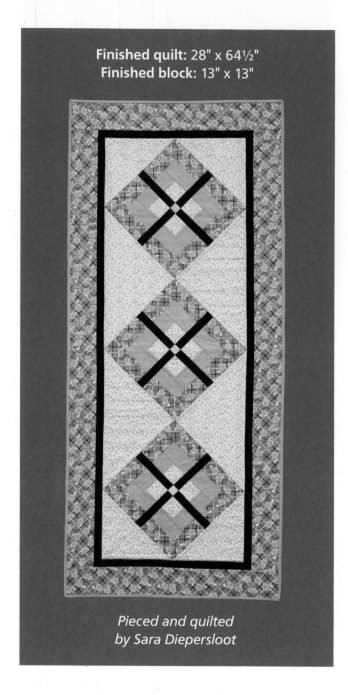

Finished quilt: 28" x 64½"
Finished block: 13" x 13"

Pieced and quilted
by Sara Diepersloot

MATERIALS

Yardage is based on 42"-wide fabric.

1⅛ yards of light green print for blocks and setting triangles

1 yard of red floral print for blocks and outer border

⅔ yard of green dot print for blocks and binding

⅓ yard of dark red print for blocks and inner border

⅛ yard or scrap (2" x 6" piece) of yellow print for blocks

2 yards of fabric for backing

34" x 70" piece of batting

CUTTING

From the green dot print, cut:
3 strips, 2½" x 42"; crosscut into 12 squares, 2½" x 2½", and 12 rectangles, 2½" x 4½"
5 strips, 2¼" x 42"

From the light green print, cut:
1 strip, 2½" x 42"; crosscut into 12 squares, 2½" x 2½"
1 square, 20" x 20"; cut into quarters diagonally to make 4 triangles
2 squares, 10¼" x 10¼"; cut in half diagonally to make 4 triangles

From the red floral print, cut:
4 strips, 2½" x 42"; crosscut into 12 rectangles, 2½" x 4½", and 12 rectangles, 2½" x 6½"
5 strips, 4" x 42"

From the dark red print, cut:
6 strips, 1½" x 42"; crosscut 2 of the strips into 12 rectangles, 1½" x 6½"

From the yellow print, cut:
3 squares, 1½" x 1½"

MAKING THE BLOCKS

1. Sew a green dot 2½" square to a light green print 2½" square. Press the seam allowances toward the green dot.

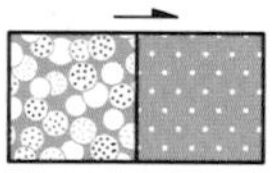

2. Sew a green dot 2½" x 4½" rectangle to the top of the unit made in step 1, making sure that the green dot is on the right and the light green print is on the left. Press toward the rectangle.

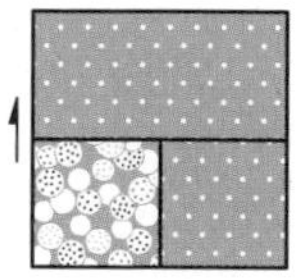

3. Sew a red floral 2½" x 4½" rectangle to the right side of the unit. Press the seam allowances toward the red floral.

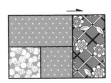

4. Sew a red floral 2½" x 6½" rectangle to the top of the unit. Press toward the red floral.

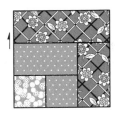

5. Repeat steps 1–4 to make six A units.

6. Sew a green dot 2½" square to a light green print 2½" square. Press the seam allowances toward the green dot.

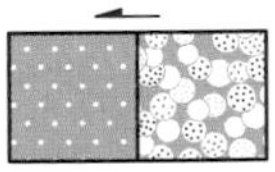

7. Sew a green dot 2½" x 4½" rectangle to the top of the unit made in step 6, making sure that the light green print is on the right and the green dot is on the left. Press.

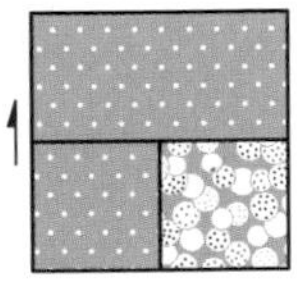

8. Sew a red floral 2½" x 4½" rectangle to the left side of the unit. Press the seam allowances toward the red floral.

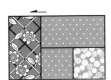

9. Sew a 2½" x 6½" red floral rectangle to the top of the unit. Press.

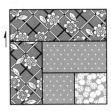

10. Repeat steps 6–9 to make six B units.

11. Sew an A unit and a B unit together with a dark red print 1½" x 6½" rectangle between them. Press the seam allowances toward the red print. Make six.

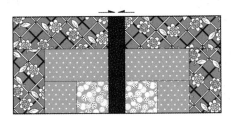

Make 6.

12. Sew a yellow 1½" square between two dark red 1½" x 6½" rectangles. Press the seam allowances toward the red. Make three. Sew one of these units together with two units from step 11. Make three blocks.

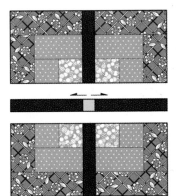

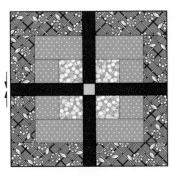

Make 3.

ASSEMBLING THE QUILT TOP

1. Sew the blocks and light green setting triangles into diagonal rows as shown. Press toward the setting triangles. Join the rows. Press. Sew two corner setting triangles to each end of the table runner. Note that the setting triangles were cut slightly oversized and will be trimmed.

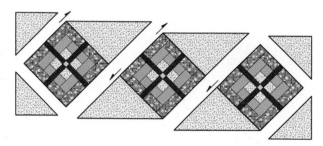

2. Referring to "Making Diagonally Set Quilts" on page 75, trim and square up your quilt top.

3. Referring to "Adding Borders" on page 76, attach the dark red inner and red floral outer borders.

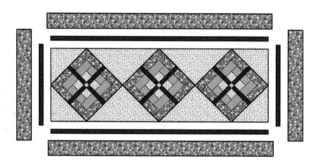

FINISHING THE QUILT

1. Layer the quilt top with batting and backing and quilt as desired.

   Quilting Note: For small table runners, you can choose to simply stitch in the ditch (see page 77) or use a quilting design that goes with your fabric.

2. Referring to "Binding" on page 77, bind the edges of the quilt using the green dot strips.

Fabric Alternatives

For a super wintertime table runner, use something similar to this pinecone fabric with coordinating prints and colors.

Summer Garden

I love the vibrant colors in this black, red, and green floral print. The extra-large blocks make it super-quick to piece and let you take full advantage of a gorgeous fabric.

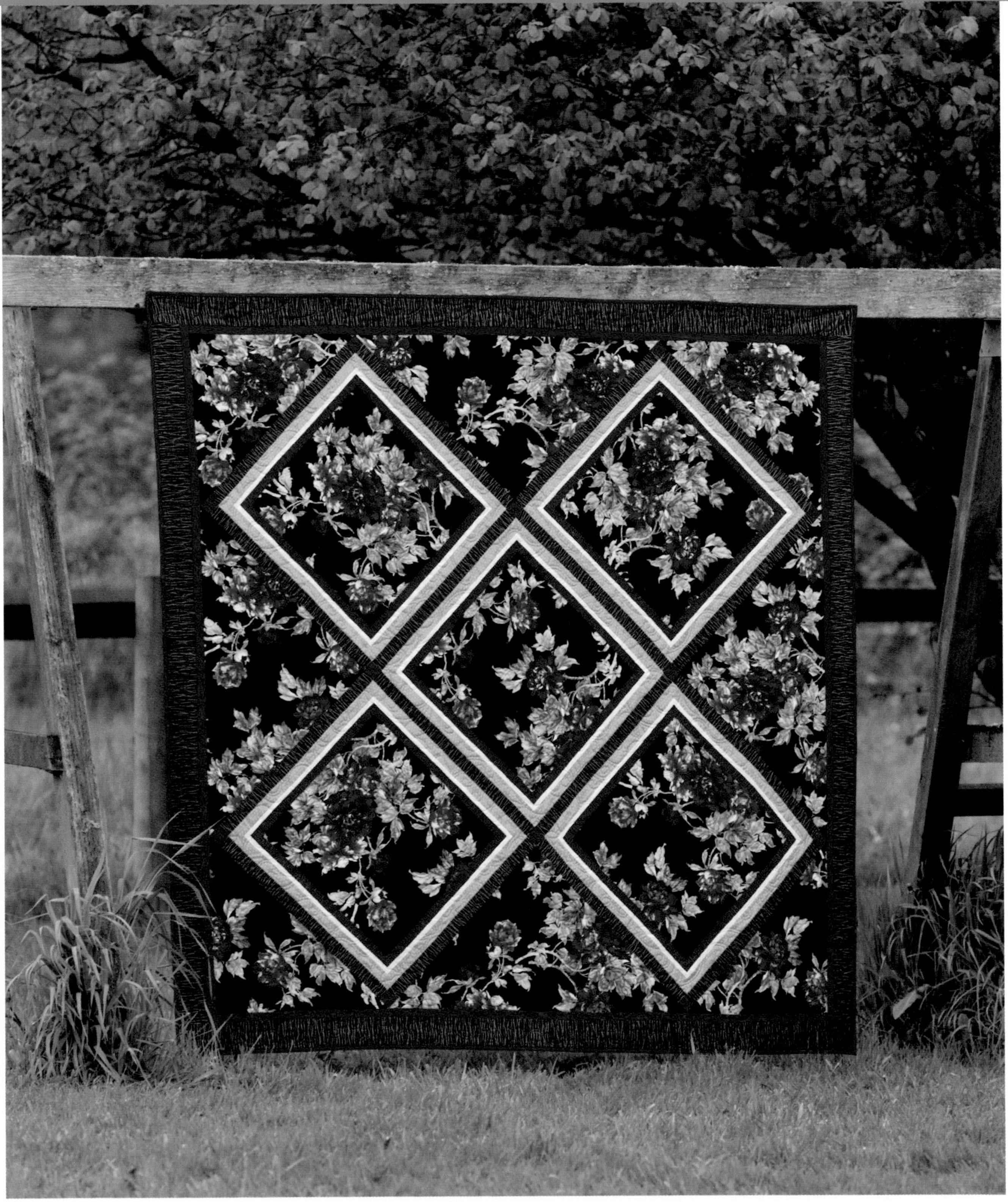

Finished quilt: 86½" x 86½"
Finished block: 25" x 25"

*Pieced by Sara Diepersloot;
quilted by Deborah Rasmussen*

MATERIALS

Yardage is based on 42"-wide fabric.

3¾ yards of black-and-red floral print for blocks and setting triangles

2⅛ yards of black striped print for sashing and outer border

1⅛ yards of green polka-dot print for blocks

1⅛ yards of red fabric for inner border and binding

⅞ yard of red striped print for blocks and corner squares

⅔ yard of white fabric for blocks

8 yards of fabric for backing

95" x 95" piece of batting

CUTTING

From the black-and-red floral print, cut:
5 squares, 20" x 20"

2 squares, 19¾" x 19¾"; cut in half diagonally to make 4 triangles

1 square, 39" x 39"; cut into quarters diagonally to make 4 triangles

From the red striped print, cut:
10 strips, 1½" x 42"; crosscut into 10 pieces, 1½" x 20", and 10 pieces, 1½" x 22"

1 strip, 2" x 42"; crosscut into 12 squares, 2" x 2"

From the white fabric, cut:
20 strips, 1" x 42"; crosscut into 10 pieces, 1" x 22", and 10 pieces, 1" x 23"

From the green polka-dot print, cut:
20 strips, 1¾" x 42"; crosscut into 10 pieces, 1¾" x 23", and 10 pieces, 1¾" x 25½"

From the black striped print, cut:
16 strips, 2" x 42"; crosscut into 16 pieces, 2" x 25½"

9 strips, 4" x 42"

From the red fabric, cut:
8 strips, 1½" x 42"

9 strips, 2¼" x 42"

MAKING THE BLOCKS

When adding the strips to the floral center square, press all seam allowances away from the center square.

1. Sew red striped 1½" x 20" pieces to opposite sides of a black-and-red floral 20" square. Press. Sew 1½" x 22" red striped pieces to the remaining two sides of the black-and-red floral square. Press.

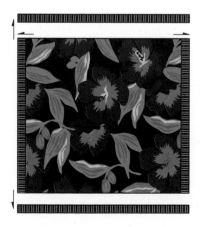

2. Sew white 1" x 22" pieces to opposite sides of the unit from step 1. Press. Sew a white 1" x 23" piece to each of the remaining sides. Press.

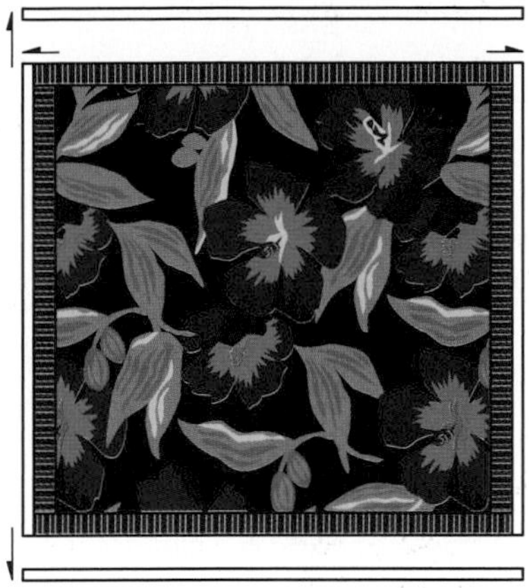

3. Sew green polka-dot 1¾" x 23" pieces to opposite sides of the block. Press. Sew a green polka-dot 1¾" x 25½" piece to each of the remaining sides. Press.

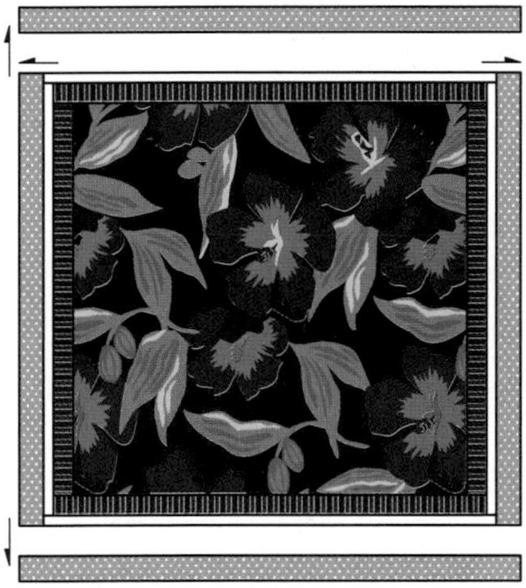

4. Repeat steps 1–3 to make a total of five blocks.

ASSEMBLING THE QUILT TOP

1. Sew a red striped 2" square to each end of a black striped 2" x 25½" sashing piece. Press the seam allowances toward the sashing. Make two.

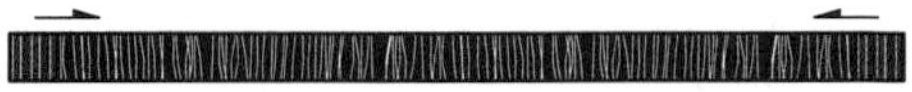

Make 2.

2. Sew four red striped 2" squares and three black striped sashing pieces together into rows. Press toward the sashing. Make two rows.

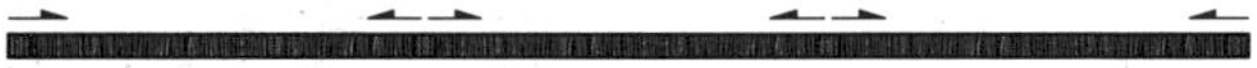

Make 2.

3. Sew two black striped sashing pieces to opposite sides of a block. Press the seam allowances away from the block. Sew a sashing piece with two red squares to the top. Press. Sew a side setting triangle cut from the 39" square to each end of the block as shown to make a row. Press the seam allowances toward the triangles. Make two rows.

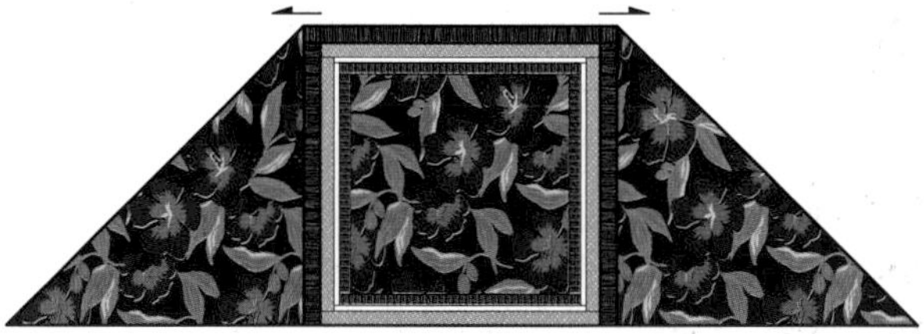

Make 2.

4. Sew four black striped sashing pieces and three blocks together into a row. Press.

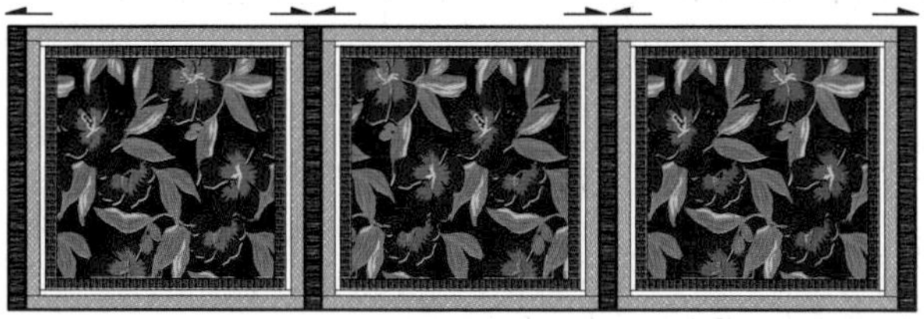

5. Sew the block rows and sashing rows together. Press the seam allowances toward the sashing. Add a corner setting triangle cut from the 19¾" squares to each corner of the quilt. Press.

6. Referring to "Making Diagonally Set Quilts" on page 75, trim and square up your quilt top.

7. Referring to "Adding Borders" on page 76, attach the red inner and black striped outer borders.

FINISHING THE QUILT

1. Layer the quilt top with batting and backing and quilt as desired.

   Quilting Note: This bold quilt needed a bold quilting pattern to complement it. Big swirling vines and bright green thread bring it all together.

2. Referring to "Binding" on page 77, bind the edges of the quilt using the red strips.

Fabric Alternatives

Try these beautiful navy and teal colors with a lime green sashing and border for a subtler version of my bold red, green, and black quilt.

Campout

Whip up this quilt and take it on your next picnic. Or cuddle up at the campfire, and then layer it over your sleeping bag when it's time to hit the sack.

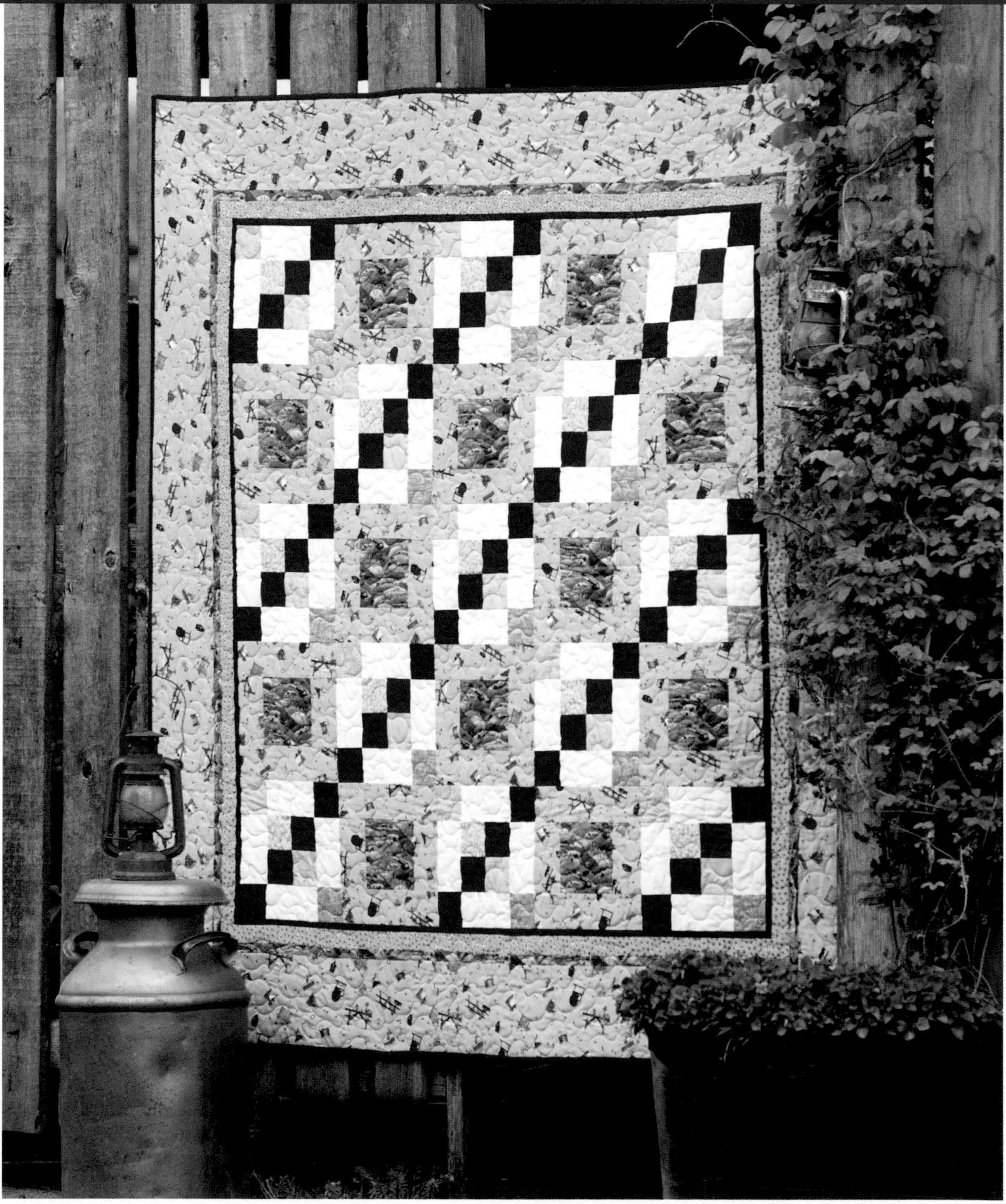

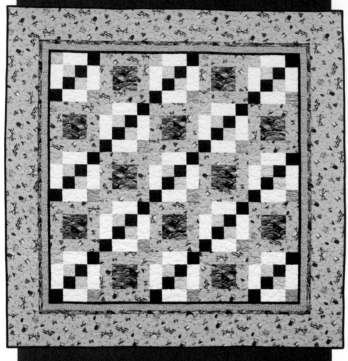

Finished quilt: 68½" x 68½"
Finished block: 10" x 10"

Pieced by Sara Diepersloot;
quilted by Deborah Rasmussen

MATERIALS

Yardage is based on 42"-wide fabric.

2½ yards of small-scale green campground print for blocks and border 4

⅞ yard of white fabric for blocks

⅝ yard of large-scale green camping print for blocks and border 3

⅛ yard *each* of 4 different red fabrics for blocks

⅛ yard *each* of 4 different green fabrics for blocks

⅜ yard of green bee print for border 2

¼ yard of red print for border 1

⅝ yard of red print for binding

4½ yards of fabric for backing

77" x 77" piece of batting

CUTTING

From *each* of the 4 different red fabrics, cut:
1 strip, 3" x 42"

From *each* of the 4 different green fabrics, cut:
1 strip, 3" x 42"

From the white fabric, cut:
8 strips, 3" x 42"; crosscut into 52 rectangles, 3" x 5½"

From the small-scale green campground print, cut:
11 strips, 3" x 42"; crosscut into 24 rectangles, 3" x 5½", and 24 rectangles, 3" x 10½"
7 strips, 7" x 42"

From the large-scale green camping print, cut:
2 strips, 5½" x 42"; crosscut into 12 squares, 5½" x 5½"
6 strips, 1¼" x 42"

From the red print for border 1, cut:
6 strips, 1" x 42"

From the green bee print, cut:
6 strips, 1¾" x 42"

From the red print for binding, cut:
8 strips, 2¼" x 40"

MAKING BLOCK A

1. From the 3" x 42" strips of reds and greens, choose the two red fabrics and two green fabrics you want to have in the center four-patch unit of the blocks. Sew one red strip to one green strip to make a strip set. Press the seam allowances toward the red. Repeat with the second red and green strips to make two strip sets. Crosscut each strip set into 13 segments, 3" wide.

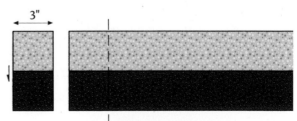

Make 2 strip sets.
Cut 26 segments total.

2. Sew the 3" segments together to make a four-patch unit. Press. Make 13 units.

Make 13.

3. Cut the remaining red 3" x 42" strips and green 3" x 42" strips into 3" squares. You'll need 13 of each color.

4. Sew a red 3" square and a green 3" square to opposite ends of a white 3" x 5½" rectangle. Press the seam allowances toward the corner squares. Make 26.

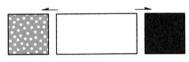

Make 26.

5. Sew 3" x 5½" white rectangles to opposite sides of a four-patch unit. Press the seam allowances toward the four-patch unit.

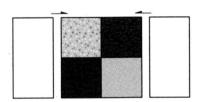

6. Join the segments from steps 4 and 5 to make block A. Make 13 of block A.

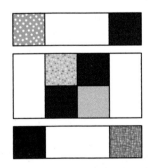 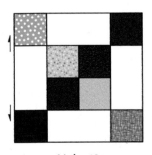

Make 13.

MAKING BLOCK B

1. Sew small-scale green campground print 3" x 5½" rectangles to opposite sides of a large-scale green camping print 5½" square. Press.

2. Sew a green campground print 3" x 10½" rectangle to the top and bottom of the center unit. Press the seam allowances away from the center square.

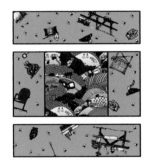 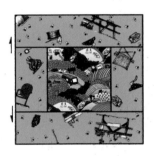

3. Repeat steps 1 and 2 to make 12 of block B.

ASSEMBLING THE QUILT TOP

1. Arrange the A and B blocks together into five rows of five blocks each, alternating the A and B blocks. Press the seam allowances toward the B blocks. Join the rows. Press the seam allowances in one direction.

2. Referring to "Adding Borders" on page 76, attach the four borders in this order: red print, green bee print, large-scale green camping print, and small-scale green camping print.

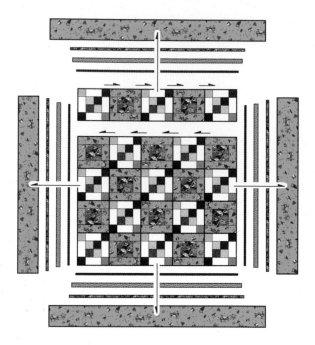

FINISHING THE QUILT

1. Layer the quilt top with batting and backing and quilt as desired.

   Quilting Note: This quilt has a simple quilting pattern that mimics the rolling hills of the fabric.

2. Referring to "Binding" on page 77, bind the edges of the quilt using the red strips.

Fabric Alternatives

Any great novelty prints can be featured in this quilt. Swap out the camping fabrics with this fun strawberry print. Coordinate with subtle prints of red, green, and black for the blocks.

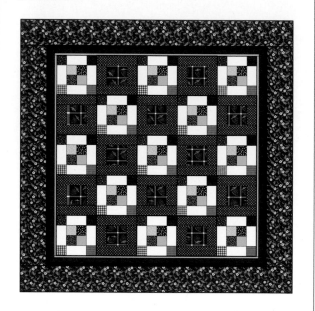

Summer Camp

Summer camp is always one of the highlights of the summer for my kids. The colorful camp print used in this quilt is perfect for a week spent away from home in a cabin or a tent. When little campers take this fun quilt along, they can wrap up in a comforting hug from home.

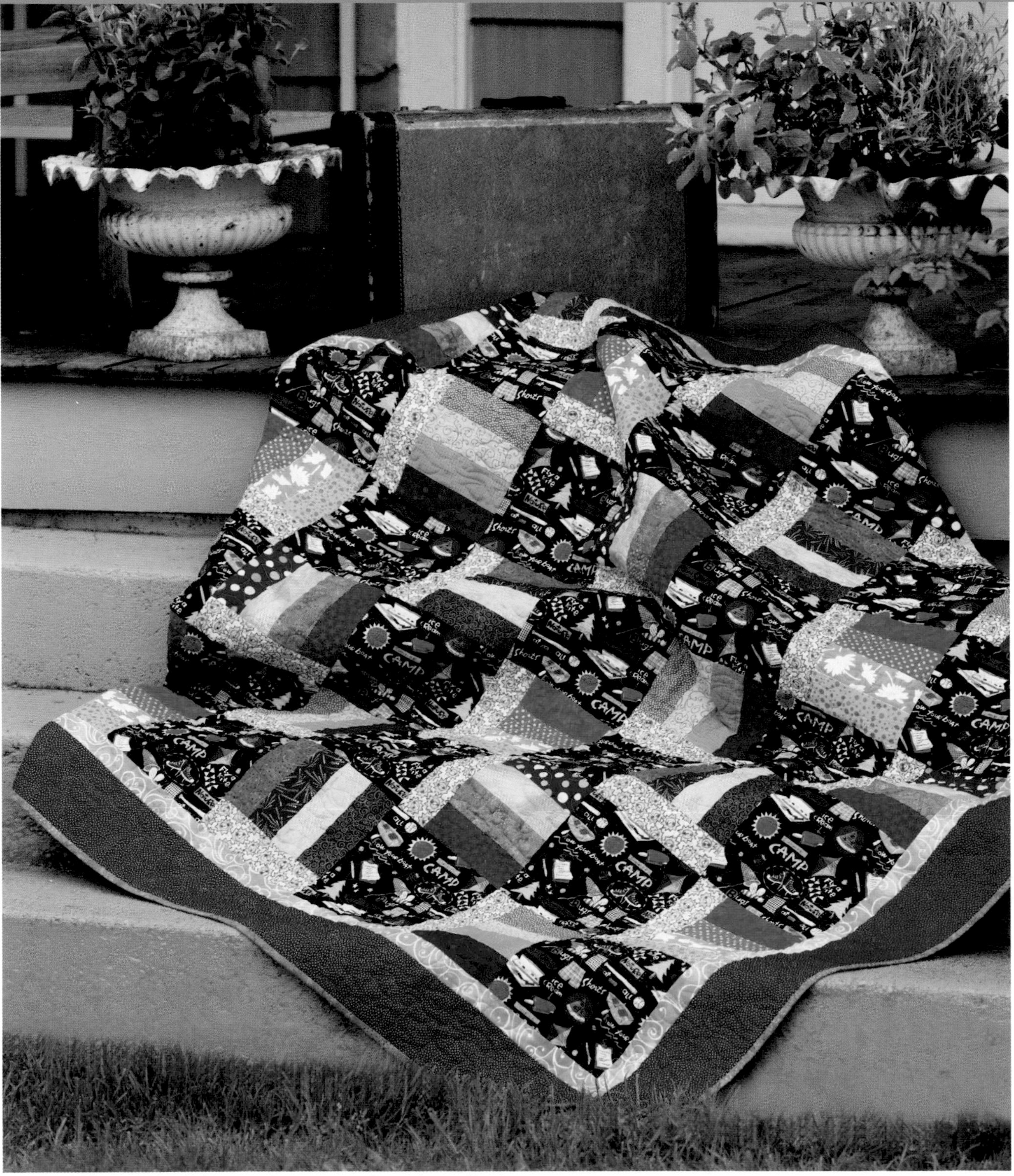
CAMP

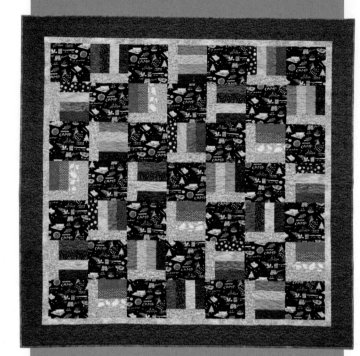

Finished quilt: 68" x 68"
Finished block: 8" x 8"

*Pieced by Sara Diepersloot;
quilted by Deborah Rasmussen*

MATERIALS

Yardage is based on 42"-wide fabric.

¼ yard *each* of 16 assorted bright prints for blocks

1⅞ yards of black summer-camp print for blocks

1⅛ yards of red print for outer border

⅝ yard of yellow sun print for blocks

⅜ yard of yellow print for inner border

⅝ yard of blue print for binding

4⅜ yards of fabric for backing

76" x 76" piece of batting

CUTTING

From the 16 assorted bright prints, cut *a total of:*
24 strips, 2½" x 42"

From the yellow sun print, cut:
7 strips, 2½" x 42"; crosscut into 24 rectangles,
    2½" x 8½"

From the black summer-camp print, cut:
7 strips, 8½" x 42"; crosscut into 25 squares,
    8½" x 8½"

From the yellow print, cut:
6 strips, 1¾" x 42"

From the red print, cut:
7 strips, 5" x 42"

From the blue print, cut:
8 strips, 2¼" x 42"

MAKING THE BLOCKS

1. Divide the 24 bright 2½" strips into six groups of four. Sew each set of four strips together to make a strip set. Press all seam allowances in one direction. Make six strip sets.

Make 6 strip sets.

2. Cut each strip set into four segments, 6½" wide, for a total of 24 units.

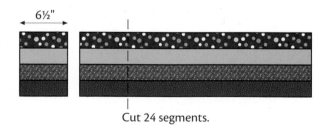

Cut 24 segments.

3. Sew a yellow sun print 2½" x 8½" rectangle to the side of each strip segment. Press toward the yellow rectangle. Make 24 blocks.

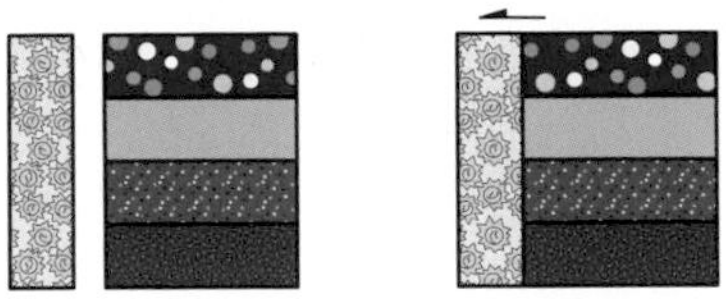

Make 24.

ASSEMBLING THE QUILT TOP

1. Arrange the pieced blocks and summer-camp print setting squares in rows, alternating the orientation of the pieced blocks as shown in the quilt diagram. Join the blocks into rows. Press the seam allowances toward the setting squares. Sew the rows together. Press the seam allowances in one direction.

2. Referring to "Adding Borders" on page 76, attach the yellow inner and red outer borders.

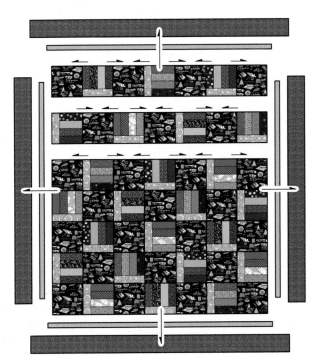

FINISHING THE QUILT

1. Layer the quilt top with batting and backing and quilt as desired.

   Quilting Note: *It's great when you can find a quilting pattern that goes with an element in your quilt. This one looks like the yellow print in the blocks.*

2. Referring to "Binding" on page 77, bind the edges of the quilt using the blue strips.

Fabric Alternatives

Replace the black summer-camp print with a cozy snowman print, change the coordinating fabrics, and you've got a great wintertime quilt!

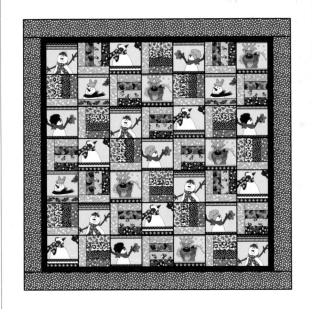

Picnic Day

Grab your picnic basket and go! Take this quilt along too, of course. It goes together quickly using a fanciful novelty print in the large, unpieced center area.

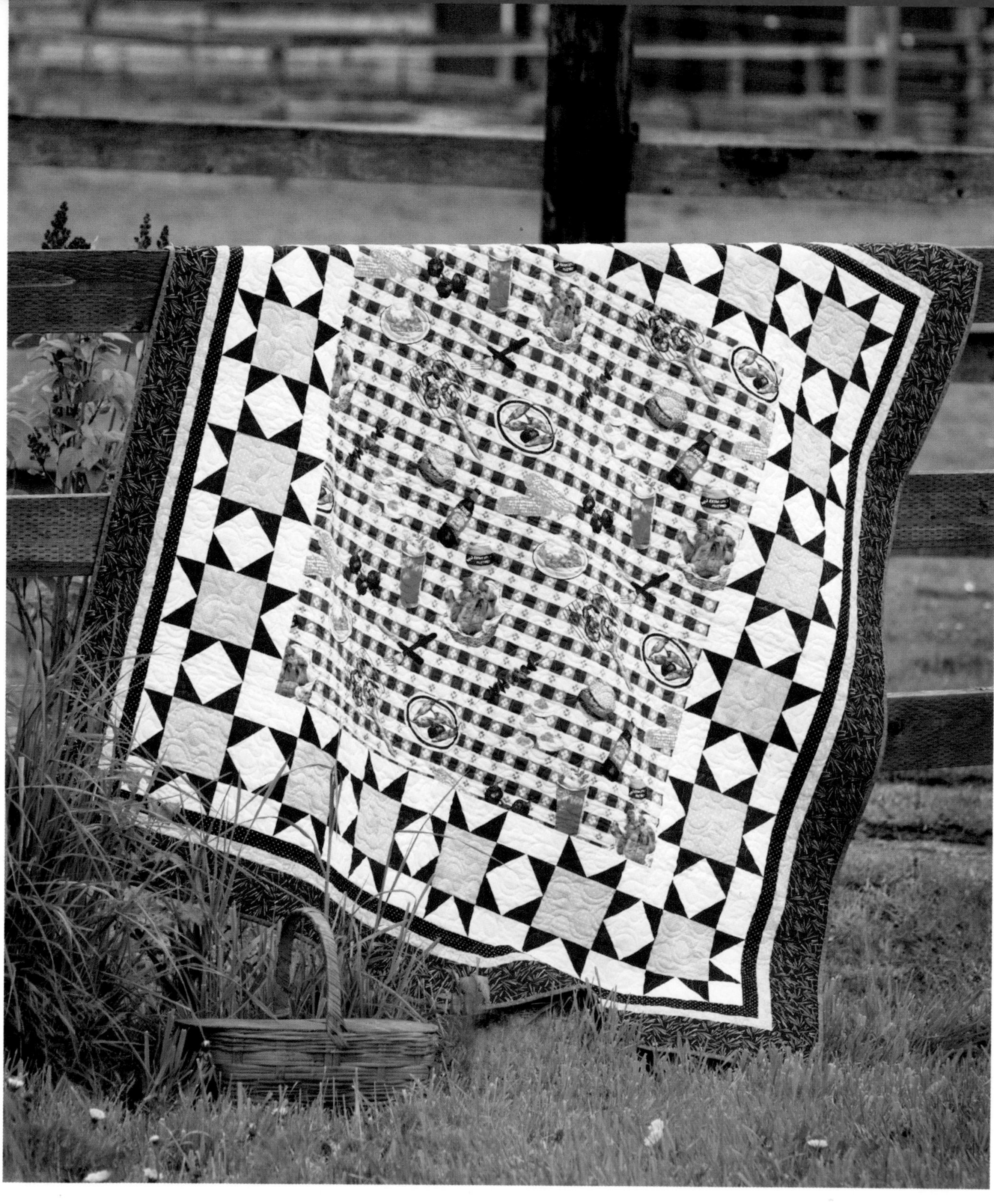

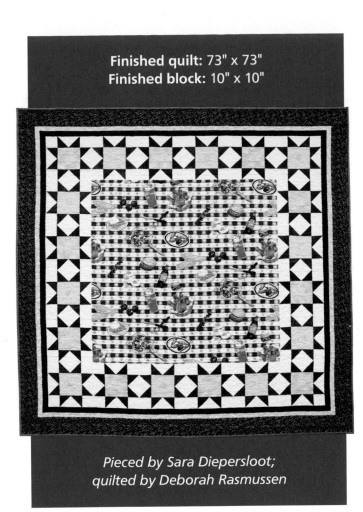

Finished quilt: 73" x 73"
Finished block: 10" x 10"

Pieced by Sara Diepersloot;
quilted by Deborah Rasmussen

MATERIALS

Yardage is based on 42"-wide fabric.

1⅔ yards of white print for blocks

1⅓ yards of blue checked picnic print for quilt center*

1 yard of red print for outer border

⅔ yard of red checked fabric for blocks

⅔ yard of red star print for blocks

½ yard of dark blue dot print for inner border

⅜ yard of yellow dot print for blocks

⅜ yard of green dot print for blocks and corner squares

⅜ yard of yellow print for middle border

⅝ yard of green fabric for binding

4¾ yards of fabric for backing

81" x 81" piece of batting

This fabric must be at least 40½" wide after washing and removing selvages.

CUTTING

From the green dot print, cut:
1 strip, 2" x 42"; crosscut into 10 squares, 2" x 2"
4 strips, 2¼" x 42"; crosscut into 20 rectangles, 2" x 2¼", and 20 rectangles, 2¼" x 5½"
4 squares, 1½" x 1½"

From the yellow dot print, cut:
1 strip, 2" x 42"; crosscut into 10 squares, 2" x 2"
4 strips, 2¼" x 42"; crosscut into 20 rectangles, 2" x 2¼", and 20 rectangles, 2¼" x 5½"

From the red star print, cut:
6 strips, 3" x 42"; crosscut into 80 squares, 3" x 3"

From the white print, cut:
18 strips, 3" x 42"; crosscut into 80 rectangles, 3" x 5½", and 80 squares, 3" x 3"

From the red checked fabric, cut:
6 strips, 3" x 42"; crosscut into 80 squares, 3" x 3"

From the blue checked picnic print, cut:
1 square, 40½" x 40½"

From the dark blue dot print, cut:
7 strips, 1¾" x 42"

From the yellow print, cut:
7 strips, 1½" x 42"

From the red print, cut:
7 strips, 4½" x 42"

From the green binding fabric, cut:
8 strips, 2¼" x 42"

MAKING STAR BLOCK A

1. Sew green dot 2" x 2¼" rectangles to opposite sides of a yellow dot 2" x 2" square. Press the seam allowances toward the green. Make 10.

Make 10.

2. Sew a green dot 2¼" x 5½" rectangle to the top and bottom of the step 1 unit. Make 10.

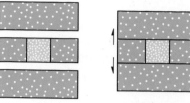

Make 10.

3. Draw a diagonal line from corner to corner on the wrong side of the red star 3" squares. Lay a square on one end of a white 3" x 5½" rectangle, right sides together. Sew on the drawn line. Trim off the excess ¼" from the stitching line. Press the seam allowances toward the triangle. Repeat on the other end of the rectangle, orienting the diagonal line in the opposite direction. Make 40 of these star-point units.

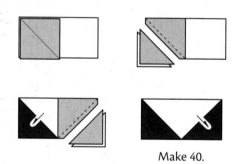

Make 40.

4. Arrange the white 3" squares, the star-point units, and the center units as shown. Join the units into rows, and then sew the rows together. Make 10 blocks.

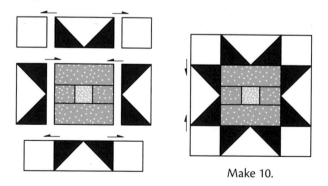

Make 10.

MAKING STAR BLOCK B

1. Sew yellow dot 2" x 2¼" rectangles to opposite sides of a green dot 2" x 2" square.

2. Sew a yellow dot 2¼" x 5½" rectangle to the top and bottom of the step 1 unit. Make 10.

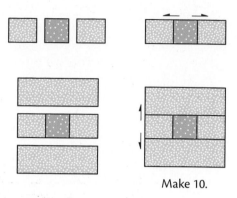

Make 10.

3. Repeat step 3 of "Making Star Block A" at left using the red checked 3" squares and the remaining white 3" x 5½" rectangles. Make 40 star-point units.

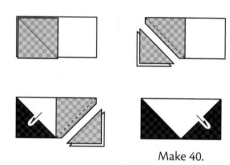

Make 40.

4. Arrange the remaining 3" white squares, the star-point units, and the center units as shown. Join the units into rows, and then sew the rows together. Make 10 blocks.

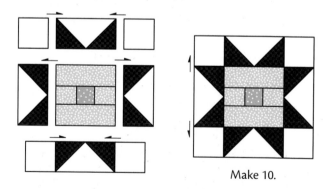

Make 10.

ASSEMBLING THE QUILT TOP

1. Arrange two of Star block A and two of Star block B in a row, alternating them as shown in the quilt diagram. Join the blocks into a row. Press the seam allowances toward block A. Make two rows and sew them to each side of

the blue checked picnic 40½" square. Press the seam allowances away from the square.

2. Arrange three of Star block A and three of Star block B in a row, alternating them as shown in the quilt diagram. Join the blocks into a row. Press the seam allowances toward block A. Make two rows and sew them to the top and bottom of the blue checked picnic square. Press the seam allowances toward the square.

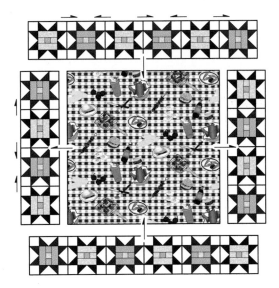

3. Referring to "Adding Borders" on page 76, attach the dark blue dot inner border.

4. Measure the length and width of the quilt and cut yellow print middle-border strips to those dimensions. Add the side borders to the quilt. Sew the green dot squares to the top and bottom borders and add them to the quilt.

5. Repeat step 3 to add the red print outer border.

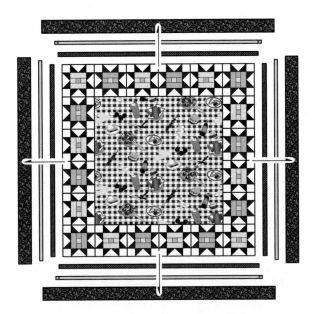

FINISHING THE QUILT

1. Layer the quilt top with batting and backing and quilt as desired.

   Quilting Note: When you have a very busy fabric, you don't want the quilting to compete with it or add to the busyness. This quilt has a subtle leafy design stitched in white thread.

2. Referring to "Binding" on page 77, bind the edges of the quilt using the green strips.

Fabric Alternatives

The center of this quilt provides a large space to show off novelty prints that can sometimes be tricky to use. Try making a beach blanket with a fun ocean print. Pull coordinating colors from the print to make the Star blocks.

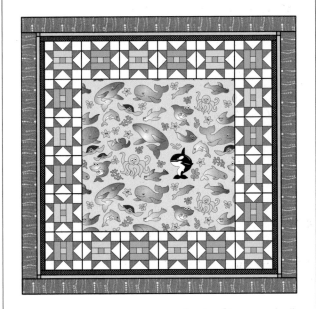

Summer BBQ

Summer BBQs, watermelon, ice cream . . . yum! The novelty print and bright colors combine to make a quilt that's perfect for a summer day outside.

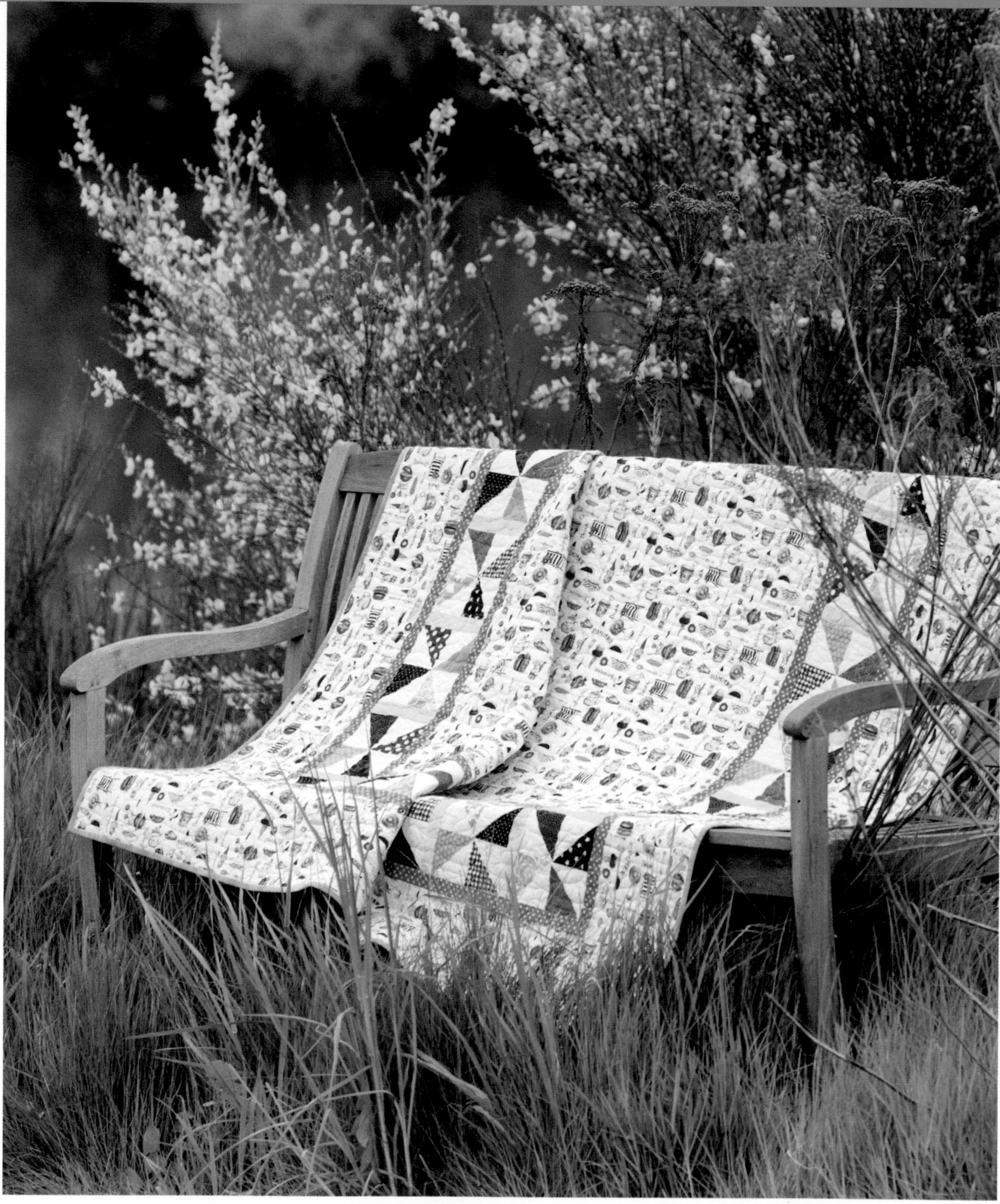

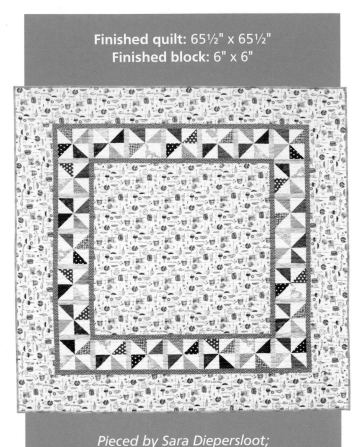

Finished quilt: 65½" x 65½"
Finished block: 6" x 6"

*Pieced by Sara Diepersloot;
quilted by Deborah Rasmussen*

MATERIALS

Yardage is based on 42"-wide fabric.

2⅝ yards of summer BBQ print for center square
and outer border

1 fat eighth *each* of 12 assorted bright prints for
blocks*

⅔ yard of white print for blocks

½ yard of blue dot print for inner and middle borders

¼ yard of light blue print for sashing

⅝ yard of green print for binding

4¼ yards of fabric for backing

74" x 74" piece of batting

Or scraps to equal 48 squares, 4" x 4".

CUTTING

From the summer BBQ print, cut:
1 square, 34½" x 34½"
6 strips, 8" x 42"

From the white print, cut:
5 strips, 4" x 42"; crosscut into 48 squares, 4" x 4"

From *each* of the 12 bright prints, cut:
4 squares, 4" x 4" (48 total)

From the light blue print, cut:
4 strips, 1½" x 42"; crosscut into 24 rectangles,
    1½" x 6½"

From the blue dot print, cut:
9 strips, 1½" x 42"; crosscut *4* of the strips into:
    2 strips, 1½" x 34½"
    2 strips, 1½" x 36½"

From the green print, cut:
7 strips, 2¼" x 42"

MAKING THE BLOCKS

1. Draw a diagonal line from corner to corner
   on the wrong side of the white 4" squares.
   Lay a square on a bright 4" square, right sides
   together. Sew ¼" away from the drawn line on
   both sides of the line. Cut directly on the drawn
   line. Press the seam allowances toward the
   bright fabric. Make 96 half-square-triangle units.

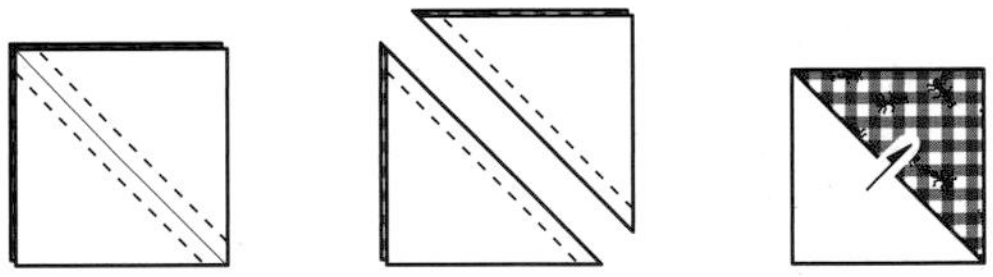

Make 96.

2. Square up each half-square-triangle unit to be
   3½" x 3½". This is a very important step; it will
   ensure that your Pinwheel blocks line up and
   come out beautifully.

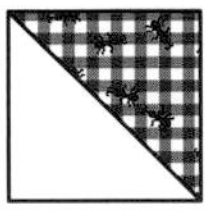

3½"

3½"

3. Sew four triangle units together to make a Pinwheel block as shown. Make 24 blocks.

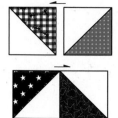 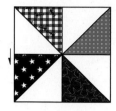

Make 24.

ASSEMBLING THE QUILT TOP

1. Sew the blue dot 1½" x 34½" strips to the sides of the BBQ print 34½" square. Press the seam allowances toward the border. Sew the blue dot 1½" x 36½" strips to the top and bottom. Press.

2. Sew five Pinwheel blocks together into a row, alternating them with six light blue 1½" x 6½" sashing rectangles as shown. Make two rows. Press the seam allowances toward the blue sashing. Sew seven Pinwheel blocks together into a row, alternating them with six light blue 1½" x 6½" sashing rectangles as shown. Press. Make two rows.

Make 2.

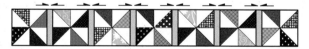

Make 2.

3. Sew the shorter block rows to the sides of the quilt. Press the seam allowances toward the blue inner border. Sew the longer block rows to the top and bottom of the quilt center. Press.

4. Referring to "Adding Borders" on page 76, attach the blue dot middle and BBQ print outer borders.

FINISHING THE QUILT

1. Layer the quilt top with batting and backing and quilt as desired.

   Quilting Note: I love the quilting on this one. Ice cream cones are subtly stitched with white thread.

2. Referring to "Binding" on page 77, bind the edges of the quilt using the green strips.

Fabric Alternatives

Try something completely different using these white, lime green, and black prints. It's amazing how different a quilt can look in another colorway.

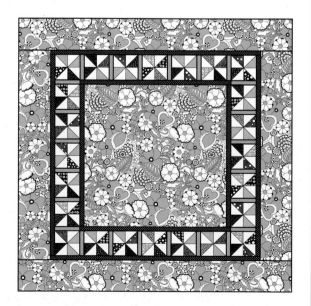

Seaside Table Runner

Keep your summer vacation memories close at hand with this beach-inspired table runner. You can make it very quickly using strip piecing, and it's a good opportunity to use up some scraps.

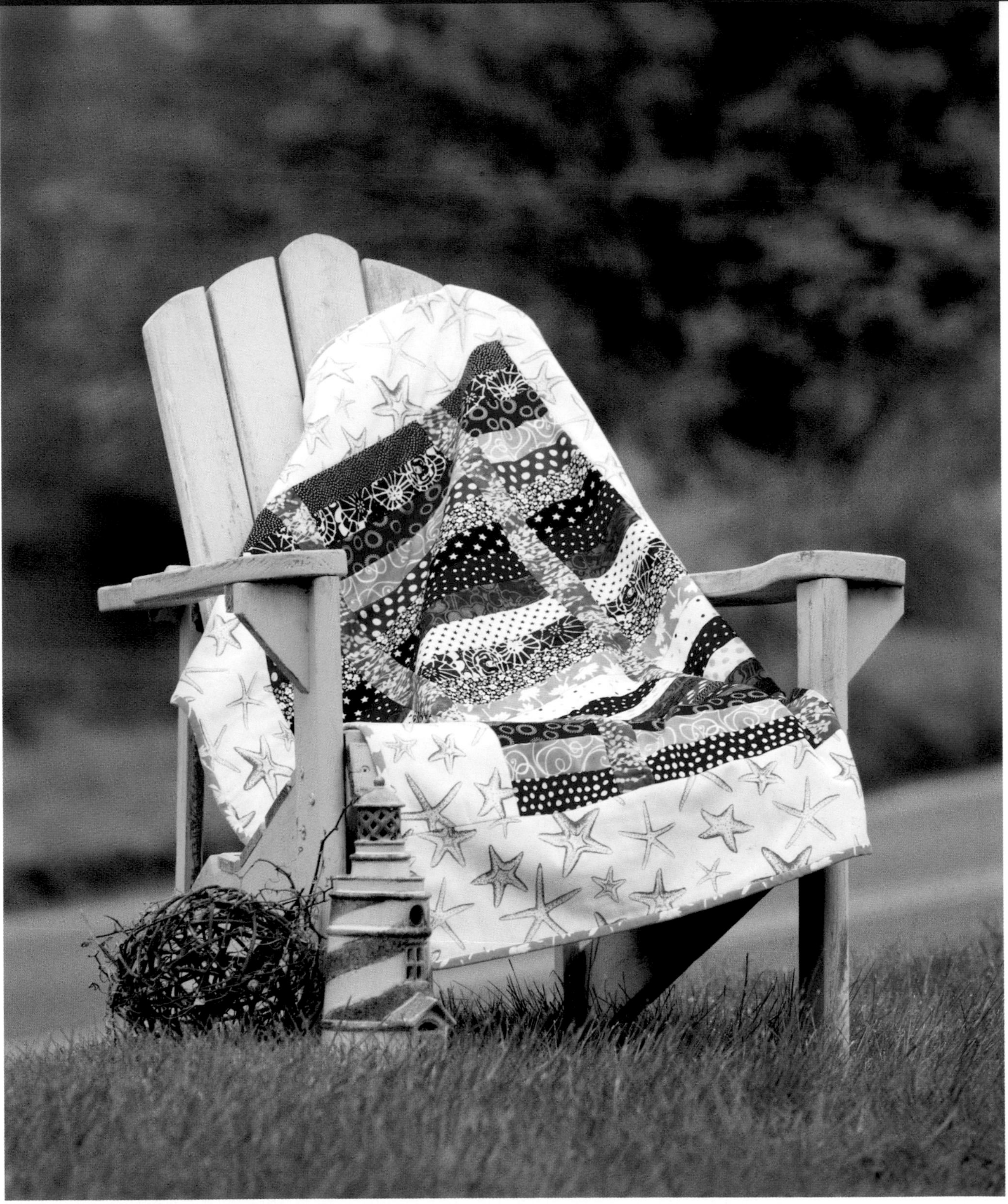

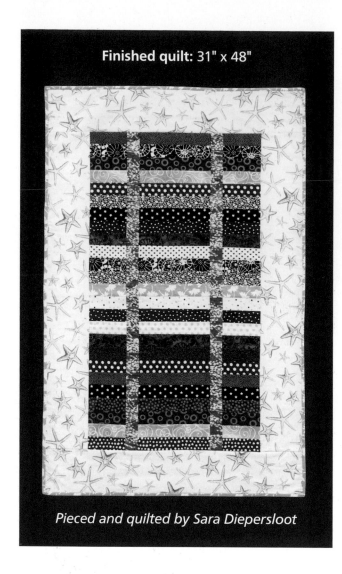

Finished quilt: 31" x 48"

Pieced and quilted by Sara Diepersloot

MATERIALS

Yardage is based on 42"-wide fabric.

¾ yard of starfish print for border

1 strip, 2" x 42", *each* of 16 assorted red, blue, yellow, and white prints for blocks

¼ yard of blue print for sashing

½ yard of yellow print for binding

1⅔ yards of fabric for backing

37" x 54" piece of batting

CUTTING

From *each* of the 16 red, blue, yellow, and white print strips, cut:
2 strips, 2" x approximately 21" (32 total)

From the blue print, cut:
2 strips, 2" x 42"; crosscut into 2 strips, 2" x 38"

From the starfish print, cut:
4 strips, 5½" x 42"

From the yellow print, cut:
5 strips, 2¼" x 42"

MAKING THE BLOCKS

1. Lay out 25 of the red, blue, yellow, and white strips to decide the order and positioning of the colors and prints. There will be seven extra strips.

2. Sew the strips together in groups of five to make five strip sets. This makes it easier to press and cut than if you made one large strip set. Press the seam allowances in one direction. Crosscut each strip set into two segments, 5" wide, and one segment, 9" wide.

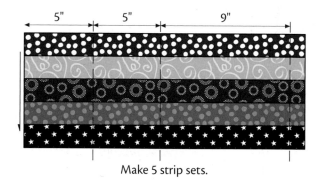

Make 5 strip sets.

3. Sew the five strip-set segments together into rows, making two 5"-wide rows and one 9"-wide row. To match the quilt shown, keep the strips in the same order for all three rows. Of course, if you prefer a design twist, mix them up!

ASSEMBLING THE QUILT TOP

1. Sew the strip-pieced rows together with the two blue 2" x 38" strips, alternating them as shown. Press the seam allowances toward the blue strips.

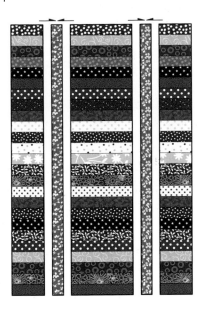

2. Referring to "Adding Borders" on page 76, attach the starfish print border.

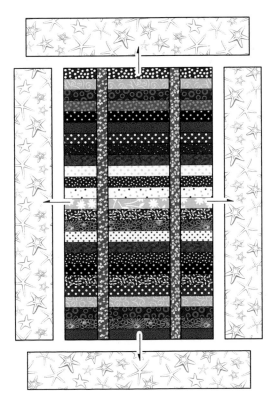

FINISHING THE QUILT

1. Layer the quilt top with batting and backing and quilt as desired.

   Quilting Note: When you use a medium- or large-scale print in the borders, you can free-motion quilt around the print and echo those shapes in the interior. Or simply stitch in the ditch (see page 77) of the strip-pieced center.

2. Referring to "Binding" on page 77, bind the edges of the quilt using the yellow strips.

Fabric Alternatives

Depending on the fabric you choose for the border, you can make this table runner for any season or occasion. How about using all red and green fabrics for Christmas?

Simple Strips

Find a black-and-white print that you love, add a few bright colors, and you're ready to make this easy strip-pieced quilt.

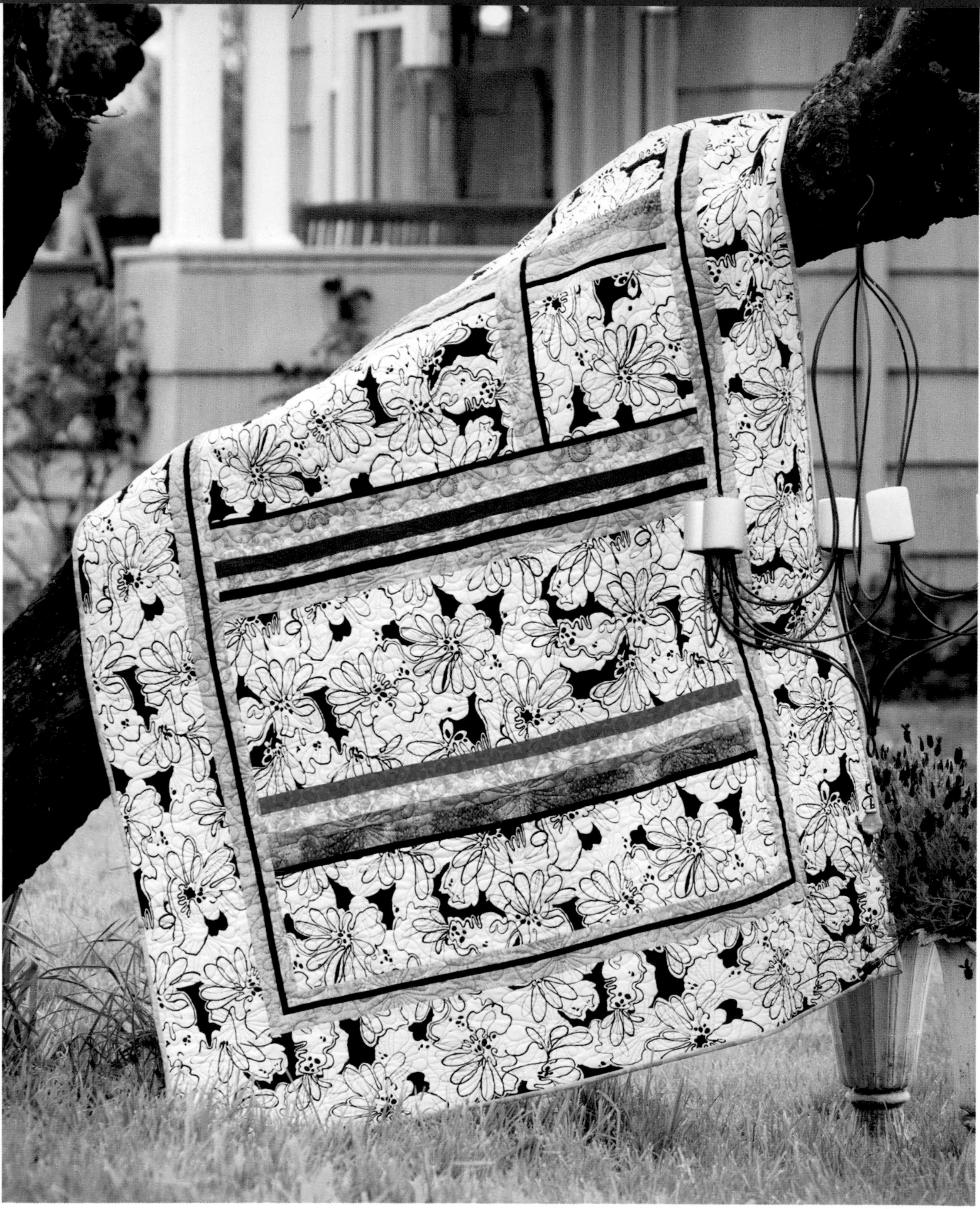

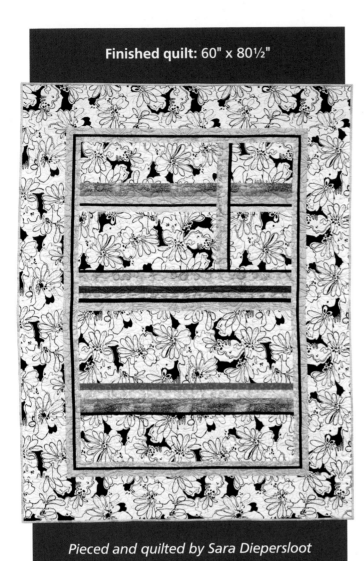

Finished quilt: 60" x 80½"

Pieced and quilted by Sara Diepersloot

MATERIALS

Yardage is based on 42"-wide fabric.

3⅛ yards of black-and-white floral print for quilt center and border 4

⅛ yard *each* of 6 assorted bright prints for quilt center (I used green vine print, yellow dot, green dot, red plaid, blue dot, and orange print.)

⅔ yard of green-and-teal print for quilt center and binding

½ yard of green-and-blue dot print for quilt center and border 3

⅜ yard of black dot print for quilt center and border 2

⅓ yard of green swirl print for quilt center and border 1

¼ yard of bright purple print for quilt center

¼ yard of bright yellow batik for quilt center

4 yards of fabric for backing

68" x 88" piece of batting

CUTTING

From the bright purple print, cut:
1 strip, 2¼" x 42"
1 strip, 2" x 42"

From the 6 bright prints, cut:
1 strip, 1¼" x 42" (green vine)
1 strip, 1½" x 42" (green vine)
1 strip, 1½" x 42" (yellow dot)
1 strip, 2" x 42" (green dot)
1 strip, 1¾" x 42" (red plaid)
2 strips, 1½" x 42" (blue dot)
1 strip, 1¾" x 42" (orange)

From the green-and-blue dot print, cut:
1 strip, 2" x 42"
6 strips, 1¾" x 42"

From the black dot print, cut:
9 strips, 1" x 42"
1 strip, 1¼" x 42"

From the black-and-white floral print, cut:
1 strip, 8" x 42"; crosscut into 1 piece, 8" x 11½", and 1 piece, 8" x 25"
1 strip, 11" x 42"; crosscut into 1 piece, 11" x 11½", and 1 piece, 11" x 25"
1 strip, 13½" x 42"; crosscut into 1 piece, 13½" x 38½"
1 strip, 9" x 42"; crosscut into 1 piece, 9" x 38½"
7 strips, 8½" x 42"

From the green swirl print, cut:
6 strips, 1½" x 42"

From the bright yellow batik, cut:
1 strip, 1½" x 42"
1 strip, 2" x 42"

From the green-and-teal print, cut:
1 strip, 2" x 42"
8 strips, 2¼" x 42"

MAKING THE BLOCKS

1. Sew the bright purple 2¼" strip, the green vine 1¼" strip, the green-and-blue dot 2" strip, a black dot 1" strip, and the yellow dot 1½" strip together. Press the seam allowances in one direction. Cut the strip set into one segment, 11½" wide, and one segment, 25" wide.

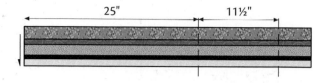

2. Sew the black-and-white floral 8" x 11½" and 8" x 25" pieces to the top of the strip-set segments. Sew the black-and-white floral 11" x 11½" and 11" x 25" pieces to the bottom of the strip-set segments. Press the seam allowances toward the strips.

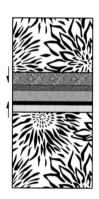

3. Sew a black dot 1" strip, a green swirl 1½" strip, and a blue dot 1½" strip together. Press the seam allowances in one direction. Cut the strip set into one segment, 24" wide.

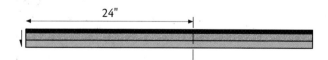

4. Sew the 24" strip-set segment made in step 3 between the 25" strip set and the 11½" strip set. Press the seam allowances toward the center.

5. Sew a black dot 1" strip, the green dot 2" strip, the yellow batik 1½" strip, the red plaid 1¾" strip, the remaining blue dot 1½" strip, the black dot 1¼" strip, and the green-and-teal print 2" strip together. Press the seam allowances in one direction. Cut the strip set into one segment, 38½" wide.

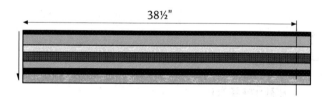

6. Sew the black-and-white floral 13½" x 38½" piece to the bottom of the strip-set segment. Press toward the strips.

7. Sew the orange 1¾" strip, the yellow batik 2" strip, the green vine 1½" strip, the bright purple 2" strip, and a black dot 1" strip together. Press the seam allowances in one direction. Cut the strip set into one segment, 38½" wide.

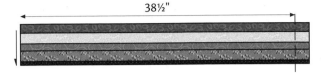

38½"

8. Sew the black-and-white floral 9" x 38½" piece to the bottom of the strip-set segment. Press the seam allowances toward the strips.

ASSEMBLING THE QUILT TOP

1. Sew the strip-pieced units together as shown in the quilt diagram.

2. Referring to "Adding Borders" on page 76, attach the four borders in this order: green swirl, black dot, green-and-blue dot, and black-and-white floral print.

FINISHING THE QUILT

1. Layer the quilt top with batting and backing and quilt as desired.

Quilting Note: The bold floral print inspired this quilting pattern. Outline or echo quilt the floral or other motifs in your featured fabric.

2. Referring to "Binding" on page 77, bind the edges of the quilt using the green-and-teal strips.

Fabric Alternatives

This easy quilt would be fantastic in batiks. Choose one that you love for the main print, and then add some of your batik scraps. They will coordinate beautifully!

Harvest Star

With fall colors and autumn-themed prints, this star quilt makes a fitting table topper or wall hanging for the fall season.

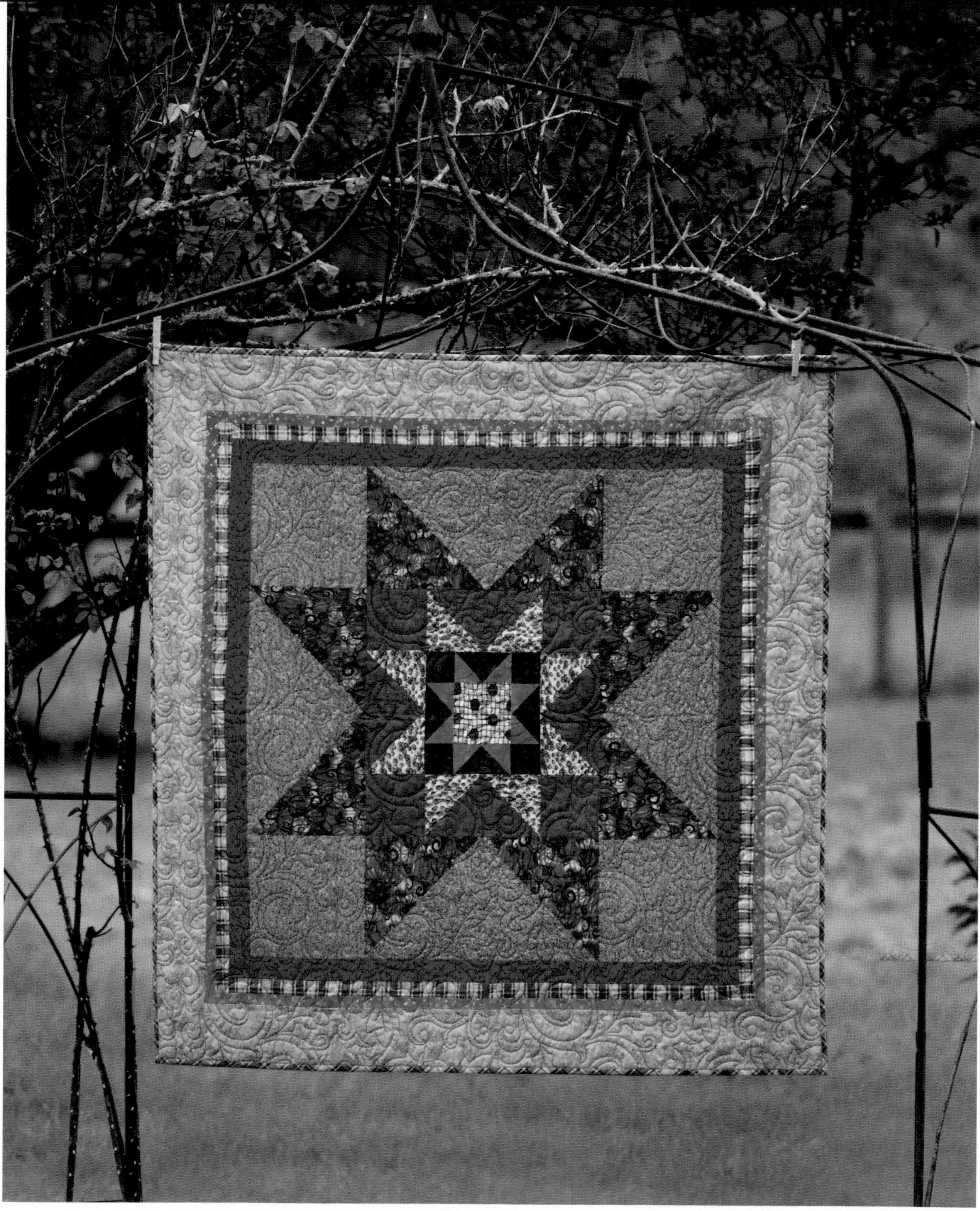

Finished quilt: 47" x 47"

*Pieced by Sara Diepersloot;
quilted by Deborah Rasmussen*

MATERIALS

Yardage is based on 42"-wide fabric.

⅞ yard of gold leaf print for blocks

¾ yard of tan leaf print for border 4

⅝ yard of large-scale pumpkin print for blocks

⅝ yard of brown plaid for border 2 and binding

⅓ yard of rust print 1 for blocks

⅓ yard of rust print 2 for border 1

¼ yard of tiny pumpkin print for blocks

¼ yard of gold star print for border 3

⅛ yard of brown pumpkin print for blocks

⅛ yard of gold dot print for blocks

1 fat eighth or 5" x 5" piece of pumpkin plaid for
   center square

3⅛ yards of fabric for backing

55" x 55" piece of batting

CUTTING

From the gold dot print, cut:
1 strip, 2½" x 42"; crosscut into 8 squares,
   2½" x 2½"

From the brown pumpkin print, cut:
1 strip, 2½" x 42"; crosscut into 4 rectangles,
   2½" x 4½", and 4 squares, 2½" x 2½"

From the pumpkin plaid, cut:
1 square, 4½" x 4½"

From the tiny pumpkin print, cut:
1 strip, 4½" x 42"; crosscut into 8 squares,
   4½" x 4½"

From the rust print 1, cut:
2 strips, 4½" x 42"; crosscut into 4 rectangles,
   4½" x 8½", and 4 squares, 4½" x 4½"

From the large-scale pumpkin print, cut:
2 strips, 8½" x 42"; crosscut into 8 squares,
   8½" x 8½"

From the gold leaf print, cut:
3 strips, 8½" x 42"; crosscut into 4 rectangles,
   8½" x 16½", and 4 squares, 8½" x 8½"

From the rust print 2, cut:
4 strips, 2" x 42"

From the brown plaid, cut:
4 strips, 1½" x 42"
5 strips, 2¼" x 42"

From the gold star print, cut:
4 strips, 1¼" x 42"

From the tan leaf print, cut:
5 strips, 4½" x 42"

MAKING THE BLOCKS

1. Draw a diagonal line from corner to corner on
   the wrong side of the gold dot 2½" squares.

2. Lay a marked square on one end of a brown pumpkin 2½" x 4½" rectangle, right sides together. Sew on the drawn line. Trim off the excess ¼" from the stitching line. Press the seam allowances toward the triangle. Repeat on the other end of the rectangle, orienting the diagonal line in the opposite direction. Make four of these star-point units.

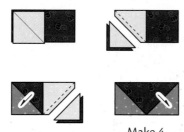

Make 4.

3. Arrange the brown pumpkin 2½" squares, the star-point units, and the pumpkin plaid 4½" square as shown. Join the units into rows, and then sew the rows together. Press, following the arrows in the diagram.

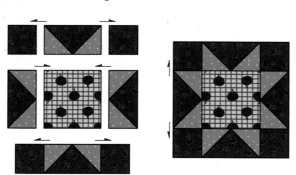

4. Draw a diagonal line from corner to corner on the wrong side of the tiny pumpkin print 4½" squares. Repeat step 2, placing the squares on a rust print 4½" x 8½" rectangle. Make four of these star-point units.

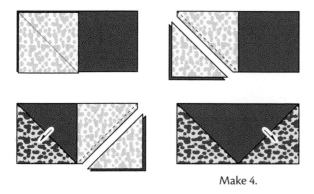

Make 4.

5. Arrange the 4½" rust squares, the star-point units, and the unit made in step 3 as shown. Join the units into rows, and then sew the rows together. Press.

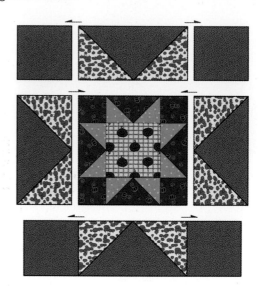

6. Draw a diagonal line from corner to corner on the wrong side of the large-scale pumpkin print 8½" squares. Repeat step 2, placing the squares on a gold leaf print 8½" x 16½" rectangle. Make four of these star-point units.

7. Arrange the gold leaf print 8½" squares, the star-point units, and the unit made in step 5 as shown. Join the units into rows, and then sew the rows together. Press.

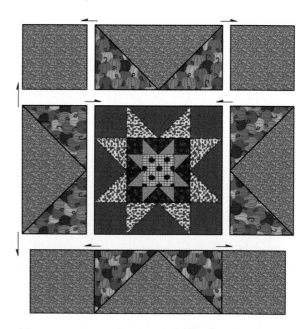

ASSEMBLING THE QUILT TOP

Referring to "Adding Borders" on page 76, attach the four borders in this order: rust print, brown plaid, gold star print, and tan leaf print.

FINISHING THE QUILT

1. Layer the quilt top with batting and backing and quilt as desired.

   Quilting Note: The quilt shown uses an overall pattern of vines and leaves to echo the seasonal theme.

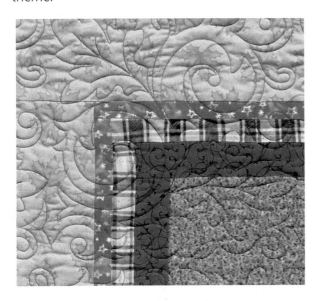

2. Referring to "Binding" on page 77, bind the edges of the quilt using the brown plaid strips.

Fabric Alternatives

While the pumpkin print in this quilt is perfect for fall, you can turn this quick quilt into the perfect spot for a little girl's tea party with sweet pink-and-brown cupcake fabric. Time for dress-up, teddy bears, and tea!

Harvest Time

I really liked the leaf print with the light background. In designing this quilt around it, I was able to use up a lot of seasonal scraps in harvest colors and fall prints.

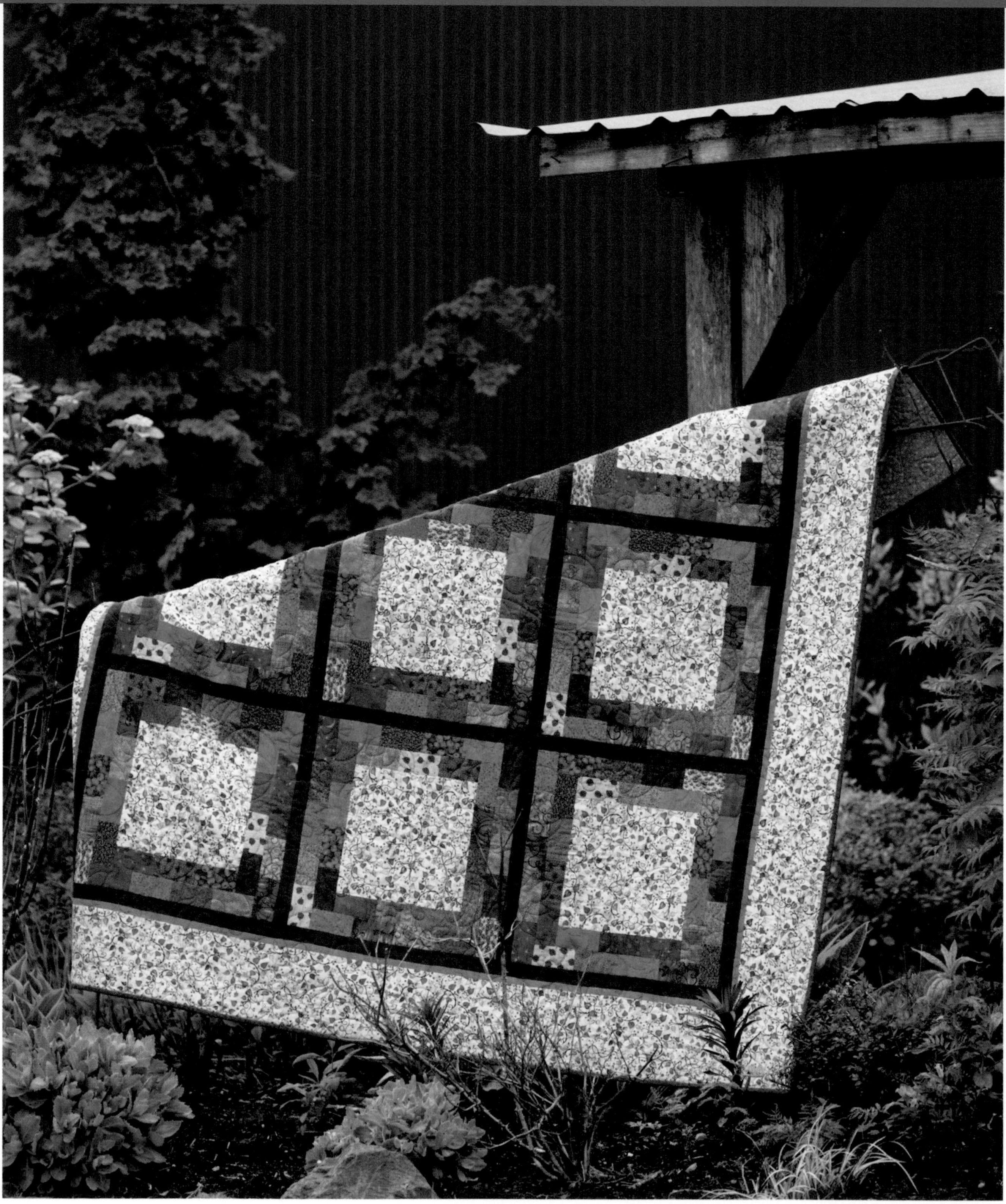

Finished quilt: 72" x 72"
Finished block: 17½" x 17½"

Pieced by Sara Diepersloot;
quilted by Deborah Rasmussen

MATERIALS

Yardage is based on 42"-wide fabric.

2½ yards of ivory leaf print for blocks and outer border

2¼ yards *total* of tan, orange, rust, and green fall prints for blocks

⅔ yard of dark brown fabric for sashing

¼ yard of gold fabric for inner border

⅝ yard of brown print for binding

4½ yards of fabric for backing

80" x 80" piece of batting

CUTTING

From the ivory leaf print, cut:
3 strips, 11" x 42"; crosscut into 9 squares, 11" x 11"
7 strips, 7" x 42"

From the tan, orange, rust, and green fall prints, cut *a total of:*
29 strips, 2¼" x 42"; crosscut into 288 rectangles, 2¼" x 4"

From the dark brown fabric, cut:
12 strips, 1¾" x 42"; crosscut 3 strips into 6 pieces, 1¾" x 18"

From the gold fabric, cut:
6 strips, 1" x 42"

From the brown print for binding, cut:
8 strips, 2¼" x 42"

MAKING THE BLOCKS

I like to use a design wall to decide the placement of my fabrics. Arrange your 2¼" x 4" fall print rectangles in a manner that pleases your eye. All nine blocks can be different, or they can all be the same. When making my blocks, I found three arrangements that I liked and made three blocks of each. When joining the rectangles to each other, press all of the seam allowances in one direction.

1. Sew three fall print 2¼" x 4" rectangles together along the short ends. Make two. Press. Sew these units to opposite sides of an 11" ivory leaf print square. Press the seam allowances away from the center.

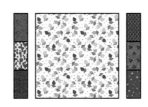 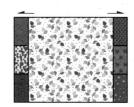

2. Sew four fall print 2¼" x 4" rectangles together. Make two. Sew these units to the top and bottom of the center unit. Press the seam allowances away from the center.

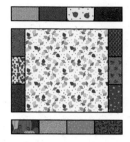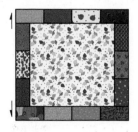

3. Sew four fall print 2¼" x 4" rectangles together. Make two. Press. Sew these units to opposite sides of the step 2 unit. Press the seam allowances away from the center.

4. Sew five fall print 2¼" x 4" rectangles together. Make two. Press. Sew these units to the top and bottom of the step 3 unit. Press the seam allowances away from the center.

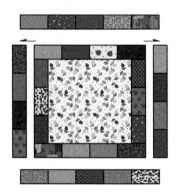

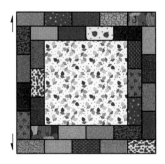

5. Repeat steps 1–4 to make a total of nine blocks.

ASSEMBLING THE QUILT TOP

1. Join three blocks into a row, alternating them with two dark brown 1¾" x 18" sashing pieces. Press the seam allowances toward the sashing. Make three rows.

2. Sew the remaining dark brown fabric strips together end to end. Crosscut into four strips, 1¾" x 55½", and two strips, 1¾" x 58".

3. Sew the three rows together, alternating them with two 1¾" x 55½" sashing strips. Press the seam allowances toward the sashing. Sew the remaining 1¾" x 55½" sashing strips to the sides of the quilt top. Press. Sew the 1¾" x 58" sashing strips to the top and bottom edges of the quilt top. Press.

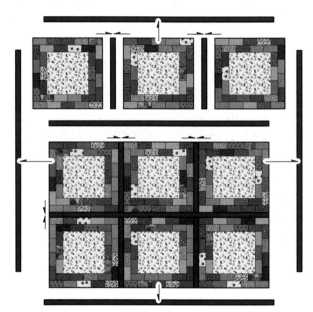

4. Referring to "Adding Borders" on page 76, attach the gold inner and ivory leaf print outer borders.

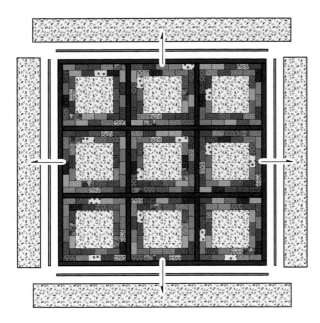

FINISHING THE QUILT

1. Layer the quilt top with batting and backing and quilt as desired.

   Quilting Note: *This quilt was calling out for a pumpkin quilting design.*

2. Referring to "Binding" on page 77, bind the edges of the quilt using the brown strips.

Fabric Alternatives

This quilt is the perfect place to show off a fabric and use it with many coordinating colors and prints. Here's a fresh print with bright blues and greens on a crisp white background. You can have fun adding lots of different blue and green prints as the coordinates.

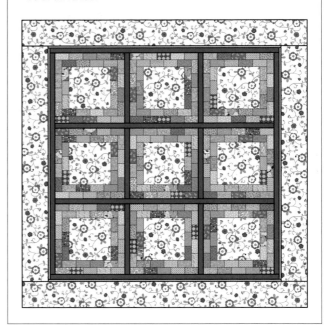

Cozy Winter Night

Grab a marvelous Jelly Roll and a 5" charm pack and go! Or, use up leftover strips and squares from your stash. Either way, have fun choosing the fabrics for the setting squares and the border, and enjoy the easy piecing. (This quilt features the Fruitcake Collection from Moda.)

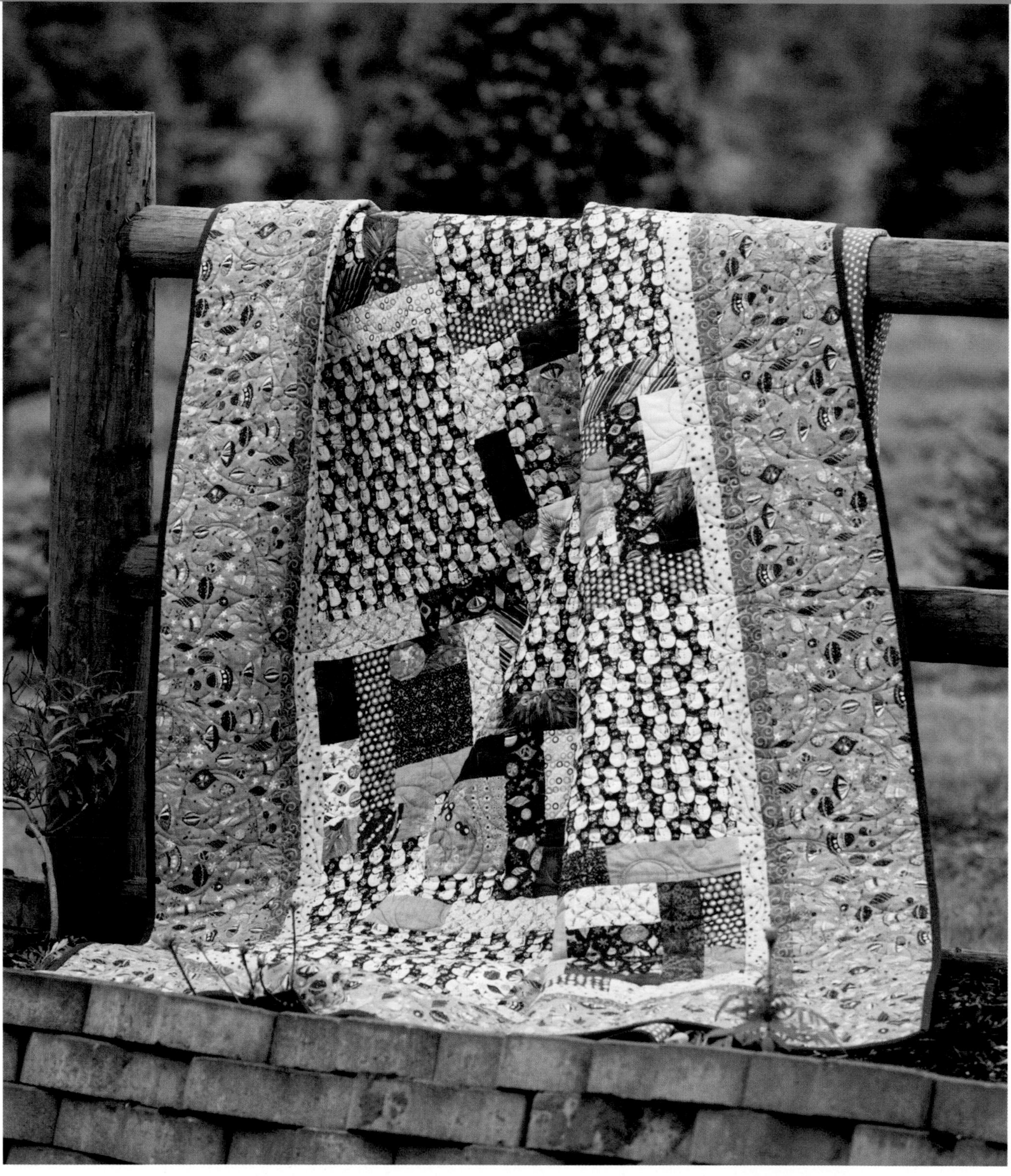

Finished quilt: 80½" x 80½"
Finished block: 12½" x 12½"

*Pieced by Sara Diepersloot;
quilted by Deborah Rasmussen*

MATERIALS

Yardage is based on 42"-wide fabric.

1 Jelly Roll for blocks*

1 charm pack or 13 squares, 5" x 5", for blocks**

1¾ yards of blue print for outer border

1⅝ yards of snowman print for setting squares

½ yard of green-and-red dot print for inner border

⅜ yard of green print for middle border

⅔ yard of brown print for binding

7½ yards of fabric for backing

90" x 90" piece of batting

A Jelly Roll is 40 strips of fabric, 2½" x 42".

**A charm pack is 35 to 40 squares, 5" x 5".*

One at a Time

When the blocks are scrappy, like those in this quilt, I use a design wall to determine the placement of my fabrics. I typically lay out and cut one block at a time.

CUTTING

From the Jelly Roll strips, cut:
26 rectangles, 2½" x 5"
26 rectangles, 2½" x 9"
52 rectangles, 2½" x 4¾"
52 rectangles, 2½" x 6¾"

From the snowman print, cut:
4 strips, 13" x 42"; crosscut into 12 squares, 13" x 13"

From the green-and-red dot print, cut:
7 strips, 1¾" x 42"

From the green print, cut:
7 strips, 1½" x 42"

From the blue print, cut:
8 strips, 7" x 42"

From the brown print, cut:
8 strips, 2¼" x 42"

MAKING THE BLOCKS

Press all seam allowances away from the center of the block.

1. Sew Jelly Roll 2½" x 5" rectangles to the top and bottom of a 5" charm square.

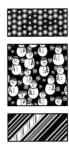 

2. Sew Jelly Roll 2½" x 9" rectangles to opposite sides of the unit.

3. Sew two Jelly Roll 2½" x 4¾" rectangles together along the short ends; make two. Sew these units to opposite sides of the block. Sew two 2½" x 6¾" Jelly Roll pieces together; make two. Sew these units to the top and bottom of the block. Repeat to make 13 blocks.

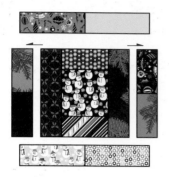

Make 13.

ASSEMBLING THE QUILT TOP

1. Arrange the pieced blocks and setting squares in rows, alternating them as shown. Join the blocks into rows. Press the seam allowances toward the setting squares. Sew the rows together. Press.

2. Referring to "Adding Borders" on page 76, attach the green-and-red dot inner, green print middle, and blue print outer borders.

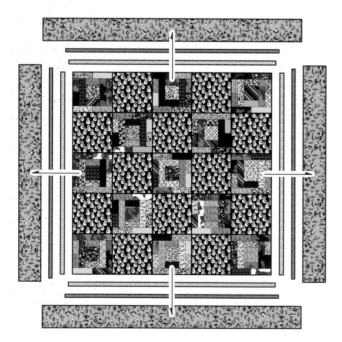

FINISHING THE QUILT

1. Layer the quilt top with batting and backing and quilt as desired.

   Quilting Note: This warm quilt has a soft, flowing floral pattern quilted on it. It blends with the busy background and doesn't distract from the fabric prints.

2. Referring to "Binding" on page 77, bind the edges of the quilt using the brown strips.

Fabric Alternatives

I love how easy it is to go to your local quilt shop and find a prepackaged set of beautiful fabrics. It takes the guesswork out of fabric selection. Try this quilt with a charming floral collection like this one.

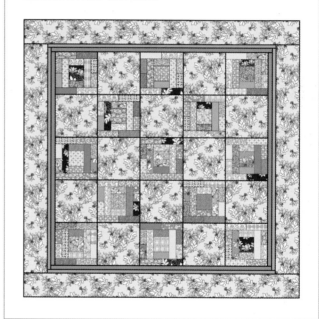

Winter Wonderland

You'll be cozy all winter long after piecing this softly colored quilt. The fussy-cut snowmen in the block centers make this quilt extra adorable. The snowman border print adds the crowning touch to create an amazing border.

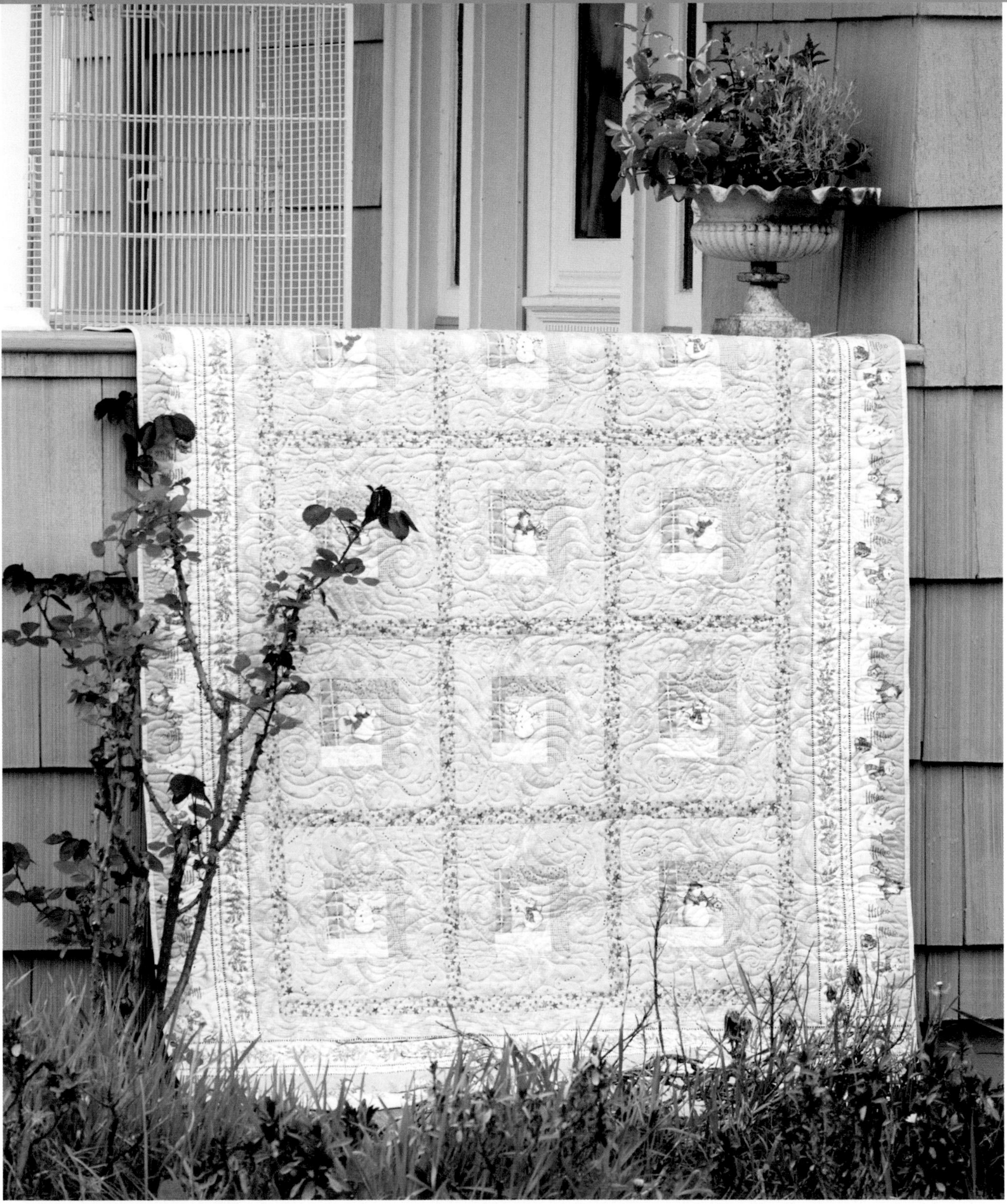

Finished quilt: 62" x 76¼"
Finished block: 13" x 13"

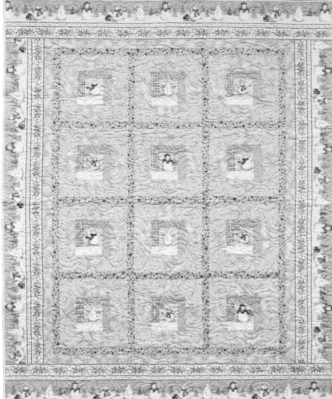

*Pieced by Sara Diepersloot;
quilted by Deborah Rasmussen*

MATERIALS

Yardage is based on 42"-wide fabric.

2 yards of snowman striped fabric for outer border*

1¼ yards of blue snowman print for blocks

1⅛ yards of gold snowflake print for blocks and inner border

¾ yard of gold star print for sashing

⅔ yard of snowman print for block centers**

¼ yard of green checked fabric for blocks

¼ yard of green plaid for blocks

¼ yard of blue floral print for blocks

¼ yard of ivory snowflake print for blocks

⅝ yard of ivory print for binding

5 yards of fabric for backing

70" x 85" piece of batting

This fabric is printed along the lengthwise grain; you'll need four repeats.

**This amount allows extra for fussy cutting; ⅓ yard is enough if you don't fussy cut these pieces.*

CUTTING

From the snowman print, cut:
12 squares, 4" x 4"

From the green checked fabric, cut:
2 strips, 2" x 42"; crosscut into 12 rectangles, 2" x 5½"

From the blue floral print, cut:
2 strips, 2" x 42"; crosscut into 12 rectangles, 2" x 5½"

From the green plaid, cut:
2 strips, 2" x 42"; crosscut into 12 rectangles, 2" x 5½"

From the ivory snowflake print, cut:
2 strips, 2" x 42"; crosscut into 12 rectangles, 2" x 5½"

From the gold snowflake print, cut:
4 strips, 5½" x 42"; crosscut into 24 squares, 5½" x 5½". Cut the squares once diagonally to make 48 triangles.
6 strips, 2¼" x 42"

From the blue snowman print, cut:
5 strips, 7½" x 42"; crosscut into 24 squares, 7½" x 7½". Cut the squares once diagonally to make 48 triangles.

From the gold star print, cut:
12 strips, 1¾" x 42"; crosscut *3* of the strips into 8 pieces, 1¾" x 13½"

From the snowman striped fabric, cut:
4 strips, 7½" x 66", from the *lengthwise* grain

From the ivory print, cut:
8 strips, 2¼" x 42"

MAKING THE BLOCKS

Press all seam allowances away from the center of the block after each sewing step.

1. Sew a green checked 2" x 5½" rectangle to the right side of a snowman print 4" square. Sew until you're 1" away from the bottom edge of the snowman square.

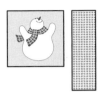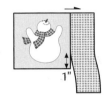

2. Sew a blue floral print 2" x 5½" rectangle to the top of the center unit.

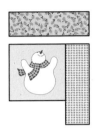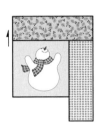

3. Sew a green plaid 2" x 5½" rectangle to the left side of the center unit.

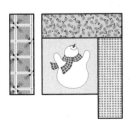

4. Sew an ivory snowflake print 2" x 5½" rectangle to the bottom of the center unit.

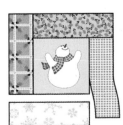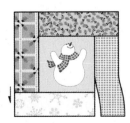

5. Sew the remainder of the seam that was left unsewn in step 1. Make a total of 12 units.

Make 12.

6. Sew a gold snowflake triangle to each side of the unit.

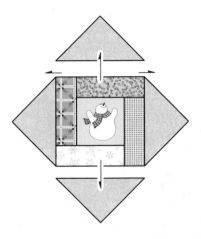

7. Sew a blue snowman triangle to each side of the unit. Make 12 blocks.

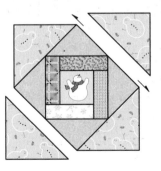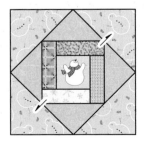

Make 12.

ASSEMBLING THE QUILT TOP

1. Join the blocks into four rows of three blocks each, alternating them with the gold star 1¾" x 13½" sashing pieces. Press the seam allowances toward the sashing.

2. Sew the remaining gold star print 1¾" x 42" strips together end to end. Crosscut into three pieces, 1¾" x 42"; two pieces, 1¾" x 56¼"; and two pieces, 1¾" x 44½".

3. Sew the rows together, alternating them with the 1¾" x 42" sashing pieces. Press the seam allowances toward the sashing. Sew the 1¾" x 56¼" sashing pieces to the sides of the quilt top. Press. Sew the 1¾" x 44½" sashing pieces to the top and bottom edges of the quilt top. Press.

4. Referring to "Adding Borders" on page 76, attach the gold snowflake inner and snowman striped outer borders.

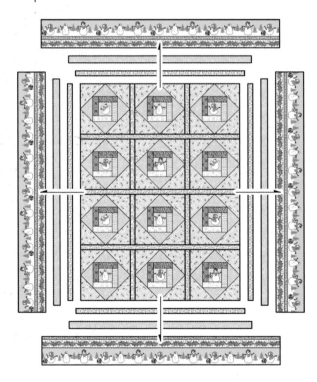

FINISHING THE QUILT

1. Layer the quilt top with batting and backing and quilt as desired.

Quilting Note: This cozy quilt has a swirly design that reminds me of snow flurries.

2. Referring to "Binding" on page 77, bind the edges of the quilt using the ivory strips.

Fabric Alternatives

The soft colors and snowmen in the photographed quilt make you want to cuddle. For a totally different look, bright pink, orange, and green florals will really make this quilt pop.

Snowmen's Forest

I used snowmen, but almost any favorite or special fabric can serve as the focal fabric in this quilt. You'll be cozy in a hurry with quick piecing and large rectanglular setting blocks.

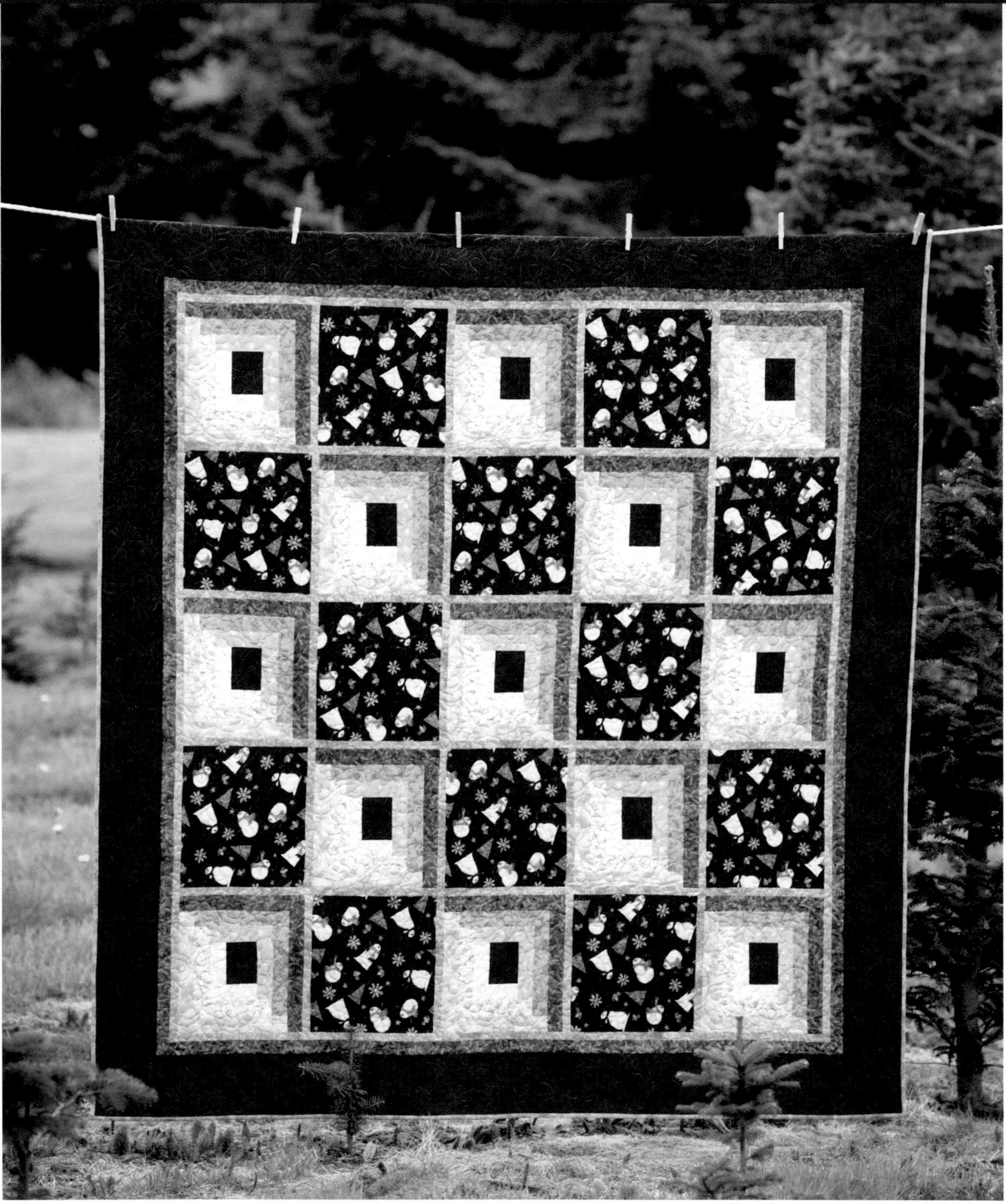

Finished quilt: 81" x 86"
Finished block: 12" x 13"

*Pieced by Sara Diepersloot;
quilted by Deborah Rasmussen*

MATERIALS

Yardage is based on 42"-wide fabric.

1⅞ yards of red snowflake print for block centers
and outer border

1⅔ yards of red snowman print for setting blocks

1⅛ yards of green holly print for blocks and inner
border

1⅛ yards of green dot print for blocks and binding

⅞ yard of gold dot print for sashing

⅝ yard of gold snowflake print for blocks

½ yard of ivory star print for blocks

⅜ yard of green snowflake print for blocks

⅓ yard of ivory snowflake print for blocks

7½ yards of fabric for backing

89" x 94" piece of batting

CUTTING

From the red snowflake print, cut:
2 strips, 4½" x 42"; crosscut into 13 rectangles,
3½" x 4½"

8 strips, 6½" x 42"

From the ivory snowflake print, cut:
4 strips, 2" x 42"; crosscut into 13 rectangles,
2" x 4½", and 13 rectangles, 2" x 5"

From the green snowflake print, cut:
5 strips, 2" x 42"; crosscut into 13 rectangles, 2" x 6",
and 13 rectangles, 2" x 6½"

From the ivory star print, cut:
6 strips, 2" x 42"; crosscut into 13 rectangles,
2" x 7½", and 13 rectangles, 2" x 8"

From the green dot print, cut:
7 strips, 2" x 42"; crosscut into 13 rectangles, 2" x 9",
and 13 rectangles, 2" x 9½"

9 strips, 2¼" x 42"

From the gold snowflake print, cut:
9 strips, 2" x 42"; crosscut into 13 rectangles,
2" x 10½", and 13 rectangles, 2" x 11"

From the green holly print, cut:
9 strips, 2" x 42"; crosscut into 13 rectangles,
2" x 12", and 13 rectangles, 2" x 12½"

7 strips, 1¾" x 42"

From the red snowman print, cut:
4 strips, 13½" x 42"; crosscut into 12 rectangles,
12½" x 13½"

From the gold dot print, cut:
21 strips, 1¼" x 42"; crosscut *7 strips* into 20 pieces,
1¼" x 13½"

MAKING THE BLOCKS

Press all seam allowances away from the center.

1. Sew an ivory snowflake 2" x 4½" rectangle to the left side of a red snowflake 3½" x 4½" rectangle.

2. Sew an ivory snowflake 2" x 5" rectangle to the bottom of the center unit.

3. Sew a green snowflake 2" x 6" rectangle to the right side of the center unit.

4. Sew a green snowflake 2" x 6½" rectangle to the top of the center unit.

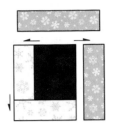 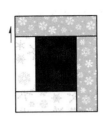

5. Sew an ivory star 2" x 7½" rectangle to the left side of the center unit.

6. Sew an ivory star 2" x 8" rectangle to the bottom of the center unit.

7. Sew a green dot 2" x 9" rectangle to the right side of the center unit.

8. Sew a green dot 2" x 9½" rectangle to the top of the center unit.

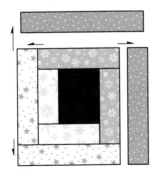

9. Sew a gold snowflake 2" x 10½" rectangle to the left side of the center unit.

10. Sew a gold snowflake 2" x 11" rectangle to the bottom of the center unit.

11. Sew a green holly 2" x 12" rectangle to the right side of the center unit.

12. Sew a green holly 2" x 12½" rectangle to the top of the center unit. Make 13 blocks.

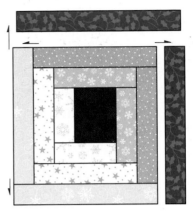

Make 13.

ASSEMBLING THE QUILT TOP

1. Arrange the pieced blocks and red snowman print rectangles in rows, alternating them as shown in the quilt diagram on page 74. Add a gold dot 1¼" x 13½" sashing piece between each block. Join the blocks into rows. Press the seam allowances toward the blocks.

2. Sew the remaining gold dot 1¼" x 42" strips together end to end. Crosscut into four pieces, 1¼" x 63½"; two pieces, 1¼" x 68½"; and two pieces, 1¼" x 65".

3. Sew the rows together, alternating them with the four 1¼" x 63½" sashing pieces. Press the seam allowances toward the blocks. Sew the 1¼" x 68½" sashing pieces to the sides of the quilt top. Press the seam allowances toward the sashing. Sew the 1¼" x 65" sashing pieces to the top and bottom of the quilt top and press the seam allowances toward the sashing.

4. Referring to "Adding Borders" on page 76, attach the green holly print inner and red snowflake print outer borders.

FINISHING THE QUILT

1. Layer the quilt top with batting and backing and quilt as desired.

   Quilting Note: The quilting design repeats a lovely holly motif from the green holly print fabric.

2. Referring to "Binding" on page 77, bind the edges of the quilt using the green dot strips.

Fabric Alternatives

Take these easy Log Cabin blocks from winter to summer using a fun sailboat print. Choosing a feature fabric with lots of color makes it easy to find coordinating fabrics for your blocks.

Quiltmaking Techniques

All of the quilts in this book are very easy and were made using standard quiltmaking techniques—rotary cutting, machine piecing, and machine quilting. If you're new to quiltmaking, you'll find that the projects are quite accessible for you.

In this section, I've included basic information on cutting, piecing, and finishing your quilts. You may also find it helpful to take a class at your local shop. Not only will you learn a great deal, but you'll also meet other people who share a passion for quilting.

SEAM ALLOWANCES

One of the most important aspects of quiltmaking is having an accurate ¼" seam allowance. If your seams aren't accurate, your quilt won't fit together well and you'll be frustrated! Many sewing machines today have a ¼" quilting foot that allows you to use the edge of the foot as a guide.

An easy test to see if your ¼" seam is accurate is to take three 2"-wide scraps and sew them together. Press the seam allowances to one side and measure the center piece. It should measure 1½" wide. If it doesn't, adjust your seam allowance accordingly.

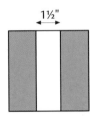

MAKING STRAIGHT-SET QUILTS

Many of the quilts in this book feature straight settings—blocks arranged in horizontal rows that are then sewn together. Follow the steps below to sew blocks together.

1. Arrange the blocks of your quilt in rows as shown in the illustrations for the project you're making.

2. Sew the blocks together into horizontal rows (with sashing pieces if called for). Press the seam allowances in opposite directions from row to row. If you have unpieced alternate setting blocks, press the seam allowances toward the setting blocks.

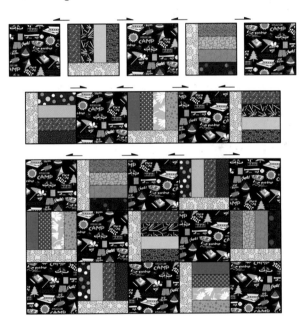

3. Sew the rows together. Press the seam allowances in one direction.

MAKING DIAGONALLY SET QUILTS

Blocks set in diagonal rows, or "on-point" quilts, require side and corner setting triangles. The cutting dimensions for all the setting triangles in this book are slightly oversized. This allows you to square up your quilt top after adding the triangles and before adding any borders.

1. Arrange the blocks and setting triangles as shown in the illustrations for the project you're making.

2. Sew the blocks together in diagonal rows. Press the seams in opposite directions from row to row (or as specified in the project instructions).

3. Sew the rows together. Press the seam allowances in one direction. Add the corner setting triangles last and press toward the triangles or as specified.

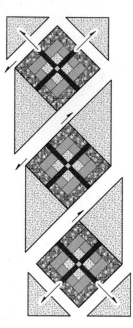

4. Square up each side of the quilt top, lining up the ¼" mark on your ruler with the block points and trimming the quilt edges. This gives you a perfect ¼" seam allowance. Square up the corners to 90° angles; a large square ruler is very helpful for this.

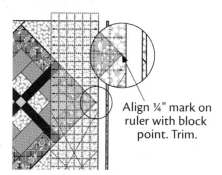

Align ¼" mark on ruler with block point. Trim.

ADDING BORDERS

When measuring your quilt to determine the length of the borders, measure through the center of the quilt. The edges of your quilt may have stretched slightly from handling and can differ in length from one side to the other. By measuring through the center of the quilt, you'll get accurate borders that lie flat and this will help to keep your quilt nice and square.

1. Measure the length of the quilt top through the center from top to bottom. Cut two border pieces this length for the sides of your quilt. Mark the center of the quilt and the center of each border strip. Match the centers and ends, pin, and then sew the border strips to the sides of the quilt, easing to fit if necessary. Press the seam allowances toward the borders.

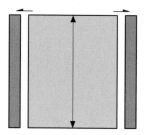

2. Measure the width of the quilt top through the center from side to side, including the side borders just added. Cut two border pieces to this length. Mark the center of the quilt and the center of the border strips. Pin and sew the borders to the top and bottom edges of the quilt, easing to fit if necessary. Press the seam allowances toward the borders.

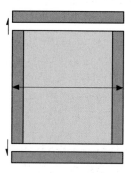

3. Repeat the steps for each border that you add.

Matching Prints When Piecing Borders

When it's necessary to piece border strips, it can sometimes be difficult to piece a large-scale print without a very obvious seam. The easiest way is to find an area in the print that's predominantly all background; add the next border strip there.

If your print is busy and there's no open background area, try to find the spot where the pattern repeats. If you can sew the strip together in the same place of the repeat on a second border strip, it will look like one long strip of fabric.

Seam in background area

Seam in repeat

LAYERING AND BASTING

Many quilters today choose to send their quilt tops to a professional long-arm machine quilter for quilting. Ask your quilter for any specific instructions on how to prepare the quilt top. Typically, you'll need to provide a backing piece that's about 4" larger than the quilt top on all sides. You won't need to layer or baste your quilt; the long-arm machine does this for you.

If you choose to do the machine quilting yourself, find a table or even a wood floor that's big enough to lay out your entire quilt. Smooth out the quilt backing, right side down, and tape it down with masking tape to hold it in place. Next, smooth the batting out over the quilt backing. Finally, center the pressed quilt top over the backing and batting and smooth it out, making sure there are no wrinkles in any of the layers.

Using quilting safety pins, pin the quilt every 4" to 6", trying to avoid placing pins where you're going to quilt.

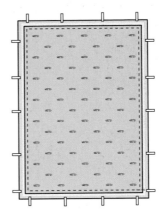

Stitch in the Ditch

An easy way to quilt is to simply stitch in the ditch. This is a straight stitch done very close to, or "in," the seam lines of the pieced elements of your quilt. The stitching should be on the side without seam allowances and it can be done by hand or machine.

BINDING

I use 2¼"-wide strips for my bindings. The instructions for each quilt in this book specify the number of binding strips you'll need to cut, typically the measurement around the quilt plus 10" to 12" for mitering corners and overlap.

1. Sew the binding strips together using a diagonal seam to create one long strip. Trim the seam allowances and press them open. Fold the

binding strip in half lengthwise with wrong sides together and press.

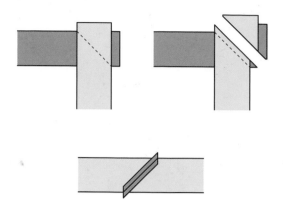

2. Place the binding about two-thirds of the way down one side of the front of the quilt, with the raw edges even. Leaving a 5" tail and using a ¼" seam allowance, sew the binding to the quilt. Sew until you're ¼" from the corner of the quilt. Backstitch and remove the quilt from the machine.

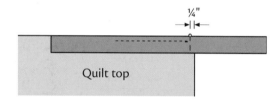

¼"

Quilt top

3. Fold the binding strip up at a 45° angle from the quilt. Then fold it back down so that it's even with the next side as shown. Start sewing at the top edge of the quilt. Continue sewing around the quilt, repeating the mitering at each corner.

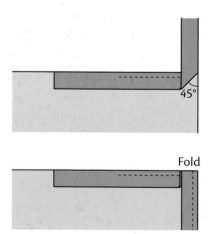

45°

Fold

4. When you're about 10" from where you started, remove the quilt from the machine. Fold back the beginning and ending tails of the binding so that they meet in the center. Finger-press the folded edges.

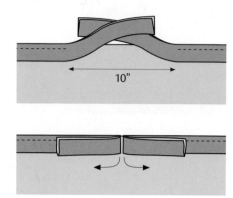

10"

5. Unfold both ends of the binding and match the center points of the two folds, forming an X as shown. Pin and sew the two ends together on the diagonal of the fold lines. Trim about ¼" away from the sewing line. Press the seam allowances open and refold the binding. Continue sewing the binding to the quilt.

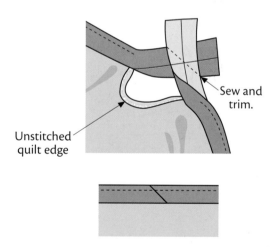

Sew and trim.

Unstitched quilt edge

6. Fold the binding to the back of the quilt over the raw edges. The corners will fold into beautiful miters. The binding should just cover the stitching line. Hand stitch the binding in place.

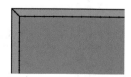

Quilt back

Acknowledgments

This book would never have been completed without the incredible work of Deborah Rasmussen and Renae Gleason. These two ladies did an incredible job. Deborah, you never cease to amaze me with your talented long-arm machine quilting. Somehow you always know the perfect way to finish off a quilt! Renae, thank you so much for your countless hours of sewing the most perfect bindings I've ever seen. I honestly don't know what I would have done without both of you.

About the Author

Sara Diepersloot lives in Scotts Valley, California, with her husband and four children. Her passion for sewing and design led her to get a degree from the Fashion Institute of Design and Merchandising in San Francisco. Sara worked as a designer and patternmaker until she started her family. While staying home with her young children, Sara began quilting and fell in love with it.

Sara is the author of *Simple Style: Easy Weekend Quilts*, also published by Martingale & Company.

There's More Online!

Visit Sara's blog at http://freshquiltdesigns.blogspot.com. *Find more great books on quilting and sewing at* www.martingale-pub.com.